Fostering Innovation and Competitiveness With FinTech, RegTech, and SupTech

Iustina Alina Boitan
Bucharest University of Economic Studies, Romania

Kamilla Marchewka-Bartkowiak
Poznan University of Economics and Business, Poland

A volume in the Advances in Finance, Accounting, and Economics (AFAE) Book Series

IGI Global
PUBLISHER of TIMELY KNOWLEDGE

Published in the United States of America by
IGI Global
Business Science Reference (an imprint of IGI Global)
701 E. Chocolate Avenue
Hershey PA, USA 17033
Tel: 717-533-8845
Fax: 717-533-8661
E-mail: cust@igi-global.com
Web site: http://www.igi-global.com

Library of Congress Cataloging-in-Publication Data

Names: Boitan, Iustina Alina, editor. | Marchewka-Bartkowiak, Kamilla, 1973- editor.
Title: Fostering innovation and competitiveness with fintech, regtech, and suptech / Iustina Alina Boitan and Kamilla Marchewka-Bartkowiak, editors.
Description: Hershey, PA : Business Science Reference, [2021] | Includes bibliographical references and index. | Summary: "This book addresses technologically innovative solutions and mechanisms from economic, financial, and legal perspectives"-- Provided by publisher.
Identifiers: LCCN 2020013013 (print) | LCCN 2020013014 (ebook) | ISBN 9781799843900 (hardcover) | ISBN 9781799856900 (paperback) | ISBN 9781799843917 (ebook)
Subjects: LCSH: Finance--Technological innovations. | Finance--Law and legislation. | Technological innovations--Economic aspects.
Classification: LCC HG173 .F677 2020 (print) | LCC HG173 (ebook) | DDC 332--dc23
LC record available at https://lccn.loc.gov/2020013013
LC ebook record available at https://lccn.loc.gov/2020013014

This book is published in the IGI Global book series Advances in Finance, Accounting, and Economics (AFAE) (ISSN: 2327-5677; eISSN: 2327-5685)

British Cataloguing in Publication Data
A Cataloguing in Publication record for this book is available from the British Library.

Advances in Finance, Accounting, and Economics (AFAE) Book Series

Ahmed Driouchi
Al Akhawayn University, Morocco

ISSN:2327-5677
EISSN:2327-5685

Mission

In our changing economic and business environment, it is important to consider the financial changes occurring internationally as well as within individual organizations and business environments. Understanding these changes as well as the factors that influence them is crucial in preparing for our financial future and ensuring economic sustainability and growth.

The **Advances in Finance, Accounting, and Economics (AFAE)** book series aims to publish comprehensive and informative titles in all areas of economics and economic theory, finance, and accounting to assist in advancing the available knowledge and providing for further research development in these dynamic fields.

Coverage

- Economics of Natural and Environmental Resources
- Field Research
- Finance and Accounting in SMEs
- Economics of Agriculture and Biotechnology
- Statistical Analysis
- Auditing
- Microeconomics
- Accounting Standards
- Labor Economics
- Stock Market

IGI Global is currently accepting manuscripts for publication within this series. To submit a proposal for a volume in this series, please contact our Acquisition Editors at Acquisitions@igi-global.com or visit: http://www.igi-global.com/publish/.

The Advances in Finance, Accounting, and Economics (AFAE) Book Series (ISSN 2327-5677) is published by IGI Global, 701 E. Chocolate Avenue, Hershey, PA 17033-1240, USA, www.igi-global.com. This series is composed of titles available for purchase individually; each title is edited to be contextually exclusive from any other title within the series. For pricing and ordering information please visit http://www.igi-global.com/book-series/advances-finance-accounting-economics/73685. Postmaster: Send all address changes to above address.

Titles in this Series

For a list of additional titles in this series, please visit:
https://www.igi-global.com/book-series/advances-finance-accounting-economics/73685

Bridging the Gender Gap in Digital Financial Inclusion
Puja Singhal (Sashakt-A Centre of Empowerment, India) and Rosy Kalra (Amity University Uttar Pradesh, India)
Business Science Reference • © 2021 • 300pp • H/C (ISBN: 9781799850120) • US $215.00

Innovative Strategies for Implementing FinTech in Banking
Yousif Abdullatif Albastaki (Ahlia University, Bahrain) Anjum Razzaque (Ahlia University, Bahrain) and Adel M. Sarea (Ahlia University, Bahrain)
Business Science Reference • © 2021 • 367pp • H/C (ISBN: 9781799832577) • US $225.00

Handbook of Research on Emerging Theories, Models, and Applications of Financial Econometrics
Burcu Adıgüzel Mercangöz (Istanbul University, Turkey)
Business Science Reference • © 2020 • 300pp • H/C (ISBN: 9781799831969) • US $275.00

Circular Economy and Re-Commerce in the Fashion Industry
Archana Shrivastava (Jaypee Business School, JIIT, Noida, India) Geetika Jain (FMS, Amity University, Noida, India) and Justin Paul (University of Puerto Rico, Puerto Rico)
Business Science Reference • © 2020 • 204pp • H/C (ISBN: 9781799827283) • US $195.00

Mapping, Managing, and Crafting Sustainable Business Strategies for the Circular Economy
Susana Serrano Rodrigues (Polytechnic Institute of Leiria, Portugal) Paulo Jorge Almeida (Polytechnic Institute of Leiria, Portugal) and Nuno Miguel Castaheira Almeida (Polytechnic Institute of Leiria, Portugal)
Business Science Reference • © 2020 • 401pp • H/C (ISBN: 9781522598855) • US $195.00

Applied Econometric Analysis Emerging Research and Opportunities
Brian W. Sloboda (University of Phoenix, USA) and Yaya Sissoko (Indiana University of Pennsylvania, USA)
Business Science Reference • © 2020 • 264pp • H/C (ISBN: 9781799810933) • US $195.00

Handbook of Research on Accounting and Financial Studies
Luís Farinha (University of Beira Interior, Portugal) Ana Baltazar Cruz (School of Management, Polytechnic Institute of Castelo Branco, Portugal) and João Renato Sebastião (Polytechnic Institute of Castelo Branco, Portugal)
Business Science Reference • © 2020 • 487pp • H/C (ISBN: 9781799821366) • US $295.00

IGI Global
PUBLISHER of TIMELY KNOWLEDGE

701 East Chocolate Avenue, Hershey, PA 17033, USA
Tel: 717-533-8845 x100 • Fax: 717-533-8661
E-Mail: cust@igi-global.com • www.igi-global.com

Editorial Advisory Board

Table of Contents

Section 2
Innovation and Digitization in Financial Markets and Economy

Detailed Table of Contents

The chapter focuses on the innovative financial technology called FinTech and explores its prospects for becoming a catalyst for financial inclusion. The novelty of the research approach resides in being the first study computing an EU FinTech index for the EU member countries. The index gathers four dimensions and provides insights on whether the FinTech environment in one country is better or worse compared to other countries in the sample. Countries' ranking based on index scores computed for two different years show that Sweden, Finland, Luxembourg, and Germany are always placed on the top of the hierarchy. Therefore, they exhibit real development opportunities in this regard. At the opposite are some countries in South-Eastern Europe that persistently record the lowest FinTech index scores; thus, there is still room for improvements in terms of market players' presence, existing regulation, access to digital financial inclusion.

The purpose of the chapter is to evaluate selected strategies and business models as key tools for competing within the financial sector in the digital environment, especially the position of banks against FinTechs and BigTechs, from the perspective of the risk culture factor. The main hypothesis says the success of the process of adapting banks to new competition rules requires the development of individual strategies and business models, taking into account an adequate organizational culture and, within it, a risk culture. To verify this assumption, the relationships between significant competitive features of banks in the digital environment, risk management, and risk culture are presented. The analyses of selected strategies and digital business models are trying to answer the question, to what extent it is possible to implement a new approach, useful in constructing effective solutions for banks to reduce the threats, especially created by FinTechs and BigTechs.

In this chapter, the authors provide some answers to the following questions: (1) To what extent can FinTech enter the market? (2) Are the markets accommodative enough for new innovative financial projects? (3) What are the main drivers of FinTech phenomenon? (4) Will FinTech shape the financial landscape going forward? By constructing four indices that can influence and drive FinTech market entry, such as (1) demand factors, (2) supply factors, (3) business environment, and (4) investment climate and by applying a z-score methodology, the results point out which economy is better prepared for a challenging wave of innovative changes in the financial sector relatively to the other economies included in the study. The authors focus on the EU countries over a period of 12 years (2007–2018). The FinTech market indices are computed by taking into account a wide variety of variables such as the level of financial inclusion, the available technology and infrastructure, the ease of starting new business, and the risk factors related to investment climate for all EU economies.

The buzz word 'RegTech' is on the rise. A financial service regulation has inflated at an astounding rate since the financial crisis and, therefore, has the price tag of regulatory compliance. Many start-ups have begun to apply digital technological knowledge including APIs, AI, RPAs, and many more to these immediate, numerous, and burdensome tasks to meet the terms and regulations, hence the emergence of RegTech. This study examines the implications for financial institutions and regulation particularly when technology poses a confront to the global banking and regulatory system. It attempts to examine the characteristics and applications of RegTech in the world of regulatory compliance. It also illustrates a model to define the transformation of present workload to proposed workload of regulatory compliance with an application of RegTech.

New technological innovation has incorporated frontier technologies in transforming the way we access and use existing products and services. The economy is becoming increasingly disrupted by revolutionary enterprises using technologies such as cloud computing, extensive use of artificial intelligence and data analytics, integration of interoperable internet of things (IoT) devices and the blockchained decentralization, including advanced materials. At the same time, regulatory and legal systems need to be strengthened in order for the ecosystem be protected from cyber risks and threats to allow for the market actors to flourish. In order to enjoy the benefits brought on by digital technologies, there are regulatory issues that come with technological adoption along with financial stability implications and consumer protection, with suggestions that regulators themselves adopt advanced technologies (RegTech) to embark on the new era of market supervision and monitoring to enhance cybersecurity.

Technological advances in data transmission and processing are an important structural factor influencing the banking sector. As they have an important impact on the cost base of banks and are characterized by large one-off costs, it is argued that investments in digital technologies enhance the positive returns to scale in the banking system. This in turn further improves the competitive position of the largest market players, creating a positive feedback loop. In the longer run, this leads to a polarization of the banking sector, between large universal banks and small specialized banks. These processes are important from the point of view of macroprudential policy, notably in the dimension of reducing the risks connected with the emergence of "too big to fail" institutions. The chapter illustrates these issues using the results of a survey on the investments of banks in digital transformation in Poland, focusing on the relationships between market structure, financial position, and investments in digital technologies.

Financial innovation and financial inclusion are helping countries to achieve inclusive economic growth by mitigating poverty. The purpose of the chapter is to examine how financial innovation accelerating financial inclusion in South Asian countries. The uses of internet banking, mobile banking, short message service (SMS) banking, electronic banking (e-banking), agent banking, mobile money accounts, and mobile wallet banking is increasing at an increasing rate, which is engaging the unbanked people in the financial systems. The robust growth of the mobile ecosystem in South Asia is contributing broadly to the engagement of financial inclusion. The empirical analysis was done by using data from the Global Financial Inclusion Database (Global Findex) and Global Financial Development Database to see how automated financial products and services are conveniently receiving by the unbanked population. The results of the analysis show that many financial innovations in financial products and services delivery from financial technology is closing gaps in financial inclusion significantly.

The main objective of the chapter is to provide a comprehensive overview of the development of the digital economy in the context of foreign direct investment flows, especially from the European Union member states point of view. First, the term and conceptualization of the digital economy is introduced, followed by an overview of theoretical background and empirical findings related to the role of foreign direct investment in the digital transformation of the economy. In this regard, the nature, position, and international footprint of digital multinational enterprises are also analyzed. The level of the digital economy and society development in the context of foreign direct investment flows is evaluated specifically in the conditions of the European Union member states. The conclusion summarizes the main partial findings, evaluates them in a mutual context, and brings implications for future research.

Preface

The subject of this edited book titled *Fostering Innovation and Competitiveness With FinTech, RegTech, and SupTech* gravitates around the concept of new, innovative technologies to be applied in economics and financial fields. It is a topical issue on the European Commission's agenda, in the following being summarized the main initiatives and strategies in this regard, which advocate for the importance and need of such a book targeted to a professional audience.

The Digital Single Market envisaged by the European Commission has as a pillar the blockchain technologies which are increasingly more considered to be transformative for the decades to come due to expected improvements for the European industry (from start-ups to large corporates, administrations and citizens). Their strength relies on creating decentralised, trusted, transparent, user-centric digital services and stimulating new and improved business models, in the benefit of society and sustainable economic growth.

In this regard it can be mentioned the launch by the European Commission in February 2018 of the European Blockchain Observatory and Forum and of the European Blockchain Partnership in April 2018. In April 2019 it had been launched the International Association for Trusted Blockchain Applications.

FinTech, another pillar of the Digital Single Market, is the term used to describe the impact of new technologies on the financial services industry. It comprises a variety of products, applications, processes and business models that have transformed the traditional way of providing banking and financial services due to increased pace of technological innovation (artificial intelligence, social networks, peer-to-peer lending, crowdplatforms, machine learning, mobile applications, distributed ledger technology, cloud computing and big data analytics). In March 2018 the European Commission adopted an action plan on FinTech to foster a more competitive and innovative European financial sector. The action plan stimulates the development of innovative business models, supports the uptake of new technologies such as blockchain, artificial intelligence and cloud services in the financial sector and increases cyber security awareness in the financial system.

As regards regulatory and supervisory technologies (RegTech and SupTech), it is a novel field of debate. The most recent analysis in this regard pertains to the European Securities and Markets Authority and was released on March 2019. The results indicated that regulatory pressure and budget limitations determine financial market players to increasingly use automated software for replacing human decision-making activities. New automated tools have been implemented in areas such as fraud detection, regulatory reporting and risk management, while financial regulators use them for greater surveillance capacity and improved data collection and management.

The Regional Innovation Monitor created under the aegis of the European Commission documents about the Economy 4.0 initiative launched in 2015 by the Lower Austrian Department of Economic Affairs and updated in 2018. The specific goals of this initiative are: i) to raise awareness for digitalisation and networks, and its potential for future business growth; ii) support financial innovation, new technologies and investment solutions; iii) develop new skills and focus on qualifications that will be beneficial to the Economy 4.0. Although at the moment it is a national strategy, it can be expanded at European level with appropriate arguments, analyses and dissemination as the ones proposed through this book.

The main objective of the book is to address technologically innovative solutions and mechanisms from multiple perspectives (economic, financial, legal), as this new approach to economy and finance, which relies closely on the newest technological trends, is in the spotlight of European and national decision makers, public and financial institutions, academia and research centers. This publication aims at bringing a fresh, topical and comprehensive analysis of financial and economic development driven by new technology, as well as the survey of the most recent initiatives in this regard.

The topics addressed in this book have been structured in two main sections, each section gathering thematic chapters. The first section is titled "Emergence and Competitiveness of FinTech, RegTech, and SupTech" and aims at providing a comprehensive insight on FinTech, RegTech and SupTech issues, by reconciling qualitative-conceptual methods with statistical ones.

The chapter "EU Fintech Index: An Evaluation of Countries" Opportunity for FinTech Growth" focuses on the innovative financial technology called FinTech and explores its prospects for becoming a catalyst for financial inclusion. The novelty of this research approach resides in being the first study computing an EU FinTech index for the EU member countries. The index gathers four dimensions (the demand for FinTech-led financial inclusion, the market supply side of FinTech technologies, the political and regulatory environment, SMEs financial access) and provides insights on whether the FinTech environment in one country is better or worse compared to other countries in the sample. The aggregate index level allows making comparisons and rankings between countries in terms of FinTech environment and prospects, as well as to assess the FinTech improvements one year from another. In addition, the values recorded by each sub-index indicate which component of the overall index contributes more to FinTech advancements in a given country and, respectively, which one should be improved, through targeted public policies.

The chapter "Strategies and Business Models of Banks in Front of the FinTech and BigTech Competition" evaluates several bank strategies and business models, as key tools for competing within the financial sector in the digital environment, especially the position of banks against FinTechs and BigTechs, from the perspective of the risk culture factor. The authors have investigated the hypothesis that the successful process of banks' adaptation to new competition rules requires the development of individual strategies and business models, taking into account an adequate organizational culture and, within it, a risk culture. To verify this assumption, the relationships between significant competitive features of banks in the digital environment, risk management and risk culture are presented. The analyses of selected strategies and digital business models are trying to answer the question to what extent it is possible to implement a new approach, useful in constructing effective solutions for banks to reduce the new threats and challenges triggered by FinTechs and BigTechs.

The chapter "The FinTech Wave in the Financial Sector for European Union Countries" provides answers to the following questions: (i) to what extent can FinTech enter the market? (ii) are the markets accommodative enough for new innovative financial projects? (iii) what are the main drivers of FinTech phenomenon? (iv) will FinTech shape the financial landscape going forward? By constructing four indices that can influence and drive FinTech market entry, such as (a) demand factors, (b) supply factors, (c) business environment and d) investment climate and by applying a z-score methodology, our results point out which economy is better prepared for a challenging wave of innovative changes in the financial sector relatively to the other economies included in the study. We focus on the EU countries over a period of 12 years (2007–2018). The FinTech market indices are computed by taking into account a wide variety of variables such as the level of financial inclusion, the available technology and infrastructure, the ease of starting new business and the risk factors related to investment climate for all EU economies.

The chapter "Accelerating Financial Innovation Through RegTech: A New Wave of FinTech" performs an overview of RegTech emergence, being understood as a sub-set of FinTech that relies on new technologies for supporting the delivery of regulatory requirements more ingeniously and productively than accessible capabilities. RegTech operates in a variety of monetary spheres and has increased implications for financial services. Adopting RegTech will bring modifications in business practices and cultures and will allow the incorporation of additional skills in data science and artificial intelligence. It is emphasized the idea that RegTech is not usually projected to fully replace all human involvement in the relevant risk and obedience processes. RegTech is ideal for removing low-level, repeatable, manual processes as existing technologies are not enough to replace more ambiguous and complex decisions.

The chapter "Finding Solutions to Cyber Security Challenges in the Digital Economy" explores the statement that new technological innovation, which incorporates frontier technologies, is radically transforming the way we access and use existing products and services. The economy is becoming increasingly disrupted by revolutionary enterprises using technologies such as cloud computing, extensive use of artificial intelligence and data analytics, integration of inter-operable Internet of Things (IoT) devices and the block-chained decentralization, including advanced materials. At the same time, regulatory and legal systems need to be strengthened in order to protect the ecosystem from cyber risks and threats and to allow for the market actors to flourish. To enjoy the benefits brought on by digital technologies, there are regulatory issues that come with the technological adoption, along with financial stability implications and consumer protection, with suggestions that regulators themselves have to adopt advanced technologies (RegTech) to embark on the new era of market supervision and monitoring to enhance cyber security.

The chapter "Non-Technological and Technological (SupTech) Innovations in Strengthening the Financial Supervisory" provides guidance and support for supervisory institutions in the digitization of reporting and regulatory processes, by emphasizing international applications of innovations in financial supervision (SupTech). It presents the most popular technological and non-technological solutions along with an evaluation of their usefulness in exercising supervision over the financial market. The authors discuss the types of innovations and the reasons for implementing them by supervisory institutions. Furthermore, they describe the most important non-technological supervisory solutions and technologies that supervisors can apply in creating SupTech tools. The study uses, among other things, data from reports and elaborations by central banks, supervisory institutions and consulting companies. Authors' main focus is on the analysis of the solutions employed by European Union member states.

The second section is titled "Innovation and Digitization in Financial Markets and Economy" and gravitates around several specific topics of interest, related to virtual currencies, use of blockchain technologies for facilitating the financial inclusion on the capital market, use of various financial innovation solutions for stimulating financial inclusion, the digital transformation witnessed by the economy and banking system, the development prospects for auditing practices and leadership on the background of technological innovations.

The chapter "Blockchain-Based Tokens as Financing Instruments: Capital Market Access for SMEs?" explores the advantages of using the blockchain technology as a technological basis for supplementing corporate financing processes. The issuance of digital tokens offers several potential advantages such as tradability, efficiency, automation and cost benefits compared to traditional financial products. This transformation of financing processes and capital markets can allow small and medium-sized enterprises (SMEs) to access capital markets and at the same time closes the existing retail investment gaps. In this paper, the challenges of SMEs financing are described and blockchain-based financing (initial coin offerings - ICOs) and security token offerings (STOs) are introduced. The blockchain-based financing mechanisms are compared with conventional forms of financing and potentials and challenges are discussed. In conclusion, it is stated that potential clearly outweighs risk and that the majority of all existing challenges can be tackled through sensible and coordinated regulation.

The chapter "Legal Risks and Challenges Related to Virtual Currencies" starts from the statement that the appearance of the virtual currencies generates several legal questions beyond their economic and monetary nature. The chapter analyses the emergence of virtual currencies from a legal point of view, after a brief analysis of the concept and development of money, and discusses the related possible and probable legal risks and challenges in comparison to the operation of traditional (fiat) currencies. The author provides a brief background of the technology of virtual currencies. The chapter considers specific issues that virtual currencies raise concerning the legal regulation in several fields, e.g. exchange services, taxation, salaries, lending and borrowing in virtual currencies, law enforcement, money laundering, etc. Before the author assesses the impacts and probable functions of virtual currencies, it is indispensable to have also a look at the relations between state and money through the concept of monetary sovereignty and the related compatibility issues.

The chapter "Digital Transformation in Banks of Different Sizes: Evidence From the Polish Banking Sector" argues that technological advances in data transmission and processing are an important structural factor influencing the banking sector. As they have an important impact on the cost base of banks and are characterized by large one-off costs, it is argued that investments in digital technologies may enhance the positive returns to scale in the banking system. This in turn further improves the competitive position of the largest market players, creating a positive feedback loop. In the longer run, this leads to a polarization of the banking sector, between large universal banks and small specialized banks. These processes are important from the point of view of macro prudential policy, notably in the dimension of reducing the risks connected with the emergence of "too big to fail" institutions. The chapter illustrates these issues using the results of a survey on the investments of banks in digital transformation in Poland, focusing on the relationships between market structure, financial position and investments in digital technologies.

The chapter "Financial Innovation: Accelerating Financial Inclusion in South Asia" addresses the interplay between financial innovation and financial inclusion, as drivers for countries' achievements in terms of inclusive economic growth, by mitigating poverty. The purpose of the chapter is to examine how financial innovation is accelerating financial inclusion in South Asian countries. The use of internet banking, mobile banking, short message service (SMS) banking, electronic banking, agent banking, mobile money accounts, and mobile wallet banking is increasing at a rapid pace, which is engaging the unbanked people in the financial systems. The robust growth of the mobile ecosystem in South Asia is contributing broadly to widening financial inclusion. The empirical analysis was done by using data from the Global Financial Inclusion Database (Global Findex) and Global Financial Development Database, to uncover how automated financial products and services are conveniently accessed by the unbanked population. The results of the analysis show that many financial innovations in financial products and services delivery due to new financial technology are significantly closing the gaps in financial inclusion.

The chapter "The Digital Economy in the Context of Foreign Direct Investment Flows" performs a comprehensive overview of the development of the digital economy in the context of foreign direct investment flows, especially from the European Union member states point of view. First, the term and conceptualization of the digital economy is introduced, followed by an overview of theoretical background and empirical findings related to the role of foreign direct investment in the digital transformation of the economy. In this regard, the nature, position and international footprint of digital multinational enterprises are also analyzed. The level of the digital economy and society development in the context of foreign direct investment flows is evaluated specifically in the conditions of the European Union member states. The conclusion summarizes the main partial findings, evaluates them in a mutual context and brings implications for future research.

The chapter "The Future of Audit in Light of Technological Changes: Opportunities and Threats" addresses the topic of external audit of financial statements, which plays a key role in achieving transparent financial reporting, since its purpose is to provide reasonable assurance that the presented financial statements are free of material misstatements due to fraud or error. In the process of fulfilling this role, auditors must be adaptable, especially when it comes to technological advancements. This chapter explains the effects that new technologies have on auditing the financial statements. In addition to summarizing the technological changes that impacted the audit profession in the past and therefore introduced new generations of auditors and audit tools, the authors have identified issues and challenges in the way the audit is currently performed. Some of the new technologies that are discussed in this chapter have the potential to mitigate these issues. However, new challenges and risks may be introduced while accepting these technologies in the process of financial reporting and auditing.

The chapter "Leadership in FinTech: Authentic leaders as Enablers of Innovation and Competitiveness in Financial Technology Firms" discusses the intricacies of innovation and competitive advantage, the current leadership gap within FinTech firms, and how these occurrences are enabled and improved through the utilization of authentic leadership practices within the context of the FinTech industry. Following this discussion, it is observed the future research directions and potential areas of exploration in which other scholars may divulge. Through the exploration of the research question "How can authentic leadership behaviors enable innovation and competitive advantage in FinTech firms?", the authors have found that the importance of authentic leadership within any industry or organization may be enhanced and explored further, as it appears to have a positive impact on innovation within organizations which, in turn, has the potential to provide a variety of opportunities for growth and competitive advantage.

The book is expected to bring a significant impact to existing research and practice, as it aims at reconciling the newest theoretical, conceptual frameworks with case studies, qualitative and quantitative analyses gravitating around the core issue of innovative technology applied for finance and economy. The European Commission's recent initiatives, partnerships and analyses represent an additional argument for the added value this publication might bring.

The theme of this edited book is suitable for multiple audiences, due to increased importance gained by technological advances in the financial and economic environment. The book is expected to exert an impact especially among European Commission and national decision makers and professionals (financial and public institutions, corporate and start-up firms, entrepreneurs). It also might be of importance for academia, research centres within universities and for the use of doctoral, under-graduate and graduate students. In this respect, there are envisaged the faculties/universities providing lectures on Finance/Financial System/Banking/Economics/New Economy/Law and Economics/Law/Governance or technical specializations such as Information technology/Artificial intelligence/Blockchain and DLT/ Big Data/Machine Learning which can illustrate students real economic, financial and legal examples of applying new technology.

The added value of this book is not limited to expanding decision makers' knowledge and capabilities and broadening research in the field, but it will also contribute to increasing professionals' awareness on the need to permanently update their skills and competencies in line with the new technological and digital advances. On the background of global rapid pace technological changes, both employers and employees have to become aware of witnessing challenging, dynamic times which greatly redesign future career patterns and pathways. The changing financial landscape (development of new financial products and services, digitalization, artificial intelligence-related innovative technologies, evolving regulations in the financial field) is also requesting a shift in the traditional, conservatory mindset.

Our book aims at gathering the most influential, fresh and forthcoming analyses performed by reputed contributors with professional knowledge, in order to channel them to a specialized audience and exert a further medium-term impact on public policies and strategies, financial and economic decision makers, professionals and labor market.

It is written for decision-makers, professionals and academia who want to improve their understanding of the strategic role that technology is going to play in the future development of the economy and financial activity.

Section 1

Emergence and Competitiveness of FinTech, RegTech, and SupTech

Chapter 1
EU FinTech Index: An Evaluation of Countries' Opportunities for FinTech Growth

Iustina Alina Boitan
https://orcid.org/0000-0001-6510-5063
Bucharest University of Economic Studies, Romania

Teodora Cristina Barbu
Bucharest University of Economic Studies, Romania

ABSTRACT

The chapter focuses on the innovative financial technology called FinTech and explores its prospects for becoming a catalyst for financial inclusion. The novelty of the research approach resides in being the first study computing an EU FinTech index for the EU member countries. The index gathers four dimensions and provides insights on whether the FinTech environment in one country is better or worse compared to other countries in the sample. Countries' ranking based on index scores computed for two different years show that Sweden, Finland, Luxembourg, and Germany are always placed on the top of the hierarchy. Therefore, they exhibit real development opportunities in this regard. At the opposite are some countries in South-Eastern Europe that persistently record the lowest FinTech index scores; thus, there is still room for improvements in terms of market players' presence, existing regulation, access to digital financial inclusion.

INTRODUCTION

Increasingly more decision makers and practitioners in the financial field perceive the emergence of new, innovative financial technology, called FinTech, as a potential solution for improving a country's financial inclusion. The study conducted by McKinsey (2016) argued that digital and financial inclusion are able to trigger major macroeconomic benefits, and FinTech could boost the GDP of emerging economies by 6% in 2025 which is supposed to generate about 95 million new jobs. Nevertheless, the reality shows that country-specific initiatives meant to support financial inclusion are uneven, fragmented and focus-

DOI: 10.4018/978-1-7998-4390-0.ch001

ing mostly on financial education. Public authorities should consider designing a comprehensive and tailored financial inclusion strategy, encompassing also a digital approach, to address the identified gaps.

However, the success of FinTech initiatives is difficult to ascertain, as it is the outcome of several country-related and individual-related factors, such as economic development, the state of existing physical and technological infrastructure, supporting regulations for the business environment, demographic and financial access indicators (Frost, 2020).

In this regard, analysts from ING Bank have set up in 2016 a FinTech index, meant to assess a country's need for FinTech led financial inclusion, its FinTech infrastructure as well as country-specific governance and demographic features. This FinTech Index comprises 3 sub-indices, related to: a) the urgency or need for FinTech to financially include individuals; b) the FinTech infrastructure and ecosystem which assesses countries' business environment for FinTech companies; c) the political and regulatory environment which is a determinant of a country's investment climate. Each sub-index gathers several proxy variables, whose values have been normalized before computing the unweighted index. The scores provide insights on whether the FinTech environment in one country is better or worse compared to other countries in the sample. It has to be mentioned that this initial index was built only for low and middle-income countries across the world.

Our research relies on the same methodological steps and variables as proposed by ING's FinTech index, but we focus exclusively on European Union (EU) countries. The EU FinTech index developed within this chapter is computed distinctly for the years 2014 and 2017, due to data availability constraints for some indicators, and covers 28 EU countries. Another significant novel feature of our research resides from updating the structure of the FinTech overall index, by creating a fourth new sub-index meant to measure the financial access conditions for start-ups and small and medium sized companies (SMEs). In this respect, we employed detailed data regarding SMEs access to various bank, non-bank and capital market sources of financing, such as loans, issuance of bonds or equity, leasing and factoring.

The aggregate index level allows making comparisons and rankings between countries in terms of FinTech environment and prospects, as well as to assess the FinTech improvements one year from another. In addition, the values recorded by each sub-index will indicate which component of the overall index contributes more to FinTech advancements in a given country and, respectively, which one should be improved, through targeted public policies. By plotting on a map the results obtained, one can gain a visual insight of the best-performing countries in terms of FinTech environment.

The novelty of our research approach resides in being the first study computing an EU FinTech index for the EU member countries. Our attempt overlaps on the active debates, meetings and public consultations which take place at European level, related to identifying obstacles for financial innovation and creating prospects for FinTech developments. The momentum for quantitatively assessing FinTech opportunity of growth is outlined by the official roadmaps defined at European level. For instance, the European Commission has adopted in March 2018 an *Action Plan on FinTech* comprising 19 steps to foster the development of a more competitive and innovative European financial sector, by relying on new technologies, while the European Banking Association has published several reports on the FinTech impact on banks' business models and the risks and opportunities arising from incorporating FinTech in the regular banking business.

The remaining of the chapter is structured as follows: the literature review section outlines the existing concerns and challenges linked to FinTech, the methodology section describes the stages for computing the FinTech index score and the variables used. The next section presents and explains the findings obtained, while the last part concludes.

LITERATURE REVIEW

The information technology has witnessed a rapid pace dynamics and evolution in the past decade, which has triggered changes also in the financial system functioning, the competitive environment, features of financial products and services, risk management frameworks and relationship with customers. Digitization has a strong impact on the financial services industry as financial products are almost exclusively based on flows of information. The continuous digitization process leads to a growing automation and fundamental reorganization of the financial services value chain with new business models (e.g. robo advisers) and new players entering the market (e.g. ApplePay). The main drivers of this profond transformation are represented by the changing role of IT, shifts in consumer behavior, changing ecosystems and regulation (Puschmann, 2017).

For instance, the blockchain technology which is embedded in FinTech developments is claimed to exert ample implications if combined with secure, remote automation of financial processes (Roubini and Byrne, 2018). Peer-to-peer lending, another component of FinTech, employs a particular matching technique between borrowers and lenders (excluding the financial intermediation of a bank). They meet directly on an online platform, describe the investment project and amount of financing needed and wait for prospective lenders (individuals or businesses) to access the platform and choose the project to fund. Thus, it eliminates inefficiency and overhead transaction costs and allows borrowers with lower creditworthiness to apply for loans that otherwise would have been inaccessible to them (Foo et al, 2017).

There is widespread consensus that FinTech phenomenon represents an alternative financial model, that doesn't exclude the traditional ones. It emerges especially in developing countries and focuses on large customer segments which gain access to financing without relying on banks; hence, it fills a gap in the lending market (Blakstad and Allen, 2018). A complementary belief belonging to Nassiry (2018) argues that the range of new financial technologies, called simply FinTech, may be used also for achieving the Sustainable Development Goals and fighting against climate change effects. Specifically, there are prospects for developing green finance technologies, such as blockchain, the Internet of Things and big data. The author suggests several areas for the possible application of FinTech in green finance: blockchain applications for sustainable development, for renewable energy, for decentralized electricity market, carbon credits and climate finance.

The use of FinTech may bring several other advantages, such as: lowering the search costs involved in matching transacting partners, lowering verification costs, cheaper and secure information transmission, economies of scale (Thakor, 2019). The author further explains that FinTech development opportunities seem to be enhanced by a financial environment characterized by large percentages of banked individuals, more concentrated banking system with low to moderate banking competition, low deposit interest rates and high credit-to-GDP ratios. The same reasoning is shared by Frost et al. (2019), which claim that FinTechs use to lend more in countries with less competitive banking sectors and less stringent regulation, particularly in emerging market and developing economies.

Haddad and Hornuf (2019) have investigated a broader array of economic and technological determinants of FinTech sector emergence and development. Their findings suggested that FinTech appearance is positively influenced by an existing well-developed economic background, available venture capital, increased number of secure Internet servers and mobile telephone subscriptions.

Another strand of literature examines the evolution of the financial sector's digitization and identifies various stages. Thakor (2019) claims there are three phases in the FinTech evolution and we are currently witnessing the last phase:

i) 1866 - 1967 – use of the telegraph. This period is characterised by an increase of rapid transmission of financial information, transactions and payments;
ii) 1967 – 2008 – appearance of electronic payments and clearing systems, ATMs and online banking. Traditional financial institutions start the use of information technology for providing financial products and services;
iii) 2008 – till present – technology is employed by new market players for providing non-intermediated financial services directly to customers. The competitive landscape in the financial industry is changing.

A more nuanced evolutionary process is assumed by Puschmann (2017), which identifies five phases:

i) until 1960 - the strategically focus of the financial institution was on the single customer channel, with the aid of several support processes and no system integration;
ii) 1960 – 1980 – the focus moves on the two customer channels, complemented with back-office processes and partial internal systems;
iii) 1980 – 2020 – financial institutions put in place multi-customer channels, by relying on front-office processes and internal systems integration;
iv) 2010 – 2020 – development of cross-customer channels, relying on provider processes and integration of external financial services provider systems;
v) since 2020 – use of hybrid customer channels and integration of external non-financial services provider systems.

The FinTech sector has continuously evolved in the last years, by broadening the offering of financial services, the segments of targeted customers, expanding their global coverage and entering in direct competition with banks. Ernst & Young (2019) report observes that the use of FinTech services by individuals has rapidly increased from 16% in 2015 to 64% in 2019, most services used being related to making payments, managing money, and getting financing. As regards FinTech adoption rate by SMEs, China leads with 61%, followed by the US, with 23%.

Slower pace of FinTech adoption rate by SMEs is witnessed by Europe (with UK recording the highest growth and dominance in the European FinTech sector), although at global level the FinTech sector grows at an exponential pace. The report published by the European Investment Fund (2019) indicates that one in four European SMEs still face severe difficulties in having access to finance. Therefore, the existing bank credit market fails in meeting SMEs' financing needs, opening the way for Fintechs to involve in the SMEs financing landscape.

The range of innovative services provided to SMEs encompasses various solutions, such as: payments, financing, insurance (securing working capital), and financial management (hedging foreign exchange risk, managing cash flows, billing, accounting). The reasons individual customers bring for using FinTech are the attractive rates or fees, meanwhile SMEs are more concerned with features and functionality, round-the-clock availability of service, ease in configuring and using the service.

The consequence is that financial intermediaries felt the need to protect their market share and competitive advantage and developed their own FinTech solutions. A report published by the World Economic Forum (2017) observes that the success recorded by FinTechs has made some financial institutions to convert the potential threat of FinTech into a business opportunity. Thus, financial intermediaries reshaped their conventional business models into more agile, financial innovation-connected models, and concluded partnerships with FinTech providers in order to increase their capabilities for providing digital financial services. This trend has been noticed also by KPMG (2018): on the background of growing maturity of the FinTech sector, there is an increase in the diversity of investors. At global level, more mid-tier banks, in addition to insurance and wealth management companies, have started the cooperation with FinTech providers and are making investments either directly or through participation in accelerators, incubators or innovation consortia. Recently, the European Investment Fund (2019) summarized the three strategies used by established financial system players for reacting to the FinTech challenge, namely the imitation of FinTech way of functioning (e.g. introduction of dedicated own online platforms), cooperation/partnerships with FinTechs (joint ventures, common platforms), or a process of M&A for integrating such companies.

The European Banking Authority (2018) argues that shifts in banks' conventional business models will be driven by four main determinants, namely customers' expectations and financial behaviour, bank profitability concerns, increased competition in the financial landscape and the regulatory framework. Also, it discriminates between two different digitization trends depicted by banks' activity: digital transformation and digital disruption. Digital transformation consists of a transformation of internal processes, through automation of basic operations, digitalization and optimization of operations with customers. Digital disruption, on the other hand, represents a profound change of the traditional banking activity through the creation of new financial products and services which embed the use of innovative technologies and allow new, real time ways for customer interaction in order to enhance customers' satisfaction and loyalty.

In practice, there is a multitude of FinTech solutions that may be used by banks or other non-financial providers, such as financing, asset management, payment, insurance, loyalty programs, risk management, exchanges, regulatory technology, and other business activities. By far, the most important segment of the emerging FinTech market is financing, followed by payment, asset management, insurance, loyalty programs, risk management, exchanges, and regulatory technology (Haddad and Hornuf, 2019). To gain an insight on the size of FinTech lending market, figure 1 illustrates the total amount of loans provided to private sector in selected countries.

Figure 1. FinTech credit volume, selected countries (2017 data)
Sursa: Frost (2020)

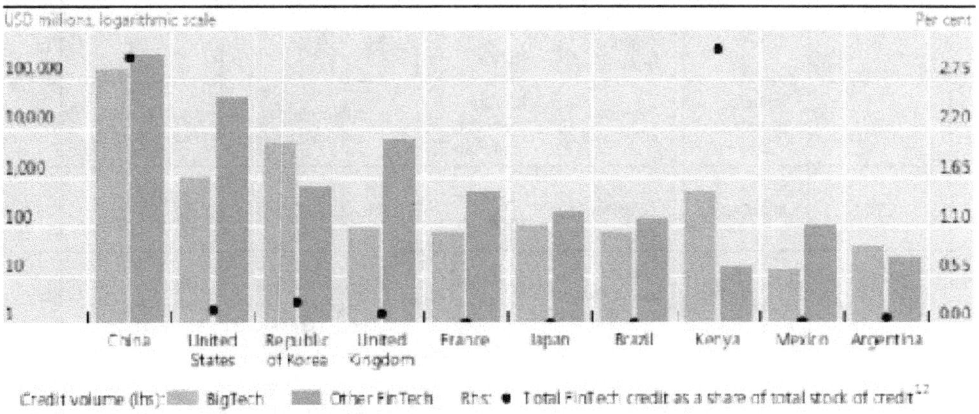

BigTech platforms hold larger market shares in the financing of small and medium enterprises operating in China, the US and UK. Fintech total credit, including credit extended by big tech platforms, is quite small in much of Continental Europe, the Middle East and Latin America (less than 1% of the outstanding credit granted by banks and other lenders). A survey having as respondents US small businesses (Schweitzer and Barkley, 2017) uncovered that firms with less than $100,000 of revenue use to apply more often for financing with an online lender or FinTech provider. Online borrowers' characteristics prove to be very much like the businesses that were denied bank credit. The findings indicated also the ordering of customer satisfaction: bank borrowers are more satisfied than online borrowers, who are more satisfied than businesses that were denied credit.

Table 1 synthesizes several practical examples of digital solutions implemented by banks and insurers, to withstand FinTech-driven competition and establish a closer connection with customers' financial and advisory needs.

Table 1. Digital solutions developed by banks, insurers and FinTechs

Provider type	Banking process					
	Interaction type	**Advice**	**Payments**	**Investments**	**Financing**	**Cross-process**
Bank	B2C	Video conferencing	Social media payment	Robo-advisory	Online credit application	Online bank account opening
	C2C	Online customer community)	Peer-to-peer payment	Community-based interest rate	Crowdlending	Social network
Non-bank	B2C	Personal finance management	Cryptocurrency	Multi-asset trading	Corporate credits	Electronic data safe
	C2C	Community-based advisory	Mobile Payment	Covesting	Crowdlending	Loyalty points marketplace
	B2B	Digital client advice	Personal finance management	Stock analysis and prediction	Crowdlending	Digital identity

Provider type	Insurance process						
	Interaction type	**Advice**	**Non-life insurance**	**Life insurance**	**Claims management**	**Risk management**	**Cross-process**
Insurer	B2C	Personalized marketing	Pay-as-you-drive	Online contracting	Drone-based claims analysis	Big data analysis of industrial accident insurances	Automated policy management
	C2C	–	Crowd-based liability insurance	–	–	–	–
Non-insurer	B2C	Digital insurance broker	Pay-how-you-drive	Life style-dependent premium	Mobile claims management	Risk data management	Online reinsurance calculation
	C2C	Online rating	Sharing economy insurance	Crowd-life insurance	No-claims bonus	Crowd underwriting	Donations from insurance premiums
	B2B	Insurance broker management	Sensor-monitored households' insurance	On-demand insurance products	Buy, compare and manage insurance policies and claims	Big data-based catastrophe models	Compliance and reporting

Source: Puschmann (2017)

Globally, the uneven adoption of FinTech across countries is conditioned by a series of country-specific demand and supply factors. Thus, in developing countries, FinTech adoption is the result of increased demand for financial services. In other economies, the adoption of FinTech is due to the increased cost of traditional financing, a favourable regulatory environment and other macroeconomic factors. The demographic factor, especially young, technologically savvy customers, plays an important role in the spread of FinTech services. Population aging and variations in people's trust in technology and FinTech may have important effects, shaping the future direction of FinTech sector development. Also, regulatory factors may play a role, but it does not appear to be a major driver of Fintech so far, at least at global level (Frost, 2020).

Kammoun et al. (2020) have investigated the impact of lending provided through FinTech on financial stability and economic performance. Empirical findings indicate, on the one hand, that it fuels inflation which may however be contained through the implementation of sound monetary regulations. By facilitating the access to affordable financial products, especially loans, for individuals and small and medium sized enterprises, it boosts financial intermediation and opens the way towards financing innovative projects, which may be rejected by banks due to higher uncertainty related to their return. The positive effect of FinTech on the economy is empirically supported, through stimulating economic growth, spending and investment. Interestingly, the relationship between FinTech and economy may be hampered by a political instability climate. A similar view on the economic implications of FinTech is shared by Nakaso (2016), which claims that, if innovation in information technology and FinTech enhance the efficiency of channelling finance to productive areas with potential, then it will eventually contribute to economic development.

Khiewngamdee and Yan (2019) have empirically assessed the impact of FinTech e-payments on the economic development, by considering variables as income growth, productivity, price volatility, and income inequality. The results show that the highest effect on these variables is exerted for countries recording a low economic development level. Hence, Fintech positively supports growth and productivity and diminishes price volatility and income inequity.

On the background of rapid pace increase of FinTech sector, several international authorities have become concerned about the implications for regulators and the financial industry. The World Economic Forum (2017) warns that increased consolidation of FinTechs market share is a source of risks for the financial sector. Consequently, regulators must define clear rules, because FinTech lending providers tend to adapt their business model and mimic the one of a bank. World Bank Group and IMF (2018) details a series of potential risks and concerns for the financial system and its customers, arising as the financial system adapts to the new digital environment: consumer and investor protection, clarity and harmonization of regulatory and legal frameworks, the potential for regulatory arbitrage and contagion, the adequacy of existing financial safety nets, including lender-of-last-resort functions of central banks, potential threats to financial integrity.

FinTech impact on financial stability, prudential supervision and regulations has been analysed by the Financial Stability Board (2017) report. The conclusions indicated 3 priority areas for international collaboration: managing operational risk from third-party service providers, mitigating cyber risks and monitoring macro-financial risks that could emerge as FinTech activities increase.

The potential of FinTechs to generate new systemic risks that need to be further addressed by regulations is investigated by Haddad and Hornuf (2019). Although market volumes in many FinTech segments are small, other segments (online factoring, online lending, payment services) exhibit the prospects for becoming soon of systemically importance and should be carefully examined by regulators.

From the standpoint of banks' business models sustainability and soundness, the European Banking Authority (2018) lists a number of factors that could significantly affect them, namely: digitization strategies that banks implement to keep up with the pace of a fast-changing environment, challenges arising from IT systems, operational capacity to implement the necessary digital changes, concerns regarding retaining and attracting technologically savvy staff that has knowledge and skills for using big data and artificial intelligence techniques, and increasing risk of competition from peers and other FinTech firms.

New regulations adopted globally during 2018, related to the implementation of Payment Services Directive 2 and General Data Protection Regulation (GDPR), are expected to drive additional FinTech investment and create the field for open banking. KPMG (2018) report suggests that open banking will cover a wide range of activities, from traditional institutions partnering with FinTechs in order to process and leverage their data to FinTechs able to use open banking for increasing their visibility and market coverage.

A pessimistic view on the adoption of FinTech is expressed by Frost (2020), which claims that the same failures of the traditional financial intermediation market will occur, namely the informational asymmetry and the adverse selection of customers and investment projects, liquidity mismatches, interconnection with financial intermediaries and systemic risk in the financial system. Therefore, adequate and proportionate regulation and supervision is needed.

In an attempt to manage the existing trade-off between fostering FinTech's benefits and mitigating its potential risks, as well as for strengthening international cooperation and guidance in addressing Fintech issues, the IMF and the World Bank (2018) have launched the Bali Fintech Agenda. The Agenda defines a series of guidelines to be considered by policymakers and the international community in order to adapt them to FinTech national circumstances.

As a follow-up of the Bali FinTech Agenda, the IMF (2019) performed a research that uncovered the persistence of important regional and national differences and gaps in regulation and infrastructure, as well as in digital financial awareness and literacy. However, countries seem to broadly explore the opportunities bring by FinTech related to stimulating economic growth and inclusion, while balancing risks to stability and integrity. Countries are willing to provide a supporting FinTech environment, that includes open and affordable access to core digital services and infrastructures, and anticipate significant gains to be first obtained from FinTech advances in payments, clearing, and settlement. An issue to be further exploited and improved by international organizations is related to strengthening the international cooperation in several key areas, such as: cybersecurity, anti-money laundering and combating the financing of terrorism, development of harmonized legal, regulatory, and supervisory frameworks, increased security of payment and securities settlement systems and cross-border payments.

METHODOLOGICAL INSIGHTS AND DATA USED

Although the role of financial technology (FinTech) occupies a core place in the international public debate on how to financially include poor people and to give start-ups, small and medium sized businesses better and cheaper access to finance, to date there is a singular approach meant to quantitatively evaluate the prospects a country depicts for FinTech advancement. Economists from ING have launched in 2016 a FinTech Index to serve as a signalling tool of the FinTech climate and raise awareness on the need for appropriate government and investment policies to improve it. Consequently, they built a

FinTech index to assess a country's need for FinTech led financial inclusion, its FinTech infrastructure as well as country risks. The index has been computed exclusively for the developing world countries.

The ING's FinTech Index comprises 3 sub-indices, represented by:

- the demand for FinTech-led financial inclusion, to account for the need or urgency for FinTech developments to financially include individuals;
- the market supply side of FinTech technologies, as a proxy of a country's supportive environment for FinTech. This dimension is further split into two components: the state of IT usage and access and the FinTech ecosystem which assesses a country's business and innovation environments;
- the political and regulatory environment, as a proxy for a country's investment climate.

All the three components determine the final index in different ways. For instance, a country may have a high need for FinTech driven financial inclusion, may show good IT infrastructure and ecosystem, but may be less attractive due to a volatile, unpredictable investment climate.

Each sub-index is calculated as the un-weighted average of the indicator values, while the overall index score is computed as the un-weighted average of the sub-indices scores. Therefore, the FinTech index provides a relative assessment of the supportive climate in each country, based on these indicators. The scores should not be interpreted in absolute terms, as their role is to give insights on whether the FinTech environment in one country is better or worse compared to other countries in the sample.

Our research approach takes an in-depth look at the FinTech environment in 28 European Union countries. In order to investigate how supportive is the existing macroeconomic, regulatory and financial environment for the development of FinTech sector, we constructed a EU FinTech Index having as starting point the methodological steps and index components proposed by ING's economists. The novelty of our approach consists in reconfiguring the structure of the initial index by adding a fourth new component, meant to signal small and medium sized businesses' access to financing. Countries that will show a low level of this sub-index suggest the need for Fintech's contribution to increase access to financing for small entrepreneurs. In our opinion, a comprehensive assessment of Fintech climate has to include not only individuals' need for financial integration, but also businesses one. Due to data availability constraints, the comparative analysis is restricted to two reference years: 2014 and 2017.

Obviously, when creating an index, the critical factors are related to the process of selecting and including the appropriate corresponding indicators. The adoption of FinTech and further opportunities for FinTech companies can be further sub-categorized in terms of different activity sectors, such as e-payments, peer-to-peer lending, enterprise tech, robo-advisory, etc., which would also illustrate gaps and opportunities in those particular segments. However, the index still cannot be built distinctly for each sub-category due to the lack of a proper track record for specific determinant indicators, transparently disclosed and harmonized across all EU countries. These are the reasons which made us to rely on the already built and validated FinTech index created by professionals in the financial system, and expand its composition with a missing component, focused on SMEs.

The list of indicators included in the computation of each sub-index, as well as the databases from which they were collected is mentioned in table 2.

Table 2. List of indicators used for computing the EU FinTech index

FinTech index component	Indicator	Data source
Demand sub-index (household financial inclusion)	Financial institution account (% age 15+)	World Bank, Global Findex Database
	Borrowed amount from a financial institution or use of a credit card (% age 15+)	
	At-risk-of-poverty rate	Eurostat
	Rural population (% of total population)	World Development Indicators
Supply sub-index	Individuals' mobile internet access	Eurostat
	Internet use by individuals	Eurostat
	Time required to start a business (days)	World Development Indicators
	Eco-innovation index	Eurostat
Investment climate sub-index	Corruption Perceptions Index	Eurostat
	Political Stability	Worldwide Governance Indicators
	Regulatory Quality	
SMEs financial access sub-index	Bank loan taken in the past 6 months	Survey on the access to finance of enterprises (SAFE), conducted by the European Central Bank and the European Commission
	Debt issuance (bonds) in the last 6 months	
	Equity capital issued in the last 6 months	
	Leasing financing obtained in the last 6 months	
	Factoring financing used in the past 6 months	

EU FINTECH INDEX: COMPUTATION AND INTERPRETATION OF RESULTS

Each time series belonging to considered indicators has been standardized through z-scores, by applying the formula $(x-x_{min})$/standard deviation. Then we computed the scores of each sub-index and finally the overall score of the EU FinTech index. In the following we discuss the scores recorded by each sub-index, in a comparative fashion (2014 versus 2017), the dynamics of the overall index and perform the ranking of European countries.

The values computed for each sub-index indicate which component of the overall index contributes more to FinTech advancements in a given country and, respectively, which one should be improved, through targeted public policies. Figure 2 exhibits each sub-index, computed for 2014-year end data, to gain an insight on its dynamics across EU countries.

By computing the basic descriptive statistics, we noticed that the investment climate sub-index registered the highest standard deviation (0.89), meaning that the raw data is widely scattered around sample's average and hence there is increased dissimilarity between countries from the standpoint of regulatory and political environment, and corruption perceptions. Countries witnessing large values for this sub-index benefit from a stable and sound regulatory framework, smooth political transitions and moderate concerns regarding the corruption phenomenon.

The second largest standard deviation belongs to the supply sub-index (0.67), indicating that FinTech existing infrastructure (internet access and use) and ecosystem (speed for launching new businesses/ start-ups, innovation capabilities) are too heterogeneous among countries. Discrepancies persist also in terms of the SMEs financial access sub-index, with a standard deviation of 0.5. Countries exhibiting

Figure 2. EU FinTech Index components (2014 year-end data)
Source: authors

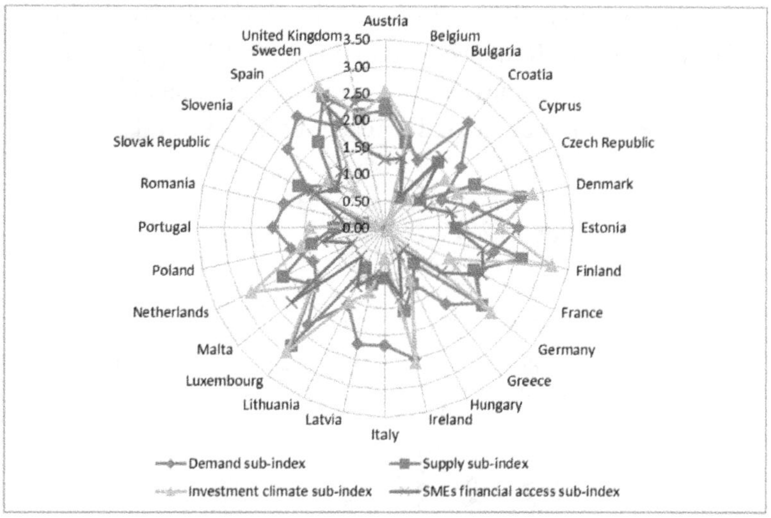

increased sub-index values depict a higher reliance of the business environment on various financing opportunities provided by the banking system or the capital market, such as issuing bonds, shares subscription, borrowing, concluding leasing or factoring agreements. Thus, the business environment is more open and knowledgeable about the various channels for attracting financing in order to ensure a smooth functioning and going concern.

The lowest standard deviation (0.41) was recorded by the demand sub-index, which signals the financial access of individuals to basic banking products. Consequently, EU countries are the least dissimilar from this standpoint, although variations are still present.

Further, the analysis may be individualized for each country to account for the component that contributes most to the overall FinTech index level. For instance, Finland records the largest value of the investment climate sub-index among all EU countries, high values for the demand and supply components, while the SMEs financial access component impacts to a lesser extent the overall index due to lower reliance on the capital market financing.

Also, similar scores of the overall index are driven by different sub-indices scores. Austria and Denmark record an identical EU FinTech index score of 2.07, but national features are relatively different. Both countries have obtained the same score for the SMEs financial access component (1.25), but in Austria this result is determined by businesses predominant use of leasing, bank loans and factoring, while in Denmark it is due to increasingly reliance on leasing contracts and equity capital. As regards the investment climate sub-index, Denmark outperforms Austria mainly because of better positioning in terms of the corruption perception. Denmark performs better also for the supply component, showing a strong evidence of internet access and use, as well as innovation capabilities and short time gaps for starting a business. Austria outperforms Denmark only in terms of the demand component.

A similar approach may be performed for each country in the sample, to identify its related peers, then to analyze the national policies, strategies and measures in comparison with the peers' ones, to make proper adjustments and recalibrations and enter into a catch-up process. Of course, there are also subjective factors that may impede the rapid development of the FinTech sector in a given country.

These factors are represented by the financial literacy, awareness and knowledge held by individuals and businesses in discriminating between the various financial products provided by the banking sector and capital market, making comparisons in terms of features and costs or return and choosing the one appropriate for their financial needs. Risk aversion and risk profile (conservative, traditional) may be another factor impeding people and businesses to turn to FinTech financing solutions.

Figure 3 synthesizes the new scores computed for each sub-index, for data reported at 2017- year end.

Figure 3. EU FinTech Index components (2017 year-end data)
Source: authors

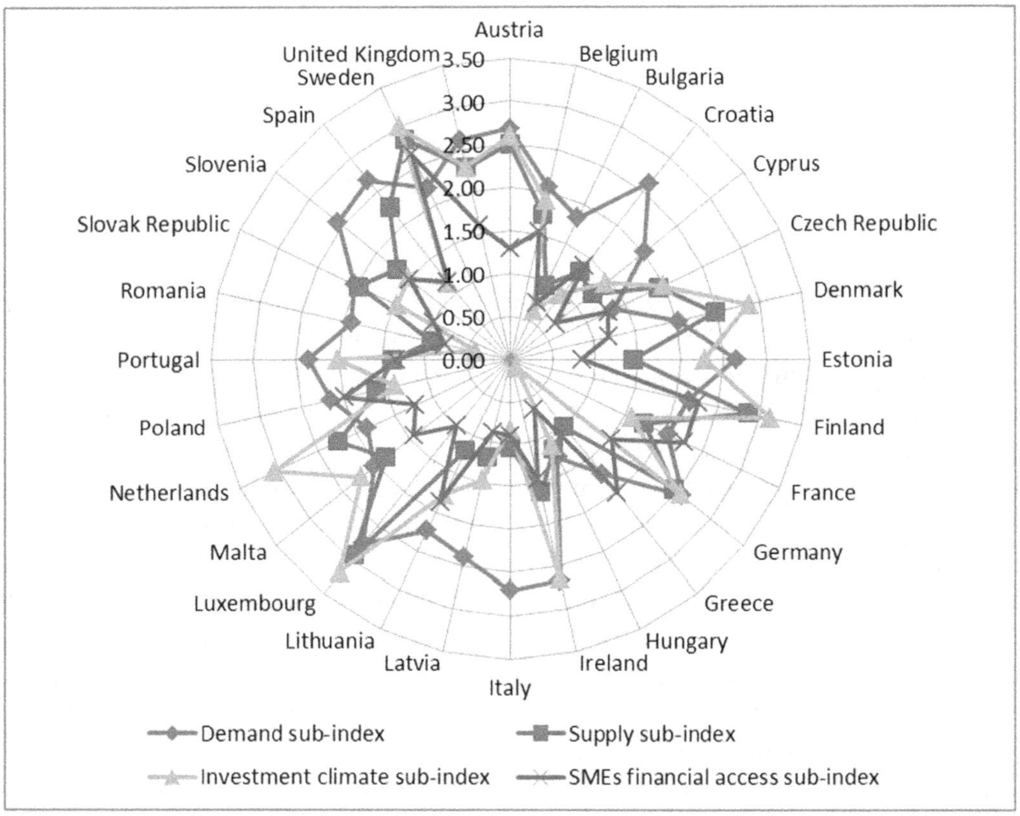

The standard deviation statistic computed for each sub-index shows that the previous classification keeps unchanged. The highest variability across countries appears in terms of the investment climate component, followed by the supply component, SMEs access and the demand component. However, the level of the statistic recorded a slight decrease, compared with the 2014 one, for 3 sub-indices and a small increase for the SMEs financial access component. Consequently, countries' national features have evolved, some indicators entering into a smooth convergence path while others being far apart.

If in 2014 Austria and Denmark registered the same FinTech index score, in 2017 Austria slightly outperforms Denmark, through better positioning in terms of demand and supply components and SMEs financial access. Three countries in the sample record the same overall index score in 2017, of 1.80

(Belgium, Estonia and Spain). When assessing the contribution of each component to the overall index score, country peculiarities appear. As regards SMEs financial access, Belgium leads with the highest score. It can be noticed that business environment in Belgium and Spain uses almost exclusively the borrowing from banks, leasing and factoring agreements, meanwhile Estonia relies on bank loans and lease contracts. None of these countries puts emphasis on the financing attracted from the capital market, through shares and bonds. The investment climate component shows that Estonia surpasses its peers due to a more even, balanced evolution in all the three indicators included in this sub-index. As regards the demand and supply sub-indices, Spain is best performing mainly due to increased individuals' reliance on financing from banks and respectively to internet use and innovation capabilities. Therefore, although the overall FinTech index level is identical for these 3 countries, the national developments are multifaceted and divergent.

Figure 4 illustrates the comparative evolution of the aggregated EU FinTech index, in two different years. In 2014, 14 countries recorded above-average index scores (1.61) while 4 countries exhibited a subunit score. In 2017, 15 out of the 28 countries registered above-average index scores (1.8) and no country shows subunit scores. Therefore, it can be noticed an improvement of the EU FinTech index score in 2017 compared with 2014, both as an average value and as absolute minimum and maximum values. All the countries considered have registered an increase of the aggregate index level in the period 2014-2017. However, the convergence path is very slow as indicated by the standard deviation statistic (from 0.48 in 2014 to 0.45 in 2017).

Figure 4. Comparison of Index scores
Source: authors

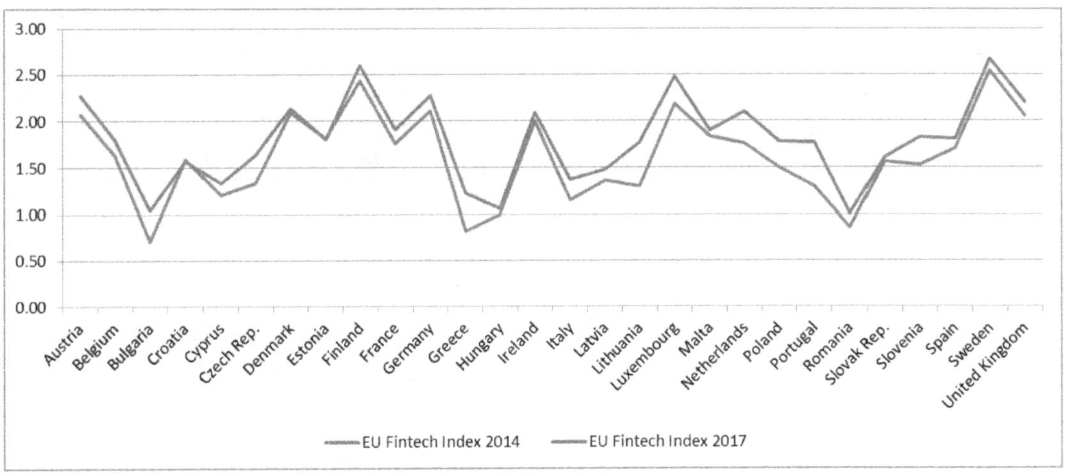

Table 3 synthesizes how the EU countries are performing based on the individual scores computed for each sub-index and overall index, by giving a snapshot on the granular ranking.

Based on the computed EU FinTech index scores we performed a descending ranking, starting from the highest / best value of the FinTech index. Sweden, Finland, Luxembourg, Germany, Spain, and Belgium have kept unchanged their place in the ranking of the EU countries in both years considered. Sweden shows the best value of the FinTech index in both years considered, so it benefits of real opportunities

Table 3. Computed scores of the sub-indices and overall index (2017 data)

Country	Demand sub-index	Supply sub-index	Investment climate sub-index	SMEs financial access sub-index	EU Fintech Index 2017	FinTech Index Ranking
Austria	2.68	2.50	2.60	1.29	2.27	5
Belgium	2.05	1.73	1.90	1.53	1.80	14
Bulgaria	1.83	0.96	0.63	0.73	1.04	27
Croatia	2.62	1.31	0.97	1.40	1.58	21
Cyprus	2.01	1.23	1.43	0.67	1.34	24
Czech Rep.	1.35	1.94	1.99	1.28	1.64	19
Denmark	2.02	2.46	2.87	1.18	2.13	7
Estonia	2.64	1.45	2.28	0.84	1.80	15
Finland	2.14	2.85	3.12	2.26	2.59	2
France	2.05	1.74	1.58	2.26	1.91	10
Germany	2.58	2.46	2.55	1.52	2.28	4
Greece	1.73	1.02	0.12	2.02	1.22	25
Hungary	1.29	1.17	1.13	0.65	1.06	26
Ireland	2.66	1.61	2.63	1.45	2.09	9
Italy	2.71	1.05	0.83	0.90	1.37	23
Latvia	2.39	1.18	1.47	0.88	1.48	22
Lithuania	2.24	1.20	1.78	1.87	1.77	18
Luxembourg	2.76	2.94	3.19	1.00	2.47	3
Malta	2.04	1.86	2.23	1.44	1.89	11
Netherlands	1.86	2.23	3.06	1.23	2.09	8
Poland	2.14	1.61	1.38	1.99	1.78	16
Portugal	2.36	1.37	2.02	1.34	1.77	17
Romania	1.91	0.94	0.41	0.78	1.01	28
Slovak Rep.	2.01	1.96	1.46	0.99	1.61	20
Slovenia	2.57	1.69	1.53	1.50	1.82	12
Spain	2.66	2.26	1.14	1.16	1.80	13
Sweden	2.21	2.84	3.00	2.64	2.67	1
UK	2.61	2.29	2.29	1.60	2.20	6

Source: authors

to further develop this segment. In the last part of the ranking a number of countries are constantly positioned, namely Bulgaria, Romania, Hungary, Greece, Italy and Cyprus. Intrinsic vulnerabilities, in terms of investment climate, SMEs financial access and supply-side factors related to infrastructure, prevent them from stimulating the FinTech sector.

In order to better discriminate between countries and to identify groups of resembling countries in terms of existing FinTech capabilities, prospects for further development and market share increase, we computed the quartiles of the EU FinTech index (the values recorded in 2017). Then, the index scores

Table 4. Countries included in each quartile range

Quartile range and code of color	EU countries	Explanation
1,01 - 1,505	Bulgaria, Cyprus, Greece, Hungary, Italy, Latvia, Romania	Countries with the lowest level of FinTech index
1,506 - 1,8	Belgium, Croatia, Czech Rep., Estonia, Lithuania, Poland, Portugal, Slovak Rep., Spain	Countries with a below-average level of FinTech index
1,81 - 2,12	France, Ireland, Netherlands, Slovenia	Countries exhibiting an above-average level of FinTech index
2,13 - 2,67	Austria, Denmark, Finland, Germany, Luxembourg, Sweden, UK	Countries with the highest level of FinTech index

Source: authors

were divided in four quartile ranges and we have classified each country within a range of variation (based on the index values), as shown in table 4 below.

Table 4 synthesizes the quartile range, the EU countries included in each range and a brief explanation on their FinTech status. 9 out of 28 countries register a below-average index level, 7 exhibit either the lowest or the highest level, meanwhile the remaining 4 countries record a good, above-average level. By summing up, most EU countries (16) are not well prepared for the FinTech challenge. The visual representation in the form of a map reveals that the core-periphery division which is present in economic literature among EU countries, in terms of economic and financial sector development, holds too when addressing the FinTech issue. The codes of color depicted in table 4 are the same with the ones in figure 5, for a better identification of countries.

Figure 5. Visual plot of the territorial spread of FinTech index scores
Source: authors

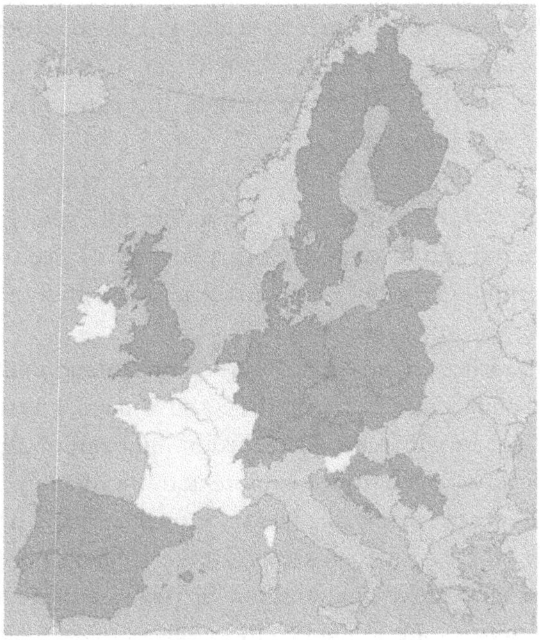

The visual findings indicate that Central and Northern Europe countries register the highest scores of the index, Western Europe countries record above-average scores, while South-Eastern European countries show the lowest development of the FinTech sector. Thus, we have obtained a visual image of the heterogeneity or different speed of implementation of FinTech innovation in Europe.

CONCLUSION

The chapter aimed to explore the potential nexus between Fintech dynamics and the process of financial integration. Existing literature (Nakaso, 2016) advocates for the enhancement of financial inclusion, due to the restructuring of financial services' features, use of smartphones for accessing financial services and providing personalized assistance and potential for globalizing basic financial services. Frost (2020) explains that Fintech can stimulate greater financial inclusion and make the financial system more inclusive and more efficient, with long-lasting beneficial effects on the economy, while the G20 report titled "G20 High-Level Principles for Digital Financial Inclusion" perceives digital financial services as essential for closing the financial inclusion gaps.

An ample report issued jointly by the World Bank Group and the IMF (2018) enumerates a series of actions that may be adopted so as to encourage the adoption of FinTech as a promoter of financial inclusion and financial markets development: i) national strategies related to financial integration and financial literacy have to be updated with a digital literacy and FinTech component; ii) increase FinTech awareness among individuals and businesses, in terms of advantages and risks, to make an informed decision making; iii) set up a dedicated authority to monitor FinTech development, promote the ease of doing business and consider international cooperation opportunities; iv) foster partnerships and promote knowledge-sharing among public and private-sector players, civil society, and other key stakeholders in the FinTech ecosystem; v) evolve toward digitized government payments, to improve revenue collection efficiency, reduce fraud and tax evasion.

This research is meant to emphasize that there is no one-size-fits-all approach for stimulating the emergence and further development of the FinTech sector in EU countries, as national dissimilarities are prevailing and catch-up is difficult to achieve. As ING (2016, p.2) argues, "there is no panacea to improve a country's FinTech supportive environment, since this is the product of a multitude of factors which are related to economic development".

The ranking of countries according to the FinTech index score indicates that few countries were able to maintain the top positions in terms of FinTech sector opportunities for growth, in the 2 years considered, while most of them recorded variations of the place held in the ranking. Another finding valid for both years is that countries occupying the last places in the hierarchy haven't succeeded to improve their scores and persistently depict the same drawbacks.

Some clustering of neighbouring countries, from a regional standpoint, is identified. Specifically, countries located in the North and Centre of Europe benefit from a domestic environment (public regulations, financial regulations, increased financial inclusion, innovation capabilities, large-scale use of internet, individuals and businesses' openness to explore and use financial services developed by other categories of providers) which acts as a catalysing factor for further FinTech boost, and hence they exhibit real development opportunities for the FinTech sector. At the opposite are the South-Eastern European countries which reveal the least attractive potential for FinTech sector development. The main vulnerabilities exhibited by these countries are related to the reduced usage of financing attracted from the capital market by businesses, the presence of unbanked population, lower standard of living as indicated by the at-risk-of-poverty-rate indicator, moderate levels of the innovation index, perceptions of unstable political climate, corruption and frequent changes in regulations.

To sum up our empirical findings, almost half of the EU countries record good prospects for further strengthening the innovative financial technology (FinTech) use by people and businesses. FinTech will hence contribute to diversifying their access to finance, by complementing the existing conventional market players, and will stimulate the financial integration through increased digital awareness and inclusion.

Our research is meant to represent only a piece in the broader FinTech framework, by mapping those countries with a similar, convergent path towards FinTech implementation and development and opening the way for future research. Emerging research directions should explore more the interplay between FinTechs and financial regulators. As Mention (2019) documents, many FinTechs have adopted consumer-centric approaches, and hence they have increased their understanding and knowledge about the local communities and their financial needs and behaviour. By strengthening collaboration between regulators and FinTech companies and transferring this specialised knowledge to financial regulators, it can be greatly enhanced the latters' awareness of financial consumer habits, behaviours, and needs. This awareness raising process, conducted in a transparent and reliable manner, creates the prospects for designing new regulatory systems in order to monitor FinTechs activity, to build consumer trust in these platforms and to develop measures for protecting these consumers of FinTech financial services.

REFERENCES

G20. (2016). *G20 High-Level Principles for Digital Financial Inclusion*. G20.

Blakstad, S., & Allen, R. (2018). Fintech Revolution, Universal Inclusion in the New Financial Ecosystem. Cham, Switzerland: Palgrave Macmillan.

Ernst & Young. (2019). *How FinTechs are a world of choice for small and medium-sized enterprises*, https://www.ey.com/en_kw/banking-capital-markets/how-fintechs-are-a-world-of-choice-for-small-and-medium-sized-enterprises

European Banking Authority. (2018). *EBA report on the impact of Fintech on incumbent credit institutions' business models*. Author.

European Commission. (2018). *Action Plan on FinTech*. Author.

European Investment Fund. (2019). *European Small Business Finance Outlook*. EIF Research & Market Analysis, Working Paper 2019/57. Luxembourg.

Financial Stability Board. (2017). *Report Financial Stability Implications from Fintech Technology*. Author.

Foo, J., Lek-Heng, L., & Ken, W. (2017). *Macroeconomics and FinTech: Uncovering Latent Macroeconomic Effects on Peer-to-Peer Lending*. https://www.researchgate.net/publication/320754864_Macroeconomics_and_FinTech_Uncovering_Latent_Macroeconomic_Effects_on_Peer-to-Peer_Lending

Frost, J. (2020). *The Economic Forces Driving FinTech Adoption across Countries*. BIS Working Papers No. 838, 2020.

Frost, J., Gambacorta, L., Huang, Y., Shin, H. S., & Zbinden, P. (2019). *BigTech and the Changing Structure of Financial Intermediation*. BIS Working Paper.

Haddad, C., & Hornuf, L. (2019). The emergence of the global Fintech market: Economic and technological determinants. *Small Business Economics*, *53*(1), 81–105. doi:10.100711187-018-9991-x

ING. (2016). *The FinTech Index. Assessing digital and financial inclusion in developing and emerging countries*. ING Economics Department.

International Monetary Fund. (2019). *Fintech, the Experience So Far.* IMF Fintech Policy Paper no. 19/024.

Kammoun, S., Loukil, S., & Loukil, Y. B. R. (2020). The Impact of FinTech on Economic Performance and Financial Stability in MENA Zone. In *Impact of Financial Technology (FinTech) on Islamic Finance and Financial Stability*. IGI Global. https://www.igi-global.com/chapter/the-impact-of-fintech-on-economic-performance-and-financial-stability-in-mena-zone/236809

Khiewngamdee, C., & Yan, H-D. (2019). The role of Fintech e-payment on APEC economic development. *Journal of Physics*, 1324.

KPMG. (2018). *The Pulse of Fintech 2018: Biannual global analysis of investment in Fintech*. KPMG.

McKinsey. (2016). *Digital Finance for all: powering inclusive growth in emerging countries*. Author.

Mention, A. L. (2019). The Future of Fintech. *Research Technology Management*, *62*(4), 59–63. doi:10.1080/08956308.2019.1613123

Nakaso, H. (2016). *FinTech – Its Impacts on Finance, Economies and Central Banking*. Remarks at the University of Tokyo - Bank of Japan Joint Conference in Tokyo on “FinTech and the Future of Money”. https://www.boj.or.jp/en/announcements/press/koen_2016/data/ko161118a.pdf

Nassiry, D. (2018). *The Role of Fintech in Unlocking Green Finance: Policy Insights for Developing Countries*. ADBI Working Paper 883. https://www.adb.org/sites/default/files/publication/464821/adbi-wp883.pdf

Puschmann, T. (2017). Fintech. *Business & Information Systems Engineering*, *59*(1), 69–76. doi:10.100712599-017-0464-6

Roubini, N., & Byrne, P. (2018). *The Blockchain Pipe Dream*. Project Syndicate. https://www.project-syndicate.org/commentary/blockchain-technologylimited-applications-by-nouriel-roubini-and-preston-byrne-2018-03

Schweitzer, M., & Barkley, B. (2017). *Is ‘Fintech’ Good for Small Business Borrowers? Impacts on Firm Growth and Customer Satisfaction*. https://www.federalreserve.gov/conferences/files/is-fintech-good-for-small-business-borrowers.pdf

Thakor, A. V. (2019). *Fintech and Banking*. Available at SSRN: https://ssrn.com/abstract=3332550

World Bank Group & IMF. (2018). *The Bali Fintech Agenda*. Chapeau Paper, September 2018.

World Economic Forum. (2017). *Beyond Fintech: How the successes and failures of new entrants are reshaping the financial system.* Available at: http://www3.weforum. org/docs/Beyond_Fintech_-_A_Pragmatic_Assessment_of_ Disruptive_Potential_in_Financial_Services.pdf

ADDITIONAL READING

European Central Bank. 2019. A binary future? How digitalisation might change banking, https://www.bankingsupervision.europa.eu/press/speeches/date/2019/html/ssm.sp190311~2af7fb032e.en.html

European Central Bank. 2019. Financial markets and the digital revolution, https://www.bankingsupervision.europa.eu/press/speeches/date/2019/html/ssm.sp191126~0a1bb2038c.en.html

European Commission. 2020. Digital Finance, https://ec.europa.eu/info/business-economy-euro/banking-and-finance/digital-finance_en

International Monetary Fund. 2018. Digitization of Money and Finance: Challenges and Opportunities, https://www.imf.org/en/News/Articles/2018/05/08/sp050818-digitization-of-money-and-finance-challenges-and-opportunities

International Monetary Fund. 2019. Framing the Debate on Fintech: Current Trends and Continuing Policy Concerns, https://www.imf.org/en/News/Articles/2019/04/01/sp040119-framing-the-debate-on-fintech-current-trends-and-continuing-policy-concerns

OECD. 2018. Financial Markets, Insurance and Private Pensions: Digitalisation and Finance, http://www.oecd.org/finance/Financial-markets-insurance-pensions-digitalisation-and-finance.pdf

PriceWaterhouseCoopers. 2016. Blurred lines: How FinTech is shaping Financial Services, https://www.pwc.com/il/en/home/assets/pwc_fintech_global_report.pdf

PriceWaterhouseCoopers. 2019. Global FinTech Report 2019, https://www.pwc.com/gx/en/industries/financial-services/fintech-survey.html

Tanda, A., & Schena, C.-M. (2019). *FinTech, BigTech and Banks.* Digitalisation and Its Impact on Banking Business Models, Palgrave Macmillan Studies in Banking and Financial Institutions. doi:10.1007/978-3-030-22426-4

KEY TERMS AND DEFINITIONS

Alternative Lenders: A broader category of intermediaries (e.g. online platforms providing crowd funding services), apart from traditional financial intermediaries in the banking and stock market.

Digital Transformation in Financial Services: Reliance on digital technologies by financial intermediaries, to innovate and improve the customer experience in accessing and using financial services.

Financial Ecosystem: Encompasses the entire range of market players in the financial system, having a role in efficient and sound capital allocation to sustainable, value adding projects, by matching savers and investors.

Financial Inclusion: Smooth access to appropriate and affordable financial products and services that meet the needs of individuals and businesses.

FinTech: Financial innovation emerged due to technological developments.

FinTech Supportive Environment: A combination of country-specific factors, related to economic, financial, regulatory, political and demographical issues that determine the further development of FinTech sector.

Green Finance: Designates the financing channeled particularly to investment projects that bring not only economic and financial value, but also environmental and/or social benefits.

Peer-to-Peer Lending: Loans provided directly between lenders and borrowers (individuals or businesses), by using an online platform which connects them, instead of applying for a bank loan.

RegTech: Reliance on FinTech in the process of verifying the compliance of the periodic reports and of the activity of a bank with the regulations in force.

SupTech: Use of new analytical technologies (FinTech) for improving the efficiency, timeliness and accuracy of the prudential supervisory activity.

Chapter 2
Strategies and Business Models of Banks in Front of the FinTech and BigTech Competition

Lech Kurkliński
Warsaw School of Economics, Poland

Stanislaw Kasiewicz
Warsaw School of Economics, Poland

ABSTRACT

The purpose of the chapter is to evaluate selected strategies and business models as key tools for competing within the financial sector in the digital environment, especially the position of banks against FinTechs and BigTechs, from the perspective of the risk culture factor. The main hypothesis says the success of the process of adapting banks to new competition rules requires the development of individual strategies and business models, taking into account an adequate organizational culture and, within it, a risk culture. To verify this assumption, the relationships between significant competitive features of banks in the digital environment, risk management, and risk culture are presented. The analyses of selected strategies and digital business models are trying to answer the question, to what extent it is possible to implement a new approach, useful in constructing effective solutions for banks to reduce the threats, especially created by FinTechs and BigTechs.

INTRODUCTION

The purpose of this chapter is to evaluate selected banks' strategies and business models as key tools for competing in the digital environment, especially towards FinTechs and BigTechs, from the perspective of the risk culture factor.

The process of banks' transformation forced by growing competition from non-bank financial institutions and the wave of new technologies as well as the occurrence of many negative external conditions has serious consequences. It makes majority of banks lost and unaware of how to compete

DOI: 10.4018/978-1-7998-4390-0.ch002

in these circumstances. This is due to the fact that "New competition rules bring to the world of strategy a murderous pace, uncertainty and chaos, global competition, pressure to constantly improve and transform the business model of an enterprise." The functioning of modern companies reminds travelers of the nineteenth century, who try to break through the Amazon jungles with only a compass at their disposal (Obłój, 2002). Nevertheless banks are becoming aware that they must adapt to the new rules of the market game. The main hypothesis formulated in this chapter is the following: the success of the process of adapting banks to new competition rules requires developing individual strategies and business models, while taking into account not only new technologies but also an adequate organizational culture, including a risk culture. The relationships between significant competitive features of banks in the digital environment, risk management based on new technologies and risk culture are presented. For this purposes, the analysis of selected strategies and digital business models was conducted, on how to create a new approach in constructing effective solutions for banks to reduce the risks, especially created by FinTechs and BigTechs.

Authors try to present an original methodological value, first of all based on the logical coherence between three issues: role of strategy, digital competition and risk culture. Secondly, it is related to the differentiation of approach to traditional banks' business models in the face of contemporary challenges. Thirdly, underestimating the risk culture, as is the case in many financial institutions, generates threats of weakening their market position. T. R. Viscelli, D.R. Hermanson, M.S. Beasley (2017) discuss issues such as poor integration of risk in strategy, weak risk culture and lack of clarity in roles and risk reporting.

The well-known models of strategy, built in the second part of the 20th century, are no longer adequate for the present business world. The competition is becoming more complex, dynamic, discontinuous and uncertain. Industry boundaries are blurring. The life cycles of products and companies are becoming dramatically shorter. Technological progress and a changing environment are quickly transforming business activities. High economic and political uncertainty are becoming increasingly apparent. This trend is likely to continue in the foreseeable future. Under these circumstances, there are various recommendations, how to meet the contemporary challenges of the competition. First-class consulting companies provide advice. For example, BCG proposes (Kimura, Reeves & Whitaker, 2019):

- increasing the self-learning pace of the organization,
- the use of ecosystems with the participation of many companies,
- combining competition in the physical and digital world,
- preference for new ideas and their quick implementation,
- increasing resistance in the face of growing uncertainty.

In the further part of the chapter, authors are trying to develop an answer to the question, how banks' digital strategies and business models can meet these challenges and fit into the conditions of the contemporary competition.

DIGITAL BANKING STRATEGIES AND BUSINESS MODELS

The transformation of financial institutions to the digital age is an issue more widely deliberated on, which is confirmed by the increasing number of publications (Ismail, Khater, & Zaki, 2017). They include challenges related to the development of business strategies and models, their implementation and impact assessment. Each of these thematic areas concerns in particular issues such as future conditions and induce the involvement of management boards and employees, where to start, how to proceed, what evaluation systems to use, etc. Answers for many of these questions were found by the strategic management academics quite a long time ago . The proposed prescriptions were created for typical conditions of competing at the end of the 20th century, not in the environment of online and mobile competition. This "old" approach loses from sight a key aspect in formulating contemporary digital strategies and models, i.e. the role of technology. However, the analysis of technological solutions alone is not enough, it should be supplemented with factors determining the success or failure of its implementation, as shown by various types of strategies contained in Table 1.

Table 1. Digital transformation management strategies

Strategy type	Explanation
Spin-Off	Independent spin-off or a separate organizational unit to ensure adequate staffing and help follow potentially disruptive innovations.
Lender	Early preparation and market entry to gain a first-mover advantage.
Expert opinion	Gathering information from a wide range of sources like technological staff, cooperation partners, customers and external experts to support the transformation process despite internal resistance from stakeholders.
Trial and Error	Testing products and markets to achieve fully developed software, especially for high-quality products.
Recruitment	Recruiting innovative and experienced staff to help with the transformation process or cooperating with universities and lead customers.
Direct Sales	Distributing on-demand software directly or by financially incentivizing resellers to promote on-demand sales.
Step-by-Step	A ramping-up approach by focusing on smaller solutions in the beginning and expanding the customer base with time.
Partnership and Ecosystem	Gaining access to technology expertise through a strong technological partner to adapt to disruptive technology faster.
Visionary Top Management	Top management vision communication can accelerate the transformation process and motivate employees.

Source: Ismail, Khater, & Zaki, 2017, p. 21.

In the digital competition of financial institutions, the strategy is built by blocks that cover various aspects, including database management, changes in the organizational structure, differences in risk, and finally taking into account an adhesive (kind of glue) bonding these elements, i.e. the appropriate organizational culture. That is why it is so important that the way the organization works is coherent and contributes not only to survival, but also to development. Ultimately, the final decision is made by the customer who makes a decision whether to buy or not given services or products. Hence, building the future must be based on creating benefits for customers and their positive experience. Such an approach can be found in emerging proposals for digital transformation strategies. They often have many common features and can be divided into four different dimensions (Matt, Hess & Benlian, 2015):

a) usage of technology,
b) changes in value creation,
c) structural changes,

d) financial aspects.

It is understandable that the digital strategy should refer to these cross-sections serve as a key concept for: integration, coordination, setting priorities and shall be a guide for the bank's transformation. Therefore, it should go beyond processes and include the essence of the value proposition provided to the client. The use of new technologies in the bank's strategy illustrates its ability to independently create or assimilate innovation. On one hand, it is connected to an improvement of operational efficiency, but on the other hand, banks should guarantee an increase in the satisfaction of final recipients. This leads to the determining the key role of IT and to the bank's technological ambitions. At first it must decide whether a particular financial institution wants to become a market leader in the usage of technology with the possibility of developing its own standards or whether its strategy will be based on deeper and multilateral cooperation with other entities. Each of these two scenarios implies different types and levels of risk. The usage of technology has a fundamental impact on the creation of a new formula for positioning the bank in the value chain addressed to customers. As always in the face of change, there are dilemmas with determining selection criteria between existing solutions and new - proposed ones. Structural changes are needed when an organization wants to implement different technologies and forms of value creation. This kind of action relates to the organizational structure, but also products, processes or competences. If the scope of modifications is modest, it may be more reasonable to integrate new operations with existing corporate structures. In case of significant changes, it would be effective to create a separate bank subsidiary. Mainly this is due to the problem with organizational culture, because the current one creates serious barriers, blocking efficient digital transformation. The high level of uncertainty and associated risks are forcing a different approach and therefore a new risk culture. Usually, large banks have the resources to implement new business models. What are the biggest obstacles to their progress? It depends on the current global and local environment. Often new solutions are not accepted eventually, because they are becoming replaced by even newer ones, the costs of their implementation exceeds the benefits, or do not reach the sufficient scale, e.g. due to a lack of standardization, etc. A proper concept is required to provide a structural move in this chaos and stimulate the transition to bolder thinking while maintaining minimum security. S. Khanna and H. Martins have identified six strategies for banks which can fuel their future growth and ensure success (Khanna & Martins, 2018, p. 2):

a) develop your core business into the right ecosystem,
b) build a financial supermarket,
c) expand your value proposition on a customer's journey,
d) monetize your data,
e) become a factory supplying products or infrastructure,
f) become a digital competitor.

In the face of increasing uncertainty, it is an open question whether these strategies can be victorious, or whether they might be implemented autonomously, or whether it will be necessary to build a strategic hybrid consisting of some of the options mentioned above.

The first type of strategy (a) raises some doubts about success. It is based on abandoning the provision of classic customer services directly provided by a bank. It is aimed at gradually building the banking ecosystem based on external, not fully controlled suppliers. The problematic nature of such proceedings stems from the fact that significant risks related to synchronization of the inherited infrastructure with the new one, required structural changes, regulatory regime and management system as well as organizational culture are often ignored. Digitization changes sustained pillars of the bank, but introduces other management rules and mechanisms, e.g. employee liability issues, new reporting system, resource allocation, etc. The next strategies of S. Khann and H. Martins present some advantages, but also weaknesses. The construction of a financial supermarket means providing a wide range of more or less developed own and external services through own distribution channels. It is a proposal that most financial institutions strive to implement in the digital environment. Like in the first strategy, there are doubts whether it will be possible to ensure high quality and integrity of bank's offer, especially having the number of own and external services on a scale not previously observed. These services can be offered by entities with different regulatory, technical or risk management cultures. In relation to the third strategy, this type of threat seems to be less important, as it focuses on the client, forcing a higher level of service integration and quality. The issues contained in the popular concepts of customer experience and customer journey fit this strategy. The idea of monetizing data by banks is slowly becoming common. However, due to the bank's formal status, some forms of monetization related to data are not allowed by regulatory systems or may be treated as too controversial. In relation to the fifth strategy (e), it means weakening the main advantage which is the relationship with the customer. Finally, moving towards a digital competitor's strategy seems much easier for entities that are not limited by a regulatory bound, e.g. technology companies. Especially giants from the group of GAFA, or BAT have huge advantages. The number of legislative limitations is pretty low and it seems that they have enormous lobbying power. In this situation, banks will find it difficult to compete with BigTechs, when they fully decide to enter the financial services market.

The above-presented review of the strategies for the digital transformation of banks clearly indicates how important the differences between the current functioning of traditional institutions (such as banks) are in relation to the present digital revolution. First of all the attention is focused on the pace of action (speed of change), flexibility (responding to volatility and uncertainty) and approach to these new conditions, i.e. organizational culture, including creativity, ability to learn, making decisions and accepting risks (see figure 1).

Figure 1. What is the biggest difference between working in a digital environment versus a traditional one?
Source: Kane, Phillips, Copulsky & Andrus, 2019.

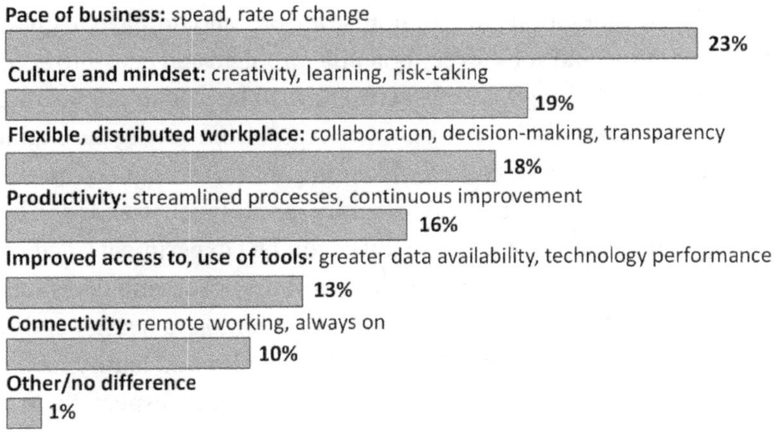

These circumstances pose new challenges for managers, in particular in such traditional institutions as banks (see figure 2).

Figure 2. What is the most important skill organizational leaders should have to succeed in a digital workplace?
Source: Kane, Phillips, Copulsky & Andrus, 2019.

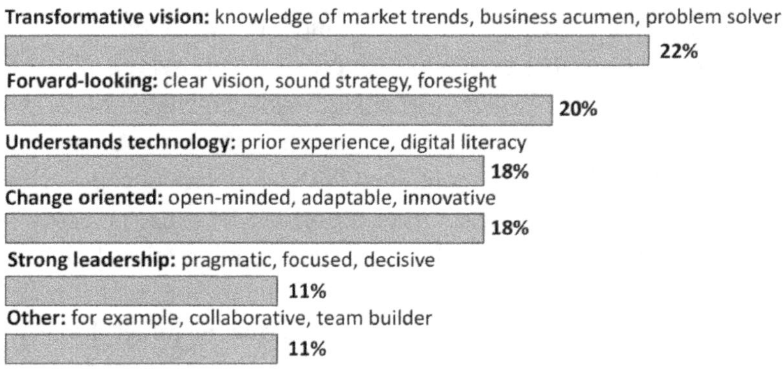

The challenges facing organizations are standing in front of leaders. In such complex and changing conditions, it is difficult to fix troublesome problems, especially when cultural barriers appear. Only real, genuine leaders can handle it. Authentic leadership concept shows how it is possible to achieve success. This kind of people is self-aware (about e.g. their strengths, limitations, and emotions) and they are not focused on a social engineering. They show their real selves to their followers. and don't hide their mistakes or weaknesses. What is coherent with agile and ethic approach. Authentic leaders realize that being self-actualized is an endless journey, never complete. They are mission driven and result-oriented, ahead of their own self-interest. They lead with their heart (showing emotions, direct communication), not just pure calculations. The key role is played by motivation of followers to achieve goals through sincerity and positive moral attitude. Authentic leaders have in mind the long-term, not in just beating quarterly estimates. It is visible at the Amazon case and the role of J. Bezos. Leaders must realize that to nurture individuals and a company requires hard work and patience, but this approach pays large dividends even in such turbulent time (Kruse, 2013).

Summing up the above considerations, the digital strategies should have a smaller range of issues considered, not striving to capture and solve every potential problem and take into account all conditions. Being aware of the key role of technology, attention should also be paid to other factors determining the success or failure of implementing digital transformation. Apart from having the engineering knowledge, it is important to have the ability to assess the holistic impact of technology on the bank's operation (including social issues), demonstrate the ability to identify development trends and the behaviour of key market players (especially outside the sector), be ready to conduct experiments, determine the individual responsibility of employees for the risk, as well as the possibility of wrong decisions.

The management boards of banks are paying much more attention to quarter and annual results. This is due to the fact that the future becomes uncertain, highly complex and hardly recognizable. It is more difficult to determine which decision will become a success or failure, especially in relation to the long time horizon. That is why the efforts for an improvement of a market position as well as the efficiency of operations are determined by short-term assessments. Mainly for these reasons, the key management tool, which was the bank's strategy, covering a long period (often over 5 years), is gradually losing its importance. Under these conditions, the business model is a new concept of company management. It has started to be more often used in practice since the beginning of the 21st century, because it helps to generate income in these turbulent conditions, primarily determined by the digital revolution. This tool is defined differently by individual researchers. R. Amit and C. Zott (2001, p. 493) assume that "the business model presents content, structures and management that allow for building the value through the use of existing business opportunities and opportunities. The business model of the company is an important tool for implementing innovation and a key source of value creation for the company as well as for its suppliers, partners and clients." Due to the recent downward trend in banks' income and profit margins, much attention is paid to cost reduction as a factor leading to increased efficiency. Structurally, employees' salaries constitute almost 60% of banks' costs, the IT-sphere occupies the second place with an approximate 20% share (Gopalan, Jain, Kalani & Tan, 2012, pp. 30-35). In general, banks have the highest IT spending among all sectors of the economy in relation to their revenues. Moreover, their expected further growth is equally important. The second major factor affecting the operation of banks is the recent regulatory tsunami. More precisely, a wave of severe regulations, is imposing many restrictions on the operation of banks, also affecting the cost side. Regulatory requirements absorb IT resources significantly. At the same time, adapting to new legislation is becoming the highest priority for banks. But these regulations can be compared to the Swiss cheese. On one hand, they are very intense and severe, on the other, serious gaps are created, such as unregulated new phenomena caused by the wave of technology changes. But it isn't easy to regulate the digital business. Some legislative ideas are controversial and they are scaring companies (Howard, 2019).

A characteristic feature of most banks is the tendency to control almost all aspects of their business, visible in a high degree of reliance on their own products and distribution channels. This means that despite step by step wide-spreading outsourcing, banks still use the services of partners to a small extent, opposite to the automotive industry. The banks are accused of poor performance results because of the low level of industrialization and standardization. Research shows that for 700 comprehensive banking processes, approx. 50% can be automated. It means that banks' operational and business models will evolve towards intelligent automation, cooperation and industrialization by 2025 (Gasser et al. 2017, p. 8).

A slightly neglected area that affects not only the development, but also the implementation of the bank's business model is its organizational culture, especially the risk culture (Agarwal, Kallapur, 2018). This is due to the pressure of the influx of many innovations. The level of actual creation and absorption of innovations depend very much on the prevailing culture - values, beliefs and assumptions are considered to be the key elements in both enhancing and inhibiting innovation. While ad hocratic cultures (more common in FinTechs) could enhance the development of new products or services, hierarchical cultures (typical in incumbent banks) inhibit innovation (Valencia, Valle, Jiménez, 2010). What matters is not only the invention of a new technology or proposing streamlining organizational solutions, but, above all, the ability to implement them successfully.

The business scheme (template) proposed by A. Osterwalder and Y. Pigneur in 2012 is well known. According to them, "A business model describes the rationale of how an organization creates, delivers, and captures value." (Osterwalder & Pigneur, 2010, p. 14) The main elements of this model are presented below (see figure 3).

Figure 3. Business model according to A. Osterwalder and Y. Pigneur
Source: Osterwalder & Pigneur, 2010, pp. 18-19.

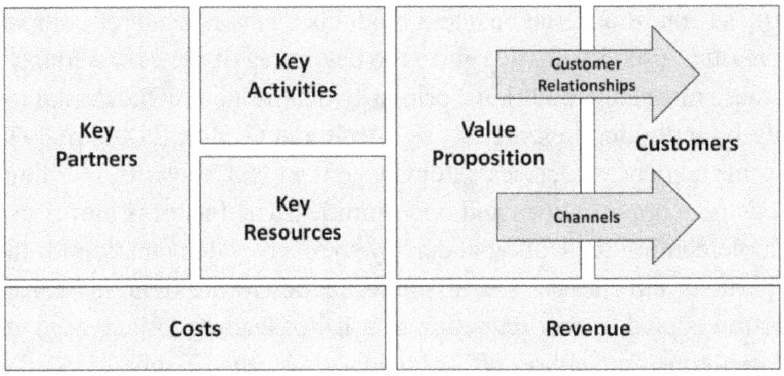

Business models for digital banks should consist of the same components. They differ in approaches, accents and the detailed description. According to Ch. Skinner (2018), the essence of the digital model of the bank boils down to the fact that the following functional areas (divisions) are separated: back office, data transformation and transaction unit and front office.

In the case of a new generation bank, its specificity is based on an extensive digital platform, which uses inter-operational applications and programming interfaces. In addition, data analytics and various algorithms are used. It is open to other banks and third parties. It is moving away from closing customers in a cage of outdated technological and management solutions directed towards the interior of the bank as well as giving up the pursuit of full control of all service processes. New generation bank focuses on developing a culture of cooperation, partnership and harmonization of activities in the external environment. The digital bank may become the main conductor in this ecosystem. The sources of income mainly come from being a curator and integrator. There is no doubt that traditional business model, management architecture, IT infrastructure and organizational culture must change.

One of the proposals of business models for the digital bank was proposed by B. Robinson (2016). According to him, there are 4 strategic options open to banks (figure 4). They differ in the scope of the bank's own operations (X-axis) and in terms of profitability (Y-axis).

The **traditional-universal banking model** is characterized by the fact that it provides a rich product offer and requires a high level of assets, which makes it unattractive and unprofitable. The same applies to the **infrastructure provider**, which is also burdened with a significant balance sheet scope. It generates low profitability because of low-interest margins and high fixed costs. The **aggregator** gives the possibility of very high profitability based on the low intensity of assets. The success of its implementation is determined by the ability to aggregate and adapt offers delivered by various partners to the variety of customer' needs. Therefore, the open **model of the electronic platform**, acting to a large extent analogous to the integrated platforms operated by BigTechs, probably constitutes the best way to obtain satisfactory results. The stabilizing element is vertical integration and the scale of operations, based on an own offer as well as offer from third parties. However, there are still existed threats associated with ensuring homogeneity and quality.

An alternative business model proposal for digital banks was presented by Capgemini (2018). It is a kind of ecosystem (see figure 5 and figure 6).

Figure 4. Business models according to B. Robinson
Source: Robinson, 2016, p. 2

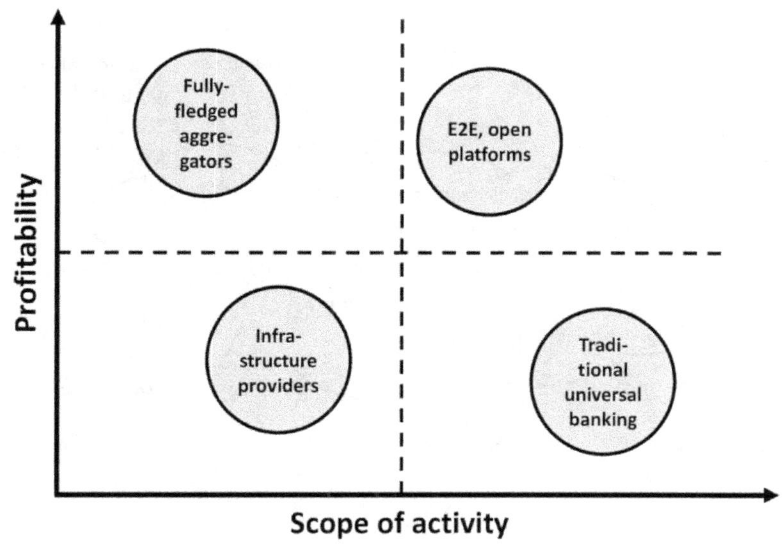

Figure 5. Today and tomorrow bank in transition
Source: Capgemini, 2018, p.1.

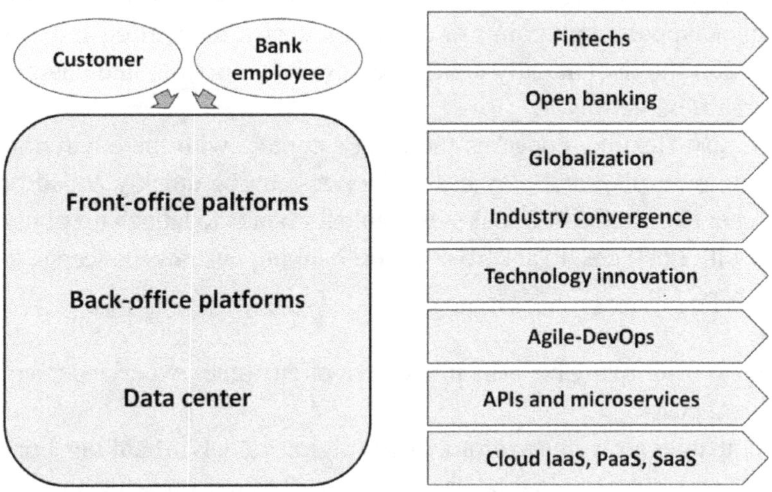

DevOps - a methodology for integrating development and operation as well as quality assurance; API - application programming interface; IaaS - Infrastructure as a service - one of the cloud computing models. The supplier is providing the entire IT infrastructure, such as e.g. virtualized equipment, adjusted to the user's needs; PaaS - Platform as a service is one of the cloud computing models too. It means the provision of a virtual work environment by the supplier; SaaS - Software as a service - one of the cloud computing models in which the application is stored and executed on the computers of the service provider and it is made available to users via the internet.

Figure 6. Bank of the future ecosystem player
Source: Capgemini, 2018, p.1.

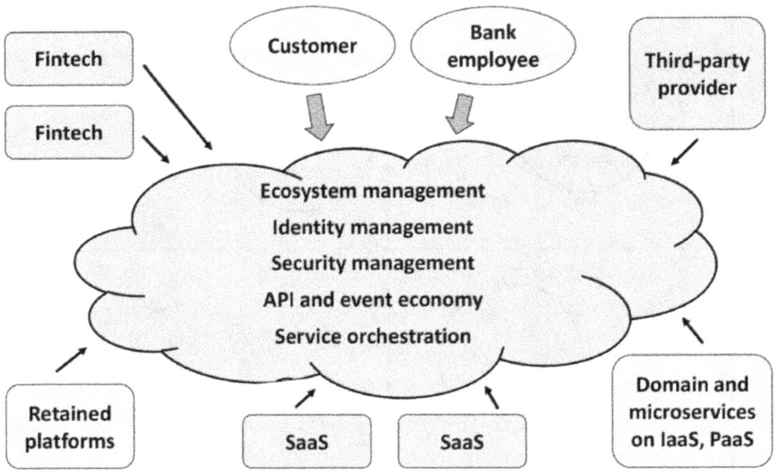

Capgemini recommends a three-layer banking model:

1. The first, simplified bank layer (core), with minimal functionality, is reduced to the basic ledger.
2. The second one is agile with non-linear or limited digital functions such as customer management and multi-channel support at all points of contact, security, integration and analysis. In this layer, it is possible to add the dynamically configured products, pricing and charging prices (fees and interest rates) in a flexible way.
3. The third layer, also flexible, concerns the bank's contact with the environment. It allows third parties to operate on a plug-and-play basis. Services can be quickly added or removed to meet changing customer expectations. It makes possible for banks to launch new business models based on cooperation with FinTechs, to absorb new non-banking business concepts, leading to increased value for customers.

This model seems to offer many benefits in the area of customer experience, agile architecture and reduction of operational costs.

Some software companies are trying to promote new digital models in banking. For example, Backbase recommends three variants of business models (see figure 7) to meet new technological and regulatory challenges, especially resulting from the expansion of open banking and the usage of API (Backbase, 2017).

Revenue-Sharing Models

This applies to entities using APIs for external service providers and it is based on the business model and applications developing outside the bank. The sharing concept may include a split of margins or sales revenues. Numerous versions of this type of model can be applied because of different methods of dividing revenues between banks and third parties: in a fixed way, flexible or hybrid.

Figure 7. Business models according to Backbase
Source: Backbase, 2017, p. 10.

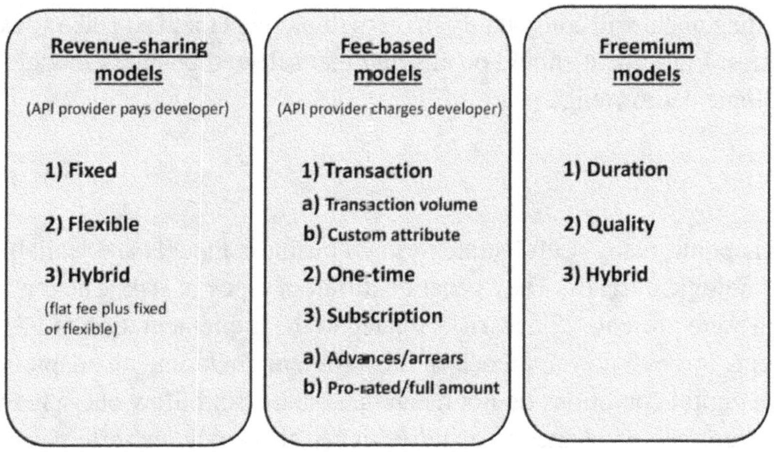

Fee-Based Models

This model is popular in the payment industry. It is used, for example, by PayPal or appears in the usage of credit cards. Acting as an intermediary of banking services offered by means of API requires the appropriate allocation of charges. Their level may depend on the type of transaction and size. The billing structure can evolve. Generally, it depends on the type of payment: one-off or a subscription.

Freemium Models

This model is an experiment. Freemium is based on offering services free of charge temporarily or permanently. For example, when customers collect a limited number of points, a bank is changing their status. The goal is to achieve a situation when a customer becomes dependent on a particular institution's services and then some forms of fees are introduced. The implementation of this model requires conducting a verification, which form of application will ultimately bring the most beneficial effect for the bank. There is a certain analogy here to the business models of integrated digital platforms (e.g. from the GAFA group).

The company PwC also dealt with digital business models (Sandrock, & Fringes, 2016). Based on an analysis of six cases: Buddybank, Number26, Treefin, Satispay, the Open Bank project and Figo, eight recommendations were made:

First of all, banks can't develop their business models without having a strategy. Secondly, it would be the best to combine preparations of strategy together with business. These works should be carried out simultaneously and teams involved in these tasks should work closely together. This would ensure their consistency. Thirdly, the digital strategy ought to be made as synthetic as possible. Fourthly, for creating a business model, it is useful to implement the CANVAS template (the mentioned business model according to A. Osterwalder and Y. Pigneur). Fifthly, from the beginning a bank should try to diagnose a desire organizational culture as thoroughly as possible, including a culture of bank's own risk, identify how to manage it. Sixthly, it is important not only to develop subsequent versions of the business model, but also to perform experiments to determine how to achieve the goals in the most effective way.

Seventhly, the components of the business model delivering success in the first stage of implementation should be prioritized. At the same time, it should be clear for employees that conducted activities are not apparent, and the management will consistently strive to implement them and take advantage of emerging business opportunities. Eighthly, it should be ensured that selected business model is developed using professional technological knowledge.

* * *

Summarizing this point, many useful strategies and business models are available for banks trying to adapt to new technological trends. They generate different types of risk. The report prepared for the Warsaw Banking Institute presents 22 new risks related to the implementation of PSD2 (Kostro, 2020). Such variety of threats forces a new approach to this problem, including an adaptation of an appropriate risk culture. The digital conditions do not mean that banks can follow one scheme or a template of conduct. A management has no chance to achieve higher efficiency and effectiveness if the sense of implementing an appropriate strategy for a bank is rejected by the organization itself (e.g. employees). Because of new, contemporary conditions, a bank's conduct should not duplicate the patterns according to which a strategy was developed for a stable and mature banking market (like in the 20th century). The strong recommendation relates to the necessity to adapt not only to new technological conditions, but also to uncertainty (Courtney, Kirkland, & Vigueri, 1997; Krupski, 2007; Koźmiński, 2004). Despite adverse and turbulent conditions banks should have a proper strategy, It helps to keep the consistency of whole activity, adapt to technological and market challenges, verify progress according to accepted measures etc. But of course, it requires a higher level of flexibility and ability to change.

FINTECHS AND BIGTECHS AS THE MAIN COMPETITORS FOR THE DIGITAL BANK

The subject of this part will be companies in the FinTech sector, including BigTechs, which have become new, flexible and aggressive players. They accelerate the transformation of the financial services market. There is the controversy around the definition of FinTech term concerning objective and subjective approach. According to treating FinTechs as firms, it is important to present the dynamics of the development of this kind of entities. Generally, they can adopt three main strategies of competing with banks on the financial market. The first is based on cooperation with banks by providing fragmentary solutions geared to the front or back office. The second means coopetition, i.e. simultaneous competition and cooperation. The third strategy is the autonomous offering of selected banking services (competition). FinTechs are highly diversified, micro and small entities dominate. However, global technology companies called BigTechs are becoming more active and threaten incumbent banks.

Generally goals, management systems, as well as regulatory culture and risks are different for banks and FinTechs. As a result, their partnership and cooperation often do not go harmoniously, which was openly admitted by the ING high representative at the Banking Risk Congress in Poland in 2019. Within a competitive approach, the perception of competition between FinTechs and banks has evolved over time, since the predictions of the potential, complete failure of banks to the point of reaching a certain structural balance. Today, it is still difficult to determine who will prove to be the winner in the long run: banks or FinTechs, or maybe BigTechs.

Determining the FinTech sector has not come to a precise and universally accepted definition. It raises some controversy and translates into difficulties in studying the current state of the size of this market, forecasting its potential growth, as well as categorizing services provided by FinTechs. Generally, the term FinTech comes from the abbreviation for financial technologies dedicated to the latest IT and telecommunications technologies, improving the process of providing financial services (Czugan, 2017, pp. 28-29). It is closer to a subjective approach. Such a definition is proposed by the Financial Stability Board (2017), where FinTechs are "financial innovations based on new technologies, which may result in new business models, applications, processes or products that may have a significant impact on financial markets and institutions and the way of providing financial services". According to the objective approach, the FinTech is a new sector of financial services, which consists of companies that are not traditional financial service providers, using innovative technologies. R. S. Freedman (2006) describes these entities as involved in building modelling systems, pricing and processing financial products. P. Schueffel (2016) has defined the FinTech as a new financial sector that uses technology to improve financial activity, which has resulted from a review of over 200 scientific research over the past forty years. The definition of the FinTech sector according to the company EY refers to the industry, which includes companies starting operations at an early stage, but also entities with increased scale of operations, high degree of maturity, and even firms providing services from outside the financial sector (EY, 2017). This definition includes BigTechs – the giant technological corporations. The most common opinions are that FinTech is a sector of entities using modern information technologies in the area of financial services (Solarz, 2017, pp. 235-236). The service offered by the FinTech company meets at least one of the following criteria (Carmona, et al, 2018, p. 47):

a) it is a technology service addressed to financial institutions,
b) it provides a new business model in the sphere of financial services,
c) it offers added value for any of the financial services market stakeholders (mainly customers).

Such characterization of FinTechs allows to include in this group: licensed banks, new small technological companies (start-ups), large corporations, as well as other entities operating in the shadow economy.

The importance of the FinTech sector can be considered in two aspects: in the perspective of the development of the whole financial services industry and its digitization. Innovations transform various types of existing services, modifying them or introducing new ones, including loans, deposits, investments, payments, affecting the sphere of risk, cost, price management, etc. Advanced digital technologies are becoming destructive for traditional services and banks themselves. The key role is played by blockchain, cloud technology, analysis of large data sets, Internet of Things, robo-advisory and artificial intelligence. Requirements such as flexibility, transparency, in-depth adaptation to customer needs and ensuring maximum comfort are becoming very important. Simultaneously they also change the client's psychological attitude to the financial industry.

The wave of financial innovation is expanding because technological advances allow for a deeper recognition of consumer behaviour and preferences. Understanding how people buy services or products, acquire and use the information to make purchasing decisions is the foundation for success for any type of business. The demand for financial innovations has roots arising from the growing expectations of customers in terms of higher personalization and convenience. Step by step entry barriers are being reducing and the implementation of new technologies is accelerating. The issue of competing FinTechs

Figure 8. New emerging FinTech trends
Source: Mohamed & Ali, 2019, p. 23.

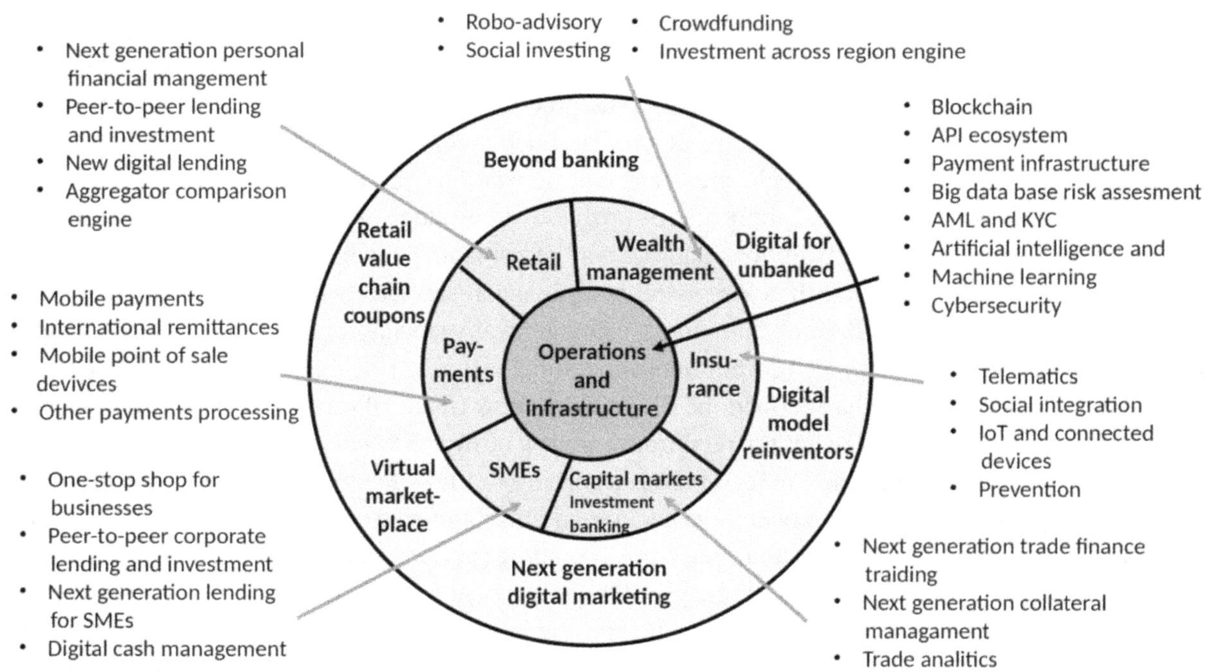

with traditional banks is fascinating and multi-threaded. The huge scale of changes and new initiatives caused by FinTechs on the financial services market can be observed at the figure 8.

However, the most important determinants for the development of the FinTech sector are customer reviews. Reports prepared on this topic indicate a large potential for the future growth of this sector. The possibilities of accelerating the development of the FinTech sector may be evidenced by the example that in the United Kingdom there was an increase in digital clients in the entire financial sector in the years 2015 - 2017 from the share of 10% of total clients to 30% (EY, 2017, p. 3). In general, the entire European alternative finance market is growing at an incredible pace, as illustrated in the figure 9.

According to data from 2015, among the European countries on the alternative finance market, the Great Britain has just gained a great advantage (5608 million Euro). The next countries are: France (EUR 444 million), Germany (EUR 322 million) (Carmona et al, 2018, p. 24). However, the United States has a global leadership position in the FinTech sphere, with a total investment of approximately USD 43 billion (2017). China, already mentioned the Great Britain and India occupy the next positions. The European Union (excluding the UK) was in the 5th position with investments at USD 3.6 billion, which represents 12% of the total amount invested in the USA (Carmona et al, 2018, p. 34).

The 2018 report prepared by Capgemini (2018, p. 4) presents current trends on the financial market from the digital transformation point of view. It is claimed that FinTechs are becoming more important. However, traditional financial services companies will not disappear from the market soon. Step by step they are solving problems with the help of innovations. In many cases, this process is slow but happens. Their customers' journey is gradually redefined with the support of creative and more efficient new technologies. On one hand, not only FinTechs, but also banks are beginning to understand the benefits of technological solutions. On the other hand, the value of having customers and their trust has been

Figure 9. The European online alternative financial market in 2013 - 2016 (excluding the United Kingdom), in EUR million
Source: Carmona et al, 2018, p. 23.

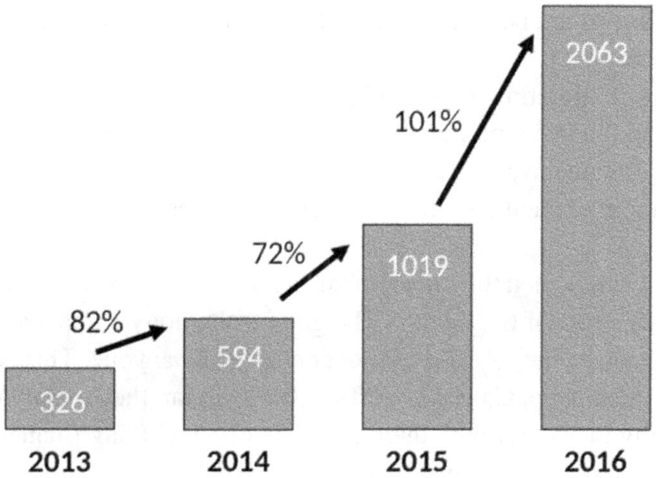

strengthened. The market has seen several successes in which partnership (which is not easy and very often fails) of existing financial institutions and FinTechs has generated significant growth. According to the research conducted by PwC, only 17% of banks in Poland and 31% in the world buy ready products or services from FinTechs. This report says that 44% banks declare cooperation, but still very often (56% responses) their only response to growing competition is monitoring FinTech activities (PwC, 2017). Generally, the opinion about the perception of incumbent operators as inefficient and unwilling to cooperate with FinTechs dominates. The management cultures of these two groups are radically different. Traditional institutions - with their current systems and slowly changing rigid, hierarchical structures - are increasingly struggling to break through the confusion generated by the several thousand newly established FinTechs. Often the cooperation between traditional financial service providers and new ones ends at a very early stage. It is like a short-lived business affair. Completely different organizational cultures are playing key role. In this case, even a well-prepared action does not help, because, as P. Drucker said, “Culture eats strategy for breakfast” (Moore & Rose, 2000).

The cultural differences can be identified including the approach to risk management in banks and in FinTechs. The maturity of risk management competencies of FinTechs is limited, sometimes very poor. They do not have enough experience and there are problems with the risk culture.

Particular attention should be paid to the principles and mechanisms of competing on the FinTech services market. The special European Parliament report is explaining this competition affected by supply and demand factors (Carmona et al, 2018). The supply side includes the provision of services via online platforms and the intensive usage of data. The demand factors are: access and usage of technology, as well as perception and behaviour of users. The great importance is attached to the new competition tools such as business models. The authors of the report see a much weaker role of traditional competition measures, i.e. market share or prices . Due to the continuous changeability of services offered by FinTechs, it is difficult to specify new rivalry rules and mechanisms. Such a situation creates huge problems for the regulators. This situation provokes the desire to use anti-competitive practices. It is especially true for BigTechs. For example, the European Commission has formulated a broad list of allegations against Google (Vestager, 2017):

a) using market position from one market for profitable entry into other markets;
b) blocking market access;
c) preventing users from migrating to other platforms;
d) acting as a judge and the main market player at the same time when it comes to measuring viewership and providing online advertising;
e) collecting data without explicit control of proper authorities.

This kind of problems arise when the same global operator sets its own access rules and principles of cooperation on a very large part of the market. The giant technology companies are playing the role of a controller and simultaneously they are almost not controlled by anyone. This is how global, integrated digital platforms work (Cusumano, Gawer & Yoffie, 2019). So far, they mainly mediate among various entities, but systematically they enter with their own services, including financial ones such as Google Pay or Apple Pay. This is a serious challenge for banks.

* * *

Banks will not give up their market position against FinTechs so easily. For example Ch. Skinner says" I got fed up with people saying that banks would be destroyed and disrupted by technology. Banks are very challenged by technology but they're not going to be destroyed by technology. We've had that discussion for a long time. It is not going to happen. As I say, banks are now integrating and collaborating with new technologies, to integrate those into their structures and become something different, to become digital banks" (Skinner, 2020). It seems that FinTechs aren't the biggest threat. It may be different with BigTechs. This rivalry should motivate banks to proper preparation for competitive struggle even more. Due to the weakness of the fair competition regulatory system in the digital age, including financial markets, the need for banks to meet this challenge is growing. The use of modern technology is not enough to win this battle. The changes must also concern the sphere of their organizational culture. Traditional financial institutions should become agile entities, flexibly behaving towards the client and contemporary development trends. These challenges are facing barriers related to difficulties with hierarchical, formalized structures and procedures. The new approach and strategies should also relate to one of the most important competences of banks - risk management, largely determined by the risk culture.

RISK CULTURE AND ITS DIGITAL DETERMINANTS

Because of high changeability of the economic, social and political environment, it is impossible to carry out an effective bank's digital transformation and an effective competitive fight, limiting only to the development of strategies and business models. It is necessary to confront these tools with the organizational culture. The starting point should be the assessment of the current culture with the desired one, against the features of digital competition and scale of risks. Unfortunately, many companies (banks) ignore the importance of this issue.

The cultural context is clearly seen within the concept of an agile approach to business. It was born in connection with the adoption of the programming manifesto, which has been focused on such issues (Agile Manifesto, 2014; Ambler, 2017):

- Tools and processes are useful, but it is more important to have competent people working together effectively.
- Proper software documentation is valid, but it isn't a purpose itself.
- A formal contract should be agreed but it doesn't substitute close cooperation with customers.
- A project plan is important, but it must flexible because of changes in technology, the environment, stakeholders' priorities etc.

If these requirements are transferred to the entire organization, the chances of innovation and the ability to create solutions tailored to the needs of customers can become an important ally of the competitive struggles. This remark is especially true under the conditions of the digital economy. In addition, the increasing scale of uncertainty has further emphasized the significance of flexibility. It has underlined the importance of agility approach in the activities of modern companies. This kind of philosophy creates better opportunities for survival and victories in the market game. Banks have also noticed these new conditions. It's not just about small financial institutions, which can easily apply this approach in a natural way. Even large corporations such as Bank of America, Merrill Lynch, JP Morgan, Citibank, Credit Suisse, Deutsche Bank, Barclays have started experiments. Already gained experience shows this is a method for better adaptation to customer requirements, more suited to quickly changing external factors, and complex regulations. It helps to face the competitive threats created by destructive technology companies. While aiming at reducing uncertainty, new risks associated with the digital world should also be avoided. Therefore the successful implementation of the agile approach will be determined by the change in the organizational culture of financial institutions. Until now banks have been operating in a completely different (stable, hierarchical, formalized, etc.) world. Now they have to establish the ability to cope with risk management in decentralized, flexible structures. To achieve this goal they need to solve the problem with culture. For many companies, especially those with traditional organizational culture (like banks), the ability to change is the biggest challenge in digital transformation. How can a company become more agile and innovative, adapted to a turbulent environment without discouraging its employees or destroying the best practices developed over the years, and without losing existing customers? This situation is overlapped by a huge dose of uncertainty, requiring a modified approach to risk management. This is a discussion not only about new tools for risk identification, measurement, mitigation, etc., but also about the appropriate skills and behaviours of all staff and management. Such transformation can't be done without changes in risk culture. Preparing a strategy focused on transforming a company (bank) into an agile institution is relatively simple. The biggest problems arise with its implementation. Therefore, even the best and ambitious plans will fail without cultural transformations. It turns out that culture is more difficult to change than strategy, because to a large extent it is not very conscious. Managers and leaders must understand and diagnose the company's current culture, identify the differences between the existing and the desired one. If suddenly people start to be ordered to do things contrary to deeply rooted values, beliefs, customs, this failure is certain. (Kasiewicz & Kurkliński, 2019)

Research on cultural differences between traditional and technological successful companies has allowed distinguishing four key recommended features of digital culture: impact, speed, openness and autonomy (see table 2).

Table 2. The four key values of digital culture

Impact	Speed	Openness	Autonomy
Change the world radically through constant innovation.	Move fast and iterate rather than waiting to have all the answers before acting.	Engage broadly with diverse sources of information and insight. Share advice and information openly rather than keeping knowledge to oneself.	Allow people high levels of discretion to do what needs to be done rather than relying on formally structured coordination and policies.

Source: Westerman, Soule & Eswaran, 2019.

The first feature relates primarily to the creation and then implementation of innovation, with a strong faith in the success of the actions. Some of these innovations are able to revolutionize entire industries and win the competition with existing major players who are not changing quickly enough. Therefore, the second feature is speed. It helps companies to stay ahead of the competition and to keep up with rapidly changing customer expectations. The openness encourages employees to question the status quo and to innovate. The autonomy gives people the freedom to do what is right for the company and its clients without waiting for formal permission. Together, all these values can support the entire staff. Regular employees feel personally responsible for the company and continuous change. The values of high-performance digital companies shape their basic practices: rapid experimentation, self-organization, decision making based on a variety of data, and obsession about customers and results. They strengthen each other when they manage to integrate them. Creating a unified culture is an effective expression of four key digital values (Westerman, Soule & Eswaran, 2019).

These requirements should be imposed on an organizational and risk culture of traditional financial institutions, especially banks. The distance, which in most cases appears to be huge, is noticeable without the need for extensive research. To a large extent, FinTechs do not have this problem. Nevertheless, the awareness of changes and digitization of business models is steadily rising in most traditional banks. However, innovations in banks are so far focused on customer experience, journeys (acquisition, service) and operations (cost reductions). Only recently banks have more intensively extended their transformations to other parts of the organization, including the risk function. That's why the awareness of the importance of risk culture is also slowly breaking through. They began to recognize that various aspects of risk management, previously underestimated e.g. a human resource area. This applies to the recruitment and training of personnel with digital experience, fluent in risk and business language, operating in agile culture, who value innovation and experimentation. Professionals linking the digital world with risk management are recognized as critical. There is no conviction yet that all employees and all managerial staff should be characterized by an appropriate risk culture located in the agile culture of the organization. In order for the bank to meet the challenges of modern digitization. The lesson of using very advanced quantitative risk management models before the 2007+ financial crisis is already being studied but these modern, sophisticated tools did not contribute to avoiding the global financial collapse. Why? Because the risk culture has just failed, as defined by the Institute of Risk Management (2012, p. 7) "... values, attitudes and behaviours shared in the bank that allows deeper, broader understanding, identification and management of risk." When risk management goes down to all levels of the organization, it means that a bank creates the risk culture which can be the key to success, especially in front of FinTech or BigTech competition. (Kasiewicz & Kurkliński, 2019)

CONCLUSION

The selected bank's digital strategies and business models described in this chapter attach great importance to technological and organizational determinants. This should be assessed positively, but there are other effects of the extraordinary rate of change, which implies the necessity to present a high level of adaptability. This mainly applies to behavioural and psychological limitations affecting management boards and employees. The human factor depends to a great extent on cultural aspects in which risk culture plays a prominent role. Therefore, banks should look at the difference between the current and desired cultures. On this basis, the bank's digital transformation strategy can be formulated. The outline, probably still fragmentary, of the proceedings aimed at meeting the challenges of competition between banks and FinTechs/BigTechs was presented. The new conditions practically undermine the canons of strategic management from the 20th century. One of the most important aspects of the modern competition is the technology race. Banks are already greatly aware in this respect. However, there is a dichotomy. On one hand, the types of technology, at least those that seem to dominate the financial services market in the coming years, are more or less recognized. On the other hand, the dynamics of change and the degree of uncertainty remain high. For the preparation of business strategies and models, it can be used a version that fits into a one page of paper (simplicity) with a large creative participation of managers having positive experience in digital transformation. The degree of effectiveness of strategy implementation depends on a risk management perspective. That's why a bank's digital strategy should also include aspects of risk culture. After studying innovation among 759 companies based in 17 major markets G. J. Tellis, J. C. Prabhu and R. K. Chandy (2009) found that corporate culture was a much more important driver of radical innovation than labor, capital, government or national culture. Usually there are no official (tangible) requirements to create a proper culture. Therefore it can be postponed for a more convenient time, specially under the pressure of other, urgent problems related to new mechanisms of digital competition. There is no doubt, the market players' attention should be paid to their behaviour, in particular increasing flexibility and demonstrating market intelligence. Especially for banks, it is important not to lose their main advantage - customer trust. Unfortunately, this confidence was seriously damaged by the recent global financial crisis, opening the field for the activity of new players - technology companies (FinTechs). In addition, the lack of clarity and volatility of market competition rules means that there is a certain model of the strategic game that can be observed. Some of the players do not reveal their attitudes and behaviour, and the basics of making decisions are not fully clear and predictable. This phenomenon can be described as "silent market war". Every day and place a new, unexpected competitor may appear and successfully take over a part of the banking services market (e.g. Revolut case).

After all, banks are not without a chance to win a market battle with at least FinTechs (especially niche ones), but the bigger problem is competition with companies from the BigTech sector. Perspectives are much worse here. Technology giants operate in a system of digital platforms, have easier access to new technologies (their investment budgets are gigantic) and have direct relationships with clients. They are also slowly collecting the trust of customers. Currently, as operators, they are already acquiring knowledge through partnerships with large financial institutions, including banks. Their development is not as dependent on regulators as it is in the case of traditional banks. Therefore, the final result of the competition is not known.

Risk management plays an important role in the process of competing banks and FinTechs. For the first time in the history of banks' operations, there has been a huge flood of new types of risk (e.g. pandemic, climate, environmental, technological, social or even political). In this situation it is necessary not only to have specialist knowing and understanding technological trends but also to have authentic leaders as enablers of innovation and competitiveness together with professional risk management.

REFERENCES

Agarwal, R., & Kallapur, S. (2018). Cognitive risk culture and advanced roles of actors in risk governance: A case study. *The Journal of Risk Finance*, *19*(4), 327–342. doi:10.1108/JRF-11-2017-0189

Agile Manifesto. (2014). *Manifesto for Agile Software Development*. Available from https://agilemanifesto.org/

Ambler, S. (2017). *Examining the Agile Manifesto*. Available from http://www.ambysoft.com/essays/agileManifesto.html

Amit, R., & Zott, C. (2001). Value Creation in E-Business. *Strategic Management Journal*, *22*(6-7), 493–520. doi:10.1002mj.187

Backbase. (2017). *The PSD 2. Playbook*. Available from http://www.backbase.com/wp-content/uploads/2017/04/Backbase_The_PSD2_Playbook.pdf

Capgemini. (2018a). *The bank of the future: an ecosystem of services*. Available from https://www.capgemini.com/2018/04/the-bank-of-the-future-an-ecosystem-of-services/

Capgemini. (2018b). *World Fintech Report*. Available from https://www.capgemini.com/wp-content/uploads/2018/02/world-fintech-report-wftr-2018.pdf

Carmona, A. F. (2018). *Competition issues in the Area of Financial Technology (FinTech)*. Policy Department for Economic, Scientific and Quality of Life Policies. Directorate-General for Internal Policies. Available from https://www.europarl.europa.eu/RegData/etudes/STUD/2018/619027/IPOL_STU(2018)619027_EN.pdf

Courtney, H., Kirkland, J., & Viguerie, P. (1997). Strategy Under Uncertainty. *Harvard Business Review, 1*. Available from https://hbr.org/1997/11/strategy-under-uncertainty

Cusumano, M. A., Gawer, A., & Yoffie, D. B. (2019). *The Business of Platforms: Strategy in the Age of Digital Competition, Innovation, and Power*. Harper Collins Publishers.

Czugan, M. (2017). Problemy otoczenia regulacyjnego rozwoju sektora fintech. In Regulacje finansowe: fintech - nowe instrumenty finansowe –resolution. Warszawa: C.H. Beck.

EY. (2017). *EY FinTech Adoption Index 2017. The rapid emergence of FinTech*. Available from https://www.ey.com/Publication/vwLUAssets/ey-fintech-adoption-index-2017/$FILE/ey-fintech-adoption-index-2017.pdf

Financial Stability Board. (2017). *Financial Stability Implications from FinTech. Supervisory and Regulatory Issues that Merit Authorities' Attention*. Available from https://www.fsb.org/wp-content/uploads/R270617.pdf

Freedman, R. S. (2006). *Introduction to Financial Technology.* Academic Press. Available from https://booksite.elsevier.com/samplechapters/9780123704788/Sample_Chapters/01~Frontmatter.pdf

Gasser, U., Gassmann, O., Hens, T., Leifer, L., Puschmann, T., & Zhao, L. (2017). *Digital Bank 2025.* Available from https://www.alexandria.unisg.ch/publications/253962

Gopalan, S., Jain, G., Kalani, G., & Tan, J. (2012). Breakthrough IT Banking. *The McKinsey Quarterly, 26*(2). https://www.mckinsey.com/business-functions/mckinsey-digital/our-insights/breakthrough-it-banking

Howard, A. (2019). The Regulation of AI— Should Organizations Be Worried? *MIT Sloan Management Review*, (July), 29.

Institute of Risk Management. (2012). *Risk Culture. Under the Microscope Guidance for Boards.* Available from https://www.primo-europe.eu/wp-content/uploads/2017/06/Risk_Culture_A5_WEB15_Oct_2012.pdf

Ismail, M. H., Khater, M., & Zaki, Z. (2017). *Digital Business Transformation and Strategy: What Do We Know So Far?* University Cambridge. Available from https://cambridgeservicealliance.eng.cam.ac.uk/resources/Downloads/Monthly%20Papers/2017NovPaper_Mariam.pdf

Kane, G. C., Phillips, A. N., Copulsky, J., & Andrus, G. (2019). How Digital Leadership Is(n't) Different. *MIT Sloan Management Review.* Available from https://sloanreview.mit.edu/article/how-digital-leadership-isnt-different/

Kasiewicz, S., & Kurkliński, L. (2019). Konkurencja cyfrowa a kultura ryzyka w sektorze finansowym. In Bankowość emocjonalna. Cyfrowa transformacja banków a oczekiwania klientów. Warszawa: Wydawnictwo Poltext.

Khanna, S., & Martins, H. (2018). *Six digital growth strategies for banks.* McKinsey. Available from https://www.mckinsey.com/business-functions/mckinsey-digital/our-insights/six-digital-growth-strategies-for-banks

Kimura, R., Reeves, M., & Whitaker, K. (2019). *Winning the '20s: The New Logic of Competition.* BCG Henderson Institute. Available from https://bcghendersoninstitute.com/winning-the-20s-the-new-logic-of-competition-7c1500c5a187

Kostro, M. (2020). *Bezpieczeństwo usług opartych o otwarte interfejsy programistyczne (API) w kontekście implementacji Dyrektywy PSD 2.* WIB Warszawa.

Koźmiński, A. (2004). *Zarządzanie w warunkach niepewności.* Wydawnictwo Naukowe PWN.

Krupski, R. (Ed.). (2007). *Planowanie strategiczne w warunkach niepewności.* Prace Naukowe Wałbrzyskiej Wyższej Szkoły Zarządzania i Przedsiębiorczości.

Kruse, K. (2013). What is Authentic Leadership? *Forbes*, (May), 12.

Matt, C., Hess, T., & Benlian, A. (2015). Digital Transformation Strategies. *Business & Information Systems Engineering, 57*(5), 339–343. doi:10.100712599-015-0401-5

Mohamed, H., & Ali, H. (2019). *Blockchain, Fintech, and Islamic Finance.* Walter de Gruyter Inc. doi:10.1515/9781547400966

Moore, B., & Rose, J. (2000). Recovered paper trading—ready for the Web? PIMA's North American Papermaker: The Official Publication of the Paper Industry Management Association, 82(9).

Obłój, K. (2002). *Tworzywo skutecznych strategii.* PWE.

Osterwalder, A., & Pigneur, Y. (2010). *Business model generation: a handbook for visionaries, games changers, and challengers.* Wiley.

PwC. (2017). *Na współpracy banków i fintech-ów skorzystają klienci.* www.pwc.pl›media›2017-06-08-na-wspolpracy-bankow-i-fintech-

Robinson, B. (2016). *4 banking business models for the digital age.* Temenos. Available from https://www.linkedin.com/pulse/4-banking-business-models-digital-age-ben-robinson/

Sandrock, J., & Fringes, A. (2016), *Catalyst or threat? The strategic implications of PSD 2 Europe's banks.* Available from http://www.vivanest.com/wp-content/uploads/2016/09/Catalyst-or-threat-The-strategic-implications-of-PSD2-for-Europes-banks-.pdf

Schueffel, P. (2016). Taming the Beast: A Scientific Definition of FinTech. *Journal of Innovation Management, 4*(4), 32–54. doi:10.24840/2183-0606_004.004_0004

Skinner, C. (2018). Digital Human: The Fourth Revolution of Humanity Includes Everyone. Singapore: Marshall Cavendish International (Asia) Pte Ltd.

Skinner, C. (2020). *Doing Digital.* https://calendly.com/chris_skinner/30min

Solarz, M. (2017). FinTech – innowacje w obszarze usług finansowych. *Prace Naukowe Wyższej Szkoły Zarządzania i Przedsiębiorczości z siedzibą w Wałbrzychu, 43*(4), 233-250.

Tellis, G. J., Prabhu, J. C., & Chandy, R. K. (2009, January). Radical Innovation Across Nations: The Preeminence of Corporate Culture. *Journal of Marketing, 73*(1), 3–23. doi:10.1509/jmkg.73.1.003

The Telegraph. (2017). *The future of fintech.* Available from https://www.telegraph.co.uk/content/dam/business/spark/Fintech/Telegraph_Fintech_Report%202017.pdf

Valencia, J. C. N., Valle, R. S., & Jiménez, D. J. (2010). Organizational culture as determinant of product innovation. *European Journal of Innovation Management, 13*(4).

Vestager, M. (2017). *Google has to follow European rules.* Available from http://f24.my/youtubeEN

Viscelli, T. R., Hermanson, D. R., & Beasley, M. S. (2017). The integration of ERM and strategy: Simplications for corporate governance. *Accounting Horizons, 31*(2), 69–82. doi:10.2308/acch-51692

Westerman, G., Soule, D. L., & Eswaran, A. (2019). Building Digital-Ready Culture in Traditional Organizations. *MIT Sloan Management Review.* Available from https://sloanreview.mit.edu/article/building-digital-ready-culture-in-traditional-organizations

KEY TERMS AND DEFINITIONS

Ad Hocratic Culture: Dominance of dynamics, entrepreneurship, creativity, direct communication, typical for a flat organization. People are not afraid of risk. Innovations and experiments are promoted. It's the opposite of hierarchical culture.

API: Application programming interface.

Artificial Intelligence: Creating models of intelligent behavior as well as programs and systems simulating these behaviors.

BigTech: Major technology companies such as Apple, Google, Amazon, Facebook, Microsoft or Baidu, Alibaba, Tencent.

Canvas: Concept of business model created by A. Osterwalder and Y. Pigneur, consisting from the following elements: key partners, key activities, key resources, cost, value propositions, customers, revenues and interconnectedness.

BAT: Group of Chinese technological giants Baidu, Alibaba, and Tencent.

Blockchain: Distributed register of operations carried out in a given digital network, to which all users have access.

Cloud Technology: Transferring and using data or applications from computers belonging to the users to servers maintained by external companies providing these services. An access is available by remote mode.

Digital Transformation: Organizational change, covering both technology and management model, which aims to increase efficiency through the use of digital technologies.

FinTech: Financial technology or innovations but the same term is also used as the name of companies that offer innovative solutions for the financial sector and its customers.

GAFA: Group of American technological giants Google, Amazon, Facebook, and Apple.

Internet of Things: A system in which objects (things), equipped with special sensors, communicate and exchange data with computers and other devices, using a variety of network solutions.

Risk Culture: Norms, forms, and traditions of the behavior of individuals or groups within a given organization. It determines how risk is perceived and managed.

Robo-Advisory: A form of automated financial consulting about e.g. investment services, loans and insurance, etc., based on advanced algorithms using artificial intelligence and analysis of large data sets (Big Data).

Chapter 3
The FinTech Wave in the Financial Sector for European Union Countries

Alina-Nicoleta Radu
Faculty of Finance and Banking, Bucharest University of Economic Studies, Romania

Anca Mihaela Copaciu (Paraschiv)
National Bank of Romania, Romania

ABSTRACT

In this chapter, the authors provide some answers to the following questions: (1) To what extent can FinTech enter the market? (2) Are the markets accommodative enough for new innovative financial projects? (3) What are the main drivers of FinTech phenomenon? (4) Will FinTech shape the financial landscape going forward? By constructing four indices that can influence and drive FinTech market entry, such as (1) demand factors, (2) supply factors, (3) business environment, and (4) investment climate and by applying a z-score methodology, the results point out which economy is better prepared for a challenging wave of innovative changes in the financial sector relatively to the other economies included in the study. The authors focus on the EU countries over a period of 12 years (2007–2018). The FinTech market indices are computed by taking into account a wide variety of variables such as the level of financial inclusion, the available technology and infrastructure, the ease of starting new business, and the risk factors related to investment climate for all EU economies.

1. INTRODUCTION[1]

Over the last few years, the financial sector has witnessed a major transformation, undergoing a steady process of customizing and implementing the new technologies. According to the Bank for International Settlements (BIS, 2017), how technology-driven innovation in financial services (Financial Technology - FinTech) is defined is important from the perspective of supervisory authorities' approaches. Even though there are several definitions for FinTech, the most commonly used is considered to be that of the

DOI: 10.4018/978-1-7998-4390-0.ch003

Financial Stability Board (FSB), namely "technologically enabled financial innovation that could result in new business models, applications, processes, or products with an associated material effect on the provision of financial services".

In 2017, the European Banking Authority (EBA) conducted a FinTech mapping exercise and identified four clusters of financial products or services under the scope of financial technology innovations: (i) credit, deposit, and capital raising services; (ii) payment, clearing and settlement means and services; (iii) investment services/investment management services; and (iv) other financial-related activities. At the same time, according to a study developed by Bruegel (2017), the impact of FinTech development on the financial system may be considerable, as technological innovation has the potential to reconfigure the current structure of the system. The advantages of FinTech underlined are: (i) deepening of financial inclusion due to easier access to financial services via secure communication environments; (ii) decentralization and diversification of financial intermediation services; (iii) more efficient and faster banking services; and (iv) reduction of information asymmetries and the enhancement of risk analyses by broadening the type of data used in this sense.

A very important key is played by the banks' business models. Due to both the increasingly fast-paced development of financial technology innovations, and the structural changes in the social, economic and demographic sectors, banks had to redefine their strategies as regards not only the products and services provided, but also the interaction with clients. One advantage of FinTech relates to the opportunities of reducing operational costs, by transforming the activity in a more efficient one.

European Commission (2016) and other European competent authorities have engaged in talks on establishing a legal framework allowing each Member State to test the new technologies in a regulated environment. In this context, the European Supervisory Authorities (ESAs) take into consideration all FinTech-specific aspects in the activities carried out by them. Simultaneously, in order to support innovation hubs and testing environments, the authorities have enriched the prudential supervisory framework. Moreover, ESAs will promote FinTech-specific technological education along with the exchange of data on information security (cyber threats, incidents and attacks), and will coordinate the strategies on information security and safeguarding cyber-resilience with a view to ensuring the enhancement of the security and integrity of the European financial system (FSR, 2017).

In the context of implementing measures on fighting money laundering and terrorist financing, initiatives on the cooperation between public and private sectors were developed. Their main aim is twofold, first, to enhance the exchange of information and to set up a more effective compliance system, and second, to create a secure environment enabling the testing of innovative solutions for financial products and services.

Research performed by G20 (2016) shows that the use of internet and of mobile telephony services, at large scale, alongside with the availability of high-speed computers and the advance in cryptography and other technological innovations have reduced entry barriers on the financial services market. These have enabled the access to the market of different financial institutions, including non-bank entities, mobile telephony operators or IT companies. At the same time, taking into consideration the role of FinTech as a catalyst for global efforts towards financial inclusion, it can also trigger additional concerns about the fact that some FinTech products might acquire systemic importance. According to the Financial Stability Board (FSB) the risks generated by FinTech on financial stability into two broad categories: (i) macro-financial risks and (ii) micro-financial risks. FSB (2017) considers that there are currently no compelling signs of materialisation of the main risks to financial stability from FinTech developments, given the still contained magnitude of this domain. Nevertheless, FinTech warrants increased scrutiny considering the pace at which it advances.

The role of FinTech as a tool for financial inclusion was also discussed by the European Parliament (European Parliament Motion, 2016). In this context, it was underlined the need for better financial education of consumers and investors alike, so as to enable these participants to make sound financial decisions autonomously. Digitalization is enabling consumers and businesses to transfer value instantaneously, technology platforms to scale up rapidly in payments, and new digital currencies to facilitate these payments. By transforming payments, digitalization has the potential to deliver greater value and convenience at lower cost. But there are risks. Some of the new players are outside the financial system's regulatory guardrails, and their new currencies could pose challenges in areas such as illicit finance, privacy, financial stability, and monetary policy transmission.

The chapter adds to the literature by providing some answers to the following questions: (i) to what extent can FinTech enter the market? (ii) are the markets accommodative enough for new innovative financial projects? (iii) what are the main drivers of FinTech phenomenon? (iv) will FinTech shape the financial landscape going forward? By constructing four indices that can influence and drive FinTech market entry, such as (a) demand factors, (b) supply factors, (c) business environment and d) investment climate and by applying a z-score methodology, our results point out which economy is better prepared for a challenging wave of innovative changes in the financial sector relatively to the other economies included in the study. Most euro area countries provide good capacity of innovation, good entrepreneurial business climate and sound infrastructure to develop further FinTech solutions, while in lower-income countries (mostly non-euro area) both infrastructure and business environment require improvement to make Fintech-led financial inclusion a success.

The paper is structured as follows. Section 1 presents briefly the literature review, section 2 presents the challenge, the risks and opportunities of FinTech, section 3 the finTech versus Financial Inclusion, section 4 describes the case study, section 5 the data and methodology, section 6 describes the main results and section 7 concludes.

2. THE CHALLENGE, THE RISKS AND OPPORTUNITIES OF FINTECH

2.1. General Overview

Examples of innovations that are central to Fintech today include various applications of blockchain technologies, new digital advisory and trading systems, artificial intelligence and machine learning, peer-to-peer lending, equity crowd funding and mobile payment systems. Given the stakes, the public sector must engage in order to ensure that the payments infrastructure is safe as well as efficient and fast, assess whether regulatory perimeters need to be redrawn or new approaches are needed in areas such as consumer data and identity authentication, and explore the role of central bank digital currencies in ensuring sovereign currencies stay at the center of each nation's financial system. These issues are complicated and consequential. Digital Players Technology firms—from BigTechs to FinTechs—are driving the digital transformation of payments. Not only are the new players bringing innovation to the way payments are made between businesses and consumers and peer-to-peer, but they are bringing new business models that bundle payments with other activities in novel ways.

Payments have traditionally been a service provided by trusted intermediaries such as banks. The operations of banks and some related financial service providers, such as card companies, are subject to regulatory oversight for sound risk management. Banks offer important consumer protections, including deposit insurance, error resolution, and fraud protection. In addition to providing payments services, banks generally provide credit, with deposits providing stable funding. Many banks rely at least in part on legacy technology.

In contrast, BigTechs tend to be established platforms with massive user networks that provide payments in support of core nonfinancial services—ranging from commercial transactions to social engagement to mobile apps to search engines. In China, the majority of consumers and businesses participate in two mobile payment networks, Alipay and WeChat Pay, which by some accounts handled more than $37 trillion in mobile payments in 2018. BigTechs and FinTechs typically leverage cloud-based platforms and computing power, along with mobile applications, often to provide different combinations of services and enhanced user experiences.

They generally benefit from network effects: the more users they have, the more convenience and benefit new users derive from joining. These network benefits may be augmented by leveraging economies of scale and scope in user data for a host of purposes, from prioritizing which information is pushed to users to allocating and pricing credit to sharing reviews. The entrance of BigTech and FinTech into payments may drive competition; enhance product offerings, and lower transactions costs. It has the potential to enhance financial inclusion by expanding the number and diversity of ways people gain access to financial services and by creating more consumer friendly offerings. A Federal Deposit Insurance Corporation (FDIC) study found that 8.4 million households are unbanked and an additional 24 million are underbanked. These households often rely on more-expensive means of payments, including nonbank providers and bank money orders. Many have smartphones, which could facilitate access to payment apps.

The entry of big technology networks into payments brings risks as well as benefits. Statutory and regulatory protections on bank accounts in the United States mean that consumers can reasonably expect their deposits to be insured up to a limit; their banks to be held to strong data security standards; many fraudulent transactions to be the liability of the bank; transfers to be available within specified periods; and clear, standardized disclosures about account fees and interest payments to be readily available. Consumers may not appreciate that nonbank providers might not provide the same protections. Further, the integration of payments with a variety of consumer services that rely intensively on user data raises the urgency of questions surrounding data security, how consumers' financial data are used, and the circumstances under which the data are disclosed to third parties.

Unlike many foreign central banks, the Federal Reserve does not have plenary authority over payment systems. No federal agency does. The Federal Reserve has broad authority over payment systems that are designated as systemically important by the Financial Stability Oversight Council or that are chartered as entities for which the Federal Reserve is the primary supervisor. These authorities cover two large-value interbank payment systems but no retail payment system to date. The banking agencies may oversee certain aspects of a nonbank payment system to the extent there is a bank nexus, under the Bank Service Company Act, or bank affiliation, under the Federal Deposit Insurance Act. However, this oversight will be quite limited to the extent that nonbank players reduce or eliminate the nexus to banks, such as then technology firms develop payments services connected to digital wallets rather than bank accounts and rely on digital currencies rather than sovereign currencies as the means of exchange.

Given the growing role of nonbank technology players in payments, a review of the nation's oversight framework for retail payment systems could be helpful to identify important gaps. A good place to start may be contrasting the U.S. oversight framework for retail payment systems with other jurisdictions. Many foreign central banks, for example, have explicit authority for general retail payments oversight. Moreover, most jurisdictions require that payment systems obtain a license and/or registration before commencing operations. A 2018 World Bank study found that the large majority of jurisdictions have some sort of license and/or registration requirement for mobile money platforms, payment card networks or switches, or clearinghouses. The United States requires registration of a money transmitter at the federal level for purposes of Bank Secrecy Act/Anti-Money-Laundering compliance, but it does not require broader federal oversight of payment system operators.

In contrast to other jurisdictions where there is explicit responsibility for broad regulation of payment systems, the Federal Reserve's role as an operator has instead long formed the basis of the U.S. approach to promoting accessible, safe, and efficient payments. Since the Federal Reserve Banks opened for business around the country in 1914, as directed by the Congress, they have provided payment and settlement services in competition with private-sector providers.

At the same time, central banks across the world have quickened the pace with which they are looking at issuing their own digital currencies, also known as CBDCs. Facebook's (FB.O) push to launch its Libra cryptocurrency has added fuel to questions over whether nation states will continue to control money in the decades ahead. Of the major central banks, China's has emerged as the frontrunner in the drive to create its own digitized money, though details of its project are still scarce. In the United States, Fed Chairman Jerome Powell said in November 2019 he was monitoring the digital currency debate but not actively considering its own amid a host of legal, regulatory and operational questions. But Philadelphia Federal Reserve bank president Patrick Harker said a month earlier it was "inevitable" that central banks, including the Fed, would start issuing digital currency.

CBDCs are traditional money, but in digital form, issued and governed by a country's central bank. By contrast, cryptocurrencies such as bitcoin are produced by solving complex maths puzzles, and governed by disparate online communities instead of a centralized body. The common denominator is that cryptocurrencies and CBDCs, to a varying degree, are based on blockchain technology, a digital ledger that allows transactions to be recorded and accessed in real time by multiple parties. Last year BoE Governor Mark Carney took aim at the U.S. dollar's "destabilizing" role in the world economy and said central banks might need to join together to create their own replacement reserve currency. The best solution would be a diversified multi-polar financial system, something that could be provided by technology, Carney said. Facebook's Libra is the most high-profile proposed digital currency to date but it faces a host of fundamental issues that it has yet to address, he added.

2.2. The Challenge

Central banks play one of the most critical roles in the global economy, from managing price stability and monetary policy, to safeguarding the domestic financial system through oversight of commercial banks. Their decisions about implementing distributed ledger and digital currency technologies in the future will have far-reaching consequences on financial and monetary systems, domestic economies, and the welfare of citizens. Distributed ledger technology (DLT) has the potential to enhance efficiency, financial inclusion, resiliency, and security in financial systems. At the same time, any imprudent DLT or digital currency implementation poses significant risks to financial stability on a domestic or even international scale.

Central banks across the world have been formally or informally experimenting with DLT. However, they are often conducting this research independently without efficient ways to share insights, coordinate, or scale work. Further, they may be reluctant to publicly share their activities because of the impact such signalling may have on markets. The result is that research is poorly disseminated and may be duplicated, and there are missed opportunities to collaborate over high-potential research topics.

Central banks across economies also have difficulty closely following rapidly evolving developments in DLT and digital currency technology in order to fully understand their implications, possibilities, and risks. They must at once understand and evaluate technology capabilities available now and in the future, determine their value and applicability to financial systems and central bank operations, and critically study any and all risks and challenges posed by implementing DLT.

Finally, experimentation of DLT in the financial sector to-date has primarily been driven by large and well-resourced financial institutions seeking to replace or retro-fit privately operated financial infrastructure for the benefit of their clients and shareholders. This focus may overlook significant opportunities to improve publicly operated financial infrastructure or to deploy new, collaborative public-private efforts of DLT-based financial infrastructure.

2.3. The Opportunity

Convening a community of technologists from central banks across diverse countries to coordinate and scale experimentation efforts is very important. The community will capture lessons from current research and pilot projects following appropriate levels of privacy and anonymization to avoid potentially harmful market signalling. These insights will be synthesized into trusted governance frameworks that can help central banks around the world understand salient issues and experiment with and potentially deploy blockchain for proven use cases in an effective, safe, responsible, and inclusive manner.

The community will co-design frameworks to support investigation and potential deployment of relevant use cases such as cross-border inter-bank settlements; wholesale or retail central-bank issued digital currency (“CBDC”); and know-your-customer/anti-money-laundering topics. It will partner with forward leaning jurisdictions and cross-sector stakeholders to pilot these frameworks with high-potential use cases, testing key assumptions and implementation risks and challenges. In so doing, it will help to scale responsible experimentation globally and assure that any future implementations are validated by robust research and diverse test cases.

Relevant institutions, start-ups, and experts have the opportunity to engage in this process and shape the exploration and experimentation of DLT for global financial and monetary systems. Importantly, they can ensure that potential DLT implementation does not result in increased stratification and systemic risk, but instead lays the groundwork for truly stable, efficient, and inclusive global systems.

2.4 The Risks

In banking, managing risks is very important, especially in the context of an increasing FinTech financial industry. If not managed in a proper and effective manner, liquidity, credit, market, and, especially, operational risks could affect financial stability. This might trigger a loss of confidence and even bank-runs. The precise nature of the risk should be very well identified and established, in order to develop the adequate models to measure and quantify them. For smaller economies, there may be material effects on monetary policy from private-sector digital currencies, as well as foreign central bank digital currencies. In many respects, these effects may be the digital version of "dollarization," with the potential for a faster pace and wider scope of adoption.

Operational risk gained notoriety as a distinct risk category in the mid to late 1990s, following events such as the case of Nicholas Leeson, the "rogue" trader often credited with the undoing of Barings bank. Not long after, the Basel II standards introduced operational risk capital requirements, with operational risk defined as "the risk of losses resulting from in adequate or failed internal processes, people, systems or from external events" (Basel Committee on Banking Supervision (2003)). Measuring and understanding operational risk is critical for both banks and public authorities. Operational risk currently represents a significant portion of banks' risk-weighted assets, second only to credit risk. Regulators, central banks and international organizations, in turn, place the understanding and mitigation of operational risk – and subcomponents such as cyber risk – high in their agendas. Despite this focus, the paucity of data and analysis on operational risk means that discussions on the topic lack a proper empirical grounding. A consortium by banks was founded with the aim of sharing operational loss risk data in an anonymized fashion in order to benchmark operational risk models. It was found that after a notable increase post-Great Financial Crisis (GFC), operational risk losses in bank share been declining strongly since 2015. Digging deeper into the type of event behind this aggregate rend shows that one category in particular is responsible for the pattern in cost, namely "Clients, Products& Business Practices". This category includes improper business practices like fiduciary breaches, aggressive sales, and breaches of privacy, account churning and misuse of confidential information. These are the type of operational risks that characterize periods of financial excess, with mis-selling of mortgage-backed securities in the mid-2000s being a prime example. Towards the peak of the GFC there is a significant increase in the occurrence of this type of event (especially in North America), which were then recognised in the books of banks a few years later. Importantly, this pattern is observed only in terms of loss amounts and not in terms of frequency of occurrence.

Cyber and IT-related risks can be seen as a subset of operational risks and are frequently cited as a prominent there at to the financial system (see Kaffenberger et al. (2017); Kashyap and Wetherilt (2019). This threat extends well beyond finance as the interest in cyber has gradually increased over time, as shown for example by web search queries. In March2017, the G20 Finance Ministers and Central Bank Governors noted that "the malicious use of information and communication technologies (ICT) could disrupt financial services crucial to both national and international financial systems, undermine security and confidence, and endanger financial stability". In December 2018 the Basel Committee on Banking Supervision published a report on the range of cyber-resilience practices (Basel Committee on Banking Supervision (2018)). An accurate quantification of cyber risks using the ORX database is challenging, as there is no precise definition of cyber events.

Cyber losses represent a small fraction of total losses in terms of gross amount and frequency. More recently, however, the share of cyber losses in terms of amounts has been increasing, with a strong spike in particular around 2016. The effect of the financial crisis is not as evident as it was for the larger operational risk class, indicating that cyber costs are less correlated with macroeconomic conditions. Indeed, in unreported results we find that the stance of monetary policy and the credit-to-GDP gap are not associated with higher cyber losses in the future. On the contrary, as shown in Table VIII, stronger supervision can influence the incidence of cyber losses at least to the same extent as it does broader operational risk losses

3. FINTECH VS. FINANCIAL INCLUSION

In the financial sector, digital innovations and technology-enabled business model innovations are also covered by FinTech. According to Philippon (2020), these types of innovations can change the industry structures that are in place, by facilitating strategic disintermediation, revolutionizing the way in which different firms create and deliver products and services, providing new openings for entrepreneurship, and democratizing access to financial services. At the same time, these activities generate significant privacy, a few challenges in the regulatory and field and they could increase the scope for some forms of discrimination.

A first question addressed in the literature is whether there has been any material change in financial intermediation in recent years. To clarify this, Philippon (2020) updated the work of Philippon (2015) with post-crisis U.S. data. The problem underlined in the previous research was that the unit cost of financial intermediation was very close to 200 basis points for more than one hundred years, despite advances and investment in the information and communication technologies. The post-crisis information show that this problem might be decreasing and the recent analyses show that the unit cost of financial intermediation has declined over the past 10 years.

At the same time, Philippon (2020) develops an analysis related to two main issues: access to finance and discrimination. On one hand, he underlines that FinTech brings efficiency gains to financial intermediation, but, he also stresses that a very important question that rises is: how will these gains be shared? And Will FinTech democratize access to financial services or will it increase inequality? Philippon (2020), identifies two elements that will help shaping the answer to the questions. The first elements relates to increasing returns to scale brought by technology; the nature of fixed versus variable costs has changed in a way that is likely to improve access to financial services, although it may not reduce inequality among all groups. The second element relates to the use of big data and machine learning. According to his research, this technology might reduce unjustified human biases against minorities, but there are chances that it will probably reduce the effectiveness of current regulations. An intermediate conclusion that can be drawn is that FinTech can bring widely-shared welfare benefits but changes in existing policies and regulations are necessary to achieve its full potential.

Recent literature has assessed FinTech and financial inclusion and the conclusions are very interesting. In Buchak et al. (2018) the growth is analyzed as a percentage of the market share of shadow bank and FinTech lenders. The results show that FinTech lenders serve more creditworthy borrowers (relative to shadow banks) but charge higher interest rates (14-16 basis points). This outcome supports the idea that a consumer is ready to pay for better user experience and quick decisions. At the same time, Fuster et al. (2019) analyze the differences between FinTech and traditional lenders in the mortgage market and find that the former is quicker in processing applications (20% faster), without increasing loan risk. The paper also demonstrates that FinTech lenders adjust supply more elastically to demand shocks and increase the propensity to refinance, especially among borrowers that are likely to benefit from it. Their results suggest that FinTech companies have improved the efficiency of financial intermediation in mortgage markets.

Taking these into consideration, it can be underlined that the introduction of FinTech is often seen as a promising avenue for reducing inequality in access to credit. This was studied by Bartlett et al. (2018). Analyzing the role of FinTech lenders in alleviating discrimination in mortgage markets, the authors identify that all lenders, including FinTech, charge minorities more for purchase and refinance mortgages, but that Fintech algorithms discriminate 40% less than face-to-face lenders. Therefore, to the extent that minorities were affected by bias or negative stereotyping, these minorities should gain from the use of alternate data sources.

Berg et al. (2019) analyze the use of new technologies in credit markets, more precisely the information content of the "digital footprint" for predicting consumer default. The data is from German e-commerce sector and, they find that they methodology equals or exceeds the predictive power of traditional credit bureau scores. The results suggest that new technologies and new data might bring a superior ability for screening borrowers. This comes to support the idea that alternate data sources are likely to reduce non-statistical discrimination, but, on the other hand, there is the risk that new data can reduce the effectiveness of existing regulations.

A role of FinTech can also be seen in the market for wealth management. In 2017, the market for robo-advisors in the United States accounted for more than half of all investments in robo-advisors (Abraham et al., 2019). However, robo-advisors manage a small portion of assets of total assets under management, with average client wealth much smaller than the average in the industry (Economist, 2017). Abraham et al. (2019) considers that robo-advisors can reduce minimum investment requirements and charge lower fees because they save on fixed costs. Moreover, robo-advisors are likely to improve participation by relatively less wealthy household.

4. CASE STUDY

Technological innovation has registered a major evolution in many business sectors in recent years. The financial field is no exception, being subject to a constant process of development and implementation of new technologies. Digitalisation and technological innovations in the financial and banking sector pose a challenge, as well as an important concern for both credit institutions and the relevant supervisory and regulatory authorities. Digitalisation and FinTech are a major challenge for credit institutions, given that the developments that appear are extremely lively and banks which do not adapt most likely will disappear. The impact of FinTech segment development on the financial system can be considerable as technological innovation has the potential to reconfigure the current structure of the system. Some of the main benefits driven by FinTech may refer to: (i) faster and more efficient financial services; (ii) easier access to financial services can lead to increased financial inclusion and (iii) decentralization and diversification of financial intermediation services.

FinTech adoption is taking place across markets at global level, but not evenly. At European level, on average, the FinTech segment has been on the rise over the past years and European Union (EU) countries have improved their digital performance. According to the Digital Economy and Society Index (DESI) developed by the European Commission[2], Finland, Sweden, the Netherlands, and Denmark scored the highest ratings in 2019 and are among the global leaders in digitalisation. However, the low degree of financial inclusion, along with the social and economic asymmetries, may play a part in the sluggish digitalisation of the financial and banking sector in some of the less developed EU countries, such as Bulgaria, Romania, Greece or Poland.

Even though credit institutions have been striving to develop new banking technologies and products and directing customers towards the on-line environment, some European countries still have a long way to go to allign to more developed EU countries. Some of the main challenges the credit institutions may face may refer to: (i) adjusting the business models by improving the cost efficiency in a financial environment characterized by pressures of profitability and by redefining strategies regarding not only the products and services provided, but also the interaction with customers, by transferring them to the online environment; (ii) increased competition (competition in this area is generated not only by FinTech companies, but also by non-specialized entities that provide FinTech products or services, some of them being large, globally active companies (such as Alibaba, Amazon or, more recently, Apple); (iii) further consolidation of the banking sector and (iv) new and more challenging regulatory and supervisory activities.

The main objective of the proposed case study is to provide some answers to the following questions: (i) to what extent can FinTech enter the European market? (ii) are the European markets accommodative enough for new innovative financial projects? (iii) what are the main drivers of FinTech phenomenon? (iv) will FinTech shape the financial landscape going forward? By constructing four indices that can influence and drive FinTech market entry, such as (a) demand factors, (b) supply factors, (c) business environment and d) investment climate. By applying a z-score and a 1 to 10 ranking methodologies, our results point out which economy is better prepared for a challenging wave of innovative changes in the financial sector relatively to the other economies included in the study.

5. DATA AND METHODOLOGY

In terms of data and timespan, we focus on the 28 European Union countries over a period of 12 years (2007 – 2018). As FinTech activity is driven by a range of demand-side and supply-side factors, the authors build four indices that can influence and drive Fintech market entry as follows: (i) demand factors, aiming to surprise the level of financial inclusion, (ii) supply factors, focusing on the available technology and infrastructure, (iii) business environment, capturing the ease of starting new businesses and (iv) investment climate, aiming to point out the main risk factors related to investment environment for all EU economies. The variables used to construct the four indices, their impact in the composition of the indices and the data sources are presented in the Table 1.

The methodologies used to construct the ranking scoring are based on z-scores and 1 to 10 ranking:

$$z_{year\ t}^{country\ i} = \frac{x_{year\ t}^{country\ i} - mean\left(x_{year\ t}^{EU\ countries}\right)}{std\left(x_{year\ t}^{EU\ countries}\right)} \tag{1}$$

$$z_{year\ t}^{country\ i} = -\frac{x_{year\ t}^{country\ i} - mean\left(x_{year\ t}^{EU\ countries}\right)}{std\left(x_{year\ t}^{EU\ countries}\right)} \tag{2}$$

$$Index_{year\ t}^{country\ i} = 9 * \frac{x_{year\ t}^{country\ i} - min\left(x_{year\ t}^{EU\ countries}\right)}{max\left(x_{year\ t}^{EU\ countries}\right) - min\left(x_{year\ t}^{EU\ countries}\right)} + 1 \tag{3}$$

$$Index_{year\ t}^{country\ i} = (-9) * \frac{x_{year\ t}^{country\ i} - min\left(x_{year\ t}^{EU\ countries}\right)}{max\left(x_{year\ t}^{EU\ countries}\right) - min\left(x_{year\ t}^{EU\ countries}\right)} + 10 \tag{4}$$

Table 1. Data

Variables	Impact
Demand factors (financial inclusion)	
Unbanked population (% of population without a bank account)	Negative
Ease of access to loans* (index)	Positive
People at risk of poverty or social exclusion (% of total population)	Negative
Rural population (% of total population)	Negative
Supply factors (available technology and infrastructure)	
Automated Teller Machines (ATMs) per 100,000 adults	Positive
Usage of internet (% of Individuals using the internet)	Positive
Technological readiness* (index)	Positive
Mobile-cellular telephone subscriptions per 100 inhabitants	Positive
Quality of electricity supply* (index)	Positive
Business environment (ease of starting new business)	
Capacity for innovation* (index)	Positive
Number of procedures to start a business	Negative
Number of days to start a business	Negative
Availability of scientists and engineers* (index)	Positive
Financial services meeting business needs* (index)	Positive
Investment climate (risk factors)	
Corruption perception* (index)	Positive
Burden of government regulation* (index)	Positive
Property rights* (index)	Positive
Legal rights* (index)	Positive

Note: * higher value of the indicator means a more positive outcome
Sources: World Bank, Eurostat, international Monetary Fund, United Nations specialized agency for ICTs, Global Competitiveness Index

Scores provide insights whether the FinTech environment in one country is better or worse compared to the rest of the countries in the sample. Sub-indices are built following two rules: (i) if a higher value of the indicator leads to a positive outcome, equations (1) and (3) are applied and (ii) if a lower value of the indicator leads to a positive outcome, equations (2) and (4) are applied. The two methodologies are consistent and the results provide the same country rankings. National indices were computed as unweighted averages of sub-indices. EU overall index was computed as population weighted average of the national indices. The meaning of the scores for the four constructed market indices is presented in Table 2.

6. RESULTS AND MAIN TAKE-AWAY

The resulted scores provide insights whether the FinTech environment in one country is better or worse compared to the rest of the countries in the sample.

Table 2. Interpretation of the resulted scores

Market indices	Meaning of resulted scores
Demand factors (financial inclusion)	1 / low z = low financial inclusion 10/high z = high financial inclusion
Supply factors (available technology and infrastructure)	1 / low z= low infrastructure 10 / high z = high infrastructure
Business environment (ease of starting new businesses)	1 / low z= difficult environment to start a new business 10 / high z = friendly environment to start a new business
Investment climate (risk factors)	1 / low z= high risks 10 / high z = low risks

Source: Authors' estimations

Looking at the demand factors related to financial inclusion and supply factors referring to available technology and infrastructure (Figure 1), the results show that lower - income countries (such as Romania, Bulgaria, Greece) face low financial inclusion and low technology and infrastructure, while higher - income countries (mainly euro area countries, Great Britain and Denmark) show a better level of financial inclusion and more supportive technology and infrastructures. However, on average, the European Union is characterized by a relatively good level of financial inclusion and supportive technology and infrastructure.

Judging by the relation between financial inclusion and the investment climate (Figure 2), the results show that most EU countries may have a high need for more financial inclusion, however, the investment climate may not be very friendly. In general, there is a good level of financial inclusion in the EU, but the investment environment is still risky. There are also countries such as Great Britain, Germany, the Netherlands, Finland or Denmark which face a low risk environment for investments and register a good level of financial inclusion as well. However, there is still a pretty high number of countries (such as Romania, Bulgaria or Greece) characterized by both low financial inclusion and high risk investment climate.

Figure 1. Country rankings based on demand and supply factors (2018)
Note: The dimension of the country bubbles is calculated based on the countries' population.
Source: Authors' estimations

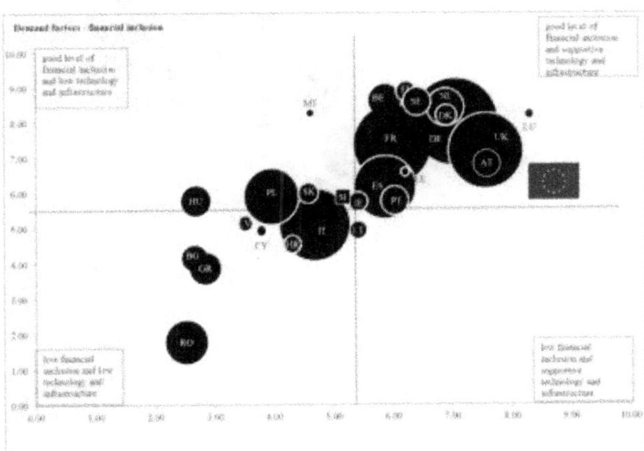

Figure 2. Country rankings based on demand factors and investment climate (2018)
Note: The dimension of the country bubbles is calculated based on the countries' population.
Source: Authors' estimations

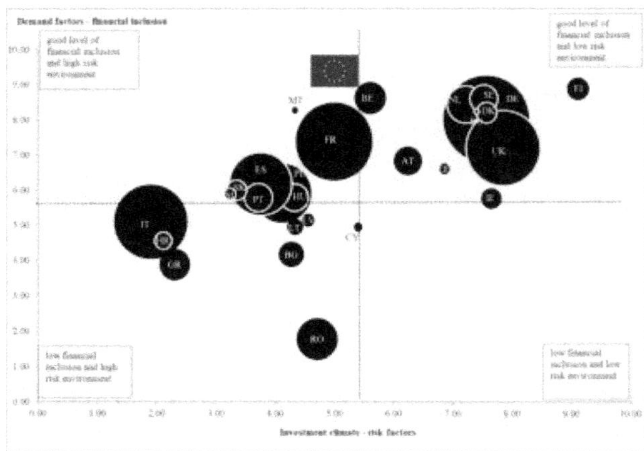

Figure 3 presents the relation between the supply factors (available technology and infrastructure) and the business environement (ease of doing business). Most euro area countries, Great Britain and Denmark provide good capacity of innovation, good entrepreneurial business climate and sound infrastructure to develop further FinTech solutions, while in lower - income countries, mostly non - euro area countries such as Romania, Bugaria, Hungary or Poland, both infrastructure and business environment require improvement to make Fintech - led financial inclusion a success. On average, the European Union is characterized by both supportive technology and infrastructure and a friendly environment to start new businesses.

Figure 3. Country rankings based on supply factors and the business environment (2018)
Note: The dimension of the country bubbles is calculated based on the countries' population.
Source: Authors' estimations

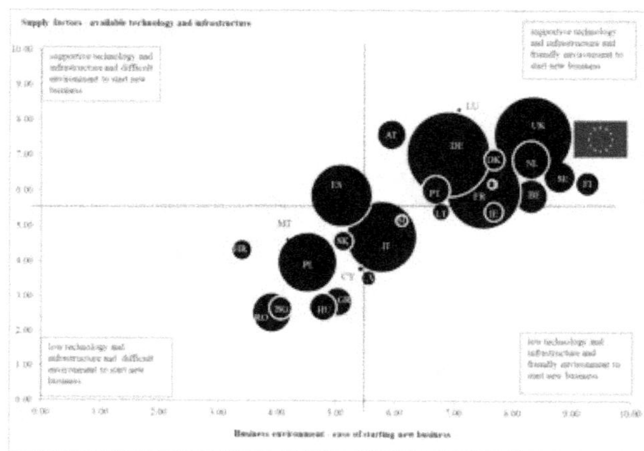

In order to foster an easier FinTech access on the markets, countries which resulted to be situated at the end of the rankings (such as Romania or Bulgaria) should focus on improving the digital and financial inclusion, make further steps to advance in new technologies and infrastructures, accommodate a more friendly investment climate and improve the ease of starting new business on their territory.

7. CONCLUSION

The estimated overall European Union index and national sub-indices provide a relative assessment of the EU countries with regards to the markets' environment for FinTech. The case study results show that the adoption of FinTech across the EU countries is not evenly distributed and that it has been greater in higher - income countries reflecting economic development (mostly euro area countries) compared to lower - income countries (mostly non - euro area countries).

The sustainable development of digitalisation and technology-driven innovation in financial services (FinTech) requires an adequate competitive environment, which can be ensured by introducing a set of internationally-applicable standards and rules. Moreover, establishing a clear and comprehensive regulatory framework governing the new technological progress in the financial field is a key prerequisite for the harmonized integration of FinTech products worldwide. The new set of rules should address technological and operational requirements, from the perspective of both the business environment and the supervisory authorities, with a view to containing the materialization of risks to financial system stability. At the same time, steps should be taken to narrow the gap between the prudential regime applied to credit institutions and that governing the new companies which will act as providers of FinTech products and services.

Moreover, it is worthwhile to develop an educational thread, namely the PFM (Pesonal Finance Management) applications. This can be done by synthetic analysis of banking applications, non-banking apps. (like. Mint, Quicken, Spendee, Bilo, Acorns, Wallet, Fuelio, etc. and social apps. (like. social bookmarking, facebook, youtube banking). According to official reports, the rates of PFM consider the use of personal finance management systems integrated into the banking software. They don't include the use of stand-alone apps, like Mint (budget tracker and planner) or Acorns - (savings automation and investment tool) with 20 and 30-40 million users in the US, correspondingly. Therefore PFM is a must-have for banks, who must transform static platforms into attractive and cooperation-driven digital products, helping them to create new business models.

REFERENCES

Ajao, O. S., Jayeoba, O., & Ajibade, A. (2016). Evolution and development of auditing. *Unique Journal of Business Management Research*, *3*(1), 32–40.

Association of Chartered Certified Accountants – ACCA. (2019). *Audit and technology. Professional insight report.* Retrieved from https://www.accaglobal.com/content/dam/ACCA_Global/professional-insights/audit-and-tech/pi-audit-and-technology.pdf

Association of Chartered Certified Accountants – ACCA. (n.d.). *Data analytics and the auditor. Technical articles*. Retrieved from https://www.accaglobal.com/in/en/student/exam-support-resources/professional-exams-study-resources/p7/technical-articles/data-analytics.html

Bowrin, A. R., & King, I. I. J. II. (2010). Time pressure, task complexity, and audit effectiveness. *Managerial Auditing Journal*, *25*(2), 160–181. doi:10.1108/02686901011008963

Chartered Professional Accountants of Canada - CPA Canada & American Institute of CPAs – AICPA. (2017). *Blockchain technology and its potential impact on the audit and assurance profession*. Retrieved from https://www.aicpa.org/content/dam/aicpa/interestareas/frc/assuranceadvisoryservices/downloadabledocuments/blockchain-technology-and-its-potential-impact-on-the-audit-and-assurance-profession.pdf

Dai, J., & Vasarhelyi, M. A. (2016). Imagineering audit 4.0. [Editorial]. *Journal of Emerging Technologies in Accounting*, *13*(1), 1–15. doi:10.2308/jeta-10494

Deloitte. (2015). *Industry 4.0 – Challenges and solutions for the digital transformation and use of exponential technologies*. Retrieved from https://www2.deloitte.com/content/dam/Deloitte/ch/Documents/manufacturing/ch-en-manufacturing-industry-4-0-24102014.pdf

Han, S., Razaee, Z., Xue, L., & Zhang, J. H. (2016). The association between information technology investments and audit risk. *Journal of Information Systems*, *30*(1), 93–116. doi:10.2308/isys-51317

Holotescu, C. (2018). *Understanding blockchain opportunities and challenges*. Paper presented at The 14th International Scientific Conference "eLearning and software for education", Bucharest, Romania. Retrieved from https://www.researchgate.net/profile/Carmen_Holotescu/publication/324209739_Understanding_Blockchain_Opportunities_and_Challenges/links/5dac4f2c299bf111d4bf50f9/Understanding-Blockchain-Opportunities-and-Challenges.pdf

IDEA. (n.d.). *Big data and audit*. Retrieved from https://idea.caseware.com/big-data-and-audit/

International Federation of Accountants – IFAC. (2009). *International Standard on Auditing 240*. Retrieved from https://www.ifac.org/system/files/downloads/a012-2010-iaasb-handbook-isa-240.pdf

International Federation of Accountants – IFAC. (2019a). *Introduction to: ISA 315 (Revised 2019) Identifying and assessing the risks of material misstatement*. Retrieved from https://www.ifac.org/system/files/publications/files/IAASB-Introduction-to-ISA-315.pdf

International Federation of Accountants – IFAC. (2019b). *Technology and the future-ready auditor*. Retrieved from https://www.ifac.org/system/files/publications/files/IAASB-Tech-Talk-November-2019.pdf

Jensen, M. C., & Meckling, W. H. (1976). Theory of the firm: Managerial behaviour, agency costs and ownership structure. *Journal of Financial Economics*, *3*(4), 305–360. doi:10.1016/0304-405X(76)90026-X

KMPG. (2018). Three technologies that will change the face of auditing. *Forbes Insights*. Retrieved from https://www.forbes.com/sites/insights-kpmg/2018/07/16/three-technologies-that-will-change-the-face-of-auditing/

Lee, T.-H., & Ali, A. M. (2008). The evolution of auditing: An analysis of the historical development. *Journal of Modern Accounting and Auditing*, *4*(12), 1–8.

Li, Z. (2017). Will blockchain change the audit? *China-USA Business Review*, *16*(6), 294–298.

Lord, S. (2018). The future of the audit - The enduring importance of professional scepticism. *Accounting Today*. Retrieved from https://www.accountingtoday.com/opinion/the-enduring-importance-of-professional-skepticism-in-auditing

Massachusetts Department of Revenue – Computer Assisted Audit Group. (n.d.). *A guide to computer assisted audit techniques*. Retrieved from http://www.mtc.gov/uploadedFiles/Multistate_Tax_Commission/Audit_Program/Resource/caat.pdf

Mujawar, S., & Joshi, A. (2015). Data analytics types, tools and their comparison. *International Journal of Advanced Research in Computer and Communication Engineering*, *4*(2), 488–491.

Organisation for Economic Co-operation and Development – OECD. (2018). *OECD Blockchain Primer*. Retrieved from https://www.oecd.org/finance/OECD-Blockchain-Primer.pdf

Organisation for Economic Cooperation and Development – OECD. (2015). *G20/OECD Principles of Corporate Governance*. Paris: OECD Publishing. Retrieved from https://www.oecd.org/daf/ca/Corporate-Governance-Principles-ENG.pdf

Perić, E. (n.d.). *Industrija 4.0* [Industry 4.0]. Croatian Chamber of Economy. Retrieved from https://www.hgk.hr/documents/hgk-industrija-4058d8c59722f1e.pdf

Sever Mališ, S., Tušek, B. & Žager, L. (2012). *Revizija - načela, standardi, postupci* [Audit - principles, standards, procedures]. Zagreb: Hrvatska zajednica računovođa i financijskih djelatnika [Croatian Association of Accountants and Financial Professionals].

Svanström, T. (2016). Time pressure, training activities and dysfunctional audit behaviour: Evidence from small audit firms. *International Journal of Auditing*, *20*(1), 42–51. doi:10.1111/ijau.12054

The Institute of Chartered Accountants in England and Wales – ICAEW & Dubai Financial Services Authority – DFSA. (2018). *Understanding the impact of technology in audit and finance*. Retrieved from https://www.icaew.com/-/media/corporate/files/middle-east-hub/understanding-the-impact-of-technology-in-audit-and-finance.ashx

Voshmgir, S., & Kalinov, V. (2017). *Blockchain – A beginners guide*. BlockchainHub. Retrieved from https://s3.eu-west-2.amazonaws.com/blockchainhub.media/Blockchain+Technology+Handbook.pdf

Wen Ooi, J. (2018). Big data and analytics will transform the audit profession - Here's what you must know. *Prospects*, *7*. https://www.prospectsasean.com/big-data-analytics-transform-audit-profession/

ADDITIONAL READING

American Institute of Certified Public Accountants – AICPA. (2015). Audit analytics and continuous audit: looking toward the future. Retrieved from https://www.aicpa.org/interestareas/frc/assuranceadvisoryservices/downloadabledocuments/auditanalytics_lookingtowardfuture.pdf

Arens, A. A., Elder, R. J., Beasley, M. S., & Hogan, C. E. (2017). Auditing and Assurance Services. Sixteenth Edition. Global Edition: Pearson.

Boynton, W. C., & Johnson, R. N. (2006). *Modern auditing: assurance services and the integrity of financial reporting* (8th ed.). John Wiley & Sons.

Centre for Financial and Reporting Reform – CFRR. (2017). Audit data analytics: opportunities and tips. World Bank Group. Retrieved from http://siteresources.worldbank.org/EXTCENFINREPREF/Resources/4152117-1427109489814/SMPs_spreads_digital.pdf

Deloitte (2018). Auditing the risks of disruptive technologies: Internal audit in the age of digitalization. Retrieved from https://www2.deloitte.com/content/dam/Deloitte/us/Documents/finance/us-rfa-auditing-the-risks-of-disruptive-technologies.pdf

KPMG. (2017). Harnessing the power of cognitive technology to transform the audit. Retrieved from https://assets.kpmg/content/dam/kpmg/us/pdf/2017/02/harnessing-the-power-of-cognitive-technology-to-transform-the-audit.pdf

KPMG & Forbes Insights. (2017). Audit 2025: The future is now. Retrieved from https://assets.kpmg/content/dam/kpmg/us/pdf/2017/03/us-audit-2025-final-report.pdf

Public Company Accounting Oversight Board - PCAOB. (2017). Technology and the Audit of Today and Tomorrow. Retrieved from https://pcaobus.org/News/Speech/Pages/Harris-statement-PCAOB-AAA-4-20-17.aspx

Salijeni, G., Samsonova-Taddei, A., & Turley, S. (2018). Big Data and Changes in Audit Technology: Contemplating a Research Agenda. *Accounting and Business Research*, *49*(1), 95–119. doi:10.1080/00014788.2018.1459458

Vasarhelyi, M. A., & Romero, S. (2014). Technology in audit engagements: A case study. *Managerial Auditing Journal*, *29*(4), 350–365. doi:10.1108/MAJ-06-2013-0881

ENDNOTES

1 The views expressed in the chapter are those of the authors and do not necessarily reflect those of the National Bank of Romania nor the Bucharest University of Economic Studies. The authors would like to thank for useful comments to the participants of the Annual Regional Seminar on Financial Stability jointly organized by the National Bank of Romania and the International Monetary Fund and the High Level Roundtable on Resolution and Financial Stability, which was held on 26 -27 October 2017 in Bucharest, Romania.

2 https://ec.europa.eu/digital-single-market/en/desi

Chapter 4
Accelerating Financial Innovation Through RegTech:
A New Wave of FinTech

Shilpa Narang
https://orcid.org/0000-0001-8037-6822
Guru Gobind Singh Indraprastha University, Delhi, India

ABSTRACT

The buzz word 'RegTech' is on the rise. A financial service regulation has inflated at an astounding rate since the financial crisis and, therefore, has the price tag of regulatory compliance. Many start-ups have begun to apply digital technological knowledge including APIs, AI, RPAs, and many more to these immediate, numerous, and burdensome tasks to meet the terms and regulations, hence the emergence of RegTech. This study examines the implications for financial institutions and regulation particularly when technology poses a confront to the global banking and regulatory system. It attempts to examine the characteristics and applications of RegTech in the world of regulatory compliance. It also illustrates a model to define the transformation of present workload to proposed workload of regulatory compliance with an application of RegTech.

INTRODUCTION

"RegTech is redefining the future for financial services. New digitization technologies are changing the way risk management and regulatory compliance requirements are addressed and delivered. However, for this to happen, collaboration across a number of actors is crucial, particularly across the banks, the regulators, the RegTech firms, and the large consultancies." **-Subas Roy,** *Partner , RegTech, Digital risk & compliance*

The word "RegTech" was proposed in 2015 by the Financial Conduct Authority, which portrayed it as a sub-set of FinTech that relies on technologies that may support the delivery of regulatory requirements more ingeniously and productively than accessible capabilities.

DOI: 10.4018/978-1-7998-4390-0.ch004

RegTech takes on a selection of meanings depending on the individuals defining it. Usually, the portmanteau refers to any company rising agile technology that can help financial companies to enhance comply with regulations. In the period of 2008 financial crisis, financial regulators wanted to make sure the industry would not face the same troubles again. New system was put in place to develop risk controls, maintain capital and create a more transparent financial sector.

With an enlarged focus on managing risk and complying with stricter rules, the financial industry needed to find new ways to adjust. On top of this, knowledge was advancing; significance much more was possible. The growth of FinTech has stretched in three stages. The first and foremost stage is distinguished as FinTech 1.0. A period that stretches from the laying of the transatlantic cable to the development of the global telex association and which captures long-standing connections between technology and finance.

The second stage, FinTech 2.0, encompasses the pre-GFC time underpinned by the digitization of customary financial services, opening with the first ATM and culminating in e-banking. Since the GFC is rapidly developing and the production of startups and IT firms is categorized with financial services. The era of FinTech 3.0, the speedy evolution of FinTech weight a similar evolution of RegTech. "RegTech", has been derived from 'regulatory' and 'technology', depicts the usage of technology, primarily information technology (IT), in the scaffold of regulatory scrutinizing, reporting and thus, compliance too.

To elaborate, the development of RegTech is defined in a chain of stages. RegTech 1.0, a pre-2008 replica, was mainly determined by industry but insisted a partnership with regulators that focused on an over-reliance on a quantitative internal risk organization structures. This stage was pursued by RegTech 2.0, an epoch that is commencing to be encouraged by financial advertise participants and regulators who are using technological expertise to progress regulatory compliance and renovate its component processes.

CONCEPTUAL VIEW: FINTECH AND REGTECH

Explaining FinTech

FinTech is not a new conception. The term "FinTech" can be traced to the early 1990s and now refers to a quickly developing evolutionary process across financial services. This development only began to attract the attention of regulators, industry participants, consumers, and academics in 2014 (Anagnostopoulos 2018).

EXPLAINING REGTECH

Evolution and Significance of RegTech

RegTech refers to technological solutions that modernize and improve regulatory processes. Like FinTech, RegTech has stretched in three stages. The initial stage, RegTech 1.0, was directed by massive financial institutions that embraced know-how into their internal methods to fight against rising compliance fees and complications, as characterized in the Base principal Accord.

The second stage, RegTech 2.0, has been determined by new post-GFC regulatory necessities and the costs to the financial industry of their achievement (Barberies et.al 2017). At the same time, regulators are looking for mirror the increasingly digitized nature of the markets they observe and to improve their capacity to analyze the escalating volumes of data generated by post-GFC exposure obligations.

In the future, RegTech will display its furthermost prospective in the third stage of its growth RegTech 3.0, in which knowledge will help us reconceptualize finance and its guideline to construct a better financial system (Beall, 2019). Eventually, it is quarreled that the increasingly data centric environment of both FinTech and RegTech has the latent to prompt a shift from a KYC example to a KYD mindset. Instead of being seen as a growing subcategory of FinTech, RegTech should be viewed as a detach phenomenon.

FEATURES OF REGTECH

Advanced Analytics Usage

Advanced modelling and machine learning helps in real time analytics capabilities and supports accelerated assessment of emerging regulations. Big data competencies helps in integrating diverse data from different sources. Robust tools like Tableau, Hadoop and Pentaho are used to in-built automated compliance assurance.

Robust Technology Architecture

Open Network and platforms provide users data sharing, format of standardization and common processes. Robust application programming interface allows legacy system to communicate with upcoming systems and among each other. Cloud-based solutions are flexible and cost efficient and promote remote and secure data management. Additionally, robust risk data warehouses and other enterprises have wide risk aggregation; it also performs risk data management and scenario analysis. Automated due diligence processes can be tailored according to FI's risk based approaches (Butler, 2018). Robust technology architecture accurate timely and secure extraction data capabilities. Data presented is standardized and have to be sliced and diced in multiple formats.

Effective Tools

Robust risk management tool includes analysis tool like regulation gap, complaint for health check and provides management information system tools, monitoring tool, regulatory reporting tool, case management tool, consumer management tool, validation tool and many others. System risk management tools make sure that real-time analysis works properly in financial crime risk monitoring, trade surveillance, AML, and customer profiling (Butler & O'Brien, 2019). Bio metrics and social media analysis tools helps to tackle the financial of terrorism and for KYC / AML compliance. RegTech provides powerful tools aid visualization, understanding and reporting of various heterogeneous data sources. To interact directly with regulatory reporting system there is innovative accounting tool. Robo-advise tools provide regulated and custom advice.

Agility and Flexibility

Agility and flexibility provides short implementation time frames. In RegTech new features can be easily added, customized and can be removed. It helps in generating new configuration regulatory reports (CBInsights 2017). In RegTech data controllable is depended on organisation.

Significance of RegTech

- Scalable and sustainable solutions, providing flexibility and growth
- Reduces cost of compliance and need for manual checks
- Improved governance and transparency of regulatory reporting
- Streamlines risk management processes, using scenario analytics
- Using advanced data analytics to enhance business confidence
- Increased market stability, protects health of financial institutions

Scope of RegTech

The scope and difficulty of regulation has extended to include almost all areas of commerce, and effectively managing guideline has never been so complicated and critical to business (CBInsights 2018). As we've seen with the FinTech revolution, when problems are huge enough, startups are usually the first to respond. As a result, a range of companies are moving up to help businesses reduce the cost and risk of obedience while concurrently identifying new business opportunities that arise in the wake of changing guideline (Deloitte, 2019).

Guideline, of course, is nothing new. One of the essential tasks of governments has always been to protect the rights of the many, regularly by limiting the actions of the few (Deloitte, 2017a). Though, recent trends have increased the controlling burden on companies to such an extent that a new industry is forming to deal with this difficulty. As a result, "RegTech" is expanding its footprint far outside its traditional association with FinTech, and reaching all types and facets of businesses (Deloitte, 2017b).

Applications of RegTech

RegTech operates in a variety of spheres of the monetary and narrow space. A numeral of projects that Regtech automates comprises employee observation, fulfillment data management, deception prevention, and audit track capabilities (Ernst & Young, 2015a).

A RegTech production can't just work together with any financial institution or narrow authority as it may have dissimilar goals and strategies that may be different from the other parties (Ernst & Young, 2015b). For example, a RegTech that seeks to recognize credit card deception in the digital payments bionetwork may not expand a relationship with an asset firm concerned with its employees' behavior online or the Securities and Exchange Commission (SEC) whose present issue may be an augment in insider trading actions (Fathi, 2018).

However, the major reflective transformation could emerge from the application of digital technology. According to the standard principle, financial regulations could be written into managerial supervisory systems that banks easily plug into Institute of international finance (2016). Automation of compliance in bank processes and adaptation to regulatory could make regulatory compliance easy to implement.

Table 1. RegTech will transform compliance by four means

S.No.	Areas of RegTech	How it helps redefine the future of compliance
1	Technology that permits more competent techniques of sharing information	Alternative regulatory reporting methods including data provision, collection and predictive analytics. Shared utilities via. cloud or other online, on-demand platforms. Including capabilities that permit the banks and FIs to communicate among each other, and also with the regulator(s) thereby removing the need for lengthy reviews and investigations (Friedman, 1996).
2	Technology that makes effectiveness by bridging the gap between intention and interpretation.	Data ontology standards to enable risk-theme based (e.g. credit risk, misconduct, cyber, fraud) regulatory interpretations, assessment and reporting at a real-time (Goertzel, 2007). Diminish / eradicating the requirement for post-trade scrutiny and transactions monitoring including implementation of machine readable and machine-executable regulations
3	Technology that simplifies data, allows improved decision making and facilitates cognitive automation.	Alternative, secondary regulatory data architecture with open-source APIs to allow simplified, real-time reporting and assessments (Hill, 2018). Cognitive automation enables reading and performing risk and compliance tasks and design of innovative models
4	Technology that allows regulation and compliance processes to be looked at differently, proactively.	Holistic digital compliance such as data integration, verification and visualization (Huber, 2018). Demand for incorporated, utility based risk management and reporting covering an extensive array of regulations, across both financial and non-financial risks.

RegTech can improvise the efficiency of compliance (Kavassalis, 2018). The analytical data needed to satisfy regulators' demands is also vital for business decision-making. For instance, they can be utilized to spot not only customers who are probable money launderers or fraudsters but who are likely to default on loans, run large deposit balances or otherwise act in ways favorable or unfavorable to the bank's earnings (Nicoletti, 2017). This technology can also aid a bank recognize where "macro risks" are budding – for instance, from political or economic developments in countries where it has coverages – thereby, notifying not only tactical but deliberate decision making (Panisi & Perrone 2018).

The proposed model reflects the transformation of the present workload to the proposed workload with an application of RegTech. The fragmented or manual processed data environments will be transformed into digitally-enabled and automated data environments, complying with the leading regulatory compliance frameworks (Roy et.al., 2018). This will result in rapid scalability and reconfiguration. Adopting RegTech will provide pivotal bedrock not only to the banks' processes but also, result in a change in staff requirements. Standardized and relatively low-level roles now employed in compliance and control will need to be replaced by some data scientists and systems engineers (Shäubli, 2018). Banks will need to collaborate more effectively, not only with the specialist organizations that supply the technology but with the wider industry. Initiating alone, banks can apply RegTech to minimize their compliance costs. But the major gains will be given by digitization of regulations themselves and their incorporation into the structure of financial services (Thomson, 2017). Therefore, moving towards this target will require an unparalleled group effort between banks and their regulators, not only on their data interfaces but on the foundational structure of banking regulation itself.

Figure 1. Common RegTech players around the world

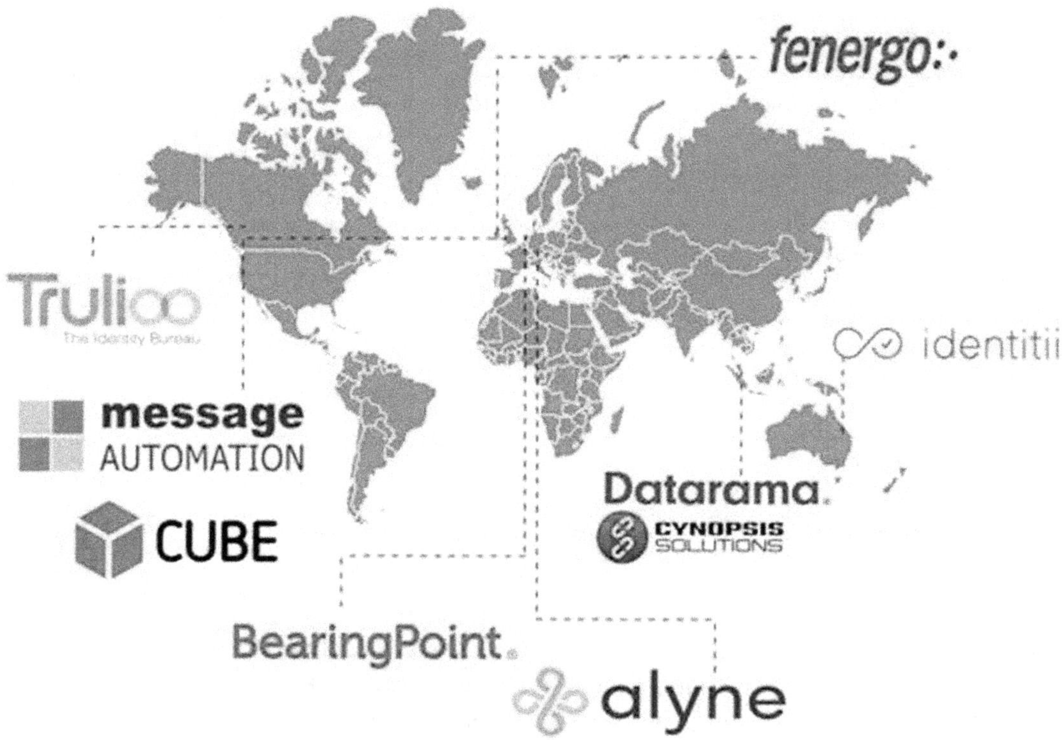

Figure 2. Model to signify RegRech's assist to minimize the regulatory workload

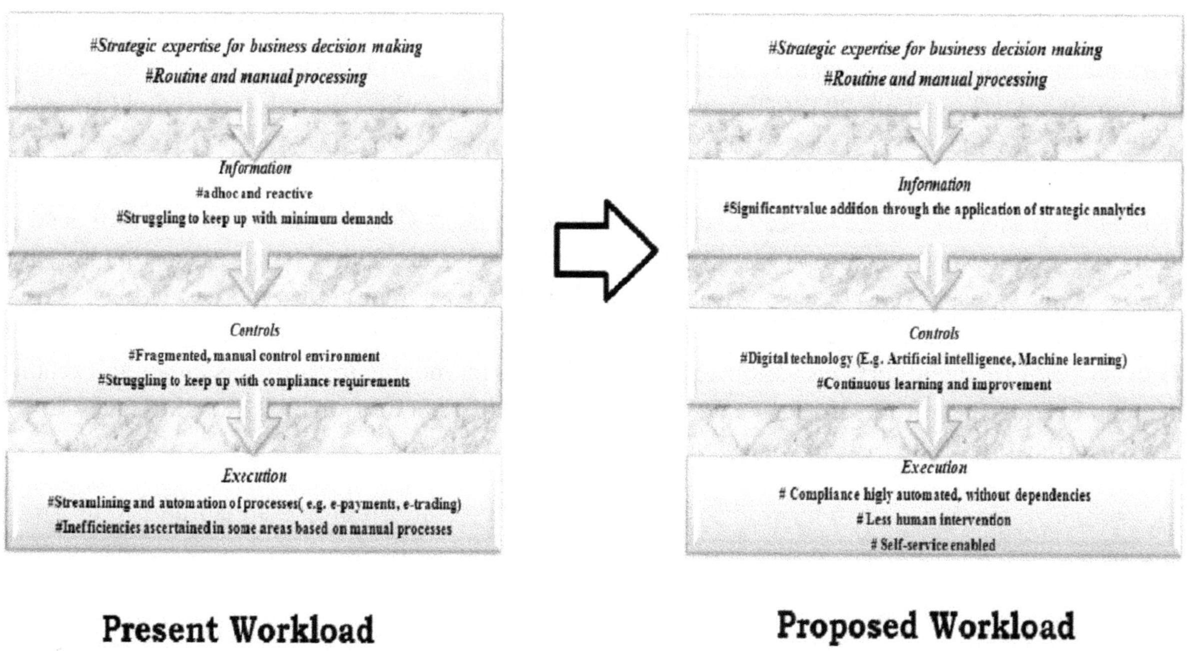

IMPLICATIONS OF REGTECH FOR FINANCIAL SERVICES

Adopting RegTech will bring modifications in their business practices and cultures and, to incorporate additional skills in data science and artificial intelligence. This is a prolonged effort but financial services firms can take certain steps now to commence moving in the correct route:

- Preset digital and innovation - a top priority for the organization (Thomson, 2019).
- Mobilizing a team that will prioritize, monitor, assess, and measure the innovation pipeline based on value generation.
- Use an incremental method to tackle complex issues such as data quality and accessibility issues.
- Implement a mechanism to learn from previous digitization projects and programs.
- Embed an innovation-based culture and digital escalation.
- Create a diverse and cross-functional group of stakeholders that will congregate to drive efforts forward.

SOME CASES DISCUSSED

The following cases have been illustrated to display real-life applications of regulation technologies. These companies put forward regulatory compliance solutions for audit and assurance purposes (Treleaven, & Bogdan, 2017).

Aigine GDPR Compliance

The General Data Protection Regulation (GDPR) plans to guard personal information of individuals (Burgess, 2019). The new regulation affects companies, and potentially pushes them to hire additional staff to be able to conform with GDPR accordingly (Burgess, 2019). Burgess (2019), claims that GDPR has already replenished the way firms grip the personal data issues. Aigine offers a solution that might minimize the requirement for new staff hired for GDPR compliance purposes.

Solution: Makes it easier and more effective to detect unstructured personal information to comply with GDPR

Benefits: Reduces the human contribution - The review can be done without a lawyer

Limitations:

- Companies need to "teach" cognitive computing with their own data
- It takes time for a client to get started with the product

Apiax Tax Product

Apiax is a RegTech company that provides advanced tools for compliance of financial regulations. The objective is to make compliance of regulations efficient (Apiax, 2019). Ralf Huber (2018), Legal Lead and Co-Founder of Apiax, outlines the possibilities of the Tax Product as "Financial institutions can efficiently make usage of tax calculations in their advisory processes. This is the missing bit in the riddle of value-added, personalized investment advice."

Solution: Allows focusing on tax adjusted returns globally without knowing national tax laws and regulations

Benefits:

- ◦ Financial institutions may use tax adjusted returns in their advisory procedure.
- ◦ The price of tax consultancy may fall.

Limitations: Responsibility issues and challenges in case of judicial proceeding

Mindbridge AI-Auditor

Mindbridge Ai is a company that provides the first AI-powered auditing global solution. (MindBridge, 2018). Mindbridge Ai auditor practices machine learning and AI tools and techniques to alter the auditing procedure more effortless and efficient (MindBridge, 2018). They offer digital solutions for companies in audit and assurance and internal audit purposes. They have tailored product also for companies that present financial services.

Solution: AI-motorised solution for audit and internal audit, which permits the company to analyse their whole dataset in minutes

Benefits:

- ◦ The quality of audit raises substantially
- ◦ Reduces the human role

Limitations: Relatively high price

Interpretation Based on Above Cases

- The first company delivers solution that complies with GDPR and spots unstructured personal evidence.
- The second company operates with a software solution which permits direct determination of tax outcomes of an investment, without additional calculations.
- The third company proposes an artificial-intelligence-powered-solution for auditing and internal audit processes.

REGTECH- A NEW FINTECH: THE CASE OF SINGAPORE AS A REGIONAL INNOVATION SANDBOX

Singapore and FinTech signify a perfect tie in bliss. The combo of finance and technology have fused up to boost the future finance industries. With the great efforts of Singaporeans since decades, they have achieved an edge in global finance Asia-Pacific and have sketched their place as a well-established regional hub for FinTech.

RegTech, a blend of 'regulatory technologies' addresses the regulatory issues and challenges through innovative elucidations (Yang, 2018).. This new FinTech is influencing and transforming regulatory monitoring, reporting and compliance practices globally and prominently in Singapore. FinTech is acting as a big comrade to guide the success path to RegTech. Since 2016, the Singaporean Government had already been proactively committed to utilize FinTech developments to enrich the regulatory capacity.

The Monetary Authority of Singapore (MAS) is in the process of merging money exchange and remittance systems law into single legislation which would empower the inclusive regulation of old and new payments services (Finriskalert, n.d.).

A huge hurdle in other countries involved in such generalizations of legislation and having corrected that issue very easily is evidencing to be a prodigious edge in the worldwide RegTech insight. Managing director of the MAS focused on mission to construct an electronic payments society and this vision shadows the relief of a consultation paper for a regulatory-governed sandbox, based on the one customed by the Financial Conduct Authority, UK. This resourcefulness aims to confirm that any financial know-how is publicly reachable and is a best exercise (Vysya & Kumar n.d.).

This consultation paper admits that the planned sandbox cannot eradicate all risks completely, "as failure is an inherent characteristic of innovation". It aims to minimize the adverse bearing of any such incidence. At the global reach, the MAS has also joined services with French regulators Autorité de Contrôle Prudentiel et de Résolution (ACPR) and the Autorité des Marchés Financiers (AMF), along with a conglomerate with the Swiss Financial Market Supervisory Authority (FINMA).

According to "Report of the Committee on the Future Economy", the authorities have highlighted the matter of keeping pace with technological know-how in their regulatory practices and procedures multiple times, appealing that "..the Government should identify and focus on areas with high potential for technological and industry innovation… providing clear and updated regulations will be particularly important for the development of these emerging industries, such as MedTech, FinTech and food and nutrition. The *regulatory agencies* should then systematically collaborate to review existing regulations".

Besides its administrative and legislative use, RegTech permits agile and scalable solution keys for corporations, as it supports their acquiescence with cumulatively increasing stringent and endlessly fluctuating regulations (Kraft, n.d.). The chief technology planner of Hitachi Data Systems stated in a report that the firm has been using the MAS sandbox to examine blockchain technologies that issue and settle checks in Singapore. BearingPoint, one of the European tech consulting firm developed a software called "Abacus360 Banking", an integrated platform for reporting, risk calculation, monitoring and controlling regulatory KPIs. The software helps in overcoming the challenges for banks and financial institutions such as scalability and achieving efficient reporting (Luca, 2018). A formidable task of handling massive volume of transactions across numerous banks and national borders and irregular compliance challenges can be resolved easily with such technologies.

Even, many startups in Singapore have emerged with imaginative RegTech solutions. Local tech companies can now provide risk management platforms which make more efficient and affordable. They are also advancing in complex screening and monitoring tools linked with blockchain technology to streamline compliance-driven due diligence processes and procedures and thus, making new corporations administered and funded.

Therefore, Mindfulness and responsiveness of RegTech is fairly high in Singapore as compared to many other counties in the world.

CHALLENGES OF REGTECH

The Human Resource Challenge

Rigorous human efforts are essential to develop the quality of data and large organizations have employed thousands of heads for this purpose. It is expected that 10-15% of the total work force is currently committed to risk management and agreement activities. Going forward, with an increase in volumes of data and obedience requirements, the human resource necessities will also multiply manifold (KPMG, 2018). However, skilled specialists with the relevant experience will be hard to find and it will be the organizations that will need to train the labor force.

Regulators

Regulatory technology "RegTech" includes new technologies to help financial service providers reorganize back-office functions, improve productivity, and overcome regulatory challenges, such as the risks and costs related to obedience requirements (Kroll et.al. 2017).

RegTech for Regulators also called "SupTech" involves technology-based clarifications and data science that can help financial establishments regulate and supervise the marketplace more effectively and professionally. RegTech for Regulators solutions can support financial establishments to implement their obligations related to financial stability, integrity, presence, and consumer protection. Some of these solutions are critically needed to monitor competition and enable revolution, and to facilitate more cross-sectoral and cross-jurisdictional teamwork between supervisory authorities (Linström, 2018).

The Data Woes

While RegTech is a promising solution for obedience woes, not everything is as smooth as it may seem at the surface. There are challenges that still need to be determined. The biggest challenge appears to be data. Mechanization can deliver the anticipated results only when the input data is clean and balanced, else the results are assured be off-track. The same data that makes RegTech effective is also its nemesis, as not all data is usable and it must be managed to make it use-worthy.

Increased Complexity

The sheer number of rule changes is cumulative — Even with the current U.S. management taking steps to reduce the number of guidelines. For example, by making a new rule that any new "economically significant" guideline needs to be offset by the repeal of two existing guidelines — the total number of guidelines continues to increase (Mankesiöld, 2018).

Guideline is broadening and impacting more companies — Guideline has long focused on industry verticals: medications, financials, automotive, food, etc. In the information age, though, companies are seeking to gain a competitive advantage from technology. Data, in particular, has become a planned asset for those companies that can digitize it, structure it, and create a layer of value on top of it with software and analytic solutions powered by AI.

The global nature of commerce — the full range of globalization is obvious in the supply chains of even the smallest businesses (Micheler & Whaley, 2018). The reality is that international companies must adopt the standards of the harshest jurisdiction they operate in and often apply those standards across their operations to ensure stability.

Regulation as a driver of growth — Regulation is now often seen by governments as tool to help create new businesses, not just to police current ones (Nicoletti, 2017). Consider the special economic development zones in China, the Silicon Indirect initiative in London, or the green energy creativities in the U.S. Through regulation and tax incentives, governments are driving growth by removing fences for emerging companies. The result is that companies will need to monitor guideline not just to reduce risk, but also to find new opportunities.

High Cost

Competitions are complex if they rise from unpredicted industries, and this might create chaos and disturbances. New FinTech players are the developing competitions to the traditional institutions and these newbies are increasing the market scope but resulting in bigger obedience scrutiny. This evolving risk situations leads all market participants to fulfil with more guidelines and ends up with higher obedience cost.

The system can do anything but to teach the system and to predict the guidelines, domain expertise is essential. Few organizations depend on the external investigators for industry contributions. Many big financial firms are paying heavy amount for researching and domain proficiency consulting. For instance, Europe's MiFID II has guideline on external research spending and it has to be reported as research unbundling reports. So, domain expertise is the new black.

Stringent Timelines

Being strict is not the worst thing in the world except it needs lot of manual workloads and error-prone procedures to be tracked and reported. This will influence investor security and avoids business risks but coping with stringent guidelines is costing heavily in terms of spending among FinTech firms.

Standardization of Data

Another challenge for RegTech is the adjustment of data. Data is fast substituting documents. But, although managers have subjected documents to audit, the same is not true for data. As a step towards adjustment, regulators around the globe can take a cue from the Standard Business Reporting (SBR) in Australia. The Australian government has made important efforts to provide a list of data fields and classification for reporting to multiple agencies, while also working with the software industry to get software built using these data fields. The result is increased mechanization, savings of millions of dollars yearly, and a data-centric obedience model.

SOLUTIONS OF REGTECH

Balanced Consulting Approach

IBM verified the need for the arrangement of regulatory and technical expertise when they planned to purchase influential regulatory consulting firm, which was Promontory Financial Group for about $300 million in 2016. Cape was purchased only for the sole purpose of partnering with IBM's existing AI platform and this combination helped in providing IBM with a viable go to market strategy for breaking industry into RegTech. Yet for FI's were not planning to get hold of a consulting firm to solve their talent gaps and individuals with the mandatory regulatory and technological knowledge are in high demand with short supply.

To concentrate on the shortage supply, FI's will have three primary options:

1. Industry needs to train and up skill their existing workforce.
2. Should contract with outside firms to help out with the implementation of RegTech.
3. Last thing industries can do is outsource certain functions.

Upskilling

Upskilling will fabricate the best lasting results because it will result in training and long-term internal workforce. Moreover experience is gained while Upskilling because it proves value for upcoming future with some opportunities and obstacles. However, Upskilling is a long-lasting process; requiring important investments are required in training and hiring. For many FI's, their hazard and conformity problems are imperative, and many FI's simply do not have the capacity to wait until their workforce has been amply Up skilled before solving the problems.

Outsourcing

Lastly, FI's is likely to determine that certain functions and processes are sufficiently standard enough to carry out outsourcing procedure of the existing RegTech providers. This is tab that will make fl's forgo the ability to maintain expertise and direct supervision over the outsourced functions. But on the other hand this approach can also make resources available for more mission critical items.

The truth so far has been that, most of the Fls will tend to leverage a hybrid approach, i.e. outsourcing what they can and bring in third parties to provide short to medium term solutions, while simultaneously improving the skills of the internal staff for the long term functionality. This is supported by a Thomson Reuters study that eas conducted in 2017 and found out that 41% of fls would use a mixed approach to RegTech adoption, as compared to 22% that was planned to handle this work entirely internally and 20% which would exclusively focus on outsourcing. Even though entirely outsourcing has its own advantages, the balanced approach of improving the skills of internal resources for long term sustainability while also everything the existing knowledge and experience from outside the firm for the implementation of short to medium term solutions, will help in producing the most valuable results.

Contracting Implementation

For more instantaneous results, FI's are expected to turn with outside firms, including with both consulting firms and outer technology providers, this process was already requisite with knowledge to quickly put together RegTech with existing inner procedures and systems. Exterior firms can be tasked with the help of implementation of short to medium-term solutions and while the FI can influence the outside firm's knowledge to assist with the Upskilling process and expansion towards long-term sustainability.

Cappitech

Cappitech's reporting can be measured with Dashboard which helps FI's to exchange traded derivatives and over the counter derivatives by using Capptivate platform.

Captivate platform launched by Cappitech helps in connecting client's to trade data. It helps in guiding the clients to the required fields for European regulatory report and the data is validated during trade repositories.

Risk officers gain timely gain timely and valuable insights on their EMIR regulation reporting with easy drill down capabilities with the help of dashboard.

Cappitech can enhance user experience through a web or mobile based friendly dashboard. It shows visual reports and provides capabilities to user's to search orders using trade, identifiers and divide into categories according to asset class and counterparty source.

Next Angles

Process encoding is used to convert data to machine intelligible data and process modeling is used to define organization and relationship between the transaction and department.

Models that encompass on business knowledge, regulatory requirements and other policies are Computer comprehensible.

Flexible solutions are now scalable across business lines and other asset classes. It shows efficient and innovative real-time liquidity, cash flow projection and classification of assets.

Timely identification of counterparty risk has to go through the cross examination of asset data and knowledge models with reference to some public data sources.

OPPORTUNITIES OF REGTECH

Monitoring New and Changing Regulations

A 2017 survey showed that obedience officer's foremost concern for the year was the "volume and pace of monitoring change." Traditionally, FIs have been dependent upon both internal staff and external vendors to track monitoring changes and analyze their impact on existing organizational processes and standards. As previously stated, certain global FIs could be held responsible for obedience with regulations that are changing every twelve minutes.

Luckily, document and process reviews, which are key components of monitoring change management, were among the first domains where artificial intelligence (AI), and more specifically natural language processing (NLP) algorithms, were effectively applied. RegTech companies have been quick to embrace this technology, with their solutions capable of reading and reviewing multiple monitoring sources and automatically identifying and alerting FIs of any recent changes or additions.

Using Robotic Process Automation to Streamline KYC, CDD, and AML Workflows

For most FIs, Know Your Customer (KYC) and Anti-Money Laundering (AML) guidelines have resulted in a difficult customer onboarding process. FIs typically require their front offices to collect and manually review various documents and enter relevant customer information across various systems. Back offices are concurrently asked to conduct their own reviews and functions to ensure obedience and consistency. Once on boarded, customers require current Customer Due Diligence (CDD), resulting in similar labor-intensive processes to those used in onboarding. Mutually, these processes require substantial resource hours by both front and back office staffs and are exposed to the human error factor, which includes everything from simple typos to intentional process deviance.

Robotic process automation (RPA), sometimes stated to as robotics or digital labor, is a type of RegTech that provides FIs an effective substitute. Bots, the "workforce" of RPA, are software programs that follow defined internal business rules and policies and can be trained on fundamentally any repeatable process. By training bots to follow consistent compliance-related processes, FIs can improve effectiveness, increase throughput, and reduce errors.

Using Robotic Process Automation to Streamline KYC, CDD, and AML Workflows

By automating much of the onboarding workflow through bots, FIs can importantly reduce the amount of time spent devoted to manual, repeatable processes. Moreover, RPA can help better meet quality standards by ensuring that every customer follows the same standard process without the risk of human error or deviance. RPA is not partial to automating onboarding, however. As implementation actions continue, FIs tasked with large-scale remediation or look back efforts can efficiently deploy RPA to more efficiently handle workloads and reduce their dependence on both external vendor staff and internal support staff. By design, implementation actions generally require FIs to complete work either deemed incorrect or unsatisfactory by regulators, and this work is equally manual. Rather than scrambling to identify external vendors, and the relevant internal employees needed to support them, FIs can consume RPA to accomplish many of these same remediation tasks, expressively reducing costs and increasing productivity.

Improving Rules-Based Transaction Monitoring and Fraud Detection Systems with Machine Learning

Presently, most FIs take a rules-based approach for producing unusual transaction alerts and cases. This has caused in significant volumes of false positives which require at least some level of inquiry, with many FIs averaging 90 to 95% false positive rates of their total alerted transactions.

With such inadequacies, even marginal improvements will result in important savings, both in investigative time and overall obedience spend. To tackle this problem, firms have begun executing machine learning solutions, with most focusing on managed machine learning algorithms as their starting point. By training managed algorithms on prior alerted activity, FIs can fine-tune rules to decrease the number of false positives. Instead of relying on unwieldy periodic reviews, feedback loops - which include all reviewed transactions - will allow managed algorithms to compare current rules and investigatory results, using the delta to make recommended changes. This process runs frequently in the background, and as the delta decreases and the FIs become more confident in the supervised algorithm's reference, the pace of rule modification can increase accordingly.

Solution Maturity

To be clear, the solutions defined are not yet complete. To reach their full capabilities, additional research, testing and overall progress is still required. It is also important to note that as of now, RegTech is not usually projected to fully replace all human involvement in the relevant risk and obedience processes. RegTech is ideal for removing low-level, repeatable, manual processes, however, existing technologies are not enough to replace more ambiguous and complex decisions. In truth, a certain level of human observing of RegTech solutions will always be required. The ideal future-state FI will have applied RegTech to replace most if not all its manual, repeatable risk and obedience processes, and will have freed up its efficient obedience staff to conduct more meaningful, targeted work. Overall, RegTech implementation is more a matter of when, not if, and represents opportunities for considerable cost-savings and process restructuring. In fact, the adoption of RegTech is closer than many may think, and midsize banks may represent the most promising spectators for adoption.

EPILOGUE

The extensive position matrimony of technology and finance has been incessantly evolving. This paper has traversed the three stages of FinTech's growth and the two stages, to date, of RegTech's growth. FinTech nowadays exhibits great assure in both rising economies, where quite a lot of original factors—rising Smartphone infiltration, unproductive customary financial systems, and behavioral shifts amongst consumers—present fertile earth for FinTech expansion, and residential economies, where existing speculation in FinTech is growing at an amazing pace.

Enforcd stated a "short" summary that traces the difficulty to catch the right people:

"Here is the short summary: Enforcd has been fortunate in that we have not encountered too many barriers to adoption of our tech; the main reason for this is two fold – firstly we are SaaS and secondly we use no customer data, so are low risk from this perspective. Where we have suffered is in getting the attention of the right people – because compliance and risk staff (our primary sponsors) often say they are simply 'too busy' to consider new solutions. This is frustrating, as the whole point of Enforcd is to save money and time! It's an understandable lament however – given the current regulatory environment and ever increasing Brexit uncertainty. We have noticed some characteristics that are shared by the firms and organisations we have worked with most successfully, namely: a dedicated innovation and/or regtech scout, who has budget and a mandate to go into the market and find effective solutions for

company problems. These people can act as 'intrapreneurs' and hold the hands of more risk averse staff in firms, who are wary of sticking their neck out to work with a new, small vendor. The scouting team, who quite often have a tech background so are in a strong position to assess the viability of a platform or a solution, are well placed to advocate for start-up and scale-up vendors, and to run small scale, low risk pilots to create a strong business case, which can then be used to support wider engagement. It's a model that works well for both sides. senior managers who are serious about finding good new solutions and are not afraid to suggest their teams take a look at these things. It's amazing how quickly a deal can proceed when someone of sufficient seniority gets behind the concept. All in all though, in London especially, we have found we are pushing at an open door with Enforcd. The financial services industry is increasingly receptive to new solutions."

REFERENCES

Anagnostopoulos, I. (2018). Fintech and regtech: Impact on regulators and banks. *Journal of Economics and Business*, *100*, 7–25. doi:10.1016/j.jeconbus.2018.07.003

Arner, D. W., & Barberies, J. N. (2017). FinTech and RegTech in a Nutshell, and the Future in a Sandbox. *SSRN Electronic Journal*. DOI: doi:10.2139srn.3088303

Beall, A. (2019). *What is regtech? The latest wave of startups hitting the fintech industry*. Wired.co.uk. Available at: https://www.wired.co.uk/article/regtech-next-fintech

Butler, T. (2018). On the role of ontology-based regtech for managing risk and compliance reporting in the age of regulation. *Journal of Risk Management in Financial Institutions*, *11*(1), 19–33.

Butler, T., & O'Brien, L. (2019). Understanding RegTech for Digital Regulatory Compliance. In Disrupting Finance (pp. 85-102). Palgrave Pivot.

CBInsights. (2017). *Regtech 101: What It Is, Why Now, & Why It Matters*. Available: https://www.cbinsights.com/research/regtech-four-phases-expert-intelligence/

CBInsights. (2018). *Regtech 102: The Evolution of Regtech and The Future of Regulatory Compliance*. Available: https://www.cbinsights.com/research/regtech-four-phases-expert-intelligence/

Deloitte. (2017a). *The Future of Regulatory Productivity, powered by RegTech. RegTech position paper, Financial Service*. Available: https://www2.deloitte.com/content/dam/Deloitte/us/Documents/regulatory/us-regulatory-future-of-regulatory-productivity-powered-by-regtech.pdf

Deloitte. (2017b). The RegTech universe on the rise. *Inside Magazine- Edition*. Available: https://www2.deloitte.com/content/dam/Deloitte/lu/Documents/technology/lu_inside-regtech-universe-on-rise.df

Deloitte. (2019). *RegTech Universe. Website*. Available: https://www2.deloitte.com/lu/en/pages/technology/articles/regtech-companies-compliance.html

Ernst & Young. (2015a). Innovating with RegTech. *EY's 2015 Global Governance, Risk and Compliance Survey*. Available: https://www.ey.com/Publication/vwLUAssets/EY-Innovating-with-RegTech/$FILE/EY-Innovating-with-RegTech.pdf

Ernst & Young. (2015b). Financial regulation of FinTech. *EY Global Financial Services Institute Article, 3*(3). Available: https://www.ey.com/Publication/vwLUAssets/ey-financial-regulation-of-fintech/$FILE/ey-financial-regulation-of-fintech.pdf

Fathi, E. (2018). *How artificial intelligence can help mend the UK's broken audit system*. Available: https://thefintechtimes.com/artificial-intelligence-audits/

Friedman, B., & Nissenbaum, H. (1996). Bias in computer systems. *ACM Transactions on Information Systems, 14*(3), 330–347.

Goertzel, B., & Pennachin, C. (2007). *Artificial General Intelligence*. Springer.

Gurung, N., & Perlman, L. (2018). *Use of Regtech by Central Banks and Its Impact on Financial Inclusion*. Available SSRN: https://ssrn.com/abstract=3285985

Hill, J. (2018). *Fintech and the remaking of financial institutions*. Available: https://ebookcentral.proquest.com

Huber, R. (2018). *Apiax at Swiss Asset Management Day 2018: Introducing tax efficient investing*. Available: https://blog.apiax.com/apiax-at-swiss-asset-management-day-2018-introducing-tax-efficient-investing-4055b5c4bb49

Institute of International Finance. (2016). *Regtech in Financial Services: Technology Solutions for Compliance And Reporting*. Available: https://www.iif.com/Portals/0/Files/private/iif-regtech_in_financial_services_-_solutions_for_compliance_and_reporting.pdf?ver=2019-01-04-142943-690

Kavassalis, P. (2018). An innovative RegTech approach to financial risk monitoring and supervisory reporting. *The Journal of Risk Finance, 19*(1), 39–55.

Kavuri, A. S., & Milne, A. K. L. (2019). *Fintech and the Future of Financial Services: What Are the Research Gaps?* CAMA Working Paper No. 18/2019. Available SSRN: https://ssrn.com/abstract=3333515

KPMG. (2018). *There's a revolution coming- Embracing the challenge of RegTech 3.0*. Available: https://home.kpmg/content/dam/kpmg/uk/pdf/2018/09/regtech-revolution-coming.pdf

Kroll, J., Huey, J., Baroca, S., Felten, E., Reidenberg, J., Robinson, D., & Yu, H. (2017). Accountable algorithms. *University of Pennsylvania Law Review, 165*(3), 633–707.

Linström, K. (2018). *Kommuner tar hjälp av AI I GDPR-jobbet*. Available: https://computersweden.idg.se/2.2683/1.697727/gdpr-kommuner-ai

Mankesiöld, P. (2018). *Kommuner tar hjälp av AI I GDPR-jobbet*. Available: https://computersweden.idg.se/2.2683/1.697727/gdpr-kommuner-ai

Micheler, E., & Whaley, A. (2018). *Regulatory Technology*. Available SSRN: https://ssrn.com/abstract=3164258

Nicoletti, B. (2017). *The future of fintech: Integrating finance and technology in financial services*. Available https://ebookcentral.proquest.com

Nizan Geslevich Packin. (2018). RegTech, Compliance and Technology Judgment Rule. *Chi.-Kent L. Rev., 193.*

Panisi, F., & Perrone, A. (2018). Systems So Perfect That No One Will Need to be Good'? RegTech and the 'Human Factor'. *Orizzonti del Diritto Commerciale*. Available: SSRN: https://ssrn.com/abstract=3284636

Roy, S. (2018). *Regtech on the rise: Transforming Compliance into Competitive advantage*. Oliver Wyman. Available at: https://www.oliverwyman.com/our-expertise/insights/2018/may/the-rise-of-regtech.html

Shäubli, T. (2018). *Apiax launches tax product, addresses key challenges of banks and wealth managers.* Available: https://blog.apiax.com/apiax-launches-tax-product-addresses-key-challenges-of-banks-and-wealth-managers-9bd0615aa9ff

Straessle, A. (n.d.). *FAQ - Business benefits - Do you offer an efficient solution for cross-border compliance? The Digital Marketplace.* MindBridge AI Auditor. Available: https://www.digitalmarketplace.service.gov.uk/g-cloud/services/464121930318123

Reuters, T. (2017). *Regtech 2020 and Beyond – What Does the Future Hold?* Author.

Thomson Reuters. (2019). English S. & Hammond S., Fintech, Regtech and the Role of Compliance in 2019. Thomson Reuters Report 2019.

Treleaven, P., & Batrinca, B. (2017). Algorithmic Regulation: Automating Financial Compliance Monitoring and Regulation Using AI and Blockchain. *Journal of Financial Transformation, Capco Institute, 45*, 14–21.

Yang, D. (2018). Evolutionary Approaches and the Construction of Technology-Driven Regulations. *Emerging Markets Finance & Trade, 54*(14), 3256–3271.

Finriskalert. (n.d.). *Mercati, intermediari, istituzioni*. Retrieved from https://www.finriskalert.it/regtech-get-onboarding-the-challenges-of-compliance/

Vysya, V. N., & Kumar, A. (n.d.). Regtech: A magical entity from the fintech ecosystem. *Infosys*, 1–8. https://www.infosys.com/industries/financial-services/white-papers/Documents/magical-entity-finTech-ecosystem.pdf

Kraft, O. (n.d.). Financial RegTech: Opportunities and Obstacles. *CapTech*, 1–18. https://www.captech-consulting.com/uploads/whitepapers/financial-regtech-ebook-opportunities-and-obstacles-final-compressed.pdf

Luca. (2018, January 28). *Financial Supervisors and Regtech: Four Roles and Four Challenges*. Retrieved from https://poseidon01.ssrn.com/ delivery.php?ID= 6871 0106 7008 1020 1701 7029 0040 6408 7090 0960 5505 8047 0230 4303 1088 0131 0908 7104 0290 8901 7121 0610 5300 0000 0330 9705 2117 0781 1803 1019 1080 6500 9094 0100 4501 4112 1170 0811 3118 0720 2509 5087 0410 0110 2031 0161 2208 2121 0900 8410 7122 0870 2511 9118 0070 0411 2102 0650 9300 4103 1020 8912 7&EX T=pdf

KEY TERMS AND DEFINITIONS

AML: Anti-money laundering (AML) refers to accessible laws or procedures intended to diminish illegally obtained income.:

API: Application programming interface (API) represents the functionalities of a positive program. These are central because they allow other programmers to use machinery of existing software: allowing for quicker and more consistent software development - a main element of the FINTECH group.

Crypto Currency: A digital money using cryptography for guideline and safety. It's a decentralized scheme, meaning no essential unit exists to manage the processes. In its place, it uses a block chain. There are quite a few dissimilar kinds of crypto currency, together with Bitcoin, Ethereum, and Ripple.

Bitcoin: The majority accepted crypto currency, frequently deemed the initial of its type. The unlock basis of software comes with an indefinable and strange history.

Block Chain: Where crypto currency dealings get recorded. It operates like a public ledger where in order, once entered, can't be distorted. Block chain technology also has quite a lot of non-crypto currency applications together with smart contracts and the copy of digital assets.

Collaborative Consumption: A financial model based on the allocation: exchange, and renting of services. The allocation economy or joint economy can be seen in platforms like Airbnb or Kickstarter and is growing in FINTECH solutions via solutions like peer-to-peer lending.

Chapter 5
Finding Solutions to Cybersecurity Challenges in the Digital Economy

Hazik Mohamed
Stellar Consulting Group, Singapore

Hassnian Ali
International Center for Research in Islamic Economics, Pakistan

ABSTRACT

New technological innovation has incorporated frontier technologies in transforming the way we access and use existing products and services. The economy is becoming increasingly disrupted by revolutionary enterprises using technologies such as cloud computing, extensive use of artificial intelligence and data analytics, integration of interoperable internet of things (IoT) devices and the blockchained decentralization, including advanced materials. At the same time, regulatory and legal systems need to be strengthened in order for the ecosystem be protected from cyber risks and threats to allow for the market actors to flourish. In order to enjoy the benefits brought on by digital technologies, there are regulatory issues that come with technological adoption along with financial stability implications and consumer protection, with suggestions that regulators themselves adopt advanced technologies (RegTech) to embark on the new era of market supervision and monitoring to enhance cybersecurity.

INTRODUCTION

Since there are rotten apples and black sheep even in the virtual world, cybersecurity has become an important component in protecting digital rights and associated digital assets. This will be an important area of development which is constantly evolving because of the creativity of hackers and cyber-criminals. That challenge has been prevalent for the police in the physical world, and it continues to be a challenge in the virtual world. There are many factors behind the increasing number of cyberattacks including lack of right and skilled talent in cybersecurity, especially for exchanges. The attacks expose massive security

DOI: 10.4018/978-1-7998-4390-0.ch005

concerns on crypto-exchange systems, and their lack of protection for the assets on their platforms and robustness to respond to attacks and reduce loopholes within their systems. This requires a clear strategy of cybersecurity to decipher and defend from attacks in a decentralized anonymous network.

Any financial scheme or economic system has to be protected by a sound legal and enforcement system that protects the rights of individual, not only property rights, but also intellectual property. When the objectives of financial inclusion are set and rules are framed to achieve them, an effective mechanism must be implemented to make sure that the rules are enforced and observed. Effective enforcement requires a mechanism to detect the violation and proper sanctions to deter anyone from violating the rules to, for instance, intellectual property. These include enforcing contracts through the mechanism of prevention and the mechanism of remediation.

In this chapter, we first discuss the frontier technologies that will determine the extent of digital transformation to the economy. We then review the different types of cybersecurity lapses and cyberattacks that has happened over the last few years to grasp the extent of the problem and its challenges. At the same time, regulatory and legal systems need to be strengthened in order for the ecosystem to be protected from cyber risks and threats to allow for the market actors to flourish. As many nations have already implemented a national cybersecurity strategy, we provide suggestions for improvements and enhancements to current strategies with continual review and assessments as technology changes rapidly.

DIGITAL TRANSFORMATION IN THE ECONOMY: FRONTIER TECHNOLOGIES

Currently, financial services institutions are increasing their investment in digital technologies as it brought various benefits such as providing better customer service. Data collected through the cloud system, AI and robotics could help the financial services institutions to predict and understand their customer's behaviour and expectation better. It provides opportunities to the financial institutions to develop new or personalise products and services to cater to their customers' needs. Similarly, digital technologies could help to perform fraud management. According to PwC (2016), financial institutions are using AI to spot abnormal behaviour to detect market abuse and rogue trading. Also, AI and robotics were used to defend cyberattack through monitoring possible threats and identifying potential security risk. These technologies allowed financial institutions to react immediately in order to protect their customers' personal and account details. Apart from that, blockchain technologies started to be widely adopted by financial services institutions. Although blockchain technologies are often related to cryptocurrencies, however it could benefit the financial services institutions. Blockchain technologies allow a distributed database that holds a growing number of records and the distributed ledgers are continually updated and synchronised across multiple computers in a network. It helps to reduce the costs spending on infrastructure as authorised participants could perform without relying on an intermediary or authority, increase efficiency and reduce errors. These digital technologies also help to improve the service quality as manual processes are automated, employees could focus on providing more specialised services such as planning, budgeting, tax and treasury.

Beyond finance, there are a host of technologies divided into four categories threaten to disrupt and reshape growth strategies for emerging economies. According to a convenient categorization by the OECD these are: digital, biotechnology, advanced materials, and energy and environment. (See Figure 1 below).

Technologies that could cause the most disruption by narrowing some opportunities for emerging economies while also opening alternative avenues for development are: (i) robotics and the automation not only of repetitive manual tasks but also of cognitively more demanding tasks with the help of intelligent/learning software systems capable of performing knowledge work of increasing sophistication[1]; (ii) additive (3D) manufacturing that permits rapid prototyping, as well as small lot, resource conserving, customized, and dispersed production; (iii) the industrial internet of things that will further reduce the labor intensity of production, monitoring, and maintenance and multiply the numbers of "lights out" factories and warehouses[2]; (iv) the mobile Internet and increased connectivity that will permit the use of mobile devices to access a wide range of banking, transport, medical, and other services; (v) Big Data and advanced data analytics; and (vi) cloud technology that delivers hardware and software over the Internet as a service (SaaS), a platform (PaaS) or an infrastructure as a service (IaaS)[3].

These and other technologies already making inroads are being refined and extended largely by advanced economies and are attuned to their factor endowments and capabilities. They reinforce the comparative advantage of high-income countries in manufacturing and services for which demand will be rising. The new technologies could widen the divergence in technologies and in productivity between the advanced and emerging economies (Haldane 2017). In fact, emerging economies are threatened by a perfect storm unless they come to grips with the new technological realities, adjust policies, upgrade human capital, and adapt institutions[4].

These and other technologies already making inroads are being refined and extended largely by advanced economies and are attuned to their factor endowments and capabilities. They reinforce the comparative advantage of high-income countries in manufacturing and services for which demand will be rising. The new technologies could widen the divergence in technologies and in productivity between the advanced and emerging economies (Haldane 2017). In fact, emerging economies are threatened by a perfect storm unless they come to grips with the new technological realities, adjust policies, upgrade human capital, and adapt institutions.

CYBER-ATTACKS WITHIN THE ECONOMY

The consequence of the digital economy is the use of internet at scale. Every transaction is recorded and almost everything is available at your fingertips on your mobile. This high and extensive use of internet has created concerns of personal data loss, information leakages or loss of money through cyberattacks. The pattern of cyberattacks are now changed from practical jokes to intentional attacks, that are pre planned and most severe in order to hurt someone badly through loss of money or by blackmailing due to loss of personal information. In order to save themselves from destruction the companies have to take the multiple and serious steps to get protection from cyberattacks. The companies have to make sure that it is not only the responsibility of IT departments or selected individuals, rather the responsibility of all employees.

The companies are increasing the usage of disruptive technologies to gain customer's attention. According to Hess, Benlian, Matt and Wiesböck, (2016) almost 90% of the market leaders in USA and UK want their IT professionals to use the internet in every model and scheme. They want to have immediate access to their customers to get better product views. However, they are potentially exposing themselves, as companies are becoming increasingly connected through wireless technologies in their models. Having such access, cyber-attacks can result in the loss of sovereignty of the companies. Ac-

Figure 1. The four categories of frontier technologies
[Source: OECD (2016) STI Outlook 2016.]

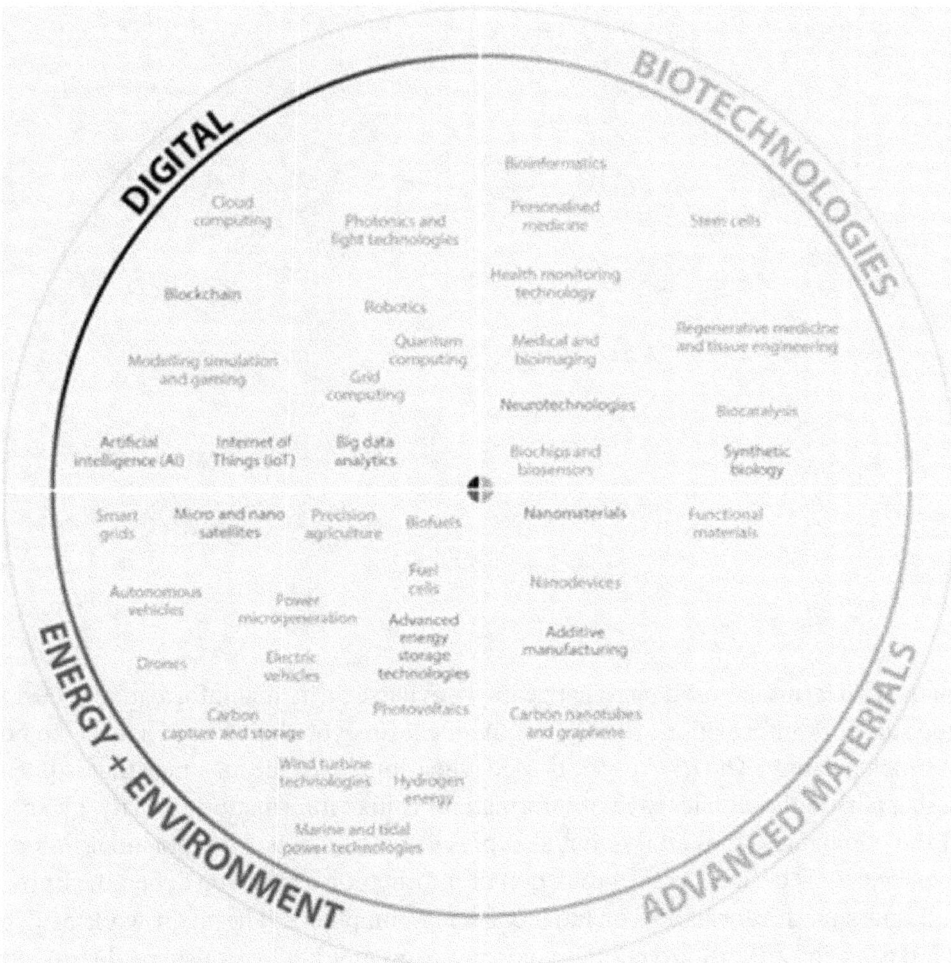

cording to a survey by (PwC, 2015) they estimated that companies who face the cyberattacks loss their value by 2.1% annually with US$1.6 billion loss on per incident. Such incidents may create losses that are hard to recover from.

A report by the World Economic Forum (2017) have rated the large-scale cyber-attacks as one of the five most dangerous attacks on this planet. It is also estimated (Morgan, 2017) that the loss from cyber-attacks and loss of data will reach to US$6 trillion until 2021, double that of 2015. Figure 2 shows that the worldwide spending on cybersecurity has been increased from US$75.6 billion in 2015 to US$124 billion in 2020 (Statista, 2020).

Figure 3 shows the timeline of cyber incidents that happened involving financial institutions during the period of May 2019 to March 2020.

There are different types of cyberattacks experienced by financial institutions. Of them, web-based attacks, people-based attacks, ransomware are those categories that are on the rise. An exclusive report "Cost of Cybercrime Study in Financial Services" by (Accenture, 2019) compiled the common types of cyberattacks in terms of their occurrence for 2017 and 2018.

Figure 2. Cyber security Spending (2015-2020)
Source: Modified from (Statista, 2020)

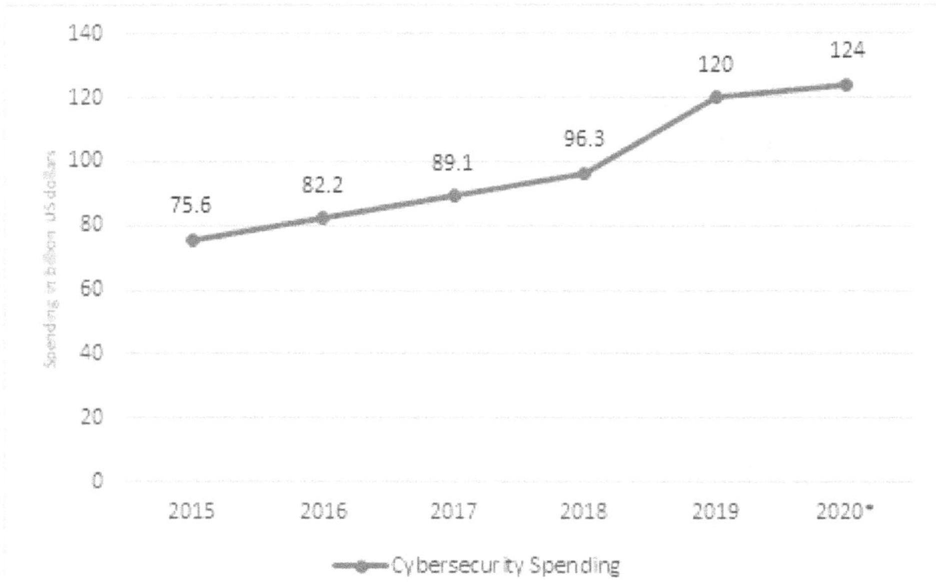

Although the two terms are used interchangeably—cybersecurity and information security— cybersecurity is the subset of information security despite the term cyber being used across the board due to its vast and complex nature. The term cyber is used when someone face an attack that is intentional and want to hurt that person through leakage of information. Unlike information security, cybersecurity not only protect the companies from attacks but also preserves the assets from potential loss due to these attacks. Cybersecurity is defined as the protection of information asset from cyberattacks by protecting the processed and stored information of interconnected computers. The main work of cybersecurity is to set up a design in order to protect the company from any kind of mishaps due to cyberattacks. Ponemon Institute calculated that in 2017, the direct cost of any cyberattack is US$3.62 million while the A. Report (2015) by ISACA found out that both direct and indirect cost of any cyberattack make up a loss of around US$5.5 million.

Due to the crucial role of financial institutions as intermediators, the financial sector is especially vulnerable and prone to cyber-attacks. As ambition and scale of cyberattacks and breaches within global financial institutions continues to grow and escalate, the management of cybersecurity is now viewed as a critical priority by the financial institutions and regulatory bodies (Camillo, 2017). In the modern financial system, where institutions are increasingly being automated, cybersecurity has become one of the pressing issues linked to the future of global financial intermediation (Lin, 2015). The dated models of computer security used in the financial institutions are no longer fit to handle the modern risks of cybersecurity.

Furthermore, cyberattacks result in number of problems like loss of privacy, inability to implement business models, loss of reputation, loss of sovereignty, loss of wealth and loss of public interest and confidence on these firms. In July 2017, there was a cyberattack in a Sweden on a very large level where data is stolen from cloud computing, it results in loss of personal information, threat to national security, big international scandals got leak, weakening of government and even resignation of ministers as well. Again, in July 2017, the British Airways got hacked result in cancellation of 100 flights from London Airport resulting in massive losses in the tune of 114 million Euros. Investigations into these attacks show that these attacks are carefully planned and executed, while they are difficult to detect and prevent.

IMF estimates globally, the financial institutions face potential losses due to cyberattacks valued from 9% of their net income up to approximately half of their net income in worst case scenario (Lagarde, 2018).

No doubt, economy with full of digitalization made our lives easier but it also causes serious concern on our privacy because, everyone can be a victim of these cyberattacks.

Figure 3. Timeline of Cyber Incidents Involving Financial Institutions (May 2019-March 2020)
Source: (Carnegieendowment.org, 2020)

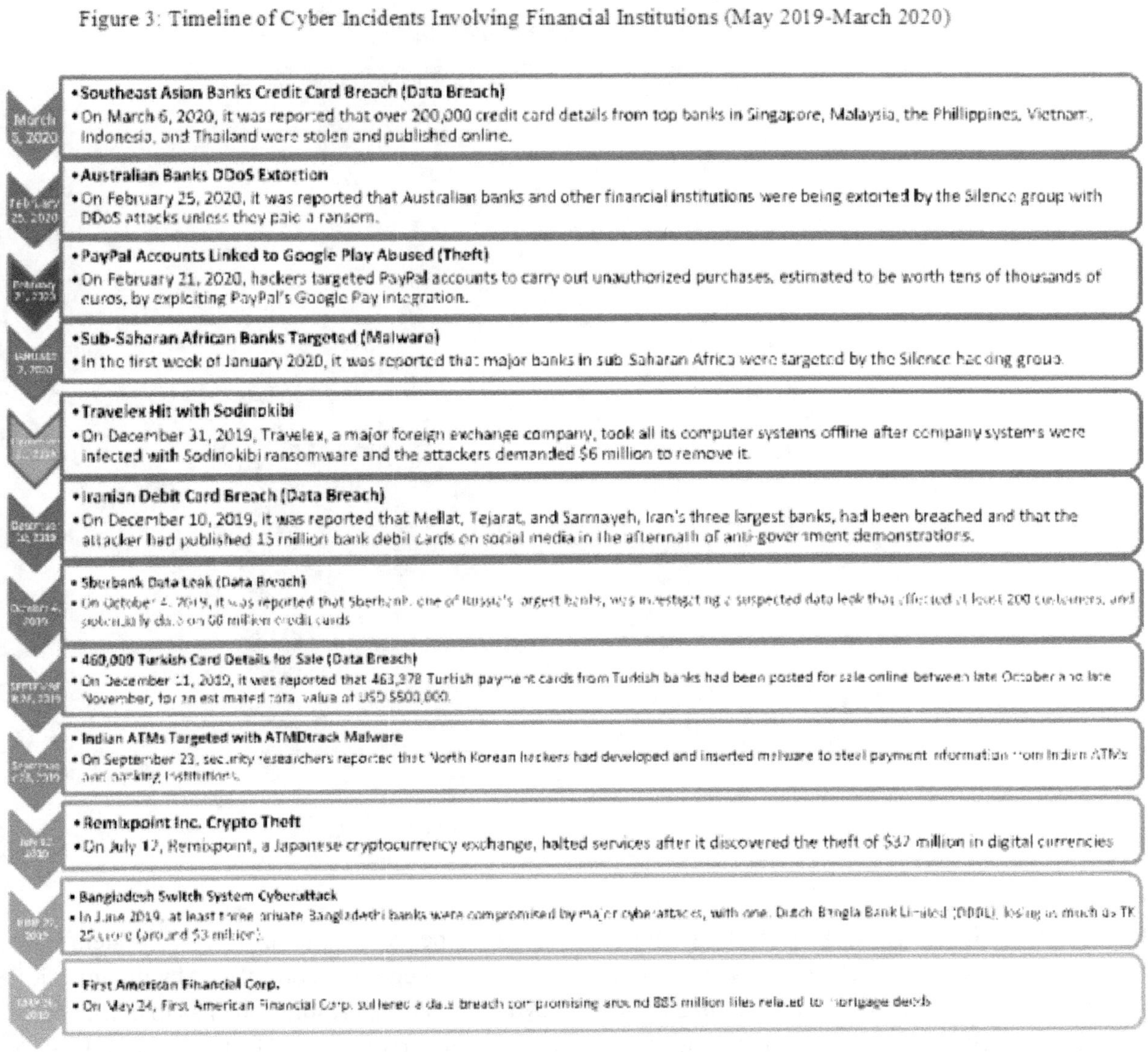

Figure 4. Types of cyberattacks experienced by Financial Services companies (% increase 2017–2018)
Source: (Accenture, 2019)

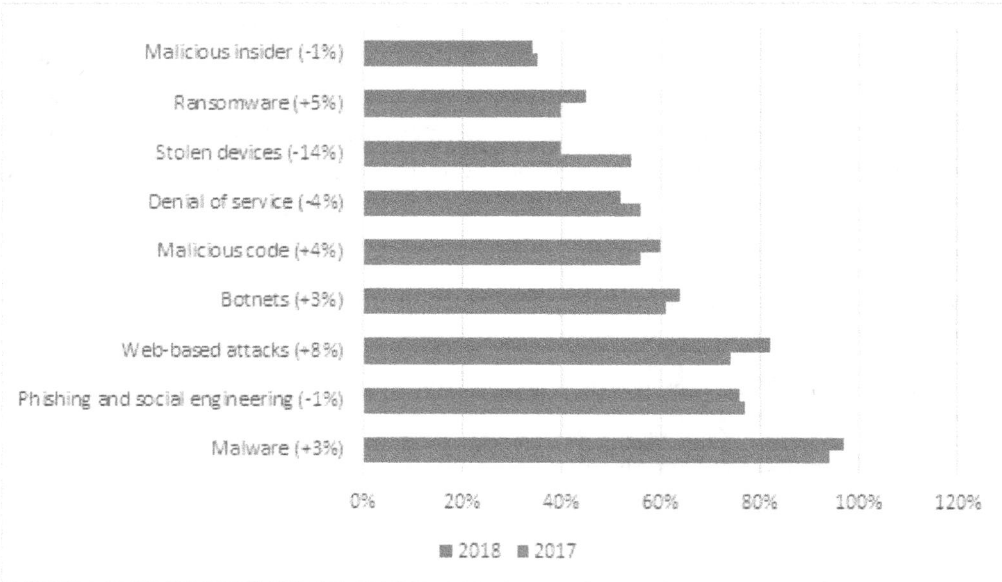

Figure 5. Potential Impact on Banks Profit (percent of net income)

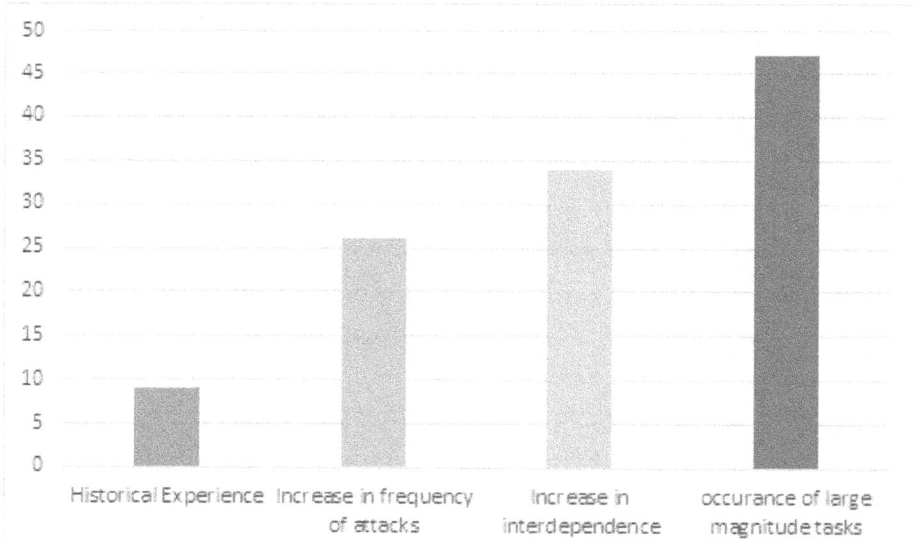

Operationally, cyberattacks reflect the failure of the whole network system. Every IT system have embedded controls and tools that save it from these attacks. The better the controls set by organization for prevention the better the result will be. So, for achieving the optimal results, one has to consistently update its security controls and perform checks to identify any vulnerable areas. The Report from ISACA (A. Report, 2015) shows that almost 97% of the total cyberattacks can easily be prevented if company had invested in its cyber well-being.

There are many factors behind the increasing number of cyberattacks including lack of right and skilled talent in cybersecurity, especially for exchanges. The attacks expose massive security concerns on crypto-exchange systems, and their lack of protection for the assets on their platforms and robustness to respond to attacks and reduce loopholes within their systems. This requires a clear strategy of cybersecurity to decipher and defend from attacks in a decentralized anonymous network.

REGULATORY ISSUES CONCERNING NEW TECHNOLOGIES

Technological disruption is accelerating at a scale that presents quickly apparent benefits to the economy and society collectively, but as in anything in economics, it incurs potential risks from unintended consequences. Some of such concerns are:

i. Regulation and Supervision

By and large, regulators are aware that technological disruption "has the potential to deliver immense economic benefits, by lowering the cost of operations and enhancing competition, and societal benefits, by boosting financial inclusion and delivering more convenient financial services" (Beck et al., 2018). However, risk and failure are an integral part of innovation in any experimentation for tech solutions. Therefore, Mohamed and Ali (2019) advises that it is "critical for regulators to ensure safeguards are in place to manage the risks (such as institution-specific micro-financial risks and system-wide macro-financial risks). Providing parameters and regulatory clarity through a framework (for Technological disruption business models) is essential for technological disruption's mass adoption in order to ensure the financial stability of the system". They point out that "regulatory sandboxes are only one of the approaches to manage Technological disruption and may not fit circumstances in different situations and jurisdictions". As such, they emphasise that "market supervisors will have to ensure that financial institutions or firms have robust governance frameworks and (such) surveillance" could be complemented by data-driven supervision.

Other risks include those associated with the usage of such digital currency, which the public may not be aware of. Securitized Token Offerings (STOs) have much improved regulatory oversight which evolved from the absence of regulations for Initial Coin Offerings (ICOs) when ICOs was a new method of raising capital through decentralised means, which has the potential to side-step rigorous monitoring requirements for funds-raising established by authorities.

Another critical risk management issue is the operational risk that manifests in cyber-security, fraud and theft, data privacy and legal issues. The Basel Committee on Banking Supervision (BCBS) prescribes a capital regime for operational risk which does not really address risk-related operational issues. Mohamed (2020) notes that "while regulatory instruments such as BCBS capital requirements can create incentives to address certain operational risks, such as business continuity, capital is not sufficient to restore operations if a financial institution suffers a cyber-attack". Hence, cyber-security and the safeguard of Critical Information Technology Infrastructure (CITI) have to be now top priority for the market conduct and supervisory authorities, particularly the banking and financial sectors.

In addition, there is grave apprehension on the risk of money laundering and financing of terrorism, termed as AML/CFT, which requires financial institutions including banks to have adequate measures to counter the risk of AML/CFT.

As new business models and services emerge, such as sharing services (e.g. Airbnb and Grab) and ICOs/STOs, government agencies are challenged with updating regulatory toolkits or modifying regulations, enforcing them, and working with market players that they watch over, relaying such information to stakeholders, while still working within legacy frameworks that will be outdated in the next decade, and knowing so, strive to foster innovation for fair competition.

ii. Financial Stability and Consumer Protection

It is incumbent on market supervisors will need to ensure is that financial institutions including banks have in place robust plans for scenarios that could threaten their own stability or the larger macroeconomic stability. For instance, robo-advisory services that automatically recommend investment portfolios for clients which rely on AI algorithms fed with investors' data, need to be within approved products or companies offering such services need to be compelled to disclose more information when required (Baker & Dellaert, 2018). Similarly, third-party service providers or vendors to financial institutions may need to be regulated in order to manage related operational risks, which may impact financial stability indirectly.

Under financial stability, consumer protection including personal data protection is one of the areas that are highly focused on. The danger of cyber-attacks and hacking, as well as the need to protect sensitive consumer and corporate financial data, raises many issues including data privacy, ownership and administration, and legal liability. In order to avoid any undesirable situations, much work needs to be done on boosting cyber-security and alleviating cyber risks. And we make recommendations and discuss that in greater depth in following sections on RegTech.

iii. Local and Cross-Border Arrangements

A common approach and strategy need to be in place to address technological disruption issues at the national and also the international levels. Hence, regional cooperation will be integral in regulating technological disruption that scale beyond borders. Furthermore, innovations in cross-border lending, trading and payment transactions, including via smart contracts, raise questions about the cross-jurisdictional disputes and enforceability issues. Domestically for Technological disruption developments, there has to be coordination among the monitoring and supervisory agencies regulating financial institutions under a digital economic framework.

It is an obvious fact that the scourge of the digital economy comprise cyber threats and attacks on critical infrastructure. Empirical evidence on NCSS shows that it is necessary for success and continuous growth in digital economy (Teoh & Mahmood, 2017). For a start, many nations have launched national cybersecurity strategies (NCSS) but these need to be reviewed and enhanced on a yearly basis. This continual review and assessment are needed to balance the changing nature of digital technology and to ensure the security and reliability of the cyber-economy.

iv. Expertise and Capacity Building

Talent and the right expertise are one of the areas that requires attention and needs to be addressed moving forward. As traditional roles within some areas of the economy become automated, forward-thinking planning for capacity building and innovation-related expertise has to be part of the overall strategy in order to provide proper market supervision.

Hence, to benefit from digital technologies, firms need to attract the best talent that could apply and enhance digital technologies in the financial sector. Towards that, economies need to reduce skills mismatch between talent demand from the financial sector and talent supply from the education system. Skills mismatch, in simple terms, is where skills offered by workers and jobseeker do not match the skills required by the financial sector. Skills mismatch results in lower productivity utilization of the individual talent in the financial sector. Hence, the educational systems need to impart the skills required for the new generations to fully participate in digitised financial market. To do that, a qualification framework for the financial services related educational sector can be jointly developed between training institutions and industry players.

Secondly, economies need to address the skills shortages or skills gap concern. This is where demand for talent with a particular skill exceeds the supply of workers do not have the right skills to meet the financial sector requirement towards digitization. To overcome this concern, the authority needs to assess future skills demands for the digitized financial sector. For example, finance students need to be exposed to technology areas like virtual reality, IoT, big data analytics, artificial intelligence, 3D printing and cloud computing that will soon become relevant. This helps improve students' digital literacy on top of their technical skills and knowledge to be applied in their occupations.

Thirdly, to have the best talent, the financial services industry needs to have a competitive wage, incentive and reward system. This is to avoid skills shortages of digital financial specialists in the domestic economy and talent international migration. The globalization of labour markets had increased the movement of employees of multinational companies from one country to another. Talents are seeking for employment prospects and better wages. For example, higher wages paid in Singapore had induced Malaysian digital financial specialists to seek employment abroad.

REGTECH: DIGITAL REPORTING AND COMPLIANCE

Around the world, regulators are facing the challenges of the rapid emergence of new Technological disruption technologies and non-traditional market entrants, all at extraordinary speed. Authorities are faced with the task to develop regulatory approaches that do not hamper development and innovation while still limiting risks to consumers and financial stability.

RegTech is largely seen as a category that focuses on technologies that may facilitate the delivery of regulatory requirements more efficiently and effectively than existing capabilities[5]. However, Arner et al (2016) view RegTech as more than just an efficiency tool but rather a pivotal change leading to a paradigm shift in regulation. To them, RegTech holistically represents the next logical evolution of financial services regulation and should develop into a foundational base underpinning the entire financial services sector.

The "application of technology to monitoring and compliance offers massive cost savings to established financial companies and potentially massive opportunities to emerging Technological disruption start-ups, IT and advisory firms"[6]. From a regulator's perspective, RegTech will enable the prospect of continuous monitoring that would improve efficiency by both liberating excess regulatory capital, decreasing the time it takes to investigate a firm, fostering competition and upholding their directives for financial stability (both macro and micro) and market integrity.

CYBERSECURITY STRATEGIES

While regulators regulate prescribed market behaviors, there is a need for an independent agency that enforces and acts when there is a security breach in the Critical Information Technology Infrastructure (CITI) within corporations and government information systems. Hence, a National Cybersecurity Agency (NCsA) is recommended to establish a legal framework for the oversight and maintenance of national cybersecurity in the country. The agency will also be responsible to develop and enforce cyber-secure framework to be used in conjunction with any existing Systems Development Lifecycle (SDLC) methodologies adopted by organisations, as well as complementing government policies, standards, guidelines and directives.

Mohamed and Ali (2019) notes that "while most organisations acknowledge that security is an important consideration in developing computer systems, costs and business performance often take precedence over security. Even though awareness has been elevated on security issues, most organisations focus on applying security only at the commissioning stage of the system development and try to force-fit security into the final design, resulting in ineffective application of security". In this case, the financial institutions are able to detect the coming cyberattacks but not capable enough to prevent them. According to a survey by Deloitte (2019), more than 50% of surveyed respondents are of the view that the theft of customer data or system failures are due to insecure technology or software implemented within organizations. Moreover, this study also notes that financial organizations are comparatively more effective in detecting cyberattacks than in preventing them.

Despite the significant benefit of digital transformation, there are forces that will disrupt these benefits such as cyber-attacks and hackers, system breakdown, cloud data leakages etc. Cybersecurity is the top priority for institutions due to the rapid evolvement of complex technologies, cross boarder data exchanges, emerging usage of Internet of things (IoT). It has been canvassed in a survey conducted in the Conference of State Bank Supervisors (CSBS) that more than 70% of respondents ranked cybersecurity as their top priority and critical risk among other risks (CSBS, 2019). It is supported by the study of Boston Consulting Group (BCG) which revealed that the financial industry is 300 times more vulnerable to cyberattacks (Zakrzewski et al., 2019) when compared to other industries.

With these forces took place in the upcoming business environment, it is mandatory for financial institutions to be capable of developing resilience cybersecurity framework in order to be sustainable in the long run. The main function of newly developed cybersecurity framework is to detect cyber threats and efficiently respond to cyber events. With this adoption of cybersecurity framework, it will help financial institutions to minimize financial losses occurred due to business disruption. In relation to this, it is highly recommended for the management to focus on 6 main areas which are to (1) proactively manage cyber risk and regulation, (2) build and execute strategic cyber security roadmap, (3) establish commercially reasonable cyber security capability, (4) develop world class cyber response, (5) acquire, develop and retain key talent, and (6) align cyber security team with business risk. New tools to fight cybercrime can be developed based on the cybersecurity framework. With the right tools in place, cyber threats arise from digital transformation of financial sector can be mitigated thus, enable financial institutions to maximize its exploitation on the benefit of digitalisation of financial sector. Besides, regulations must be modernised to encourage innovation, investments and participation in the digitisation of financial market ecosystem. Privacy and cybersecurity issues must be addressed to instil trust including control over data use to manage privacy concerns. To some extent, it is appropriate to consider developing a legal framework on data protection as the cybersecurity breach causes wide economic, social and sovereign implications, such as cyberattacks on a country's banking system.

An effective way to protect computer systems against cyber threats is to integrate security into every step of the SDLC, from initiation, to development, to deployment and eventual disposal of the system (NIST, 2008). Control Gates or decision points are specific milestones where the security implementations are evaluated. They specify to the corporation that "security considerations are addressed, adequate security controls are built in, and identified risks are clearly understood before the system development advances to the next lifecycle phase". The Agile approach can be adopted to continuously update and improve on standards.

Security planning is to be conducted as part of integrating security in SDLC, and should include:

- Identifying and confirming key security roles in the system development project
- Outlining key security milestones and activities for the system development.
- Connecting the use of secure design, IT architecture and coding standards.
- Warranting all key stakeholders have a shared understanding of the goals, implications, considerations and requirements of performing security

These values integration is crucial in responding to potential security threats as it highlights to key stakeholder important areas of systems development progress, and that critical decisions made will have security implications.

In addition, an updated Bill or an Act can be improved to:

A. Enhance NCsA to Prevent Threats and Respond to Cybersecurity Incidents

The Act has empowered authorities (e.g. a national cybersecurity agency like NCsA) "to investigate cybersecurity threats and incidents to determine their impact and prevent further harm or cybersecurity incidents from arising. The powers that may be exercised are adjusted to the severity of the cybersecurity threat or event and the appropriate measures required for response". CITI sectors are: Banking and Finance, Emergency Services, Health (hospitals, etc.), Transport (air, land and sea), Information Communications (media, etc.), Power and Water.

B. Maintain and Enforce a Framework for Sharing Cybersecurity Information

The Act can improve "information sharing, which is critical as timely information helps the government and owners of computer systems identify vulnerabilities and prevent cyber incidents more effectively". The Act needs to be maintained and enforced "as a national cybersecurity agency to request information, and for the protection and sharing" of private, restricted or sensitive information.

Yip et al. (2012) found that due to attraction of a huge bounty, cybercriminals have now collaborated with each other in trading and exchanging information and skills to achieve their goals. In addition to this, they also have social networks for recruiting talents from colleges and universities. Similarly, authorities and financial institutions can also make the sharing of data and information mandatory in order to break the chains within a cybercrime network and ultimately, dismantle it.

C. Review Licensing Frameworks for Cybersecurity Service Providers Periodically

NCsA can act to license different types of "service providers, namely cyber-threat penetration testing, cyber-defence and managed security operations monitoring. These services are prioritised because providers of such services have access to sensitive information and hence have a significant impact on the overall security landscape. The licensing framework allows for a balance between security needs and the development of a vibrant cybersecurity ecosystem" (NIST, 2010).

INSTITUTION-SPECIFIC MICRO-FINANCIAL RISKS

An effective way to protect computer systems against cyber threats is to integrate security into every step of the SDLC, from initiation, to development, to deployment and eventual disposal of the system, which is called the Security-by-Design (SBD) approach (NIST, 2010).

In 2008, the National Institute of Standards and Technology published guidelines for a Security-by-Design approach to "software and hardware development that seeks to minimise systems vulnerabilities and reduce the attack surface through designing and building security in every phase of the SDLC" (NIST, 2008). This includes incorporating security specifications in the design, continuous security evaluation at each phase and adherence to best practices. The values of integrating security into SDLC include:

- Early identification and mitigation of security vulnerabilities and misconfigurations of systems.
- Identification of shared security services and devices that reduce cost, improves security through proven methods and best-known practices.
- Improved systems operability that would otherwise be hampered by isolated security of systems.
- Records of critical security decisions throughout the lifecycle of the system, ensuring that security was top-of-mind at every stage.
- Enabling informed key stakeholder decisions through thorough risk management in a judicious fashion.

Specific to cybersecurity, SBD addresses the cyber protection considerations throughout a system's lifecycle. This includes security design specifically for the identification, protection, detection, response and recovery capabilities to strengthen the cyber resiliency of the system.

CONCLUSION

In order to maintain fairness where all market participants are treated equally, the market needs to adopt and apply the best practices and codes of conduct, transparent in reflecting the price and activity, open and accessible. Financial technology which is the technology and innovation that improves and automates the delivery of financial services will able to overcome the challenges related to fairness.

Money-laundering, terrorism financing and cybersecurity are among the security challenges issues in the financial markets and these challenges can be addressed using the blockchain technology. Cloud security on the other hand is one of the ways to combat cybersecurity. Many fintech companies utilize cloud services to provide consistent and scalable performance with lower upfront costs.

Upholding integrity of markets is very important and identifying criminal cyber activities will help to overcome the issue of data breaches involving service firms among others apart from developing the legal national framework to enable the local law-enforcement agencies to cooperate with law-enforcement agencies abroad.

REFERENCES

Accenture. (2019). *Cost of Cybercrime Study in Financial Services: 2019 Report*. https://www.slideshare.net/accenture/cost-of-cybercrime-study-in-financial-services-2019-report

Arner, D. W., Barberis, J. N., & Buckley, R. P. (2016). FinTech, Regtech and the Reconceptualization of Financial Regulation. *Northwestern Journal of International Law & Business*, *37*(3).

Baker, T., & Dellaert, B. (2018). Regulating Robo-advice Across the Financial Services Industry. Iowa Law Review, 103(2), 713–750. doi:10.2139srn.2932189

Beck, R., Müller-Bloch, C., & King, J. L. (2018). Governance in the Blockchain Economy – A Framework and Research Agenda. *Journal of the Association for Information Systems*, *19*(3), 1020–1034. doi:10.17705/1jais.00518

Brummer, C., & Gorfine, D. (2014). FinTech: building a 21st century Regulator's Toolkit. Milken Institute.

Brynjolfsson, E., & McAfee, A. (2017). *Machine, Platform, Crowd: Harnessing our digital future*. W.W. Norton.

Carnegieendowment.org. (2020). *Timeline of Cyber Incidents Involving Financial Institutions - Carnegie Endowment for International Peace*. https://carnegieendowment.org/specialprojects/protectingfinancial-stability/timeline#click-hide

CCN. (2018, July 4). *$731 Million Gained by Hacking Crypto Exchanges in 2018, Can it be Prevented?* Retrieved August 6, 2018, from https://www.ccn.com/731-million-stolen-from-crypto-exchanges-in-2018-can-hacks-be-prevented/

Christine, L. (2018, June 22). *Estimating Cyber Risk for the Financial Sector – IMF Blog*. IMF. https://blogs.imf.org/2018/06/22/estimating-cyber-risk-for-the-financial-sector/

CSBS. (2019). *Community Banking in the 21st Century: Seventh Annual Community Banking Research and Policy Conference*. https://www.communitybanking.org/~/media/files/publication/cb21publication_2019.pdf

Deloitte. (2019). *The Future of Cyber Survey 2019*. file:///F:/ali/hazik/us-the-future-of-cyber-survey.pdf

Ezell, S., & Swanson, B. (2017). *How Cloud Computing Enables Modern Manufacturing*. AEI/ITIF. http://www2.itif.org/2017-cloud-computing-enables-manufacturing.pdf?_ga=2.218587289.1802769062.1498483609-1058723113.1488819082

Haldane, A. (2017). *Productivity Puzzles. Bank of England.* http://worldmanagementsurvey.org/wp-content/uploads/2017/03/boespeech_220317.pdf

Hess, T., Benlian, A., Matt, C., & Wiesböck, F. (2016). *Options for Formulating a Digital Transformation Strategy*. Academic Press.

International Labor Organization. (2016). *ASEAN in Transformation*. http://www.ilo.org/public/english/dialogue/actemp/downloads/publications/2016/asean_in_transf_2016_r1_techn.pdf

Lin, T. (2015). Infinite Financial Intermediation. *Wake Forest Law Review*, *50*, 643–669.

Mark, C. (2017). Cybersecurity: Risks and management of risks for global banks and financial institutions Mark Camillo. *Journal of Risk Management in Financial Institutions*, *10*(2), 196–200.

Mohamed, H., & Ali, H. (2018). *Blockchain, Fintech and Islamic Finance: Building the Future of the New Islamic Digital Economy*. DeIG Press, De Gruyter.

Mohamed, H. (2020). The Future of FinTech in ASEAN. In M. Anshari, M. Almunawar, & M. Masri (Eds.), *Financial Technology and Disruptive Innovation in ASEAN* (pp. 63–79). IGI Global. doi:10.4018/978-1-5225-9183-2.ch003

Morgan, S. (2017). *2017 Cybercrime Report*. Academic Press.

National Institute of Standards and Technology. (2008). *Special Publication 800-64 Revision 2 - Security Considerations in the System Development Life Cycle*. Author.

National Institute of Standards and Technology. (2010). *Special Publication 800-37 Revision 1 - Guide for Applying the Risk Management Framework to Federal Information*. Author.

National Institute of Standards and Technology. (2014). *Special Publication 800-88 Revision Systems. 1 - Guide for Media Sanitisation*. Author.

OECD. (2016). *Science Technology and Innovation Outlook, 2016*. http://www.oecd.org/sti/STIO%20 10%20key%20technology%20trends%20for%20the%20future.pdf

PwC. (2016). *Turnaround and Transformation in Cybersecurity*. Retrieved from https://www.pwc.com/sg/en/publications/assets/pwc-global-state-of-information-security-survey-2016.pdf

Roh, C. (2018, July 5). *Cryptocurrency Exchange Theft Rising in 2018 According to CipherTrace*. Retrieved August 6, 2018, from https://cryptoslate.com/cryptocurrency-exchange-theft-rising-in-2018-according-to-ciphertrace/

Statista. (2020). *Global cyber security & insurance spending 2020*. Statista. https://www.statista.com/statistics/387868/it-cyber-securiy-budget/

Teoh, C. S., & Mahmood, A. K. (2017). National Cyber Security Strategies for Digital Economy. *International Conference on Research and Innovation in Information Systems*. 10.1109/ICRIIS.2017.8002519

Thomson, D. (2017). The Silent Crisis of Retail Employment. *Atlantic*. https://www.theatlantic.com/business/archive/2017/04/the-silent-crisis-of-retail-employment/523428/

Villasenor, J. (2016). *Ensuring Cybersecurity in FinTech: Key Trends and Solutions*. Retrieved May 11, 2018, from https://www.forbes.com/sites/johnvillasenor/2016/08/25/ensuring-cybersecurity-in-FinTech-key-trends-and-solutions/

World Economic Forum. (2017). *The Global Risks Report* (12th ed.). Author.

World Economic Forum. (2018). Agile Governance Reimagining Policy-making in the Fourth Industrial Revolution. Author.

Yip, M., Shadbolt, N., Tiropanis, T., & Webber, C. (2012). *The Digital Underground Economy: A Social Network Approach to Understanding Cybercrime*. https://www.sigma.com.pl/pliki/albums/userpics/10007/Virtua

Zakrzewski, A., Tang, T., Appell, G., Renaud, F., Andrew, H., Nicole, H., Michael, K., Martin, M., Federico, M., & André, X. (2019). *Global Wealth 2019: Reigniting Radical Growth*. https://image-src.bcg.com/Images/BCG-Reigniting-Radical-Growth-June-2019_tcm9-222638.pdf

ADDITIONAL READING

Carey, M. J., & Jin, J. (2019). *Tribe of Hackers: Cybersecurity Advice from the Best Hackers in the World*. Threatcare Press. doi:10.1002/9781119643395

Moallem, A. (2019). *Human-computer interaction and cybersecurity handbook*. CRC Press.

Moschovitis, C. J. P. (2018). *Cybersecurity Program Development for Business: The Essential Planning Guide*. John Wiley & Sons. doi:10.1002/9781119430018

Parenty, T. J., & Domet, J. J. (2019). *A Leader's Guide to Cybersecurity: Why Boards Need to Lead–and How to Do It*. Harvard Business Review Press.

Rohmeyer, P., & Bayuk, J. L. (2019). *Financial Cybersecurity Risk Management: Leadership Perspectives and Guidance for Systems and Institutions*. Apress. doi:10.1007/978-1-4842-4194-3

KEY TERMS AND DEFINITIONS

AI: Artificial intelligence (or AI) is intelligence demonstrated by machines through algorithms, in contrast to the natural intelligence displayed by humans and animals.

AML: Anti-money laundering (or AML) rules help authorities detect and banks to report suspicious activity including the predicate offenses to money laundering and terrorist financing, such as securities fraud and market manipulation.

CITI: These are critical infrastructure sectors whose assets, systems, and networks, whether physical or virtual, are considered so vital that their incapacitation or destruction would have a debilitating effect on security, national economic security, national public health or safety, or any combination thereof.

CTF: Combating the financing of terrorism (CFT) involves investigating, analyzing, deterring, and preventing sources of funding for activities intended to achieve political, religious, or ideological goals.

ICO: An initial coin offering (ICO) is the cryptocurrency industry's equivalent to an initial public offering (IPO). ICOs act as a way to raise funds, where a company looking to raise money to create a new coin, app, or service launches an ICO.

SDLC: Systems development lifecycle (SDLC) is a process for planning, creating, testing, and deploying an information system. The systems development life cycle concept applies to a range of hardware and software configurations, as a system can be composed of hardware only, software only, or a combination of both.

STO: STOs can be viewed as a hybrid approach between cryptocurrency ICOs and the more traditional initial public offering (IPO) because of its overlap with both of these methods of investment fundraising. A security token represents an investment contract into an underlying investment asset, such as stocks, bonds, funds and real estate investment trusts (REIT).

ENDNOTES

1 Stuart Armstrong (2014, pp.14-15) observes that computers far exceed human capacity in an increasing number of areas because of focus, patience, processing speed, and memory. "In 2009, a robot named Adam became the first machine to formulate scientific hypotheses and propose tests for them- and it was able to conduct experiments whose results may have answered a long-standing question in genetic. An AI that became adequate at technological development would soon become phenomenally good: unlike humans, the AI could integrate and analyze data from across the whole Internet. It would do R&D simultaneously in hundreds of subfields and relentlessly combine ideas among fields".

2 Until recently, jobs lost in retailing were being offset by increased employment in warehouses established by companies selling online. But as online businesses are less labor intensive than bricks and mortar stores and warehouse-based fulfilment centers are becoming more automated, it is unlikely that a continuing decline in retail jobs will be made good by online commerce. (Thompson 2017). Amazon's warehouse robots take a fraction of the space required by humans and can pick and pack an order in a fourth of the time.

3 See McKinsey Global Institute (2013) https://www.mckinsey.com/business-functions/digital-mckinsey/our-insights/disruptive-technologies; Cloud computing can facilitate design, prototyping and fabrication. Moreover, it enables firms to make use of 3D manufacturing the IoT, and industrial robots. It can be tailored for firms of all sizes and lowers the entry barriers for firms because it is scalable, obviates the need to purchase expensive equipment and software and provides data security. Ezell and Swanson (2017).

4 In their recent publication, McAfee and Brynjolfsson (2017, p.24) examine the implications for the business world and the risks for those companies that do not "bring together minds and machines, products and platforms and the core and crowd" in innovative ways.

5 Feedback Statement, Financial Conduct Authority, Call for Input on Supporting the Development and Adopters of RegTech, (July 2016).

6 Adrian Shedden and Gareth Malna, "Supporting the Development and Adoption of RegTech: No Better Time for a Call for Input," (Burges Salmon, 2016) https://www.burges-salmon.com/-/media/files/publications/open-access/supporting_the_development_and_adoption_of_regtech_no_better_time_for_a_call_for_input.pdf

Chapter 6
Non-Technological and Technological (SupTech) Innovations in Strengthening the Financial Supervision

Marcin Flotyński
Adam Mickiewicz University, Poznań, Poland

Kamilla Marchewka-Bartkowiak
Poznań University of Economics and Business, Poland

ABSTRACT

The application of non-technological and technological innovations provides support to supervisory institutions in the digitization of reporting and regulatory processes. This chapter deals with international applications of innovations in financial supervision (SupTech). The aim of the chapter is to present the most popular technological and non-technological solutions along with an evaluation of their usefulness in exercising supervision over the financial market. The authors discuss the types of innovations and the reasons for implementing them by supervisory institutions. Furthermore, they describe the most important non-technological supervisory solutions and technologies that supervisors can apply in creating SupTech tools. The study utilizes, among other things, data from reports and elaborations by central banks, supervisory institutions, and consulting companies. The authors' main focus is on the analysis of the solutions utilized by European Union member states.

INTRODUCTION

The financial sector is highly competitive and innovative. However, the current stage of implementation of new technological solutions indicates that traditional financial institutions are now beginning to face not only intra-sector competition but also the emerging market of financial technologies, the so called FinTech. Under the definition by the Financial Stability Board, the term FinTech is applied to describe

DOI: 10.4018/978-1-7998-4390-0.ch006

innovations in financial services based on technologies that can lead to the creation of new business models, applications, processes and products, thus having a significant impact on the financial market and institutions and the way financial services are rendered (Financial Stability Board, 2017).

The increased competition between the financial sector and FinTech serves as a catalyzer of their growth and often also leads to cooperation between them. Therefore, it is becoming increasingly difficult to exercise supervision over institutions the operations of which may contribute to the increased risk of financial system stability. Hence, financial supervision, mostly national, is facing a major challenge and is required to launch new supervision methods and tools. In this regard, new terms: RegTech and SupTech have been introduced. They both refer to applications of innovative technologies which support the activities of financial supervision. Consequently, they are both cases of financial technology (FinTech) use. However, there are some differences. RegTech constitutes any tool or platform that facilitates regulatory compliance, making it more efficient. It usually leads to costs decrease and to higher level of process automation in fulfilling reporting and regulatory requirements. On the other hand, SupTech denotes technologies applied by supervisory agencies in order to improve supervision (CNBV, 2018; Ascent, 2020; Broeders and Prenio, 2018, p. 3).

Technological advances and an enormous amount of data available are conducive to the development of tools for maintaining financial supervision and stability based on information analyses. Thus, SupTech provides support to supervision institutions in the digitization of reporting and regulatory processes. SupTech solutions can be categorized into two groups on the premise of gathering and analyzing data. Depending on institutions' requirements they can be aimed at prudential supervision, malpractice analysis, market supervision, fraud monitoring, money laundering prevention and risk control. Additionally, SupTech has also been reported to prevent manipulations on the market and confidential information exchange.

This chapter deals with international applications of innovations in financial supervision. First, the authors discuss the types of innovations and the reasons for implementing them by supervisory institutions. Next, the authors present the most important non-technological supervisory solutions and technologies that supervisors can apply in creating SupTech tools. As regards both technological and non-technological solutions, the authors point to the impact they exert on the future changes in the approach to financial supervision practice.

The aim of this chapter is to present the most popular technological and non-technological solutions along with an evaluation of their usefulness in exercising supervision over the financial market.

The study utilizes, among other things, data from reports and elaborations by central banks, supervision institutions and consulting companies spanning the years 2017-2020. The authors' main focus is on the analysis of the solutions utilized by European Union member states.[1]

SUPERVISORY INNOVATIONS

The development of financial technologies brings about new challenges in terms of the supervision over the financial services market in the context of reducing both micro- and macro-prudential risks. For more than a decade public supervisors (including central banks and specialized agencies) have been adjusting their operations to the continuous growth of competition among subordinate institutions and sectors. The new approach to supervision relying on supervisory innovations has not replaced the traditional approach yet, but it is becoming complementary to it. This does not mean, however, that some of the tools dedicated to technological services today will not, in the future, cover all of the supervised institutions in terms of monitoring their communication with clients, data reporting, or timely responding to identified irregularities.

Hence, "supervisory innovations" can be construed as regulatory, institutional, procedural and technological solutions aimed at enhancing the effectiveness of the supervision over financial technologies market and minimizing the risks involved.

From the perspective of the chapter's subject area, supervisory innovations could be categorized into two groups, i.e. non-technological and technological innovations. The former group includes:

- special regulations and licensing processes,
- innovations offices or hubs,
- innovation accelerators or labs,
- regulatory sandboxes.

The other group of supervisory innovations encompasses all the solutions applied within the so called SupTech (*supervisory technology*), such as artificial intelligence (AI), application programming interface (API), blockchain, Natural Language Processing etc. They are described in the next subsections.

NON-TECHNOLOGICAL SUPERVISORY INNOVATIONS

In response to the growing significance of the FinTech sector a number of supervisors set out to adjust their own tools. First, those actions meant introducing regulatory-procedural changes, and then institutional changes.

According to a 2019 report by the International Monetary Fund and the World Bank, about 65% of the countries included in the Global FinTech Survey conduct a specific form of supervision over the FinTech sector, 76% have made changes in their approach to regulating the sector, and as many as 87% have taken due actions to keep up with the development of new technological innovations (International Monetary Fund & World Bank, 2019). The findings of the survey confirm that many countries are highly aware of the need for implementing reforms and adjusting the regulators and supervisors to the fast changing environment of the technology-based sectors. Those adjustments result from extensive analyses into the role of the financial innovations sector in the national financial sector and the national economy as such. It is also becoming a common practice to create FinTech Maps[2] and, based on them, evaluate the influence of particular technologies on the further development of traditional sectors and industries. Very often, those studies include analyses into the barriers that public administration, including supervisory institutions, is facing.

As mentioned above, the actions taken by financial supervisors can be divided into four major groups of non-technological solutions.

The first group includes **special regulations and licensing processes**. Although in many countries national regulators still remain technologically neutral, there also exists a trend to adopt new regulatory solutions. They can be both "hard" legal acts and "soft" supervisory regulations dedicated to specific technologies, business models and innovations, or dedicated sets of regulations for the FinTech sector. Another approach is modifying the regulations already in force.

The first example action is two regulations introduced in the USA in 2019 concerning token and the blockchain technology, based on which the tokenization process is taking place (the Token Taxonomy Act of 2019 – HR 2144 and the Digital Taxonomy Act of 2019 – HR 2154) (Library of Congress, 2019a; Library of Congress, 2019b). These regulations use new definitions of "digital token" and "digital unit", and introduce new rules regarding their sales and trading. Another issue is new business models, including the operations of the so called "digital banks". Under a number of local jurisdictions, supervisory institutions set out the guidelines for the FinTech sector on the application of standard (traditional) criteria. Some other, including Hong Kong (The Hong Kong Monetary Authority, 2018a; The Hong Kong Monetary Authority, 2018b) or Singapore (The Monetary Authority of Singapore, 2018), drew up specific license requirements for banks specializing in digital services. Similar approach was also applied in such areas as investment counseling (robo-advisors) or insurance services (the so called InsurTech). Specific requirements concerning licensing and running business activity have also been formulated in terms of a range of actions, such as e-money issuance, payment services and community fund raising. In most cases, regulatory requirements focus on protecting the rights of consumers and investors (mainly on protecting clients' funds), Anti Money Laundering (AML), and Combating the Financing of Terrorism (CFT). Other practices regard cryptocurrencies. In this instance, authorities often issued warnings and explanations concerning the regulations that apply to issuers, owners and intermediaries on the crypto currency market. Additionally, a number of supervisory institutions imposed a ban on conducting operations involving crypto currencies (e.g. China, India, Mexico).[3] Another instance is a bottom-up approach to financial technologies introduced in Mexico, where the authorities launched a comprehensive set of regulatory tools for the development of the new financial technologies sector (SEGOB, 2018).

To sum up, as far as the FinTech sector is concerned, regulators/supervisors can apply a number of regulatory solutions, including legal acts and sets of legal acts, guidelines, special licenses, and also news releases, warnings and bans.

Innovation offices or hubs can be defined as dedicated centers of contact for firms to raise enquiries with competent authorities on FinTech-related issues and to seek non-binding guidance on the conformity of innovative financial products, financial services or business models with licensing or registration requirements and regulatory and supervisory expectations (European Supervisory Authorities, 2018).

According to a report for the United Nations, innovation offices aimed at serving FinTech are organized in a number of ways. For instance, a supervisory institution can set office hours, telephone number, email address dedicated to innovators or start a special website and group of experts for personalized contacts. Offering office hours is usually an approach that requires least resources, while providing the assistance of office staff is certainly much more resource-demanding and costly (while still generating more benefits). Innovation offices also gather the obtained information in the context of the proposed regulatory changes or evaluation of the so far applied legal instruments. It is worth noting that owing to innovation offices supervisors can extend their knowledge about the types of financial innovations and the scope of the new technologies applied. Furthermore, many innovation offices set special criteria under which entities can use their services. The criteria include as follows: type of innovation (the so called primary innovations), influence on the client, solving the issue of financial exclusion, market scope of innovation, generating risk, and so forth. Therefore, an entity that wishes to contact the supervisor must first fulfill all the requirements. In 2019, innovation offices were operational in more than 30 countries (UNSGSA, 2019).

Along with the development of the FinTech sector and the increased significance of the innovator-supervisor contacts, there has also emerged a greater need for launching new solutions, including the controlled testing of financial innovations. Such a possibility was first offered by **innovation labs or accelerators**. They are special one-off or long-term programs established by public institutions in cooperation with external partners (Di Castri, Hohl, Kulenkampff & Prenio, 2019). Basically, innovation accelerators allow sponsors (also from the financial sector) to finance and test prototypes of new technological products in a safe supervisory environment.

Table 1. Benefit-cost analysis of regulatory sandboxes

Benefits	Costs
• reducing the barriers in entering the market for FinTech innovations, • creating safe pace for FinTech, • ensuring continuous dialogue between the regulator/supervisor and FinTech sector entities, • reducing legal risk and building trust in the FinTech sector, • reduction of operational and financing costs for FinTech sector entities, • limiting the time required to obtain license by launching priority procedures, • the possibility to "loosen" regulatory requirements for FinTech in order to strengthen the sector, • launching the process of mutual teaching of commercial and public entities with further benefits for FinTech regulatory processes, • improving the image of both new FinTech businesses and the regulator/supervisor as a public entity open to dialogue and cooperation, • streamlining subsequent stages (reforms) of the regulatory process (e.g. towards *smart regulation*).	• mitigating market competition by regulators/supervisors through deliberate actions steering in terms of innovations (e.g. special selection criteria of sandbox beneficiaries) • priority given to FinTech sector entities with selective approach to improving regulatory effectiveness in other sectors, • delegating too many tasks to too few staff at public institutions (in the regulatory and supervision) in the area of innovativeness, • transferring part of the testing obligations within regulatory sandboxes onto entities outside the founding institutions (regulators/supervisors), and facing the risk of losing control over the testing process and its results, • forced risk minimization (decrease in credibility, safety) within FinTech by means of licensing, which might have indirect impact on the banking sector's increased risk levels (as regards the financing of FinTech sector entities), • impaired performance of regulatory sandboxes, resulting from the diminished effect of scale, • relatively high financial costs of running sandboxes for regulators and high costs of testing for FinTech, • regulators'/supervisors' jeopardized reputation due to the materialized risk of numerous FinTech sector entities going bankrupt.

Source: based on Marchewka-Bartkowiak (2020).

Innovation accelerators and hubs in financial supervision institutions are not as popular as **regulatory sandboxes**, i.e. specially organized environments of legal supervision created by financial supervisor (or regulator) for testing possible effects of new technological solution implementation in an isolated environment (e.g. a group of clients). The testing procedure can concern innovative products, financial services or business models created on the basis of new technologies. Regulatory sandboxes are mainly dedicated to the FinTech sector, but also to innovations developed in the traditional banking sector or insurance sector.

Since the first regulatory sandbox was created in 2015 in the UK, more and more countries have been showing their interest in this solution.[4] However, the assessment of regulatory sandboxes is still varied as they involve not only benefits but also direct and indirect costs of their implementation (Table 1).

NON-TECHNOLOGICAL SUPERVISORY INNOVATIONS: THE CASE OF EU COUNTRIES

The FinTech sector in Europe has seen a steady growth. In 2018, investment in financial technological innovations amounted to USD 38.9 bn, with the biggest growth in five years reported in the first quarter (KPMG, 2019). Although the European Union takes only third place in the technological race (following the USA and Asia), the quick pace of the new technologies sector development triggers an increased activity of EU regulators and supervisors.

EU institutions have been involved in the adjustment process for a number of years. The changes include Directive 2000/31/EC (regarding e-commerce), Directive 2002/65/EC (regarding distance marketing of consumer financial services), Directive 2009/110/EC (regarding electronic money), Directive (EU) 2015/2366 (regarding payment services), Directive 95/46/EC (regarding personal data protection). Proposals are being made towards taking joint actions at the EU level (European Commission's March 2018 FinTech Action Plan) (European Commission, 2018a), but also new legal solutions, such as the General Data Protection Regulation (EU) 2016/679 (GDPR) and the Proposal for a Regulation of the European Parliament and the Council on European Crowdfunding Service Providers (ECSP) for Business (European Parliament, 2018), and institutional solutions, e.g. launching the EU FinTech Lab (European Commission, 2018b) and the EU Blockchain Observatory and Forum (European Commission, 2019).

The institutions active in this forum are European Supervisory Authorities (ESAs), including the European Banking Authority (EBA), the European Securities and Markets Authority (ESMA) and the European Insurance and Occupational Pensions Authority (EIOPA). Some of the reports, guidelines, standpoints and statements of the representatives of these institutions concern the issues of technological and non-technological supervisory solutions, e.g. "A Report: FinTech: Regulatory sandboxes and innovation hubs", and also the Final Report to the European Commission's Expert Group on Regulatory Obstacles to Financial Innovation (ROFIEG) Thirty Recommendations on Regulation, Innovation and Finance. The latter study proposes enhancing supervisors' knowledge on new technologies (Recommendation 3) by, among other things, such initiatives as the European Forum for Innovation Facilitators (EFIF) (European Supervisory Authorities, 2019) and the EBA's FinTech Knowledge Hub (European Banking Authority, 2020b).

EU member states[5] have been introducing both national and supranational solutions. However, the area distribution of the actions taken is not even. Table 2 compiles the scope of utilizing non-technological supervisory innovations across EU member states. As the comparison shows, at the end of 2019 six states (Denmark, France, Hungary, the Netherlands, Spain and Great Britain) implemented three solutions each. At the same time, there is a group of states which has not yet launched the new solutions (Croatia, the Czech Republic, Finland, Greece, Luxembourg, and Slovenia).

It is worth drawing attention to regulatory sandboxes. This solution, first used in Great Britain, is becoming increasingly popular worldwide, including EU member states. By the end of 2019, this innovation had been launched by seven EU member states. However, there also instances of turning away from this solution. One of such countries is Poland, where the financial supervisor dropped this tool and is now developing the Innovation Hub Programme, even though sandbox had already been worked upon and planned for implementation by the end of 2019 (KNF, 2019b).

Table 2. Non-technological innovations in EU member states

Country	Supervisory authority (acronyms)	Non-technological supervisory innovations			
		Special regulations/ licensing process	**Innovation office/hub**	**Innovation accelerators/lab**	**Regulatory sandbox**
Austria	OeNB FMA	+	+		
Belgium	NBB FSMA	+	+		
Bulgaria	BNB FSC		+		
Croatia	CNB HANFA				
Cyprus	CBC Cosec ICCS		+		
The Czech Republic	CNB				
Denmark	DFSA	+	+		+
Estonia	FI		+		
Finland	FIN-FSA				
France	ACPR AMF	+	+	+	
Germany	BaFIN	+	+		
Greece	BoG HCMC		+		
Hungary	MNB		+	+	+
Ireland	CBI		+		
Italy	BI CONSOB IVASS	+	+		
Latvia	FKTK		+		
Lithuania	LB		+		+
Luxembourg	CSSF CAA				
Malta	MFSA				
The Netherlands	DNB AFM	+	+		+
Poland	KNF		+		
Portugal	BP CMVM ASF			+	
Romania	BNR ASF	+	+		
Slovakia	NBS				
Slovenia	BoS ATVP AZN				

continues on following page

Table 2. Continued

Country	Supervisory authority (acronyms)	Non-technological supervisory innovations			
		Special regulations/ licensing process	Innovation office/hub	Innovation accelerators/lab	Regulatory sandbox
Spain	BDE CNMV DGSFP	+	+		+
Sweden	FI	+	+		
The United Kingdom	PRA FCA	+	+		+

Source: based on data and information included on websites and reports of national supervisory agencies and UNSGSA (2019) and Ehrentraud, Ocampo, Garzoni & Piccolo (2020).

SUPTECH SOLUTIONS: DEFINITIONS, TOOLS, FEATURES

New solutions in financial supervision (the so called *SupTech*) concern a dozen or so technologies. The aim of this subchapter is to present the most often used tools which can be helpful to supervisors.

Artificial Intelligence (AI) and Machine Learning (ML)

Artificial intelligence is a field of IT that allows computer programs to perform such operations as speech recognition, visual perception, problem solving, language translations and decision-making. In other words, it is a set of technologies enabling computers to perceive, learn, reason and offer help in making decisions so as to solve problems in a manner that imitates the human way of thinking. AI has multiple applications and it is being increasingly often used in the financial sector (e.g. in the so called robo-advice and transactions authenticating). In recent years, the increased memory and power of data processing, as well as machine learning, contributed to a broader use of AI (Toronto Centre, 2017a, p. 4). Those systems are already used in everyday life for language translations, running factories, answering questions, writing messages, making medical diagnoses, driving vehicles and energy consumption optimization. AI technologies, like automation before, allow scaling possibilities with machines across the ever expanding world of data. The rapid increase in computing powers owing to cloud computing in connection with the growing amount of data created, reduced the limitations of entry for both developing and exploiting AI technologies in finance. This in turn allowed big and small institutions to experiment with AI systems. Artificial Intelligence can be built on human intelligence through recognizing anomalies and patterns in huge amounts of data, which is important e.g. in such applications as detection of fraudulent transactions. AI is also capable of scaling and automating repetitive tasks. Artificial Intelligence can be applied to making even very complex calculations, for instance in assessing risks levels on the financial market (UK Finance & Microsoft, 2019, pp. 4-7).

Machine learning is a subset of artificial intelligence aimed at enabling computers to analyze and learn from huge amounts of data with a view to making forecasts. Machine learning uses various techniques including deep structured learning and neural networks. In the past, artificial intelligence tried to imitate human behavior by means of methods based on rules, i.e. algorithms based on logic. At present, machine learning is based on data, i.e. computers analyze huge amounts of miscellaneous data in order to detect patterns which do not have to be intuitive, rational or translated into programming languages.

This type of machine learning exerts a significant impact on financial supervision and financial services (Toronto Centre, 2017a, p. 4).

Neural Networks

Neural network is a set of interconnected units or nodes which are similar in functioning to the animal neuron. The processing ability of the network is achieved due to learning from training patterns (Gurney, 1997, p. 13). It is modelled on the structure of the human brain and can be used to solve problems in such fields as economics, statistics and technology. Before they are used, they should be trained how to solve problems. It is often used for machine learning and artificial intelligence. Neural networks can be typically utilized in forecasts for complex systems, early warning systems, economic models and time series analysis (Mijwel, Esen and Shamil, 2019, p. 1).

Data Pull Approach

Data pull approach is a technology controlled by the financial supervisors used to gather business data directly from the institutions' operational systems. It is useful for reporting process and it ensures good quality information for decision making (IAIS, 2019, p. 3; Broeders and Prenio, 2018, p. 6-7).

Random Forest

Random forest algorithm is a popular algorithm for machine learning. It can be used as regression and classification algorithm. It creates multiple decision trees and merges them together to make predictions (Newgenapps, 2018).

Application Programming Interface (API)

API interfaces are definitions, protocols and tools that determine the way various applications interact with each other. They allow developing computer programs, such as applications for managing personal finance, which gain access to information about individuals' bank accounts with a view to ensuring a number of conveniences for the recipients of financial services (Toronto Centre, 2017a). Open API interfaces allow third parties to access the systems of financial institutions, e.g. opening internal information systems and data for program access by external service providers or their partners in a transparent and well documented way. Effective implementation of open APIs renders it possible to aggregate information and products and services of various banks within the same website and application for making easy comparisons and financial planning by users. Open information can also be used to offer unique products and new experience to their clients (HKMA, 2019).

Business or network API interfaces are easy to learn interfaces for business assets, e.g. client bases, accounts, product catalogues, prices, orders, etc. They are a public image of financial institution making specific resources, data or service available to be used by selected recipients inside and outside the organization. Application authors can gain access to business API interfaces in an approachable way. They increase the opportunities of the enterprise and open up new markets. Additionally, not being difficult to learn they allow application programmers to easily exploit, advertise and aggregate the resources of financial institutions for extending their customer base (IBM, 2016, p. 2).

Cloud Computing

Cloud computing is using remote and co-shared host servers on the Internet for storing, managing and processing data. Under the traditional approach, institutions (e.g. banks) keep their data on local computers and servers. Cloud computing is thus a completely new approach which increased significantly the capability of financial institutions and other organizations to generate, store, manage and use data with more flexibility and lower costs (Toronto Centre, 2017a, p. 5).

Cloud computing enables users to access virtual computing options – from net memories, storing data and programming environments to fully functional applications. In this way, data and applications do not have to be stored on local servers or 'on premises'; they are hosted and managed by external cloud service providers (CSPs). Enterprises commission CSPs with different levels of IT functionality, and all users have to do is simply connect to the Internet to gain access to data and applications though virtual servers. By relocating to the cloud, financial institutions can significantly reduce or even eliminate the cost of their IT function, thus transforming their business model (EY, 2015, p. 4).

Blockchain and Distributed Ledger Technology and Smart Contracts

Blockchain is a type of database used for transaction recording. It is copied to all of the computers in a participating network. Data is stored in 'blocks' which are fixed structures (Deloitte, n.d., p. 2). Distributed Ledger Technology (DLT) is a data base shared by a great many parties (nodes) with a view to conducting jointly agreed transactions based on the so called consensus mechanism. The key feature of DLT is that all knots share identical data versions, without a central trusted party (e.g. clearing house). This feature helps fight cyberattacks and data manipulation. In the case of cryptocurrencies, such as Bitcoin, transaction ledger is like a series of data blocks connected with each other by means of cryptography (blockchain) based on the work of "miners" (nodes which continuously solve cryptographic puzzles to check the correctness of transactions embracing blockchain). There are a great many potential applications of DLT, including digital currencies of central banks, crypto currencies, smart contracts and public registers (e.g. identity register, proprietorship register, birth register). DLT exerts immense impact on the financial sector by changing the market infrastructure and the roles of central counterparties or enhancing efficiency (e.g. streamlining the work of the back-office). The terms 'blockchain' and 'DLT' are used interchangeably (blockchain is a kind of distributed ledger technology) (Toronto Centre, 2017a).

Smart contract is an intelligent (digital) contract, which can perform itself automatically on fulfilling specified conditions. It uses DLT to draw up and execute contracts which offer potential benefits, such as inter-operationality and enormous processes and costs efficiency. Ethereum and Corda – a consortium of international banks developing DLT for financial services – are examples of DLT used as smart contracts platforms (Toronto Centre, 2017a, p. 5).

Tokenisation

Traditional transactions on the financial market are settled by means of updating balances in the accounts record of a centralized register, such as general ledger. However, new technologies, such as the Distributed Ledger Technology (DLT), allow creating digital tokens that could potentially be used as clearing assets. Token is a digital representation of the rights to all types of material (financial) or non-material assets (ASIFMA, 2019, p. 9; Bank for International Settlements, 2019, pp. 1-5). It offers an increased flexibility and liquidity of the underlying instrument. In order to transfer the ownership of tokens, a simple exchange is conducted using a tokenized clearing medium. In order to harmonize the types of money in circulations, central banks can provide necessary backing to new financial ecosystems which are based on tokens. It has become a particularly popular idea for central banks to have their own digital money (Accenture, 2019, pp. 4-5).

The tokenization of assets is a process of token issuance, based on the blockchain technology. The process involves digital mapping of real assets. In some aspects, it is similar to securitization. Tokens are created by means of Initial Coin Offering, and then traded in on the secondary market. The greatest advantages of using tokens include high liquidity, the speed and low cost of transactions, transparency and easy access to a broad circle of investors (Laurent, Chollet, Burke & Seers, 2018, p. 2).

There are two different concepts: security tokens and tokenized securities. Tokenized securities are traditional securities listed on regulated markets. They are characterized by digital wrapper. Examples include traded stocks and bonds registered in distributed ledgers. Security tokens can cover a broader spectrum. They are designed to represent a certain type of underlying asset, such as stakes in companies, profit streams, the right to dividend or interest payment (or a combination of these). Tokens of this type can be classified as stocks, bonds, derivatives or collective investment schemes – depending on the economic function they perform (ASIFMA, 2019, p. 9).

The tokenization of financial assets can help satisfy the needs of the financial market in terms of, among other things, reducing the limitations of the existing wholesale market infrastructure. Tokenization can help to streamline the processes of simultaneous payment and delivery, foreign exchange transactions, and boost resistance to market manipulations (Beau, 2019, p. 3).

Predictive Modeling

Predictive modeling is a mathematical and computing technique for predicting events or results. In the mathematical approach an equation-based model describes the phenomenon under analysis. The model is used to predict a result in a different state or time based on the changes in the model's entry data. Model parameters help to explain how model's entry data impact the final result (MathWorks, n.d).

Big Data

Big data is a term referring to huge amounts of unstructured data (e-mail messages, Internet traffic, etc.) and structural data (e.g. data bases) the analysis of which is not possible by means of traditional analytical tools. It includes data gathered via nets (such as the Internet or corporate intranets), and other data that is generated and stored by organizations. Big Data analysis deals with, among other things, finding correlations, trends and patterns in data, or clients' preferences. The analysis of Big Data uses machine learning or other technologies (Toronto Centre, 2017a).

Chatbots, Text Mining, Dashboards and Web Scraper

Chatbot is a program utilizing artificial intelligence, which interacts with another chatbot or a human being, giving the impression of interacting with a human being (Zemčík, 2019).

Text mining is a multidisciplinary field involving information mining, text analysis, categorizing, grouping, visualization, data exploration and machine learning. There are five basic steps of text mining:

- gathering information from unstructured data,
- transferring the obtained information into structured data,
- identifying patterns on the basis of structural data,
- pattern analysis,
- abstracting valuable information and storing it in data base (Dang & Ahmad, 2014).

Dashboards are configurable, dynamic tools for interactive reporting, which download and visualize data automatically. They are tools which enable adjusting business processes and strategies execution (Di Castri, Hohl, Kulenkampff & Prenio, 2019).

Web scraping is a technique of mining data from the Internet and saving it in the system or data base for future download or analysis. Net data is usually downloaded by means of the http protocol or a web browser. The process is automated and conducted by a bot or net robot, or manually by user (Zhao, 2017, pp. 1-3; Mooney, Westreich & El-Sayed, 2015; Bar-Ilan, 2001).

Data Cubes and Data Lake

Data cubes are used to evaluate data aggregated from different viewpoints. They can be described as multidimensional extension of two-dimensional tables. Data cubes are used to represent data that is too big and complex to be described with a table of columns and rows. They can exceed three-dimensionality and comprise a great number of other dimensions (Techopedia, n.d.).

Data lake is a repository for storing unstructured and structured data that is downloaded in its raw form and stored by a highly scalable, distributed files system known as *open source*. Additionally, it is also possible to make parallel calculations and service a number of access methods. The final effect is a new approach to analysis which makes it possible to identify data, patterns and queries to perform. As a result it is easier for institutions to detect relationships, trends and patterns, which otherwise would not be possible to identify. It allows analysts to think out of the box and identify spots where unpredicted risks could materialize. Data lake is an implementation pattern suitable for organizations that are well aware of the data to be processed. The most important advantages of data lakes include the low cost of gathering and analyzing data, as well as the possibility to store multiple types of contents (OVUM n.d., p. 9-10).

Geographic Information Systems

The Geographic Information System (GIS) is a computer system covering analyzing, managing, intercepting, hardware, software and displaying information in the geographic context. GIS can help accelerate performing everyday procedures delivering up-to-date data for supporting the decision-making. GIS supports public and private institutions worldwide in their decision-making processes and can help develop administration and management procedures that are more efficient, more transparent and more customer friendly while at the same time ensuring high quality of the data used in making management decisions. The advantages of GIS include: a quick insight into spatial data, more effective allocation of resources and more effective communication between the departments of public and private institutions, plus quicker identification of the sought after investment targets on the financial market (Gunawardena, 2014, p. 2; Wehrmann & Glavina, 2009, pp. 1-6).

Natural Language Processing

Natural Language Processing (NLP) is an area covering Artificial Intelligence and linguistics. It involves processing the information saved in a computer's database so as to make it comprehensible for human beings. NLP was developed with a view to streamlining the work of users and satisfying the need to communicate with the computer in a natural language. NLP techniques can be used to make report summaries, find key words in press articles, as well as sense the context and mood in which they were written. Next, these functions can be used to make a conscious decision on the basis of latest reports and market sentiment (Khurana, Koli, Khatter, & Singh, 2017, p. 2; Khant, & Mehta, 2018).

Network Analysis

Network analysis is a process of examining structures by means of networks and graphs theory. It is a set of integrated techniques for presenting the relationships between specific entities and analyzing the structure. The basic assumption is that an effective explanation of phenomena is possible though data analysis concerning the system of network between entities (data collected in the form of matrix). If institutions are represented as knots, and their relations as lines between couples of knots, the network concept becomes an operational tool that exploits the mathematical language of the theory of graphs as well as matrix and relational algebra (Di Castri, Hohl, Kulenkampff & Prenio, 2019; Chiesi, 2001).

Robotic Process Automation (RPA) and Self-Organizing Maps (SOM)

Robotic Process Automation (RPA) is a method of automating repetitive processes with software which works like a human being and performs tasks on computers. Transactions processes of this type are often performed in financial institutions at the back office or at shared services centers. The software is used to process data and conduct communication between different IT systems. This type of activities, following strictly defined supervisor rules, can be performed successfully by robots instead of human beings (Jovanović, Đurić, & Šibalija, n.d.; Martino, Laurent, Hauman, Gavray, n.d.).

Self-organizing maps (SOMs) are a type of neural network which uses an unsupervised training algorithm and a process known as self-organization. This technique is capable of "teaching itself" without any supervision (SOM "training"). By the end of the training SOM enables analysts to review new relationships, patterns and structures at entry vector. In contrast to traditional methods, SOMs ensure an easy visualization, imposing only a few assumptions and limitations. Additionally, it is capable of serving huge datasets. SOMs are being increasingly often used for exploring data in finance (Shanmuganathan, Sallis, & Buckeridge, 2004; Deboeck & Kohonen, 1998; Deboeck, 2000).

THE CAPABILITIES OF TECHNOLOGICAL SUPERVISORY INNOVATIONS (SUPTECH)

Another tool often used by supervisory institutions is a technology for conducting information analysis into the identification and evaluation of money laundering and the risk of terrorism financing. The process involves challenges concerning the quality of huge datasets in terms of, among other things, collecting and completeness of the data. Automation of the processes of collecting and verifying data solves some of the challenges. Supervisors develop tools for data analysis with a view to conducting efficient information processing from various sources and obtaining a complete and consistent insight into the risk of money laundering and terrorism financing (AML/CFT), for the compliance evaluation or irregularities detection (Coelho, De Simoni & Prenio, 2019). To this end, supervisory institutions focus their attention on payment institutions.

The Financial Transactions and Reports Analysis Centre of Canada (FINTRAC) uses the heuristic model for evaluating the overall risk of money laundering. The tool utilizes risk factors that are determined on the basis of huge amounts of data. The aim of the tool is to evaluate the risk profile of each reporting institution so as to help set priorities in the "on-premises" research. The model results are checked against the results of supervised learning (Coelho, De Simoni & Prenio, 2019, p. 8).

Additionally, FINTRAC also uses text mining. By means of trends and patterns analysis it can identify suspicious operations, the detection of which can lead to further investigation and developing warnings for auditors (Coelho, De Simoni & Prenio, 2019).

For comparison, the CNBV (*Comisión Nacional Bancaria y de Valores*) applies machine learning for transaction data analysis. Anomalous transactions are used to train algorithms. Next, the tool scans the whole dataset to detect other transactions of similar patterns. The number of detected unreported anomalous transactions helps conduct an assessment of banks' regulatory compliance and determine the list of priority institutions to be controlled on-premises. Such tools help detect suspicious activities in a number of ways including: detecting networks of entities involved in suspicious activities, the assessment of money laundering probability, and the identification of patterns and trends in criminal activity. It is worth noting that this tool uses the network analysis (similarities are identified on the basis of network structure) and scans the transactions database (e.g. involving gold) in search of behaviors "resembling" the pattern of frauds already investigated (Coelho, De Simoni & Prenio, 2019, p. 10).

Machine learning for supervisory purposes is also used by ROSFIN, for identifying transactions similar to transactions involving money laundering (Coelho, De Simoni & Prenio, 2019).

Predictive modeling rely on supervised ML algorithms (powered with training data marked as honest or dishonest), which can learn patterns based on past frauds with a view to detecting similar transactions and, consequently, new frauds. Machine algorithms for detecting anomalies in the behavior of market participants (reflecting rare or anomalous patterns) can be combined with predictive models without supervision in order to ensure sufficient predictive capability and accuracy in fraud detection. Predictive modeling can be used in real time for preventing fraudulent transactions. The model receives a stream of business data as entry data to be checked and gives back an estimate of potential fraud possibility for each entry in the stream. When a result given by the model for a specific entry reaches a pre-defined threshold, the entry is considered suspicious. Next, alarm is raised and the financial transaction is quarantined until a public institution officer (e.g. a compliance inspector) can control it manually. If the model is accurate, the compliance inspector will have fewer transactions to control and, thus, more time to work on the transactions marked as potentially fraudulent. The inspector takes his or her decision on the basis of an *ad hoc* investigation. For further enhancing the performance of the model new recognized patterns found in the frauds detection process can be applied for regular model requalifying (the feedback loop) (Coelho, De Simoni & Prenio, 2019; MathWorks, n.d).

A document by the Bank of International Settlements (BIS) (Auer, 2019) offers the concept of the so called embedded supervision based on tokenization. The concept fits within a legal framework which provides for automatic compliance monitoring by accessing market ledger. This solution reduces the administrative burden on companies and increases the quality of data accessible to supervisory institutions. As a result, there is a smaller need for investment companies to actively gather, verify and deliver data. DLT allows decentralized trade in security tokens (which are secured by tangible or intangible assets), and decentralized token-based financial engineering by means of self-executing ("intelligent") contracts. If such innovations become popular, they will drive financial markets development owing to their transparency and data credibility.

Such credibility of DLT can be achieved due to a decentralized data structure based on economic consensus. DLT effectively urges market participants to utilize the new manner of data verification, which is not based on the intermediaries' activity. In such an instance, monitoring compliance with requirements would be automated owing to the mechanism of building trust in decentralized markets to supervisory purposes. For instance, compliance with Basel III capital standards could be verified automatically by banks that have security tokens. The verification could happen by balance reconciliation (of loans allowed and taken out) and related risk weights in appropriate distributed ledgers (Auer, 2019, p. 1).

The four basic ideas behind embedded supervision are (Auer, 2019, p. 2):

- promoting low compliance costs and equal operations conditions for small and big businesses,
- applying to decentralized markets
- developing in the context of financial market consensus, taking account of the market's response to automated supervision,
- functioning as a part of the overall regulatory framework, supported by an effective legal system and supporting institutions.

DLT allows proving the transfer of the ownership of asset-backed tokens from one entity to another. Nevertheless, the connection between the underlying asset and digital token must have legal grounds. For instance, if there is a bond based on the tokens of a particular company, which does not participate in the distributed market, there should also exist an institution to enforce interest and principal payment. A high level of trust could be generated by a system in which the distributed market offers an economic incentive for reaching consensus on ledger update. In that event, a supervision institution would confirm the consensus if proved irreversible (Auer, 2019, p. 15).

An example application of digital tokens are the so called stablecoins. Trade in them is conducted by means of distributed ledger and cryptographic verification techniques in order to achieve stable values in relation to fiduciary currencies. Such a solution allows users to protect the face value of their capital assets. The application of stablecoins usually involves a trusted intermediary or some other centralized infrastructure (Bank for International Settlements, 2019).

At present, whole sale tokens are being researched into utilizing them to settling payments. They could also be used under token platforms for settling payments concerning transactions involving other digital assets, including secured tokens and tokenized currencies. However, at this stage it is too early to prejudge the direction the possible applications can take (Bank for International Settlements, 2019, p. 1).

Inbuilt supervision can mitigate the conflict between data availability, data collection / verification costs, and privacy. The costs towards ensuring compliance with rules are a huge burden for financial institutions, small and medium-size institutions in particular. Thus, supervision institutions are facing the issue of obtaining required data on the one hand, and keeping compliance costs at reasonable levels on the other. The embedded supervision can also help ensure the privacy of businesses and their clients as cryptographic tools can serve to report aggregated financial sheets to supervision institutions without disclosing transactions behind particular settlements. Although regulations ought to remain technologically neutral, supervision must develop along with technology development. Even though DLT does not eliminate basic risks, it can give way to new forms of supervision over those threats. Instead of attempting to adjust cryptographic sets to the existing regulations (e.g. the regulations on securities, formulated long before the emergence of DLT), it is worth considering how the new technologies could be utilized to monitor risk in financial markets (Auer, 2019, pp. 1-2).

The compliance process today involves reporting at multiple levels of data specificity. In their accounts, banks include millions of individual transactions. This information must be gathered, aggregated and delivered to supervisory institutions and a great number of internal stakeholders (internal auditor, compliance inspectors, managers, traders, etc.). Thus, compliance costs grow very high. DLT-based innovations can help transform financial markets considerably as they offer new forms of market transparency. The prime advantage of this technology is automation (e.g. of the transaction process) which reduces the costs and risks of non-compliance and streamlines the execution of operational targets (Auer, 2019, pp. 5-8). The operational targets of launching technological solutions in supervision include, among other things, reduction of the marginal cost of running a business by providing easier access to credible information, reducing fixed compliance costs (i.e. offering equal conditions for big and small financial institutions), and streamlined resolving of market disputes. Regulatory and supervisory institutions should consider how using technologies can evolve along with the development of the finance industry. The key principle of the inbuilt supervision is also the mechanism of building trust in decentralized markets for regulatory purposes. The development of DLT-based markets could change the trade in assets and sophisticated financial products. As the information embedded in blockchain is verified by the decentralized consensus, it can replace the current processes of data verification and delivery. At present, in the compliance verification process, data credibility is guaranteed by the legal system and relevant institutions. In order to have inbuilt supervision implemented regulatory institutions will also have to acquire extensive technological know-how and show willingness to adjust their operational approach to the technology developed by the finance sector (Auer, 2019, pp. 19-21).

SUPTECH CASES IN EUROPEAN UNION MEMBER STATES

In the EU, as far as technological solutions in financial supervision are concerned, leaders in this field are the Euro zone states (Table 3). The biggest number of SupTech tools are used in the following states: Germany, France, Italy, the Netherlands, Spain, Malta, Lithuania and Latvia. As far as non-Euro zone states are concerned, the leaders are Great Britain, Sweden and the Czech Republic. Poland, too, is working on solutions aimed at supporting innovativeness of supervision (KNF, 2019a).

The most often used tools include machine learning, big data analysis, blockchain/DLT and artificial intelligence. An analysis of the data in Table 3 reveals that the EU is not quite homogeneous in terms of the technological development of financial supervision. Many states have still not taken any decisive actions towards SupTech implementation. In contrast, Italy is the country where this solution is regarded as significant as confirmed by new publications on this subject.

One of the examples of institutions implementing the new solutions is the Central Bank of the Netherlands which developed a tool for preventing the risk of money laundering and terrorism financing. The tool uses machine learning for detecting anomalous money transfer patterns. Suspicious transfers depend on a transaction and customer profile. The task of the supervisor is to check whether payment institutions detect and report a sufficient amount of suspicious money transfers. Additionally, the aim is to increase the efficiency of the analysis of many long documents. DNB detects suspicious transfers by combining a great number of different data sources (Broeders, 2019). DNB also analyses reports by replying to specific questions. The technology is trained in participation of supervision institutions which check the feedback provided and sent in by the tool in use (Coelho, De Simoni & Prenio, 2019).

Table 3. SupTech tools in EU member states

Country/Institution	API	ML	Big Data	Cloud computing	Chatbots	AI	Blockchain and DLT	Text mining	Other
Austria		+	+			+			
Lithuania			+						
Italy		+	+						
The Netherlands		+	+	+		+			
Sweden		+	+						
The UK		+	+			+			
Ireland						+	+		
Malta			+				+		
Latvia	+		+	+		+	+		+
Poland						+	+		
EIOPA		+							+
Spain		+			+	+			
France		+				+			

Source: own elaboration.

A report by the European Banking Authority (European Banking Authority, 2020a) proposes an approach to detecting market malpractices. The tools differ depending on the types of malpractice (internal fraud, payment fraud, identity theft, loan extortion, etc.). For more accuracy, the institution depends on the predictive model, previously "trained" on the retrospective data concerning customer behavior, and complementary data, such as transactions data. In order to enrich the model, it is possible to configure certain additional features, such as rules highlighting an obvious fraud model (e.g. the speed feature combining the time mark and seller's localization for future transactions on one credit card: the higher the speed feature value, the higher the probability that falsified cards are being used).

Another example of SupTech facility used by EBA is the European Centralized Infrastructure of Data comprising the data of several hundred biggest banking groups across the European Union. The base is accessible to tools based on big data and machine learning. The advantages of enhanced analysis scope include: benchmarking and market discipline, better risk comprehension, proportionality in banking regulations, business models analysis, and conducting regulation impact analyses without incurring additional reporting costs. Additionally, EBA also uses a tool for data visualization (Eley, 2018).

The Bank of Sweden is working on the application of machine learning in predicting speculative bubbles on the property market, detecting frauds in the finance sector, and assessing the risk of debtor insolvency (Hull, 2019).

Machine learning is also used in supervision for minimizing the risk of losing stability by the real economy and financial system. In 2019, the Bank of Italy published an article on utilizing machine learning for predicting the risk of companies' bankruptcy. The author compared traditional statistics models against machine learning models using decision trees (*Random Forest* and *Gradient Boosted Trees*) (Moscatelli, 2019; Moscatelli, Narizzano, Parlapiano & Viggiano, 2019).

Predicting bankruptcies is key for several financial entities: financial institutions (e.g. verification of potential borrowers, developing new loans requirements), micro-prudential bodies (e.g. supervision over aggregated insolvency risk), investors (e.g. in the context of corporate bonds purchase and portfolio management). The article looks at the issue of how the process of predicting bankruptcy could be streamlined by applying machine learning models which can fully utilize big data sets by intercepting complex non-linear interactions between the economy, finance and credit variables. The subject of the comparison was the traditional approach to predicting bankruptcy (applying traditional statistical models, i.e. logistic regression and linear discriminative analysis) and the approach utilizing machine learning based on the Gradient Boosted Trees. A data base was established comprising financial and credit information, indicators, and a variable denoting the execution, or not, of a financial obligation (Moscatelli, 2019; Moscatelli, Narizzano, Parlapiano & Viggiano, 2019).

Next, a training was conducted involving statistical models (linear discriminative analysis, logistic regression) and machine learning models by applying a dataset. Another step required applying the models to make predictions and compare their accuracy. An advantage of machine learning is picking up on the relations between the dependent variable and independent variables. Overall, machine learning based models are more effective in predicting bankruptcies than traditional statistical models. The advantage is even greater if the information available is of worse quality (e.g. information accessible to external credit analysts) (Moscatelli, 2019; Moscatelli, Narizzano, Parlapiano & Viggiano, 2019).

SupTech solutions can be implemented with a view to increasing timeliness, the scope and detailedness of the collected data and reducing the dependence on manually performed processes. The systems of uploading and downloading data take the burden of data aggregation off the shoulders of financial service providers. Owing to this solution, supervision bodies gain access to "raw" data. An example usage of these tools for uploading data is the market behavior control system used by supervision bodies in Austria. Oesterreichische Nationalbank (OeNB), in cooperation with Austrian commercial banks, developed an innovative platform for regulatory reporting for uploading data. The platform provides a direct interface between the banks' information systems. The initiative depends on a deeper data harmonization and integration with the information systems of the supervisory body and supervised entities. It operates through a joint tool called Austrian Reporting Services GmbH (AuRep) – a joint venture of Austria's major bank groups. AuRep runs a joint regulatory reporting platform based on ABACUS/GMP which serves as the central interface between the supervised banks and the OeNB. The platform allows banks to send data in a normalized format, in accordance with central bank requirements, which can next convert the data into "intelligent cubes" or datasets comprising specific data and information that is useful to various departments of the supervisory institution. The new model releases banks from the obligation to draw up separate reports for different departments under the supervision bodies. This allows a joint and equal division of costs between the supervised sector and public institutions. Additionally, the solution ensures more consistency and high quality data (World Bank, 2018; Bearing Point, n.d.).

The Bank of Lithuania launched an electronic system with a view to allowing consumers to lodge complaints and settle disputes with financial institutions online. The data is then stored and sent under a single database. Thus, supervision over solving issues is much easier. Prior to the system launch, all complaints and notifications were sent by traditional mail, e-mail, or in person. Consumer complaints were handled manually. Such a solution hampered solving disputes in a timely manner and reduced the updateness and usefulness of such data in supervisory activities. The registered data is included in the supervisory assessment of institutional risk and market risk. The Bank of Lithuania issued a statement in which it announced that the system improved efficiency and effectiveness of supervisory processes. In order to conduct market supervision the institution assumed a risk-based approach. This means that main assets go towards the cost of controlling the major players of the financial market and services or financial products of the highest risk for consumers. The bank conducts assessments of service risk and financial products risk almost entirely on the basis of statistical data in the electronic data base. In this circumstance, systems risk is not taken account of. The focus is on possible threats to consumers on the basis of complaints lodged against financial institutions for selling specific financial products. Once a significant risk has been identified, the supervisor will conduct inspection "on premises" for further threats identification. The process is conducted regardless of the size of the institution (World Bank, 2018; Bank of Lithuania, 2017).

All the above instances of SupTech application across many countries confirm that the technology makes it possible to increase efficiency and reduce costs while still facing operational, legal and reputational types of risk. SupTech increases efficiency by improving existing processes, enabling swift supervisory activities. As regards data collection, the new technologies are faster and more flexible in capturing data from supervised companies than the traditional approach based on templates. This in turn allows supervision bodies to further improve their monitoring activities and early detection of potential threats. As regards data analysis, SupTech solutions cut the time spent on conducting analyses significantly. For instance, the identification of potential problems involving money laundering in transactions data base takes only a few minutes rather than weeks (Broeders & Prenio, 2018).

SupTech applications cut costs thanks to the automation of the processes which usually put a bad strain on the staff. In particular, the benefits concern the process of gathering data. It reduces the role of traditional quality control and the ensuing communication between supervision bodies and financial institutions for correcting errors in reporting. As a result, data analysis also becomes less time consuming. SupTech apps increase supervisory capabilities by doing things that human beings can not do, For instance, securities market supervisory bodies receive thousands of documents from supervised entities. Supervision inspectors can hardly manage to scan them all. SupTech apps can scan all legal acts and identify potential supervisory issues. Having said that, we can not overlook the legal issues arising from using SupTech, especially in terms of data collection. Supervisory bodies must confirm having all the necessary legal authority to use data for supervisory purposes (Broeders & Prenio, 2018, pp. 19-21).

Financial supervisors apply various technologies for developing a selection of very useful tools that support them in their work for more efficient performance. The researched cases of SupTech application focus mainly on the analysis of malpractice, reporting and data management. In most cases, conducting supervision and the work of financial analytics departments comes down to analyzing huge amounts of unsorted data. To this end, supervisors can take advantage of the emergence of big data architecture and

AI tools. Subsequently, they can be used in micro-prudential analysis, macro-prudential analysis and market supervision analysis. Most of SupTech initiatives are still in the development and trial phase (Di Castri, Hohl, Kulenkampff & Prenio, 2019, pp. 5-6,13,19). According to the authors of this Chapter, the rapid development of SupTech tools means that more and more supervision bodies will consider applying those technologies across various segments of the finance market.

Most often in practice are used tools based on artificial intelligence and machine learning. Nowadays, supervisory institutions have to deal with exponentially growing amount of data. This is a huge challenge for them which requires high-performing tools and strong analytical capacity. Big data technologies enable using not only traditional structured data but also alternative data sources. They are known to be very effective in realizing supervisory tasks (Bruno, Jani, Schmidt & Tissot, 2020).

Above-mentioned and other innovations contribute to strengthening the financial supervision in several aspects (CNBV, 2018, p. 2):

- automatic communication to the authority and fulfilling reporting obligations,
- high-quality analytics of big data,
- easier real-time monitoring of the low quality and large amounts of data,
- automatic monitoring of compliance with various regulations as well as vulnerability identification,
- identity management with the use of biometrics or blockchain,
- forecasting, modelling and scenario analysis useful for risk management and stress testing which is sophisticated – it must embrace many variables, risks and potential shocks,
- risk management in terms of liquidity or capital,
- implementation of a risk based approach that ensures financial integrity and promotes financial inclusion,
- reduction of time spent on on-site inspections,
- improvement the quality of analysis, thus the chances to find money laundering or fraud cases are higher,
- reduction of compliance costs.

Notwithstanding this, authorities must take into account potential risks that emerge. One of the technical challenges is linked with supplier and concentration risk. Normally, market participants will utilize infrastructure set up by supervisory institutions. Relying on one solution or supplier only would be risky in cases it fails. Another matter is keeping cyber risk at control. Its significance is steadily growing since the number of hacking attacks surges around the world. Moreover, the sensitive character of users' data makes it potentially prone to leakage outside the systems. This, in turn, generates significant legal risk. Above considerations show that introducing new platforms is a complex issue which requires at least know-how and large IT expenses. Therefore, such solutions are often constrained by the available resources.

Best practices within SupTech include the following (Bruno, Jani, Schmidt & Tissot, 2020):

- employing specialists: staff with specialized statistical and IT skills, an analytical mindset as well as data scientists, economists, lawyers and mathematicians in order to cope with big data,
- when SupTech projects are considered to be introduced, there are some key elements to take into account: technological needs, security, use cases (business requirements), system complex-

ity, financial costs, performance and reliability of a tool and operating model (Lambe, Micic and Sosnovsky, 2019),

- ensuring cooperation between business (economic, financial) and IT departments to promote a data-driven culture,
- establishing medium- to long-term SupTech objectives,
- paying attention to data governance framework,
- periodical monitoring of the progress, reviewing the plan and learning from any successes or failures,
- keeping international cooperation and knowledge-sharing between financial supervisors in terms of the fast-changing and heterogeneous technological landscape. As the result, the experience will be shared and the synergies can be met.

The analysis of SupTech use cases allow to formulate some other recommendations. First and foremost, supervisors should concentrate on tools and techniques which can deal with a large and constantly growing amount of data. Solutions based on artificial intelligence and machine learning are particularly useful. Efficient application of such tools requires high-quality IT infrastructure. Without significant investments in this field it would be difficult for authorities and supervised entities to meet the complexity of systems. Secondly, supervisors ought to be opened to new technological opportunities that are continuously emerging. Obviously, supervisory technology, particularly at the initial stage, can present a lot of bugs and misconcepts which generate various sorts of risk. Before full-scale application they should be thoroughly tested. Helpful in this regard can be getting to know other supervisors' experiences, sharing expertise and introducing systems which gave interesting results in other jurisdictions. The another thing is keeping security at high level. Effective and safe systems have to be at utmost importance.

CONCLUSION

This chapter deals with the multiple applications of technological and non-technological innovations in financial supervision. Over the past years, innovative technologies utilized by supervision bodies (SupTech) for ensuring efficient financial supervision have enjoyed increased popularity. The introduction of new technological solutions helps achieve basic supervisory goals by the existing and also new financial market players. The biggest changes occurred in the field of data collection/analysis and preventing malpractice. This has led to an evolution in the approach to financial supervision and created new possibilities in, e.g. predicting and signaling risk.

Nowadays, supervisory institutions are facing a great number of challenges in terms of exercising control over the financial market and ensuring a satisfactory level of its stability. For them to fulfill the legally imposed obligations it is necessary to ensure a proper regulatory and technological environment. In their current activity, supervisory institutions are increasingly forced to collect big datasets provided by financial institutions. Processing and analyzing huge amounts of information is a complex task which requires engaging a lot of resources (human resources, in particular). To this end, new solutions must be developed for achieving higher quality standards of supervision work.

The authors of this chapter have provided numerous instances of the application of innovations and new technologies that will boost the performance of supervision inspectors significantly. The attempts at launching the innovations have been found to be successful. According to the authors, in the future it will be possible to reduce some of the threats on the financial market. However, as new ideas and solutions emerge, there also emerge new threats. At the same time, the risks already recognized and researched on can build up and escalate. Therefore, it is essential for supervisors to utilize the new solutions without blindly following the fashion to apply them. The key is to weigh the benefits against possible costs and potential risks.

It is worth researching all new emerging SupTech solutions and the fast developing regulatory environment. It will be particularly interesting to see how the solutions described in this paper are implemented in various countries and how this process affects the transformation of the currently existing financial supervision models. It is also essential to analyze the possible development trends in this respect, including the scope of coordination of the activities of EU member states.

Another field of research is the use of artificial intelligence and machine learning in detecting potential problems in supervised entities. It would be particularly useful for continuous monitoring of legal requirements fulfilling such as capital or liquidity buffers. Therefore, the study will check whether it helps to achieve safer and more sound financial system.

SupTech cases are based on the numerous technologies and techniques described in this chapter. It would be desirable to distinct the most popular and useful ones from the viewpoint of the supervisors. Consequently, a study can predict in which direction will the utilized tools evolve. It would be especially interesting to emphasize the amendments to the currently utilized methods so as to make them more efficient data gathering and analysis.

Application of new technological tools will probably open new ways to financial oversight. It can also lead to new possibilities in the sphere of financial regulation. Therefore, further research can answer the question how financial institutions can be regulated in the context of SupTech tools application.

The legislation environment, along with innovation accelerators, innovation hubs and regulatory sandboxes, is highly likely to grow and perfect itself. However, it is an open question whether legal acts will be capable of keeping up with the fast changing technologies and whether supervisors will actually decide to utilize innovations. In many countries, supervisory institutions still lack a mission, strategy, or a clear vision of SupTech development. Furthermore, one of the conclusions drawn from this study is that supervisory institutions often take technologically neutral positions. If they can apply the new solutions to a broader extent, the new technologies will develop rapidly. The change will not occur any time soon. In this context, the following words by Bill Gates make perfect guidelines for financial supervision decision-makers (Banque de France, 2019, p. 10):

We always overestimate the change that will occur in the next two years and underestimate the change that will occur in the next ten. Don't let yourself be lulled into inaction.

ACKNOWLEDGMENT

The chapter was prepared through the project financed within the Regional Excellence Initiative program of the Minister of Science and Higher Education of Poland, years 2019-2022, grant no. 004/RID/2018/19, financing 3,000,000 PLN

REFERENCES

Accenture. (2019). *The (r)evolution of Money II, Blockchain Empowered Central Bank Digital Currencies.* Author.

Ascent. (2020). *What is SupTech and How Will it Change Compliance?* Retrieved from https://www.ascentregtech.com/blog/what-is-suptech-and-how-will-it-change-compliance/

ASIFMA. (2019). *Tokenised Securities. A Roadmap for Market Participants and Regulators.* Retrieved from https://www.asifma.org/research/tokenised-securities-a-roadmap-for-market-participants-and-regulators/

Auer, R. (2019). *Embedded supervision: how to build regulation into blockchain finance.* BIS Working Papers No 811. Monetary and Economic Department. Bank for International Settlements. Basel.

Bank for International Settlements. (2019). *Wholesale Digital Tokens.* Committee on Payments and Market Infrastructures.

Bank of Lithuania. (2017). *Supervisory Activities.* Retrieved from https://www.lb.lt/en/supervisory-activities

Banque de France. (2019). *Financial regulation and supervision issues raised by the impact of Tech firms on financial services, Speech by Denis Beau –First Deputy Governor of the Banque de France.* Banque de France.

Bar-Ilan, J. (2001). Data collection methods on the web for infometric purposes – A review and analysis. *Scientometrics, 50*(1), 7–32. doi:10.1023/A:1005682102768

Bearing Point. (n.d.). *Regulatory reporting platform for Austrian banks.* Retrieved from https://www.reg.tech/en/our-solutions/banks-other-financial-institutions/regulatory-reporting-for-austrian-banks/

Beau, D. (2019). *Denis Beau: What policy framework to help building innovation and growth into Europe's capital market?* Speech by Mr Denis Beau, First Deputy Governor of the Bank of France, at the AFME (The Association for Financial Markets in Europe) Annual Capital Markets Technology and Innovation Conference, Paris.

Broeders, D. (2019). *Digital Supervision at DNB. Workshop on "Big Data & Machine Learning Applications for Central Banks".* DeNederlandscheBank. Eurosystem. Retrieved from https://www.bancaditalia.it/pubblicazioni/altri-atti-convegni/2019-bigdata/Broeders_Suptech_BoI_2019.pdf

Broeders, D., & Prenio, J. (2018). *Innovative technology in financial supervision (SupTech): The experience of early users. FSI Insights on policy implementation, (9).* Bank for International Settlements.

Bruno, G., Jani, H., Schmidt, R., & Tissot, B. (2020). *Computing platforms for big data analytics and artificial intelligence.* Bank for International Settlements.

Chiesi, A. M. (2001). The International Encyclopaedia of the Social &. *Behavioral Science.*

CNBV. (2018). *RegTech and SupTech: Where do we see the frontier?* Retrieved from http://pubdocs.worldbank.org/en/841991528990787287/04062018-RegTech-y-SupTech-Foro-Bernardo-Gonzalez.pdf

Coelho, R., De Simoni, M., & Prenio, J. (2019). *Suptech applications for anti-money laundering. FSI Insights on policy implementation No 18. Financial Stability Institute.* Bank for International Settlements.

Dang, S., & Ahmad, P. H. (2014). Text mining: Techniques and its application. *The International Journal of Engineering & Technology Innovations*, *1*(4), 866–2348.

Deboeck, G., & Kohonen, T. (1998). *Visual Explorations in Finance with Self-organizing Maps*. Springer Finance. doi:10.1007/978-1-4471-3913-3

Deboeck, G. J. (2000). Financial applications of self-organizing maps. *Neural Network World*, *8*(2), 213–241.

Deloitte. (n.d.). *What is blockchain*. Retrieved from https://www2.deloitte.com/content/dam/Deloitte/uk/Documents/Innovation/deloitte-uk-what-is-blockchain-2016.pdf

Di Castri, S., Hohl, S., Kulenkampff, A., & Prenio, J. (2019). *The SupTech generations*. Bank for International Settlements.

Ehrentraud, J., Ocampo, D. G., Garzoni, L., & Piccolo, M. (2020). *Policy responses to fintech: a cross-country overview*. Financial Stability Institute BIS.

Eley, S. (2018). *RegTech and SupTech: Innovation, Risks and Opportunities*. 18th Annual WBG-IMF-FRB Conference on Policy Challenges for the Financial Sector, Washington, DC. Retrieved from http://pubdocs.worldbank.org/en/692151528989872128/2018-06-07-Session4-RegTech-SupTech-Slavka-Eley.pdf

ESMA. (2019). *ESAs publish joint report on regulatory sandboxes and innovation hubs*. Retrieved from https://www.esma.europa.eu/press-news/esma-news/esas-publish-joint-report-regulatory-sandboxes-and-innovation-hubs

European Banking Authority. (2017). *Regulatory sandboxes. A proposal to EBA by the Banking Stakeholders Group*. EBA.

European Banking Authority. (2020a). *EBA report on big data and advanced analytics.*

European Banking Authority. (2020b). *FinTech Knowledge Hub*. Retrieved from https://eba.europa.eu/financial-innovation-and-fintech/fintech-knowledge-hub

European Commission. (2018a). *FinTech action plan: For a more competitive and innovative European financial sector*. Retrieved from https://ec.europa.eu/info/publications/180308-action-plan-fintech_en

European Commission. (2018b). *First meeting of the EU FinTech Lab*. Retrieved from https://ec.europa.eu/info/publications/180620-eu-fintech-lab-meeting_en

European Commission. (2019). *EU Blockchain Observatory and Forum*. Retrieved from https://ec.europa.eu/digital-single-market/en/eu-blockchain-observatory-and-forum

European Parliament. (2018). *The Proposal for a Regulation of the European Parliament and the Council on European Crowdfunding Service Providers (ECSP) for Business*. Author.

European Supervisory Authorities. (2018). *FinTech: Regulatory Sandboxes and Innovation Hubs*. EBA, ESMA, EIOPA. Retrieved from https://www.esma.europa.eu/file/49963/download?token=fN2J9ilC

European Supervisory Authorities. (2019). *European Forum for Innovation Facilitators (EFIF)*. Retrieved from https://esas-joint-committee.europa.eu/Pages/Activities/EFIF/European-Forum-for-Innovation-Facilitators.aspx

EY. (2015). *When finance moves into the cloud, will CFOs sleep better at night? Finance in the cloud.* Retrieved from https://www.ey.com/Publication/vwLUAssets/EY-finance-in-the-cloud/$FILE/EY-finance-in-the-cloud.pdf

Finance, U. K. Microsoft. (2019). *Artificial Intelligence in Financial Services*. Retrieved from https://www.ukfinance.org.uk/system/files/AI-2019_FINAL_ONLINE.pdf

Financial Stability Board. (2017). Financial Stability Implications from Fintech: Supervisory and Regulatory Issues that Merit Authorities' Attention. Basel: Author.

FinTech Australia. (2017). *Booming Australian fintech scene shown in new member ecosystem map.* Retrieved from https://fintechaustralia.org.au/newbooming-australian-fintech-scene-shown-in-new-member-ecosystem-map/

Fintechmap. (n.d.). *Explore the Swiss FinTech startup ecosystem*. Retrieved from https://fintechmap.ch/

Gunawardena, N. K. (2014). *Introduction to geographic information system.* Retrieved from https://www.researchgate.net/publication/264742771_INTRODUCTION_TO_GEOGRAPHIC_INFORMATION_SYSTEM

Gurney, K. (1997). *An introduction to neural networks*. CRC press. doi:10.4324/9780203451519

Hull, I. (2019). *Big Data*. Machine Learning, and Quantum Computing at the Riksbank, Sveriges Riksbank.

IAIS. (2019). *RegTech and SupTech: Implications for Supervision Report of the A2ii – IAIS Consultation Call*. IAIS.

IBM. (2016). *Identifying API use cases: Banking industry*. Retrieved from https://www.ibm.com/downloads/cas/G4DVGRQJ

International Monetary Fund & World Bank. (2019). FinTech: The experience so far. Washington, DC: Authors.

Jovanović, S. Z., Đurić, J. S., & Šibalija, T. V. (n.d.). *Robotic Process automation: overview and opportunities*. Academic Press.

Khant, A., & Mehta, M. (2018). *Analysis of Financial News Using Natural Language Processing and Artificial Intelligence*. Conference: International Conference on Business Innovation 2018, Sri Lanka.

Khurana, D., Koli, A., Khatter, K., & Singh, S. (2017). *Natural language processing: State of the art, current trends and challenges*. arXiv preprint arXiv:1708.05148

KNF. (2019a). *Departament Innowacji Finansowych FinTech (DFT)*. Retrieved from https://www.knf.gov.pl/o_nas/urzad_komisji/dane_teleadresowe_struktura?articleId=61228&p_id=18

KNF. (2019b). *KNF Regulatory Sandbox*. Retrieved from https://www.knf.gov.pl/en/MARKET/Fintech/Regulatory_Sandbox

KPMG. (2019). *The Pulse of Fintech*. Retrieved from https://home.kpmg/xx/en/home/campaigns/2020/02/pulse-of-fintech-h2-2019.html

Lambe, E., Micic, D., & Sosnovsky, X. (2019). *BIS initiative to build a big data Platform, presentation given at a workshop on computing platforms for big data and machine learning*. Bank of Italy.

Laurent, P., Chollet, T., Burke, M., & Seers, T. (2018). The tokenization of assets is disrupting the financial industry. Are you ready? *Inside Magazine*, *19*(2). Retrieved from https://www2.deloitte.com/content/dam/Deloitte/lu/Documents/financial-services/lu-tokenization-of-assets-disrupting-financial-industry.pdf

Library of Congress. (2019a). *H.R.2144 — 116th Congress (2019-2020)*. Retrieved from https://www.congress.gov/bill/116th-congress/house-bill/2144/text?format=txt

Library of Congress. (2019b). *H.R.2154 - Digital Taxonomy Act of 2019*. Retrieved from https://www.congress.gov/bill/116th-congress/house-bill/2154/text

Marchewka-Bartkowiak, K. (2020). *Rola piaskownic regulacyjnych w ograniczaniu ryzyka prawnego sektora FinTech, In Bankowość emocjonalna. Cyfrowa transformacja banków a oczekiwania klientów*. Poltext.

Martino, P., Laurent, P., Hauman, S., Gavray, G. (n.d.). Process automation for the financial industry. *Inside Magazine, 13*.

MathWorks. (n.d.). *Predictive Modeling*. Retrieved from https://www.mathworks.com/discovery/predictive-modeling.html

Mijwel, M. M., Esen, A., & Shamil, A. (2019). *Overview of Neural Networks*. Academic Press.

Mooney, S. J., Westreich, D. J., & El-Sayed, A. M. (2015). Epidemiology in the era of big data. *Epidemiology (Cambridge, Mass.)*, *26*(3), 390. doi:10.1097/EDE.0000000000000274 PMID:25756221

Moscatelli, M. (2019). *Corporate Default Forecasting with Machine Learning*. Bank of Italy.

Moscatelli, M., Narizzano, S., Parlapiano, F., & Viggiano, G. (2019). *Corporate default forecasting with machine learning (No. 1256). Economic Research and International Relations Area*. Bank of Italy.

Newgenapps. (2018). *Random Forest Analysis in ML and when to use it*. Retrieved from https://www.newgenapps.com/blog/random-forest-analysis-in-ml-and-when-to-use-it/

OVUM. (n.d.). *Assessing the role of Big Data in tackling financial crime and compliance management. Examining real use cases and its potential*. Retrieved from http://www.oracle.com/us/industries/financial-services/fs-big-data-fccm-wp-2861557.pdf

PWC. (2018). *Canadian FinTech market map*. Retrieved from https://www.pwc.com/ca/en/industries/technology/canadian-fintech-market-map.html

SEGOB. (2018). *Law to Regulate Financial Technology Institutions*. Diario Oficial de la Federación. Retrieved from http://www.dof.gob.mx/nota_detalle.php?codigo=5515623&fecha=09/03/2018

Shanmuganathan, S., Sallis, P., & Buckeridge, J. (2004). Self-organising maps for integrating data across multiple scales. In *Bridging scales and epistemologies; Linking local knowledge with global science in multi-scale assessments International Conference by Millennium Ecosystem Assessment (MEA).* Bibliotheca Alexandrina.

Techopedia. (n.d.). *Data Cube*. Retrieved from https://www.techopedia.com/definition/28530/data-cube

The Hong Kong Monetary Authority (HKMA). (2018a). *Authorization of Virtual Banks*. Retrieved from www.hkma.gov.hk/media/eng/doc/key-functions/banking-stability/guide-authorization/Chapter-9.pdf

The Hong Kong Monetary Authority (HKMA). (2018b). *Guide to Authorization*. Retrieved from https://www.hkma.gov.hk/eng/regulatory-resources/regulatory-guides/guide-to-authorization/

The Hong Kong Monetary Authority (HKMA). (2019). *Open Application Programming Interface (API) for the Banking Sector*. Retrieved from https://www.hkma.gov.hk/eng/key-functions/international-financial-centre/fintech/open-application-programming-interface-api-for-the-banking-sector/

The Law Library of Congress. (2018). *Regulation of Cryptocurrency Around the World. Global Legal Research Center*. Retrieved from https://www.loc.gov/law/help/cryptocurrency/world-survey.php

The Monetary Authority of Singapore. (2018). *Eligibility Criteria and Requirements for Digital Banks.* Retrieved from www.mas.gov.sg/-/media/Digital-Bank-Licence/Eligibility-Criteria-and-Requirements-for-Digital-Banks.pdf?la=en&hash=502B26B6D52B499200B4E95FA90ADDC983778655

Toronto Centre. (2017a). *FinTech, RegTech and SupTech: What They Mean for Financial Supervision.* Retrieved from http://res. torontocentre. org/guidedocs/FinTech% 20RegTech% 20and% 20SupTech, 20, 20.

Toronto Centre. (2017b). *Regulatory Sandboxes*. Retrieved from https://res.torontocentre.org/guidedocs/Regulatory%20Sandboxes%20FINAL.pdf

Ukrainian Association of Fintech. (2019). *The Ukrainian Fintech Catalog 2019*. Retrieved from https://map.fintechua.org/en

UNSGSA. (2019). *Early Lessons on Regulatory Innovations to Enable Inclusive FinTech: Innovations Office, Regulatory sandboxes and RegTech*. Retrieved from https://www.unsgsa.org/files/2915/5016/4448/Early_Lessons_on_Regulatory_Innovations_to_Enable_Inclusive_FinTech.pdf

Wehrmann, B., & Glavina, J. (2009). *Geographic Information Systems (GIS): the spatial dimension to development cooperation*. GT.

World Bank. (2018). *From Spreadsheets to SupTech: Technology Solutions for Market Conduct Supervision*. Retrieved from http://documents.worldbank.org/curated/en/612021529953613035/pdf/127577-REVISED-Suptech-Technology-Solutions-for-Market-Conduct-Supervision.pdf

Zemčík, M. T. (2019). *A Brief History of Chatbots. DEStech Transactions on Computer Science and Engineering*. 2019 International Conference on Artificial Intelligence, Control and Automation Engineering (AICAE 2019).

Zhao, B. (2017). *Web scraping. In Encyclopedia of big data*. Springer.

KEY TERMS AND DEFINITIONS

Application Programming Interface (API): Definitions, protocols and tools that determine the way various applications interact with each other.

Artificial Intelligence (AI): A set of technologies enabling computers to perceive, learn, reason, and offer help in making decisions so as to solve problems in a manner that imitates the human way of thinking.

Big Data: Huge amounts of unstructured data (e-mail messages, internet traffic, etc.) and structural data (e.g., data bases) the analysis of which is not possible by means of traditional analytical tools.

Blockchain: A kind of distributed ledger technology. Blockchain is a type of database used for transaction recording. It is copied to all of the computers in a participating network. Data is stored in 'blocks' which are fixed structures.

Chatbots: A program utilizing artificial intelligence, which interacts with another chatbot or a human being, giving the impression of interacting with a human being.

Cloud Computing: Facility using remote and co-shared host servers on the Internet for storing, managing and processing data.

Dashboards: Configurable, dynamic tools for interactive reporting, which download and visualize data automatically.

Data Cubes: A tool used to evaluate data aggregated from different viewpoints.

Data Lake: A repository for storing unstructured and structured data that is downloaded in its raw form and stored by a highly scalable, distributed files system known as open source.

Data Pull Approach: A technology controlled by the financial supervisors used to gather business data directly from the institutions' operational systems. It is useful for reporting process and it ensures good quality information for decision making.

Distributed Ledger Technology (DLT): A data base shared by a great many parties (nodes) with a view to conducting jointly agreed transactions based on the so called consensus mechanism.

FinTech: Innovations in financial services based on technologies that can lead to the creation of new business models, applications, processes and products, thus having a significant impact on the financial market and institutions and the way financial services are rendered.

Geographic Information Systems (GIS): A computer system covering analyzing, managing, intercepting, hardware, software and displaying information in the geographic context.

Innovation Lab/Accelerator: Special one-off or long-term programs established by public institutions in cooperation with external partners. Basically, innovation accelerators allow sponsors (also from the financial sector) to finance and test prototypes of new technological products in a safe supervisory environment.

Innovation Office: Dedicated centers of contact for firms to raise enquiries with competent authorities on fintech-related issues and to seek non-binding guidance on the conformity of innovative financial products, financial services or business models with licensing or registration requirements and regulatory and supervisory expectations.

Machine Learning (ML): A subset of artificial intelligence aimed at enabling computers to analyze and learn from huge amounts of data with a view to making forecasts.

Natural Language Processing: An area covering artificial intelligence and linguistics which involves processing the information saved in a computer's database so as to make it comprehensible for human beings.

Network Analysis: A process of examining structures by means of networks and graphs theory. It is a set of integrated techniques for presenting the relationships between specific entities and analyzing the structure.

Neural Network: A set of interconnected units or nodes which are similar in functioning to the animal neuron with the ability to learn from training patterns. It is modelled on the structure of the human brain and can be used to solve problems in such fields as economics, statistics, and technology.

Predictive Modeling: A mathematical and computing technique for predicting events or results.

Random Forest Algorithm: Is a popular algorithm for machine learning. It can be used as regression and classification algorithm. It creates multiple decision trees and merges them together to make predictions.

RegTech: A tool or a platform that facilitates regulatory compliance, making it more efficient.

Regulatory Sandbox: Specially organized environments of legal supervision created by financial supervisor (or regulator) for testing possible effects of new technological solution implementation in an isolated environment (e.g., a group of clients).

Robotic Process Automation (RPA): A method of automating repetitive processes with software which works like a human being and performs tasks on computers.

Self-Organizing Maps (SOM): A type of neural network which uses an unsupervised training algorithm and a process known as self-organization.

Smart Contracts: An intelligent (digital) contract, which can perform itself automatically on fulfilling specified conditions.

SupTech: Technological tools used in financial supervision.

Text Mining: A multidisciplinary field involving information mining, text analysis, categorizing, grouping, visualization, data exploration and machine learning.

Tokenization: A process of digital token issuance, based on the blockchain technology.

Web Scraper: A technique of mining data from the Internet and saving it in the system or data base for future download or analysis.

ENDNOTES

1 The analysis also includes Great Britain which left the European Union on 1 January 2020.

2 Examples of FinTech Maps:
for Switzerland: (Fintechmap, n.d.),
for Canada: (PWC, 2018),
for Ukraine: (Ukrainian Association of Fintech, 2019),
for Australia: (FinTech Australia, 2017).

3 More in: (The Law Library of Congress, 2018).

4 More in: European Banking Authority (2017), Toronto Centre (2017b), European Supervisory Authorities (2018), UNSGSA (2019), ESMA (2019).

5 As of the end of 2019 the analysis covers 28 EU states.

APPENDIX

Table 4. Special regulations and licensing process, innovation offices/hubs/lab/accelerators and regulatory sandboxes in EU member states

Country	Supervisory authority	Special Regulations / licensing process	Innovation office/hub	Innovation accelerators/lab	Regulatory sandbox
Austria	OeNB FMA	Crowdfunding	FMA FinTech Point Contact and FMA FinTech Navigator		
Belgium	NBB FSMA	Cryptoassets	NBB Contact Point for FinTech and FSMA Fintech Contact Point		
Bulgaria	BNB FSC		Innovation Helpdesk		
Cyprus	CBC Cosec ICCS		CySEC Innovation Hub		
Denmark	DFSA	Cryptoassets			FT Lab
Estonia	FI		Innovation Office		
France	ACPR AMF	crowdfunding cryptoassets	AMF FinTech, Innovation and Competitiveness division and ACPR FinTech-Innovation Unit	Le Lab Banque de France	
Germany	BaFIN	Cryptoassets	BaFin FinTech		
Greece			FinTech Innovtion Hub		
Hungary	MNB		MNB Innovation Hub	MKB FinTech Lab	Regulatory Sandbox
Ireland	CBI		Innovation Hub		
Italy	BI CONSOB IVASS	Crowdfunding	Canale Fintech		
Latvia	FKTK		Innovation Centre		
Lithuania	LB		Innovation Office		Regulatory Sandbox Blockchain sandbox (LB Chain)
Malta	MFSA				Cryptocurrency Sandbox
The Netherlands	DNB AFM	crowdfunding robo advice cryptoassets	AFM and DNB Innovation Hub		
Poland	KNF	Cryptoassets	Innovation Hub Programme		

continues on following page

Table 4. Continued

Country	Supervisory authority	Special Regulations / licensing process	Innovation office/hub	Innovation accelerators/lab	Regulatory sandbox
Portugal	BP CMVM ASF			Startup Lisboa	
Romania	BNR ASF	Cryptoassets	InsureTech Innovation Hub		
Spain	BDE CNMV DGSFP	Crowdfunding	FinTech/Innovation Portal		Regulatory Sandbox
Sweden	FI	crowdfunding robo advice	Finansinspektionen's Innovation Centre		
The United Kingdom	PRA FCA	crowdfunding robo advice	FCA Innovate		Regulatory Sandbox

Source: based on data and information included on websites and reports of national supervisory agencies and UNSGSA (2019); Ehrentraud, Ocampo, Garzoni & Piccolo (2020).

Section 2

Innovation and Digitization in Financial Markets and Economy

Chapter 7
Blockchain-Based Tokens as Financing Instruments:
Capital Market Access for SMEs?

Lennart Ante
Blockchain Research Lab, Universität Hamburg, Germany

ABSTRACT

Blockchain technology represents a technological basis with which existing corporate financing processes can be supplemented. The issuance of digital tokens offers several potential advantages such as tradability, efficiency, automation, and cost benefits compared to traditional financial products. This transformation of financing processes and capital markets can allow small and medium-sized enterprises (SMEs) to access capital markets and at the same time close existing retail investment gaps. In this chapter, the challenges of SME financing are described and blockchain-based financing (initial coin offerings [ICOs] and security token offerings [STOs]) is introduced. The blockchain-based financing mechanisms are compared with conventional forms of financing and potentials and challenges are discussed. In conclusion, it is stated that potential clearly outweighs risk and that the majority of all existing challenges can be tackled through sensible and coordinated regulation.

INTRODUCTION

The phenomenon of blockchain-based financing is complementing traditional funding mechanisms with innovative technology, which offers various potential benefits. At a time when small and medium sized enterprises (SMEs) are subject to financing constraints (Carpenter and Petersen 2002; European Central Bank 2018), blockchain-based financing can possibly help to close these financing gaps and enable SMEs to access the capital market (Ante et al. 2018; Organisation for Economic Co-operation and Development 2019). However, it should be borne in mind that there are various forms of financing using so-called tokens (token sales), each of which is suitable for specific applications.

DOI: 10.4018/978-1-7998-4390-0.ch007

The aim of this chapter is to show readers the problem of financing constraints (and retail investment gap) using Europe as an example and then to introduce them to blockchain-based financing, i.e. Initial Coin Offerings (ICOs) and Security Token Offerings (STOs), how the it differs from traditional forms of financing and where exactly the advantages and challenges lie. Even if these markets are only just emerging and a large number of challenges still need to be solved, the potential and efficiency gains clearly outweigh the risks. The purpose of the following chapter is to present blockchain-based financing in its various forms and to describe the impact it can have on SMEs. To this end, a distinction is first made between token sales and other forms of financing for SMEs. Subsequently, the potential and challenges of blockchain-based financing are discussed before concluding remarks are stated.

The following text is structured as follows: Section 2 examines SME financing constraints and retail investment gap. In the first step this is done on the basis of scientific principles/basics and in the second step on the basis of existing facts on the European market. Section 3 presents the two blockchain-based financing methods - ICOs and STOs - and Section 4 compares them with traditional forms of financing. Finally, potentials and challenges of token sales are discussed in Section 5 before a short conclusion is made (Section 6).

SME FINANCING CONSTRAINTS AND RETAIL INVESTMENT GAP

Ever since the seminal work of (Coase 1937), economic theory has been debating the determinants of optimal firm size. SMEs employ much of the world's human capital but often face serious obstacles to their growth, among which limited access to finance is an important one (Beck and Demirguc-Kunt 2006). The corporate finance literature has consistently shown a higher leverage ratio for larger firms (Booth et al. 2001; Fama and French 2002; Kurshev and Strebulaev 2015; Rajan and Zingales 1995; Titman and Wessels 1988). Hennessy and Whited (2007) find substantially higher external financing costs for smaller firms, which implies that that these firms face a greater risk of default. It is much costlier for small firms to issue new equity or long-term debt, which suggests that smaller firms may prefer short term debt in the form of bank loans due to lower fixed costs (Smith 1977; Titman and Wessels 1988). One reason for these higher costs is a risk premium for the greater volatility of company assets in smaller firms, which are likely to grow faster and to be located in volatile industries (Fama and French 2002). Kurshev and Strebulaev (2015) offer the additional explanation that the degree of information asymmetry in capital markets may be lower for large firms due to greater investor acuity. A third reason is that fixed costs decline with company size, leading for example to smaller time frames between refinancing rounds (Kurshev and Strebulaev 2015).

Compared to large businesses, SMEs tend to have higher ratios of fixed to total assets, trade debt to total assets and current liabilities to total assets. They rely more heavily on retained profits to finance their investment flows, with bank loans covering most of the remaining financing needs. SMEs are financially riskier than large businesses, which is reflected in higher failure rates (Evans 1987; Hughes 1997). These differences can in part be explained by the pecking order hypothesis, which says that firms prefer finance from trade debt and retained profits, followed by debt and then equity. Another reason for these differences in the financial structure of smaller and larger firms is asymmetric access to capital markets. (Carpenter and Petersen 2002) show that access to capital markets is a major determinant of the capital structure of small firms. Long-term debt only becomes available after a firm's flotation, which reduces the relevance of collateral. For listed companies, age and profitability are no longer determinants of liquidity. Agency theory (Jensen and Meckling 1976) may also provide a fitting explanation for differences between SMEs and larger firms. SMEs must choose between debt-financing against collateral and the costs of going public. Long-term financing of unlisted small firms is provided through collateral, rather than through profitability. (Carpenter and Petersen 2002, p.67) state that "these less than optimal outcomes suggest a need to continue to find ways of reducing barriers to entry to the stock market for small firms".

SMEs are an essential factor for the European economic area. An estimated 24.5 million small and medium-sized enterprises (SMEs) existed in 2017, of which the majority (22.8m) can be classified as micro firms (less than 10 employees). They achieved an estimated €4.156 billion on value added, representing a total share of about 56.8% and employed 94.8 million people, representing a total share of 66% (European Commission 2019). As a result, SMEs are frequently referred to as the backbone of the European economy. However, SMEs continue to face limited funding choices, for example, as they have difficulties accessing capital markets (Carpenter and Petersen 2002). Therefore, SMEs heavily rely on bank financing, which accounts for about 70% of the average external funding of European SMEs. By comparison, this share is only 30% in the USA. Gaps between loan demand and supply should therefore lead to constraints in overall economic growth (Euler Hermes 2019).

Initial start-up financing mainly relies on savings of founders, while friends and family, government funding and business angels are involved in 20% of financing processes of start-ups.

Figure 1. Major sources of startup funding (adapted from German Startups Association 2015)

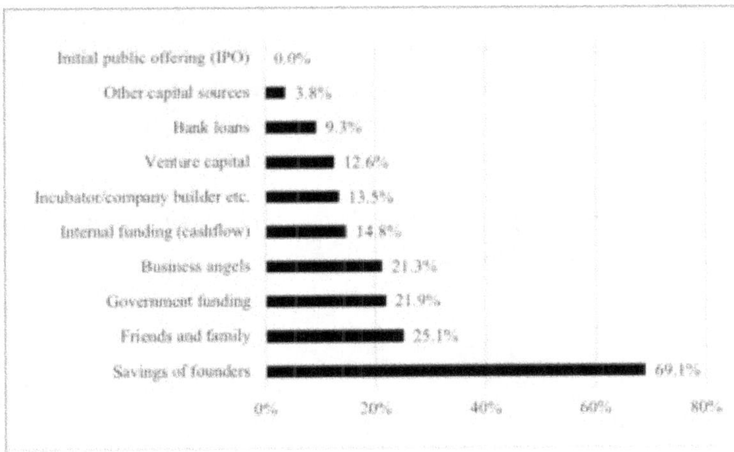

Furthermore, an average of 80% of all loan requests are rejected by banks. This finance gap can hamper the overall economic growth. Contrary to access to financing options, however, companies plan to collect an average of €3.3 million in further rounds (German Startups Association 2015). A systematic problem can be identified here, which could possibly be solved in part by enabling SME access to the capital market. Yet in the post-crisis economy characterized by low interest rates, bank lending will become increasingly scarce for SMEs. Banks in many EU member states frequently impose tough conditions on SMEs - either by making funding practically unavailable or by stifling the business after having obtained funding (Boata and Gerdes 2019). For micro and small firms, the only other funding alternative often becomes partnering with venture capital firms or business angels. Strict screening and participation requirements, as well as large regional and sectorial inequalities in such funding, not only often make these options extremely burdensome, but also result in loss of control of their venture – assuming that funding is even available.

In addition, markets for venture capital and business angel funding remain underdeveloped in comparison to the demand for funding and are also subject to hurdles for certain institutional investors. The European Commission noted that alternatives, such as capital markets, have historically been less developed in Europe than in other parts of the world. It has therefore become a political priority to help SMEs, and in particular start-ups, to obtain easier and more accessible funding for their projects (European Commission 2015). Due to the current number of intermediaries required to access capital markets, accessing European capital markets is cumbersome and a costly way of financing. Most SMEs are not only unable to bear the costs linked to a public issuance of securities, but also struggle to deal with the requirements imposed by exchanges (e.g. track record and restrictions relating to the business strategy) (Deutsche Börse Cash Market 2019). On the other hand, large corporates generally have easier access to capital markets, with bigger resources for initial offerings and also for ongoing compliance obligations.

Retail investor participation in European capital markets remains very low compared to other parts of the world – while huge amounts of potential capital sits in old-fashioned savings accounts at banks. Cash and bank deposits amount to 30% of total EU household assets, compared to 12.3% in the US. On the other hand, equity and debt securities in Europe claim a share of 25%, compared to 40.7% in the US. In Luxembourg (13%), Germany (11%), the UK (9%), and the Netherlands (8%), the proportion of equities in cumulated household financial assets is even lower (European Central Bank 2013, 2018; European Commission 2018).

Figure 2 shows that the gross disposable income in the euro area has been growing steadily since about 2013 at between 2 and 3 percent, while the growth of gross fixed capital has increased sharply since 2016 and has grown at new highs in 2019. The investment rate is - understandably - also rising with the growth of disposable income and will be at around 8.3% in 2019.

Figure 2. Growth of gross fixed capital formation and nominal growth disposable income of households and the investment rate (adapted from Eurostat 2019)

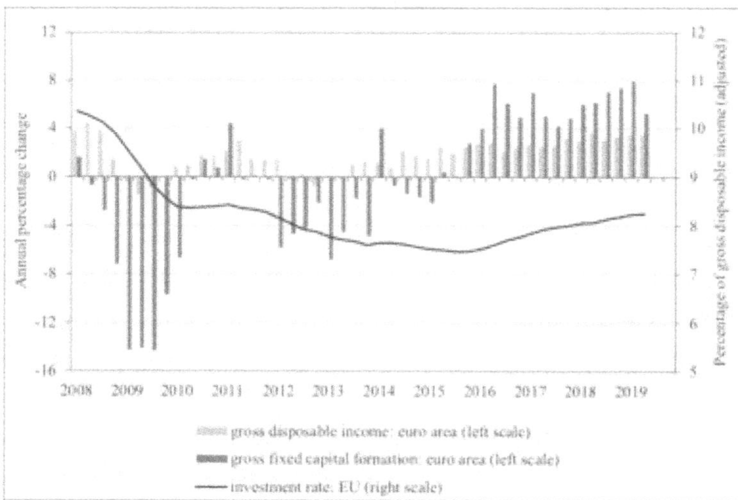

Where is this capital allocated to (apart from consumption)? Figure 3 shows the net acquisition of financial assets and net incurrence of liabilities of EU households. It can be seen that the share of investments in shares and other equities has steadily decreased until 2019 - in the fourth quarter 2018 this value amounted to 0.2% of the disposable income. The clearly highest share was at currency and deposits (4.5%) and other financial assets (2.5%; insurance reserves, financial derivatives, loans granted). If one now considers return characteristics of different asset classes, a potentially systematic problem emerges. Between 2013 and 2017, cash achieved a return of around 0.2%, bonds 3.2% and stocks between 7.9 and 15.8% (Morningstar Inc. 2018). If one now considers return characteristics of different asset classes, a potentially systematic problem emerges. Between 2013 and 2017, cash achieved a return of around 0.2%, bonds 3.2% and stocks between 7.9 and 15.8%. European households run the risk of generating long-term losses in value.

A basic explanation, among others, may be that individual investors are not able to invest in projects and companies at an early stage. They simply lack investment alternatives, as they can only invest in very large established companies.

SMEs are rarely publicly traded and, even when they are, such investments are restricted to qualified investors. Even indirect investments into SMEs via investment funds are rarely available in smaller denominations and to retail investors. Furthermore, consumers are overwhelmed by the complexity and uncertainty of investment products and lack general financial education. This results in little or no investment. These challenges accumulate when looking into the needs of the new generation of self-directed investors who are more tech savvy and demand for digital tools or social media rather than classic intermediaries, such as banks and financial advisors (European Commission 2018).

Even if the current wealth of the younger generation (millennials) may have no significant impact on the financial industry yet, it will shape the landscape of how investing will function in the coming years.

Figure 3. Net acquisition of financial assets, net incurrence of liabilities (adapted from Eurostat 2019)

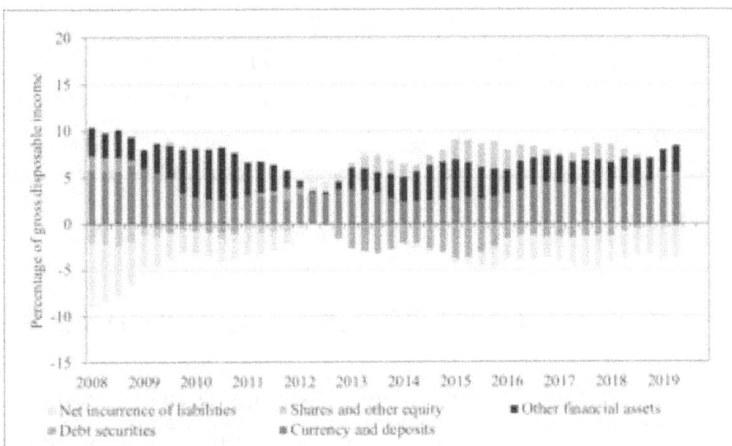

BLOCKCHAIN-BASED FINANCING: ICOs AND STOs

In a token sale, tokens are generated on a blockchain and are sold to investors. These tokens can represent virtually any value or property and are characterized by the fact that users can hold and transfer them directly. In a figurative sense, Bitcoin represents a token with the value or use case of a currency. In the same way, any type of value can be represented in a token on the blockchain. This can be a currency, vouchers, software licenses, governance rights, digital twins (e.g. in the supply chain) or regulated financial instruments.

Blockchain-based financing has gained considerable momentum in the context of so-called initial coin offerings (ICOs), which were a very successful means of financing for blockchain startups between 2013 and 2018 (Adhami et al. 2018; Ante et al. 2018; Ante and Meyer 2019; Chen 2019; Fisch 2019; Meyer and Ante 2020; Zetzsche et al. 2017). With progressive regulation of the market, various cases of crime (Ante 2018) and the weakening of an initial hype cycle, the concept of ICOs, the sale of tokens on the blockchain, which have certain rights (e.g. vouchers or software licenses), is used significantly less. Nevertheless, the phenomenon has shown that existing financing processes such as crowdfunding or initial public offerings (IPOs) can be improved by the addition of blockchain technology (Ante 2019a) and automation via smart contracts (Ante 2020), which enables transferability and thus secondary markets.

The basic mechanism of blockchain-based financing is by no means new. Initial public offerings (IPO) s represent a similar solution for larger firms and equity crowdfunding represents a similar mechanism. The main benefits come with the use of blockchain technology, which allows for 1) transparency, 2) pseudo-anonymity (or defined degrees of anonymity), 3) finality, i.e. no need for clearing and settlement processes, 4) automation via the use of smart contracts and 5) security. Compared to traditional settlement, which can take up to three business days, blockchain-based transactions are immediately settled. A blockchain-based clearance system updates the register of ownership instantly, which could save stock markets costs and could prevent abuse in the form of dividend stripping, like so called cum-ex deals (Fiedler et al. 2018). Tokens are immediately transferable, can be traded 24/7 on secondary markets, can be held personally, i.e. brokers and custody accounts are no longer required and the underlying blockchain ensures transparency of all transactions (Ante and Fiedler 2019).

Security token offerings (STOs) represent the sale regulated securities in the form of blockchain tokens. Companies are able to issue and sell tokens in an STO to investors under the applicable regulations for emitting securities (e.g. MiFID II in the European Union), as STOs fall under the financial regulation of the specific jurisdiction where they are issued. The technical protocols for security tokens, legal structures and secondary markets continue to evolve. As tokens can represent all kinds of things, a security token can in theory also (additionally) serve as a means of payment or as a utility token. The financing round thus allows the issuer to gain direct access not only to investors but also to potential customers (Ante and Fiedler 2019).

COMPARISON OF SME FINANCING OPTIONS: BLOCKCHAIN VS "TRADITION"

In order to understand the concept and the special features of blockchain-based financing, conventional forms of financing are compared with blockchain-based financing. This helps to better differentiate between the alternatives and to understand that blockchain-based financing means nothing more than adding technology, which in turn leads to various advantages and challenges - which will be discussed later.

Crowdfunding represents a type of corporate financing, where retail investors are able to fund specific projects. It can be 1) donation-based, without any actual rewards, 2) rewards-based, with non-financial rewards in the form of promotion or services, 3) lending-based, with a financial return like interest payments, or 4) equity-based with financial returns like dividends (Griffin 2012). Yet, Hornuf and Schwienbacher (2018) use the term "quasi-equity" for equity crowdfunding, as investors oftentimes acquire mezzanine financial instruments. Blockchain-based financing may be a promising solution to issue real equity instruments for retail investors.

In principle, crowdfunding and token sales can be compared very well, since exactly the existing forms of crowdfunding also exist in the market for token sales. A basic comparison is shown in Table 1. STOs can be assigned to both equity-based and rewards-based crowdfunding, each of which is characterised by the fact that the offering is generally only made by companies and regulated under securities law. ICOs can be assigned to both rewards- and donation-based crowdfunding, as the level of regulation is lower – usually trade law applies.

Table 1. Comparison between crowdfunding and token sale types

Underlying purpose or rights	Investor motivation	Crowdfunding equivalent	Token sale equivalent	Relative level of regulation
Equity or participation rights (e.g. profit- or revenue-sharing rights)	• Stake of ownership • Participation in a venture	equity-based	STO	high
Debt instruments	• Interest payments • Repayment	debt-based	STO	high
Access rights (e.g. to a blockchain network), goods & services	• Rewards in terms of access • Services or goods	rewards-based	ICO	low
Reputation gain or support for valuable ideas	• Support of ideas worth supporting • Charitable actions	donation-based	ICO	low

Both forms of financing are based on the use of technology: crowdfunding on the Internet and token sales on the Internet and blockchain technology. In addition, payments (or donations, investments etc.) are processed online in the respective campaigns. In principle, both forms are suitable both for the very early financing of ventures and for later financing rounds.

A significant difference between crowdfunding and conventional ICOs is that crowdfunding was usually carried out via platforms such as Kickstarter or Companisto. This means that there is a mediating entity between projects and investors (or backers), which carries out processes such as due diligence – also due to reputation risks for the platform. This means that morally hazarded projects in the crowdfunding area would potentially be rejected by platform operators before the start of the financing campaigns, whereas this was not the case with ICOs. Accordingly, ICOs are and have been considered with high information asymmetry, fraud and risk (Ante 2018; Chen 2019; Momtaz 2020; Roosenboom et al. 2020).

The process of so-called Initial Exchange Offerings (IEOs) is a special form of ICOs, where crypto-currency exchanges conduct token sales directly on their platforms and tokens can therefore be handled directly after the campaign. Here one could assume that due diligence is carried out by exchanges similar to crowdfunding. In fact, however, this leads to another agency problem, since exchanges are not necessarily interested in the long-term success of an ICO token - tokens can be traded on other exchanges after a certain period of time. In addition, they are often paid in tokens of projects, which they then want to sell themselves.

The great 'success' of ICOs can probably be explained by a special feature (that crowdfunding does not possess, or only to a limited extend) that represents an essential aspect for future potentials: Access to secondary markets. Individual ICO tokens have achieved enormous returns on the secondary market in the short term – without a finished product. This resulted in great attention being paid to the form of financing and rapid market growth. Token sales can be described as an innovative but less mature alternative to crowdfunding.

Now how do blockchain-based financing mechanisms and IPOs compare? Essentially, STOs represent IPOs for ventures of any size. Ventures of any size can issue securities digitally and make use of more efficient processes, like lower cost or a wider investors' base. The OECD's (2019) study list various differences between ICOs and IPOs that are presented in Table 2:

Table 2. Different characteristics of IPOs and ICOs (in part adapted from OECD 2019)

	IPO (in part also STO)	ICO
Financing type	• Risk capital • Exit possibilities for investors	• Risk capital • Early-stage
Venture type	• Mature ventures • Proven track record • All industries and sectors	• No track records • Concept stage • Oftentimes blockchain products
Regulation	• Regulated financial instruments, i.e. securities law	• Unclear framework, oftentimes trade law applies
Cost	• 3-7%	• 3%
Speed of execution	• Long preparation and execution	• Fast execution
Rights attached	• Ownership stakes • Dividends • Governance / voting rights	• Anything possible (e.g. software licenses, vouchers, currency) • Multiple functions of one token possible
Investor types	• Mostly accredited	• Any entity or individual
Valuation mechanisms	• Financial basis	• Unclear
Legal obligations	• Disclosure obligations • Reporting obligations	• None
Trading / liquidity	• Regulated markets	• Markets with less regulation • 24/7 trading

POTENTIALS AND CHALLENGES ASSOCIATED WITH BLOCKCHAIN-BASED FINANCING

Table 3 provides an overview of potentials associated with blockchain-based financing. These can be divided in the four different groups 1) (cost) efficiency, 2) global access / decentralization, 3) investor participation / network value and 4) financial innovation.

The disintermediation of processes in the financing process represents an essential basis for the efficiency potential of token sales. Corresponding conditions of a financing campaign can be easily created by means of scripts (smart contracts) anchored decentrally on the block chain and subsequently act autonomously. As a token sale, it is not necessary to submit documents and applications in a form comparable to that of an IPO and to engage middlemen. The initial cost and effort threshold are therefore

Table 3. Potential benefits of token sales.

Benefit	Description
(Cost) Efficiency	• Costs can be saved, as processes are disintermediated • Smart contracts allow for the automation of processes and thus efficiency gains (Ante 2020) • Cap table management can be automated • Transfer restrictions can be hard coded and automatically executed • Notifications to regulators can automatically be triggered • Risks like dividend stripping can be prevented, as clearing and settlement processes are eliminated – tokens can be directly transferred, thus ownership is always clear (Fiedler et al. 2018)
Global access / decentralization	• Cryptographically secured ownership (Roth et al. 2019) • Programmability of assets (Roth et al. 2019) • Global investors can be accessed and targeted for the financing campaign (Organisation for Economic Co-operation and Development 2019) • A multitude of different exchanges can be used to enable trading of the token • 24 hours a day, seven days a week trading and thus access to liquidity (Ante and Fiedler 2019) • Standardization and open ecosystems (Roth et al. 2019)
Investor participation / network value	• Investors do not only invest but become part of a network, i.e. a token sale can be both financing and marketing (building of customer base) (Catalini and Gans 2018) • Downstream network effects • Tokens can be held personally, i.e. brokers and custody is not required (technically) (Ante and Fiedler 2019)
Financial innovation	• Investors can purchase fractions of tokens (Organisation for Economic Co-operation and Development 2019) • Peer-to-peer transfers / trading • Financial inclusion for investors of any size • Capital raising without the need to transfer ownership rights (Ante et al. 2018; Organisation for Economic Co-operation and Development 2019) • Startup and SME capital market access (Ante and Fiedler 2019) • Liquidity for investment in SMEs (Ante and Fiedler 2019; Benedetti and Kostovetsky 2018) • Financing of open source projects (Ante et al. 2018)

no longer an obstacle for SMEs to issue equity. Additionally, the speed of a financing campaign can be increased, allowing entrepreneurs to refocus on their business more quickly.

Risks associated with the management, control and governance of existing tokens can be minimized because processes can be hard coded and automated using smart contracts. If a fictitious investor were to acquire more than 25% of all tokens, the smart contract token protocol could immediately perform the corresponding disclosure requirements.

Investors own assets and do not have to hold them with brokers. They can transfer them directly - clearing and settlement processes become superfluous (Fiedler et al. 2018). This in turn also leads to SMEs being able to establish direct contact with investors. Investors are not silent partners but can be actively involved in processes, for example by voting on smart contracts for token owners.

Of course, there are also many challenges for such a new form of financing and emerging markets. These can be roughly classified into three aspects: 1) project-related, 2) regulatory and 3) secondary market-related risks. An overview of the main topics is shown in Table 4.

Especially due to the comparatively low level of regulatory supervision and the lack of review bodies and platforms, projects have incentives for misconduct, such as sending the wrong quality signals to investors (Ante and Fiedler 2019; Momtaz 2020; Spence 1973). Since the quality of projects without a track record can to a large extent only be identified or assessed via signals, this results in downstream negative effects. Projects are not necessarily required to disclose financial plans and reporting and may change the design of the token they emit, as contributions are often only legally classified as donations (Ante et al. 2018). The low level of regulation also leads to problems with related secondary markets where negative effects such as insider trading and wash trading occur (Alameda Research 2019; Ante 2019b; Ante and Meyer 2019; Feng et al. 2018).

However, it can be said that all challenges are absolutely solvable. A sensible and selected application of established legal frameworks can regulate projects, platforms and exchanges accordingly, so that critical factors can be excluded. What remains are issues such as the right of oblivion or the scalability of systems, which is only of limited relevance for applications such as corporate finance. In this respect, a successful transformation of the markets for corporate finance can only be achieved if there is a sensible legal basis and a more mature market.

Table 4. Challenges associated with token sales.

Benefit	Description
Project-related risks	• Moral hazard risks due to immaturity of the market and lack of control mechanisms in the financing process (Ante and Fiedler 2019; Momtaz 2020) • Lack of reporting requirements for ICOs, as contributions were regulated as donations • Conflicts of interest, as project founders also own tokens • Uncertainty regarding the underlying value of the token (token economics), how are tokens, open source projects etc. valued? (Organisation for Economic Co-operation and Development 2019)
Regulatory risks	• Lack of regulatory oversight / unclear regulatory framework (e.g. SEC 2019) • Lack of disclosure requirements for unregulated token sales • Uncertainty regarding legal issues related to technical characteristics of the blockchain, e.g. (pseudo) anonymity, irreversibility, right to be forgotten (Ante 2018) • Uncertainty regarding legal and technical characteristics related to smart contracts, e.g. enforceability, can code represent legalese? • Know-your-customer (KYC), anti-money-laundering (AML) and counter-terrorist-financing (CTF) mechanisms may not be adequate (Organisation for Economic Co-operation and Development 2019)
Secondary market risks	• Highly volatile, high-risk investments at this stage of market maturity • Lack of regulatory oversight of cryptocurrency exchanges (wash trading, insider trading, pump-and-dump schemes, front running etc.) (Alameda Research 2019; Ante 2019b; Ante and Meyer 2019; Feng et al. 2018) • Moral hazard risks (e.g. exchanges receiving listing fees in tokens) (Meyer and Ante 2020)

CONCLUSION

Blockchain-based financing represents a financial innovation that has the potential to make capital markets accessible to companies of all sizes. The markets and service providers of token sales are just emerging, so obvious potentials cannot yet be tapped to a large extent. Nevertheless, it is obvious and desirable that future financing will be provided by the block chain (or a comparable technology). This allows automation, cost reduction, transparency and integration of formerly excluded participants (SMEs and retail investors).

Distributed technology, such as blockchain or similar technologies, will form the basis for the representation, transfer and management of financial products. The only question is when technology, law and the market will be sufficiently developed to fully exploit their potential.

REFERENCES

Adhami, S., Giudici, G., & Martinazzi, S. (2018). Why do businesses go crypto? An empirical analysis of initial coin offerings. *Journal of Economics and Business*, *100*, 64–75. doi:10.1016/j.jeconbus.2018.04.001

Alameda Research. (2019). *Investigation into the Legitimacy of Reported Cryptocurrency Exchange Volume*. https://ftx.com/volume-report-paper.pdf

Ante, L. (2018). Cryptocurrency, Blockchain and Crime. In K. McCarthy (Ed.), *The Money Laundering Market: Regulating the Criminal Economy* (pp. 171–198). Agenda Publishing. doi:10.2307/j.ctv5cg8z1.10

Ante, L. (2019a). *A Place Beside Satoshi – Scientific Foundations of Blockchain and Cryptocurrency in Business and Economics*. doi:10.13140/RG.2.2.27208.67842

Ante, L. (2019b). *Market Reaction to Exchange Listings of Cryptocurrencies*. doi:10.13140/RG.2.2.19924.76161

Ante, L. (2020). *Smart Contracts on the Blockchain – A Bibliometric Analysis and Review*. doi:10.13140/RG.2.2.23964.03207

Ante, L., & Fiedler, I. (2019). *Cheap Signals in Security Token Offerings (STOs)*. doi:10.2139srn.3356303

Ante, L., & Meyer, A. (2019). *Cross-listings of Blockchain-based Tokens issued through Initial Coin Offerings: Do Liquidity and specific Cryptocurrency Exchanges matter?* doi:10.13140/RG.2.2.27494.37442

Ante, L., Sandner, P., & Fiedler, I. (2018). Blockchain-Based ICOs: Pure Hype or the Dawn of a New Era of Startup Financing? *Journal of Risk and Financial Management*, *11*(4), 80. doi:10.3390/jrfm11040080

Beck, T., & Demirguc-Kunt, A. (2006). Small and medium-size enterprises: Access to finance as a growth constraint. *Journal of Banking & Finance*, *30*(11), 2931–2943. doi:10.1016/j.jbankfin.2006.05.009

Benedetti, H., & Kostovetsky, L. (2018). *Digital Tulips?* Returns to Investors in Initial Coin Offerings., doi:10.2139srn.3182169

Boata, A., & Gerdes, K. (2019). *European regulatory changes will make banks less willing to lend to SMEs*. https://www.eulerhermes.com/content/dam/onemarketing/euh/eulerhermes_com/erd/publications/pdf/20190529-TheView-EuropeanRegulatory.pdf

Booth, L., Aivazian, V., Demirguc-Kunt, A., & Maksimovic, V. (2001). Capital structures in developing countries. *The Journal of Finance*, *56*(1), 87–130. doi:10.1111/0022-1082.00320

Carpenter, R. E., & Petersen, B. C. (2002). Is the growth of small firms constrained by internal finance? *The Review of Economics and Statistics*, *84*(2), 298–309. doi:10.1162/003465302317411541

Catalini, C., & Gans, J. S. (2018). Initial Coin Offerings and the Value of Crypto Tokens. *SSRN Electronic Journal*, 1–37. doi:10.2139srn.3137213

Chen, K. (2019). Information asymmetry in initial coin offerings (ICOs): Investigating the effects of multiple channel signals. *Electronic Commerce Research and Applications*, *36*, 100858. doi:10.1016/j.elerap.2019.100858

Coase, R. H. (1937). The Nature of the Firm. *Economica, 4*(16), 386–405. doi:10.1111/j.1468-0335.1937.tb00002.x

Deutsche Börse Cash Market. (2019). *Eigenkapitalfinanzierung für kleine und mittlere Unternehmen (KMU)*. https://www.deutsche-boerse-cash-market.com/scale/

Euler Hermes. (2019). *European SME's: Filling the bank financing GAP*. https://ehrg.de/ver/studien/Studie_20190409.pdf

European Central Bank. (2013). Economic and Monetary Developments. *Monthly Bulletin*, 15–19.

European Central Bank. (2018). *Survey on the Access to Finance of Enterprises in the euro area*. https://www.ecb.europa.eu/pub/pdf/other/accesstofinancesmallmediumsizedenterprises201512.en.pdf?2c146594df6fe424c7adb001e1306c73

European Commission. (2015). *Communication from the European Commission on action plan on building a capital markets union*. https://eur-lex.europa.eu/legal-content/EN/TXT/PDF/?uri=CELEX:52015DC0468&from=EN

European Commission. (2018). *Distribution systems of retail investment products across the European Union*. https://ec.europa.eu/info/sites/info/files/180425-retail-investment-products-distribution-systems_en.pdf

European Commission. (2019). *2018 SBA Fact Sheet & Scoreboard*. https://ec.europa.eu/docsroom/documents/32581/attachments/1/translations/en/renditions/native

Eurostat. (2019). *Households and non-profit institutions serving households*. https://ec.europa.eu/eurostat/documents/499359/6246888/EN-Charts-and-Tables.xlsx/ed769615-8aa4-4f00-954e-550e765919a8

Evans, D. S. (1987). The Relationship Between Firm Growth, Size, and Age : Estimates for 100 Manufacturing Industries. *The Journal of Industrial Economics, 35*(4), 567–581. doi:10.2307/2098588

Fama, E. F., & French, K. R. (2002). Testing Trade-Off and Pecking Order Predictions About Dividends and Debt. *Review of Financial Studies, 15*(1), 1–33. doi:10.1093/rfs/15.1.1

Feng, W., Wang, Y., & Zhang, Z. (2018). Informed trading in the Bitcoin market. *Finance Research Letters, 26*, 63–70. doi:10.1016/j.frl.2017.11.009

Fiedler, I., Ante, L., Steinmetz, F., & Häseler, S. (2018). Distributed Ledger Technology: A Possible Way Forward for Securities Clearing. *Binary District*. https://journal.binarydistrict.com/distributed-ledger-technology-a-possible-way-forward-for-securities-clearing/. Accessed 8 September 2019

Fisch, C. (2019). Initial coin offerings (ICOs) to finance new ventures. *Journal of Business Venturing, 34*(1), 1–22. doi:10.1016/j.jbusvent.2018.09.007

German Startups Association. (2015). *European Startup Monitor*. https://europeanstartupmonitor.com/fileadmin/presse/download/esm_2015.pdf

Griffin, Z. (2012). *Crowdfunding: Fleecing the American Masses*. doi:10.2139srn.2030001

Hennessy, C. A., & Whited, T. M. (2007). How costly is external financing? Evidence from a structural estimation. *The Journal of Finance*, *62*(4), 1705–1745. doi:10.1111/j.1540-6261.2007.01255.x

Hornuf, L., & Schwienbacher, A. (2018). Market mechanisms and funding dynamics in equity crowdfunding. *Journal of Corporate Finance*, *50*, 556–574. doi:10.1016/j.jcorpfin.2017.08.009

Hughes, A. (1997). Finance for SMEs: A U.K. Perspective. *Small Business Economics*, *9*(2), 151–168. doi:10.1023/A:1007971823255

Jensen, M. C., & Meckling, W. H. (1976). Theory of The Firm Managerial Behaviour, Ageny Costs and Ownership structure. *Journal of Financial Economics*, *3*(4), 305–360. doi:10.1016/0304-405X(76)90026-X

Kurshev, A., & Strebulaev, I. A. (2015). Firm Size and Capital Structure. *The Quarterly Journal of Finance*, *5*(3), 1550008. Advance online publication. doi:10.1142/S2010139215500081

Meyer, A., & Ante, L. (2020). *Effects of Initial Coin Offering Characteristics on Cross-listing Returns*. doi:10.13140/RG.2.2.10972.33920

Momtaz, P. P. (2020). Entrepreneurial Finance and Moral Hazard: Evidence from Token Offerings. *Journal of Business Venturing*. doi:10.1016/j.jbusvent.2020.106001

Morningstar Inc. (2018). *2018 Fundamentals for Investors*. https://advisor.mp.morningstar.com/resourceDownload?type=publicForms&id=3f9dff3c-f085-47a1-98ba-0bc008df9f25

Organisation for Economic Co-operation and Development. (2019). Initial Coin Offerings (ICOs) for SME Financing. *Organisation for Economic Co-operation and Development*, 1–72. http://www.oecd.org/finance/ICOs-for-SME-Financing.pdf

Rajan, R. G., & Zingales, L. (1995). What Do We Know about Capital Structure? Some Evidence from International Data. *The Journal of Finance*, *50*(5), 1421–1460. doi:10.1111/j.1540-6261.1995.tb05184.x

Roosenboom, P., van der Kolk, T., & de Jong, A. (2020). What Determines Success in Initial Coin Offerings? *Venture Capital*, *23*(2), 1–23. doi:10.1080/13691066.2020.1741127

Roth, J., Schär, F., & Schöpfer, A. (2019). The Tokenization of Assets: Using Blockchains for Equity Crowdfunding. *SSRN Electronic Journal*. doi:10.2139srn.3443382

SEC. (2019). *SEC Sues Alleged Perpetrator of Fraudulent Pyramid Scheme Promising Investors Cryptocurrency Riches*. https://www.sec.gov/news/press-release/2019-74

Smith, C. W. Jr. (1977). Alternative methods for raising capital. Rights versus underwritten offerings. *Journal of Financial Economics*, *5*(3), 273–307. doi:10.1016/0304-405X(77)90040-X

Spence, M. (1973). Job Market Signaling. *The Quarterly Journal of Economics*, *87*(3), 355–374. doi:10.2307/1882010

Titman, S., & Wessels, R. (1988). The Determinants of Capital Structure Choice. *The Journal of Finance*, *43*(1), 1–19. doi:10.1111/j.1540-6261.1988.tb02585.x

Zetzsche, D. A., Buckley, R. P., Arner, D. W., & Föhr, L. (2017). *The ICO Gold Rush: It's a Scam, It's a Bubble, It's a Super Challenge for Regulators*. doi:10.2139srn.3072298

Chapter 8
Legal Risks and Challenges Related to Virtual Currencies

Zsolt Halász
Péter Pázmány Catholic University, Hungary

ABSTRACT

The appearance of the virtual currencies provokes several legal questions beyond their economic-monetary nature. The chapter focuses primarily from a legal point of view on the emergence of virtual currencies after a brief analysis of the concept and development of money, and analyses the related possible and probable legal risks and challenges in comparison to the operation of traditional (fiat) currencies either. The author provides a brief background of the technology of virtual currencies. The chapter considers specific issues that virtual currencies raise concerning the legal regulation in several fields, for example, exchange services, taxation, salaries, lending and borrowing in virtual currencies, law enforcement, money laundering, etc. Before the author assesses the impacts and probable functions of virtual currencies, it is indispensable to have also a look at the relations between state and money through the concept of monetary sovereignty and the related compatibility issues.

INTRODUCTION

Since the appearance of Bitcoin, the first and currently most popular virtual currency, no single day has passed away without market news, references and commentaries on the developments of the virtual currency operations, markets and technology. In 2019, key players of the financial markets and social networks also launched a project, which aimed to establish a virtual currency to be used by billions around the globe (Libra-project – White Paper). Even if the implementation of this projects is delayed or even derailed, it seems there are significant public and market interests towards the virtual currencies, which could challenge the dominance of the traditional or fiat currencies and may raise serious questions related to the monetary sovereignty of the states.

Besides the remarkable enthusiasm, there are several essential questions not yet answered on nature and operation of the virtual currencies. Some examples of these questions:

DOI: 10.4018/978-1-7998-4390-0.ch008

- Can virtual currencies be regarded as money or what are the intrinsic features and preconditions to be met for the recognition of any of them as money?
- Can they be credible alternatives to traditional currencies?
- What would be the consequences of legal recognition as money of any of them?
- Do they need to be regulated and what aspects of them can be regulated?

Besides these fundamental issues, one can endeavour specific related legal topics like the usage of virtual currencies in taxation, lending and borrowing, savings, payment of salaries, law enforcement, etc.

Both lists can be further extended.

According to the Coinmarketcap database, in January 2020, there were more than 5000 existing virtual currencies; however, this number can change at any time, due to the unregulated and uncontrolled creation and issuance of them. Practically, anyone can create their own one. At the same time, the market capitalisation of the virtual currencies was around USD 238 bn. Bitcoin's share of the whole market is around 65%. The number and market of the virtual currencies are constantly growing. Since the beginning of 2018, their number has grown by 3500!

I predicted that there was a significant number of legal risks and uncertainties around these new assets. The purpose of this chapter to provide an insight primarily into these legal issues and – where it was possible – to give also answers and/or formulate possible solutions either. Due to the close relevance, in certain cases, I also refer to economic aspects of the topic, however, my primary intention was to give a legal assessment.

BACKGROUND

Currently, virtual currencies are legally not regulated in general, neither by domestic nor by international laws. They are designed to be digital forms of money based on the internet, mainly but not exclusively on the blockchain and the distributed ledger technology (DLT). Issuers or creators are not central banks entitled to issue banknotes and coins on behalf of the state. Creators are developer groups without any central authority. In many cases (e.g. in the case of Bitcoin) the developers' or creators' identity is unknown. Users of the virtual currencies are members of the internet's virtual community.

To understand better their economic and legal background, it is necessary to find proper definitions and to examine their functions and forms. Monetary sovereignty is a substantial part of the concept of state sovereignty. Since the emergence of virtual currencies as privately created money raises several questions in this relation, this heading also analyses the scope of the monetary sovereignty and the impacts of virtual currencies on it. For a more precise understanding, it is also necessary to gain a brief insight into the technology either.

Concept of Money

It is often complicated to formulate an appropriate definition for the terms habitually used in everyday life. This is the case for example for certain essential terms of finances as 'tax' or 'money'. In the case of money, we will see below, how complicated is it to find a legal definition of money that fits the needs of everyday life either.

Economic and Legal Definitions of Money

From an economic point of view, it is common to define money in the light of its economic functions: medium of exchange, means of payment, unit of account, store of value. Evidently, the different economic functions imply different legal aspects related to the operation of money.

The medium of exchange (or means of payment) means, that money is the asset, which is paid for the purchase of goods, services or discharge of obligations. Fox (2008) referred to the theories of Menger and Jevons, according to whom money emerged to overcome the barter transactions. In practice, the substantial question is what single kind of commodity was to be selected for general exchange purposes. A variety of different commodities was used as money from see-salt to gold coins (or other coins having intrinsic value). They had to be homogenous, stable in preserving its value, easily recognisable and its value had to be apparent to anyone (p. 7.) However, today's corporeal money (coins and banknotes) have no intrinsic value.

The unit of account function means expressing the value of goods, services, rights or obligations.

The store of value function arises from the potential use of money in exchange for other commodities.

Proctor (2012) mentions as fourth the measure of value function either (p. 10).

Max Weber (1922, p. 97-99.) classified money as means of circulation and means of exchange. Money becomes a means of payment through state regulation. According to Weber, money is emerged by state will and state regulation. The modern state keeps in its hands the monopoly of monetary system regulation and money issuance. Money is kept alive by legal state force. The key function of money is to settle various debts (paying taxes to the state, paying interest payments by the state, etc.). Since the usage of money as a universal means of exchange is provided by legal state force, its main function will be the payment function.

The European Central Bank (2015) analysed the operation of virtual currencies in the light of the following main functions of money: medium of exchange, store of value, and unit of account.

The legal definition of money reflects according to Proctor (2012) primarily to the economic functions of it, however, the law focuses primarily on the private rights and the discharge of monetary obligations (p. 10.). Secondly, the law makes distinctions between money and currency. Lastra (2015) points out, that the concept of money is broader than the concept of currency: under the concept of currency, physical banknotes and coins are to be understood. The central bank usually has the monopoly of currency issue (on behalf of the State), but the creation of money is not exclusively a monopoly of the State (p. 13.). Public law focuses on currency status, the issuance of money and the related central bank competences, while private law focuses on the payment functions of money. For a generalised legal definition of money, Mann (2012, p. 11.) proposes the following elements:

a) with a primary focus on the medium of exchange role, the law must require creditors accept payments through that medium, in other words, if a medium is declared as legal tender payments must be accepted through it;
b) the unit of account must be prescribed by law to ensure its permanence;
c) to be able to fulfil the 'store of value' function, money must be expressed by reference to an identified unit of account, which preserves the nominal value of it.

A general conclusion by Mann (2012, p.15.) and Zimmermann (2013, p. 12-13.) based on Knapp (1923) is that a legal definition of money must recognise both the functions of money and the legal framework within it was created.

From a legal point of view, the ruling of the Supreme Court of Canada in the Alberta Statutes case (in 1938) gives a clear direction, as the court declared „money as commonly understood is not necessarily legal tender. Any medium which by practice fulfils the function of money and which everybody will accept in payment of a debt is money in the ordinary sense of the words even although it may not be a legal tender".

Forms of Money

Money can appear in various forms. Metallic coins were minted earlier in the history and since the 19th-century banknotes have also been issued. At the time, when banknotes were introduced, the holders had the right to redeem them in metallic coins. Later this right was abolished. Banknotes were initially issued by commercial banks as proof of metallic coin deposits. The notes were transferable like the coins. Nowadays, issuing coins and banknotes is an exclusive right of the state conferred usually to the central banks. Money (in the form of banknotes and coins) issued by the central banks enjoys the quality of being legal tender. Besides the corporeal forms, money also exists in incorporeal forms like bank account and credit balances, deposits. As Fox (2008) drew up, incorporeal money or bank money is a legal claim to be paid in corporeal money (p. 16.).

Theories of Money

Among the different definitions and concepts, three pronounced theories of money are also to be highlighted, since they emphasise the main different characteristics of money.

State theory defines money in a strictly formal sense: as Proctor (2012) emphasised, only those chattels are to be considered as money, which are recognised as such by laws of the State, denominated by reference to a unit of account and serves as universal means of exchange in the State of issue (p. 15). The State theory of money is generally recognised by modern constitutions (Some examples: US Constitution Art. I. § 8., German Basic Law (Grundgesetz) Art. 73. (1) 4., French Constitution Art 34.). The *Lex monatae* principle means according to Proctor (2012) that each State has the competence, the exclusive sovereign power to decide which currency it will use and the units of accounts of the currency is determined by the laws of the State in question, however, earlier the right of coinage had been recognised as a part of Crown's prerogatives (p. 17.). Lastra (2015) points out the State's sovereign powers to determine what constitutes *legal tender* (what coins and notes have a character of money) within its territory (p.15.) while Proctor (2012) adds that the State has the right to define the nominal value attributed to them (p. 366). Money having legal tender status is to be accepted for settling a financial obligation, or when offered (tendered) in payment of a debt, it extinguishes the debt. Coins and banknotes are usually defined as legal tender, but cheques, cards, and similar cash substitutes are not. Payments made by other means than legal tender are usually not restricted, but in certain cases, such restrictions may happen. The State theory neither obstructs introducing a common currency by a group of States (e.g. EU - European Monetary Union) nor prevents double currency systems (e.g. China – Hong Kong).

Proctor (2012, p. 23.), Zimmermann (2013, p. 13.) and Lastra (2015, p. 18.) describe the societary theory of money as it considers the attribution of the character of money or the recognition of it derives from the usages of commercial life and practices of the society and the confidence of people. It is not a formal decision by the State, but the attitude taken by the society is relevant in deciding what counts as money. As an early follower of the theory, Carl Friedrich von Savigny (1851) pointed out (cited recently Rahmatian (2020)), „it's not the state which founds and creates money and fixes its (market) value, but the state is an intermediary, which seeks to bring about a certain faith by issuing coins in a considerate way (p. 407-408). One hundred years later Arthur Nussbaum (1950) highlighted „the Societary process which gives life to money is not exactly a process of 'customary law'" (p. 8.). For economists, public acceptance and confidence are substantial criteria. Proctor (2012) underlines that the theory plays a significant role in inflation periods and times of monetary turbulences (p. 25).

In the institutional theory most recently elaborated by Vicuña (2010), money is not limited to cash (coin and banknotes) but as Lastra (2015) underlines it encompasses the dematerialized or incorporeal forms (e.g. demand deposits, positive account balances) either (p. 17.). In other words, formulated by Vicuña (2010), it is no longer a chattel, but transferable credit within an institutional framework. The theory highlights the value of money is not determined by gold, but the monetary policy of central banks and market developments. It also notes the significant reduction of the role and volume of physical or corporeal money. For the creation, the functionality and the determination of the value of the money in the absence of gold (or other assets) institutional agreements are substantial. The money consists of primarily of claims against the issuing central bank but also includes credit/deposit balances with commercial banks.

Monetary Sovereignty

The State's sovereignty over its own currency is traditionally recognised by public international law; however, as Zimmermann (2013) points out, this recognition was never expressed in basic instruments of international law (p. 2). The Permanent Court of International Justice in 1929 declared the State's competence to regulate its own currency as a generally accepted principle in the Brazilian Loans Case (1929) and the Serbian Loans Case (1929). According to Zimmermann (2013, p. 3-4) and Lastra (2015, p. 19.) the following regulatory competencies fall within the conceptual scope of monetary sovereignty:

- the right to create money within the territory of the issuing state through the issuance of currency (coins and banknotes);
- the right to conduct monetary policy (control the money supply and interest rates);
- the regulation of the banking and payment system;
- the right to determine the exchange rate policy and control the exchange rate;
- the right to control the extra-territorial use of the currency (decision on convertibility, the imposition of exchange and capital controls)
- the organisation of financial regulation and supervision.

Mann (2012) adds three further elements (p. 526-527):

- the right to peg the own currency to another one;
- the prohibition of the use of foreign currencies within the State borders;
- the right to devaluate the currency.

Bodin (1576) was the first who gave a systematic description of the abstract principle of sovereignty as a key foundation for the exercise of the state power. Bodin regarded coinage, the issuance of money as a royal prerogative, a substantial attribute of sovereignty. „There is nothing of more moment to a country, after the law, than the denomination, the value, and the weight of the coinage". In other words, according to Bodin, the definition and issuance of the money – as a part of sovereignty – is an exclusive and non-transferable right of the state, the sovereign (p.47.).

Monetary sovereignty is generally described as a substantial element of a State's sovereignty, however as Zimmermann (2013) points out, certain limitations can be applied to it, especially on a voluntary basis. These kinds of limitations are known e.g. as monetary unions, like the European Monetary Union (p. 144). Involuntary limitations on a stand-alone basis without limitations on further parts of sovereignty do not occur. Lastra (2015) underlines, however, some other specific forms of limitation, e.g. the financial effects of globalisation have a clear impact on the prevalence of the principle of territoriality (p. 24). Lastra (2015) also refers to the deterritorialization of money as well as to the role of the banks and other financial institutions in the creation of money. The power of a State to issue a currency can be emptied quite rapidly in case of loss of public confidence in such conventional money. The use of alternative currencies can be subject to permission or even punished, but in case of loss of trust, the State is less able to control processes. In the current digital world, such situations may culminate in the emergence of new, private, from state independent, digital and virtual currencies (p. 25.).

Although monetary sovereignty with all of its consequences has been regarded as an unchallenged fact, a notable reference has to be made to the theories of Nobel laureate Friedrich August von Hayek (1976), who – four centuries after Bodin – elaborated on the concept of private – non-state issued – money. Hayek advocated the free choice of currency with opening up the provision of currency to the competition of issuers from the private sector either. Hayek's concept preceded by three decades the factual appearance of the first virtual currency. According to Hayek's concept, the state's right for money issuance would be abandoned, and the monetary policy as we know it would not exist.

In the last decade, we have seen the preliminary steps of this competition prognosticated by Hayek became reality. The emergence of virtual currencies will most likely create such a competition between the central banks and the private money creators.

Despite these arguments and the recent technical opportunities, the current legal frameworks are still not in favour of the creation of private money.

In the Brazilian Loans case and the Serbian Loans case the Permanent Court of International Justice declared the State's competence to regulate its own currency as a generally accepted principle.

The US Constitution mentions among the powers of the Congress „To coin Money, regulate the Value thereof, and of foreign Coin, and fix the Standard of Weights and Measures; to provide for the Punishment of counterfeiting the Securities and current Coin of the United States" (Art. I. § 8.). According to the US Constitution, the coinage (money issuance) is kept at the federal level, since the Constitution prohibits the States to coin Money (Art. I. § 10.).

Within the EU-Zone, the constitutions kept the State competences on monetary affairs, although the power to issue the currency (the Euro) has already been transferred to the European Union (precisely to the European Central Bank). The German Basic Law declares: „[T]he Federation shall have exclusive legislative power with (...) currency, money and coinage, weights and measures, and the determination of standards of time" (Art. 73. (1) 4.). According to Art. 34. of the Constitution of France „[S]tatutes shall determine the rules concerning: (...) the base, rates and methods of collection of all types of taxes; the issuing of currency".

Despite all specific features and details of the monetary sovereignty and the development of it, one has to note, that the notion of sovereignty has changed significantly during the centuries (especially since 1929). E.g. substantial State competences have been privatised: private armed forces are active at several points of the globe, and – for us more importantly – private (virtual) money emerged and spread unstoppably.

Virtual currencies have emerged as a kind of criticism on the traditional monetary systems. This criticism erodes one of the fundamental elements of state sovereignty, financial sovereignty, including the right to issue the own currency.

Concerning the application of Blockchain technology, some initial steps have already been done by the governments. For example, the Government of Germany has published its Blockchain Strategy (2019), in which, the German Government evaluates the Blockchain technology in the context of digital sovereignty.

The Technology of Virtual Currencies

Before all else, one has to make clear that the virtual currencies' concept and their issuance are different from that of electronic money, even if both operate in an electronic environment and based on digital technology. Virtual currencies are different from and independent of fiat currencies. Electronic money is issued against traditional money. The value and accounting of the virtual currencies are independent of that currency from which the exchange has happened.

Blockchain and the distributed ledger are the fundaments of virtual currency technology. This technology, unlike a traditional centralised monetary system, operates in decentralised IT systems, in other words in a shared database. The distributed ledgers are usually public databases spread across multiple sites. Blockchain represents a type of distributed ledger. The blockchain includes the transactions (or stores decisions of the virtual currency owners), which are verified as legitimate. Through the legitimation process, additional blocks containing the verified data are added next to each other in the chain. As Abramovicz (2016) underlines, blockchain as a tool of general applicability can be an authoritative and chronologically ordered record of any type of legal decision. In the case of blockchain type databases, any number of copies may exist, and the protocol ensures they are synchronised (p. 371-372).

The blockchain as a fundament of the functioning of the virtual currencies necessarily contains the entire history of transactions. Each new transaction is validated by reference to this public history. Without analysing its details here, I would only emphasise one main characteristic of this system, namely compared to the computational operations performed on the traditional IT systems where the operations can be subsequently modified, it is not possible in the blockchain, where the system is unbreakable (until no one possesses at least 50%+1 of computers attached to the system). This feature undoubtedly promotes the use of technology in payment transactions. The possibility of creating a non-manipulable and – within the system – cheaper payment system through the virtual currencies is undoubtedly an important positive factor. (The cheapness is to be understood within the system only because commission fees are routinely added to the exchange operations between traditional and virtual currencies and there are certain differences between bid and sell rates either.)

The operation of the blockchain requires public-key cryptography, in which two keys (a public and a private) are generated by a mathematical technique. The public key is the virtual currency address and the transactions are signed by the private key corresponding to the public one. In possession of the public key, any person can encrypt the data, which can be decrypted by the private key. The possession of the private key provides control over the coins.

The storage location of the private key is the so-called 'wallet'. A wallet can be software on a computer or mobile device, but it can exist as hardware or even a piece of paper. One's mind can also serve as a wallet, however, it is not easy the keep a long alphanumeric key in it.

Each transaction is designed to be anonymous. Participants are not identified by their names. There is neither a central authority nor any bank-type financial intermediary institution exist, which could identify the virtual currency users. The addresses or public keys to and from which a transaction is concluded are however stored in the ledger; therefore, the identity of the counterparts can be revealed. Consequently, virtual currency transactions are factually not anonym; they are rather a pseudonym.

LEGAL CHALLENGES RELATED TO VIRTUAL CURRENCIES

Can Virtual Currencies Be Recognised as Money?

According to the economic theory of money described for example by Fox (2008), the emergence and status of any asset as money is a social fact. The state or the law cannot simply confer the status of money on a certain kind of asset. It requires a certain level of general acceptance in the community (p. 3). As Proctor (2012) underlines, in the framework of the societary theory of money, anything can be money if it functions as such, but in case of a crisis such money can lose its character quite quickly and, in such situations, no money can be created (p. 24). We have also seen the State theory on money, where only those chattels are to be considered as money, which are recognised as such by laws of the State. Directly related, the concept of monetary sovereignty clearly describes the State's competencies related to the definition and regulation of its own currency and monetary system. But as Proctor (2012) points also out, one also has to keep in mind that states in the modern world are frequently unable to control the external value of their currencies and the sovereignty of the state over its monetary system is currently relatively limited (p. 24). The above-mentioned ruling in the Alberta Statutes case (1938) gives a clear direction, as not only legal tenders can be regarded as money, but anything which everybody accepts in payment of debt.

Virtual currencies are neither a commodity currency (backed by gold or another commodity) nor fiat currency. As it is demonstrated below, there is no consensus on the legal characterisation of virtual currencies.

According to the definition adopted by the European Banking Authority (2014), virtual currencies are a digital representation of value that is neither issued by a central bank or a public authority nor necessarily attached to a fiat currency but is accepted by natural or legal persons as a means of payment and can be transferred, stored or traded electronically. The main actors are users, exchanges, trade platforms, inventors, and e-wallet providers.

European Central Bank (ECB) uses a very similar definition in its report on virtual currencies. ECB (2015) underlines, that key actors of the virtual currencies are neither regulated nor supervised and users do not benefit from legal protection such as redeemability or a deposit guaranty scheme and are more exposed to the various risks that regulation usually mitigates.

Concerning value-added taxation (VAT), the European Court of Justice also had to analyse the nature and operation of the virtual currencies in the Hedquist case (C-264/14). In a preliminary ruling procedure, the Court had to answer the question: whether transactions, which consist of the exchange of traditional currency for units of the 'bitcoin' virtual currency and vice versa, in return for the payment of a sum equal to the difference between, on the one hand, the price paid by the operator to purchase the currency and, on the other hand, the price at which he sells that currency to his clients, constitutes the supply of services for consideration within the meaning of the relevant article of the VAT Directive? In its ruling, the Court declared „bitcoin virtual currency, being a contractual means of payment, cannot be regarded as a current account or a deposit account, a payment or a transfer. Moreover, (…) the 'bitcoin' virtual currency is a direct means of payment between the operators that accept it. Transactions involving non-traditional currencies, that is to say, currencies other than those that are legal tender in one or more countries, in so far as those currencies have been accepted by the parties to a transaction as an alternative to legal tender and have no purpose other than to be a means of payment, are financial transactions. It is common ground that the 'bitcoin' virtual currency is neither a security conferring a property right nor a security of a comparable nature.

It should be noted that the European Central Bank (2015) represents an opposite view on virtual currencies. According to the ECB virtual currencies are not used widely to exchange value, they are not legally money, and – in the absence of minted versions – they are not currency either, and no virtual currency is a currency. However, it does not exclude to use virtual currencies as contractual forms of money between private parties (p. 24.).

Specific Legal Issues Related to Virtual Currencies

Basic Issues

The legal issues related to the virtual currencies are particularly focused on the legal consequences and risks associated with the unregulated nature of this issue and whether it is possible and/or necessary to create any kind of regulation.

The current global monetary system operates on the fundament of several important factors; however, this system has undergone many profound changes, including the legal basis, in the not too distant past. Let us just refer here e.g. to the Bretton Woods rules and the elimination of the gold standard.

The approach of governments around the globe towards virtual currencies is significantly divers. Construction of a comprehensive regulatory regime would be undoubtedly necessary, but due to the complexity and difficulty of the issues and aspects to be regulated, it requires considerable time. The significant number and especially the diversity of virtual currencies do not help the completion of the legislation process. Particular difficulties of proper regulation arise from among others the lack of central register, the lack of responsible issuer/creator. In many cases even the identity of the creator is unknown.

Official currencies are not exclusive means of payment; however certain payments (e. g. tax-payments) generally have to be implemented in official currencies. While legal regulation is difficult to be disrupted, a financial crisis can easily lead to a distrust in the traditional monetary and banking system. After the 2008 crisis, the trust was partially lost, which might have initiated the creation of the first virtual currencies. However, as mentioned above, the idea of private money was not new even at that time.

The most substantial risks associated with virtual currencies stem from their unregulated nature and the officially uncertified technology. The system promises fast, safe and cheap payments. This promise is based on the new technology described above that allows financial transactions to be implemented directly between virtual wallets bypassed the traditional banking system. The basis of the operations is the – blind – confidence in the unknown creator/issuer, and/or the technology created by it, without any kind of legal guarantee or assurance. Furthermore, as Firth-Butterfield, Brent and Grant (2017) underlined virtual currencies didn't give rise to any legal right vis-a-vis another. There is neither a contractual basis nor any regulatory protection for cases if any unexpected loss or damage occurs related to the transactions with virtual currencies. The state regulation of the traditional monetary system lends – stronger or weaker, and sometimes varying – confidence in the legal tender in the course of history (p. 548-549).

A substantial feature of virtual currencies' system and technology is the global accessibility, even if the freedom of usage and mining of virtual currencies is diverse around the world. (In Europe or the USA, they are not banned or restricted, but the regulatory climate is different e.g. in certain other countries like China or India.)

Virtual currencies conceptually different from fiat money as they are created by private entities, they are not issued by the sovereign (by any central bank). States are not involved in the creation of virtual currencies and transfers of virtual currencies don't pass through the banking system, consequently, transfers can be relatively cheaper, and they can be executed without state supervisory control. As Bamford (2015) points out this bypassing of the governmental and regulatory controls creates potential risks of money laundering and the destabilizing of the banking system (p. 17-18).

Since the creation of new virtual currencies is not regulated in most countries, there are no legal obstacles or limits to the creation of further currencies besides existing ones. By January 2020, the number of virtual currencies reached 5000 and no one can predict the potential further increase. The purpose and background of the emergence of this large number of various virtual currencies are not clear. It is impossible to predict which ones will exist in the future and until when. It is also unforeseeable for what reasons (loss of users' interests or upon creators will) will any of them cease to exist. A further generic consequence of the non-regulated nature is the possible spontaneous exit from the market.

States can regulate their own currency; however, the regulation of creation or issuance of virtual currencies is practically impossible on a standalone basis. Consequently, it may be easier to regulate the access to them and the various transactions related to them. Since different transactions bear different risks, differentiated regulatory responses would be needed.

Despite this regulatory challenge, one can see some serious attempts for effective regulation. The most comprehensive regulatory response has been set up in Malta. The Maltese Parliament has adopted three laws establishing the legal basis of DLT based businesses and setting up the relevant safeguards: the Virtual Financial Assets Act (VFA Act), the Innovative Technology Arrangements and Services Act (ITAS Act), and the Malta Digital Innovation Authority Act (MDIA Act). In Switzerland, the Federal Government has already tabled the bill on the Federal Law on Adaptation of federal law to developments in the technology of distributed electronic registers (DLT Bill). The consultation on the proposal started in March 2019, but the bill has not been endorsed yet.

The Promise of Anonymity

The particular operation features based on the technology of the virtual currencies promise anonymity to the users equivalent to cash. The virtual currency system allows anonymous ownership and anonymous transfers between virtual wallets. The identification requirements determined by law are less strict than requirements to be met in the traditional financial services. Such a liberal system can be easily used for tax evasion, money laundering, terrorism financing and other illicit purposes. Furthermore, anonymity is just pseudo-anonymity in case if many virtual currencies (e.g.: Bitcoin) and technically the users can be traced back in most cases. However, some other virtual currencies (e.g.: Monero, Z-cash) using specific technologies provide real anonymity, which makes serious the above-mentioned concerns especially in the light of global accessibility and usage.

Impacts on Traditional Monetary Policy

By the emergence of the virtual currencies – especially if the significance of them compared to the current levels gains more importance –, the control capacity of states and central banks may weaken substantially over the monetary systems and processes. Additionally, if a significant amount of liquidity flows from traditional currencies to virtual ones, this can harm the financial situation of the traditional banking sector. Virtual currencies are outside the scope of the central bank's monetary policy toolbox, and concerning them, neither the central bank's interest rate policy (virtual assets is conceptually interest-free) nor the exchange rate policy can have any impact.

Payments in Virtual Currencies

One of the most important questions is which payments can be implemented by a virtual currency. Certain types of payments require specific attention, e. g. payment of taxes or payment of salaries. Traditionally state treasuries accept tax payments in their own fiat currency. Waiving tax payments in their own currency would practically mean waiving and cessation of own currency either.

This restriction is a serious constraint itself for the conversion of any other transactions into virtual currency since the conversion immediately involves a significant exchange rate risk for merchants, service providers and other taxpayers, as well for the states themselves collecting taxes in virtual currencies.

In case of businesses based and implemented in virtual currencies, it may be however reasonable to make the tax payments possible in virtual currencies. Based on such considerations certain tax (registry fee) payments in virtual currencies are made possible in Canton Zug in Switzerland.

Payment of wages in virtual currencies raises specific issues. Salary payments virtual currency may make it convenient to employ and pay remote workers globally since payments can be made almost instantly around the globe, even without access to the local banking institutions. On the other hand, besides the possible significant exchange rate fluctuation and related risks, there are legal issues employers and employees have to face. Firstly, for the reason of defence of wages, several jurisdictions require the payments of wages in local currency (e.g. in Hungary), but there are countries (e.g. Japan, Australia, New-Zealand and Denmark), where employers can pay wages in virtual currencies. In case of salary payments, there are two different options to be examined: in the first option salaries defined and contracted in fiat currency and changed (on the choice of the employee as a fringe benefit) to virtual currency before payment; in the second option salaries defined and contracted in virtual currency. The second option has not been widespread yet. Although virtual currency payments – even salary payments – can be used globally, one has to keep in mind that taxation of these assets and payments differs country by country.

Lending and Borrowing Activities

It may be surprising, but virtual currency lending services already exist. They can be a simple means of peer-to-peer (P2P) lending platforms. In the case of P2P platforms, no bank type intermediary institution is needed, the platform itself connects the creditor and the borrower. Since virtual currencies are not recognised as money, lending in virtual currency does not constitute money lending service and banking laws (neither prudential requirements nor customer protection rules are not applicable). Financing operations are well-known risky services. However, these services implemented in virtual currencies must be regarded as even riskier operations. To illustrate the associated risks, it is perhaps enough to mention the FX-based lending, which resulted in the most serious domestic financial disaster of the last two decades in Hungary and some other countries in the CEE region.

A related question is the virtual currency backed lending. Even currently lending services backed by virtual assets are also available. These operations are less risky than lending, but the fluctuation of exchange rates may make the provision of additional coverage necessary.

Virtual Currencies as Financial Instruments

Applicable regulations (e.g. EU MiFID II) consider neither traditional nor virtual currencies as financial instruments, as a subject of investment services. Virtual currencies do not pay interest or dividends. Financial benefits, returns on them may solely arise from their exchange rate fluctuations. However, this is known to show significant shifts. Concerning traditional convertible currencies, the convertibility and the financial gains arising from the exchange rate changes are not restricted.

Money Laundering and terrorism financing

Virtual currencies present a remarkable risk of financial crime especially in the field of money laundering and terrorism financing due to the anonymity or pseudonymity of the transactions related to them. It is not completely impossible but relatively difficult to trace the transactions and the users of them since they enable the users to avoid contact with the regulated traditional financial intermediaries. Virtual currencies cannot be regulated in the same way as fiat currencies as most of the trading businesses happen on online platforms without the involvement of third parties as Firth-Butterfield, Brent & Grant (2017) underlined (p. 540-541). They also referred to specific methods (e. g. bitcoin debit cards or even more delicate if such cards are linked to a Paypal account) in which cryptocurrencies can be used for money laundering and terrorism financing activities either. Furthermore, it also has to be highlighted, that there are certain types of virtual currencies (e.g. Monero, Z-cash), which provide real anonymity for their users.

A special related issue is the legal status of the exchange service providers, who provide currency exchange services related to virtual currencies. The relevant EU banking legislation (CRD, CRR) defines currency exchange as auxiliary financial service provided by a bank (or by its agent). However, by definition, foreign exchange transactions (and services) mean only the sale of foreign currency (money issued by a foreign state/central bank) against a domestic or foreign currency and vice versa. The sale/exchange of virtual currencies against traditional (foreign or domestic) currency is outside the concept of currency exchange service and as such does not fall under the scope of the banking regulations. Consequently, this activity doesn't require any license to be issued by the financial supervisory authority and it is not supervised either. In the lack of legal regulation and protection, the operation of virtual currency trading platforms and wallet service providers can carry serious security risks.

In July 2016, the European Commission has tabled a proposal on the amendment of the Anti-Money Laundering (AML) Directive (COM(2016) 450 final), proposing the list of so-called obliged entities defined by the Directive to be complemented by virtual exchange platforms and custodian wallet providers. The proposal also includes a definition of the term "virtual currency": a digital representation of value that is not issued or guaranteed by a central bank or a public authority, is not necessarily attached to a legally established currency and does not possess a legal status of currency or money, but is accepted by natural or legal persons as a means of exchange and which can be transferred, stored and traded electronically. The proposal aims to counterbalance the anonymity related to the transactions in comparison with traditional currency transfers, with particular emphasis on the fact that public administrations (in and outside EU) are currently not monitoring the payments in virtual currencies. The proposal has been approved by the Council and the European Parliament after 2 years of discussion in May 2018 (Directive (EU) 2018/843). It had to be transpositioned by the Member States until 10 January 2020, but the Directive cannot be regarded as a comprehensive answer for the issues raised.

Taxation

In the field of taxation, at least three essential questions require deeper analysis.

The first question on payment of taxes in virtual currencies has already been mentioned above. As the example of Canton Zug in Switzerland showed, certain duties to the Commerce Registry Office have been payable in virtual currencies either. The technology behind this payment option is the involvement of a selected intermediary payment agent. The payment obligation and amount are determined in CHF and always the actual exchange rate used. The recipient doesn't take any risk related to the use of virtual currencies.

In the case of revenue taxation, among others, the taxation of mining activities, salaries received in virtual currencies and gains from exchange activities can be put in the focus. The principal issue in the taxation of private individuals is how to define the appropriate revenue type/category according to the local laws. In corporate taxation, revenues from mining activities may be regarded as financial revenues if the relevant virtual currency was recognised as money. An additional question is, however, how to apply the rules on provisions? What conversion rate is to be applied in the determination of the relevant market value? In the case of salary taxation, the last question is equally relevant.

At the time of writing this chapter in January 2020 virtual currencies are not universally recognised as money. No official exchange rates are defined either and definition exists for the timing of acquisition of revenues: the date of exchange or year-end or an average rate was to be applied.

In the field of VAT, the most problematic issue is the calculation of the tax base. According to the EU Directive (2006/112/EC) on VAT the tax base, the taxable amount is the counter-value: everything which constitutes consideration. This counter-value can be settled even in virtual currencies. The first related question is how to define such transactions in the VAT system? Can settlements in virtual currencies be regarded as payments? The above mentioned Hedquist ruling of the ECJ doesn't give guidance in this question. According to the VAT Directive, transactions in fiat currency – transactions, concerning currency, banknotes and coins used as legal tender – are exempt from VAT (based on Art. 135), but virtual currencies are not on the exemption list. Consequently, transactions settled in virtual currencies are to be regarded as an exchange of goods, and tax base (taxable amount) is to be determined based on market value. The determination of the market value could be based on an actual exchange rate, but the Directive defines neither official exchange rates nor exchange rate providers.

Law Enforcement

In the case of traditional currencies and their storage on bank accounts the law enforcement measures (e.g. enforcement of claims, administrative decisions, court rulings, seizures, etc.) can easily be applied and executed. These measures can be implemented by the application of certain obligations imposed by law enforcement authorities on banks and other relevant financial institutions.

In the case of virtual currencies, the applicability of various law enforcement measures may become at least questionable. For law enforcement authorities the legal regulation technically cannot provide such direct access to virtual currency storage facilities (e.g. wallets) as to traditional bank accounts. For example, in the case of Bitcoin, the owner's access to his/her wallet can be limited by law enforcement and/or forensic measure, but the success of the coercive measures depends in many cases on the owner's willingness to cooperate. In case of other, yet less popular currencies as Monero or Zcash, the identifying and tracing of the owner is much more complicated or even declared impossible.

Effective law enforcement is the foundation of legal certainty, therefore this is one of the most crucial legal issues related to virtual currencies. The virtual currency schemes as a whole, however, cannot be regulated effectively. The regulation can focus on the activities (e. g. exchange services) and the intermediaries. The regulation cannot cover the whole scheme – especially the creation and the cessation – due to the lack of central authority governing the system. If once exchange services were not needed anymore due to the spread of any virtual currency, the regulation was even more extremely difficult.

SOLUTIONS AND RECOMMENDATIONS

No total quality solution exists. As described above, first of all for the reason of maintaining a stable monetary system states of the world cannot afford to ignore this issue of virtual currencies and not to provide an adequate regulatory response within the foreseeable future.

Why should virtual currencies be regarded as money? The answer offered by the societary theory of money on this question is remarkable: if the acceptance of a chattel as money is a social fact, it should be recognised as money. However, it cannot be declared, that all of the more than 5000 virtual currencies are accepted by society as money (the vast majority of them are even not known at all). The state factually cannot stop the emergence, development, and usage of these new virtual currencies. Nevertheless, the state legislation should define the basic parameters and requirements for recognition of any virtual currency as money and additionally all the legal consequences of the recognition as money should be determined. Ideally, these laws should be globally accepted and applied, since the global accessibility can be a major advantage (e.g. in many places allowing a reduction in the number of conversion transactions between different fiat currencies), however, it also poses serious threats due to the easy transfers of money stemming from crimes or other illicit activities.

Interestingly, central banks of Europe, the USA, or Canada don't see the appearance and development of the virtual currencies as a threat to the traditional monetary system. Central banks issue only notices on the risks of their usage.

The anonymity or pseudonymity should be addressed as one of the most complex issues of the virtual currencies. The usage of cash (coins and banknotes) provides anonymity for the users. The usage of non-cash type money (money on bank accounts, e-money, etc) is never anonymous. The complexity of the anonymity derives from the hybrid nature of the virtual currencies. They do not exist physically but at the same time, the users are not identified directly. Even if the anonymous usage of virtual currencies cannot be eliminated, service providers can be encouraged or obliged for comprehensive identification parallelly with discouraging or persecuting any kind of services related to virtual currencies providing real anonymity for its users.

As for the payments, it does not appear necessary to introduce limitations on transactions of private parties related to the usage of virtual currency instead of using a traditional one/fiat (similarly as it is possible to use different fiat currencies). The task of the states and central banks to draw the attention of the users on the risk related to the volatility of the exchange rates and other legal uncertainties. Prohibitions and restrictions should only be considered if the stability of the monetary and financial system was compromised, or specific legal interests are to be defended e.g. in taxation or payment of salaries.

The lack of recognition of virtual currencies as money causes the most problematic situation in the field of salary payments and taxation. In the case of salary payments, legislation had to ensure the protection of the value of salaries paid in virtual currency, especially if it opens up the possibility of salary payments in virtual currency. In taxation, the non-recognition leads to serious legal uncertainties.

For a proper creditor and borrower protection within lending services through P2P platforms, special regulation would be needed, independently from the type of currencies (fiat or virtual) they use. Borrowing in virtual currency should only be allowed if the incomes of the borrowers involved are predominantly originating in virtual currency. Until that happens, this activity should be restricted.

For virtual currencies used as financial instruments of investment services, there is no apparent reason for any restriction on the conversion or redemption of traditional currency into virtual currency or vice versa, even if it is for any gainful purpose. Prohibitions and restrictions are only to be considered if the stability of the financial system is compromised.

The timing of the regulatory answers in the field of anti-money laundering and counter-terrorism -financing is extremely slow. Within the European Union, it took a decade, and the situation is not even better in the rest of the world. As a solution, an identification level equivalent to financial services provided in fiat currencies should be required. (Alternatively, the recognition of virtual currencies as money would also serve as a solution). The regulation of exchange service activity would also possible and justified in line with the traditional currency exchange services, especially if one considers the unregulated trade of these instruments can be a simple tool for covering various illicit activities or criminal offences and/or the gains originating from them.

For the reason of legal certainty, the State always has to ensure the enforceability of the law. The appearance of virtual currencies challenges this foundation, through its technology (transaction validation by private key), the anonymity/pseudonymity provided by the system and the lack of the central authority and intermediaries. The most challenging question is whether appropriate regulatory answers can be found before the virtual currencies gain significantly more ground.

FUTURE RESEARCH DIRECTIONS

In this chapter, I have described the most important elements of legal issues related to virtual currencies. However, this topic can be examined in a considerably broader context in many aspects, which would worth more and deeper research.

Among others, the further details of challenges, which the traditional concept of monetary sovereignty has to face can be examined. Central banks are also interested in creating their own digital currencies, however, their relevant projects, which will be surely analysed, are still in early stages.

Besides virtual currencies, the local currencies used in smaller regions are also existing alternatives of fiat currencies, even if they are of various types. Experiences with local currencies may serve as valuable inputs for the analyses of virtual currencies.

This chapter covered numerous areas of relevant legislation, which are affected by virtual currencies. There is a general need for the monitoring of the whole legal system to discover further affected territories of it.

CONCLUSION

We have seen the fundamental question related to the effective functioning of the current financial and legal system is not whether it is necessary to regulate the virtual currencies (both their issuance and usage), but all the more how can this be achieved and how can we ensure the proper operation and of our monetary, financial and also legal system in case of a surely occurring further proliferation of the virtual currencies? The usage of virtual currencies cannot be abolished. Taking down any computers of the P2P network has a very limited effect over the whole system.

The task, therefore, is not simple but requires a global regulatory response. For the requirement of legal certainty, the consistency of law – especially in the field of taxation and financial-type services – a clear regulatory framework has to be ensured. The protocol of virtual currencies cannot be modified without the cooperation of nearly all its users, who choose what software they use. Assigning special rights to state authorities in the rules of the global Bitcoin network is not a practical possibility. The situation can be even more complicated by the creation and use of further less well-known virtual currencies that might also help illicit purposes.

The most urgent step would be the regulation and monitoring of the traditional/virtual currency exchange/intermediary activities (not solely AML-CTF) – by transnational or rather global regulatory measures.

In addition to the necessity of a regulation, a further question is whether the blockchain system underlying the operation of the virtual currencies can be adapted to the development of the traditional financial system? Since this new technology has undoubted advantages either, and it cannot be ruled out that a virtual currency operating without the above-mentioned issues might emerge in the future, the state and central bank decision-makers should consider in the development and regulation of the financial system.

The non-recognition of virtual currencies as money results in several open questions especially in the field of taxation but also in other fields of legislation. Virtual currencies used for payments should, therefore, be recognised as money.

Having a look at the regulatory trends and developments around the world, one can observe serious steps in the direction of the adaptation of the legal framework to the new features and opportunities of the distributed ledger technology. One of the most advanced examples is the Swiss draft distributed ledger technology (DLT) law (2019) currently under discussion by the Swiss Federal Parliament. The new Swiss draft law doesn't focus on virtual currencies exclusively, but certain elements are also important and may be applicable for virtual currencies either. It intends to define the regulatory framework and to increase legal certainty for business models based on DLT. The new law will increase legal certainty for the digital transfer of rights. It will create a new category of securities with substantially the same features as certificated securities that allow the digital transfer. These are similar to asset tokens, e.g. shares or bonds registered on the blockchain. Furthermore, it creates a new licence category for blockchain-based financial market infrastructures and confirms the application of the AML law to decentralised trading platforms.

ACKNOWLEDGMENT

This research received no specific grant from any funding agency in the public, commercial or not-for-profit sector. The research was completed by utilising the facilities of Péter Pázmány Catholic University, Faculty of Law, Budapest, Hungary.

REFERENCES

Abramovicz, M. (2016). Cryptocurrency-Based Law. *Arizona Law Review*, *58*(2), 359–420.

Act CXXXIX of 2013 on the National Bank of Hungary

Act I of 2012 on the Labour code of Hungary. art. 154

Banford, C. (2015). *Principles of International Financial Law* (2nd ed.). Oxford University Press.

Basic Law (Grundgesetz) of the Federal Republic of Germany. art. 73. (1) 4.,

Blockchain-Strategie der Bundesregierung. (2019). *Bundesministerium für Wirtschaft und Energie, Bundesministerium für Finanzen*. Retrieved from: https://www.bmwi.de/Redaktion/DE/Publikationen/Digitale-Welt/blockchain-strategie.pdf?__blob=publicationFile&v=10

Bodin, J. (1576). *Six books on the Commonwealth*. Basil Blackwell.

C-264/14. Skatteverket v David Hedqvist ECLI:EU:C:2015:718 [22], [42], [49], [55]

Constitution of the Republic of France. art 34.

CRD: Directive 2013/36/EU of the European Parliament and of the Council of 26 June 2013 on access to the activity of credit institutions and the prudential supervision of credit institutions and investment firms, OJ L 176, 27.6.2013, p. 338–436

CRR: Regulation No 575/2013 of the European Parliament and of the Council of 26 June 2013 on prudential requirements for credit institutions and investment firms, OJ L 176, 27.6.2013, p. 1–337

Directive (EU) 2018/843 of the European Parliament and of the Council of 30 May 2018 amending Directive (EU) 2015/849 on the prevention of the use of the financial system for the purposes of money laundering or terrorist financing, and amending Directives 2009/138/EC and 2013/36/EU, OJ L 156, 19.6.2018, p. 43–74

EBA Opinion on 'virtual currencies'. (2014). EBA/Op/2014/08. London: European Banking Authority.

Firth-Butterfield, K., Brent, R., & Grant, T. (2017). Virtual Currencies, Artificial Intelligence and Emerging Legal Questions. In Banks and Financial Crime (2nd ed.). Oxford University Press.

Fox, D. (2008). *Property rights in money*. Oxford University Press.

Hayek, F. A. (1976). *Denationalisation of Money*. Institute of Economic Affairs.

Knapp, G. F. (1923). *Staatliche Theorie des Geldes (4. Ausgabe)*. Duncker und Humblot.

Lastra, R. M. (2015). *International Financial and Monetary Law* (2nd ed.). Oxford University Press.

Libra project – White Paper. (2019). *An Introduction to Libra – White Paper*. From Libra Association Members.

MiFID II: Directive 2014/65/EU of the European Parliament and of the Council on markets in financial instruments, OJ L 173, 12.6.2014, p. 349–496

Nussbaum, A. (1950). *Money in the Law – National and International*. The Foundation Press.

Payment in Gold of Brazilian Federal Loans Contracted in France (Fr. v. Braz.), 1929 P.C.I.J. (ser. A) No. 21 (July 12)

Payment of Various Serbian Loans Issued in France (Fr. v. Yugo.), 1929 P.C.I.J. (ser. A) No. 20 (July 12)

Proctor, C. (2012). *Mann on legal aspect of money* (7th ed.). Oxford University Press.

Proposal for a Directive of the European Parliament and of the Council amending Directive (EU) 2015/849 on the prevention of the use of the financial system for the purposes of money laundering or terrorist financing and amending Directive 2009/101/EC COM(2016) 450 final

Rahmatian, A. (2020). *Credit and Creed: A Critical Legal Theory of Money*. Routledge.

Savigny, C. F. (1851). *Obligationsrecht I. als Theil des heutigen Römschen Rechts*. Berlin Veit und Comp.

Alberta Statutes - The Bank Taxation Act; The Credit of Alberta Regulation Act; and the Accurate News and Information Act, 1938 CanLII 1 (SCC), [1938] SCR 100

Swiss DLT-Bill: Bundesgesetz Entwurf zur Anpassung des Bundesrechts an Entwicklungender Technik verteilter elektronischer Register, https://www.admin.ch/opc/de/federal-gazette/2020/329.pdf

U.S. Const., art. I. § 8., § 10.

VAT Directive: Council Directive 2006/112/EC of 28 November 2006 on the common system of value-added tax, OJ L 347 11.12.2006, p. 1.

Vicuña, A. S. (2010). An Institutional Theory of Money. In M. Giovanoli & D. Devos (Eds.), *International Monetary and Financial Law: the Global Crisis*. Oxford University Press.

Virtual Currency Schemes – further analysis. (2015). European Central Bank.

Weber, M. (1922). *Wirtschaft und Gesellschaft*. Mohr.

Zimmermann, C. D. (2013). *A contemporary concept of monetary sovereignty*. Oxford University Press. doi:10.1093/acprof:oso/9780199680740.001.0001

ADDITIONAL READING

Brito, J., Shadab, H., & Castillo, A. (2014). Bitcoin Financial Regulation: Securities, Derivatives, Prediction Markets and Gambling. *The Columbia Science and Technology Law Review*, *16*, 144–221.

Cvetkova, I. (2018). Cryptocurrencies legal regulation. *BRICS Law Journal*, *5*(2), 128–153. doi:10.21684/2412-2343-2018-5-2-128-153

Kaplanov, N. M. (2012). Nerdy Money: Bitcoin, the Private Digital Currency, and the Case Against its Regulation. *Loyola Consumer Law Review*, *25*(1), 111–174.

Kiviat, T. I. (2015). Beyond Bitcoin: Issues in regulating blockchain transactions. *Duke Law Journal*, *65*, 569–608.

Krover, M. R., Pelker, A. & Poteat, E. (2019) Attribution in Cryptocurrency Cases. *DOJ Journal of Federal Law and Practice*, 2019(2), 233-262.

Nabilou, H. (2019). The Dark Side of Licensing Cryptocurrency Exchanges as Payment Institutions. *Law and Financial Markets Review*, *13*(4), 1–19.

Nabilou, H., & Prüm, A. (2019). Ignorance, Debt and Cryptocurrencies: The Old and the New in the Law and Economics of Concurrent Currencies. *Journal of Financial Regulation*, *5*(1), 1–35. doi:10.1093/jfr/fjz002

Rueckert, C. (2019) Cryptocurrencies and fundamental rights. *Journal of cybersecurity*, 1-12.

KEY TERMS AND DEFINITIONS

Blockchain: A specific type of distributed ledgers, which are usually public databases spread across multiple sites.

Central Bank: An institution that manages the currency and the money supply of a state or several states forming a monetary union, and usually oversees the commercial banking system. It has a monopoly on issuing the national currency as legal tender.

Electronic Money: A currency stored in banking computer systems and backed by fiat currency, which distinguishes it from cryptocurrency.

Fiat Currency: Currencies issued by states (central banks) are regarded as real or 'fiat' currency. Fiat currency has value based on its market assessment.

Legal Tender: A medium of payment recognised by a state to be valid for meeting financial obligations on its territory.

Virtual Currency: Digital representation of value that is neither issued by a central bank or a public authority, nor necessarily attached to a fiat currency, but is accepted by natural or legal persons as a means of payment, and can be transferred, stored or traded electronically.

Chapter 9
Digital Transformation in Banks of Different Sizes:
Evidence From the Polish Banking Sector

Teresa Czerwińska
European Investment Bank, Luxembourg & University of Warsaw, Poland

Adam Głogowski
https://orcid.org/0000-0002-2135-1163
Narodowy Bank Polski, Poland

Tomasz Gromek
Narodowy Bank Polski, Poland

Paweł Pisany
Narodowy Bank Polski, Poland & Polish Academy of Sciences, Poland

ABSTRACT

Technological advances in data transmission and processing are an important structural factor influencing the banking sector. As they have an important impact on the cost base of banks and are characterized by large one-off costs, it is argued that investments in digital technologies enhance the positive returns to scale in the banking system. This in turn further improves the competitive position of the largest market players, creating a positive feedback loop. In the longer run, this leads to a polarization of the banking sector, between large universal banks and small specialized banks. These processes are important from the point of view of macroprudential policy, notably in the dimension of reducing the risks connected with the emergence of "too big to fail" institutions. The chapter illustrates these issues using the results of a survey on the investments of banks in digital transformation in Poland, focusing on the relationships between market structure, financial position, and investments in digital technologies.

DOI: 10.4018/978-1-7998-4390-0.ch009

INTRODUCTION

Technological advances in data transmission and processing are an important structural factor influencing the banking sector. As they can affect the cost base of banks, investments in digital technologies influence the competitive position of individual banks, the competitive landscape – and in medium term – the market structure of the banking sector.

Rapid technological changes challenge the role of banks in the economy. Advances in data processing and data transmission allow financial services to be delivered remotely, with limited need for in-person contact between the financial institution and the customer. This can be seen as the way in which the so-called "Fourth Industrial Revolution" - as described e.g. by Schwab (2016) manifests itself in the banking sector. Advances in information analysis and processing, driven by technology companies and developed in non-financial industries – such as e-commerce or tailored advertising based on search results or social media content – mean that banks are no longer the industry which has the competitive advantage in processing information for business purposes. This lowers the barriers to entry into the markets of some financial services[1].

As a result, banks face increased competitive pressure from fintechs, technology firms entering into finance ("bigtechs") as well as other banks or financial institutions operating cross-border. In order to stay competitive, banks are starting to look for new ways to reduce costs or new sources of income and find them in providing innovative services and solutions for their clients, like mobile banking, new channels of communication with clients, big data analytics coupled with artificial intelligence algorithms, robo-advisory, etc. Banks need to adapt to the new competitive environment and use flexible and innovative technologies.

The digital transformation of the banking sector is not without challenges for financial stability, as the importance of cyber risk increases in the operational risk profile of banks. Thus public policies have a role to play in ensuring a sustainable development path of financial system. Public authorities and financial supervisors should reconcile various goals and balance different values in their activity, i.e. supporting innovation in the banking sector, but also protecting competition and consumer rights as well ensuring level playing field for different agents and preventing regulatory arbitrage. In the context of microprudential supervision cybersecurity issues have received increased attention, notably through the issuance of guidelines on managing cybersecurity risks[2]. As far as macroprudential perspective is concerned, potential structural changes, for example increasing concentration in the tech-suppliers markets, need to be monitored[3]. A trade-off between development pace and sustainability exists and well-balanced regulatory scheme may slow down financial innovation in the short term, while maximizing benefits versus risks ratio in the long-term.

As investments in digital technologies are characterized by large one-off costs, their implementation is easier for banks which are characterized by a large scale of operations and sound financial position. Given that many of these innovations result in lower long-term operational costs, it is argued that they enhance positive returns to scale in the banking system. This, in turn, further improves the competitive position of the largest market players, creating a positive feedback loop. Furthermore, this amplifies the "demise of the middle tier" in the banking sector – i.e. medium sized universal banks are less able to compete with the largest players, as the mid-tier banks find it hard to invest in digitalization at the same pace as the largest ones and thus are at risk of being stuck with higher cost ratios and lower profitability. In the longer run, this leads to a polarization of the banking sector between large universal banks and small specialized banks. Another factor accelerating this process is the growing role of remote (internet and mobile) banking, giving the most technologically proficient banks the ability to compete for clients without the need to scale up their physical network. The role of remote transaction channels is particularly important during disruptions in the functioning of the economy which make it difficult to use face-to-face communication, such as during public health emergencies or natural disasters. Of course these solutions can function only when the telecommunications infrastructure is operational and is not affected by the disruption in question.

These processes are important from the point of view of macroprudential policy, notably in the dimension of reducing the risks connected with the emergence of institutions "too big to fail". The evolving operational profile of banks, notably the increasing role of cloud computing, has also potential implications for microprudential supervisors, changing the composition of risks to which banks are exposed.

The purpose of this chapter is to investigate how banks, which are driven by the need to respond to the ongoing "fintechisation" of financial services, invest in innovative technology. We base our research on the Polish banking, drawing conclusions about the impact this investment has on the competition and structure of the banking sector.

The scale of a bank's business is likely to affect its response to the emergence of competition from fintech, as well as the actual reaction of the bank to the technological challenges arising from the operating environment. To support this statement, we show that innovation, technological profiles and business objectives of specific asset size peer-groups of big, medium and small banks are structurally different with potentially fundamental consequences for their future competitive position and, consequently, for the market structure.

We investigate these relationships using the results of a survey[4] about the investments banks make in the digital transformation in Poland, focusing on market share, financial position and investments in digital technologies of individual banks. The results of the survey were published by NBP[5], however in this chapter we try to contribute by interpreting the results of the survey in a broader scientific context, pointing to potential interlinkages between technology investments and market structure in the banking sector.

Banks in Poland are aware of the growing digitization of the financial sector and the increasing competition from both fintechs and large technology companies - bigtechs. For this reason, they have been investing in new IT solutions and modern technologies. Some of them see themselves explicitly as transforming into "technology companies with a banking license"[6]. While the empirical work has been focused on the Polish market, banks in many markets worldwide face, and respond to, similar challenges, as their business have to face both smaller fintech firms and large technology companies (see e.g. World Economic Forum (2017) for an overview of the processes disrupting the traditional business models of finance).

LITERATURE REVIEW: INNOVATION AND BANK PERFORMANCE

The finance and banking sector, like all competitive industries, has market participants striving to outcompete their peers through increased operational efficiency, development of new products and processes in order to increase market shares and incomes. This can be analysed from the point of view of Schumpeter's "creative destruction" approach, whereby technological advances allow firms to introduce new products, services and organizational processes thus gaining market share at the expense of their non-innovating competitors. Some are then able to leverage their new competitive position and gradually accumulate "monopolistic rents", increasing their profitability still further (see e.g. Schumpeter (1943), Cainelli, Evangelista & Savona (2006) and the discussion on productivity impact of ICT adoption summarized by Scott, Van Reenen & Zachariadis (2017)).

In this context, the economic literature investigates the link between innovation in banking and the various aspects of the functioning of the banking system (e.g. cost efficiency, stability, risk taking)

One has to acknowledge that innovation – despite being an intuitively easy term – does not seem to have a universal definition in economic literature. Beck, Chen, Ling & Song (2016) document this disparity by pointing out that studies of innovation in banking do not focus on measures widely used in other industries, such as patents, as innovations in banking rarely result in patents.

Frame & White (2002) propose a grouping of innovations in financial industry into: new financial products, new services (or modes of delivery, such as internet or mobile channels of access to financial services), new processes in provision of financial services (an analogy to production processes in manufacturing) and new organizational forms. Most empirical studies focus on one of these areas, such as new forms of financial securities (Grinblatt & Longstaff, 2000), the adoption of credit scoring techniques (Frame & White 2009), (Akhavein, Frame & White. 2005), new organizational forms, such as banks focusing on the Internet as their distribution channel (e.g. DeYoung (2005), Cyree, Delcoure & Dickens (2008)), or new forms of mortgage lending (Gerardi, Rosen & Willen, 2010).

There are also country-specific studies on the influence of adoption of specific ICT solutions on bank performance and cost efficiency (e.g. Ardizzi, Crudu & Petraglia (2019) for use of ATMs by Italian banks, Holden & El-Bannany (2004) for ATMs in UK banks, Gündoğdu & Taskin (2017) for Turkey), or cross country studies on the impact of specific innovations (e.g. Scott et al (2017) for SWIFT adoption). These generally suggest that the implementation of ICT innovations improves cost efficiency at individual banks.

Relatively few studies (such as Beck et al., 2016) try to use a wider measure of bank innovation (in their case, R&D expenditure and value of off-balance sheet items) and track its impact on financial stability and economic growth. This research tries to assess the relative merit of competing views on macro effects of financial innovation. The view of innovation which seems to be dominant in the literature in 1990s and early 2000s is sometimes called the innovation-growth view, which emphasizes the positive impact of financial innovations on the quality of banking services, risk sharing, financial inclusion and efficiency of resource allocation. Financial innovation is thus seen as enhancing economic growth. On the other hand, the experience of the global financial crisis of 2007-2009 and its aftermath led to the reappreciation of fragilities generated in the financial sphere through excessive debt - as earlier suggested by Minsky (1992) - and the role of financial innovation (especially new financial instruments) in excessive risk taking – the so-called innovation-fragility hypothesis.

In the context of the relationship between investment in innovative technology and market structure, an important question is whether this investment influences economies of scale and scope in banking. Boot (2017) shows that the discussion on the economies of scale and scope resulted in changing conclusions over time. Studies prior to 2000, as reviewed e.g. by Berger, Demsetz & Strahan (1999), did not offer conclusive results, although at that point in time most studies were based on data from relatively restrictively regulated banking systems. The more recent literature, such as Wheelock and Wilson (2011), find positive economies of scale in banking. An important strand of the research, notably inspired by bailouts of financial institutions during the global financial crisis of 2007-2009, focuses on funding cost advantages driven by implicit government guarantees as a cause of economies of scale (the "too-big-to-fail premium"). However, other authors, such as Boot (2003), point to information technology-related economies as another potential source. On this point, empirical research yields mixed results – as Boot (2017) reports, researchers do not identify a stable relationship between investment in information technology and bank efficiency. However, he also notes the potential of IT to enable scope economies with multiple product offerings to customers, using remote distribution channels. These developments might intensify competition as physical presence in local markets becomes less important.

A stronger role of ICT in banking also increases the importance of cyber risk for the functioning of the banking system. For example, Kopp, Kaffenberger & Wilson (2017) provide an overview of systemic aspects of cyber risk for financial services, while Bouveret (2018) proposes a quantitative framework for the assessment of cyber risk. A study of a large dataset of cyber risk incidents by Aldasoro, Gambacorta, Giudici & Leach (2020) shows that the financial sector experiences attacks more frequently than other sectors, although the costs of cyber incidents are not as high as in other sectors, perhaps due to the higher investment in cyber resilience by financial firms in comparison to other sectors. However, a detailed assessment of the cyber risk exposure consequences of investment in innovative ICT solutions by banks is beyond the scope of this chapter as it has not been covered by the survey addressed to banks which constitutes the basis for this research.

In summary, while multiple dimensions of innovation in banking have been explored in economic literature, the impact on competition and market structure in banking has received a little less attention. However, some research suggests that investments in IT innovations have the potential to improve cost efficiency of banks as well as enable economies of scale and scope in reaching new clients and thus improve the competitive position of banks developing their digital capabilities.

INNOVATIONS IN THE FINANCIAL SECTOR: TYPES REACTIONS PRESENTED BY BANKS

Innovative financial services are an area where multiple types of financial institutions compete. Financial innovations are developed and offered by smaller specialized companies grouped under the "fintech" label (including start-ups), large technology companies entering into finance (so-called "bigtechs") and traditional financial institutions like banks and insurance companies.

As an illustration of the scope of activity of fintechs, and consequent competitive pressures for incumbent financial institutions, market research in Poland (see Figure 1) shows that fintechs offer their products and services in 11 categories of activity.

The most important field of activity is payments. More than 50% of fintech companies report offering payment services. The second biggest field of activity is credit and loans provided online. And the third one encompasses sales channels, which include services supporting online sales processes used by financial firms. Platforms aggregating offers of banking products are an example of this category of fintechs.

Fintech companies direct their products mainly to small and medium enterprises and financial institutions (see Figure 2). This shows that many fintechs aim to cooperate with established financial companies. This mirrors the findings e.g. of the World Economic Forum report (WEF, 2017) which shows that established financial institutions are attempting to change the competitive threat of fintechs into opportunity for development. Cooperation with fintechs allows incumbents to partially outsource the development of innovative products, as well as use the market experience of fintechs as a testing ground to investigate market demand for new products.

Figure 1. Products and services offered by fintechs in Poland
Source: Cashless.pl & Accenture (2018). Based on a survey conducted in April 2018 (respondents could select more than one category of client/product).

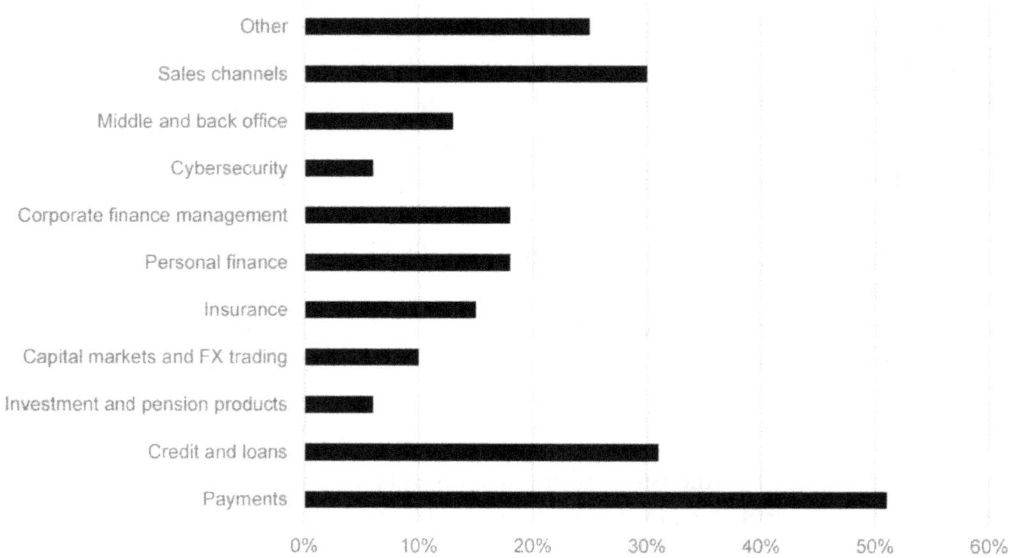

Figure 2. Target markets for fintechs in Poland
Source: Cashless.pl & Accenture (2018). Based on a survey conducted in April 2018 (respondents could select more than one category of client/product).

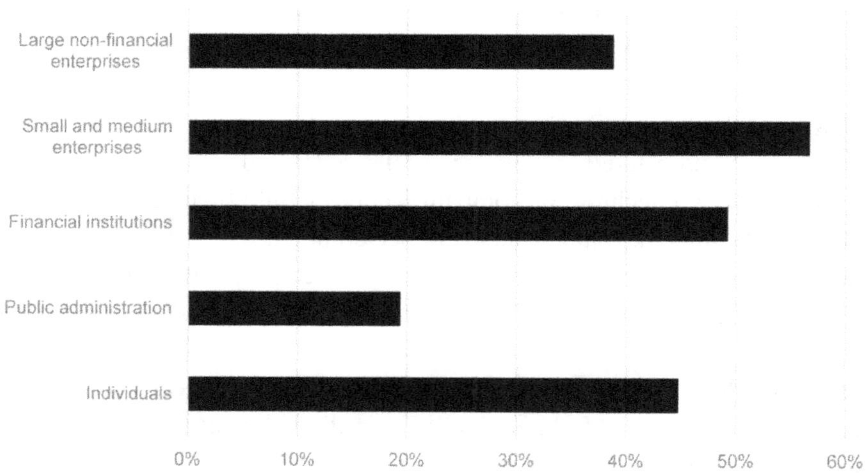

Fintech activity varies across countries. Frost (2020) finds that fintech activity is higher in countries where there is a significant unmet demand for financial services (i.e. financial inclusion gaps) and where financial services are costly, possibly pointing to limited competition between incumbent institutions. Against these criteria, the Polish market offers relatively limited opportunities for the development of fintechs. The Polish banking sector does not exhibit significant concentration[7], and the level of financial inclusion is high. As of 31 December 2018, 87% of the population in Poland has a bank account, there are 41.5m current bank accounts in a population of 38m people. There are also more than 41m payment cards. Moreover, the universal banking model gives banks a good base to offer a wide-range package of financial services including financial innovation.

The Polish banking sector made a huge technology leap in the 1990s and the 2000s, adopting what used to be the modern technology at the time. For example, the sector introduced modern card payments, bypassing other standards, such as cheques. Poland is also one of the leaders in implementing contactless card payments[8].

Due to the strong position of the banking sector in the Polish financial market, fintechs can only find relatively small market gaps, in which banks are either generally not interested or they are not yet interested. The niches where fintechs can develop their activity include:

- small-value loans to high-risk individuals,
- electronification of small-value purchases (bus tickets, train tickets, parking fees etc.),
- small and micro enterprise factoring and debt-collecting services,
- FX exchange services,
- price comparison of financial services and development of distribution platforms offering products from multiple providers,
- small-scale market funding for enterprises (debt and equity crowdfunding),
- internet payments and their extensions such as deferred payments.

Moreover, banks do not stand still in the face of fintech phenomena. In Poland we can distinguish five main types of the banks' responses to the fintech sector.

The first one relies on increasing the banks' expenditures on innovative technologies, either through in-house development, or through joint work with IT providers. One such area of investment is cloud computing which, according to many bankers, has the potential to significantly change the operations of financial institutions. In Poland, 63% of enterprises are interested in using solutions offered by cloud platforms.[9] The advantages of the cloud are: flexibility of operations, reduction of capital expenditure, improvement of remote working and faster circulation of information and documents, as well as easier data recovery. Banks and other financial institutions are preparing for the expansion of fintechs and bigtechs and have been investing in the infrastructure enabling the provision of modern services based on digital technologies for a number of years already. For large banks, in-house development of technology takes an important role (see Figure 3 below) but, in one form or another, almost all banks, even small cooperative ones, respond in this way[10].

The second type of response involves the banks' incubation and acceleration programs. They rely on co-financing of a fintech by the bank at an early stage of its development and on providing business mentoring in the form of consultations with bank experts. During the acceleration program, fintechs can test their solutions using the bank's research facilities. Approximately 10 biggest banks in Poland have launched such programs. These banks have the strongest financial position in the Polish banking sector, generating the vast majority (more than 80%) of the sector's financial results.

The third type of response is cooperation with fintechs and bigtechs. Examples of such cooperation include banks offering payment solutions developed by technology companies (such as GooglePay, ApplePay or GarminPay), or distributing their products through fintech-developed platforms aggregating offers for consumers[11]. Startup-scale fintechs find it hard to compete with banks, especially if their products face competition from traditional institutions, which have the advantage of customer trust and an established client base. For these fintechs, the choice to cooperate with traditional financial institutions in order to offer improved services may be a rational choice (a win-win situation)[12].

The fourth type involves a takeover or investment in a fintech company. As the WEF (2017) report summarizes, the growth of fintechs has provided financial institutions with an external supply of innovation which they can use through acquisitions and partnerships. This activity is visible both in large global institutions[13] as well as more local banks[14].

The fifth type of reaction is simply entering into a competition with fintech sector. An example of such a project which aims to provide a product which can compete with fintech solutions is the development of the BLIK payment system which has been operational since 2015 and can be used for retail internet payments, as well as for peer-to-peer instant transfers (NBP 2019). The system was developed by a consortium of Polish banks, and is a relatively rare example of a common product being developed by competing institutions. Another example is the increasing digitization of the loan origination process by banks, especially in the case of consumer loans, where banks face competition from non-bank internet lenders which offer loans at higher interest rates, but in a quicker, fully digitized, origination process.

The types of responses presented by banks to fintech sector can be illustrated by the most popular channels banks get their innovative solutions through. Figure 3 presents the percentage of technology-based innovative use cases implemented by the surveyed banks that have been sourced through particular channels: in-house, intra-capital group transfers, Business-to-Business services (B2B), and acceleration programs. Despite the fact that in-house efforts as well as B2B are important sources of innovative solutions in all peer groups, survey results reveal some important structural differences. In-house work is the main way for realizing innovative projects in the biggest banks as they possess enough resources to develop technology-driven innovations themselves. It means that they are able to work on tailored solutions which may boost efficiency of their processes in comparison to other peer groups. Moreover, only big banks in the Polish sector can successfully conduct accelerators for start-up ventures and then incorporate their selected ideas into the banking business model. Medium and small banks are focused primarily on market sourcing (B2B) and off-the-shelf solutions. Intra-group transfers are relatively less popular and are used by some banks which are part of multinational financial groups.

Summing up, the relations between banks and fintech sector in Poland are complex, but it seems that cooperation elements prevail over pure competition. The significance of B2B sourcing suggests that technology companies are focused on delivering solutions to banks and it is consistent with the abovementioned results of the *Map of Polish FinTech* (Cashless.pl & Accenture, 2018), where financial institutions have been indicated as one of the two main target clients for financial innovation sector. In-house work that prevails in the biggest banks may be the source of efficient, tailored solutions and it shows that technology is becoming the core strategy in the most competitive banks.

BACKGROUND: MARKET STRUCTURE AND PROFITABILITY IN POLISH BANKING SECTOR

In a very competitive environment of rather deconcentrated structure – as is the case of the Polish banking system – reactions to direct competition from other entities requires banks to invest in highly cost efficient technologies so that they can keep or regain their market position. The need to react to competition from fintechs imposes a further strain on banks, as all five responses to fintech listed above are costly.

Figure 3. The main sources of innovative solutions for Polish banks in peer-groups
Source: NBP and PFSA survey.

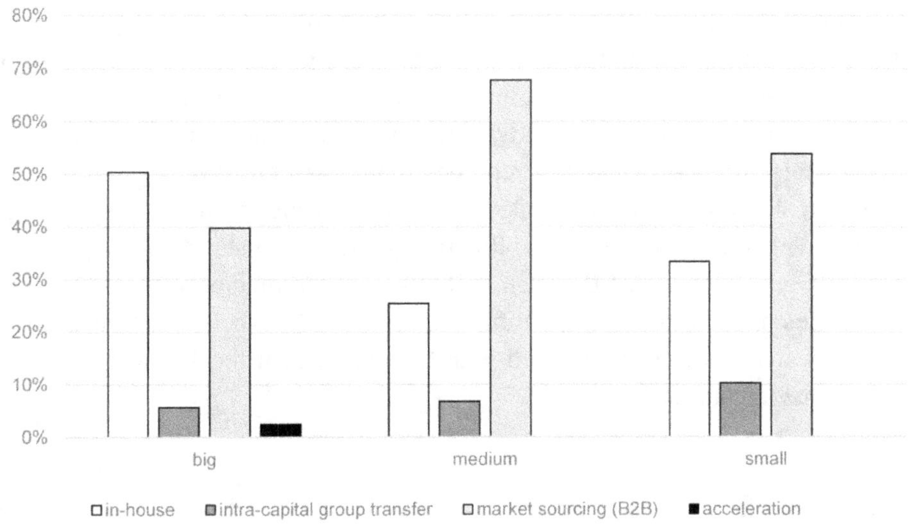

The economic literature suggests that economies of scale are present in banking. But they concern and benefit the biggest entities mostly via the most prominent channel, namely by funding costs and the "too-big-to-fail" premium. Active regulatory policy tries to soften some of these scale effects by introducing, for example, specific capital buffers to the systemically important banks. Consequently, the strength of scale effects may evolve over time, to the extent that policies aiming to lower the effects of "too big to fail" phenomena achieve their goals.

Figure 4. ROA, weighted average (peer-groups, share of total assets weighting)
Source: NBP

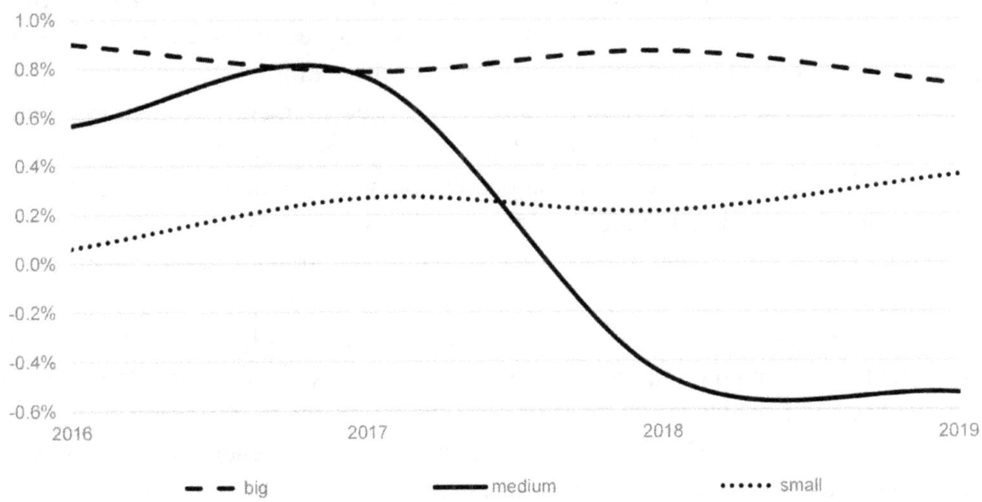

Over the 2016-2019 period, a vast majority of institutions achieved positive financial results. The Polish banking sector shows consistently higher profitability among large banks. Some medium-sized banks posted losses in 2018 and 2019. Even though the number of banks with negative profitability and their share in the sector's assets remained low, their results weighted significantly on respective peer-group's profitability since 2018[15]. The biggest and most profitable banks have more ability to invest in modern technologies and gain an innovative advantage over competitors and thus – if they manage the investment process well – are best placed to strengthen their market position.

As shown in Figure 4, the ROA for big banks is substantially higher than that of medium and small banks. Big banks manage to create a safe profitability margin which translates into a significant advantage over other direct competitors on which they can build their strong market position by investing in new innovative technologies and solutions. Even more importantly though, as illustrated above, medium-sized and small banks may soon be confronted with financial constrains because their profitability is low or negative in some instances.

DATA AND METHODS

Information and Communication Technologies (ICT) influence financial services sector globally. They affect the efficiency and stability of the banking sector also in Poland. To investigate the scope and scale of ICT spending, as relevant data – beyond IT spending under national FINREP reporting – was scarce, the Polish Financial Services Authority and the NBP conducted a targeted survey regarding innovation amongst commercial banks. We use the data from this survey to investigate the differences in innovative investments between groups of banks.

The following questions were part of the exercise:

- Question 1 concerned expenditure on innovation in 2016-2019 period, and the use of IT and ICT innovation tax deductions by banks
- Question 2 looked into the main sources of innovations, including in-house, acceleration, acquisitions of FinTech companies, import and implementation of technologies used within the parent group, purchase of external products and services. It also examined the projects where specific investments and technologies were implemented (e.g. development of e-banking platforms and channels; implementation of API; cooperation with e-commerce entities or platforms; remote identification, including biometrics; development and implementation of tools to identify and fraud-prevention; automation and digitization of business processes).
- Question 3 looked at the expenditure, its time structure and individual sources of innovation defined in Question 2.
- Question 4 delved into the technological structure and amounts of their investments in IT infrastructure, the roll out and the implementation of cloud services; use of Big Data solutions; artificial intelligence and machine learning; remote identification and biometrics; DLT as well as automation and digitization as well as other specific technologies implemented by banks. Respondents were also asked to provide a self-assessment as to what extent their initiatives were gradual or revolutionary and whether they were geared at cost reduction, revenue increase, risk reduction, improvement of client experience.

- Question 5 concerned the use of innovation in individual areas and business processes (risk management, sales and support functions within organizations).
- Question 6 looked at the scope and scale of cloud computing, outsourcers and outsourcees.

The survey was conducted by the NBP (central bank of Poland) and the Polish Financial Supervision Authority in the third quarter of 2019. The survey covered 26 commercial banks (including universal, specialist and associating banks), whose total assets exceed 79% of the total assets of the Polish banking sector. The survey covered expenditure on both simpler development activities and solutions allowing banks to reduce costs, often referred to as "digital transformation", as well as more innovative applications of information technology, which could potentially change the business models of banks. Banks reported total investments, with additional breakdown into channels (e.g. internal development, outsourcing) through which the obtained the relevant products or services. Banks were also asked to report the innovative IT investments broken down by technologies used, objectives that they wanted to attain, as well as business areas in which investments were made. The survey used a written questionnaire with predefined lists of possible answers, but banks could also augment the responses with additional explanations.

CASE STUDY: INVESTMENTS IN INNOVATION IN THE POLISH BANKING SECTOR

Polish commercial banks surveyed by the authorities in 2019 (see previous section for the details on the survey) reported that expenses on innovative ICT had increased steadily over the preceding years. Their declared ICT spending amounted to EUR 268m in 2016 and expanded by 46% to EUR 391m in 2019.

In our analysis we tried to disentangle growth patterns in innovative ICT spending into potential trends specific to particular peer-groups of banks based on size. We have compared three peer-groups of small, medium-sized and big entities and found tangible evidence of spending expansion in all groups driven by innovation needs.[16] As shown in Figure 5, over the period 2016-2019 within the sample, big banks increased their annual innovative ICT expenditure from ca. EUR 219m in 2016 to EUR 305m in 2019, i.e. by 40%. Simultaneously, while medium-sized banks ICT investments rose by 70%, from EUR 32m to 54.5m, small banks boosted spending figures even more, namely by 81%.

In nominal and aggregate terms, ICT spending was by far the largest among big banks. Yet expenditure growth rates were substantially stronger among medium and the highest in small banks, where expenses accelerated notably in 2018 and 2019 (see Figure 5). These patterns illustrate some sort of "catching-up" efforts of medium-sized and small banks and an indication of their attempt to keep up with the general pace of innovation among financial market competitors and new market entrants, either bigtech or fintech companies. However, based on the evidence gathered, such catching-up process over a longer term horizon may be materially constrained by a falling or even a negative profitability (return-on-assets) in some instances, as shown in Figure 3.

In order to cross-check the answers provided by banks in the survey, we considered potential proxies to compare overall survey results with available micro-prudential reporting data. We used national financial reporting dataset on "general management costs" incurred by banks on solo basis[17] and its item 4 data ("IT costs"). With all caveats which the data entails, we have found that IT expenditure was a robust proxy to compare a bank's ICT spending declared in the survey with the real spending reported by banks.[18] The declared spending growth and overall rates of the ICT spending budget expansion are confirmed by official financial reporting data within the banking system and among peer-groups of banks. They show a broadly continuous trend of increasing spending on IT both over the 2016-2019 period, as well as over the longer horizon (see Figure 6). Since 2011, IT expenditure has been rising in the banking sector, with small and medium banks recording higher growth rates than big banks. Nevertheless, the expenditure of big bank still dominated by an overwhelming margin.

Figure 5. Innovative ICT spending declared by banks (per peer-group, EURm, current prices)
Source: NBP and PFSA survey.

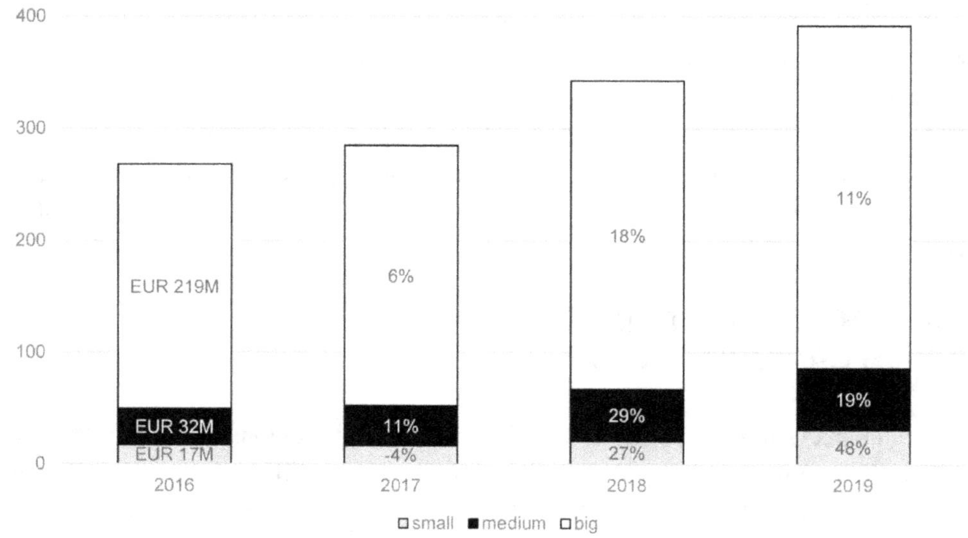

Figure 6. IT costs per peer group (EURm, left-hand scale, current prices) and their yearly growth rate (right-hand scale)
Source: Official financial reporting data (FRN009.4), authors' calculations

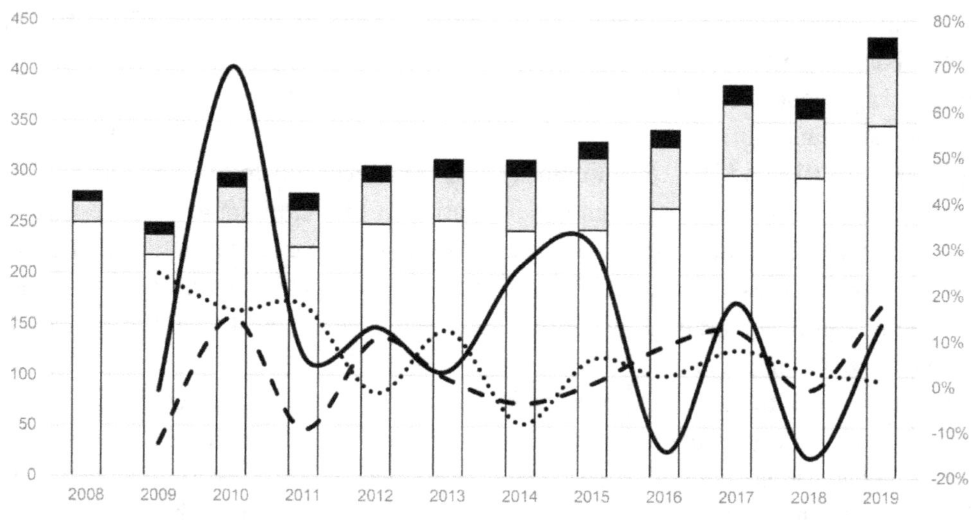

As shown in Figure 6, over the period 2016-2019, the big banks included in the sample increased their annual IT expenditure from ca. EUR 242m in 2016 to EUR 353m in 2019, i.e. by 46%, although its share to total banking system assets dropped by 10% (from 0.20% in 2016 to 0.18% in 2019). Simultaneously, medium-sized banks' IT costs rose by 19%, from EUR 60m to 71m, and small banks boosted their spending figures by 12%.

All in all, total ICT spending declared by big banks in the survey amounted to EUR 1033m throughout the four year period, medium sized – EUR 168m, and small – EUR 86m. Share of big banks' in total declared ICT spending of the sample during the 2016-2019 period exceeded 80%, with medium and small at the level of 13% and 7%. The ICT costs reported by banks amounted to EUR 1535m, big banks' IT expenditure stood at EUR 1203m (78% share) in the last four years since 2016, medium – EUR 258m (17% of the total), and small – EUR 74m (i.e. 5% share). Thus, we see clear evidence of a bi-polar structure, a two-tier banking system, where largest institutions are clearly most profitable and, therefore, able to invest consistently in ICT development over long-term horizon. They should be able to withstand competition from outside, fintech and bigtech companies in particular, and from direct competitors in the banking system. At the same time, there is a large portion of the sector, involving medium and small banks, that over the last few years reinforced substantially its ICT development efforts and increased IT costs to catch-up with recent instantaneous market- and competition-driven pressure to innovate. However, such efforts may be constrained by very low or negative profitability among smaller institutions.

It is interesting to note that despite rapid asset expansion throughout the last decade, per peer-group, medium and small banks invested more – relatively to total banking system assets – than the 10 biggest banks shown in Figure 7 below. The difference suggests that large banks enjoy some benefits of scale. However, the large gap of innovation-driven IT investments of medium and small banks and 10 biggest entities seen since 2010, narrowed down considerably in recent years. Using micro-prudential reporting data on IT costs, we observed the relative IT costs drop among the small banks from 0,25% in 2013 to 0,18% in 2019 . This is most probably due to the looming profitability constraints within this peer-group. Medium-sized banks recorded a lesser drop (namely from 0,21% in 2015 to 0,16% in 2019). Consequently, the gap between peer-groups closed by a significant margin, either because the competition pressures that big banks faced were not that intense, or the effects of earlier investments were vast and proportionate as their more recent response was feeble and postponed (in 2015 and 2018).

Catching-up process is further evidenced by a comparison of the share of each bank group in innovative ICT spending, IT costs and assets, as provided in Figure 8 below. Whereas the share in declared spending and IT costs among big banks decreased somewhat in recent years, it was generally lower by 2 to 8 p.p. compared to their share in total assets. For medium-sized and small banks, the share of declared spending and IT costs were generally higher than their share in total assets and it increased somewhat within the period analyzed, 2016-2019. We consider these as another piece of evidence of the "catching-up" efforts among medium and small banks, in particular since 2018.

In the next step we strive to take a closer look at the technology structure of expenditures and goals of innovations in the Polish banking sector. Figure 9 presents the expenditure of banks on innovative technologies broken down by technology type. The responses show that vast majority of technology expenses in the whole sector is related to the improvement and optimization of the already used, well-established bank systems. The second most important category is automation and digitization of processes that until now were implemented mostly without the support of ICT solutions. A significant amount of expenses was directed to the development of the IT resources and infrastructure that should allow for the implementation of cloud computing in the coming years. The fourth most important expenditure category was Big Data, however it accounted for a relatively small proportion of the investments.

In order to understand the way and reason for technology investments in the sector, we have asked the surveyed banks for indication of the main objectives of these innovations. In the analyzed period, expenditure on innovative technologies in the Polish banking sector was primarily used to reduce costs. In 2019, 19 banks indicated that cost reduction was the goal of investments in innovation. The following objectives were of lesser importance: improving the quality of customer experience (in 16 banks); increase in revenues (in 15 banks) and risk mitigation (in 15 banks).

Figure 7. Banks' IT costs (per peer groups) as percentage of total assets of each peer group
Source: Official financial reporting data, authors' calculations

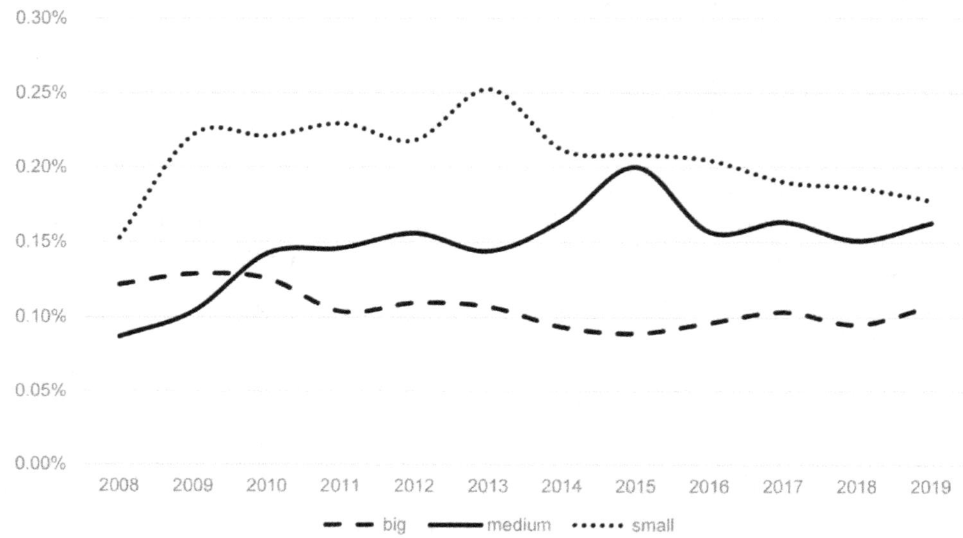

Figure 8. Banks' share in total assets, innovative ITC spending and IT costs (per peer-groups)
Source: NBP and PFSA survey.

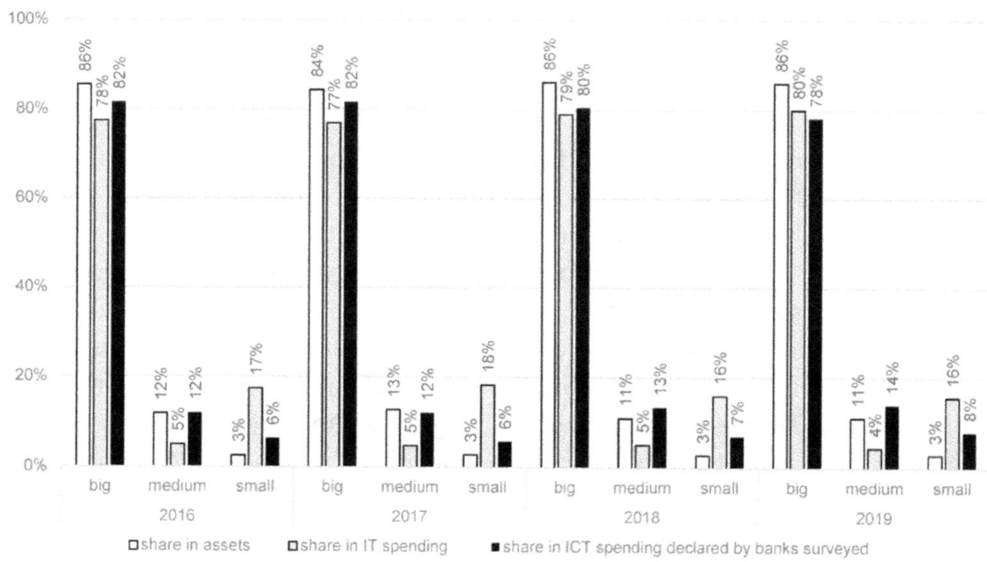

Figure 9. Banks' expenditures on technology innovations (EUR million, current prices)
Source: NBP and PFSA survey.

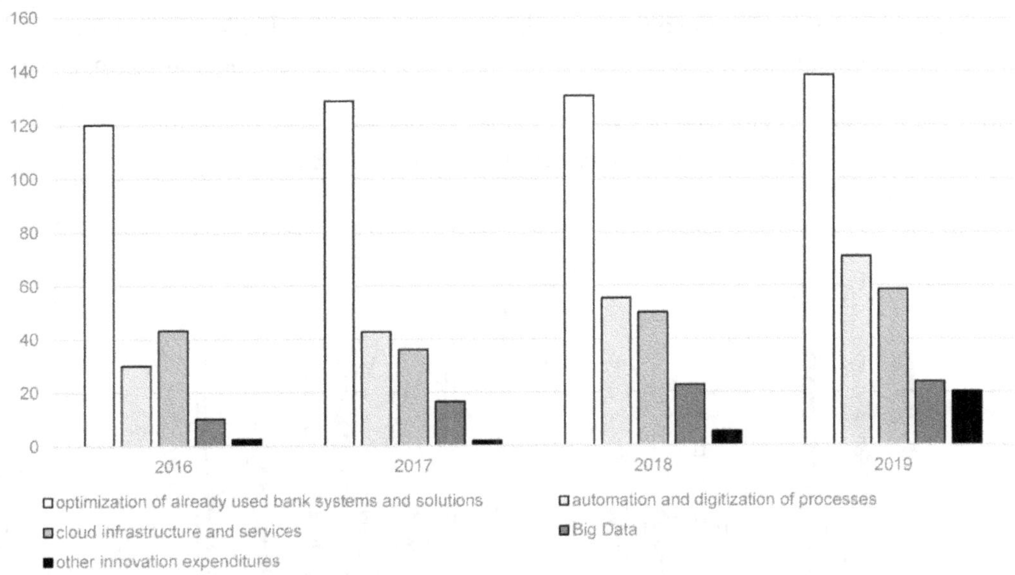

Figure 10 presents the percentage of banks in peer groups that reported innovations aiming to achieve a given goal. In the biggest banks two goals of innovations prevail, i.e. cost reduction and revenue increase. Client experience improvement is the third most important area, and may be linked to the response of banks to changes in client expectations driven by new market entrants, as well as by providers of digital non-financial services. Corroborating evidence can be seen in a report by Deloitte[19] which classifies the Polish banking system (based on the assessment of 5 largest banks) among leaders in the quality of consumer digital banking.

In the medium banks, cost reduction is the most vital motivation for innovative projects. The relative significance of other goals, in particular revenue increase and client experience improvement, is weaker. For small banks, the *other goals* category prevails. Qualitative answers provided by banks in this question allow to associate this answer with expenses for operational support and maintenance of existing systems and gradual digitization of subsequent processes. Moreover, the figure shows that the percentage of small banks indicating cost reduction as a goal of innovations has risen since 2016. One can assume that this is the first phase of going into technology projects by financial institutions. Boosting revenues as a target in innovative venture comes later. It seems that the next phase of technology leap may be once again associated with back office processes and migrating into cloud computing solutions.

In general, Figure 10 illustrates the advantages of big banks in Poland over the rest of sector that comes from more sophisticated implementation of technology innovations, in particular focus on revenues and client experience. Their investments go beyond cost savings and streamlining operations and aim to strengthen their market position.

Furthermore, we have identified significant and structurally different innovation profiles of all three peer-groups analyzed. Their technological development paths diverge substantially.

Figures 11-13 show the percentage of banks in each peer group reporting use of a particular technology in a particular business area. Large banks reported using more advanced technologies more often than other groups. Their business lines more frequently used and implemented technologies that are considered more sophisticated (e.g. BigData Analytics, Data Science, AI&ML) and forward-looking so that they would likely develop additional technological advantage over smaller competitors. Consequently, innovative capacities would allow big banks to make a more fundamental leap into cloud-based banking and use fully the potential of BigData and AI&ML, with multiplying effects for their competitive position.

Figure 10. Percentage of banks in peer groups that indicated a given technology expenditure goal
Source: NBP and PFSA survey.

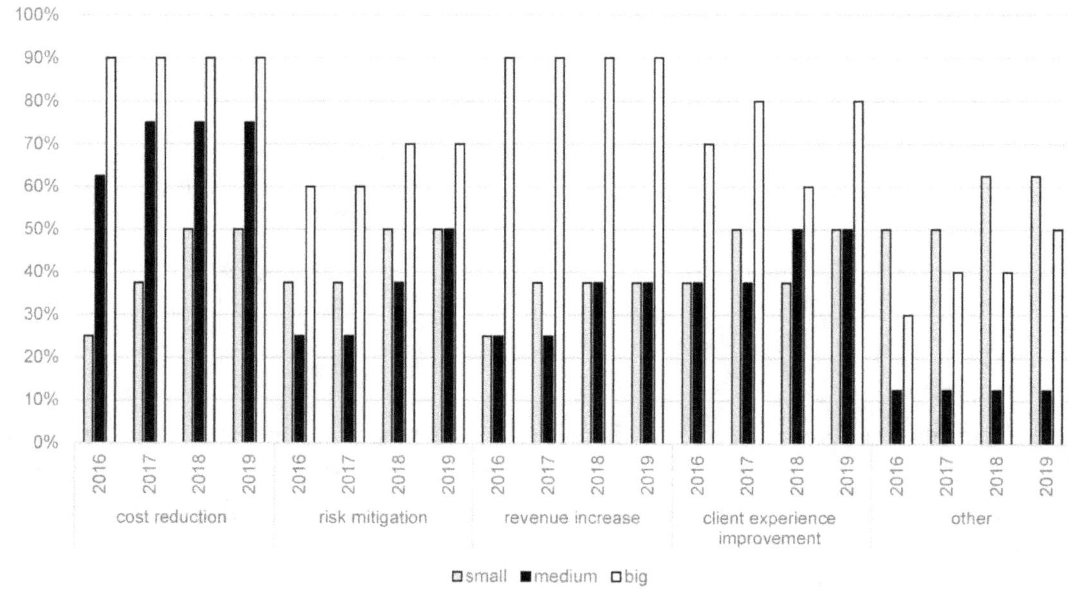

Figure 11. Innovation profile, technologies implemented by risk management function (percentage of banks per peer-group)
Source: NBP and PFSA survey.

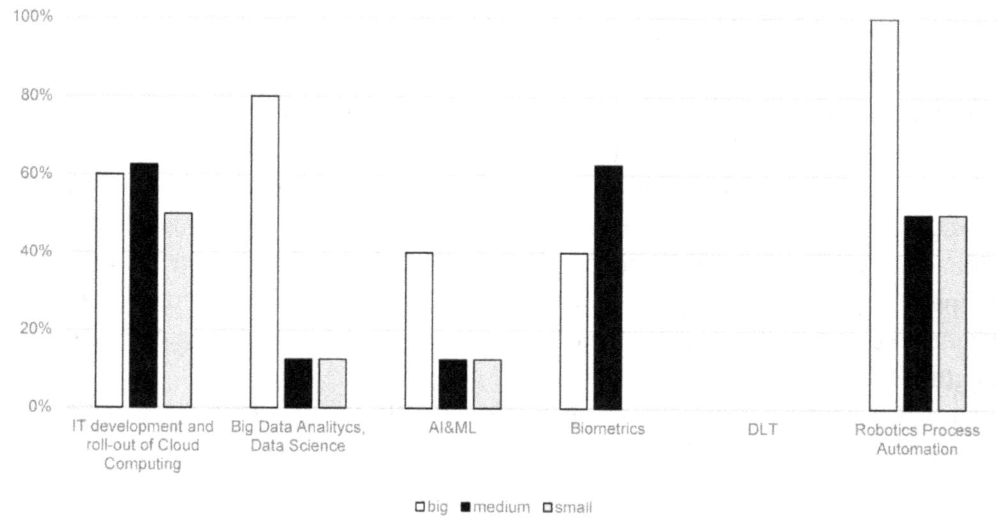

Medium-sized and small banks were significantly less advanced, despite few instances where efforts to innovate (e.g. biometrics in risk management) were substantial. These may mean that medium and small banks could remain technologically impaired and structurally trapped with their long-term business plan viability and expansion at stake.

Overall, banks used RPA technologies and solutions most widely and commonly as part of their innovation schemes during the period 2016-2019 regardless of specific business lines prescribed and analyzed in the survey. Along all business lines (i.e. risk management[20], internal support functions within organizations[21] and sales functions[22]) RPA dominated among all peer groups of banks. Significant innovative efforts were also reported by many banks in all three peer-groups in IT development and Cloud Computing roll-out measures. Expansion of risk management business line was most technology intensive. Sales and client management functions were slightly less innovation-demanding but Big Data, AI&ML and biometrics application was relatively frequently reported.

Figure 12. Innovation profile, technologies implemented by HR and compliance functions (percentage of banks per peer-group)
Source: NBP and PFSA survey.

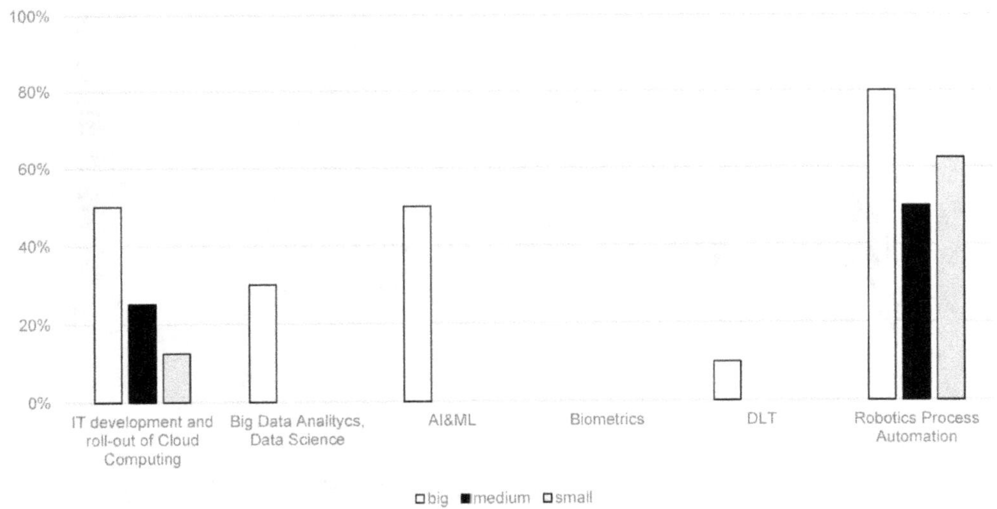

The use of cloud solutions in the banking sector is quite low. 16 out of 26 banks did not report using this technology. However, the scale of innovation expenses in the sector, especially on the ICT infrastructure, indicates that propensity to use cloud computing may significantly rise in the coming years. The development path of cloud solutions will strongly depend on regulatory environment, among others Financial Stability Authority outsourcing soft law acts. The regulatory requirements shape the perspectives for cloud computing significantly and direct the dialogue between banks, technology providers and supervisors is essential to reach potential benefits coming from migration to cloud computing. In 2019, the Polish Cloud Platform (*Operator Chmury Krajowej*) started a joint venture with Google as its main technology partner[23], with the aim to provide cloud services for Polish commercial and government entities. Cooperation with a large technology company creates the possibility to meet data protection standards and opens wide opportunities for Polish banks in the future. One can assume that the biggest banks, being the most efficient and technology-oriented, will be the first to benefit from the new possibilities.

The survey conducted by NBP does not currently indicate any risk of a concentration of cloud services providers. However, it still should be treated as a potential threat as the market is evolving. As the analysis by FSB (2019) shows, cloud technology may offer security and operational resilience benefits, yet significant failures of cloud service providers are not impossible. Such a failure may compromise the integrity or confidentiality of data, disrupting the operations of a financial institution, or resulting in penalties under data protection rules. In concentrated cloud services markets, these risks could be further amplified, potentially leading to system-wide disruptions or even stability risks if financial institutions were to increase their reliance on cloud technology for core operations. These risks underscore the need to require cloud service providers to fulfill high security and (financial and technical) resilience standards.

Figure 13. Innovation profile, technologies implemented by sales and client management functions (share of banks per peer-groups)
Source: NBP and PFSA survey.

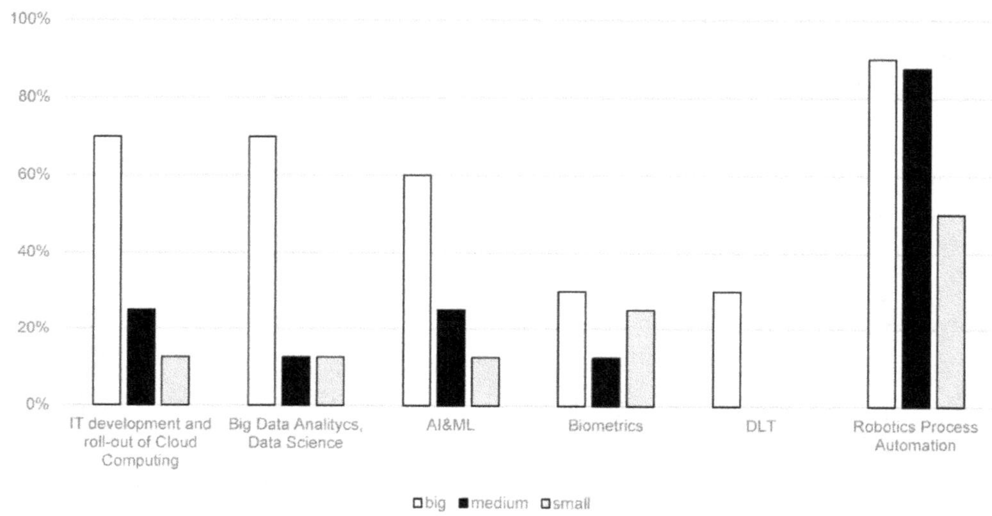

Summing up, the technological structure of expenses and declared goals suggest that technology change in the Polish banking sector is rather gradual and still focused on well-established ICT technologies. In terms of expenditure volumes, ML&AI, Big Data and blockchain play a minor role. However, in the next few years gradual investments should allow banks to make a significant back-office technology leap, associated mainly with the cloud computing.

CONCLUSION

Investments in digital technologies are characterized by significant, initial one-off costs. Their implementation is easier for banks with a large scale of operations and a sound financial position. Many of these innovative technologies drive long-term operational costs down for banks and bring positive returns based on scale in the banking system, and further improve the competitive position of largest market players by creating a positive feedback loop. However, conducting a technological transformation of a complex entity such as a bank is costly, and these costs can be an important burden for some banks with already low profitability. This amplifies the "demise of the middle tier" in the banking sector – i.e. medium-sized universal banks are less able to compete with the largest players, as the mid-tier banks find it hard to invest in digitalization at the same pace as the largest ones and thus become trapped with higher cost ratios and lower profitability. In the longer run, this leads to a polarization of the banking sector, between large universal banks and small specialized banks, which may have structural consequences for the entire sector via M&As and further lead to market concentration. A challenge for financial stability may arise when there is a need to ensure an orderly market exit of unviable mid-tier banks.

An increase in market concentration, both through organic growth of large banks as well as through M&As, is not without consequences for systemic risks. The growing market share of largest institutions increases the potential of "too-big-to-fail" risks. This presents challenges for deposit guarantee schemes and resolution authorities in the case of problems of large banks. Large institutions, especially ones which were created as a result of mergers, can also increase in complexity of their operations, making them more difficult both to manage and supervise effectively. Regulatory instruments available to address this risk are at present focused on ensuring additional capital buffers of systemically important banks, but other actions, such as enhanced supervisory attention to these institutions, can play an important role.

The complexity of the largest institutions is likely to increase in line with the deployment of advanced technologies, such as AI, as large banks aim to obtain similar proficiency in the use of data to "bigtech" firms. As it has been observed by the FSB (2017) in its preliminary assessment, the use of these tools can result in a more efficient processing of information and thus increase the efficiency of the financial system. However, there are important challenges related to the lack of interpretability or "auditability" of AI and machine learning methods, data privacy and unintended market dynamics, for example arising from the common use by various institutions of previously unrelated data sources. Supervisors will need to acquire skills sufficient to challenge the use and governance of these advanced models by financial firms in order to limit risks and maximize benefits.

The scenario of an increasing polarization of the banking sector is likely to materialize in Poland. In recent years we have experienced a significant increase in ICT and IT investments driven by innovation needs and competitive pressure. In nominal terms, the expenditure of big banks was dominant, yet some catching up efforts were noticeable among medium-sized and small banks, attempting to close the innovation gap and strengthen the competitive position vis-à-vis other banking sector players and new market entrants. There are noticeable differences in technology and innovation profiles between peer-groups. Less advanced and less sophisticated profiles of medium-sized and small banks could put an additional drag on their declining competitive position. We see clear evidence of a bi-polar, two-tier system, where the largest institutions are more profitable and consistently invest more in innovative technologies. Should big banks continue to invest heavily in line with their capacities and historical evidence, they will remain highly competitive and gain further micro-economic advantage over the smaller banks. Medium and small banks may remain trapped in a negative feedback loop where low-profitability constraints innovative ICT investments and further reduces growth prospects and negatively affects the competitive position.

Certain structural changes within the system may be unavoidable. Mergers with better-off competitors may prove the most viable option for small and least profitable banks which are under the biggest pressures. Acquisitions by big banks could also be an alternative. However, M&A's would impact the market concentration and competition. These changes in the structure of the banking system deserve to be closely monitored by the financial stability authorities.

ACKNOWLEDGMENT

This research was produced while all the authors were employed by the Narodowy Bank Polski. The authors would like to thank Robert Jagiełło for useful suggestions and discussion. The views in this chapter are those of the authors and should not be interpreted to represent the official view of the Narodowy Bank Polski, the European Investment Bank or any other organization.

REFERENCES

Akhavein, J., Frame, W. S., & White, L. (2005). The diffusion of financial innovations: An examination of the adoption of small business credit scoring by large banking organizations. *The Journal of Business*, *78*(2), 577–596. doi:10.1086/427639

Aldasoro, I., Gambacorta, L., Giudici, P., & Leach, T. (2020). *The drivers of cyber risk*. BIS Working Paper 865.

Ardizzi, G., Crudu, F., & Petraglia, C. (2019). Innovation and Cost Efficiency in the Banking Industry: The Role of Electronic Payments. *Economic Notes by John Wiley & Sons Ltd*, *48*(1), 12121. Advance online publication. doi:10.1111/ecno.12121

Beck, T., Chen, T., Lin, C., & Song, F. (2016). Financial innovation: The bright and the dark sides. *Journal of Banking & Finance*, *72*, 28–51. doi:10.1016/j.jbankfin.2016.06.012

Berger, A. N., Demsetz, R. S., & Strahan, P. E. (1999). The consolidation of the financial services industry: Causes, consequences and implications for the future. *Journal of Banking & Finance*, *23*(2-4), 135–194. doi:10.1016/S0378-4266(98)00125-3

Boot, A. (2003). Consolidation and strategic positioning in banking with implications for Europe. Brookings-Wharton Papers on Financial Services, 37-83. doi:10.1353/pfs.2003.0001

Boot, A. (2017). The Future of Banking: From Scale & Scope Economies to Fintech. *European Economy*, *2017*(2).

Bouveret, A. (2018). *Cyber Risk for the Financial Sector: A Framework for Quantitative Assessment.* IMF Working Paper WP/18/143.

Cainelli, G., Evangelista, R., & Savona, M. (2006). Innovation and economic performance in services: A firm-level analysis. *Cambridge Journal of Economics*, *30*(3), 435–458. doi:10.1093/cje/bei067

Cashless.pl & Accenture. (2018). *Map of Polish FinTech 2018*. Retrieved from: https://www.cashless.pl/system/uploads/ckeditor/attachments/1908/Mapa_Polskiego_Fintechu_2018.pdf

Cyree, K. B., Delcoure, N., & Dickens, R. (2008). An examination of the performance and prospects for the future of internet-primary banks. *Journal of Economics and Finance*, *33*(2), 128–147. doi:10.100712197-008-9048-0

Deloitte. (2018). *Digital Banking Maturity 2018*. Retrieved from: https://www2.deloitte.com/Digital-BankingMaturity

DeYoung, R. (2001). The financial performance of pure play internet banks. *Economic Perspectives Federal Reserve Bank of Chicago*, *25*(1), 60–75.

DeYoung, R. (2005). The performance of internet-based business models: Evidence from the banking industry. *The Journal of Business*, *78*(3), 893–947. doi:10.1086/429648

DeYoung, R., Lang, W. W., & Nolle, D. L. (2007). How the Internet affects output and performance at community banks? *Journal of Banking & Finance*, *31*(4), 1033–1060. doi:10.1016/j.jbankfin.2006.10.003

European Banking Authority. (2019). *Guidelines on ICT and security risk management*. European Banking Authority.

Financial Stability Board. (2017). *Artificial intelligence and machine learning in financial services. Market developments and financial stability implications*. Financial Stability Board.

Financial Stability Board. (2019). *Third-party dependencies in cloud services. Considerations on financial stability implications*. Financial Stability Board.

Frame, W. S., & White, L. (2002). *Empirical Studies of Financial Innovation: Lots of Talk, Little Action?* Federal Reserve Bank of Atlanta Working Paper 2002(12). doi:10.2139srn.325800

Frame, W. S., & White, L. (2009). *Technological Change, Financial Innovation, and Diffusion in Banking*. Federal Reserve Bank of Atlanta Working Paper 2009(10). doi:10.2139srn.1434235

Frost, J. (2020). *The economic forces driving fintech adoption across countries*. BIS Working Paper 838.

Gaidosch, T., Adelmann, F., Morozova, A., & Wilson, C. (2019). *Cybersecurity Risk Supervision*. IMF Departmental Paper No. 19/15.

Gambacorta, L., Huang, Y., Qiu, H., & Wang, J. (2019). *How do machine learning and non-traditional data affect credit scoring? New evidence from a Chinese fintech firm*. BIS Working Paper 834.

Gerardi, K. S., Rosen, H. S., & Willen, P. S. (2010). The impact of deregulation and financial innovation on consumers: The case of the mortgage market. *The Journal of Finance*, *65*(1), 333–360. doi:10.1111/j.1540-6261.2009.01531.x

Grinblatt, M., & Longstaff, F. A. (2000). Financial innovation and the role of derivative securities: An empirical analysis of the Treasury STRIPS program. *The Journal of Finance*, *55*(3), 1415–1436. doi:10.1111/0022-1082.00252

Gündoğdu, A., & Taskin, F. (2017). Analysis of the relationship between financial innovation and the performance of the Turkish banking system. *International Review of Economics and Management*, *5*(3), 16–32. doi:10.18825/iremjournal.280341

Henderson, B. J., & Pearson, N. D. (2011). The dark side of financial innovation: A case study of the pricing of a retail financial product. *Journal of Financial Economics*, *100*(2), 227–247. doi:10.1016/j.jfineco.2010.12.006

Holden, K., & El-Bannany, M. (2004). Investment in information technology systems and other determinants of bank profitability in the UK. *Applied Financial Economics*, *14*(5), 361–365. doi:10.1080/0960310042000211623

Konkel, M. (2020). Polskie firmy nie boją się sięgać obłoków (Polish companies are not afraid to reach the clouds). *Puls Biznesu*, *2020*(19), 16.

Kopp, E., Kaffenberger, L., & Wilson, C. (2017). *Cyber Risk, Market Failures and Financial Stability.* IMF Working Paper WP/17/185.

Minsky, H. P. (1992). *The Financial Instability Hypothesis.* The Jerome Levy Economics Institute Working Paper 74. doi:10.2139srn.161024

Narodowy Bank Polski. (2019a). *Instrukcja uzupełniająca pakiet FINREP jednostkowy (FINPL) (Supplementary manual for solo FINREP reporting FINPL).* Retrieved from: https://www.nbp.pl/statystyka/sprawozdawczosc/form/instrukcja-FINREP.pdf

Narodowy Bank Polski. (2019b). *Ocena funkcjonowania polskiego systemu płatniczego w I półroczu 2019 roku (Assessment of the functioning of the Polish payment system in the first half of 2019).* http://www.nbp.pl/homen.aspx?f=/en/system_platniczy/Assessment_summary.html

Narodowy Bank Polski. (2019c). *Financial Stability Report. December 2019.* Retrieved from: https://www.nbp.pl/en/systemfinansowy/fsr201912.pdf

Narodowy Bank Polski. (2019d). *Financial Stability Report. June 2019.* Retrieved from: https://www.nbp.pl/en/systemfinansowy/fsr201906.pdf

Narodowy Bank Polski. (2020). *Innowacje w sektorze banków komercyjnych w Polsce. Raport z badania 2019 r* [Innovations in the Polish commercial banking sector. Report from 2019 survey]. Retrieved from https://www.nbp.pl/systemfinansowy/Ankieta_innowacje.pdf

Rooney, K. (2019). *Wall Street banks are upping bets on their potential fintech competitors.* Retrieved from: https://www.cnbc.com/2019/09/15/wall-street-banks-are-upping-bets-on-potential-fintech-competitors.html

Schumpeter, J. A. (1943). *Capitalism, Socialism and Democracy*. Routledge.

Schwab, K. (2016). *The Fourth Industrial Revolution: what it means, how to respond.* Retrieved from: https://www.weforum.org/agenda/2016/01/the-fourth-industrial-revolution-what-it-means-and-how-to-respond/

Scott, S., Van Reenen, J., & Zachariadis, M. (2017). The long-term effect of digital innovation on bank performance: An empirical study of SWIFT adoption in financial services. *Research Policy*, *46*(5), 984–1004. doi:10.1016/j.respol.2017.03.010

Stec, A., & Rudke, M. (2018). *Prezes PKO BP Zbigniew Jagiełło: Będziemy firmą technologiczną z licencją bankową* [PKO BP CEO: we will be a technological company with a banking license]. Retrieved from: https://www.rp.pl/Banki/311139892-Prezes-PKO-BP-Zbigniew-Jagiello-Bedziemy-firma-technologiczna-z-licencja-bankowa.html?cid

Tomaszewski, R. (2019). *Adam Marciniak, PKO Bank Polski – O Chmurze Krajowej i jej współpracy z Google Cloud.* Retrieved from: https://fintek.pl/pko-bp-chmura-krajowa-google-cloud-wywiad/

Wheelock, D., & Wilson, P. (2011). *Do Large Banks have Lower Costs? New Estimates of Returns to Scale for U.S. Banks.* Federal Reserve Bank of St. Louis Working Paper 2009(054E), doi:10.2139srn.1493261

World Economic Forum. (2017). *Beyond Fintech: A Pragmatic Assessment Of Disruptive Potential In Financial Services.* Retrieved from: http://www3.weforum.org/docs/Beyond_Fintech_-_A_Pragmatic_Assessment_of_Disruptive_Potential_in_Financial_Services.pdf

ADDITIONAL READING

Basel Committee on Banking Supervision. (2018). *Sound Practices: implications of fintech developments for banks and bank supervisors.* Retrieved from: https://www.bis.org/bcbs/publ/d431.htm

Drasch, B. J., Schweizer, A., & Urbach, N. (2018). Integrating the 'Troublemakers': A taxonomy for cooperation between banks and fintechs. *Journal of Economics and Business, 100*, 26–42. doi:10.1016/j.jeconbus.2018.04.002

Financial Stability Board. (2019). *FinTech and market structure in financial services: Market developments and potential financial stability implications.* Retrieved from: https://www.fsb.org/wp-content/uploads/P140219.pdf

Frost, J., Gambacorta, L., Huang, Y., Shin, H., & Zbinden, P. (2019). BigTech and the changing structure of financial intermediation. BIS Working Paper 779.

Komisja Nadzoru Finansowego. (2017). *Report on the activities of the Special Task Force for Financial Innovation in Poland.* Retrieved from: https://www.knf.gov.pl/knf/en/komponenty/img/Raport_KNF__ANG_11_2017_60291.pdf

Stulz, R. M. (2019). FinTech, BigTech, and the Future of Banks. *Journal of Applied Corporate Finance, 31*(4), 86–97. doi:10.1111/jacf.12378

Tanda, A., & Schena, C.-M. (2019). *FinTech, BigTech and Banks.* Palgrave Macmillan Studies in Banking and Financial Institutions., doi:10.1007/978-3-030-22426-4

Vives, X. (2019). Digital Disruption in Banking. *Annual Review of Financial Economics, 11*(1), 243–272. doi:10.1146/annurev-financial-100719-120854

KEY TERMS AND DEFINITIONS

Artificial Intelligence and Machine Learning (AI & ML): AI may be broadly defined as the application of computational tools to address tasks traditionally requiring human sophistication (Financial Stability Board, 2017). In the view presented by FSB, ML is a sub-category of AI and refers to the method of designing a sequence of actions to solve a problem, known as algorithms, which optimize automatically through experience and with limited or no human intervention. In other words, ML is a science that is aimed at providing computers with ability to learn directly from the data, without applying a program created ex-ante.

Big Data: The use of very large and complex data sets for business analytics. Big Data sets are usually defined by their size (exceeding the capability of common statistical software and metods), complexity (as they can contain data of multiple types, including numbers, text, image, etc.), velocity (as these sets can be collected and analyzed in a continuous fashion, e.g. in case of data capturing the patterns of use of an application by clients).

Cloud Computing: An online network ("cloud") of computer system resources, available on- and/or off-site, scalable, and flexible that can be accessed on a pay-as-you-go basis. Cloud service providers offer a wide range of services, namely: storage space, computing power, developer platforms or software and web applications. This model enables convenient access to a shared pool of configurable hardware and software (e.g. networks, servers, storage facilities, applications, and services) swiftly called up and released with minimal management effort or service provider interaction.

Digital Transformation: The process by which an organization increases the role of digital processes in its activities. In this research this term is used to describe gradual changes in business models of banks as a result of increased use of ICT both in internal operations of banks as well as in the customer interaction channels.

Distributed Ledger Technology (DLT): A type of database where data is stored in multiple synchronized copies and is updated and replicated using a consensus algorithm, which ensures that only entries that are accepted by a majority of participants can be entered into the database. Blockchain systems are a form of DLT.

Fintech: Technology-enabled innovation in financial services that could result in new business models, applications, processes, or products with an associated material effect on the provision of financial services. The term is used to refer both to the phenomenon as a whole and to companies, especially in start-up or growth phase, which aim to deliver financial services in new ways, heavily relying on ICT.

Robotic Process Automation (RPA): A business automation technology, where within digital systems, routine tasks are partially or fully performed by software solutions or "bots" that automate manual, laborious, rule-based, high-volume, repeatable tasks and repetitive activities originally executed by humans.

ENDNOTES

1 For example, the use of non-traditional data for credit risk assessment available to new entrants – such as e-commerce platforms and internet lenders – allows them to expand access to credit to some underbanked SME and individual customers. See e.g. World Economic Forum (2017), Gambacorta, Huang, Qiu & Wang (2019).

2 See for example guidelines on managing risks related to information and communication technology issued by the EBA (European Banking Authority, 2019) which apply to credit institutions, investment firms and payment service providers. An overview of supervisory practices in this area is provided by Gaidosch, Adelmann, Morozova & Wilson (2019). Apart from supervisory guidelines, technical standards such as ISO 27005 are used to support cyber risk management.

3 As pointed out e.g. by the Financial Stability Board (2019).

4 See section "Data and Methods" for details on the survey.

5 A partial description of the results was included in NBP (2019c) as Box 2.3 "Expenditure on technological innovation in the Polish banking sector – survey results". A full set of results was published as NBP (2020).

6 As stated by the CEO of the largest bank in Poland (PKO BP) in a November 2018 newspaper interview (Stec & Rudke, 2018).

7 As of 2018, the Herfindahl index for the Polish banking sector (calculated by assets) amounted to 0.068 and was the eight-lowest in the EU. Source: ECB, Banking structural statistical indicators.

8 As of June 2019, 85.7% of cards in Poland supported contactless payments, as did 100% of point-of-sale terminals. In the first half of 2019 76.7% of card transactions by value were contactless (Narodowy Bank Polski, 2019b).

9 See Konkel (2020).

10 As an example of even small institutions using advanced technology, the Cooperative Bank in Torun has implemented blockchain technology, in cooperation with a local IT firm, for both internal document circulation and communication with clients (using blockchain to certify electronic documents to a "durable medium" standard), allowing to simplify administrative processes and reduce costs.

11 Examples of such "marketplace" platforms include Bancovo for loans or Raisin for bank deposits.

12 Examples of such cooperation on the Polish market include the integration of ticket purchase services developed by start-up moBilet into the mobile banking application of PKO BP, the biggest Polish bank.

13 Between 2012 and 2019, large US banks made more than 110 equity investments in fintech companies, using them to expand their capabilities. See Rooney (2019).

14 Examples from the Polish market include the equity investment of the international ING group in Twisto, a payments start-up operating on Czech and Polish market, as well as an acquisition of a deferred payments start-up PayPo by Alior Bank – a Polish bank.

15 A more detailed discussion of the profitability of the Polish banking sector can be found in NBP (2019c, 2019d).

16 We have grouped banks into three distinctively separate asset-sized peer-groups of small, medium and big entities. They included – respectively – 8 small banks with total assets below EUR 2,5 billion; 8 medium banks with assets below EUR 7 billion, on top of the first group; and 10 big banks with assets exceeding EUR 12 billion.

17 The details on the definitions are available in Narodowy Bank Polski (2019a).

18 Whereas item FRN009.4 ("IT costs") incorporates goods and services on maintenance, development of IT systems and ICT innovation, it excludes ICT outsourcing expenses and ICT (own and external) staff costs. Differences originate from survey input data inaccuracies where banks declared their spending in broad terms, but also from evident omissions in the "IT cost" reporting proxy, where staff and IT outsourcing costs are not included. They structurally skew the results and calculations on both ends: the survey results and the financial reporting proxies we used to compare our results.

19 See Deloitte (2018).

20 Risk management function encompassed: credit risk, liquidity risk, market risk, operational risk, IT-risk and cybersecurity.

21 HR and talent management.

22 Sales functions and client management.

23 See Tomaszewski (2019).

Chapter 10
Financial Innovation: Accelerating Financial Inclusion in South Asia

Md. Humayun Kabir
https://orcid.org/0000-0002-5648-197X
East West University, Bangladesh

ABSTRACT

Financial innovation and financial inclusion are helping countries to achieve inclusive economic growth by mitigating poverty. The purpose of the chapter is to examine how financial innovation accelerating financial inclusion in South Asian countries. The uses of internet banking, mobile banking, short message service (SMS) banking, electronic banking (e-banking), agent banking, mobile money accounts, and mobile wallet banking is increasing at an increasing rate, which is engaging the unbanked people in the financial systems. The robust growth of the mobile ecosystem in South Asia is contributing broadly to the engagement of financial inclusion. The empirical analysis was done by using data from the Global Financial Inclusion Database (Global Findex) and Global Financial Development Database to see how automated financial products and services are conveniently receiving by the unbanked population. The results of the analysis show that many financial innovations in financial products and services delivery from financial technology is closing gaps in financial inclusion significantly.

INTRODUCTION

Technologic advances, globalization, modernization is fostering the growth of financial innovation that is ultimately adding more and more people to the digital financial platform. Financial transactions can be made quickly and conveniently as well as at low cost because of the innovative financial products and services offered by the financial service providers like the bank, non-bank financial institutions, microfinance institutions (MFIs), insurance companies, mobile services providers. Those providers are providing services to their clients at ease that no one thought a decade back. Currently, in South Asian countries: Afghanistan, Bangladesh, Bhutan, India, Pakistan, Maldives, Nepal, and Sri Lanka, the sce-

DOI: 10.4018/978-1-7998-4390-0.ch010

nario for financial inclusion is notable. Every day more and more people are opening their accounts with financial services providers to receive hassle-free services from a different area. Technological advances in the financial sector are enabling the financial services providers to provide services in rural areas. Because of the high growth of financial technology (fintech), people in this part of the world is joining with the financial services industry by receiving and providing value that is ultimately helping the counties of this region to achieve the sustainable development goals and inclusive economic growth. Financial inclusion is also alleviating poverty by providing opportunities to the poor and unbanked people of this region. An efficient and inclusive financial system could provide a wide range of financial products from savings and loans to risk management to the poor and unbanked people. Access to formal financial products and services by the poor and unbanked people can impact positivity to the economy because they can invest in education and development (Demirgüç-Kunt & Klapper, 2013). Nowadays, unbanked people can receive formal financial services like a loan from a bank's agent to start a business that fosters entrepreneurship. Besides loans, unbanked people did not have the opportunity to save their money in a financial institution a few years back. Now they can save their disposable income in the financial services providers company to earn some return on their surplus money.

Digital technology is the game-changer in the financial services industry like many other industries, and it is also enabling the financial services industry to gain an increased amount of revenue. Digital financial services (DFS) are showing the growing evidence in some African markets. They have the potential to grow and accelerate financial inclusion globally, especially in developing countries (Wyman, 2017). Similarly, Saksonova and Kuzmina-Merlino (2017) stated that competition between banks and financial technology (fintech) companies are growing in advanced economies as well as in emerging markets. The author also identified digital financial services offered by financial technology companies, discussed the benefits and shortcomings of innovative financial services and the traditional financial services, and investigated the degree of usage knowledge of the customers for using those fintech based financial services.

Globalization played a crucial role in the development of fintech because of the interaction between finance and information technologies (IT). Small and micro businesses are developing fintech based services without the help of the bank and offering formal financial services to their customers efficiently, conveniently, and safely (Saksonova & Kuzmina-Merlino, 2017). Besides, Bateman, Duvendack, and Loubere (2019) identified that financial technology (fintech) is seen as an essential tool for alleviating poverty and economic development. The authors discussed Kenya's mobile wallet M-Pesa company, which facilitates digital financial transactions through mobile phones. Particularly, fintech firms are changing the nature of the financial services industry and offering customer-oriented financial products and services by adding speed and flexibly to traditional financial products and services (Nicoletti, 2017). On the other hand, financial technology has a positive impact on the banking system of Asia because a bank can access a large market at a low cost (Alexander, Shi, & Solomon, 2017). In emerging markets, approximately 2 billion people are unbanked, and provision for financial technology companies is to create secure, convenient, and affordable products for those unbanked future clients (Alexander et al., 2017). The usage of banking services is much lower in South Asian countries, especially online banking or electronic banking (e-banking) or internet banking (i-banking) services. Besides, the demand for mobile banking (m-banking) is gaining extensive popularity because of the easy access to the mobile phone (Mani, 2016).

However, Aron (2018) examined mobile money's development and its role in accelerating financial inclusion and reviewed the broader economic impact of mobile money. Mobile money helps the financial services providers and receivers in many ways. It can reduce the transaction costs, decrease the asymmetric information, improved transparency, increase the level of savings, improve the risk and return trade-off, change the nature of savings, allow micro-insurance, improve the efficiency of an economy (Aron, 2018). Moreover, Kim, Zoo, Lee, and Kang (2018) investigated the existing literature review about the connection between mobile financial services (MFS) and financial inclusion. The researchers found that current research on MFS and FI is at a nascent phase. The driving tool of financial inclusion developing countries is the mobile financial services that can quickly engage the unbanked population in the financial system (Kim et al., 2018).

Merton (1992) viewed financial innovation act as a driving force "engine" of the financial systems to achieve the goal of the real economy. Financial innovation can help access the formal financial services, especially payments, and savings services by the unbanked people and can help the poor and underprivileged population to smooth income shocks and add to the modern market economy (Ayyagari & Beck, 2015). Likewise, Qamruzzaman and Jianguo (2018) examined the nexus between financial inclusion and economic growth in four South Asian countries (Bangladesh, India, Pakistan, and Sri Lanka) from 1975 to 2016 by using autoregressive distributed lag (ARDL) bounds test and nonlinear ARDL (NARDL) test. The researchers found that in the long run, there is a cointegration of financial innovation and economic growth and a positive correlation between financial innovation and economic growth. On the other hand, in the short run, the relationship between financial innovation and economic growth shows mixed behaviours. Additionally, Mani (2016) found that among all the South Asian countries, Sri Lanka is in the highest level of financial inclusion, on the other hand, Bangladesh, Bhutan, Nepal, and India has a moderate level of financial inclusion and Afghanistan, and Pakistan is in the lowest levels. The authors correlated economic growth, economic and financial stability, and income inequality with financial inclusion and proved that financial inclusion led to higher economic growth.

Park and Mercado (2015) studied how various factors are affecting the degree of financial inclusion in different Asian countries. In addition, the authors also investigated the relationship between financial inclusion, poverty, and income inequality. The authors found that there is a strong correlation between the rates of poverty and financial inclusion; also, financial inclusion can help reduce income inequality. The authors suggested that policymakers and the pertinent government body should take definite measures to accelerate financial inclusion. Similarly, Qamruzzaman and Jianguo (2017) also proposed that the policymakers of Bangladesh should introduce and boost financial innovation in their financial systems so that financial services will be conveniently received by consumers and also can contribute to the sustainable, equitable economic growth. The researchers also proposed that the government of Bangladesh should introduce and boost financial innovation in the capital market, giving the borrower a chance to finance long-term funds from the stock market and for investment, which will accelerate economic growth.

Access to accessible, affordable, convenient, and safe formal financial products and services by the poor, unbanked, underprivileged, vulnerable households and enterprises is the pre-condition for the growth of financial inclusion that will reduce income inequality and alleviate poverty (Swamy, 2014). However, Kumar (2013) examined the financial inclusion status and also studied its status from an Indian perspective. The author analysed the determinants of financial inclusion by using panel fixed effects and dynamic panel generalised methods of moments (GMM) methodologies. The study indicated that an employment generating scheme could mitigate poverty, improve income level, and accelerate financial inclusion. Similarly, Chibba (2009) claimed that financial inclusion provides the most extensive and robust solution for poverty mitigation, for inclusive economic development and the Millennium Development Goals (MDGs). The author also offered some useful approaches for the planner and the policymakers regarding the strength of financial inclusion, poverty reduction, and the Millennium Development Goals (FI-PR-MDG).

Furthermore, Qamruzzaman and Wei (2019) also investigated the relationship between financial innovation and financial inclusion, including the remittance inflows and financial development for Bangladesh, India, Pakistan, Nepal, Bhutan, and Sri Lanka. The researchers found a positive relationship between financial innovation and financial inclusion in both the short-term and in the long-term by using symmetry assumption. In contrast, the asymmetry assumption shows that both positive and negative shocks in financial innovation show a positive relationship with financial inclusion. However, it is proved that the intertwined connection between financial innovation and financial inclusion is critically required for the development of financial sectors.

This study engaged in identifying how financial innovation accelerating financial inclusion in Afghanistan, Bangladesh, Bhutan, India, Pakistan, Maldives, Nepal, and Sri Lanka. The empirical analysis shows the degree of financial inclusion in South Asian countries over the years.

MOTIVATION AND LITERATURE REVIEW

According to Tufano (2003), financial innovation is the process of developing and commercialising fintech based on financial products and services, financial markets, and institutions. Digitisation of financial services means developing innovative financial products and services that reach the unbanked population (Alexander et al., 2017). However, financial innovation accelerates economic growth by stimulating capital accumulation, financial service expansion, financial efficiency, and efficient financial intermediation in the long run. Those factors are required for sustainable economic growth (Qamruzzaman & Jianguo, 2018).

Zavolokina, Dolata, and Schwabe (2016) defined financial technology or fintech as the combination of finance and technology that is categorised as a novel, innovative, and emerging field. According to Buckley and Webster (2016), financial technology is giving a new path for financial innovation. The designer of fintech needs to think about the customers' needs and wants before designing innovative products and services for customers. Zavolokina et al. (2016) pointed out that the nature of the banking business is changing because of digital technologies. In every part of the traditional banking, there is a change now because of the technological innovation, namely fintech. Digital technologies, simply fintech, are changing the banking business and reforming the whole financial sector. Venet (2019) presented several potentials of digital finance. Those are accelerating economic growth, increase the efficiency and effectiveness of the financial system, reduce the spending of government on revenue collection, boost financial inclusion, provide affordable, easy and convenient banking services, and reduce opportunity costs of the lender. Efficient financial systems and diversified financial products and services can help achieve economic growth. Countries should develop innovative financial products and services to achieve sustainable and inclusive economic growth. The financial services industry should introduce innovative companies to create innovative products and services. The government should formulate policies that will reduce the risk and help achieve stability in the financial sector. Besides, financial innovation will only yield maximum benefits when the policymakers effectively and efficiently proceed with the bank-based and market-based financial developments (Qamruzzaman & Jianguo, 2018). Digital finance, like fintech, is growing at a significant rate. Still, the underprivileged or poor people do not receive the value of fintech; the digital financial elite receives most of the benefits.

Arner and Panton (2013) recognised that financial innovation is boosting economic growth and development, but possesses some risk because of the lack of adequate supervision and regulation. Johnson and Kwak (2012) argued, "A better understanding of the costs and benefits of financial innovation is essential to protecting ourselves from the next financial crisis." However, in the next financial crisis, the poor will suffer the most because the expense of the poor is enriching the digital financial elites (Bateman et al., 2019). Additionally, Mustafa et al. (2018) found that political stability is the prerequisite for the moderating effect of financial crunch on the performance of microfinance institutions (MFIs). The author also revealed that countries practising sound political practices and regulations are less severely affected by the global financial crisis. In the financial sector, financial stability risk decreases when strong regulation is ensured, and the risk increases when there is a lack of proper control. So strong supervision and management can reduce financial stability risk and accelerate financial inclusion. Except for credit access, other formal financial services does not affect financial stability adversely (Sahay et al., 2015). However, Hannig and Jansen (2010) identified that financial innovation could have an overwhelming systematic impact on the time of the financial crisis. The researcher suggested that if financial innovation is used to accelerate financial inclusion, then the process may help strengthen the financial systems instead of weakening them.

Aron (2018) defined mobile money as a recent financial innovation that is used for financial transactions through mobile phone wallet of the user and including the global unbanked people to the formal financial system. Similarly, Demirguç-Kunt, Klapper, Singer, Ansar, and Hess (2017) defined that the combination of the internet and mobile phone provides the world with a new generation of financial services. Allen, Carletti, Cull, Qian, Senbet, and Valenzuela (2014) argued that mobile money wallet or mobile banking has only succeeded in receiving and sending money. Furthermore, Akhter and Khalily (2017) investigated mobile financial services (MFS) impact on Bangladesh's financial inclusion and concluded that for the growth of financial inclusion, mobile financial services are a vital tool. Also, the researchers' analysis showed a positive nexus between MFS and financial inclusion. The bank and microfinance institutions (MFIs) should use mobile financial services as their vehicle to provide financial services in the inaccessible area for the unbanked people (Akhter & Khalily, 2017). Mobile financial services (MFS) has changed the financial products and services of banks, non-bank financial institutions, and other traditional service providers. The proper usage of MFS to the unbanked poor and underprivileged will have a broader impact on economic growth and poverty reduction (Akhter & Khalily, 2017).

Financial inclusion means providing formal financial services to enterprises and households at reasonable prices (Ayyagari & Beck, 2015). It also means providing financial products and services to all the people without considering their financial and economic situation (Wyman, 2017). Mani (2016) defined financial inclusion as to providing financial products and services to the weaker and underprivileged people who cannot access the formal financial services conveniently and efficiently at a low and reasonable cost. Sahay et al. (2015) defined: "financial inclusion is the access to and use of formal financial services by households and firms." Besides, financial inclusion is a process that ensures the easy accessibility, accountability, and usage of formal financial products and services by the members of an economy. Ease of accessibility, accountability, and usage of financial products and services are the dimension of financial inclusion, and those dimensions can be blend together to build an inclusive financial system. Besides those dimensions, banking inclusion is considered a vital aspect of financial inclusion because most financial services are delivered through the banking channel (Sarma, 2008).

Policymakers view financial inclusion as the way of alleviating poverty, improve the livelihood of people, and the inclusive and broader economic development. Wyman (2017) stated that financial inclusion through financial technology or digital financial services is explicit, and it will impact the unbanked people and help countries to achieve inclusive economic growth. Financial inclusion is considered a critical element that helps the poor and people living below the poverty line to access the formal financial services and ultimately mitigate poverty and reduce income inequality (Park & Mercado, 2015). Moreover, Information and Communications Technology (ICT) can boost financial inclusion by reducing transaction costs (Andrianaivo & Kpodar, 2011). Similarly, Andrianaivo and Kpodar (2011) investigated the impact of ICT in economic growth by using GMM estimator for African countries and concluded that the need for ICT in financial inclusion in economic development is vigorous. Llanto and Badiola (2011) explained that because of financial inclusion, poor and unbanked people can participate in the financial system and can change their economic status.

Sarma (2008) examined the connection between financial inclusion and development through a cross country analysis and found that level of human development and income is closely related to financial inclusion. Likewise, Laha (2015) concluded that the level of human development and ranking of financial inclusion has a positive relationship in India. For other South Asian countries, the ranking of human development widely follows the pattern of financial inclusion of India. Sarma (2008) pointed out "countries having low GDP per capita, relatively higher levels of income inequality, low rates of literacy, low urbanisation and poor connectivity seem to be less financially inclusive." Koh et al. (2018) argued that digital financial inclusion could provide benefits to broader branches of financial services beyond microcredit, savings, and payment services. Four key pillars are required to strengthen the financial inclusion process: the private sector (both financial and non-financial), financial knowledge, microfinance, and government or public sector support (Chibba, 2009). Mani (2016) investigated and analysed the level of financial inclusion by considering eight or nine parameters in South Asian countries and found that the level of financial inclusion is modest in South Asian countries comparing other regions of the world. The author concluded that financial inclusion is closely related to the sustainable economic growth of this region. Financial inclusion is becoming an internationally essential issue with the amplified initiative from different international bodies, governmental and non-governmental organisations, to help the poor and underprivileged global population (Koh et al., 2018).

While reviewing those studies, it was found that significant studies have proved that there is a positive correlation between financial innovation and financial inclusion. It was also found that financial inclusion is helping countries achieve economic growth and mitigation of poverty level. However, no study was conducted for South Asian countries by using the Global Financial Inclusion Database and Global Financial Development Database of the World Bank to examine the degree of financial inclusion.

IMPACT OF FINANCIAL INNOVATIONS ON FINANCIAL INCLUSION

Methodology

This study is a descriptive study where quantitative data has been collected from secondary sources to examine how financial innovation accelerating financial inclusion in Afghanistan, Bangladesh, Bhutan,

India, Pakistan, Maldives, Nepal, and Sri Lanka. The secondary data was collected from the World Bank, articles, and reviewing numerous literature. The World Bank's Global Findex database and the Global Financial Development Database from 2011 to 2017 is used to analyse the impact of financial innovations on financial inclusion indicators for South Asian Countries. Besides, the poverty headcount ratio at $1.90 a day from 2005-17, and Gross Domestic Product (GDP) growth rate data from 2004-18 was collected from the World Bank.

Analysis of Financial Inclusion Indicators

In the South Asian region, 70 per cent adult has an own or joint account in any types of financial institutions including bank and non-bank financial institutions or have a mobile money account. In just three years, the percentage of account opening in the bank and other financial services providers by an adult rose from 47 percentage point to 70 per cent in this region due to the acceleration of financial innovation in mobile financial services. Among all South Asian countries, each country's account ownership by an adult has increased from 2011 to 2017. The popularity of financially innovative products and services has helped the growth. The growth of accounts in Bangladesh is 61 per cent in just three years; also, India has a growth of 51 per cent. Moreover, all South Asian countries' ownership of accounts has increased except Sri Lanka. While comparing with world data in 2017, South Asia is 1 per cent ahead of account ownership by an adult.

Figure 1. Percentage of adults having an account in financial institutions or in mobile financial services providers
Source: Global Findex Database, 2017
Note: No data are available for the Maldives in the Global Findex Database

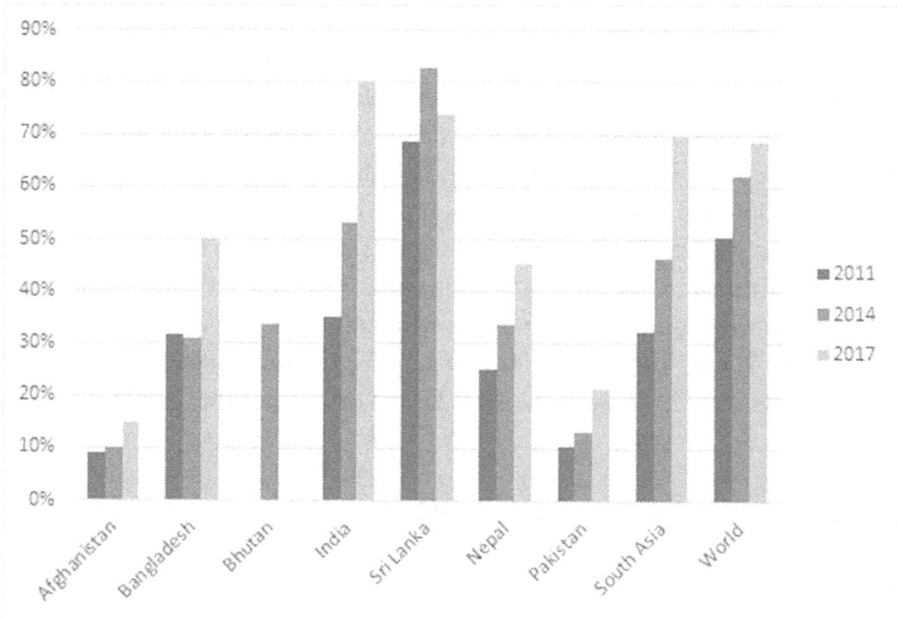

Figure 2. Percentage of adults living in rural areas having an account in financial institutions or other financial services providers
Source: Global Findex Database, 2017
Note: No data are available for the Maldives in the Global Findex Database

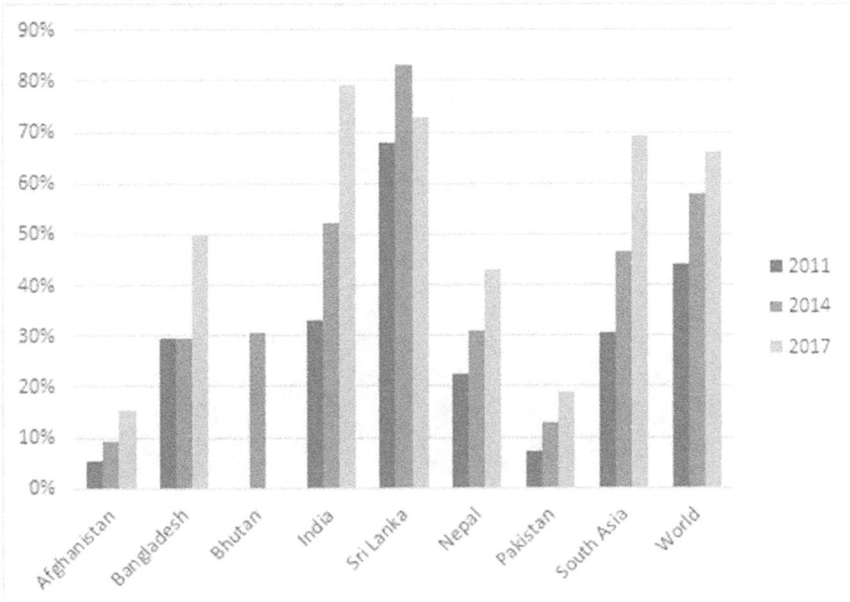

The account ownership by an adult of the rural area is also increased by 123 per cent in South Asia, and globally it has risen by 50 per cent from 2011 to 2017. The reason behind the rise of ownership in the rural area is the mobile financial services offered by financial institutions and other fintech companies in the South Asian region. India, Sri Lanka, and Bangladesh are successfully implementing the fintech policy to achieve a high degree of financial inclusion.

India and Sri Lanka are topping the chart in the financial institutions' account ownership chart. While comparing South Asia with the world, it can be seen that South Asia is 1 per cent ahead of the world. Nepal, Bangladesh, and Pakistan have seen the growth in account ownership in financial institutions. Financial technology, or simply fintech, is triggering financial inclusion in South Asia. The account ownership in the bank and other financial institutions rose from 46 percentage points to 68 percentage points from 2014 to 2017. The high growth in account ownership is because of the availability of internet banking and mobile banking.

The account ownership in a financial institution by the rural population has increased over the years in India, Sri Lanka, Nepal, and Pakistan because of massive investment in financial technology and digital finance. Financial institutions are providing agent banking, internet banking, mobile banking, short message service (SMS) banking, and agent banking services to their clients. That is engaging the poor and unbanked people of rural areas to the financial systems. Agent banking is playing an essential role in financial inclusion because the agent of a bank is offering innovative financial products and services to the poor, unbanked, and underprivileged people. A customer from the rural area can avail of all banking services from an agent of a bank or other financial institutions.

Figure 3. Percentage of adults having an account in financial institutions
Source: Global Findex Database, 2017
Note: No data are available for the Maldives in the Global Findex Database

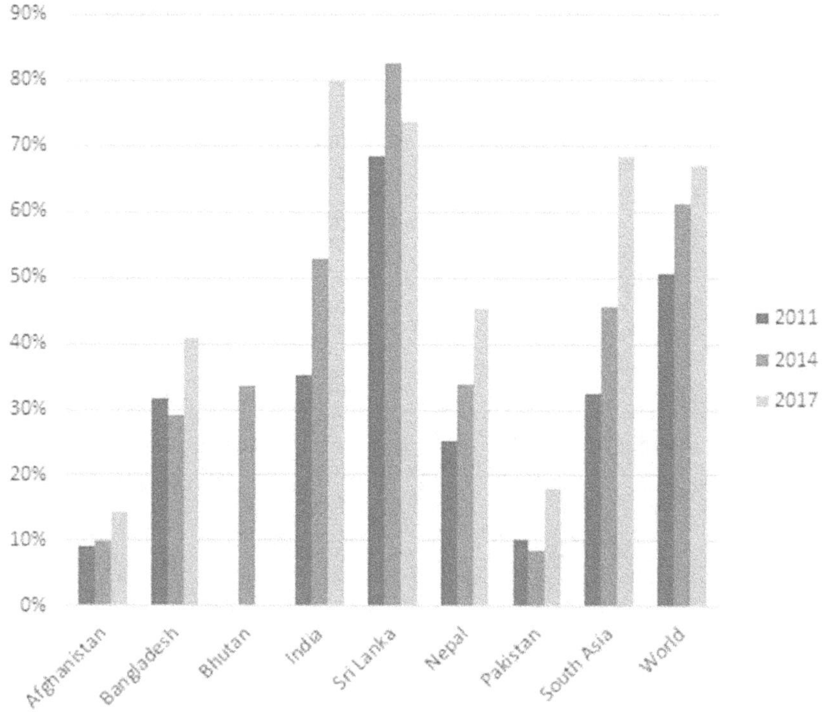

Figure 4. Percentage of adults living in rural areas having an account in financial institutions
Source: Global Findex Database, 2017
Note: No data are available for the Maldives in the Global Findex Database

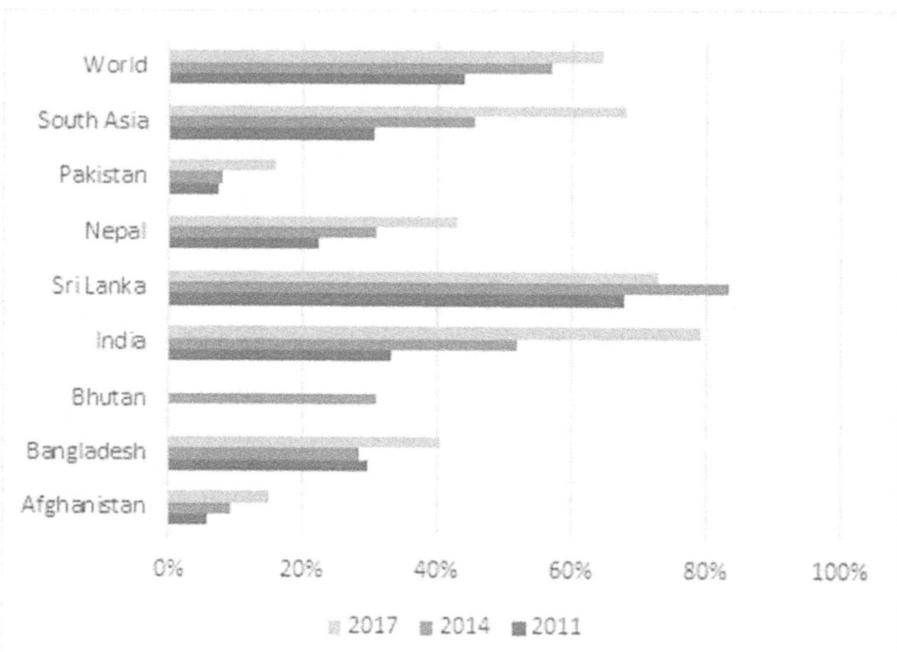

Figure 5. Percentage of adults living in rural areas saved at a financial institution
Source: Global Findex Database, 2017
Note: No data are available for the Maldives in the Global Findex Database

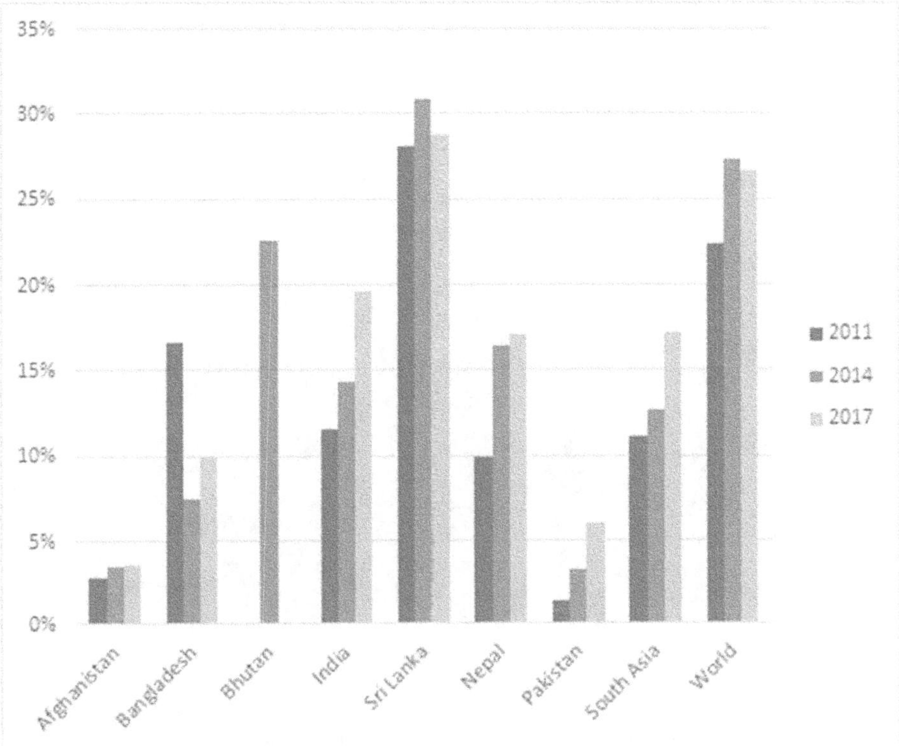

The amount of savings by an adult of the rural area is much lower in South Asian countries because the per capita income of rural people is lower than the urban people. However, some South Asian countries' amount of savings by people living in a rural area have increased over the year. In Bangladesh and India, the accumulated savings rose by 43 per cent from 2014 to 2017 because rural areas population can save in microfinance institutions. In this indicator, the performance of Sri Lanka is better than the overall performance of South Asia and World.

The amount of lending has decreased from 2011 to 2017 in most South Asian countries because of the high regulation and supervision after the Asian and global financial crushes. The rural area population is not creditworthy, generally insolvent. That is why microfinance institutions are not lending widely among customers. In Bangladesh, the amount of loans in the rural area has decreased by 64 percentage points from 2011 to 2017. The data of Afghanistan, Pakistan, and India are unchanged, but in Nepal, it has increased from 11 per cent to 15 per cent in seven years.

The digital financial revolution engaged more and more unbanked people to the financial systems, and they are receiving the benefits of digital payment services from their providers. Bangladesh has seen high growth in digital payments through credit cards, debit cards, app banking, internet banking, online banking, mobile banking, and mobile money wallet. Among South Asian countries, Afghanistan has the lowest digital payments, but Sri Lanka and Bangladesh have shown a significant percentage growth. Bangladesh's growth rate is 400 per cent, and Sri Lanka has a growth rate of 164 per cent in just three years.

Figure 6. Percentage of adults living in rural areas borrowed from a financial institution
Source: Global Findex Database, 2017
Note: No data are available for the Maldives in the Global Findex Database

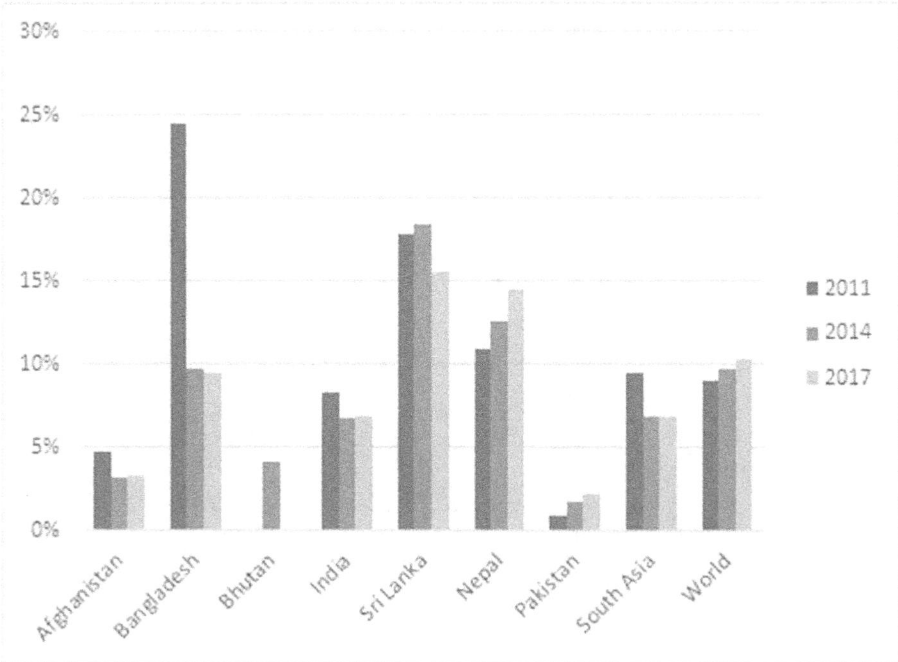

Figure 7. Percentage of adults made digital payments in the past year
Source: Global Findex Database, 2017
Note: No data are available for the Maldives in the Global Findex Database

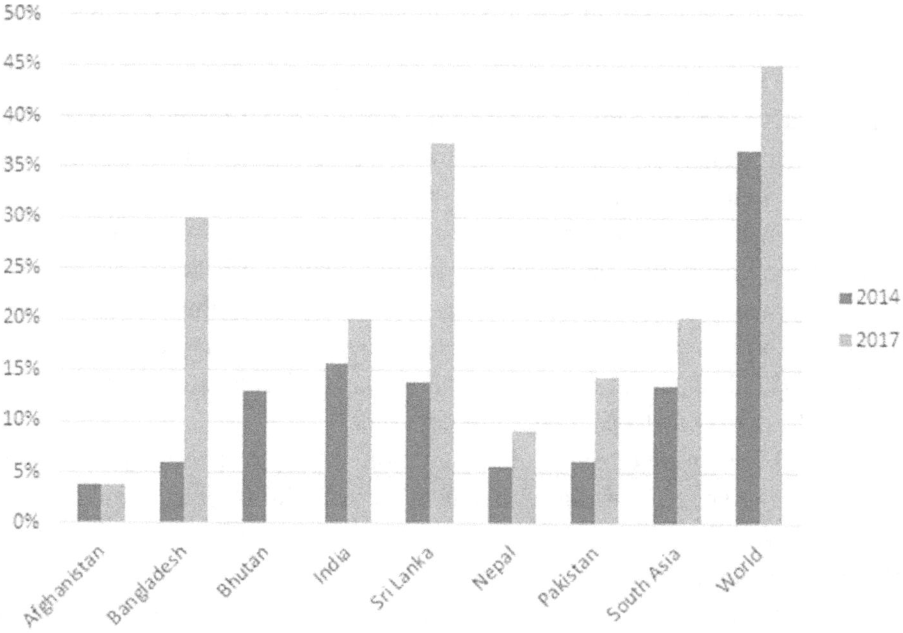

Figure 8. Percentage of adults living in rural areas made digital payments in the past year
Source: Global Findex Database, 2017
Note: No data are available for the Maldives in the Global Findex Database

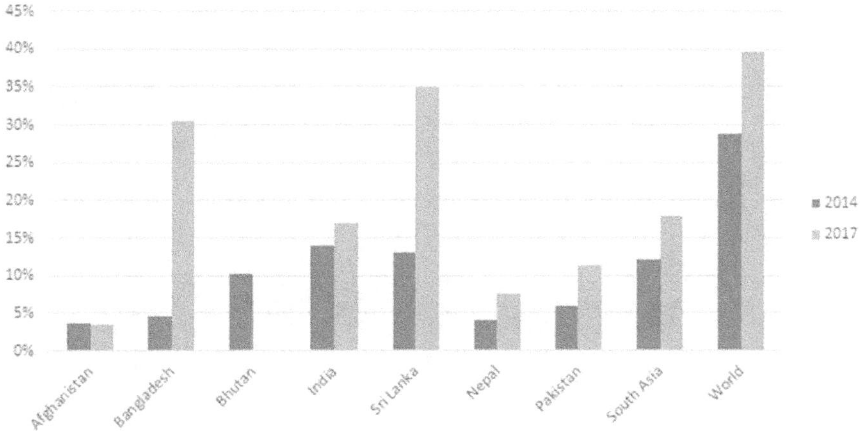

Since the rural areas people are mostly unbanked, to achieve inclusive financial inclusion, financial institutions and fintech companies should offer affordable and accessible financial products and services to the customers of rural areas. The financial services providers of Bangladesh, Sri Lanka, India, and Pakistan have successfully raised the digital payments culture in rural areas. On the other hand, the digital payments made by the percentage of adults living in rural areas of Afghanistan, Bhutan, and Nepal in the past year are inadequate.

The uses of digital financial services also helping people to receive their salaries, incentives, and other benefits from their employer, government, and other sources through the digital channel. All South Asian countries have shown an upward trend for the receipt of digital payments because companies are disbursing their salaries through mobile money account; also, the government is paying their citizens in the digital channel.

The digital payments received by rural area people are also rose from 2011 to 2017 in most of the South Asian countries due to the digitization of financial products and services. Digitization of financial products and services is the key to financial inclusion that can also help achieve the nations' sustainable economic growth. Policymakers need to identify institutions and help them digitize those institutions' products and services so that the financial inclusion goal will be achieved sooner.

In Mobile money account by an adult category, Bangladesh is topping the chart because several banks have introduced mobile money account. Besides, some fintech companies are providing an app that is used as a mobile wallet for bill payment, receipt of payment, payment of any purchase, and so forth. In just three years, the mobile money account has increased by 600 per cent in Bangladesh. Other South Asian countries lag in this indicator. In South Asia, only 4 per cent of the adult has a mobile money account that is the same as the global picture.

The scenario of mobile money accounts in rural areas is noticeable for Bangladesh as well. The mobile money account ownership in Bangladesh has risen from 2 percentage points to 22 percentage points because of the mobile financial providers. Other South Asian countries are lag behind in these particular indicators. Since the subscribers of mobile phones in this region growing, banks and other financial services providers can design mobile-based financial products and services for the poor and underprivileged population, which will accelerate financial inclusion.

Figure 9. Percentage of adults received digital payments in the past year
Source: Global Findex Database, 2017
Note: No data are available for the Maldives in the Global Findex Database

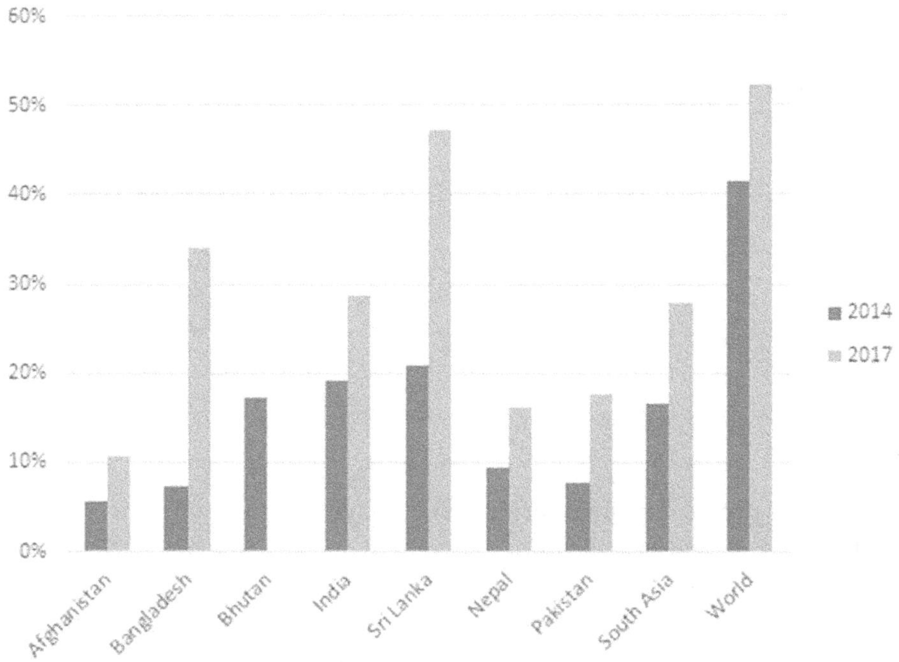

Figure 10. Percentage of adults living in rural areas received digital payments in the past year
Source: Global Findex Database, 2017
Note: No data are available for the Maldives in the Global Findex Database

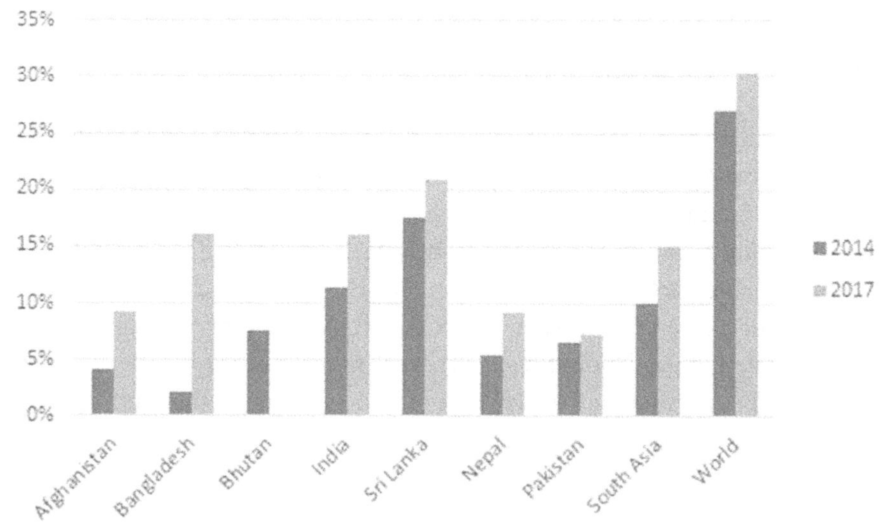

Figure 11. Percentage of adults having a mobile money account
Source: Global Findex Database, 2017
Note: No data are available for the Maldives in the Global Findex Database

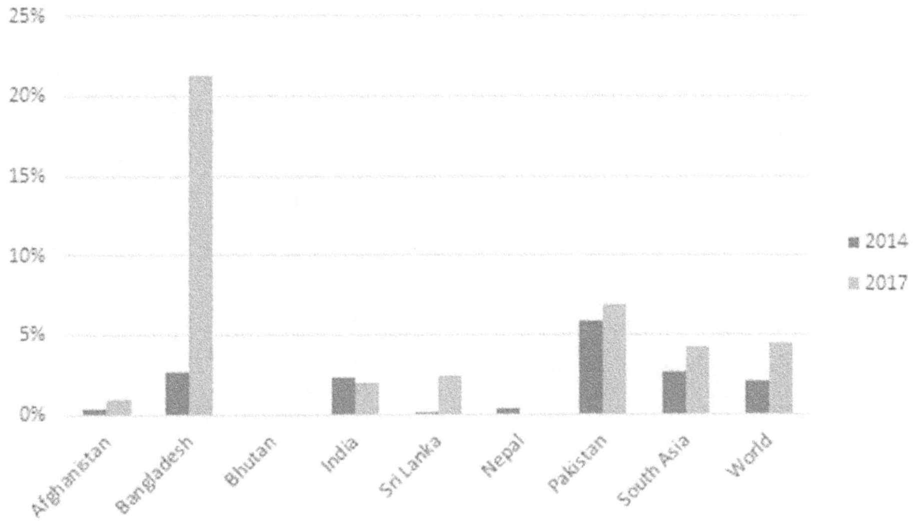

Figure 12. Percentage of adults living in rural areas having a mobile money account
Source: Global Findex Database, 2017
Note: No data are available for the Maldives in the Global Findex Database

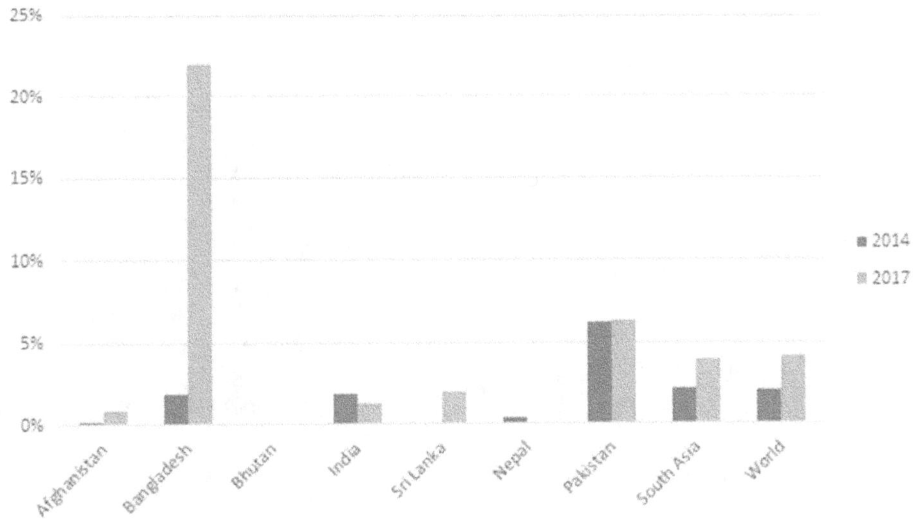

In 2017, among 1000 adults, 715 adults had a bank account in Bangladesh that is quite remarkable compared with Pakistan and Afghanistan. If the number of bank accounts increases in an economy over the years, then the goal of financial inclusion can be achieved way faster than policymakers estimated. Bank and other non-bank financial institutions can accelerate economic growth by easing the process of account opening so that the number of account ownership by the unbanked population will rise at the highest rate.

Figure 13. Number of bank accounts per 1,000 adults
Source: Global Financial Development Database, 2019
Note: No data are available for Bhutan and Maldives in the Global Financial Development Database

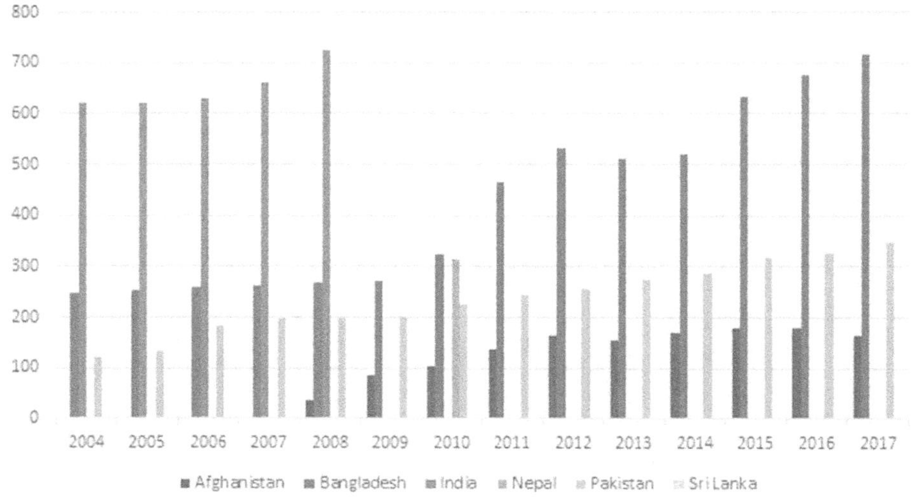

Figure 14. Number of bank branches per 100,000 adults
Source: Global Financial Development Database, 2019
Note: No data are available for Bhutan and Maldives in the Global Financial Development Database

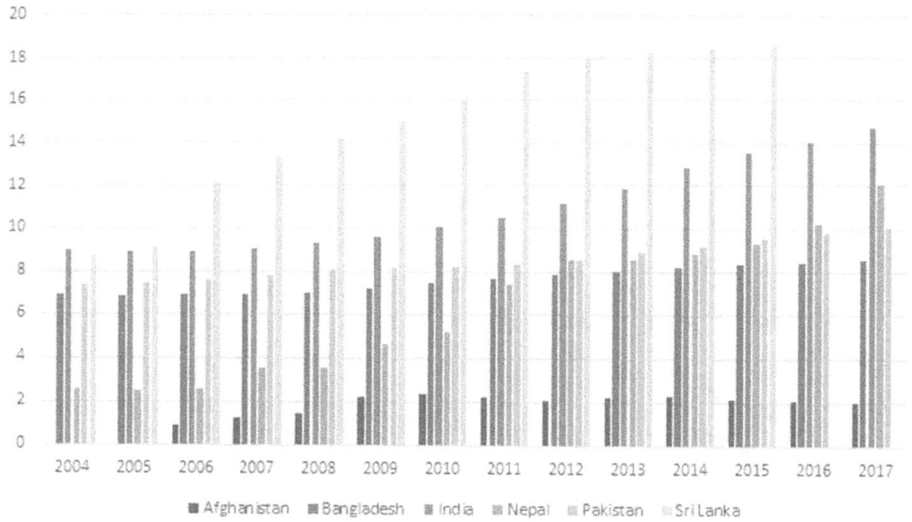

The number of bank branches for 0.10 million people in Sri Lanka was 18 in 2015. India, Nepal, Pakistan, and Bangladesh are in a favourable position, but there is still scope for the bank to expand its network and add more population to the financial systems. Banks play an essential role in the financial system and the economy. Banks provide different types of financial services, and these services help to make the overall economy more efficient. In the South Asian region, banks should open more branches to provide formal financial services for the unbanked, poor and underprivileged population who are especially living in rural areas.

Figure 15. Number of automated teller machines per 100,000 adults
Source: Global Financial Development Database, 2019
Note: No data are available for Bhutan and Maldives in the Global Financial Development Database

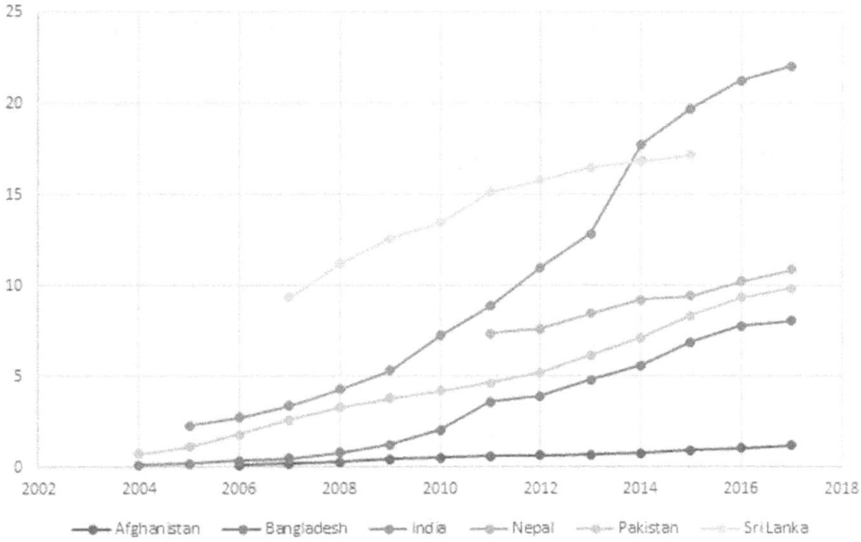

Automated teller machines, ATM, can serve as an indicator of financial inclusion. As the number of ATMs increases, the withdrawal process of money is becoming easy and convenient. The more accessibility to the ATM services the more easily and quickly the depositors can withdraw their funds that held in their bank account. In terms of the number of ATM for 0.10 million people, India is topping the chart, but Sri Lank has shown progress in setting up the ATM. Other countries banks should set up more ATM for rapid service delivery to their clients.

Figure 16. Per capita gross domestic products of South Asian countries
Source: Global Financial Development Database, 2019
Note: No data are available for Bhutan and Maldives in the Global Financial Development Database

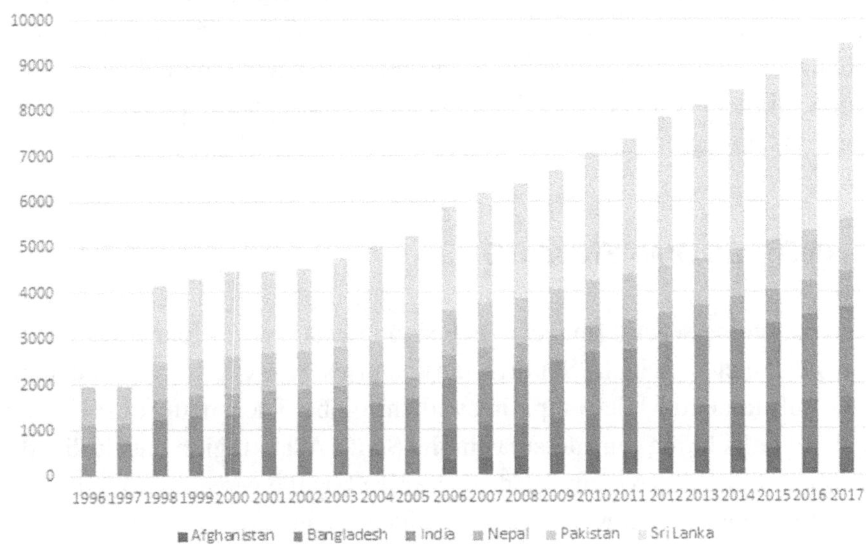

Sarma (2018) stated that income, as measured by the per capita GDP, can be used as an indicator to explain the degree of financial inclusion in a country. The analysis has shown that the per capita GDP of Sri Lanka is highest among South Asian countries. In the financial inclusion index, Sri Lanka is at the top position among eight South Asian countries. So, we can conclude that the level of financial inclusion is higher in Sri Lanka because of the higher per capita GDP.

Figure 17. Poverty headcount ratio at $1.90 a day
Source: The World Bank

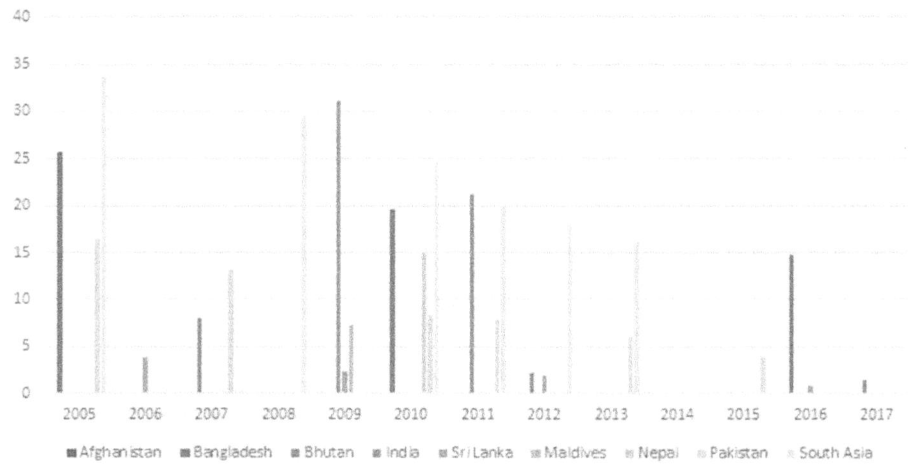

The poverty headcount ratio of $1.90 a day by the percentage of the population shows that 14.8 per cent of the population of Bangladesh was below the poverty line in 2016, which had decreased by 25 per cent from 2010 to 2016. In Sri Lanka, only 0.8 per cent population was living below the poverty line in 2016. However, the scenario for South Asia is improving; more and more people are getting a chance to escape poverty. Financial innovation is helping the population of rural areas to receive formal financial services and giving a chance to improve their livelihood.

The annual growth rate of GDP shows that the economy of Bangladesh is booming. The growth rate is 7.86 per cent. India, Maldives, and Nepal have a growth rate of above 6 per cent. Financial innovation is accelerating financial inclusion by engaging more and more people in the financial systems. Among many factors, financial inclusion is one of the main factors for consistent and considerable economic growth in the South Asian region.

SOLUTIONS AND RECOMMENDATIONS

In this study, after examining several financial inclusion indicators, it is found that financial innovation is accelerating financial inclusion in the South Asian countries. However, few financial inclusion indicators performance is substandard while comparing with the globe. The amount of savings and borrowings by the percentage of adults living in rural areas in the South Asian region has declined over the years. Similarly, the number of digital payments made or received by the percentage of adults in the past year in the South Asian region is much lower. Banks, non-bank financial institutions, and financial technol-

Figure 18. GDP growth rate of South Asian Countries
Source: The World Bank

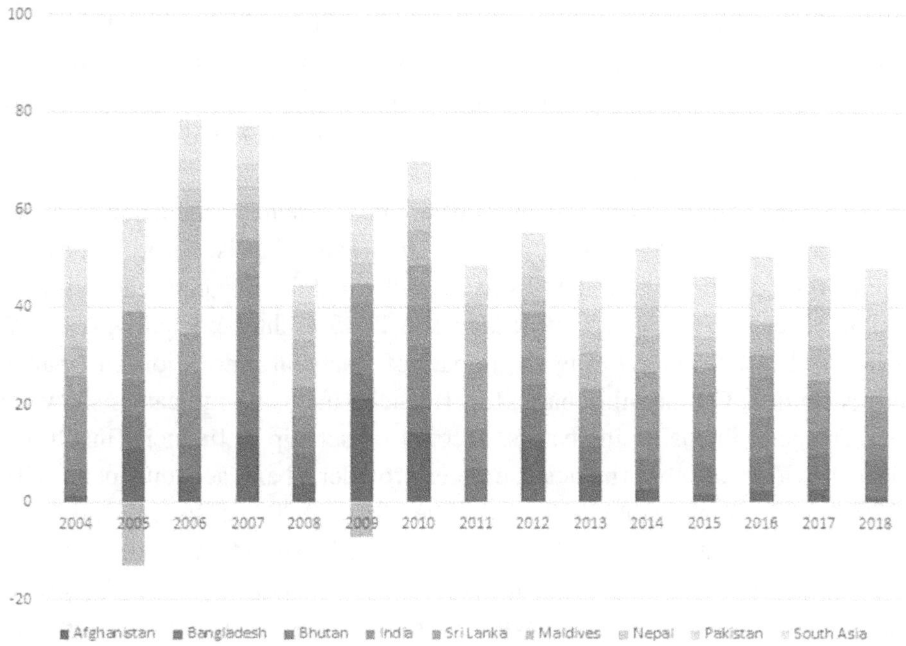

ogy companies should introduce new fintech based financial products and services to solve the problem mentioned above. If financial companies accept small amounts of deposits from the savers and provide loan at an affordable interest rate with flexible tenure to the unbanked population who are living in rural areas, then the amount of savings and borrowing by poor and unbanked population will increase. Likewise, if financial institutions lend more money to the poor and underprivileged people, then they will get a chance to way out of poverty. Besides, policymakers need to implement new policies to engage more and more unbanked people to formal financial systems. Furthermore, the number of digital payments can be increased through the extensive usage of mobile money account. If electronic commerce sites and online businesses accept payments from mobile wallets, then the number of online transactions and payments will surge. Besides saving, borrowings and digital payments, the percentage of mobile money account ownership by the percentage of adults need to rise for higher engagement in the financial system. The government of South Asian countries needs to issue policy so that the financial institutions will design technology-based financial products and services to engage the low-income unbanked population in the digital economy through accessible, affordable and convenient mobile money account.

FUTURE RESEARCH DIRECTIONS

This chapter presented the relationship between financial innovation and financial inclusion of South Asian countries. Researchers can analyse the socio and economic impact of financial innovation, financial technology, and financial inclusion in broader aspects.

CONCLUSION

In this chapter, it was aimed to identify how financial innovation accelerating financial inclusion in South Asian countries. Within this scope, eight South Asian countries were analysed in this study. Furthermore, World Bank's Global Findex database and the Global Financial Development Database from 2011 to 2017 and poverty headcount ratio at $1.90 a day from 2005-17, and GDP growth rate data from 2004-18 were taken into consideration.

In the analysis process, the empirical analysis of eighteen financial inclusion indicators was done on the collected data. According to the results of the empirical analysis, it was identified that most of the financial inclusion indicators showed a positive result which is financial innovation is accelerating financial inclusion. Several researchers (Park & Mercado, 2015; Akhter & Khalily, 2017; Wyman, 2017; Qamruzzaman & Wei, 2019) in exploring the impact of financial innovation on financial inclusion, acknowledged this finding. On the other hand, few financial inclusion indicators showed poor results. Among eighteen financial inclusion indicators, account ownership in financial institutions or mobile financial services providers or other financial services providers, bank accounts per 1,000 adults, bank branches per 100,000 adults, automated teller machines per 100,000 adults, per capita gross domestic products, poverty headcount ratio, and GDP growth rate showed satisfactory results since those indicators are accelerating the financial inclusion in South Asia over the years. However, the amount of savings and borrowings and the number of digital payments indicators has indicated poor results because the amount of savings and borrowings and the number of digital payments is much lower in this region. Due to this aspect, it was recommended that financial institutions should accept a small amount as deposits and provides easy access to the loan. Besides, financial institutions should design fintech based financial products and services, and policymakers need to issue the policy for the integration of mobile wallet account with payment systems so that the number of digital payments will yield upward trend.

Arora (2010) examined the level of financial inclusion in South Asian countries by using the World Bank and Consultative Group's Database to Assist the Poor (CGAP). The study showed that among the eight South Asian countries, Sri Lanka ranked at the top. Additionally, Sarma (2008) proposed a multidimensional index for financial inclusion (IFI) that is easily measurable and comparable across countries. The financial inclusion index of Sarma (2008) showed that Bangladesh ranked 69th, India ranked 50th, Pakistan ranked 67th, and Sri Lanka ranked 63rd among 100 countries as per the dimension of Ease of availability and usage of financial systems. This study confirmed that among all the South Asian countries, the degree of financial inclusion is high in Sri Lanka. On the other hand, Bangladesh, India, and Pakistan's level of financial inclusion is in a moderate position. Practitioners can be benefited from the findings of this study. Practitioners can be assured that the investment in fintech can be an effective idea because financial innovation is accelerating financial inclusion, and still, there is a large number of unbanked population in South Asian Countries. In Asia, more than half of the world population lives. India is at the top among the South Asian countries in unbanked population with 20.6%, Pakistan is in the second position with 5.2%, and Bangladesh ranked third with 3.7% (Alexander et al., 2017).

Economic growth can be even higher than the country's current growth if greater access to financial services by business and household, and participation of the unbanked population in the financial sector can be ensured (Arandara & Gunasekera, 2020). Access to financial services can help poverty reduction as well as can trigger the economic growth of a country. Financial technology is helping financial institutions and other financial services providers to design easy and accessible products and services. Financial institutions are offering those new innovative products and services to the unbanked population. After engaging with the financial system, the previously unbanked population is contributing to the nation's gross domestic products, and they are also getting the chance to improve their livelihood as their income increases by investing in small and medium businesses. The per capita gross domestic products and GDP growth rate have increased over the years in this region because of the high degree of financial inclusion. Several researchers (Mani, 2016; Qamruzzaman & Jianguo, 2017; Qamruzzaman & Jianguo, 2018; Bateman et al., 2019) proved that financial inclusion led to higher economic growth. Besides, the poverty headcount ratio at USD 1.90 a day by the percentage of the population has decreased over the years. Many researchers (Chibba, 2009; Swamy, 2014; Park & Mercado, 2015) acknowledged that financial inclusion is an essential tool for poverty alleviation. Financial innovation is providing many opportunities for the unbanked population through digital financial services. If the growth of financial inclusion remains at the current level, South Asia will achieve sustainable economic development.

ACKNOWLEDGMENT

This research received no specific grant from any funding agency in the public, commercial, or not-for-profit sectors.

REFERENCES

Akhter, N., & Khalily, B. (2017). *Impact of Mobile Financial Services on Financial Inclusion in Bangladesh.* Institute for Inclusive Finance and Development (InM), Working Paper, (52).

Alexander, A. J., Shi, L., & Solomon, B. (2017). *How fintech is reaching the poor in Africa and Asia.* Academic Press.

Allen, F., Carletti, E., Cull, R., Qian, J. Q., Senbet, L., & Valenzuela, P. (2014). The African financial development and financial inclusion gaps. *Journal of African Economies*, *23*(5), 614–642. doi:10.1093/jae/eju015

Andrianaivo, M., & Kpodar, K. (2011). *ICT, financial inclusion, and growth: Evidence from African countries.* Academic Press.

Arandara, R., & Gunasekera, S. (2020). *Financial Inclusion and Inclusive Growth: What Does It Mean for Sri Lanka?* World Bank Policy Research Working Paper, (9204).

Ardic, O. P., Heimann, M., & Mylenko, N. (2011). *Access to financial services and the financial inclusion agenda around the world: a cross-country analysis with a new data set.* The World Bank.

Aron, J. (2018). Mobile money and the economy: A review of the evidence. *The World Bank Research Observer*, *33*(2), 135–188. doi:10.1093/wbro/lky001

Arora, R. U. (2010). *Measuring financial access.* Griffith Business School Discussion Papers Economics, (7).

Ayyagari, M., & Beck, T. (2015). *Financial inclusion in Asia: An overview.* Asian Development Bank Economics Working Paper Series, (449).

Bateman, M., Duvendack, M., & Loubere, N. (2019). Is fin-tech the new panacea for poverty alleviation and local development? Contesting Suri and Jack's M-Pesa findings published in Science. *Review of African Political Economy*, *46*(161), 480–495. doi:10.1080/03056244.2019.1614552

Buckley, R. P., & Webster, S. (2016). FinTech in developing countries: Charting new customer journeys. *Journal of Financial Transformation*, 44.

Buckley, R. P., Arner, D. W., & Panton, M. (2013). Financial Innovation in East Asia. *Seattle UL Rev.*, *37*, 307.

Chibba, M. (2009). Financial inclusion, poverty reduction and the millennium development goals. *European Journal of Development Research*, *21*(2), 213–230. doi:10.1057/ejdr.2008.17

Demirgüç-Kunt, A., & Klapper, L. (2013). Measuring financial inclusion: Explaining variation in use of financial services across and within countries. *Brookings Papers on Economic Activity*, *2013*(1), 279–340. doi:10.1353/eca.2013.0002

Demirguç-Kunt, A., Klapper, L., Singer, D., Ansar, S., & Hess, J. (2017). *Measuring financial inclusion and the fintech revolution*. The Global Findex Database, World Bank Group.

Gabor, D., & Brooks, S. (2017). The digital revolution in financial inclusion: International development in the fintech era. *New Political Economy*, *22*(4), 423–436. doi:10.1080/13563467.2017.1259298

Goyal, A. (2012). The future of financial liberalization in South Asia. *Asia-Pacific Development Journal*, *19*(1), 63–96. doi:10.18356/81ba4404-en

Hannig, A., & Jansen, S. (2010). *Financial inclusion and financial stability: Current policy issues.* ADBI Working Paper, No. 259.

Johnson, S., & Kwak, J. (2012). Is financial innovation good for the economy? *Innovation Policy and the Economy*, *12*(1), 1–16. doi:10.1086/663153

Kim, M., Zoo, H., Lee, H., & Kang, J. (2018). Mobile financial services, financial inclusion, and development: A systematic review of academic literature. *The Electronic Journal on Information Systems in Developing Countries*, *84*(5), e12044. doi:10.1002/isd2.12044

Koh, F., Phoon, K. F., & Ha, C. D. (2018). Digital financial inclusion in South East Asia. In Handbook of Blockchain, Digital Finance, and Inclusion, Volume 2 (pp. 387-403). Academic Press. doi:10.1016/B978-0-12-812282-2.00015-2

Kumar, N. (2013). Financial inclusion and its determinants: Evidence from India. *Journal of Financial Economic Policy*, *5*(1), 4–19. doi:10.1108/17576381311317754

Laha, A. (2015). Association between financial inclusion and human development in South Asia: A cross-country analysis with special reference to India. *Journal of Economic Policy and Research*, *10*(2), 69.

Lenka, S. K., & Bairwa, A. K. (2016). Does financial inclusion affect monetary policy in SAARC countries? *Cogent Economics & Finance*, *4*(1), 1127011. doi:10.1080/23322039.2015.1127011

Llanto, G. M., & Badiola, J. A. R. (2011). *Rural Finance Environment in Asian Countries: Policies.* Innovations, Financial Inclusion.

Mani, M. (2016). Financial Inclusion in South Asia—Relative Standing, Challenges and Initiatives. *South Asian Survey*, *23*(2), 158–179. doi:10.1177/0971523118783353

Merton, R. C. (1992). Financial innovation and economic performance. *Journal of Applied Corporate Finance*, *4*(4), 12–22. doi:10.1111/j.1745-6622.1992.tb00214.x

Mustafa, F., Khursheed, A., & Fatima, M. (2018). Impact of global financial crunch on financially innovative microfinance institutions in South Asia. *Financial Innovation*, *4*(1), 13. doi:10.118640854-018-0099-8

Nicoletti, B. (2017). Financial services and Fintech. In *The Future of FinTech* (pp. 3–29). Palgrave Macmillan.

Park, C. Y., & Mercado, R. (2015). *Financial inclusion, poverty, and income inequality in developing Asia*. Asian Development Bank Economics Working Paper Series, (426).

Qamruzzaman, M., & Jianguo, W. (2017). Financial innovation and economic growth in Bangladesh. *Financial Innovation*, *3*(1), 19. doi:10.118640854-017-0070-0

Qamruzzaman, M., & Jianguo, W. (2018). Nexus between financial innovation and economic growth in South Asia: evidence from ARDL and nonlinear ARDL approaches. *Financial Innovation*, *4*(1), 20.

Qamruzzaman, M., & Wei, J. (2019). Financial Innovation and Financial Inclusion Nexus in South Asian Countries: Evidence from Symmetric and Asymmetric Panel Investigation. *International Journal of Financial Studies*, *7*(4), 61. doi:10.3390/ijfs7040061

Sahay, R., Čihák, M., N'Diaye, P. M. B. P., Barajas, A., Mitra, S., Kyobe, A., . . . Yousefi, S. R. (2015). Financial inclusion: Can it meet multiple macroeconomic goals? (No. 15/17). Washington: International Monetary Fund.

Saksonova, S., & Kuzmina-Merlino, I. (2017). Fintech as financial innovation–The possibilities and problems of implementation. *European Research Studies*, *20*(3A, 3A), 961–973. doi:10.35808/ersj/757

Sarma, M. (2008). *Financial inclusion and development: A cross country analysis*. Academic Press.

Sarma, M. (2008). *Index of financial inclusion* (No. 215). Working paper. Indian Council for Research on International Economic Relations (ICRIER).

Swamy, V. (2014). Financial inclusion, gender dimension, and economic impact on poor households. *World Development*, *56*, 1–15. doi:10.1016/j.worlddev.2013.10.019

Tufano, P. (2003). Financial innovation. In *Handbook of the Economics of Finance* (Vol. 1, pp. 307–335). Elsevier.

Venet, B. (2019). FinTech and financial inclusion. In *A Research Agenda for Financial Inclusion and Microfinance*. Edward Elgar Publishing. doi:10.4337/9781788114226.00024

Wyman, O. (2017). *Accelerating Financial Inclusion in South-East Asia with Digital Finance*. Asian development bank working paper series.

Zavolokina, L., Dolata, M., & Schwabe, G. (2016). *FinTech–What's in a Name?* Academic Press.

Zavolokina, L., Dolata, M., & Schwabe, G. (2016, December). FinTech transformation: How IT-enabled innovations shape the financial sector. In *FinanceCom 2016* (pp. 75–88). Springer.

ADDITIONAL READING

Demirguç-Kunt, A., Klapper, L., Singer, D., Ansar, S., & Hess, J. (2017). *Measuring financial inclusion and the fintech revolution.* The Global Findex Database, World Bank Group.

Gabor, D., & Brooks, S. (2017). The digital revolution in financial inclusion: International development in the fintech era. *New Political Economy*, *22*(4), 423–436. doi:10.1080/13563467.2017.1259298

Koh, F., Phoon, K. F., & Ha, C. D. (2018). Digital financial inclusion in South East Asia. In Handbook of Blockchain, Digital Finance, and Inclusion, Volume 2 (pp. 387-403). Academic Press. doi:10.1016/B978-0-12-812282-2.00015-2

Nicoletti, B. (2017). Financial services and Fintech. In *The Future of FinTech* (pp. 3–29). Palgrave Macmillan.

Park, C. Y., & Mercado, R. (2015). Financial inclusion, poverty, and income inequality in developing Asia. *Asian Development Bank Economics Working Paper Series*, (426).

Qamruzzaman, M., & Wei, J. (2019). Financial Innovation and Financial Inclusion Nexus in South Asian Countries: Evidence from Symmetric and Asymmetric Panel Investigation. *International Journal of Financial Studies*, *7*(4), 61. doi:10.3390/ijfs7040061

Saksonova, S., & Kuzmina-Merlino, I. (2017). Fintech as financial innovation–The possibilities and problems of implementation. *European Research Studies*, *20*(3A, 3A), 961–973. doi:10.35808/ersj/757

Sarma, M. (2008). *Index of financial inclusion* (No. 215). Working paper. *Indian Council for Research on International Economic Relations (ICRIER)*

Venet, B. (2019). FinTech and financial inclusion. In *A Research Agenda for Financial Inclusion and Microfinance*. Edward Elgar Publishing. doi:10.4337/9781788114226.00024

Wyman, O. (2017). Accelerating Financial Inclusion in South-East Asia with Digital Finance. *Asian development bank working paper series.*

KEY TERMS AND DEFINITIONS

Digital Financial Services: Financial products and services that can be delivered and received through digital channels.

Economic Growth: The increase in the production of goods and services in an economy in comparison with last year.

Microfinance Institutions: Institutions provide financial services to the low-income population.

Mobile Financial Services: Any financial products and services that can be accessed or received via mobile phone.

Mobile Wallet Account: It is a digital wallet that used for storing digital money and payment to the merchant.

Poverty Mitigation: Reducing poverty level and permanently lifting poor and underprivileged people out of poverty.

Traditional Financial Services: Regulated financial institutions products and services including, home loan, auto loan, checking account, savings account, and so forth.

Unbanked Population: Adults without an account in financial institutions or mobile financial services providers.

Chapter 11
The Digital Economy in the Context of Foreign Direct Investment Flows

Aneta Bobenič Hintošová
University of Economics in Bratislava, Slovakia

ABSTRACT

The main objective of the chapter is to provide a comprehensive overview of the development of the digital economy in the context of foreign direct investment flows, especially from the European Union member states point of view. First, the term and conceptualization of the digital economy is introduced, followed by an overview of theoretical background and empirical findings related to the role of foreign direct investment in the digital transformation of the economy. In this regard, the nature, position, and international footprint of digital multinational enterprises are also analyzed. The level of the digital economy and society development in the context of foreign direct investment flows is evaluated specifically in the conditions of the European Union member states. The conclusion summarizes the main partial findings, evaluates them in a mutual context, and brings implications for future research.

INTRODUCTION

The first concept of the digital economy emerged in the last decade of the 20th century, and many conceptual approaches to defining the digital economy have emerged since then. In general, the digital economy is a product of the development of digital technologies and information society and it is also referred to as the Internet Economy, New Economy, or Web Economy. It offers many new opportunities for sustainable development; however, it also comes with serious investment policy challenges, as it fundamentally changes the way companies produce and trade goods and services across borders. The weight of digital multinational enterprises (MNEs) within international production has increased dramatically in the last few years. Due to their digital communication with and selling to customers abroad, these companies are not so dependent on a large amount of physical investment in foreign markets. Hence, their economic impact on host countries is less directly visible in productive capacity generation and

DOI: 10.4018/978-1-7998-4390-0.ch011

job creation. The digital economy development is thus expected to have significant impact on changing patterns of foreign direct investment due to changes in the internalization of business models. On the other hand, however, the investment activity seems to be crucial for digital development as well. These important bidirectional relationships between digital economy and investment activity has already been suggested by UNCTAD (2017) in their *World Investment Report*. It has been indicated within a report that the digital economy is no longer just about the technology sector and digital firms, however it increasingly concerns the digitalization of supply chains across all sectors of the global economy.

In line with the presented issues, the main objective of this chapter is to provide a comprehensive overview of the development of the digital economy in the context of foreign direct investment (FDI) flows, especially from the European Union (EU) member states point of view. Similarly, as it was pointed out by Götz (2020), the author also finds it important to reevaluate the attractiveness and the readiness of countries to be engaged in the international capital movements in the light of already happening transformation to the digital economy. To meet the main objective of the chapter, the following sub-objectives are formulated: 1) introduction of the term and conceptualization of the digital economy, 2) overview of related theoretical and empirical works dealing with the problem of digital transformation of the economy and the foreign direct investment flows, 3) identification of the nature, position and international footprint of digital multinational enterprises, 4) comparison of the development of the digital economy and society in the context of foreign direct investment performance in the conditions of the European Union member states. For the comparison purposes the Digital Economy and Society Index as well as Inward/ Outward FDI Performance Indexes are used. The structure of the chapter corresponds to the outlined continuity of the presented sub-objectives.

CONCEPT OF THE DIGITAL ECONOMY

The concept of the digital economy is associated with the work by Tapscott (1996) titled *The Digital Economy: Promise and Peril in the Age of Networked Intelligence.* It was pointed out that since the old economy was typical for physical information now, in the new (so-called digital) economy, information in all its forms becomes digital, i.e. reduced to bits stored in computers and racing at the speed of light across networks. Thus, central point of this notion of the digital economy is *networking of technology* as well as *networking of humans through technology.*

Further definitions highlighted the important role of Internet (e.g. Lane, 1999) through which electronic business and electronic commerce is stimulated (e.g. Mesenbourg, 2001). In this regard, the term Internet Economy or Web Economy is also used to describe the New Economy. The development of Internet enabled the expansion of information- and knowledge- based assets connected with digital transformation of all sectors of the economy. Further definitions dealing with technological aspects pointed out digitized innovations, such as mobile services, cloud computing, big data and artificial intelligence that has boosted changes significantly and provided us extraordinary services and welfare never anticipated before (Watanabe et al., 2018b).

The digital economy has thus cross-sectoral nature, based primarily on computer- based manufacturing and/ or service provision processes. In this regard, Kling & Lamb (2000) included into the digital economy also goods and services whose development, production, sale, or provision is critically dependent on digital technologies. Besides this, the authors also explicitly recognized the segment of the information and communication technology (ICT) industry (production of ICT goods and services including telecommunications) as part of the digital economy. Finally, the authors provided one of the first segmentations of the digital economy, consisting in particular of: highly digital goods and services, mixed digital goods and services, IT-intensive services or goods production, the segments of the IT industry that support these three segments of the digital economy.

Subsequently, Mesenbourg (2001) distinguished two broader parts of the digital economy, namely production of ICT infrastructure and the use of ICTs for other economic processes. Following this concept, Asen & Blechschmidt (2016) simply suggest that there are two main areas that make up the concept of the digital economy, namely the use of digital technologies vs. placing them at the core of all business processes. Hence, newer definitions of the digital economy are broader; pointing out that the digital economy is based on dynamics, not static efficiency. Carlsson (2004) in this regard highlighted the wide use of the Internet and new level and form of connectivity among multiple heterogeneous actors, giving rise to a vast new range of combinations.

The recent definitions are trying to cover all digitally supported economic activities in their definition. What is the digital economy according to Deloitte (2020)? *It is the economic activity that results from billions of everyday online connections among people, businesses, devices, data, and processes. The backbone of the digital economy is hyperconnectivity, which means growing interconnectedness of people, organizations, and machines that results from the Internet, mobile technology and the Internet of Things (IoT).* International Monetary Fund (2018) aware of the breadth of areas and activities that the digital economy concerns distinguishes two definitions. A narrow one describes the digital economy as *online platforms, and activities that owe their existence to such platforms,* and a broader one covering *all activities that use digitized data that are part of the digital economy: in modern economies, the entire economy.*

However, despite plenty of existing definitions of the digital economy there is no universally accepted one. Instead, many authors try to perform detailed conceptualization of the notion of the digital economy distinguishing several aspects that it covers. Tsyganov & Apalkova (2016) mention macroeconomic (impact on society in general), managerial (creation of digital economy on all levels of public and private business management), structural (change of the structure of the national economy in favor of sectors related to information technologies) and technological (application of information and communication technologies) aspects.

Authors Bukht & Heeks (2017) provide further, slightly different conceptualization of the digital economy identifying three elements, namely:

- *Core scope:* Digital (IT/ICT) sector, i. e. a combination of manufacturing and services industries that capture, transmit and display data and information electronically.
- *Narrow scope:* Digital economy that represents all extensive applications of digital technologies plus their production and it would cover also some parts of emergent phenomena – the platform economy, the gig economy, the sharing economy.
- *Broad scope:* Digitalized economy, which covers e-business (ICT-enabled business transactions) and its subset, e-commerce (ICT-enabled external business transactions), algorithmic decision-making in business, use of digitally automated technologies in manufacturing and agriculture including Industry 4.0 and precision agriculture, etc.

Based on this distinction, authors provide their definition of the digital economy as *that part of economic output derived solely or primarily from digital technologies with a business model based on digital goods or services.*

Going out from the various conceptualizations of the notion of the digital economy, the clear overlap of the above mentioned approaches can be recognized, in terms of technological and structural/ sectoral aspects. This issue was pointed out also by Babaev et al. (2020) who noticed that the concept of the digital economy itself shall be interpreted in two ways, namely as a set of information and communication tools and as a sector (segment) of the economy.

In addition to various definitions and conceptualizations of the digital economy, it is possible to derive some typical features of the digital economy, which describe its nature in more detail (adopted from the work by Watanabe, 2018a):

- ICT diffusion at a tremendous pace,
- possible free of charge value provision,
- decrease of ICT prices,
- mobility and intangibility of digital goods,
- creation of different business models and digital business strategies,
- narrowing the boundaries between consumer and producer (consumers are becoming "prosumers"),
- lowering barriers of entry,
- seamless innovation activities of companies,
- using network externalities by companies,
- self-propagation phenomenon embedded in ICT products and services,
- huge monopolization of digital companies,
- these new monopolies are enhancing convenience.

FOREIGN DIRECT INVESTMENT IN THE DIGITAL ECONOMY

Important role in the process of digital transformation of the particular economy is attributed to the foreign direct investment flows (e.g. Zekos, 2005). In this regard, various so called development theories of foreign direct investment have been formulated. These theories explain the economic development of the country in connection with FDI flows, namely inward and outward FDI, where the direction of investment is evaluated from the reporting (home) economy point of view. As the most influential, Japanese FDI theories and Investment Development Path introduced by John Dunning, can be considered.

The foundations of Japanese FDI theories were laid by Kiyoshi Kojima (1975) and subsequently developed by Ozawa (1992), who described stages-based evolutionary progression of FDI on the example of transformation of the Japanese economy. According to him, the nature and direction of FDI, both inward and outward, is changing in accordance with the structural transformation of the economy. At the beginning of the factor-driven stage the resource-seeking or labor-seeking inward FDI is attracted. For the transition to the investment-driven stage outward investments towards lower-wage countries in labor-intensive manufacturing sectors are typical and at the same time inward investments in capital and intermediate goods industries are attracted. Similarly, the transition from investment-driven to the innovation-driven stage brings about simultaneously inward investments in technology-intensive sectors and outward investments in intermediate goods sectors. The economy is thus constantly evolving and developing new comparative advantages by moving from less technologically sophisticated products with low productivity to more sophisticated industrial activities with higher productivity.

The Investment Development Path developed by Dunning (1981) relates a country's net international direct investment position to its stage of development that is proxied by its GDP per capita. The theory suggests that countries tend go through five main stages of development according to their propensity to be outward and/ or inward direct investors. For the most developed countries in the last stage, it is typical that outward and inward foreign direct investments are more balanced because countries converge in the structure of their competitive advantages. These advantages are connected with the ability of countries to create and efficiently organise technological and human assets. These phenomena represent a natural and predictable progress of the structural development of economies associated with foreign direct investment flows. With the development of digital markets, the basic principles of the FDI theories seem to work well, however, according to Dunning & Wymbs (2001) the operational application of a few essential parts and the context in which they are considered must be redefined in the light of some unique characteristics of the Internet.

There are many works that have subsequently examined the relationship between foreign direct investment and the level of economic development of countries. These studies, however, have come to ambiguous results. As concluded by Carbonell & Werner (2018), the empirical literature seems to agree that positive effects of FDI on economic development and growth are largest in the case of developed countries due to their higher absorptive capacity to benefit from FDI. The studies conducted in conditions of developing economies show rather opposite results. In this regard, the study by Herzer (2012) conducted on a sample of 44 developing countries found that FDI has, on average, a negative effect on growth in these countries, but there are large differences in the effect across countries explained mainly by cross-country differences in the level of economic freedom. Similarly, Jude & Levieuge (2017) on a large sample of developing countries proved that FDI alone has no significant effect on growth; the growth-enhancing effect is obvious only beyond a certain threshold of institutional quality. Most of the studies examining the relationship between FDI and economic development and growth used the GDP indicator based on statistical data. However, the measurement of the GDP through statistics in the digital economy has been challenged e.g. by Watanade et al. (2018b). The authors point out the significance of increasing dependence on uncaptured GDP by postulating that Internet promotes a free culture, the consumption of which provides utility and happiness to people that is beyond economic value added.

Hence, in addition to these findings, it is necessary to study separately the link between FDI flows and the digital economy development taking into account appropriate measures. As noticed by Noorbakhsh & Paloni (2001) important effects connected with FDI inflows to host country are usually connected with boosting of economic growth and technology transfer, however development of technological infrastructure and human capital are critical prerequisites and so antecedents for FDI. One of the first general reviews that analyzed the role of foreign direct investment in the emergence and development of the digital economy was a work by Zekos (2005). Author concluded that FDI is focused on locations offering cheap high skilled workforce, clustering of information companies, and that the creation of joint ventures and licensing is the new form of FDI applied by MNEs. At the same time, he pointed out that the development of the digital economy does not mean that all tangible goods are transformed into digital ones but that the prevailing element is the digitization of all the other aspects that can be digitized.

One of the few recent studies in this field by Ciuriak (2018) concluded that motives to pursue inward foreign direct investment in knowledge-based and data-driven economy are different from the traditional motives in many industrial and services sectors. In the first case, the FDI are mainly realized through mergers and acquisitions (M&A) that are aimed at targeting knowledge assets, such as perspective start-ups, patents or research-intensive hubs. The author also evaluates the advantages and disadvantages associated with this type of FDI from the host economy point of view, as follows: The advantages resulting from connection with a multinational enterprise, in case the activities remain in the host country, can usually be seen in generating sufficient capital for growth, access to global markets for local products, creation of further employment opportunities for local researchers who might otherwise move abroad or provision of attractive incentive framework for local start-ups. On the other hand, the disadvantages are often connected with anticompetitive behavior of the acquirer who may block the emergence of a future competitor, relocate the knowledge-generating activities to their own headquarters abroad or outward the flow of knowledge assets.

Although there is a strong theoretical framework explaining such a behavior, empirical studies that would prove this are relatively scarce. Casella & Formenti (2018) in this regard also stated that little systematic analysis has been done to investigate the investment patterns of digital multinational enterprises. According to Götz (2020) even less is known about the digitally induced transformation of the investment promotion policies especially with respect to the countries interested in engagement in new forms of foreign direct investment. Hence, still much unknown remains about the role that foreign direct investment play in digital transformation of the economy a vice versa.

POSITION OF THE DIGITAL MNES

The importance of digital and technology-oriented multinationals is directly linked to the rapid growth of the digital economy. Not only do digital MNEs gain an excessive role in the global economy, but they also apply other internationalization patterns compared to traditional multinationals. In this regard, UNCTAD in 2017 developed a comprehensive framework for mapping firms operating in the digital economy. Two basic groups of companies are distinguished:

- Digital MNEs that perform activities based on or strictly linked to the Internet. These include:
    - *purely digital players* that operate purely in a digital environment, such as internet platforms (search engines, social networks, other platforms as sharing economy platforms and open source platforms) and providers of digital solutions (electronic and digital payments, other digital solutions in the cloud as cloud hosting and computing, web hosting and email services);
    - *"mixed" players* that combine a digital dimension with a physical one, such as e-commerce (internet retailers, other e-commerce such as online travel and booking agencies) and digital content providers (digital media and entertainment including music, video, e-books, online magazines, online courses, video games, mobile games, multiplayer interactive games as well as information and data providers such as 'big data' providers and providers of marketing and customer intelligence).
- ICT MNEs that provide the enabling infrastructure supporting the Internet. These include:
    - *IT hardware and software companies* that cover the broad categories of manufacturers of ICT hardware and components as well as software developers, providers of assistance and IT consultancy and major software houses;

- ◦ *Telecom players* that are owners of the telecommunication infrastructure on which Internet data is carried.

For practical purposes, the group of digital and the group of ICT multinational enterprises are collectively referred to in this chapter as digital multinationals. In order to compare these companies, the novel database of the 100 largest digital MNEs was introduced by UNCTAD (2017). In order to be included in the database, companies had to meet simultaneously the following criteria:

- Fulfil specific definition of "multinational company" by meeting one of these criteria:
    - ◦ Its foreign revenues or foreign assets (or both) are more than 10 per cent of the total, or
    - ◦ It has a significant number of subsidiaries outside the home economy (excluding affiliates in offshore financial centers).
- Be a corporate legal entity listed on stock exchanges worldwide. This condition helped to prevent the double-counting of consolidated accounts within the same corporate group, because few subsidiaries of listed parents are listed on their own.
- Companies should provide relevant information on the geographic distribution of sales (or operating revenues) and assets. This type of information is not part of required financial reporting and in case the company do not report any information on foreign sales or foreign assets, it is excluded from the database.

According to UNCTAD (2017), unlisted companies usually do not satisfy these minimal reporting requirements. Examples of unlisted MNEs that do not report any information on the geographic distribution of operations and on their global ownership structure are Uber, Spotify, Airbnb and Snap (Snapchat). Even among listed companies, geographic information may not be available, depending on reporting standards in the home country.

In addition, to evaluate the international footprint of these enterprises within the digital economy the new measure was introduced and applied by UNCTAD (2017). It is so called "lightness indicator" that is computed as a ratio of the share of sales generated by foreign affiliates (FS) to the corresponding share of their foreign assets (FA). It shows, in what extent the MNE is able to generate sales abroad based on the ownership of foreign assets. High values of the indicator (above 1) show "light" footprint because for the generation of particular share of foreign sales the lower share of assets is needed. On the other hand, low values (between 0 and 1) indicate "heavy" footprint meaning that the share of foreign assets is higher than the share of foreign sales. Table 1 shows top 10 digital MNEs ranked by lightness indicator.

These companies are typical for their high level of lightness that can be explained by words of Goodwin (2015): *Uber, the world's largest taxi company, owns no vehicles. Facebook, the world's most popular media owner, creates no content. Alibaba, the most valuable retailer, has no inventory. And Airbnb, the world's largest accommodation provider, owns no real estate… Something interesting is happening.*

The analysis conducted by Casella & Formenti (2018) showed that MNEs in internet-intensive sectors exhibit a highest FDI lightness ratio (a share of foreign sales is more than 2.5 times higher than share of foreign assets) against roughly the same share for traditional MNEs (value of lightness ratio equals 1). It can be explained by the tendency of digitalization to break the operational nexus between foreign sales and foreign assets. Not only have the highly digital MNEs tendency to generate more foreign sales with less foreign assets, there is in fact no correlation between the two, suggesting that commercial presence in foreign markets has no apparent association with international market entry strategies.

Table 1. Top 10 digital MNEs ranked by lightness indicator

	Company name	Sector/ classification	Share of FS (%)	Share of FA (%)	Lightness indicator
Top 10 digital MNEs by lightness indicator					
1.	VeriSign	Other digital solutions	40	3	14.67
2.	Sabre	Internet retailers	60	4	14.23
3.	eBay	Other platforms	58	7	8.89
4.	PayPal	Electronic payment	50	7	7.61
5.	CBS	Digital media	14	2	7.17
6.	Twitter	Social networks	35	7	4.93
7.	Priceline Group	Other e-commerce	80	17	4.77
8.	Sky	Digital media	30	7	4.55
9.	Expedia	Other e-commerce	44	11	3.95
10.	Netflix	Digital media	29	8	3.60
Top 10 ICT MNEs by lightness indicator					
1.	Taiwan Semiconductor Manufacturing	Components	89	3	31.30
2.	Samsung SDS	IT software & services	47	4	11.07
3.	Lite-On Technology	Components	30	3	9.76
4.	Mediatek	Components	95	16	6.00
5.	Qualcomm	IT software & services	98	18	5.61
6.	SK Hynix	Components	94	19	5.01
7.	Innolux	Components	72	16	4.38
8.	Asml Holding	Components	100	24	4.14
9.	NEC	IT software & services	21	5	3.95
10.	Nvidia	Components	87	22	3.90

Source: UNCTAD (2017)

However, none of these companies due to their relatively low amount of foreign assets is listed in the ranking of top 100 largest MNEs by volume of foreign assets, introduced every year by UNCTAD. In the recent year, following other digital MNEs were ranked among top 100 largest MNEs according to UNCTAD (2019). Beside the list of these companies, table 2 shows also calculation of lightness indicator of these companies.

Table 2 shows that 19 digital MNEs were included in the list of top 100 non-financial MNEs ranked according to the volume of foreign assets in 2018 that is the latest available data published by UNCTAD (2019). The lightness indicator for 2018 shows that their footprint is heavier than in case of companies listed in the table 1 due to establishment a tangible presence in the foreign countries where they operate. This is typically a case of telecommunication companies, which has a lightness indicator bellow 1, because they require telecommunication infrastructure to achieve capillary coverage. The last column presents values of lightness indicator of these companies in 2010 calculated on the basis of data provided by UNCTAD (2011). Only 6 of these digital MNEs belonged to the major MNEs and their footprint was

Table 2. Top digital MNEs included in the top 100 MNEs in 2018

Company	Country	Sector	Share of FS (%)	Share of FA (%)	Lightness indicator 2018	Lightness indicator 2010
Softbank Group Corp	Japan	Telecommunications	51	74	0.70	---
Apple Computer Inc	United States	Computer Equipment	63	42	1.50	---
Vodafone Group Plc	United Kingdom	Telecommunications	85	89	0.95	0.95
Amazon.com, Inc	United States	E-Commerce	39	71	0.55	---
Microsoft Corporation	United States	Computer and Data Processing	49	44	1.11	---
Deutsche Telekom AG	Germany	Telecommunications	67	68	0.99	0.92
Hon Hai Precision Industries	Taiwan Province of China	Electronic components	98	96	1.01	---
Telefonica SA	Spain	Telecommunications	74	77	0.96	0.83
Samsung Electronics Co., Ltd.	Republic of Korea	Communications equipment	61	28	2.21	2.29
Nippon Telegraph & Telephone Corp	Japan	Telecommunications	18	41	0.45	---
Tencent Holdings Limited	China	Computer and Data Processing	3	65	0.04	---
Orange SA	France	Telecommunications	56	63	0.89	---
International Business Machines Corporation	United States	Computer and Data Processing	54	56	0.96	1.44
Intel Corporation	United States	Electronic components	80	44	1.82	---
SAP SE	Germany	Computer and Data Processing	85	94	0.91	---
Alphabet Inc	United States	Computer and Data Processing	54	23	2.35	---
Altice Europe NV	Netherlands	Telecommunications	92	96	0.95	---
Sony Corporation	Japan	Consumer electronics	70	24	2.95	1.50
Oracle Corporation	United States	Computer and Data Processing	52	32	1.61	---

Source: author´s calculation based on data from UNCTAD (2019) and UNCTAD (2011)

slightly heavier (except for Samsung and International Business Machines Corporation) in comparison to the latest data.

Table 2 thus confirms rapid expansion of digital MNEs in terms of number as well as tendency to asset-lighter generation of sales. It seems that digital MNEs represent by far the most dynamic players among the largest global multinationals. As stated by Bolwijn et al. (2018) their fast growth is a result of multiple and interrelated factors, such as strong technological and market dynamics triggered by the digital revolution, financial stability and ability to cover expenditures due to high margins and liquidity, as well as a corporate culture oriented towards investment and innovation. As a result, not only have digital MNEs gained market dominance in their core segments, they have also successfully expanded in related digital areas. Over the next few years, some of them have become digital hubs operating across the wide spectrum of the digital economy. The changing nature of MNEs toward digital ones modifies also corporate strategies and attractiveness of target locations that is according to Götz (2020) happening simultaneously and being induced by the digital transformation. As indicated by Meyer et al. (2020) MNE subsidiary management works at the same time at key interfaces of technological paradigm shifts and disruption of the political and institutional environment.

Bolwijn et al. (2018) further point out to the different nature of foreign investment of digital MNEs in comparison to traditional ones, because of the different sources of value that are moving from tangible assets to intangibles and cash. This structural shift in the sources of corporate value caused that traditional approach to investment and growth based on high capital expenditures, stretched liquidity, high fixed costs and squeezed margins, is not the case of digital MNEs. There is an obvious tendency of these companies to operate on the global marketspace faster (taking into account that most of born-global companies are digital/ technological in nature) and with limited foreign investment to tangible assets. However, the development of digital MNEs may have a reverse effect on growth of global economy due to concentration of digital MNEs in a few large developed economies accompanied by limitations of outward foreign direct investment. Another obvious tendency is connected with the diversification of the activities of leading digital MNEs to other areas outside typical digital markets that is forcing also other traditional companies to use benefits of more intensive digitalization, for example by introducing online sales channels. All of these tendencies should lead to reformulation of traditional internalization strategies and introduction of new multinational business models that could form agenda of future theoretical as well as empirical research.

THE DIGITAL ECONOMY AND FDI IN THE EUROPEAN UNION MEMBER STATES

Going out from the conceptualizations of the digital economy introduced above, the progress in development of the digital economy should be examined from at least two perspectives. First, from the point of view of implementation and usage of information and communication tools not only in business but also in a wider society, and second, as a particular sector of economy that covers especially digital and ICT companies. According to the first broader context the evolution of the countries´ performance within digital economy development is evaluated by the Digital Economy and Society Index (DESI) introduced by European Commission in 2014. It is a composite index that summarizes, on an annual basis, selected relevant digital performance indicators of EU Member States in the context of the Digital Single Market Strategy. DESI is composed of five principal dimensions, each divided into a set of sub-dimensions, which are in turn composed by 44 individual indicators. The five dimensions of the DESI are following:

1. *Connectivity* – looks at both the demand and the supply side of fixed and mobile broadband and includes sub- dimensions as fixed broadband, mobile broadband, fast and ultrafast broadband and prices.
2. *Human capital* – covers two sub-dimensions as internet user skills (number and complexity of activities involving the use of digital devices and/or the Internet) and advanced skills and development (includes indicators on ICT specialist employment and ICT graduates).
3. *Use of Internet* – captures such activities as active use of Internet to get news, browse social networks, communicate, shop and other Internet services as well as use of online banking services.

4. *Integration of digital technology* – covers share of enterprises using business digitization (i.e. electronic information sharing, social media, big data analysis and cloud solutions) and e-commerce (e.g. selling online and selling online cross-border).
5. *Digital public services* – includes e-Government and e-health, i.e. e-services that reduce the time spent in public administrations and thus encourage people to use them.

Detailed explanation of the DESI construction can be found in DESI (2019) *Methodological Note*. As concluded by European Commission within DESI (2019) all EU countries improved their digital performance over the past years. The highest ratings in DESI 2019 achieved Finland, Sweden, the Netherlands, and Denmark, which also belong to the global leaders in digitalization. These countries are followed by the United Kingdom, Luxembourg, Ireland, Estonia, and Belgium. Some other countries, including all Visegrad countries (namely the Czech Republic, Hungary, Poland and Slovakia), however still have a long way to go, and the EU as a whole needs improvement to be able to compete on the global stage. In this regard, a study by Stavytskyy et al. (2019) also concluded that a more prosperous society leads to more advanced digital services. The authors at the same time showed that the current value of DESI at almost 98% is determined by its previous trends, i.e. the development of the digital economy cannot be interrupted rapidly.

At the same time, the level of development of the digital economy can to some extent be considered as a factor improving location advantage of the country and thus its relative success in attracting FDI. The success in this regard can be measured through inward FDI performance index (IFDIPI) developed by UNCTAD (2002). Later, the outward FDI performance index (OFDIPI) was introduced (UNCTAD, 2004) as a measure of ownership advantage of the companies based in particular country. Both indexes relate FDI flows to the economic size of the particular country measured by GDP and has been used in several studies for the purpose of evaluation of advantages connected with FDI flows (e.g. Rodríguez et al., 2009; Lei et al., 2013). They are calculated as the ratio of a country's share in global FDI to its share in global GDP. Depending on the direction of FDI flows, an inward or outward FDI performance index is distinguished. Values above one indicate that the country receives (or allocates abroad) higher portion of FDI than its relative economic size. Values below one indicate that the country receives (or allocates abroad) lower portion of FDI than its relative economic size.

Following overview provides comparison of the European Union member states (including the United Kingdom as the EU member at the time to which the data refer) according to their level of digital development and FDI performance. For this purpose, two matrixes are constructed that put into relation inward / outward FDI performance index calculated according to formula mentioned above and the Digital Economy and Society Index. The data for calculation of FDI performance indexes were taken from the UNCTAD statistics (UNCTADSTAT), the DESI values were taken from the DESI Data. In order to capture the longer trend in the development of these indexes, average values for the three-year period, from 2016 to 2018, were used in all cases. For the purposes of both matrixes construction, the classification of countries into particular quadrants was performed on the basis of critical values of individual indexes as follows: in case of the DESI, the critical value refers to the average value of the index of all EU member states; in case of both FDI performance indexes the critical value refers to one.

Figure 1 shows position of European Union member states in terms of the development of the digital economy and society, as well as in terms of the performance of inward foreign direct investment. Cyprus and Malta are not included in the matrix due to extreme positive values of inward FDI performance index. The majority of countries (including Cyprus) belong to attractive FDI locations (values of inward

FDI performance index are above one) with below average level of the digital economy and society development. These countries attract higher portion of FDI than may be expected according to their economic size. However, it seems that these countries attract investors by other location advantages than well-developed digital environment, such as favorable investment promotion policy or low-cost business environment. On the other hand, digitally developed countries also attract considerable portion of inward FDI, but the nature of their location advantages seem to be different as in the previous case. The third group includes digitally less developed countries attracting relatively less inward FDI when compared to their economic size, possibly due to a lack of any significant location advantage. The last smallest group consists of digitally developed countries, which, however, probably due to a lack of complementary factors, fail to attract the volume of inward FDI outweighing their economic strength.

Figure 1. Inward FDI performance - DESI matrix
Source: author´s construction based on data from UNCTADSTAT and DESI Data

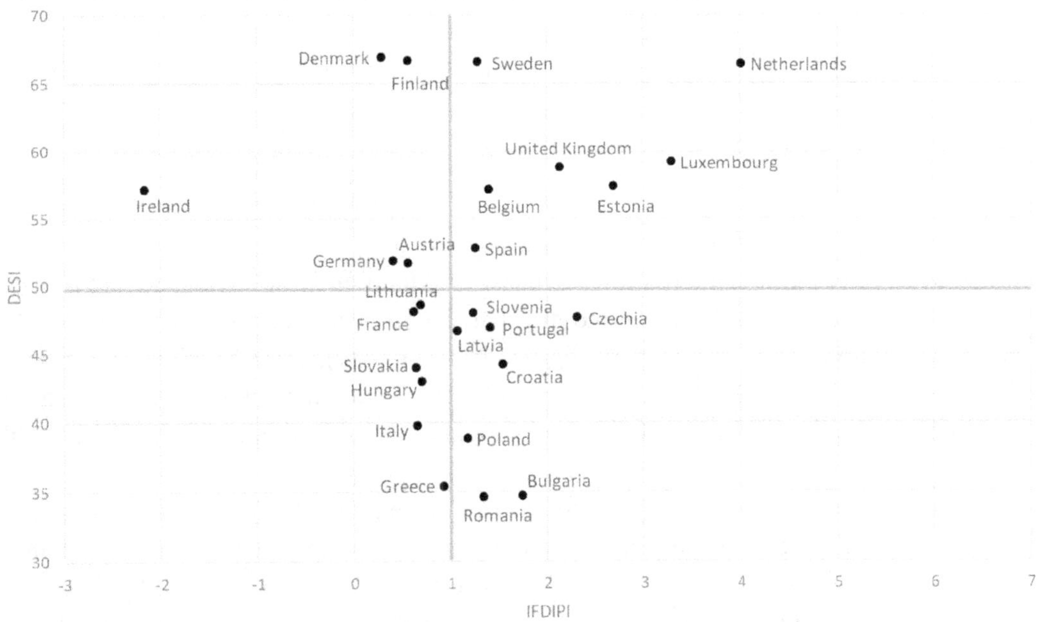

Figure 2 shows position of the European Union member states in terms of the development of the digital economy and society, as well as in terms of the performance of outward foreign direct investment. Luxembourg and Malta are not included in the matrix due to extreme values of outward FDI performance index. Most countries are those that achieve digital performance below the EU average, with a lack of local companies with strong ownership advantages. On the other hand, the least numerous group consists of digitally relatively underdeveloped countries with companies able to allocate their investments abroad. It seems that lower level of the digital development is associated with reduced ability of local companies to become carriers of international capital movements. In the case of digitally developed countries, the situation is rather opposite. Majority of these countries reached high values of outward FDI performance index suggesting that companies in the particular country have strong ownership advantages that they

Figure 2. Outward FDI performance - DESI matrix
Source: author´s construction based on data from UNCTADSTAT and DESI Data

deploy or want to amplify through international expansion. Although these advantages are firm-specific, many of them are closely related to the economic characteristics and competitive forces of the home country possibly including also high level of digitization. Another group of highly digitized countries recorded lower values of outward FDI performance index suggesting that ownership advantages of local firms (possibly including intensive use of information and communication technologies) are utilized in a home country.

To shed more light to the outlined topic, the position of individual countries within both matrixes is evaluated too. A total of 16 countries record equal positions in both matrixes. Most of them (namely Belgium, Luxembourg, Netherlands, Spain, Sweden, the United Kingdom) are digitally high performing countries and at the same time can be considered as developed countries in the last stage of investment development path. Their inward and outward investment position is significant and balanced since they can adapt investment activities to dynamic development factors. On the opposite side there are countries (namely Greece, Hungary, Italy, Lithuania and Slovakia) whose localization factors are relatively weak, apparently do not relying on digital development, accompanied by relatively weak ownership advantages of local firms. Three countries including Austria, Denmark and Ireland, despite their relatively high position in DESI ranking are underperformers in terms of inward as well as outward FDI. These countries attract and allocate abroad relatively lower portion of FDI in comparison to their size, what can indicate that local digitally advanced companies exploit their ownership advantages primarily on the local market. The remaining two countries, namely Czechia and Cyprus despite their below average position in DESI ranking, are intensively involved in international capital flows in terms of inward as well as outward FDI.

The rest of countries record different values of FDI performance indexes, namely better position in inward or outward FDI performance, with the prevalence of the first group. Countries performing better as attractive inward investment locations in comparison to outward investment (namely Bulgaria, Croatia, Latvia, Poland, Portugal, Romania, Slovenia) are attracting foreign investors by other location determinants than developed digital environment. Exemptions in this regard form Estonia and Malta that have relatively high values of DESI accompanied by relatively high values of inward FDI performance index (and below one values of outward FDI performance index). Remaining countries, namely Finland, Germany and France perform better as bearers of outward foreign direct investment. This comparative study has shown that there are significant cross-country differences in the level of digital transformation and in the rate of FDI performance within EU countries.

CONCLUSION

The digital economy can be defined and conceptualized from various points of view, however the most significant overlap is obvious within technological and structural/ sectoral aspects. The development of the digital economy can thus be considered as the consequence of qualitative transformation of wide range of economic relations that are based on intensive use of information and communication technologies. It covers also particular sector of economy aimed at production/ provision of ICT goods and services. However, the open question still remains what factors and in what direction influence the process of countries' transformation into the digital economy. In the center of the interest within this chapter was to evaluate development of the digital economy in the context of foreign direct investment flows.

The most influential FDI theories show that higher level of economic development of the country intensifies inward and outward FDI and their convergence. At the same time, however, it should be acknowledged that in the context of the development of the digital economy, some revision of FDI theories should be made, which creates interesting opportunities for future research. In this context, particular attention should be paid to the growing importance of digital MNEs in the global marketplace and their significantly changed sources of value creation. There is a structural shift from tangible assets to intangible assets as key sources of value creation. This lightness by which digital MNEs can generate high share of sales abroad without necessity of huge investments in allocation of tangible assets abroad, changes also the patterns of foreign direct investment flows. Another important feature is a geographical distribution of key global digital MNEs that are concentrated in large developed economies what can strengthen a reverse trend in direction of FDI. On the other hand, diversification of activities of digital MNEs outside their core business can motivate also other companies in traditional sectors to digitize their activities to a greater extent and consequently lead to further changes in international business models. All of these aspects, including asset-light phenomenon, changing patterns of foreign direct investment, nature of trade in goods and services as well as other global macro trends, present interesting research challenges. Despite some theoretical and descriptive analysis made in this field there is a huge space for empirical evidence creation.

Subsequent analysis of the development of the digital economy and society in the context of foreign direct investment performance in conditions of the European Union member states, showed interesting results too. The position of individual countries within both matrixes vary widely. The relationship between the level of digital development and the performance of outward foreign direct investment seems to be more pronounced, since digitally the most developed countries allocate a higher share of direct investment abroad compared to their economic size. However, this assumption would require further empirical analysis within future research. To sum up, the European Union do not form a homogenous place in terms of digital development and performance of FDI flows. Further research aimed at analyzing nature of inward and outward FDI with special emphasis on digital multinationals would shed more light on this issue. The need of future research is justified also by investment promotion policy priorities of some European countries, including Visegrad countries, to attract valuable, sustainable and technologically advanced investment. Hosting such an investment could accelerate further digitalization of local economies by various direct or spillover effects.

REFERENCES

Asen, R., & Blechschmidt, B. (2016). Making digital, real and rewarding. *Cognizanti, 9*(1), 2-13. Retrieved from https://www.cognizant.com/whitepapers/being-digital-making-digital-real-and-rewarding-cognizanti12-codex2094.pdf

Babaev, B. D., Nikolaeva, E. E., Babaev, D. B., & Borovkova, N. V. (2020). Russia: Digital economy or industrial and information economy? *Lecture Notes in Networks and Systems*, *87*, 332–341. doi:10.1007/978-3-030-29586-8_39

Bolwijn, R., Casella, B., & Zhan, J. (2018). International production and the digital economy. In International Business in the Information and Digital Age (Progress in International Business Research, Vol. 13), (pp. 39-64). Emerald Publishing Limited.

Bukht, R., & Heeks, R. (2017). Defining, conceptualizing and measuring the digital economy. In *Development Informatics* (Working paper No. 68). Manchester: Global Development Institute.

Carbonell, J. B., & Werner, R. A. (2018). Does foreign direct investment generate economic growth? A new empirical approach applied to Spain. *Economic Geography*, *94*(4), 425–456. doi:10.1080/00130095.2017.1393312

Carlsson, B. (2004). The Digital economy: What is new and what is not? *Structural Change and Economic Dynamics*, *15*(3), 245–264. doi:10.1016/j.strueco.2004.02.001

Casella, B., & Formenti, L. (2018). FDI in the digital economy: A shift to asset-light international footprints. *Transnational Corporations*, *25*(1), 101–130. doi:10.18356/cb688e94-en

Ciuriak, D. (2018). *Rethinking Industrial Policy for the Data-Driven Economy*. Retrieved from https://papers.ssrn.com/sol3/papers.cfm?abstract_id=3223072

Deloitte. (2020). *What is digital economy? Unicorns, transformation and the internet of things*. Retrieved from https://www2.deloitte.com/mt/en/pages/technology/articles/mt-what-is-digital-economy.html

DESI. (2019). *DESI Report 2019*. Brussel: European Commission. Retrieved from https://ec.europa.eu/digital-single-market/en/desi

DESI. (2019). *Methodological Note*. Brussel: European Commission. Retrieved from https://digital-agenda-data.eu/datasets/desi/visualizations

Dunning, J. H. (1981). *International Production and the Multinational Enterprise*. Allen & Unwin.

Dunning, J. H., & Wymbs, C. (2001). The challenge of electronic markets for international business theory. *International Journal of the Economics of Business*, *8*(2), 273–301. doi:10.1080/13571510110051432

Goodwin, T. (2015). *The battle is for the customer interface*. Retrieved from https://techcrunch.com/2015/03/03/in-the-age-of-disintermediation-the-battle-is-all-for-the-customer-interface/

Götz, M. (2020). Attracting foreign direct investment in the era of digitally reshaped international production. The primer on the role of the investment policy and clusters – the case of Poland. *Journal of East-West Business*, *26*(2), 131–160. doi:10.1080/10669868.2019.1692985

Herzer, D. (2012). How does foreign direct investment really affect developing countries´ growth? *Review of International Economics*, *20*(2), 396–414. doi:10.1111/j.1467-9396.2012.01029.x

International Monetary Fund. (2018). Measuring the Digital Economy. Washington: International Monetary Fund. Retrieved from file:///C:/Users/eu/Downloads/022818MeasuringDigitalEconomy.pdf

Jude, C., & Levieuge, G. (2017). Growth effect of FDI in developing economies: The role of institutional quality. *World Economy*, *40*(4), 715–742. doi:10.1111/twec.12402

Kling, R., & Lamb, R. (2000). IT and organizational change in digital economies. In E. Brynjolfsson & B. Kahin (Eds.), *Understanding the Digital Economy* (pp. 295–324). MIT Press.

Kojima, K. (1975). International trade and foreign investment: Substitutes or complements. *Hitotsubashi Journal of Economics*, *16*(1), 1–12.

Lane, N. (1999). Advancing the digital economy into the 21st century. *Information Systems Frontiers*, *1*(3), 317–320. doi:10.1023/A:1010010630396

Lei, M., Zhao, X., Deng, H., & Tan, K. C. (2013). DEA analysis of FDI attractiveness for sustainable development: Evidence from Chinese provinces. *Decision Support Systems*, *56*, 406–418. doi:10.1016/j.dss.2012.10.053

Mesenbourg, T. L. (2001). *Measuring the Digital Economy*. US Bureau of the Census. Retrieved from https://www.census.gov/content/dam/Census/library/workingpapers/2001/econ/umdigital.pdf

Meyer, K. E., Li, C., & Schotter, A. P. J. (2020). Managing the MNE subsidiary: Advancing a multi-level and dynamic research agenda. *Journal of International Business Studies*, *51*(4), 538–576. doi:10.105741267-020-00318-w

Noorbakhsh, F., Paloni, A., & Youssef, A. (2001). Human capital and FDI inñows to developing countries: New empirical evidence. *World Development*, *29*(9), 1593–1610. doi:10.1016/S0305-750X(01)00054-7

Ozawa, T. (1992). Theory of FDI as a dynamic paradigm of economic development. *Transnational Corporations*, *1*(1), 27–54.

Rodríguez, C., Gómez, C., & Ferreiro, J. (2009). A proposal to improve the UNCTAD's inward FDI potential index. *Transnational Corporations*, *18*(3), 85–114. doi:10.18356/35d71cb5-en

Stavytskyy, A., Kharlamova, A., & Stoica, E. A. (2019). The analysis of the digital economy and society index in the EU. *Baltic Journal of European Studies*, *9*(3), 245–261. doi:10.1515/bjes-2019-0032

Tapscott, D. (1996). *Digital Economy: Promise and Peril in the Age of Networked Intelligence*. McGraw-Hill.

Tsyganov, S., & Apalkova, V. (2016). Digital economy: A new paradigm of global information society. *Economic Review (Kansas City, Mo.)*, *45*(3), 295–311.

UNCTAD. (2002). *World Investment Report: Transnational Corporations and Export Competitiveness*. United Nations Publication.

UNCTAD. (2004). *World Investment Report: The Shift Towards Services*. United Nations Publication.

UNCTAD. (2011). *World Investment Report: Non-Equity Modes of International Production and Development*. United Nations Publication.

UNCTAD. (2017). *World Investment Report: Investment and the Digital Economy*. United Nations Publication.

UNCTAD. (2019). *World Investment Report: Special Economic Zones*. New York: United Nations Publication. Retrieved from https://unctadstat.unctad.org/EN/

UNCTAD. (2019). *World Investment Report: Special Economic Zones*. United Nations Publication.

UNCTADSTAT. (n.d.). Retrieved from https://unctadstat.unctad.org/EN/

Watanabe, C., Naveed, K., Tou, Y., & Neittaanmäki, P. (2018b, December). Measuring GDP in the digital economy: Increasing dependence on uncaptured GDP. *Technological Forecasting and Social Change*, *137*, 226–240. doi:10.1016/j.techfore.2018.07.053

Watanabe, C., Tou, Y., & Neittaanmäki, P. (2018a, November). A new paradox of the digital economy: Structural sources of the limitation of GDP statistics. *Technology in Society*, *55*, 9–23. doi:10.1016/j.techsoc.2018.05.004

Zekos, G. (2005). Foreign direct investment in a digital economy. *European Business Review*, *17*(1), 52–68. doi:10.1108/09555340510576267

ADDITIONAL READING

Alcácer, J., Cantwell, J., & Piscitello, L. (2016). Internationalization in the information age: A new era for places, firms, and international business networks? *Journal of International Business Studies*, *47*(5), 499–512. doi:10.1057/jibs.2016.22

Banalieva, E. R., & Dhanaraj, C. (2019). Internalization theory for the digital economy. *Journal of International Business Studies*, *50*(8), 1372–1387. doi:10.105741267-019-00243-7

Chen, W., & Kamal, F. (2016). The impact of information and communication technology adoption on multinational firm boundary decisions. *Journal of International Business Studies*, *47*(5), 563–576. doi:10.1057/jibs.2016.6

Eden, L. (2019). The fourth industrial revolution: Seven lessons from the past. In van Tulder, R., Verbeke, A., Piscitello, L. (Ed.) International Business in the Information and Digital Age (Progress in International Business Research, Vol. 13), (pp. 15-35). Emerald Publishing Limited.

OECD. (2017). *OECD Digital Economy Outlook*. Paris: OECD publishing. Retrieved from https://www.oecd-ilibrary.org/docserver/9789264276284-en.pdf?expires=1585926331&id=id&accname=guest&checksum=224158954A049A1711A4CFF9DD4C58F4

Sinha, M., & Sengupta, P. P. (2018). FDI and industry in developed and developing countries. In *Proceedings of International Conference on Soft Computing in Data Analytics* (vol. 758, pp. 463-472). Springer Nature Singapore. 10.1007/978-981-13-0514-6_46

Strange, R., & Zucchella, A. (2017). Industry 4.0, global value chains and international business. *Multinational Business Review*, *25*(3), 174–184. doi:10.1108/MBR-05-2017-0028

UNCTAD. (2019). *Digital Economy Report*. New York: United Nations Publications. Retrieved from https://unctad.org/en/PublicationsLibrary/der2019_en.pdf

Zanfei, A., Coveri, A., & Pianta, M. (2019). FDI patterns and global value chains in the digital economy. *Working Papers Series in Economics, Mathematics and Statistics No. 2019/03.*

KEY TERMS AND DEFINITIONS

Digital Economy: Consequence of qualitative transformation of wide range of economic relations that are based on intensive use of information and communication technologies.

Digital Multinational Enterprise: Enterprises that perform activities primarily based on Internet and/ or provide the enabling infrastructure supporting the Internet in more than one country.

FDI Performance Index: The ratio of a country's share in global FDI to its share in global GDP.

Inward FDI: Net inflows of foreign direct investment made by a foreign entity in business interests in another (reporting) country, in the form of either establishing business operations or acquiring business assets or property rights in the other (reporting) country.

Lightness Indicator: Indicates how many times higher share of foreign sales is generated by multinational enterprise by given share of foreign assets.

Outward FDI: Net outflows of foreign direct investment made by a domestic entity (i.e., from reporting country) in business interests in another (foreign) country, in the form of either establishing business operations or acquiring business assets or property rights in the other (foreign) country.

Visegrad Countries: A cultural and political alliance of four Central European countries, namely the Czech Republic, Hungary, Poland, and Slovakia.

Chapter 12
The Future of Audit in Light of Technological Changes: Opportunities and Threats

Sanja Sever Mališ
Faculty of Economics and Business, University of Zagreb, Croatia

Lajoš Žager
Faculty of Economics and Business, University of Zagreb, Croatia

Mateja Brozović
https://orcid.org/0000-0001-7338-7494
Faculty of Economics and Business, University of Zagreb, Croatia

ABSTRACT

External audit of financial statements plays a key role in achieving transparent financial reporting, since its purpose is to provide reasonable assurance that the presented financial statements are free of material misstatements due to fraud or error. In the process of fulfilling this role, auditors must be adaptable, especially when it comes to technological advancements. This chapter explains the effect that new technologies have on audit of financial statements. In addition to summarizing the technological changes that impacted the audit profession in the past and therefore introduced new generations of audit, the authors have identified issues and challenges in the way the audit is currently performed. Some of the new technologies that are discussed in this chapter have the potential to mitigate these issues. However, new challenges and risks may be introduced with accepting these technologies in the process of financial reporting and auditing.

DOI: 10.4018/978-1-7998-4390-0.ch012

INTRODUCTION

Financial reporting is one of the crucial mechanisms of corporate governance, aimed at reducing information asymmetry of primarily external users that are interested in the financial position and performance of a certain company. Despite the increasing importance of presenting different non-financial information, financial information still serves as a basis in a decision-making process of most of the interest groups, such as investors, creditors, financial institutions, etc. Therefore, reliable and accurate financial information on the company's operations is still essential in order to maintain the stability of the financial system. External audit of financial statements plays a key role in achieving this goal, due to its purpose of increasing confidence in the information presented in financial statements. It is inevitable that auditors must constantly adapt. First, they have to adapt to the changing environment that surrounds their clients that are subject to audit. Second, they also have to continuously improve their methods and techniques in order to keep their competitive advantage. Third, the expectations of audit users tend to change over the history, causing auditors to take on new roles. Technological changes are one of the most important drivers of changes in the audit profession, forcing auditors to adapt in all three previously mentioned areas. This chapter covers the effect that technologies such as artificial intelligence, data analytics, blockchain, etc. will have on audit of financial statements.

The evolution of modern audit profession has already been stimulated by new technologies that have been adapted over the course of history. Traditional manual audits have been replaced by IT audit that emerged in the 1970s and resulted in using computing devices, software and databases in the audit process. The output of using an increasing number of computer assisted audit techniques and tools (CAATTs) was improved efficiency and effectiveness of audit activities. Especially for large audit firms, general audit software, data-extraction software, audit reporting software, etc., are already integrated in their audit methodologies.

Despite the technology that is currently used in audit of financial statements, these advancements have still not been able to mitigate the inherent limitations of audit process. Audit of financial statements is still based on the principle of material significance, sampling and providing only reasonable assurance regarding financial statements. The question is: are the new technologies, that have the potential to be used in the audit process in the future, capable of reducing audit risk and eliminating some of the limitations that characterize the audit process today?

The main goal of this chapter is to explore the future directions in the development of audit driven by technological changes, as well as to reflect on its evolution through past and present. In line with presented main goal, the sub-goals of this chapter are: 1) to explain the importance of audit of financial statements, 2) to investigate the evolution of audit of financial statements through history and previous technological advancements, 3) to recognize potential issues and challenges in the way the audit is currently performed, 4) to identify new technologies that might shape the future of financial reporting and audit, 5) to explore the roles that auditors will assume in light of technological changes.

IMPORTANCE OF AUDIT OF FINANCIAL STATEMENTS

Information disclosure and financial transparency can be highlighted as one of the most important corporate governance mechanisms. Due to possible conflict of interest and opportunistic behavior of management responsible for financial statements, different forms of financial reporting control or supervision are required in order to enhance the credibility of the financial information presented. Therefore, the importance of auditing is also emphasized within the OECD Corporate Governance Principles, stating that an annual audit should be conducted by an independent, professional and qualified auditor in line with quality audit standards, with the purpose of providing external and objective assurance to management and other stakeholders regarding financial position and performance of the company in all material aspects (Organisation for Economic Co-operation and Development – OECD, 2015). It can be concluded that the audit of financial statements has evolved out of a need to protect the interests of financial statements users who use the information presented for business decision making.

Agent theory or agency theory has the greatest application in explaining the need for audit, but also in general corporate governance mechanisms. According to this theory, the need for audit arose when the management function of the company separated from the ownership function, meaning that the owners entrusted managing the company to professional managers (Sever Mališ, Tušek & Žager, 2012). If in such relationship both parties maximize their benefits, there is a possibility that the agent (manager) will not always act in the best interests of the principal (owner) (Jensen & Meckling, 1976). Due to this issue, owners tend to establish forms of control over managers' behavior, which causes control costs, or motivate them with monetary benefits, which can be considered as costs of bonding. However, even in such cases, there may be a discrepancy between managerial decisions and decisions that maximize wealth for owners, and these costs are called residual costs. All three types of costs are commonly referred to as agency costs (Jensen & Meckling, 1976). Audit fee can be considered as a control cost, since auditors are external and independent professionals who are hired to provide reasonable assurance regarding the truthfulness and fairness of information presented in financial statements.

The main features of audit, as a service provided by audit firms to their clients, is that it must be performed within a specified timeframe and in line with strict rules regarding the criteria and procedure for evaluating the compliance of financial statements with those criteria. As a result, the process of auditing financial statements is divided into several stages, which are intertwined and complementary. In the broadest sense, the starting point of a financial reporting framework is in accounting principles, which imply that the financial statements must be based on objective data, contain all material information, comparable to prior periods, and present the company's financial position and performance realistically. Accounting principles provide the basic guidance for the preparation of financial statements, but they are very general, which is why they are further elaborated in the form of accounting standards. Together with relevant laws, accounting principles, policies and standards, they represent basic criteria for evaluating truthfulness and fairness of financial statements. In doing so, auditors have to make sure that they comply with auditing standards, code of professional ethics and laws during every phase of the audit process.

The process of auditing financial statements can be seen as an integrated scope of various tasks that the auditor needs to perform in order to obtain sufficient and appropriate evidence, as a basis for expressing the auditor's opinion. It begins with undertaking the audit obligation and getting to know the client's business in more detail for quality audit planning and risk assessment. Appropriate planning facilities work in the later stages of the audit by helping the auditor to pay due attention to important areas, identify potential issues in a timely manner, as well as to properly allocate resources during engagement to perform audit effectively. It is essential for the auditor to be independent of management's influence when planning and defining the scope of the audit. The most important result of the audit planning phase is the design of the audit plan, which is updated and adjusted as needed during the audit. A significant segment of the financial statement audit is to become familiar with the client's internal control system, which aims, inter alia, to ensure the accuracy and comprehensiveness of the accounting records and to enable the preparation of credible financial information. In the context of auditing financial statements, the proper functioning of the internal control system can significantly reduce the scope of substantive tests that the auditor must perform. Therefore, the auditor will seek to gain an understanding of the overall system through procedures such as insights, inquires aimed at management and staff, inspection of policies, documents and instructions, followed with conducting test of controls. Based on all the information collected, the auditor assesses the risk of material misstatements in financial statements. Specifically, his duty is to obtain the audit evidence that is required to conclude that the financial statements as a whole do not contain material misstatements, which is considered as providing reasonable assurance. Depending on the assessed level of inherent and control risk, the auditor evaluates how much tests he must perform to reduce the detection risk to an acceptable level. In accordance with the principle of documentation, the auditor is required to obtain sufficient and appropriate audit evidence to express a justified opinion. Testing all population (e.g. all invoices issued) is irrational in most cases, since it would require large resources and therefore the costs usually outweigh the benefits. Therefore, the audit of financial statements is generally based on the use of a sample. The use of the sample also entails the risk of sampling, that is, the risk that the auditor will draw different conclusions from the sample compared to the conclusions that would be reached by testing all items in the population. Although the use of the sampling method in auditing has a number of advantages, primarily related to time and other resource savings, it is one of the main limitations of the audit process, allowing the auditor to provide only reasonable assurance about the reality and objectivity of the audited financial statements. The auditor's report is the final result of the entire audit process of the financial statements and the sole source of information about the audit performed for most users of the financial statements. The most important part is the auditor's opinion on whether the financial statements in all material respects comply with the applicable financial reporting framework and whether the financial statements have been fairly presented.

LIMITATIONS OF TODAY'S AUDIT - CAN NEW TECHNOLOGICAL SOLUTIONS HELP TO OVERCOME THEM?

There are certain inherent limitations in the process of auditing financial statements as it functions today. These limitations prevent the auditor from being able to provide absolute assurance that any misstatement in financial statements has been identified. In other words, even if the audit was properly planned and performed in accordance with the relevant audit standards, there is a risk that significant misstatements have not been detected. According to International Standards on Auditing, conducting an audit does not guarantee the disclosure of all material misstatements, due to the use of professional judgment of auditors, the inherent limitations of internal controls, and the fact that most of the records available to the auditor essentially create certain assurances rather than providing a final proof (International Federation of Accountants – IFAC, 2009).

The auditor is required to use professional judgment at all stages of the audit, especially when assessing audit risks, selecting audit procedures and interpreting audit evidence. While there are guidelines that should guide auditors and facilitate their professional judgment, it is still a subjective process that, due to the nature of the decisions, cannot be fully standardized or defined. It is also influenced by various factors, such as knowledge and professional skills, independence, objectivity and professional skepticism.

Professional judgment is also used during audit sampling, where, in addition to the risk of misjudgment, there is a risk of using the sample instead of the population. Namely, because of the use of the sample, it is possible for the auditor to draw different conclusions about the population in comparison to the conclusions that he would have obtained by testing all the items of the population. However, there is generally no alternative to this approach, since in the case of testing all population items, the cost of the audit would outweigh the benefits. This is the area where implementing new technological solutions might bring the most benefits by providing tools and solutions that could allow auditors to test all the items in the population efficiently.

Furthermore, the limitations of the audit process can also be found in the nature of audit evidence, which does not point to a final proof but creates a certain level of assurance. That level of assurance depends, among other things, on the source of the evidence. Although the best evidence is known to be that obtained from independent third parties, such evidence is sometimes not available for certain items, which means that the auditor must draw conclusions, for example, from management statements, which may have hidden motives and conflict of interest. This is also an area that could benefit from technological changes, which could increase the trustworthiness of audit evidence.

Financial statements and accounting records in general can additionally be distorted by fraud. The risk of detecting material misstatements due to fraud is usually greater than the risk related to unintentional errors. Frauds may be covered up by actions such as forgery, intentional omission of transaction records, or intentional submission of faulty records to the auditor. The risk is further increased when the fraud is committed by management, as management has the ability to circumvent the usual control procedures in the company. Depending on the perpetrator's abilities and the type of fraud, such misstatements can be difficult to detect by normal audit procedures.

All audit procedures necessary to reach a conclusion on the financial statements must be completed within a limited time, having regard to the statutory deadlines for the release of the financial statements. In most cases business year coincides with the calendar year, leading to seasonal pressures on auditors. Proper planning allows the auditor to schedule activities throughout the engagement period and perform as many activities as possible (such as testing internal control systems) in the so-called pre-audit. However, sometimes conditions are not ideal and time pressures are more pronounced, which can arise in a situation of limited human and technical resources or subsequent engagement by the client. Such conditions may lead to omissions or result in the issuing of an unsupported auditor's opinion. Research has shown that there is a negative correlation between time pressure and auditor performance (Bowrin & King II, 2010), and that audit quality is compromised when auditors are under severe time pressure (Svanström, 2016).

Although much intention is paid to auditor independence and the establishment of mechanisms which are aimed at timely identifying potential threats to auditor independence, due to the complexity of relationships and the human factor, it is impossible to obtain an absolute assurance that a situation that would at least partially compromise the auditor's independence will not occur. Given that the independence of the auditor is a prerequisite for all the conclusions drawn by the auditor, and especially for those involving professional judgment, compromised independence calls into question the results of the auditor's work.

Technological solutions have a potential to reduce these limitations of today's audit. "Like all transformational stories, technology in the audit story is the enabler; an enabler to renew processes that improve quality and increase efficiency. It is also a catalyst that will help shift the focus of the audit process from a retrospective view to one which is prospective, enabling much deeper insights to clients and an enriched narrative on corporate performance and its sustainability for the future" (Association of Chartered Certified Accountants – ACCA, 2019a). Potential benefits from using new technological solution and how they might overcome current limitations of audit are further described in the section of this chapter entitled "New technologies that will shape the future of audit".

GENERATIONS OF AUDIT INTRODUCED BY TECHNOLOGICAL ADVANCEMENTS

A historical overview of the development of audit and the evolution of its role leads to the conclusion that it is a profession that is constantly adapting to changes in business operations, legal environment, public expectations, political conditions and technological progress. It is technological change that is the main factor that causes changes in the audit profession in all aspects. "Technology continues to change at nearly the speed of light with no signs of slowing down. The CPA profession as a whole recognizes that its future success depends on the changes made today: but these pressures are even heavier in the field of audit" (Anderson, n.d.). "The increasing sophistication of technology as well as the progressive digitization of business have fundamentally altered the manner in which external audits are conducted" (Vasarhelyi & Romero, 2014). "What became clear is that the auditing profession has continued to see unprecedented change. The accelerating pace of change in advancing technologies relating to data, advanced analytics, robotic process automation, cognitive and emerging innovations will play a pivotal role" (Forbes Insights & KPMG, 2017). In addition to using new technologies in the audit process when collecting evidence, auditors must adapt to the changing environment their client operate in. "Our recent analysis suggests that up to 30% of UK jobs could be at risk of automation by the early 2030s, with the risk highest in sectors such as transportation and storage (56%), manufacturing (46%) and wholesale and retail (44%)" (Lord, 2017). ACCA conducted a survey with over 2,000 professional accountants and C-suite executives in order to identify the factors they expect to have the greatest impact over the next 3 to 10 years. The number one factor singled out by the respondents is the development of intelligent automated accounting systems (Association of Chartered Certified Accountants – ACCA, 2016), proving that "over the next decade information technology (IT) will be transformational" (Association of Chartered Certified Accountants – ACCA, 2016). "A Forbes Insights survey found 58% of auditors and businesses believe technology will have the single biggest impact on the audit over the next three to five years" (KPMG, 2018).

The development of audit was driven by solutions stemming from the industrial revolution. Traditional manual audit has existed for decades, based on the existence of physical work documentation and manual data processing, which were the main characteristics of the first generation of audit (Audit 1.0). Due to limited resources, primarily time and financial, many concepts have been introduced that form the basis of today's audit. Because of the significant number of transactions, the large number of corporate affiliates and the complexity of the business, it was no longer efficient to review all transactions, which is why this phase of the audit development was also marked by significant changes in the approach of the auditor. The most significant innovations included: reliance on internal company controls, use of the sampling method, gathering information from internal and external sources, reliance on the concept of materiality, physical observation of assets and paying greater attention to the income statement (Ajao, Jayeoba & Ajibade, 2016). Accordingly, many concepts and techniques of evidence gathering were introduced during this period, which today form the basis of today's audit.

The use of computer tools and techniques in auditing is a major feature of second-generation audit (Audit 2.0). The wider use of information technology meant that auditors had to adjust their approach to changes in client operations but were also able to leverage new information solutions to improve their own performance. Although the role of auditing has remained approximately the same as in the previous period, the approach of the auditor has changed from examining the books of accounts to a reliance on the enterprise information system (Lee & Ali, 2008). In this context, Computer Assisted Audit Tools (CAATs) have started to be used. CAATs tools can be divided into the following groups: 1) audit software, 2) testing data, and 3) other tools (Association of Chartered Certified Accountants – ACCA, n.d.). Audit software includes computer programs used for the purpose of conducting substantive or control tests. It may include packages that are not tailored to the needs of a specific audit firm (e.g. statistics software), purpose-written programs ordered by an audit firms, or enquiry programs which are a part of the client's accounting information system but may be used for audit purposes (e.g. if the system generates employee attendance reports on a monthly miscellaneous basis, this may also be used by the auditor to test payroll accuracy). Data testing includes methods used to test the existence and effectiveness of computer audited client internal controls. In order to perform these tests, fictitious transactions are created, which are then processed through the client's information system. In order to avoid the risk of disrupting the client's information system by recording fictitious transactions together with actual transactions, it is possible to create test accounts within the client's information system. Other computer-aided audit tools may include, for example, embedded audit facilities (EAFs) that are integrated into the client's information system, allowing the auditor to continually review the client's accounting system. The specific areas where CAATs tools have found the greatest application include:

- audit sampling – computer-aided tools allow for the application of more advanced statistical methods when selecting random samples and evaluating results,
- document management – files are combined, compared, shared and automatically ordered using generally accepted computerized file management,
- report generation – after verifying the integrity of the data, the auditor can produce various reports from the entire data population (Massachusetts Department of Revenue – Computer Assisted Audit Group, n.d.).

The third generation of audit (Audit 3.0) involves the use of tools from the second generation on the so-called big data. The term big data refers to a dataset of large quantity and complexity. "The volume of transactions and data in businesses has increased dramatically since 2016 and is expected to keep increasing in the future" (Association of Chartered Certified Accountants – ACCA, 2019a). The scope of big data is largely beyond the capacity of traditional data-processing programs, which is why analytical programs have been developed to convert raw data into meaningful decision-making information (Wen Ooi, 2018). As big data involves the use of automation, data can be processed in greater volume and at greater speed to reveal valuable insights for auditors. Some of the benefits of using big data in audit are:

- quality audit evidence,
- more relevant business insights,
- greater ability to identify fraud and operational business risks (IDEA, n.d.).

However, potential problems with the use of big data in auditing may include:

- access to data that may be considered sensitive,
- identifying what data is available and how to use it,
- combining data from different systems and adjusting them with analysis tools,
- learning how to combine structured data (e.g. transactions) with unstructured data (e.g. emails) (IDEA, n.d.).

Adopting the principles underlying third generation audit implies that audit firms have the necessary tools and techniques required to process big data, which is why the practical application in certain aspects often lag behind.

The fourth generation of audit (Audit 4.0) is supported by the basic principles of Industry 4.0. Industry 4.0 or the fourth industrial revolution refers to a new phase of the industrial revolution that focuses heavily on interconnectivity, automation, machine learning and real-time data availability. The basic principles underlying Industry 4.0 are: 1) vertical integration (the approach that involves networked production systems in the form of smart factories), horizontal integration through global value and supply chains (refers to networking of production sites, customer involvement in the production process, information exchange throughout the value chain, intelligent communication in procurement, production and logistics, etc.) (Deloitte, 2015). The digitization of the manufacturing process introduced with Industry 4.0 is expected to have many benefits, but it will also bring many implementation challenges. Benefits include: 1) orientation to individual customer requirements, 2) adaptive production, 3) reduced pressure on workers, 4) new B2B services and increased competitiveness, 5) focus on productivity and efficient use of resources, etc. (Perić, n.d.). Concerning challenges or potential shortcomings, besides the need for continuous procurement and maintenance of infrastructure, there is a problem of lack of data protection and facilitated manipulation of production systems (Perić, n.d.). In the context of the fourth generation of audit, this means that modern audit will be based and dependent on the technologies introduced by Industry 4.0. In addition to technological adaptation itself, the challenges posed by the fourth generation of the industrial revolution have the potential to provide a number of additional services to external auditors or to expand their role in the context of statutory audit. Following the main features of Industry 4.0, the main features of Audit 4.0 are:

- interoperability – technological advancements within Industry 4.0 allow for collaboration within the entities themselves as well as across the entire value chain. Collaboration between suppliers, customers, banks and other entities will enable the auditor to examine the occurrence and completeness of transactions in approximately real time and facilitate the detection of suspicious transactions,
- virtualization - involves the digitization of objects that exist in a physical sense, such that their location, properties and other features, that would be stored on the system and could be shared, searched and analyzed. This would ultimately lead to the creation of a virtual copy or mirror world, which would add transparency to the entire value chain. For auditors, this would mean a drastic reduction in the need to work in the field. As all phases of the business process would be virtually presented and stored, auditors would be able to perform much of the work continuously and remotely,

- decentralization - the increasing demands for personalization and customization of products to each customer require decentralization, which has a major impact on the internal control system of the company and therefore on the audit. Internal controls can be incorporated into any machine or device to continuously monitor accounting information and detect irregular transactions, and such a trend will require auditors to adjust their way of performing control tests,
- real-time capability - smart factories at the heart of Industry 4.0 continuously monitor the manufacturing process to identify process defects, adjust production and make real-time decisions. Audit automation leads to the creation of stand-alone tools that can identify risky or suspicious transactions and alert auditors to the need for more in-depth testing,
- service orientation - Industry 4.0 architecture implies that any resource, such as production line, workers, expertise, computer equipment, etc., can be offered to other participants in the value chain on a *pay per service* basis. One of the most important obstacles to adopting advanced technological tools in auditing is the high cost and necessity of additional training to use, which can be compensated through this way of sharing resources. In addition to using IT tools, it also involves engaging an expert in data analysis (Dai, 2016).

NEW TECHNOLOGIES THAT WILL SHAPE THE FUTURE OF AUDIT

The advancement of technology has greatly affected all stages of the accounting process as well as internal controls over financial reporting, which consequently alters the way auditors collect enough evidence to express an opinion on the reality and objectivity of financial statements. "Robotic process automation, data analytics, artificial intelligence, machine learning, distributed ledger technology… to name but a few: a seemingly endless list of transformational technologies at varying stages of evolution is already having, and will continue to have, an indelible impact on the audit process" (Association of Chartered Certified Accountants – ACCA, 2019a). "The use of advanced technologies such as AI and ML, blockchain and data analytics promises a transformation in the audit profession, changing audit from a reactive and backward-looking exercise to a proactive, constant source of forward-looking insights that can be used all the time, with the auditor as the custodian and interpreter of the underlying data foundation" (Association of Chartered Certified Accountants – ACCA, 2019a).

Sensors, drones and cloud technology are only examples of technological solutions that found their practical implementation in the audit of today. "Unmanned drones are used in a variety of commercial projects, such as power line inspection, and the Big Four accountancy firms have spotted the potential for their use in inventory inspection, particularly where physical scale or distribution is an issue", such as open cast mine or agriculture (Association of Chartered Certified Accountants – ACCA, 2019a). "The rise of cloud based systems goes back a long way: arguably, a mainframe computed connected to a dumb terminals in regional offices represented an early form of "cloud". Now, a cloud system will be hosted remotely and accessed remotely by generic devices such as tablets, PCs or smartphones" (Association of Chartered Certified Accountants – ACCA, 2019a). "Cloud-based audit platforms with integrated methodologies are available today. These will assist auditors in making the transformation to cloud technologies and will position the profession well for the audit of the future" (Anderson, n.d.). "The rise of cloud based software platforms is gradually eliminating the need for organizations to host applications within their local environment" (KMPG, 2018). "The development of cheap and reliable sensing devices that posses capabilities of vision, smell, sound detection, voice recognition, motion detection, face recognition, etc., opened the doors to a wide range of production functionalities that are also usable in the assurance function. Archives of these measures can serve as confirmatory evidence of the performance of tasks, secondary evidence of levels achieved, or as confirmation of flows" (Issa, Sun & Vasarhelyi, 2016). The same authors provide concrete examples, such as using RFID chips for production control and supply chain management, or face and voice recognition as authorization and separation of duties controls.

Some of the technologies that are expected to continue to generate changes in accounting and auditing, that we decided to analyze in more detail below, are: 1) blockchain, 2) artificial intelligence, and 3) data analytics. Data analytics was chosen as a technology that has a widespread use today, while blockchain and artificial intelligence have a huge potential, but still little practical application in audit. "Data analytics was found to be the most mature of the technologies currently used by most firms, while machine learning is still not at the stage where it is embedded in everyday practice" (Association of Chartered Certified Accountants – ACCA, 2019a). As for the blockchain, it has been claimed that "blockchain will become the industry standard for accounting and reporting" (Association of Chartered Certified Accountants – ACCA, 2019a).

Blockchain

Blockchain technology is conceived as a digitized public ledger of transactions between various participants in the network. The database or transaction book is distributed to all participants, where each participant stores an identical copy of the database. Each entry in the database represents a new transaction that involves the exchange of value between participants in the network. In doing so, all participants in the network validate the new transaction using predefined algorithms. When a transaction is verified and accepted, all copies of the transaction database are updated with new information. Multiple transactions are usually merged into a block to be added to the base or blockchain. Although participants can enter new transactions, which are timestamped, they cannot delete or modify transactions that have already been accepted by other participants and recorded in the database. This, without having to hire an intermediary, preserves the truth and completeness of the data in the database (Chartered Professional Accountants of Canada - CPA Canada & American Institute of CPAs – AICPA, 2017). In accordance with the basic method of the blockchain described above, its main principles are the following: 1) real-time processing, 2) distributed ledger of transactions, 3) irreversibility, and 4) no need for mediation. Introduced in 2009 as a key mechanism for the functioning of Bitcoin cryptocurrency, blockchain has great potential for application in a number of industries, such as finance, healthcare, education and the like (Holotescu, 2018). It should be noted that there are several types of blockchain, and they differ primarily in two characteristics: the openness of the platform and the level of permission to add information to the blockchain.

Blockchain technology has created the prerequisites for the introduction of so-called smart contracts. It is about coding a set of rules under which contract participants treat each other. If and when the predefined terms of the contract are fulfilled, the contract is automatically enforced. In the event that the contract involves the transfer of certain digitized assets, that transfer shall also be made automatically (Voshmgir & Kalinov, 2017). Apart from the fact that such a way of concluding and executing a contract reduces transaction costs, it should provide a greater level of security for participants. "Recently, IBM opened an IBM Centre for Blockchain Innovation in Singapore. The centre will initially focus on solutions for finance and trade. For example, all the parties to a transaction can be put on the blockchain, where the locations of goods are visible and terms can be executed automatically with a smart contract" (Chartered Accountants Australia and New Zealand, 2017).

As one of the basic principles of blockchain functioning is irreversibility in terms of the inability to change entered transactions that are certified and accepted by other participants in the chain, the question arises whether there is a need to audit the financial statements. In this context, it should be borne in mind that verifying that a particular transaction actually occurred is only one of the audit objectives. In other words, recording a transaction in a blockchain and authenticating it by other participants in the chain can potentially represent a sufficient level of evidence that the transaction actually occurred. However, transactions entered into the blockchain can still be: 1) unauthorized, fraudulent or illegal, 2) executed between related parties, 3) related to off-chain ancillary agreements, 4) incorrectly classified in the financial statements (Chartered Professional Accountants of Canada - CPA Canada & American Institute of CPAs – AICPA, 2017). This means that certain risks related to the nature of the transactions have not been completely eliminated by the introduction of a system such as the blockchain, so there will still be a need for an independent audit of the financial statements. While IT solutions reduce audit risk through increased business efficiency and internal controls, which reduces inherent and control risk, on the other hand, the complexity of technology creates new risks for entities and their auditors (Han, Razaee, Xue & Zhang, 2016). The following risks can be added to the list: 1) the risk of identity theft (e.g. theft of the verification key of a particular participant in the chain), 2) increased risk of money laundering, 3) hacking of the system (although it should be impossible to change once logged transactions in the chain, there is a risk of hacking programmatic codes and systems that implement blockchain technology) (Li, 2017). Moreover, while automation may reduce the risk of fraud or error, the professional judgment of the auditor will still be required in auditing management's accounting estimates that are inevitable in preparing the financial statements.

The blockchain is expected to contribute to the effectiveness of preparatory actions and information gathering in the audit. "The World Economic Forum lists blockchain as one of the top ten emerging technologies of 2016" (Andersen, 2016). As more entities and processes utilize such solutions, auditors will have continuous access to information, while eliminating many manual data collection actions that have required significant human and time resources. Accelerating access to information should consequently reduce the time gap between the end of the reporting period on the one side, and the date of the financial statements and the report of the independent auditor on the other side (Chartered Professional Accountants of Canada - CPA Canada & American Institute of CPAs – AICPA, 2017). "Beyond Bitcoin, blockchain's application as a payments and settlements mechanisms has been in banking, where reconciliations of records relating to transactions between banks can be costly and time consuming when performed via traditional channels" (Chartered Accountants Australia and New Zealand, 2017). "The use of the Blockchain for accounting use-cases is hugely promising. From simplifying the compliance with regulatory requirements to enhancing the prevalent double entry bookkeeping, anything is imaginable" (Andersen, 2016). "…as additional uses of the technology emerge over time, the full potential of the blockchain will be revealed" (Chartered Accountants Australia and New Zealand, 2017).

Artificial Intelligence

Artificial intelligence involves the use of intelligent devices designed to work and respond in a human way. The tasks that such devices can perform include learning, knowing, reasoning, creating, achieving goals, and understanding the language. It is based on machine learning and deep learning techniques, where algorithms learn how to perform certain tasks (such as object classification or value prediction) through statistical analysis of large amounts of data, rather than through explicit programming (The Institute of Chartered Accountants in England and Wales – ICAEW & Dubai Financial Services Authority – DFSA, 2018). Such technological solutions may indicate that certain systems, jobs, processes and controls can be enhanced.

A major contribution of artificial intelligence is that it enables analysis of the entire population being tested for the purpose of identifying patterns or exceptions. In addition, cognitive technology and artificial intelligence also enable the analysis of structured and unstructured data from non-traditional sources, such as social networks, television and radio. Combining this information with the information in the audited client's financial statements provides a clearer view of the risks to which the client is exposed (KMPG, 2018). In doing so, in the context of the audit of the financial statements, it may free the auditor a number of tasks, leaving more time for the training necessary to properly perform the auditor's professional judgment and interpret the results obtained. Although there have been noticeable shifts in the application of technology to areas such as language processing or sentiment analysis, professional judgment is difficult to replace with technological solutions (Association of Chartered Certified Accountants – ACCA, 2019a). In the artificial intelligence world, auditors will need to understand and be skeptical about how software works and learns, how artificial intelligence tools generate results and why they are possible, and ultimately interpret what they mean in the context of an individual and unique client situation (Lord, 2018).

Regarding the practical implications, there are several examples of applying artificial intelligence in today's audit. At PwC, they state: "Although in its infancy, AI is already being used to make the audit process better. We're using AI to spot patterns and anomalies in large bodies of structured data. Any problems identified are recognized and remembered by the machine, which then "learns" from its experience and applies the learning to the next set of data" (Lord, 2017). The same Big Four audit firms describes the artificial intelligence application by their US colleagues. "Say we're auditing company A, and we need to do an analytical review of its performance. A machine searches the web and generates a peer group of companies for company A. It then calculated and plots a series of ratios over time for company A and the peer group – for example, asset turnover, debtors days and so on. The machine is then pre-programmed to identify unusual trends, for example if company A was way out of line with the peer group benchmarks on a particular point. This data is then shared with the audit team, who can decide whether that variance is really an anomaly and if so, what caused it. The team's decision about the anomaly and its cause is then fed back to the machine, which is "taught" hot to respond to similar relationship in future. And the more this exercise is carried out, the better the machine will get at spotting real anomalies – meaning we'll be better able to identify unusual patterns and anomalies in huge amounts of data in an instant. This could help tackle the expectation gap that surrounds the auditor's ability to detect fraud" (Lord, 2017). Similarly, artificial intelligence is used by other large audit firms. "One of the best examples of AI put to use in accounting is in the review of high volume of contracts. According to Muraskin, a Deloitte team might comb through hundreds of thousands of legal documents looking for a change of control provisions during a client's sale of a business unit. This used to keep dozens of employees occupied for half a year. Now, a team of six to eight members can use an AI system to complete the same task in less than a month" (Zhou, 2017). At EY, one of the uses of artificial intelligence is in reviewing lease accounting standards and if their clients comply with the requirements of changes in the standards. They use natural language processing (NLP) to extract information instead of manually re-examining tens of thousands of leases. Another example in the same audit firm is using artificial intelligence and machine learning for anomaly detection in terms of fraudulent invoices, which is an especially valuable tool when international parties are involved (Zhou, 2017).

"The next step for auditors and finance is to apply AI and ML algorithms to improve the quality of analysis and forecasting, and increase the rate of fraud detection (Association of Chartered Certified Accountants – ACCA, 2019a). "AI has been brought to transportation, healthcare, security, home/service, and many other industries. Similarly, the Big 4 accounting firms are cooperating with AI systems providers to make those systems serve auditing purposes" (Issa, Sun & Vasarhelyi, 2016). The great potential of artificial intelligence and deep learning lies in image recognition, language analysis, natural language classification and speech recognition (Issa, Sun & Vasarhelyi, 2016), which are all areas where previous technological solutions have not made much success.

Data Analytics

Artificial intelligence is closely related to data analytics, which refers to the technique of analyzing so-called raw data to generate useful information. This allows to spot trends and signs that would otherwise be lost in the mass of data. The types of data analytics are as follows:

- descriptive data analytics - analysis that provides insight into events that have occurred in the past,
- predictive data analytics - analysis that seeks to predict future and future outcomes through statistical tools and forecasting techniques,
- prescriptive data analytics - analysis that uses optimization and simulation algorithms to provide advice on what actions to take to achieve the desired outcome (Mujawar & Joshi, 2015).

The IAASB defines data analytics for audit purposes as the science and art of detecting and analyzing patterns, discrepancies, and inconsistencies, and extracting other useful information from audit-related data through analysis, modeling, and visualization for audit planning and execution (Association of Chartered Certified Accountants – ACCA, n.d.). Large audit firms have more financial resources at their disposal and accordingly develop their own data analytics platforms, while smaller audit firms typically opt for ready-to-sell packages on the market. The main motivation for using such tools is to increase the quality of the audit, primarily due to the greater reach and scope of the data analyzed and the use of the information obtained for better risk assessment. The main advantages of using data analytics are: 1) a better understanding of the company's business through a more thorough analysis, 2) increased auditor focus on risk areas, 3) greater consistency within the same audit firm or network of audit firms, 4) improved efficiency, population focus and eliminating the risk of using the sample, 5) a greater ability to detect fraud, 6) a great ability to adapt when conducting audit testing (e.g. conducting sensitivity analysis of management estimates) (Association of Chartered Certified Accountants – ACCA, n.d.). In addition to the benefits, there are challenges to applying such tools, such as: 1) increasing the competitiveness gap between large and small audit firms, 2) the issue of data protection and client confidentiality, 3) the completeness of extracted client information cannot be guaranteed, 4) compatibility issues with client systems that may render standard tests ineffective if data are not available in expected formats, 5) audit staff's competence in working with such tools, and the need for additional training, 6) the issue of retention and subsequent restriction of access to large amounts of audit data evidence, 7) unrealistic expectations of audit users (Association of Chartered Certified Accountants – ACCA, n.d.).

As for its practical application and examples of use, “data analytics seems to be the most mature of the advances in technology and is currently used in audit practice, particularly in journal entry testing. The Big Four accountancy firms are already expanding their use of data analytics in risk assessment as well as in testing revenue, receivables, payables, and salaries. Data analytics tools are also easily accessible by SMPs at a reasonable cost” (Association of Chartered Certified Accountants – ACCA, 2019a). “Pioneers in this area like the Big Four accounting firms have started employing deep learning to harness the power of textual big data to surface deeper insights and highlight risky areas. For example, Deloitte combines its business insights in cognitive technology with Kira Systems advances in deep learning to conduct documents analysis tasks (e.g., investigations, mergers, contract management, and leasing arrangements)” (Sun & Vasarhelyi, 2018). Such tools allow auditors to use the data they were not able to use before, such as social media postings and news articles, which could point towards potential litigation risks, business risks, internal control risks and others (Sun & Vasarhelyi, 2018). “Observed examples of ADA being used to produce good quality evidence include: tracing individual revenue transactions to debtors and subsequent cash received, reproduction of inventory ageing, reproduction of debtors ageing, valuation of financial instruments, tracing supplier income to agreements and cash received, recalculation of fund managers fees based on value of assets under management” (Financial Reporting Council – FRC, 2017). At KMPG (2015) they state: “Using D&A we make the analysis of the past more insightful. Rather than sampling transactions data to test a snapshot of activities, we can now analyze all transactions processed, allowing us to identify anomalies and drill down on the items that show the greatest potential of being high risk. Our systems automate this process, increasing its ability to produce high quality evidence.”

However, the UK Financial Reporting Council claims that the application of data analytics in audit is now as widespread as it was thought (Association of Chartered Certified Accountants – ACCA, 2019a). “Audit firms and teams fell the pressure to promote the use of ADA techniques on audits to meet audit committee expectations, to achieve efficiencies and to win competitive tenders. This may result in the pace of ADA development and usage being overemphasized” (Financial Reporting Council – FRC, 2017). Regarding the examples of data analytics application, FRC also states that they “have seen ADA implemented that: analyze all transactions in a population, stratify that population and identify outliers for further examination; reperform calculations relevant to the financial statements; match transactions as they pass through a processing cycle; assist in segregation of duties testing; compare entity data to externally obtained data; manipulate data to access the impact of different assumptions” (Financial Reporting Council – FRC, 2017). Recent regulatory changes, such as mandatory audit re-tendering, help promote the development and use of data analytics of audit, but also puts a lot of pressure, since data analytics are perceived as a key competitive advantage from a standpoint of audit committees and investors. This is the reason why audit team sometimes tend to overemphasis their use of data analytic techniques when communicating with the members of audit committees (Financial Reporting Council – FRC, 2017).

FUTURE RESEARCH DIRECTIONS

As for the role of auditors in the changing environment caused by these new technologies, questions that usually arise are: 1) will auditors still be necessary?, 2) will they assume new roles regarding and beyond audit of financial statements?, and 3) how will it affect professional skepticism and judgement of auditors?. Since the technologies such as blockchain are aimed at providing real-time, reliable and transparent accounting information that cannot be altered, it could be argued that it would eliminate the need for audit of financial statements. However, others claim that the technology is simply a tool to facilitate the audit process, not the replacement. There will still be need for professional judgement, evaluation and interpretation, which are the tasks that can only be done by experienced professionals. "Human judgement and responsibility will and must remain at its heart" (Lord, 2017). Additionally, blockchain as a new technology will help auditors to confirm certain assertions such as occurrence, but other assertions still remain (e.g. valuation, classification, etc.). Although not replacing the auditors, technological changes will definitely affect the audit methodology. Increased automation and the use of advanced technologies could lead to staffing changes, by reducing the need for junior auditors who usually performed routine tasks and increasing the need for experienced auditors who are able to interpret and analyze complex and high-risk areas and evidences.

It is certain that the auditors will have to adapt in terms of their skills. "A key skill for auditors – at least during coming years – will be the flexibility to adapt to a working environment which will continue to evolve" (Association of Chartered Certified Accountants – ACCA, 2019a). All researchers agree that more work on their digital competencies will definitely be necessary, but they also emphasize the importance of communications skills. "Already important, non-technical competency areas will become even more so over the years to 2025. Knowledge of digital technologies tops the list of competency areas where professional accountants believe there are key skills gaps, followed a distant second by communication skills, with third on the list taken jointly by sector knowledge, business awareness and a global perspective" (Association of Chartered Certified Accountants – ACCA, 2016). Due to changes in technology, various technical skills will gain and lose importance, while "the requirement for professional accountants at all levels of seniority and in all roles to maintain the highest level of ethical conduct, independence and professional skepticism will remain constant" (Association of Chartered Certified Accountants – ACCA, 2016). According to a survey conducted by KMPG and Forbes Insights of CEOs, CFOs and other financial executives in large companies regarding the future of audit, it became evident that there is already a certain gap in auditors' skills from the standpoint of their clients, where clients are already "looking for increased technology skills (67%), communication skills (66%), critical thinking skills (65%) and investigative financial skills (59%)" (Forbes Insights & KMPG, 2017). International Auditing and Assurance Standards Board - IAASB (2016) agrees that "in the not too distant future, a re-skilling of a relatively large proportion of today's accountants and auditors will be necessary to realize the potential on a broad scale". In a time when technological solutions are becoming widely applied by their clients, auditors must keep track with changes in the environments, which is why the results of a study conducted by ACCA are rather concerning. "In April 2019, ACCA surveyed members and affiliates about their understanding of terms such as artificial intelligence (AI), machine learning (ML), natural language processing (NLP), data analytics and robotic process automation (RPA). On average for any given term, 62% of respondents had not heard of it, or had heard the term but did not know what it was, or had only a basic understanding. On average, only 13% of respondents claimed a "high" or "expert level" of understanding of these terms. There's a need for greater awareness of what these technologies are and their implication for the audit profession" (Association of Chartered Certified Accountants – ACCA, 2019a).

Technology could lead to questioning the auditors' ability of providing a greater level of assurance than today, due to continuous auditing, testing the entire population and using data analytics to find correlation among large amounts of data. According to the ACCA's report (2019b), 70% of the general public across 11 countries believe that the audit function should evolve to prevent corporate failure.

The potential for widening the audit expectation gap, as the gap between the benefits that auditors can provide and customer expectations, is a potentially significant problem with the use of data analytics techniques, but also in general all other technological solutions. The fact that technology allows the auditor to test the entire population, instead of the past sample testing, does not mean that the auditors will be able to increase the level of assurance from reasonable to absolute. The sampling risk is only one component of the detection risk, which is not completely eliminated by eliminating the need to perform audit on a sample. Therefore, a certain percentage of audit risk will probably still remain. On one hand, technology may decrease audit risk by decreasing inherent and internal control risk, due to the access to relevant real-time information. On the other hand, the complexity of IT introduces whole new risks for companies and their auditors, creating new ways of errors and fraud to occur.

The question that remains is should the auditors expand their assurance services beyond financial reporting, in order to offer more value to clients. Since there is an increasing importance of non-financial reporting, this is one of the areas that could potentially be included into the scope of auditors' work. According to the survey conducted by Forbes Insights and KMPG (2017), 60% of respondents think that auditors should help in assessing risks and risk management practices. During all these changes that will affect the audit profession, auditors will have to stay alert to avoid overconfidence in technology. Using standardized tools and automated solutions while assessing risks and planning audit could lead to reduced professional skepticism and caution, meaning that the auditors tend to underestimate the risk of fraud or error. Professional skepticism and awareness are the main characteristics that distinguish auditors from technological solutions, which is why the emphasis must be on these qualities during future evolution of the audit profession.

It is essential for the regulatory framework related to audit to adapt to the changes in the environment. Standard setters, such as the International Auditing and Assurance Standards Board (IAASB), have started to incorporate the use of information technology into auditing standards. For example, changes in the revised International Standard on Auditing 315 (Revised 2019) - Identifying and Assessing the Risks of Material Misstatement through Understanding the Entity and Its Environment are *intended to support auditors using the standard by incorporating guidance material that recognizes the evolving environment, including in relation to information technology* (International Federation of Accountants – IFAC, 2019a, p. 2). It is especially emphasized that *the audit risk model has not changed. However, enhancements and clarification help auditors in applying the audit risk model when identifying and assessing the risks of material misstatement* (International Federation of Accountants – IFAC, 2019a, p. 4). As already mentioned, auditors must be aware of the new risks that emerge from clients using new technologies. This is why the standard has been modernized and enhanced *to include auditor consideration in relation to IT, including new and updated appendices for understanding IT and IT general controls* (International Federation of Accountants – IFAC, 2019a, p. 5). In addition to changes incorporated into standards, the IAASB noted the importance for issuing a non-authoritative guidance in order to address the impact of technology when implementing certain parts of the ISAs. The IAASB's Audit Evidence Working Group (AEWG), founded in 2019, is currently performing information-gathering and research activities with the aim of prioritizing audit-evidence-related issues, some of which have been caused by rapid evolution in technology (International Federation of Accountants – IFAC, 2019b). The point is that the regulatory framework related to financial reporting and audit should not lag behind what happens in practice, which is not always the case. "Digitalization of the accounting system is still in its infancy compared to other industries, some of which have been massively disrupted by the advances of technology. Some of the reasons may be found in the exceptionally high regulatory requirements in respect to validity and integrity" (Andersen, 2016).

"The auditing profession is standards driven, making it impractical for the profession to adopt any new technology or methodology if not required or approved by standard-setting boards. The profession will face the challenge of adjusting the current auditing standards in order for the adoption of such a disruptive technology to prevail. An example is continuous auditing, where the adoption reluctance of external auditors seems to be driven by the current auditing standards. The standards are still based on traditional auditing procedures, which were effective when the sizes of databases where small, but became ineffective in today's real-time digital economy. These standards will have to allow and even encourage auditors to take audit effectiveness through the integration of new types of evidence…" (Issa, Sun & Vasarhelyi, 2016).

CONCLUSION

Audit of financial statements is an important internal mechanism of corporate governance, aimed at enhancing transparency of financial reporting. For auditors to be able to provide quality service, keeping up with changes in the environment is unavoidable. This includes regulatory changes, technological advancements, stakeholders' expectations, political and social issues, etc. Technological changes can certainly be singled out as one of the most important factors auditors must consider for multiple reasons. First of all, auditors have to be up to date with the technologies that are used by their clients, in order to properly assess inherent and control risks of their clients. Second, technological tools have the capability of making the audit of financial statements more efficient and effective, which is a matter of competitive advantage when compared to other audit firms, but also a national (as well as international) interest when it comes to improving audit quality.

One of the new technologies that are usually mentioned when talking about future audits include data analytics. Data analytics refers to different methods of discovering and analysing patterns, abnormalities and inconsistencies in the data, as well as extracting useful information in the data. One of the benefits of data analytics is allowing auditors to use 100% of population when performing tests, and therefore eliminates the sampling risk, i.e. the risk of reaching different conclusion based on a sample when compared to a conclusion that would result from testing the entire population. Although wider use of artificial intelligence is probably further in the future, its use has the potential to provide even more insights into the information that is hiding in huge amounts of data that are available to auditors, regarding client's performance, environment, relationships, relevant risks, etc. It would allow for auditors to examine information from non-traditional sources, such as social networks, media, radio, internet. Drone and sensor technology have a great potential in providing timely and accurate information without manual procedures of auditors, primarily when it comes to physical assets of audited subjects. Cloud-based systems improve functionality of audit teams, allowing them to access data regardless of their geographical location. In the end, there is also a blockchain technology, that is often described as *the most disruptive information technology in recent years*. Blockchain is based on distributed ledger technology, which means that every participant can enter and verify/reject the data, while the approved data is stored as a collection of blocks that cannot be altered. The use of blockchain in audit profession is still under-explored, and researchers often argue whether this new technology is an opportunity or a threat to the audit profession.

These new technologies have a potential to overcome certain limitations of today's audit. Replacing audit sampling with population testing would eliminate sampling risk, as a risk that is a part of the overall detection risk. However, this does not mean that the whole detection risk would be eliminated. Non-sampling risks, such as wrong interpretations of audit evidence, could still remain. In addition to eliminating sampling risk, certain technological solutions, such as blockchain, have the potential to increase the trustworthiness of audit evidence, promoting a system of recording transactions that is characterized by irreversibility. Moreover, technology would allow auditors to have a near real-time access to data, reduce the need for manual procedures and working in the field, provide automated or semi-automated solutions, which are all tools that could help to reduce the lag between the end of the reporting period and the date when the auditor's report is issued. One thing that would be challenging to replace by technology is professional judgment of auditors. However, use of technology could allow auditors to have more time to attend additional education aimed at improving their professional scepticism and judgment. The conclusion is that the technology is not a threat that would eliminate the audit of financial statements, but has a great potential to increase its quality.

REFERENCES

Ajao, O. S., Jayeoba, O., & Ajibade, A. (2016). Evolution and development of auditing. *Unique Journal of Business Management Research*, *3*(1), 32–40.

Andersen, N. (2016). *Blockchain technology – A game-changer in accounting?* Deloitte. Retrieved June, 10, 2020, from https://www2.deloitte.com/content/dam/Deloitte/de/Documents/Innovation/Blockchain_A%20game-changer%20in%20accounting.pdf

Anderson, A. (n.d.). *4 keys to the future of audit*. Thomson Reuters Checkpoint White Paper. Retrieved June, 10, 2020, from https://tax.thomsonreuters.com/site/wp-content/private/pdf/checkpoint/whitepapers/Checkpoint-Al-Anderson-Whitepaper.pdf

Association of Chartered Certified Accountants – ACCA. (2016). *Drivers of change and future skills*. Report. Retrieved June, 10, 2020, from https://www.accaglobal.com/content/dam/members-beta/docs/ea-patf-drivers-of-change-and-future-skills.pdf

Association of Chartered Certified Accountants – ACCA. (2019a). *Audit and technology*. Professional insight report. Retrieved June, 10, 2020, from https://www.accaglobal.com/content/dam/ACCA_Global/professional-insights/audit-and-tech/pi-audit-and-technology.pdf

Association of Chartered Certified Accountants – ACCA. (2019b). *Closing the expectation gap in audit*. Report. Retrieved June, 10, 2020, from https://www.accaglobal.com/content/dam/ACCA_Global/professional-insights/Expectation-gap/pi-closing-expectation-gap-audit.pdf

Association of Chartered Certified Accountants – ACCA. (n.d.). *Data analytics and the auditor*. Technical articles. Retrieved June, 10, 2020, from https://www.accaglobal.com/in/en/student/exam-support-resources/professional-exams-study-resources/p7/technical-articles/data-analytics.html

Bowrin, A. R., & King, I. I. J. II. (2010). Time pressure, task complexity, and audit effectiveness. *Managerial Auditing Journal*, *25*(2), 160–181. doi:10.1108/02686901011008963

Chartered Accountants Australia and New Zealand. (2017). *The future of blockchain: Applications and implications of distributed ledger technology*. Retrieved June, 10, 2020, from https://charteredaccountantsworldwide.com/wp-content/uploads/2018/07/1216-07_Future-of-Blockchain_web_FA-1.pdf

Chartered Professional Accountants of Canada - CPA Canada & American Institute of CPAs – AICPA. (2017). *Blockchain technology and its potential impact on the audit and assurance profession*. Retrieved June, 10, 2020, from https://www.aicpa.org/content/dam/aicpa/interestareas/frc/assuranceadvisoryservices/downloadabledocuments/blockchain-technology-and-its-potential-impact-on-the-audit-and-assurance-profession.pdf

Dai, J., & Vasarhelyi, M. A. (2016). Imagineering audit 4.0. [Editorial]. *Journal of Emerging Technologies in Accounting*, *13*(1), 1–15. doi:10.2308/jeta-10494

Deloitte. (2015). *Industry 4.0 – Challenges and solutions for the digital transformation and use of exponential technologies*. Retrieved June, 10, 2020, from https://www2.deloitte.com/content/dam/Deloitte/ch/Documents/manufacturing/ch-en-manufacturing-industry-4-0-24102014.pdf

Financial Reporting Council – FRC. (2017). *Audit quality thematic review – the use of data analytics in the audit of financial statements*. Retrieved June, 10, 2020, from https://www.frc.org.uk/getattachment/4fd19a18-1beb-4959-8737-ae2dca80af67/AQTR_Audit-Data-Analytics-Jan-2017.pdf

Han, S., Razaee, Z., Xue, L., & Zhang, J. H. (2016). The association between information technology investments and audit risk. *Journal of Information Systems*, *30*(1), 93–116. doi:10.2308/isys-51317

Holotescu, C. (2018). *Understanding blockchain opportunities and challenges*. Paper presented at The 14th International Scientific Conference eLearning and software for education, Bucharest, Romania. Retrieved June, 10, 2020, from https://www.researchgate.net/profile/Carmen_Holotescu/publication/324209739_Understanding_Blockchain_Opportunities_and_Challenges/links/5dac4f2c299bf111d4bf50f9/Understanding-Blockchain-Opportunities-and-Challenges.pdf

IDEA. (n.d.). *Big data and audit*. Retrieved June, 10, 2020, from https://idea.caseware.com/big-data-and-audit/

International Auditing and Assurance Standards Board – IAASB. (2016). *Exploring the growing use of technology in the audit, with a focus on data analytics*. Request for input. Retrieved June, 10, 2020, from https://www.iaasb.org/publications/exploring-growing-use-technology-audit-focus-data-analytics

International Federation of Accountants – IFAC. (2009). *International Standard on Auditing 240*. Retrieved June, 10, 2020, from https://www.ifac.org/system/files/downloads/a012-2010-iaasb-handbook-isa-240.pdf

International Federation of Accountants – IFAC. (2019a). *Introduction to: ISA 315 (Revised 2019) Identifying and assessing the risks of material misstatement*. Retrieved June, 10, 2020, from https://www.ifac.org/system/files/publications/files/IAASB-Introduction-to-ISA-315.pdf

International Federation of Accountants – IFAC. (2019b). *Technology and the future-ready auditor*. Retrieved June, 10, 2020, from https://www.ifac.org/system/files/publications/files/IAASB-Tech-Talk-November-2019.pdf

Issa, H., Sun, T., & Vasarhelyi, M. A. (2017). Research ideas for artificial intelligence in auditing: The formalization of audit and workforce supplementation [Editorial]. *Journal of Emerging Technologies in Accounting, 13*(2), 1–20. doi:10.2308/jeta-10511

Jensen, M. C., & Meckling, W. H. (1976). Theory of the firm: Managerial behaviour, agency costs and ownership structure. *Journal of Financial Economics, 3*(4), 305–360. doi:10.1016/0304-405X(76)90026-X

KPMG. (2018). *Impact of new technologies on audit and assurance*. Retrieved June, 10, 2020, from https://home.kpmg/content/dam/kpmg/ng/pdf/advisory/Impact-of-New-Tech-on-Audit-and-Assurance.pdf

KPMG & Forbes Insights. (2017). *Audit 2025: The future is now*. Retrieved June, 10, 2020, from https://assets.kpmg/content/dam/kpmg/us/pdf/2017/03/us-audit-2025-final-report.pdf

Lee, T.-H., & Ali, A. M. (2008). The evolution of auditing: An analysis of the historical development. *Journal of Modern Accounting and Auditing, 4*(12), 1–8.

Li, Z. (2017). Will blockchain change the audit? *China-USA Business Review, 16*(6), 294–298.

Lord, G. (2017). *Confidence in the future – human and machine collaboration in the audit*. PricewaterhouseCoopers. Retrieved June, 10, 2020, from https://www.pwc.co.uk/audit-assurance/assets/pdf/confidence-in-the-future-human-machine-collaboration.pdf

Lord, S. (2018). The future of the audit - The enduring importance of professional scepticism. *Accounting Today*. Retrieved June, 10, 2020, from https://www.accountingtoday.com/opinion/the-enduring-importance-of-professional-skepticism-in-auditing

Massachusetts Department of Revenue – Computer Assisted Audit Group. (n.d.). *A guide to computer assisted audit techniques*. Retrieved June, 10, 2020, from http://www.mtc.gov/uploadedFiles/Multistate_Tax_Commission/Audit_Program/Resource/caat.pdf

Mujawar, S., & Joshi, A. (2015). Data analytics types, tools and their comparison. *International Journal of Advanced Research in Computer and Communication Engineering, 4*(2), 488–491.

Organisation for Economic Co-operation and Development – OECD. (2018). *OECD Blockchain Primer*. Retrieved June, 10, 2020, from https://www.oecd.org/finance/OECD-Blockchain-Primer.pdf

Organisation for Economic Cooperation and Development – OECD. (2015). *G20/OECD Principles of Corporate Governance*. Paris: OECD Publishing. Retrieved June, 10, 2020, from https://www.oecd.org/daf/ca/Corporate-Governance-Principles-ENG.pdf

Perić, E. (n.d.). *Industrija 4.0* [Industry 4.0]. Croatian Chamber of Economy. Retrieved June, 10, 2020, from https://www.hgk.hr/documents/hgk-industrija-4058d8c59722f1e.pdf

Sever Mališ, S., Tušek, B. & Žager, L. (2012). *Revizija - načela, standardi, postupci* [Audit - principles, standards, procedures]. Zagreb: Hrvatska zajednica računovođa i financijskih djelatnika [Croatian Association of Accountants and Financial Professionals].

Sun, T., & Vasarhelyi, M. A. (2018). Embracing textual data analytics in auditing with deep learning. *The International Journal of Digital Accounting Research, 18*(1), 49–67. doi:10.4192/1577-8517-v18_3

Svanström, T. (2016). Time pressure, training activities and dysfunctional audit behaviour: Evidence from small audit firms. *International Journal of Auditing*, *20*(1), 42–51. doi:10.1111/ijau.12054

The Institute of Chartered Accountants in England and Wales – ICAEW & Dubai Financial Services Authority – DFSA. (2018). *Understanding the impact of technology in audit and finance*. Retrieved June, 10, 2020, from https://www.icaew.com/-/media/corporate/files/middle-east-hub/understanding-the-impact-of-technology-in-audit-and-finance.ashx

Vasarhelyi, M. A., & Romero, S. (2014). Technology in audit engagements: A case study. *Managerial Auditing Journal*, *29*(4), 350–365. doi:10.1108/MAJ-06-2013-0881

Voshmgir, S., & Kalinov, V. (2017). *Blockchain – A beginners guide*. BlockchainHub. Retrieved June, 10, 2020, from https://s3.eu-west-2.amazonaws.com/blockchainhub.media/Blockchain+Technology+Handbook.pdf

Wen Ooi, J. (2018). Big data and analytics will transform the audit profession - Here's what you must know. *Prospects*, 7. Retrieved June, 10, 2020, from https://www.prospectsasean.com/big-data-analytics-transform-audit-profession/

Zhou, A. (2017). EY, Deloitte and PwC embrace artificial intelligence for tax and accounting. *Forbes Media*. Retrieved June, 10, 2020, from https://www.forbes.com/sites/adelynzhou/2017/11/14/ey-deloitte-and-pwc-embrace-artificial-intelligence-for-tax-and-accounting/#4ef48ee03498

ADDITIONAL READING

American Institute of Certified Public Accountants – AICPA. (2015). *Audit analytics and continuous audit: looking toward the future*. Retrieved June, 10, 2020, from https://www.aicpa.org/interestareas/frc/assuranceadvisoryservices/downloadabledocuments/auditanalytics_lookingtowardfuture.pdf

Arens, A. A., Elder, R. J., Beasley, M. S., & Hogan, C. E. (2017). Auditing and Assurance Services. Sixteenth Edition. Global Edition: Pearson.

Boynton, W. C., & Johnson, R. N. (2006). *Modern auditing: assurance services and the integrity of financial reporting* (8th ed.). John Wiley & Sons.

Centre for Financial and Reporting Reform – CFRR. (2017). *Audit data analytics: opportunities and tips*. World Bank Group. Retrieved June, 10, 2020, from http://siteresources.worldbank.org/EXTCENFINREPREF/Resources/4152117-1427109489814/SMPs_spreads_digital.pdf

Deloitte (2018). *Auditing the risks of disruptive technologies: Internal audit in the age of digitalization*. Retrieved June, 10, 2020, from https://www2.deloitte.com/content/dam/Deloitte/us/Documents/finance/us-rfa-auditing-the-risks-of-disruptive-technologies.pdf

KPMG. (2017). *Harnessing the power of cognitive technology to transform the audit*. Retrieved June, 10, 2020, from https://assets.kpmg/content/dam/kpmg/us/pdf/2017/02/harnessing-the-power-of-cognitive-technology-to-transform-the-audit.pdf

Public Company Accounting Oversight Board - PCAOB. (2017). *Technology and the Audit of Today and Tomorrow*. Retrieved June, 10, 2020, from https://pcaobus.org/News/Speech/Pages/Harris-statement-PCAOB-AAA-4-20-17.aspx

Salijeni, G., Samsonova-Taddei, A., & Turley, S. (2018). Big Data and Changes in Audit Technology: Contemplating a Research Agenda. *Accounting and Business Research*, *49*(1), 95–119. doi:10.1080/00014788.2018.1459458

KEY TERMS AND DEFINITIONS

Artificial Intelligence: Use of intelligent devices designed to work and respond in a human way.

Audit of Financial Statements: The process of obtaining evidence that the financial statements are presented in accordance with the defined criteria and provides information about the level of compliance to interested users.

Audit Risk: Risk that the auditor expresses an unmodified opinion regarding financial statements that are materially incorrect.

Blockchain: Digitized public ledger of transactions between various participants in the network.

Computer-Assisted Audit Techniques and Tools: Techniques and tools that involve the use of technology in the audit process.

Data Analytics: Technique of analyzing so-called raw data to generate useful information.

Reasonable Assurance: A high level (but not absolute) of assurance that the financial statements are not materially misstated.

Chapter 13
Leadership in FinTech:
Authentic Leaders as Enablers of Innovation and Competitiveness in Financial Technology Firms

Tessa Campbell
Tasmanian School of Business and Economics, University of Tasmania, Australia

Matthew Knox
https://orcid.org/0000-0002-6092-071X
University of Tasmania, Australia

Josh Rowlands
https://orcid.org/0000-0002-5935-1628
Tasmanian School of Business and Economics, University of Tasmania, Australia

Zi-Ying Anna Cui
https://orcid.org/0000-0001-7199-3669
Tasmanian School of Business and Economics, University of Tasmania, Australia

Luke DeJesus
Tasmanian School of Business and Economics, University of Tasmania, Australia

ABSTRACT

This chapter discusses the intricacies of innovation and competitive advantage, the current leadership gap within FinTech firms, and how these occurrences are enabled and improved through the utilization of authentic leadership practices within the context of the FinTech industry. Following this discussion, the authors observe the future research directions and potential areas of exploration in which other scholars may divulge. Through the exploration of our research question, "How can authentic leadership behaviors enable innovation and competitive advantage in FinTech firms?" they found the importance of authentic leadership within any industry or organization may be enhanced and explored further, as it appears to have a positive impact on innovation within organizations which in turn has the potential to provide a variety of opportunities for growth and competitive advantage.

DOI: 10.4018/978-1-7998-4390-0.ch013

INTRODUCTION

Throughout the twenty-first century, organizations across all industries have experienced rapid technology growth, with greater emphasis placed on those who specialize in the production of technology and its complements. The growth is influenced by organizations seeking to develop competitive advantage in a growing global population that brings forth an increase in demand for the distribution of goods and services, as well as an increase in the incidence of purchasing technology-oriented goods and services.

There are a multitude of organizations that have identified the need for innovative ideas, which utilize contemporary technological advances to create efficient and effective services. ING Bank, UP Banking and Wildcard provide useful examples. These three FinTech affiliated firms offer diverse niche services that are executed through the utilization of technology and innovation, many that their competitors are yet to implement. Some of these services include round ups, simplistic layouts of previous and upcoming transactions, and compatibility with other banks to mitigate hidden fees (ING, 2020; Up, 2020; Wildcard, 2020). Up Banking, for example, allows its customers to create multiple savings accounts for their individual saving goals, in line with the growing 'barefoot' market segment. This service demonstrates the opportunity presented from innovation and creativity to achieve competitive advantage within the field of FinTech.

Contemporary leadership styles, such as that of authentic leadership, are needed in order to ensure the current flattening trend within organizational structures can maintain sustainable rates of growth and innovation achieved through leveraging technological development and innovative practices. Utilizing innovation to achieve competitive advantage can improve the reputation of organizations within a market but is typically only achieved if the organization can reach their strategic goals and objectives within an appropriate time frame; a time frame that outperforms competitors.

The growth and success of organizations has the potential to be reached through a manner of ethical and unethical practices. The contemporary marketplace places the consumer at the centre of organizational success metrics and key performance indicators (KPIs). From a consumer perspective, unethical practices are becoming increasingly frowned upon across a broad range of markets (Jalil et al., 2010). For example, vegan and vegetarian diets are becoming increasingly popular due to greater awareness of the unethical treatment of animals in the agricultural sector (Rowley, 2016). In this sector, ethical leadership philosophies lean into enabling socially desirable and ethical change to improve the way animal products are provided to consumers. The same is true within the FinTech industry.

This Chapter discusses the intricacies of innovation and competitive advantage, the current leadership gap within FinTech firms, and how these occurrences are enabled and improved through the utilization of authentic leadership practices within the context of the FinTech industry. Following this discussion, observations involving the future research directions and potential areas of exploration in which other scholars may divulge, are explained. Through the exploration of the research question *"How can authentic leadership behaviors enable innovation and competitive advantage in FinTech firms?"*, the explication found the importance of authentic leadership within any industry or organization may be enhanced and explored further, as it appears to have a positive impact on innovation within organizations which in turn has the potential to provide a variety of opportunities for growth and competitive advantage. This Chapter demonstrates the implementation of authentic leadership practices as being beneficial to any industry, especially that of FinTech due to the ethical dilemmas faced during the decision-making process when seeking a competitive advantage and narrowing the leadership gap.

CRITICAL REVIEW METHOD

This Chapter utilizes the method of a critical literature review, focusing on the research question: *How can authentic leadership behaviors enable innovation and competitive advantage in FinTech firms?* The aim of this Chapter is to develop a critical perspective on the role of authentic leader behaviors in enabling innovation for competitive advantage while addressing the failing leadership of FinTech firms. In doing so, it explores the role of authentic leader behaviors in a corporate setting and its effect on developing innovation to create a competitive advantage. It also explicates the role of innovation through authentic leadership on organizational success.

The rationale for engaging in a critical review over a potentially more rigorous review (e.g. systematic review) is due to the contrasting theories on authentic leadership and innovation in the organizational setting. The critical review method evaluates existing research while exploring competing ideas. This is done to provide a "launch pad" for conceptual development and "subsequent testing" (Grant & Booth, 2009, p. 93). The lack of scholarly consensus surrounding authentic leadership and the effect on innovation and competitive advantage in FinTech firms calls for a more critical and exploratory approach to the explication. Authentic leadership likewise lacks much consideration in the FinTech context and requires a critical lens to examine the potential synergies.

LITERATURE REVIEW

FinTech is an emerging industry that explores the intersection between emerging technology and disruption in the financial sector. The opportunity offered by FinTech firms is a unique optimization of the current handling and managing of a wide range of financial transactions. This can enhance the public's understanding of investment opportunities, enabling financial innovation, and ultimately enhancing the resilience of the economy, a goal that is critical to the financial system's overall health and well-being (Mayfield et al., 2008; Zavolokina et al., 2016).

Probabilistic approaches in FinTech help identify their targets and offers a framework for tracking a firm's evolution (Sironi, 2016). The financial sector, like other parts of the economy, is vulnerable to stress caused by climatic, economic, or political events. For example, consumers during the COVID-19 pandemic were uninclined to maintain investments in smaller FinTech companies who were at risk of liquidation during such an economically strenuous period (Zachariadis et al., 2020) However, emerging financial technologies, through innovative digital asset management, are offering sustainable solutions to such emergent problems.

Innovation as a source of competitive advantage is defined as the continuous effort, creativity, and initiative that allows people to go above and beyond to identify and solve problems in new ways (Lahovnik & Breznik, 2013). Successful innovation is not a short-term tool but rather a long-term strategy. The characteristics and methodologies of innovation focus on identifying and creating a culture of problem identification and subsequent solution finding. Innovation, as a source of competitive advantage, is not necessarily a matter of merely seeking to copy another's activities, but rather of doing things differently. Innovation also enhances the quality of an organization by providing a response to new and novel problems. The growth and success of a company are directly related to the enablers of innovation.

Authentic leadership within an organization is paramount to the firm's success, and so each leader must be as authentic as their team. An individual's authenticity may be gauged by their specific characteristics and behaviors as a senior leader. Other key characteristics of an authentic leader include demonstrating self-awareness, sound-morality, balanced processing of information and relational transparency with followers, as well as fostering positive self-development (Crawford et al., 2020a).

FinTech Emergence

FinTech is defined as the development of computing technologies that enhance financial services (Chen et al., 2019), and provides technologically enabled financial innovations with a direct effect on the financial markets and institutions (Schindler, 2017). The emergence of the financial services industry has experienced exponential growth in recent years, with financial technology enabling the rapid development in three key areas: i) raising capital; ii) allocating capital, and; iii) transferring capital (Gomber *et al.*, 2018; Das, 2019). Research demonstrates that the core drivers of these new systems include: i) digitalization of financial services; ii) pro-FinTech (de)regulation; iii) changing corporate needs and expectations; and iv) support for the benefits of competition (Holmes & King, 2019).

Finance and technology have a long history and have evolved rapidly over time. The three eras include the analogue age, which involved bank branch visitation to withdraw cash, followed by the digitalization of finance from the twentieth century onwards where financial banking could be conducted on computers, and finally the current era of FinTech which began in 2008 with instantaneous services on mobile banking apps, (Arner et al., 2015). Emerging FinTech encapsulates both the developed and developing world with a focus on startup organizations. While the innovation generated in the financial technology scene has real benefits for firms striving to achieve competitive advantage, the universal implications on the global economy also means regulators have had to step in and introduce new laws to counteract the risk associated with new approaches to FinTech. For example, 2017 saw Singaporean, American, Japanese and Chinese regulators implement increased oversight over cryptocurrency as innovation in this space could lead to widespread money laundering, opportunities for normally illegal financial activities such as 'painting the tape', and fraudulent financial transactions (Choudhury, 2017).

FinTech has transformed from the consumer retail sector, into a space where various stakeholders can take advantage of efficiencies of FinTech products that are continuously developing (Holmes & King, 2019). Therefore, business to consumer, consumer to consumer and business to business applications are available today and have expanded the potential for collaboration and connectivity across most industries. For example, Venmo now exists as an online tool that allows individuals to undertake financial transactions between consumers (Zhang et al., 2017). This technology offers a contemporary replacement for automated teller machine (ATM) withdrawals when splitting bills (Pinsker, 2017). Many consumers also use major payment services such as SamsungPay and ApplePay when tapping their mobile device on a pay terminal, rather than fiat currency. Finally, businesses can now complete real time bank transfers to other businesses using online payment processing providers like Dwolla who manage digital payment networks (Dwolla, 2020).

JPMorgan is an American multinational investment bank (JPMorgan Chase & Co, 2020) and Pacific Life is an American insurance company (Pacificlife, 2020). The closure of Pacific Life's investment platform, Swell, in 2019 (Miller, 2019) and JPMorgan Chase's digital banking service, Finn, in 2016 (Shevlin, 2019) are two examples of FinTech firms that have failed due to several factors. More recently, three of JPMorgan Chase's leaders have left the organization, giving the FinTech firm an opportunity to reassess its direction and leadership composition (Davis, 2020). Common shortfalls of FinTech firms are overlooking legal aspects and compliance, neglecting economic cycles and not differentiating FinTech from the technology industry (Harroch, 2019). Examples of success and failure in the FinTech industry demonstrate that sound leadership are crucial in preventing firm cessation (Davis, 2020). As such this critical review looks to identify how leadership behaviors can foster success through perpetuating components that make this pursuit possible.

Innovation

Innovation is broadly defined, however, Quintane et al. (2011) defines it as a process, an outcome, or mechanism for knowledge. In a synthesis of definitions, innovation is proposed as the application of creative or original ideas that foster new solutions to problems (Crawford et al., 2020b). This is reflected in Chell et al. (2010) research that argues the need to foster innovation as a response to challenges being faced. Innovation, technological advances and competitive advantages are multifaceted, evolving, and interlinked constructions, with the continued creation of new ideas for new and existing problems (Lengnick-Hall, 1992; Crossan & Apaydin, 2010). This leads to a competitive environment where firms must be adaptive and willing to foster new and sometimes risky undertakings (Ireland & Webb, 2007).

Schumpeter (1934) proposed innovation as generated by individuals within organizations, suggesting that large firms were the primary source of innovation (Ferreira et al., 2017), offering a key advantage over competitors. On the contrary, the application of innovation in the small to medium enterprise industry shows increasing evidence which suggests that their potential to influence growth of national economies should not be neglected (Vrgovic et al., 2012). Regardless of a firm's size, the important question remains. In what circumstances can innovation be beneficial in the FinTech industry?

Johne (1999) examines how market innovation improves the mix of target markets and provides unique motivation to explore new opportunities within organizations. FinTech examples demonstrate how skillful market innovation can provide a competitive advantage that is difficult to replicate, along with the freedom to grow and develop the organization. Business innovation excites customers, enables outperformance of out-performing competitors and facilitates new product offerings (Bowonder et al., 2010). How can companies create this competitive advantage? The following are a number of strategies Bowonder et al. (2010) suggests can be utilized: co-creation, brand value enhancement, technology leveraging, lean development, partnering, market segmentation and more. Furthermore, the adoption of innovative strategies and continuous improvement methods which contribute to operational efficiency have been found to increase profitability and further develop business performance (Bhaskaran, 2006).

Innovation is the foundation of technological evolution shaping today's FinTech communities (Cojoianu et al., 2019). The exponential rise of start-up organizations has generated pivotal technological development to fuel FinTech product innovation, from mobile payments and automated advice to cryptocurrencies and crowdfunding platforms, with smartphones assisting in offering new degrees of human access and connectivity. While financial institutions have typically held low levels of consumer trust, the opposite can be asserted for technology companies (Sapienza & Zingales, 2012; Rooney, 2018), whose marketing often includes calls for transparency, integrity, and customer-centricity. European banks alone spent an estimated 77 billion U.S. dollars on new technological investments, with the North American banking sector spending nearly 10% more (Toplensky, 2019). This extensive spending has been driven by competitive advantage and profit gained from utilizing innovative customer-centric technology designed to enable the raising, allocating, and transferring of capital (Henry, 2018; Das, 2019).

Grab was recognized by KPMG as one of the twenty-five most innovative FinTech startups in the world in 2018 (Goya, 2018). This particular organization is a Singapore-based firm, which provides ride-sharing transport services, food delivery and digital payment service solutions via mobile app (Grab, 2020). Bank Negara Malaysia has partnered with Grab to introduce Malaysia's new cashless payment system (Peyton, 2018). With the cost of cash handling and related services causing the country to be burdened by an expense of 453 million U.S. dollars per year, they claim the benefits of the electronic FinTech based payments could result in significant savings for the Malaysian economy.

SoFi (2020), another top FinTech firm, has generated interest with its private student loans and student loan refinancing scheme (D.M., 2018). The companies' innovation emerged from the need to support undergraduates, graduates and parents of students who pay for tertiary education. They offer no-fee student loans and methods in which one may consolidate an existing student loan debt without concealed fees. According to D.M. (2018), the American student loan market reaches 107 billion U.S. dollars annually. Historically it has been dominated by the US Education Department, covering 90 billion U.S. dollars in student loans each year. SoFi strived to disrupt this financial sector with new offerings. Challenges arose over time concerning their offerings including influences within the regulatory environment and consumer access to affordable bookkeeping services, however, Sofi continued to innovate and differentiate its competitive advantage through the expansion of its product range with financial services such as Home Loan, SoFi Invest and SoFi Money (SoFi, 2020).

Competitive Advantage

Competitive advantage is perhaps the most widely used term in strategic management, yet it remains poorly defined and operationalized (Ma, 2000). Competitive advantage is the ability for an entity to hold a strategy, process, or product that enables them to be superior (in at least one regard) to their competitors. To assess an organization's competitive advantage, three conditions must be met:

1. Activities in organizations are similar enough that sharing expertise is meaningful. Ability to transfer skills is likely to have little impact on competitive advantage;
2. The transfer of skill involves activities important to competitive advantage; and,
3. The skills transferred represent a significant source of competitive advantage for the receiving unit. (Porter & Kramer, 2002).

Firms are said to have obtained a competitive advantage when the entity has successfully implemented a value-creating strategy, while not simultaneously being implemented by any current or potential competitors (Flint, 2000). Since its conceptualization, the theory of competitive advantage has produced diverse schools of thought, directly relating to an organizations ability to enhance its internal and/or external strategy allowing subjective goals and objectives to be achieved.

This highlights the notion that it may be more important for an organization to focus on its ability to achieve sustainable competitive advantage over its competitors for a relatively long period of time, than it is to be able to initially manifest value creation through competitive advantage. The rationale behind this is that the required resources to gain a competitive advantage are inconsequential, unless it can be 'sustained', as the benefits of obtaining a competitive advantage cannot be experience in the short-term.

However, at their core, these theories share a common theme, that being that a firm which has achieved a sustainable competitive advantage has gained the ability to generate value creation within their specific market. This commonality raises an important question which has not yet been clearly answered and agreed upon nor reached a consensus. Who is receiving the 'value' and how are they gathering it? (Rumelt, 2003). An example of a firm having a competitive advantage and therefore demonstrating value creation, is one that is experiencing 'super-normal returns' on the basis of financial measurements and metrics. In this scenario, we must ask, does the firm have a competitive advantage, or is the industry/economy experiencing a competitive advantage?

Competitive advantage in the FinTech setting is key for consideration, given that FinTech firms can quickly ascend as unicorn start-ups and equally as quickly fold. For example, the American based company Stripe, is a successful FinTech unicorn company that develops economic infrastructure for the internet (CBinsights, 2020; Stripe, 2020). Yet, Powa Technologies was a British unicorn turned failure within three years. The leadership of Powa CEO, Dan Wagner, has been questioned after what was a rapid rise and fall of a billion-dollar company (Fletcher, 2016). FinTech is an emerging industry that is currently at its precipice and consists of an extremely small quantity of successful firms (Pollari, 2016). This Chapter looks to explore the positive impact that competitive advantage can insert into the FinTech industry, specifically to increase the probability of firms to continue or begin a successful business strategy enabling sustainable value creation. In a heavily competitive environment, strategic logistics capabilities for competitive advantage fosters organizational success (Morash et al., 1996), while ineffective leadership discourages knowledge sharing (Noe et al., 2017). FinTech companies seeking competitive advantage are looking for ways to do so sustainably, avoiding pitfalls such as emotional burnout (Brotheridge & Grandey, 2002), and ineffective leadership. This shift has driven banking institutions towards operational innovation in order to gain sustainable comparative advantage (Zhao et al., 2019).

Leadership

FinTech is one of the fastest growing industries (Romānova & Kudinska, 2016). As such the future of the industry is at a precipice. Growing industries often experience tumultuous expectations, from increased demand of service, to oversaturation of products. Among these nuances, strong leadership is needed to guide the vessel of FinTech through these new and uncharted waters. The following section explicates this importance, considers the leadership gap that exists in the contemporary organizational setting, including the FinTech industry, as well as the consequences if unaddressed. Likewise, this section will present authentic leader behavior theory, explicating its emergence as a possible antidote to unethical and ineffective leadership.

Leaders throughout organizations in all industries, showcase the importance of making crucial decisions accurately and the notion that resulting events may become detrimental if overlooked. Cases demonstrating a leadership gap can be explicated through discussion of the Global Financial Crisis (GFC) and the dot com bubble (Lloyd-Walker & Walker, 2011; Hirakubo & Friedman, 2002). Evidence from the literature suggests that, there was a lack of ethical balanced processing, one of the five behavioral traits that underpin an authentic leader. When assessing the risks associated with the business strategies involved in these scenarios, a cost-benefit analysis was not carried out to find the greatest good for the greatest number, with the negatives overlooked and resulting in operational activities implemented to maximize profits (Garicano & Posner, 2005).

Leadership Gap

Leadership is a phenomena that permeates through every aspect of day-to-day life. Effective and ethical leadership is one of the building blocks of positive organizational success and culture (Luthans, 2002). This demonstrated need is not new, with scholarly pleas for ethical and positive leadership a regular occurrence globally, not just in the FinTech industry (e.g. Crawford et al., 2017; Iszatt-White et al., 2019; Lemoine et al., 2019). A lack thereof presents its consequences in various ways. In May 2019, the National Association for Professional Triathletes in Scotland underwent an extensive review, as coaches and athletes spoke out about the significant lack of leadership (Palmer, 2020). In February 2020, the leadership of an Australian catholic school was called into question after a child grooming scandal was unearthed on national television. On a larger scale, ineffective leadership can cause wide-scale catastrophe such as the financial sector corruption leading to the Global Financial Crisis (Liu et al., 2017). From ineffective principals and coaches, to corporate corruption, the flow-on effects of unethical and failing leadership risks the very organizations that leaders are trying to guide.

Issues in relation to unethical practices and regulation within the FinTech sector can be identified throughout the world by analyzing key historical events occurring within the industry. A clear example of such occurrences is the 2008 Global Financial Crisis (GFC); to an extent this event may be contributed to both unethical practices demonstrated by individuals and the insufficient regulation of large-scale global FinTech institutions and their staff, management, and shareholders who became overly confident in the ability to manage and control risks through the application of quantitative finance and IT framework (Arner et al., 2016).

This is not to say that ineffective leaders are those who fail to demonstrate authentic leadership behaviors. Rather, leadership styles, such as authentic and transformational, promote certain behaviors that aid those in leadership positions to be better, more effective, and more ethical leaders (Crawford et al., 2017). Effective leadership has the potential to foster organizational success through a variety of means, such as competitive advantage and innovation. As such, a lack thereof often leads to long-term failure. The Australian Banking Royal Commission has created a genuine need for greater integrity within the financial services industry (Wishart & Wardrop, 2018; Atkins & Charlton, 2019). In FinTech firms, this is no exception. Engaging in the practices of ethical leadership fosters the growth of innovation and competitive advantage. Leaders in a landscape of high regulation need to have high degrees of self-awareness, sincerity, integrity, and morals to enable effective individual and organizational outcomes without compromising legal and ethical boundaries (Luthans & Avolio, 2003). At the foundation of these considerations are the means to ends.

Niccolò Machiavelli, as an early scholar in political science and leadership, articulates the need for his prince, Lorenzo de Medici, to implement the principles of an effective prince. Machiavelli (2008 [1532]) discussed the notion of city states, armies, and right-to-rule. Beyond his time, Machiavelli also explored the behavioral dimensions that lead to an effective leader. The Machiavellian leader as such, is described as an individual who puts their own self-interests above all else, often using cruel and unethical tactics under the guise of good will to boost reputation. Machiavellianism acts foundationally in contemporary literature, informing theories of unethical leadership such as, opportunism (Sakalaki et al., 2007), corporate psychopathy (Boddy et al., 2011), and apparent sincerity (Perrewe et al., 2007). The informative influence of Machiavellian leadership over corporate psychopathy is just one example of the effect unethical leadership has on the organizational setting. Machiavelli encouraged the identification and employment of wise advisors over 'yes-men', perpetuating means-to-ends styled consideration of employee's, channeling work towards the desires of leadership, rather than encouraging knowledge sharing and agency.

There are, within society, individuals who actively pursue Machiavellian behaviors. While such individuals are discouraged in organizations, they remain in number nonetheless. Siemens' corruption scandal in 2006 exemplified apparent sincerity (Venard, 2018); codes of conduct, anti-corruption norms, strict business guidelines, and membership to the Transparency International's German Chapter (a non-government anti-corruption organization) were all tactics used with underlying unethical goals. The organization received a 1.6 billion U.S. dollar fine, although this has not stopped companies from continuing such practices (Crawford et al., 2020a)

Recent FinTech emergence has galvanized a radical transformation of an old economy, connections, networks, and pace. Local newspapers and global news outlets articulate rhetoric like comments from the United Kingdom Digital Economy Minister Kate Forbes "Under Stephen Ingledew's leadership at FinTech Scotland has galvanized collaboration between Scotland's innovative SMEs, universities, financial industry and public sector" (Symon, 2020). The need for leadership expands beyond positional power, something the literature on the FinTech sector is yet to explore.

Authentic Leadership

An authentic leader is defined as an individual who has ethical core values and beliefs, and leads others in a genuine, transparent manner. Authentic leadership theory explicates positive organizational psychology, focusing on behaviors that inform positive and ethical leadership (Gardner et al., 2005; Crawford et al., 2020b). As there are many definitions of what it means to be an authentic leader, the most recent is (Crawford et al., 2020a, p. 126):

An authentic leader influences and motivates followers to achieve goals through their sincerity and positive moral perspective, enabled through heightened awareness and balanced processing.

Over the past 100 years, the term 'leadership' originated with a focus on traits rather than behaviors (e.g. Great Man Theory and Machiavelli's Prince). As a consequence, scholars are now turning their attention to better understanding individual behaviors affecting an individual's competency as a leader. This is showcased across all industries where leaders are failing the system, without education on how to lead, both emergent and established organizations are perpetuating these issues (Barbuto & Wheeler, 2006). Authentic leadership addresses this issue by facilitating self-determination of growth in areas of self-awareness, personal values, ethics and beliefs (Crawford et al., 2020a). Organizations which choose to adopt the authentic leadership style have the potential to encourage innovation from followers increasing the chance of an organization gaining a competitive advantage.

The emergence of authentic leadership came to fruition due to lack of leadership theories that were able to provide a strong response to the growing unethical trends within society (see Luthans & Avolio, 2003). In addition, authentic leaders have offered a response to unethical forms of power use that can lead to fearful employees based on hierarchical standing. In authentic leader theory, followers share the same values as this leader and are motivated to continue their ongoing support (Gardner et al., 2005). Research has shown that authentic leadership provides the moral and ethical foundation to enable an individuals' ability to make ethical decisions in the face of temptation, whereas followers of neutral or less authentic leaders may be more likely to succumb to temptation (Cianci et al., 2014). As organizations are beginning to adopt new leadership styles, authentic leadership has been viewed as; too radical, not mature enough, not politically mature enough, and not being able to think outside of the box (Nicoletti et al., 2017).

Growing evidence observes many industry leaders may mislead or exploit their supporters and employees through dishonesty, deceit and lack of transparency (Liu et al., 2017). In the fast-paced growth of the FinTech industry, it is vital that these leadership discrepancies are addressed and authentic leadership behaviors are fostered to allow for the growth of followers in the FinTech industry overall (Rego et al., 2012). Through consistent practices of authentic leadership in all levels of management, an individual's creativity and innovation in a team environment are likely to grow and develop, as authentic leaders create trust and emotional safety which allow individuals to openly express their ideas (Černe et al., 2013). The ability of an effective authentic leader to create and build confidence, hope, optimism, and resilience within each follower is paramount to gaining a competitive advantage over other FinTech companies. This is increasingly relevant within industries that are focused on innovation while operating as part of a highly competitive industry, such as that of the FinTech industry (Khan et al., 2010). The influence of authentic leadership allows individuals to bring together ideals which make the inevitable pragmatic trade-offs among multiple desired outcomes to transcend egocentric interests, conflicting roles, and practical obstacles. This mix of leadership characteristics and practical techniques can quickly amplify an innovative community's ability to adapt to change involving resources and challenges incumbent to technology leadership (Wong & Cummings, 2009). Through an improved workplace environment employees are able to cultivate innovative practices, which in turn encourage individuals to create, maximize, and measure new value within their role at their given organization in the FinTech industry.

SYNTHESIS

While Machiavellian leadership styles can lead to short-term organizational success, without effective and ethical leadership, businesses may find themselves without success in the long-term (Luthans, 2002); success that would follow the enabling of innovative practices and competitive advantage. It is observed that authentic leadership, and its behaviors, are the bonding agents when seeking to enable innovation and competitive advantage within an organization. Authentic leaders leverage awareness, sincerity, balanced processing, positive moral perspective, and informal influence to create opportunities for innovation. The theory posits the synthesis of these five areas, when applied correctly, which allow leaders within organizations to achieve innovative practices and competitive advantage. As discussed by Crawford et al. (2020a), awareness is having an insight into the behaviors of one's self, individuals, and groups. This heightened awareness may create an environment conducive to recognizing ethical issues and support an individual's ability to acknowledge poor decision-making, concepts which are paramount in business. Sincerity in the context of leadership refers to presenting one's true self to others, in a manner which is honest and open (Trilling, 2009; Crawford et al., 2020a).

Considering the potential exponential growth a newly established business may experience, demonstration of balanced processing would be advantageous during such a heated and challenging circumstance. Balanced processing is the ability of an individual to consider all relevant information available to them, and proceeding to use this information as part of their decision-making process in a manner which benefits their followers and stakeholders (Rego et al., 2012; Crawford et al., 2020a). The next component of authentic leadership, positive moral perspective, resonates the commitment to one's intrinsic ethics and the demonstration of a willingness to suppress their personal interests and ego in order to fulfill the wishes of the collective. Importantly, in FinTech, it is easy for ego to enable start-up leaders to grow an inflated sense of self-worth and make decisions to reinforce their ego rather than make considerate and holistic decisions (Block & Kremen, 1996). For example, one of the fastest growing FinTech startups in the UK, Revolut, was found manipulating recruitment applicants, not paying employees, setting unachievable targets and suffered high-staff turnover (Mellino, 2019). Finally, perhaps one of the most integral components of the leader-follower relationship; informal influence. Informal influence is an individual's ability to inspire and motivate their followers, allowing them to accomplish goals of their own volition, regardless of their position within the collective (Kellerman, 2012; Crawford et al., 2020a). With limited resources, FinTech leaders often rely on their relationship building skills and sustained informal influence to create, sustain, and enable their company's strategic competitive advantage.

FinTech Emergence

FinTech is one of many fast growing industries, as such it presents risks which require sound leadership at the helm to manage these risks. Exponential growth in any industry can present issues, specifically in FinTech the rate of growth experienced may lead to the exploitation of start-ups, inexperienced business owners, and young developers (Pollari, 2016). This is problematic as current regulations may not be up to date or implemented fast enough to monitor the advances and financial growth felt throughout the industry. The regulation is already problematic as some operating activities within the FinTech industry are falling outside the scope of traditional regulatory measures (Buchak et al., 2017). This lack of effective regulation allows issues involving cryptocurrency, fraudulent behavior, and money laundering to fall through the gaps. The presence of recurring issues reiterates the notion that ethics is an evolving concept (Fowers, 2015), one which authentic leadership behaviors would provide assistance through initiating the changing of peoples thought processes and learned behavior.

Consumers and organizations benefit from the collaboration and connectivity offered by FinTech firms. Increased connectivity enables more ways to exchange money, products, and services which benefit both consumers and organizations through diversification (Palmer & Johnston, 1996). The increased product diversification may increase exposure to the risk of data theft and tampering. The ethics and positive moral perspective present in authentic leadership behaviors would help guide individuals away from such behaviors with potentially detrimental outcomes. Given that few consumers read End User Licensing Agreements (Bakos et al., 2014), it is critical that leaders demonstrate high quality morals in upholding societal values on behalf of their consumer base. Another issue within FinTech, and its continuing emergence, is the recent decrease in investment and stakeholder interest due to the negative outcomes of the poor leadership and management of organizations within the industry. This may create further problems as it could scare away potential investors, as individuals may be less likely to invest in something that the majority are avoiding. For example, COVID-19 has seen consumers gravitate to larger financial institutions who are less susceptible to negative impact from economic busts (Zachariadis et al., 2020).

A common issue identified as directly affecting the FinTech industry is the potential ethical dilemmas faced, with the five components of authentic leadership working hand-in-hand to lead an organization and enable effective decision-making that brings individuals and groups into disrepute. The influence demonstrated by authentic leadership behaviors may aid in overcoming issues arising from egocentric interests, with such actions bringing forth the Australia Banking Royal Commission, which found four key issues that encompass unethical practices at the core (Royal Commission, 2019).

Innovation

Innovation can create a competitive business environment which may entice individuals to participate in risk taking and unethical behaviors (Tan, 2001). Authentic leadership behaviors, if correctly implemented within an organization, could reduce the likelihood of these events occurring. The demonstration of positive moral perspective and informal influence may create an environment conducive to that which brings about innovation and independent thought. Innovative practices and the encouragement of creativity can provide motivation for new opportunities, as well as contributing to efficiency and further enhancing organizational performance (Bharadwaj & Menon, 2000). This is why innovation is such a strong component within the FinTech industry. The products which are born in this industry would not come to fruition without the encouragement of innovative thought; e.g. Up Banking (Up, 2020). Innovation and the drivers of innovative practices often fill a gap in the market (Paradkar et al., 2015).

Innovation requires change, which many individuals resist when it first appears as it is often part of human nature to be conservative in the face of the new (Kotter & Schlesinger, 1989; Anderson, 2019). Change can be problematic for any industry; authentic leadership when correctly executed can reduce resistance to change through effective motivation of followers and instilling aligned values within the leader-follower relationship. The sincerity of an authentic leader may make it easier for individuals to incorporate change models such as that of Kotter's eight-step model (Kotter, 2012; Hackman, 2017), as the leader would genuinely believe in the desired outcome resulting from the change while it is happening.

Competitive Advantage

For an organization to achieve competitive advantage, they must have appropriate strategic objectives and goals, both of which are influenced by internal and external environmental factors (Nickols, 2016). Sustainable competitive advantage is of great importance, but is potentially problematic due to scarcity of resources. Authentic leadership may be the enabler which ensures these scarce resources are fairly and ethically distributed for use by both leaders and followers. An individual would achieve this via the incorporation of balanced processing and awareness, as the decision-making process of how to distribute resources may be tumultuous and present ethical challenges (Simon, 1979). There are many individuals and collectives which benefit from the achievement of competitive advantage within an organization; businesses, consumers, the market as a whole, and the economy if observed holistically. Without competitive advantage being achieved, FinTech firms can be left sitting in a tumultuous environment which poses many risks for any organization, regardless of size and age (Pollari, 2016).

Examples of success stories support the hypothesis that effective leadership, such as that of authentic leadership and its behaviors, can assist with innovation and achieving competitive advantage through the development and implementation of effective and realistic strategic goals and objectives (Porter, 2011). For example, Phillip Rosen was nominated as the best FinTech CEO in the 2019 Breakthrough Awards Program (Even Financial, 2019). Rosen was recognized for his exemplary vision and technical skills along with his ability to build a tight leadership team and execute strategy proficiently. Ethical leadership behaviors, which embody authentic leadership, bring forth innovation and competitive advantage. This may cause employees to sustain greater motivation if they know that the work they are doing is ethical and aligns with societal values. This also would motivate employees to feel safe enough to be creative and innovative, enabling organizations to continually achieve competitive advantage.

FUTURE RESEARCH DIRECTIONS

Without effective development of authentic leadership behaviors, stakeholders involved in FinTech operational activities may be at risk of exploitation, experience decreased rates of innovative growth, and have reduced opportunities to sustain their competitive advantage. Other prevalent issues which may arise are those involving a lack of ethical behavior (e.g. integrity and sincerity) and immoral decision-making (e.g. biased or unbalanced decision-making) when handling sensitive information requiring discretion within a FinTech institution.

This Chapter has the potential to spark further intrigue across all stakeholders given the present evolutionary nature of authentic leadership and its absence within FinTech institutions, which in turn may assist in the development of authentic leader behaviors while attempting to further develop innovation and enable the expansion of organizational competitive advantage. Furthermore, the incorporation of authentic leadership within organizations has the potential to create increased opportunities for the growth of innovative practices and competitive advantage across all levels of an organization.

FinTech as an individual industry, as well as the variety of organizations that utilize FinTech services during their operating activities, will perhaps find it advantageous to utilize authentic leadership methodologies in order to enhance innovative practices, which would have the potential to provide greater competitive advantage within their given market.

This Chapter may provide further insight into contemporary issues and developments arising within the realm of authentic leadership, and the influence this specific leadership style can have on the FinTech industry. The importance of authentic leadership within any industry may be enhanced and explored further, as it appears to have a positive impact on innovation within organizations which in turn has the potential to provide a variety of opportunities for growth and a greater broadening of competitive advantage.

CONCLUSION

This Chapter sought to discuss the way in which authentic leader behaviors enable innovation and competitive advantage, specifically in the context of FinTech firms. FinTech firms have experienced high growth rates and risk taking behaviors, and this critical review considered how a leader can enable innovation and competitive advantage by employing authentic leader behaviors. The literature began with explicating FinTech emergence and the problems observed across the industry. Next, considered innovation and its role in organizations, explicating specifically how it can assist in enabling competitive advantage. Followed by the explication of the way in which the five authentic leader behaviors encourage innovation and enable competitive advantage within FinTech firms.

An explanation of the chosen research method, critical review, was given, with a theoretical understanding beginning with a summary of literature behind FinTech and its emergence. The context is then followed by an explication of literature on innovation, competitive advantage, and the current leadership gap present in FinTech. Throughout the synthesis, the discussion sought to apply the behaviors of the authentic leader which encourage creativity and innovation, and enable sustainable competitive advantage within FinTech firms. To conclude, future research opportunities were briefly discussed.

REFERENCES

Anderson, D. L. (2019). *Organization development: The process of leading organizational change.* SAGE Publications, Incorporated.

Arner, D. W., Barberis, J., & Buckey, R. P. (2016). FinTech, RegTech, and the reconceptualization of financial regulation. *Nw. J. Int'l L. & Bus., 37*, 371.

Arner, D. W., Barberis, J., & Buckley, R. P. (2015). The evolution of Fintech: A new post-crisis paradigm. *Geo. J. Int'l L., 47*, 1271. doi:10.2139srn.2676553

Atkins, S., & Charlton, P. (2019). Chartered secretary: The banking royal commission final report: Culture and governance implications. *Governance Directions, 71*(2), 65.

Bakos, Y., Marotta-Wurgler, F., & Trossen, D. (2014). Does anyone read the fine print? Consumer attention to standard-form contracts. *The Journal of Legal Studies, 43*(1), 1–35. doi:10.1086/674424

Barbuto, J. E. Jr, & Wheeler, D. W. (2006). Scale development and construct clarification of servant leadership. *Group & Organization Management, 31*(3), 300–326. doi:10.1177/1059601106287091

Bharadwaj, S., & Menon, A. (2000). Making innovation happen in organizations: Individual creativity mechanisms, organizational creativity mechanisms or both? *Journal of Product Innovation Management: An International Publication of the Product Development & Management Association, 17*(6), 424–434. doi:10.1111/1540-5885.1760424

Bhaskaran, S. (2006). Incremental innovation and business performance: Small and medium-size food enterprises in a concentrated industry environment. *Journal of Small Business Management, 44*(1), 64–80. doi:10.1111/j.1540-627X.2006.00154.x

Block, J., & Kremen, A. (1996). IQ and ego-resiliency: Conceptual and empirical connections and separateness. *Journal of Personality and Social Psychology, 70*(2), 349–361. doi:10.1037/0022-3514.70.2.349 PMID:8636887

Boddy, C. R., Galvin, P., & Ladyshewsky, R. K. (2011). Corporate psychopaths. In *Ethical leadership* (pp. 17–33). Palgrave Macmillan. doi:10.1057/9780230299061_2

Bowonder, B., Dambal, A., Kumar, S., & Shirodkar, A. (2010). Innovation strategies for creating competitive advantage. *Research Technology Management, 53*(3), 19–32. doi:10.1080/08956308.2010.11657628

Brotheridge, C. M., & Grandey, A. A. (2002). Emotional labor and burnout: Comparing two perspectives of "people work". *Journal of Vocational Behavior, 60*(1), 17–39. doi:10.1006/jvbe.2001.1815

Buchak, G., Matvos, G., Piskorski, T., & Seru, A. (2017). Fintech, Regulatory Arbitrage, and the Rise of Shadow Banks, forthcoming in the. *Journal of Financial Economics.*

CBinsights. (2020). The global unicorn club. *CBinsights*. Retrieved May 23, 2020, from https://www.cbinsights.com/research-unicorn-companies

Černe, M., Jaklič, M., & Škerlavaj, M. (2013). Authentic leadership, creativity, and innovation: A multilevel perspective. *Leadership*, *9*(1), 63–85. doi:10.1177/1742715012455130

Chell, E., Nicolopoulou, K., & Karataş-Özkan, M. (2010). *Social entrepreneurship and enterprise: International and innovation perspectives*. Academic Press.

Chen, M. A., Wu, Q., & Yang, B. (2019). How valuable Is FinTech innovation? *Review of Financial Studies*, *32*(5), 2062–2106. doi:10.1093/rfs/hhy130

Choudhury, S. R. (2017, September 12). Governments want to control cryptocurrencies – but there's a danger to too many rules. *CNBC*. Retrieved March 3, 2020, from https://www.cnbc.com/2017/09/12/regulators-are-turning-their-attention-to-cryptocurrencies.html

Cianci, A. M., Hannah, S. T., Roberts, R. P., & Tsakumis, G. T. (2014). The effects of authentic leadership on followers' ethical decision-making in the face of temptation: An experimental study. *The Leadership Quarterly*, *25*(3), 581–594. doi:10.1016/j.leaqua.2013.12.001

Cojoianu, T., Clark, G. L., Hoepner, A. G., Pazitka, V., & Wojcik, D. (2019). Fin vs. tech: determinants of fintech start-up emergence and innovation in the financial services incumbent sector. *SSRN Electronic Journal*.

Crawford, J., Dawkins, S., Martin, A., & Lewis, G. (2017). Understanding the organizational climate of unethical leadership in the Australian Football League. *The Journal of Leadership Studies*, *11*(2), 52–54. doi:10.1002/jls.21525

Crawford, J., Dawkins, S., Martin, A., & Lewis, G. (2020a). Putting the leader back into authentic leadership: Reconceptualising and rethinking leaders. *Australian Journal of Management*, *45*(1), 114–133. doi:10.1177/0312896219836460

Crawford, J., Kelder, J., & Knox, M. (2020b). What does it take to be a social entrepreneur?: Authentic leaders and their effect on innovation. In C. Dogru (Ed.), *Leadership styles, innovation, and social entrepreneurship in the era of digitalization* (pp. 282–310). IGI Global. doi:10.4018/978-1-7998-1108-4.ch011

Crossan, M. M., & Apaydin, M. (2010). A multi-dimensional framework of organizational innovation: A systematic review of the literature. *Journal of Management Studies*, *47*(6), 1154–1191. doi:10.1111/j.1467-6486.2009.00880.x

Das, S. (2019). The future of fintech. *Financial Management*, *48*(4), 981–1007. doi:10.1111/fima.12297

Davis, M. F. (2020). JPMorgan hires Capital One's Haus to lead digital technology. *Bloomberg*. Retrieved May 23, 2020, from https://www.bloombergquint.com/business/jpmorgan-hires-capital-one-s-haus-to-lead-digital-technology

D.M. (2018). Sofi – an illustrative tale of why fintech disruption is so difficult. *Digital Innovation & Transformation*. Retrieved March, 3, 2020, https://digital.hbs.edu/platform-digit/submission/sofi-an-illustrative-tale-of-why-fintech-disruption-is-so-difficult/

Dwolla. (2020). The programmable payments platform. *Dwolla*. Retrieved March, 3, 2020, from https://www.dwolla.com/

Even Financial. (2019). Even financial CEO Phillip Rosen named "best fintech CEO" in 2019 fintech breakthrough awards program. *Even Financial*. Retrieved May 23, 2020, from https://evenfinancial.com/press/even-financial-ceo-phillip-rosen-named-best-fintech-ceo-in-2019-fintech-breakthrough-awards-program/

Ferreira, M., Reis, N., & Pinto, C. (2017). Schumpeter's (1934) Influence on Entrepreneurship (and Management) Research. *Revista de Empreendedorismo e Gestão de Pequenas Empresas, 6*(1), 4-39.

Fletcher, N. (2016). Dan Wagner and the fall of 'unicorn' startup Powa Technologies. *TheGuardian.com*. Retrieved May 23, 2020, from https://www.theguardian.com/business/2016/apr/18/dan-wagner-powa-technologies

Flint, G. D. (2000). What is the meaning of competitive advantage? *Journal of Competitiveness Studies, 8*(1), 121.

Fowers, B. (2015). *The evolution of ethics: Human sociality and the emergence of ethical mindedness*. Springer. doi:10.1057/9781137344663

Gardner, W. L., Avolio, B. J., & Walumbwa, F. O. (2005). Authentic leadership development: Emergent trends and future directions. *Authentic leadership theory and practice: Origins, effects and development*, 387-406.

Garicano, L., & Posner, R. A. (2005). Intelligence failures: An organizational economics perspective. *The Journal of Economic Perspectives, 19*(4), 151–170. doi:10.1257/089533005775196723

Gomber, P., Kauffman, R., Parker, C., & Weber, B. (2018). On the fintech revolution: Interpreting the forces of innovation, disruption, and transformation in financial services. *Journal of Management Information Systems, 35*(1), 220–265. doi:10.1080/07421222.2018.1440766

Goya, C. (2018). These are the 25 most innovative Fintech startups in the world, according to KPMG. *Business Insider*. Retrieved May 25, 2020, from https://www.businessinsider.com/these-are-the-25-most-innovative-fintech-startups-in-the-world-2018-10?r=AU&IR=T

Grab. (2020). Say hello to your everyday everything app. *Grab.co.sg*. Retrieved March, 3, 2020, from https://www.grab.com/sg/

Grant, M., & Booth, A. (2009). A typology of reviews: An analysis of 14 review types and associated methodologies. *Health Information and Libraries Journal, 26*(2), 91–108. doi:10.1111/j.1471-1842.2009.00848.x PMID:19490148

Hackman, T. (2017). *Leading change in action: Reorganizing an academic library department using Kotter's eight stage change model*. Academic Press.

Harroch, R. (2019). 10 Key Issues for Fintech Startup Companies. *Forbes*. Retrieved 20 May, 2020, from https://www.forbes.com/sites/allbusiness/2019/10/12/fintech-startup-companies-key-challenges/#42315493e45b

Henry, D. (2018, October 20). JPMorgan to build Silicon Valley fintech office. *Reuters*. Retrieved January, 16, 2020, from https://www.reuters.com/article/us-jpmorgan-tech-office/jpmorgan-to-build-silicon-valleyfintech-office-idUSKCN1MT2OL

Hirakubo, N., & Friedman, H. H. (2002). Dot-bombs: Lessons from the dot-com debacle. *Journal of Internet Commerce, 1*(2), 89–102. doi:10.1300/J179v01n02_07

Holmes, C., & King, R. (2019). The evolution of business-to-business FinTech: What the future holds. *Journal of Payments Strategy & Systems, 13*(3), 217–225.

ING. (2020, March 2). Retrieved from https://www.ing.com.au

Ireland, R. D., & Webb, J. W. (2007). Strategic entrepreneurship: Creating competitive advantage through streams of innovation. *Business Horizons, 50*(1), 49–59. doi:10.1016/j.bushor.2006.06.002

Iszatt-White, M., Whittle, A., Gadelshina, G., & Mueller, F. (2019). The 'Corbyn phenomenon': Media representations of authentic leadership and the discourse of ethics versus effectiveness. *Journal of Business Ethics, 159*(2), 535–549. doi:10.100710551-018-3838-x

Jalil, A., Azam, F., & Rahman, M. K. (2010). Implementation mechanism of ethics in business organizations. *International Business Research, 3*(4), 145. doi:10.5539/ibr.v3n4p145

Johne, A. (1999). Successful market innovation. In *Innovations management* (pp. 163–170). Springer.

JPMorgan Chase & Co. (2020). History of our firm. *JPMorgan Chase & Co.* Retrieved May 23, 2020, from https://impact.jpmorganchase.com/about/our-history

Kellerman, B. (2012). *The end of leadership*. Harper Business.

Khan, S. (2010). Impact of authentic leaders on organization performance. *International Journal of Business and Management, 5*(12), 167. doi:10.5539/ijbm.v5n12p167

Kotter, J. P. (2012). *Leading change*. Harvard Business Press.

Kotter, J. P., & Schlesinger, L. A. (1989). Choosing strategies for change. In *Readings in strategic management* (pp. 294–306). Palgrave. doi:10.1007/978-1-349-20317-8_21

Lahovnik, M., & Breznik, L. (2013). Innovation management and technological capabilities as a source of competitive advantage. *Management, Knowledge and Learning International Conference*.

Lemoine, G., Hartnell, C., & Leroy, H. (2019). Taking stock of moral approaches to leadership: An integrative review of ethical, authentic, and servant leadership. *The Academy of Management Annals, 13*(1), 148–187. doi:10.5465/annals.2016.0121

Lengnick-Hall, C. A. (1992). Innovation and competitive advantage: What we know and what we need to learn. *Journal of Management, 18*(2), 399–429. doi:10.1177/014920639201800209

Liu, H., Cutcher, L., & Grant, D. (2017). Authentic leadership in context: An analysis of banking CEO narratives during the global financial crisis. *Human Relations, 70*(6), 694–724. doi:10.1177/0018726716672920

Lloyd-Walker, B., & Walker, D. (2011). Authentic leadership for 21st century project delivery. *International Journal of Project Management, 29*(4), 383–395. doi:10.1016/j.ijproman.2011.02.004

Luthans, F. (2002). The need for and meaning of positive organizational behavior. *Journal of Organizational Behavior: The International Journal of Industrial. Occupational and Organizational Psychology and Behavior*, *23*(6), 695–706. doi:10.1002/job.165

Luthans, F., & Avolio, B. (2003). Authentic leadership development. In K. Cameron, J. Dutton, & R. Quinn (Eds.), *Positive organizational scholarship: Foundations of a new discipline* (pp. 241–258). Berrett Koehler Publishers.

Ma, H. (2000). Competitive advantage and firm performance. *Competitiveness Review*, *10*(2), 15–32. doi:10.1108/eb046396

Machiavelli, N. (2008). *The prince*. Hackett Publishing.

Mayfield, C., Perdue, G., & Wooten, K. (2008). Investment management and personality type. *Financial Services Review*, *17*(3), 219–236.

Mellino, E. (2019). Revolut insiders reveal the human cost of fintech unicorn's wild rise. *Wired*. Retrieved May 23, 2020, from https://www.wired.co.uk/article/revolut-trade-unions-labour-fintech-politics-storonsky

Morash, E. A., Droge, C. L., & Vickery, S. K. (1996). Strategic logistics capabilities for competitive advantage and firm success. *Journal of Business Logistics*, *17*(1), 1.

Nickols, F. (2016). Strategy, strategic management, strategic planning and strategic thinking. *Management Journal*, *1*(1), 4–7.

Nicoletti, B., & Weis. (2017). Future of FinTech. Basingstoke, UK: Palgrave Macmillan.

Noe, R., Hollenbeck, J., Gerhart, B., & Wright, P. (2017). *Human resource management: Gaining a competitive advantage*. McGraw-Hill Education.

Palmer, J. W., & Johnston, J. S. (1996). Business-tobusiness connectivity on the Internet: EDI, intermediaries, and interorganizational dimensions. *Electronic Markets*, *6*(2).

Palmer, M. (2020). Absence of leadership claim made against 'toxic' Triathlon Scotland, *The Times*. Retrieved May 22, 2020, from https://www.thetimes.co.uk/article/absence-of-leadership-claim-made-against-toxic-triathlon-scotland-mwt0tq967

Paradkar, A., Knight, J., & Hansen, P. (2015). Innovation in start-ups: Ideas filling the void or ideas devoid of resources and capabilities? *Technovation*, *41*, 1–10. doi:10.1016/j.technovation.2015.03.004

Perrewé, P. L., Ferris, G. R., Stoner, J. S., & Brouer, R. L. (2007). The positive role of political skill in organizations. *Positive organizational behavior: Accentuating the positive at work*, 117-128.

Peyton, A. (2018, May 22). Maybank makes a grab for cashless payments in Malaysia. *Fintechfutures.com*. Retrieved March 3, 2020, from https://www.fintechfutures.com/2018/05/maybank-makes-a-grab-for-cashless-payments-in-malaysia/

Pinsker, J. (2017, July 18). How in the world does Venmo make money? *The Atlantic*. Retrieved January 16, 2020, from https://www.theatlantic.com/business/archive/2017/07/venmo-makes-money-banks/533946/

Pollari, I. (2016). The rise of Fintech opportunities and challenges. *Jassa*, (3), 15.

Porter, M. E. (2011). *Competitive advantage of nations: creating and sustaining superior performance*. Simon and Schuster.

Porter, M. E., & Kramer, M. R. (2002). The competitive advantage of corporate. *Harvard Business Review*. PMID:12510538

Quintane, E., Mitch Casselman, R., Sebastian Reiche, B., & Nylund, P. A. (2011). Innovation as a knowledge-based outcome. *Journal of Knowledge Management*, *15*(6), 928–947. doi:10.1108/13673271111179299

Rego, A., Sousa, F., Marques, C., & Cunha, M. (2012). Authentic leadership promoting employees' psychological capital and creativity. *Journal of Business Research*, *65*(3), 429–437. doi:10.1016/j.jbusres.2011.10.003

Romānova, I., & Kudinska, M. (2016). Banking and Fintech: a challenge or opportunity? In *Contemporary issues in finance: Current challenges from across Europe*. Emerald Group Publishing Limited. doi:10.1108/S1569-375920160000098002

Rooney, K. (2018, September 14). After the crisis, a new generation puts its trust in tech over traditional banks. *CNBC*. Retrieved January 15, 2020, from https://www.cnbc.com/2018/09/14/a-new-generation-puts-its-trust-in-tech-over-traditional-banks.html

Rowley, J. (2016). Human Rights are Animal Rights: The Implications of Ethical Veganism for Human Rights. In *Critical Perspectives on Veganism* (pp. 67–92). Palgrave Macmillan. doi:10.1007/978-3-319-33419-6_4

Royal Commission. (2019, March 4). Retrieved from https://financialservices.royalcommission.gov.au/Pages/reports.aspx#final

Rumelt, R. P. (2003). What in the world is competitive advantage. *Policy working paper, 105*(2003), 1-5.

Sakalaki, M., Richardson, C., & Thépaut, Y. (2007). Machiavellianism and economic opportunism. *Journal of Applied Social Psychology*, *37*(6), 1181–1190. doi:10.1111/j.1559-1816.2007.00208.x

Sapienza, P., & Zingales, L. (2012). A trust crisis. *International Review of Finance*, *12*(2), 123–131. doi:10.1111/j.1468-2443.2012.01152.x

Schindler, J. W. (2017). *FinTech and financial innovation: Drivers and depth*. Academic Press.

Shevlin, R. (2019). Why did Chase Shut Down Finn? *Forbes*. Retrieved May 20, 2020, from https://www.forbes.com/sites/ronshevlin/2019/06/06/why-did-chase-shut-down-finn/#716002cf702b

Simon, H. A. (1979). Rational decision making in business organizations. *The American Economic Review*, *69*(4), 493–513.

Sironi, J. (2016). *FinTech innovation: from robo-advisors to goal based investing and gamification*. John Wiley & Sons. doi:10.1002/9781119227205

SoFi. (2020). How SoFi works. *SoFi.com*. Retrieved March 3, 2020, from https://www.sofi.com/how-it-works/

Stripe. (2020). Our mission is to increase the GDP of the internet. *Stripe*. Retrieved May 23, 2020, from https://stripe.com/au/about

Symon, K. (2020, January 9). FinTech Scotland celebrates its second birthday with growing business numbers. *Insider.co.uk*. Retrieved January 14, 2020, from https://www.insider.co.uk/news/fintech-scotland-celebrates-second-birthday-21241330

Tan, J. (2001). Innovation and risk-taking in a transitional economy: A comparative study of Chinese managers and entrepreneurs. *Journal of Business Venturing*, *16*(4), 359–376. doi:10.1016/S0883-9026(99)00056-7

Toplensky, R. (2019, September 10). Technology is bank's new battleground. *The Wall Street Journal*. Retrieved March 4, 2020, from https://www.wsj.com/articles/technology-is-banks-new-battleground-11568114378?mod=djemheard_t

Trilling, L. (2009). *Sincerity and authenticity*. Harvard University Press. doi:10.2307/j.ctvjhzrdp

Up. (2020, March 2). Retrieved from https://up.com.au

Vrgovic, P., Vidicki, P., Glassman, B., & Walton, A. (2012). Open innovation for SMEs in developing countries–An intermediated communication network model for collaboration beyond obstacles. *Innovation*, *14*(3), 290–302. doi:10.5172/impp.2012.14.3.290

Wildcard. (2020, March 1). Retrieved from https://www.wildcard.money

Wishart, D., & Wardrop, A. (2018). What can the Banking Royal Commission achieve: Regulating for good corporate culture? *Alternative Law Journal*, *43*(2), 81–88. doi:10.1177/1037969X18772153

Wong, C. A., & Cummings, G. G. (2009). The influence of authentic leadership behaviors on trust and work outcomes of health care staff. *The Journal of Leadership Studies*, *3*(2), 6–23. doi:10.1002/jls.20104

Zachariadis, M., Ozcan, P., & Dinckol, D. (2020). How is COVID-19 impacting fintech startups? *Fintech Magazine*. Retrieved May 23, 2020, from https://www.fintechmagazine.com/fintech/how-covid-19-impacting-fintech-startups

Zavolokina, L., Dolata, M., & Schwabe, G. (2016). *FinTech–What's in a Name?* Academic Press.

Zhang, X., Tang, S., Zhao, Y., Wang, G., Zheng, H., & Zhao, B. Y. (2017, May). Cold hard e-cash: Friends and vendors in the venmo digital payments system. *Eleventh International AAAI Conference on Web and Social Media*.

Zhao, Q., Tsai, P. H., & Wang, J. L. (2019). Improving financial service innovation strategies for enhancing China's banking industry competitive advantage during the fintech revolution: A Hybrid MCDM model. *Sustainability*, *11*(5), 1419. doi:10.3390u11051419

ADDITIONAL READING

Crawford, J., Dawkins, S., Martin, A., & Lewis, G. (2020a). Putting the leader back into authentic leadership: Reconceptualising and rethinking leaders. *Australian Journal of Management*, *45*(1), 114–133. doi:10.1177/0312896219836460

Jalil, A., Azam, F., & Rahman, M. K. (2010). Implementation mechanism of ethics in business organizations. *International Business Research*, *3*(4), 145. doi:10.5539/ibr.v3n4p145

Lahovnik, M., & Breznik, L. (2013). Innovation management and technological capabilities as a source of competitive advantage. In *Management, Knowledge and Learning International Conference, Zadar, Croatia.*

Luthans, F. (2002). The need for and meaning of positive organizational behavior. *Journal of Organizational Behavior: The International Journal of Industrial. Occupational and Organizational Psychology and Behavior*, *23*(6), 695–706. doi:10.1002/job.165

Porter, M. E., & Kramer, M. R. (2002). The competitive advantage of corporate. *Harvard Business Review*. PMID:12510538

KEY TERMS AND DEFINITIONS

Authentic Leader Behaviours: Authentic leader behaviors are the four specific behaviors demonstrated by an authentic leader. The four behaviors are sincerity, positive moral perspective, heightened awareness, balanced processing.

Competitive Advantage: Competitive advantage is the ability for an entity to hold a strategy, process, or product that enables them to be superior to their competitors.

Ethics: Ethics refers to an individual's concept of morals, including that of their ability to choose between right and wrong, good and bad, etc.

FinTech: FinTech involves the development of technology to enhance financial services, while enabling financial innovations through technology.

Innovation: Innovation is the process of individuals or groups using their original and creative ideas to develop solutions to problems.

Leadership: Leadership is a skill surrounding an individual or groups ability to guide an organisation, team, or other individuals towards a common goal.

Organizational Development: Organizational development is the analysis of organizational change and performance, resulting is outcomes reflecting success.

Value Creation: Value creation is any given process or change to a product or service that creates outputs of greater value than its initial inputs.

Compilation of References

Abramovicz, M. (2016). Cryptocurrency-Based Law. *Arizona Law Review, 58*(2), 359–420.

Accenture. (2019). *Cost of Cybercrime Study in Financial Services: 2019 Report*. https://www.slideshare.net/accenture/cost-of-cybercrime-study-in-financial-services-2019-report

Accenture. (2019). *The (r)evolution of Money II, Blockchain Empowered Central Bank Digital Currencies*. Author.

Act CXXXIX of 2013 on the National Bank of Hungary

Act I of 2012 on the Labour code of Hungary. art. 154

Adhami, S., Giudici, G., & Martinazzi, S. (2018). Why do businesses go crypto? An empirical analysis of initial coin offerings. *Journal of Economics and Business, 100*, 64–75. doi:10.1016/j.jeconbus.2018.04.001

Agarwal, R., & Kallapur, S. (2018). Cognitive risk culture and advanced roles of actors in risk governance: A case study. *The Journal of Risk Finance, 19*(4), 327–342. doi:10.1108/JRF-11-2017-0189

Agile Manifesto. (2014). *Manifesto for Agile Software Development*. Available from https://agilemanifesto.org/

Ajao, O. S., Jayeoba, O., & Ajibade, A. (2016). Evolution and development of auditing. *Unique Journal of Business Management Research, 3*(1), 32–40.

Akhavein, J., Frame, W. S., & White, L. (2005). The diffusion of financial innovations: An examination of the adoption of small business credit scoring by large banking organizations. *The Journal of Business, 78*(2), 577–596. doi:10.1086/427639

Akhter, N., & Khalily, B. (2017). *Impact of Mobile Financial Services on Financial Inclusion in Bangladesh*. Institute for Inclusive Finance and Development (InM), Working Paper, (52).

Alameda Research. (2019). *Investigation into the Legitimacy of Reported Cryptocurrency Exchange Volume*. https://ftx.com/volume-report-paper.pdf

Alberta Statutes - The Bank Taxation Act; The Credit of Alberta Regulation Act; and the Accurate News and Information Act, 1938 CanLII 1 (SCC), [1938] SCR 100

Aldasoro, I., Gambacorta, L., Giudici, P., & Leach, T. (2020). *The drivers of cyber risk*. BIS Working Paper 865.

Alexander, A. J., Shi, L., & Solomon, B. (2017). *How fintech is reaching the poor in Africa and Asia*. Academic Press.

Allen, F., Carletti, E., Cull, R., Qian, J. Q., Senbet, L., & Valenzuela, P. (2014). The African financial development and financial inclusion gaps. *Journal of African Economies, 23*(5), 614–642. doi:10.1093/jae/eju015

Ambler, S. (2017). *Examining the Agile Manifesto*. Available from http://www.ambysoft.com/essays/agileManifesto.html

Amit, R., & Zott, C. (2001). Value Creation in E-Business. *Strategic Management Journal, 22*(6-7), 493–520. doi:10.1002mj.187

Anagnostopoulos, I. (2018). Fintech and regtech: Impact on regulators and banks. *Journal of Economics and Business, 100*, 7–25. doi:10.1016/j.jeconbus.2018.07.003

Andersen, N. (2016). *Blockchain technology – A game-changer in accounting?* Deloitte. Retrieved June, 10, 2020, from https://www2.deloitte.com/content/dam/Deloitte/de/Documents/Innovation/Blockchain_A%20game-changer%20in%20accounting.pdf

Anderson, A. (n.d.). *4 keys to the future of audit.* Thomson Reuters Checkpoint White Paper. Retrieved June, 10, 2020, from https://tax.thomsonreuters.com/site/wp-content/private/pdf/checkpoint/whitepapers/Checkpoint-Al-Anderson-Whitepaper.pdf

Anderson, D. L. (2019). *Organization development: The process of leading organizational change.* SAGE Publications, Incorporated.

Andrianaivo, M., & Kpodar, K. (2011). *ICT, financial inclusion, and growth: Evidence from African countries.* Academic Press.

Ante, L. (2019a). *A Place Beside Satoshi – Scientific Foundations of Blockchain and Cryptocurrency in Business and Economics.* doi:10.13140/RG.2.2.27208.67842

Ante, L. (2019b). *Market Reaction to Exchange Listings of Cryptocurrencies.* doi:10.13140/RG.2.2.19924.76161

Ante, L. (2020). *Smart Contracts on the Blockchain – A Bibliometric Analysis and Review.* doi:10.13140/RG.2.2.23964.03207

Ante, L., & Fiedler, I. (2019). *Cheap Signals in Security Token Offerings (STOs).* doi:10.2139srn.3356303

Ante, L., & Meyer, A. (2019). *Cross-listings of Blockchain-based Tokens issued through Initial Coin Offerings: Do Liquidity and specific Cryptocurrency Exchanges matter?* doi:10.13140/RG.2.2.27494.37442

Ante, L. (2018). Cryptocurrency, Blockchain and Crime. In K. McCarthy (Ed.), *The Money Laundering Market: Regulating the Criminal Economy* (pp. 171–198). Agenda Publishing. doi:10.2307/j.ctv5cg8z1.10

Ante, L., Sandner, P., & Fiedler, I. (2018). Blockchain-Based ICOs: Pure Hype or the Dawn of a New Era of Startup Financing? *Journal of Risk and Financial Management, 11*(4), 80. doi:10.3390/jrfm11040080

Arandara, R., & Gunasekera, S. (2020). *Financial Inclusion and Inclusive Growth: What Does It Mean for Sri Lanka?* World Bank Policy Research Working Paper, (9204).

Ardic, O. P., Heimann, M., & Mylenko, N. (2011). *Access to financial services and the financial inclusion agenda around the world: a cross-country analysis with a new data set.* The World Bank.

Ardizzi, G., Crudu, F., & Petraglia, C. (2019). Innovation and Cost Efficiency in the Banking Industry: The Role of Electronic Payments. *Economic Notes by John Wiley & Sons Ltd, 48*(1), 12121. Advance online publication. doi:10.1111/ecno.12121

Arner, D. W., & Barberies, J. N. (2017). FinTech and RegTech in a Nutshell, and the Future in a Sandbox. *SSRN Electronic Journal.* Doi:10.2139srn.3088303

Arner, D. W., Barberis, J. N., & Buckley, R. P. (2016). FinTech, Regtech and the Reconceptualization of Financial Regulation. *Northwestern Journal of International Law & Business, 37*(3).

Arner, D. W., Barberis, J., & Buckey, R. P. (2016). FinTech, RegTech, and the reconceptualization of financial regulation. *Nw. J. Int'l L. & Bus., 37*, 371.

Arner, D. W., Barberis, J., & Buckley, R. P. (2015). The evolution of Fintech: A new post-crisis paradigm. *Geo. J. Int'l L., 47*, 1271. doi:10.2139srn.2676553

Aron, J. (2018). Mobile money and the economy: A review of the evidence. *The World Bank Research Observer, 33*(2), 135–188. doi:10.1093/wbro/lky001

Arora, R. U. (2010). *Measuring financial access.* Griffith Business School Discussion Papers Economics, (7).

Ascent. (2020). *What is SupTech and How Will it Change Compliance?* Retrieved from https://www.ascentregtech.com/blog/what-is-suptech-and-how-will-it-change-compliance/

Asen, R., & Blechschmidt, B. (2016). Making digital, real and rewarding. *Cognizanti, 9*(1), 2-13. Retrieved from https://www.cognizant.com/whitepapers/being-digital-making-digital-real-and-rewardingcognizanti12-codex2094.pdf

ASIFMA. (2019). *Tokenised Securities. A Roadmap for Market Participants and Regulators.* Retrieved from https://www.asifma.org/research/tokenised-securities-a-roadmap-for-market-participants-and-regulators/

Association of Chartered Certified Accountants – ACCA. (2016). *Drivers of change and future skills.* Report. Retrieved June, 10, 2020, from https://www.accaglobal.com/content/dam/members-beta/docs/ea-patf-drivers-of-change-and-future-skills.pdf

Association of Chartered Certified Accountants – ACCA. (2019). *Audit and technology. Professional insight report.* Retrieved from https://www.accaglobal.com/content/dam/ACCA_Global/professional-insights/audit-and-tech/pi-audit-and-technology.pdf

Association of Chartered Certified Accountants – ACCA. (2019a). *Audit and technology.* Professional insight report. Retrieved June, 10, 2020, from https://www.accaglobal.com/content/dam/ACCA_Global/professional-insights/audit-and-tech/pi-audit-and-technology.pdf

Association of Chartered Certified Accountants – ACCA. (2019b). *Closing the expectation gap in audit.* Report. Retrieved June, 10, 2020, from https://www.accaglobal.com/content/dam/ACCA_Global/professional-insights/Expectation-gap/pi-closing-expectation-gap-audit.pdf

Association of Chartered Certified Accountants – ACCA. (n.d.). *Data analytics and the auditor. Technical articles.* Retrieved from https://www.accaglobal.com/in/en/student/exam-support-resources/professional-exams-study-resources/p7/technical-articles/data-analytics.html

Association of Chartered Certified Accountants – ACCA. (n.d.). *Data analytics and the auditor.* Technical articles. Retrieved June, 10, 2020, from https://www.accaglobal.com/in/en/student/exam-support-resources/professional-exams-study-resources/p7/technical-articles/data-analytics.html

Atkins, S., & Charlton, P. (2019). Chartered secretary: The banking royal commission final report: Culture and governance implications. *Governance Directions, 71*(2), 65.

Auer, R. (2019). *Embedded supervision: how to build regulation into blockchain finance.* BIS Working Papers No 811. Monetary and Economic Department. Bank for International Settlements. Basel.

Ayyagari, M., & Beck, T. (2015). *Financial inclusion in Asia: An overview.* Asian Development Bank Economics Working Paper Series, (449).

Babaev, B. D., Nikolaeva, E. E., Babaev, D. B., & Borovkova, N. V. (2020). Russia: Digital economy or industrial and information economy? *Lecture Notes in Networks and Systems*, *87*, 332–341. doi:10.1007/978-3-030-29586-8_39

Backbase. (2017). *The PSD 2. Playbook.* Available from http://www.backbase.com/wp-content/uploads/2017/04/Backbase_The_PSD2_Playbook.pdf

Baker, T., & Dellaert, B. (2018). Regulating Robo-advice Across the Financial Services Industry. Iowa Law Review, 103(2), 713–750. doi:10.2139srn.2932189

Bakos, Y., Marotta-Wurgler, F., & Trossen, D. (2014). Does anyone read the fine print? Consumer attention to standard-form contracts. *The Journal of Legal Studies*, *43*(1), 1–35. doi:10.1086/674424

Banford, C. (2015). *Principles of International Financial Law* (2nd ed.). Oxford University Press.

Bank for International Settlements. (2019). *Wholesale Digital Tokens.* Committee on Payments and Market Infrastructures.

Bank of Lithuania. (2017). *Supervisory Activities.* Retrieved from https://www.lb.lt/en/supervisory-activities

Banque de France. (2019). *Financial regulation and supervision issues raised by the impact of Tech firms on financial services, Speech by Denis Beau –First Deputy Governor of the Banque de France.* Banque de France.

Barbuto, J. E. Jr, & Wheeler, D. W. (2006). Scale development and construct clarification of servant leadership. *Group & Organization Management*, *31*(3), 300–326. doi:10.1177/1059601106287091

Bar-Ilan, J. (2001). Data collection methods on the web for infometric purposes – A review and analysis. *Scientometrics*, *50*(1), 7–32. doi:10.1023/A:1005682102768

Basic Law (Grundgesetz) of the Federal Republic of Germany. art. 73. (1) 4.,

Bateman, M., Duvendack, M., & Loubere, N. (2019). Is fin-tech the new panacea for poverty alleviation and local development? Contesting Suri and Jack's M-Pesa findings published in Science. *Review of African Political Economy*, *46*(161), 480–495. doi:10.1080/03056244.2019.1614552

Beall, A. (2019). *What is regtech? The latest wave of startups hitting the fintech industry.* Wired.co.uk. Available at: https://www.wired.co.uk/article/regtech-next-fintech

Bearing Point. (n.d.). *Regulatory reporting platform for Austrian banks.* Retrieved from https://www.reg.tech/en/our-solutions/banks-other-financial-institutions/regulatory-reporting-for-austrian-banks/

Beau, D. (2019). *Denis Beau: What policy framework to help building innovation and growth into Europe's capital market?* Speech by Mr Denis Beau, First Deputy Governor of the Bank of France, at the AFME (The Association for Financial Markets in Europe) Annual Capital Markets Technology and Innovation Conference, Paris.

Beck, R., Müller-Bloch, C., & King, J. L. (2018). Governance in the Blockchain Economy – A Framework and Research Agenda. *Journal of the Association for Information Systems*, *19*(3), 1020–1034. doi:10.17705/1jais.00518

Beck, T., Chen, T., Lin, C., & Song, F. (2016). Financial innovation: The bright and the dark sides. *Journal of Banking & Finance*, *72*, 28–51. doi:10.1016/j.jbankfin.2016.06.012

Beck, T., & Demirguc-Kunt, A. (2006). Small and medium-size enterprises: Access to finance as a growth constraint. *Journal of Banking & Finance*, *30*(11), 2931–2943. doi:10.1016/j.jbankfin.2006.05.009

Benedetti, H., & Kostovetsky, L. (2018). *Digital Tulips?* Returns to Investors in Initial Coin Offerings., doi:10.2139srn.3182169

Berger, A. N., Demsetz, R. S., & Strahan, P. E. (1999). The consolidation of the financial services industry: Causes, consequences and implications for the future. *Journal of Banking & Finance*, *23*(2-4), 135–194. doi:10.1016/S0378-4266(98)00125-3

Bharadwaj, S., & Menon, A. (2000). Making innovation happen in organizations: Individual creativity mechanisms, organizational creativity mechanisms or both? *Journal of Product Innovation Management: An International Publication of the Product Development & Management Association*, *17*(6), 424–434. doi:10.1111/1540-5885.1760424

Bhaskaran, S. (2006). Incremental innovation and business performance: Small and medium-size food enterprises in a concentrated industry environment. *Journal of Small Business Management*, *44*(1), 64–80. doi:10.1111/j.1540-627X.2006.00154.x

Blakstad, S., & Allen, R. (2018). Fintech Revolution, Universal Inclusion in the New Financial Ecosystem. Cham, Switzerland: Palgrave Macmillan.

Blockchain-Strategie der Bundesregierung. (2019). *Bundesministerium für Wirtschaft und Energie, Bundesministerium für Finanzen*. Retrieved from: https://www.bmwi.de/Redaktion/DE/Publikationen/Digitale-Welt/blockchain-strategie.pdf?__blob=publicationFile&v=10

Block, J., & Kremen, A. (1996). IQ and ego-resiliency: Conceptual and empirical connections and separateness. *Journal of Personality and Social Psychology*, *70*(2), 349–361. doi:10.1037/0022-3514.70.2.349 PMID:8636887

Boata, A., & Gerdes, K. (2019). *European regulatory changes will make banks less willing to lend to SMEs*. https://www.eulerhermes.com/content/dam/onemarketing/euh/eulerhermes_com/erd/publications/pdf/20190529-TheView-EuropeanRegulatory.pdf

Boddy, C. R., Galvin, P., & Ladyshewsky, R. K. (2011). Corporate psychopaths. In *Ethical leadership* (pp. 17–33). Palgrave Macmillan. doi:10.1057/9780230299061_2

Bodin, J. (1576). *Six books on the Commonwealth*. Basil Blackwell.

Bolwijn, R., Casella, B., & Zhan, J. (2018). International production and the digital economy. In International Business in the Information and Digital Age (Progress in International Business Research, Vol. 13), (pp. 39-64). Emerald Publishing Limited.

Boot, A. (2003). Consolidation and strategic positioning in banking with implications for Europe. Brookings-Wharton Papers on Financial Services, 37-83. doi:10.1353/pfs.2003.0001

Boot, A. (2017). The Future of Banking: From Scale & Scope Economies to Fintech. *European Economy, 2017*(2).

Booth, L., Aivazian, V., Demirguc-Kunt, A., & Maksimovic, V. (2001). Capital structures in developing countries. *The Journal of Finance*, *56*(1), 87–130. doi:10.1111/0022-1082.00320

Bouveret, A. (2018). *Cyber Risk for the Financial Sector: A Framework for Quantitative Assessment*. IMF Working Paper WP/18/143.

Bowonder, B., Dambal, A., Kumar, S., & Shirodkar, A. (2010). Innovation strategies for creating competitive advantage. *Research Technology Management*, *53*(3), 19–32. doi:10.1080/08956308.2010.11657628

Bowrin, A. R., & King, I. I. J. II. (2010). Time pressure, task complexity, and audit effectiveness. *Managerial Auditing Journal*, *25*(2), 160–181. doi:10.1108/02686901011008963

Broeders, D. (2019). *Digital Supervision at DNB. Workshop on "Big Data & Machine Learning Applications for Central Banks"*. DeNederlandscheBank. Eurosystem. Retrieved from https://www.bancaditalia.it/pubblicazioni/altri-atti-convegni/2019-bigdata/Broeders_Suptech_BoI_2019.pdf

Broeders, D., & Prenio, J. (2018). *Innovative technology in financial supervision (SupTech): The experience of early users. FSI Insights on policy implementation, (9)*. Bank for International Settlements.

Brotheridge, C. M., & Grandey, A. A. (2002). Emotional labor and burnout: Comparing two perspectives of "people work". *Journal of Vocational Behavior*, *60*(1), 17–39. doi:10.1006/jvbe.2001.1815

Brummer, C., & Gorfine, D. (2014). FinTech: building a 21st century Regulator's Toolkit. Milken Institute.

Bruno, G., Jani, H., Schmidt, R., & Tissot, B. (2020). *Computing platforms for big data analytics and artificial intelligence*. Bank for International Settlements.

Brynjolfsson, E., & McAfee, A. (2017). *Machine, Platform, Crowd: Harnessing our digital future*. W.W. Norton.

Buchak, G., Matvos, G., Piskorski, T., & Seru, A. (2017). Fintech, Regulatory Arbitrage, and the Rise of Shadow Banks, forthcoming in the. *Journal of Financial Economics*.

Buckley, R. P., Arner, D. W., & Panton, M. (2013). Financial Innovation in East Asia. *Seattle UL Rev.*, *37*, 307.

Buckley, R. P., & Webster, S. (2016). FinTech in developing countries: Charting new customer journeys. *Journal of Financial Transformation*, 44.

Bukht, R., & Heeks, R. (2017). Defining, conceptualizing and measuring the digital economy. In *Development Informatics* (Working paper No. 68). Manchester: Global Development Institute.

Butler, T., & O'Brien, L. (2019). Understanding RegTech for Digital Regulatory Compliance. In Disrupting Finance (pp. 85-102). Palgrave Pivot.

Butler, T. (2018). On the role of ontology-based regtech for managing risk and compliance reporting in the age of regulation. *Journal of Risk Management in Financial Institutions*, *11*(1), 19–33.

C-264/14. Skatteverket v David Hedqvist ECLI:EU:C:2015:718 [22], [42], [49], [55]

Cainelli, G., Evangelista, R., & Savona, M. (2006). Innovation and economic performance in services: A firm-level analysis. *Cambridge Journal of Economics*, *30*(3), 435–458. doi:10.1093/cje/bei067

Capgemini. (2018a). *The bank of the future: an ecosystem of services*. Available from https://www.capgemini.com/2018/04/the-bank-of-the-future-an-ecosystem-of-services/

Capgemini. (2018b). *World Fintech Report*. Available from https://www.capgemini.com/wp-content/uploads/2018/02/world-fintech-report-wftr-2018.pdf

Carbonell, J. B., & Werner, R. A. (2018). Does foreign direct investment generate economic growth? A new empirical approach applied to Spain. *Economic Geography*, *94*(4), 425–456. doi:10.1080/00130095.2017.1393312

Carlsson, B. (2004). The Digital economy: What is new and what is not? *Structural Change and Economic Dynamics*, *15*(3), 245–264. doi:10.1016/j.strueco.2004.02.001

Carmona, A. F. (2018). *Competition issues in the Area of Financial Technology (FinTech)*. Policy Department for Economic, Scientific and Quality of Life Policies. Directorate-General for Internal Policies. Available from https://www.europarl.europa.eu/RegData/etudes/STUD/2018/619027/IPOL_STU(2018)619027_EN.pdf

Carnegieendowment.org. (2020). *Timeline of Cyber Incidents Involving Financial Institutions - Carnegie Endowment for International Peace*. https://carnegieendowment.org/specialprojects/protectingfinancialstability/timeline#click-hide

Carpenter, R. E., & Petersen, B. C. (2002). Is the growth of small firms constrained by internal finance? *The Review of Economics and Statistics*, *84*(2), 298–309. doi:10.1162/003465302317411541

Casella, B., & Formenti, L. (2018). FDI in the digital economy: A shift to asset-light international footprints. *Transnational Corporations*, *25*(1), 101–130. doi:10.18356/cb688e94-en

Cashless.pl & Accenture. (2018). *Map of Polish FinTech 2018*. Retrieved from: https://www.cashless.pl/system/uploads/ckeditor/attachments/1908/Mapa_Polskiego_Fintechu_2018.pdf

Catalini, C., & Gans, J. S. (2018). Initial Coin Offerings and the Value of Crypto Tokens. *SSRN Electronic Journal*, 1–37. doi:10.2139srn.3137213

CBInsights. (2017). *Regtech 101: What It Is, Why Now, & Why It Matters*. Available: https://www.cbinsights.com/research/regtech-four-phases-expert-intelligence/

CBInsights. (2018). *Regtech 102: The Evolution of Regtech and The Future of Regulatory Compliance*. Available: https://www.cbinsights.com/research/regtech-four-phases-expert-intelligence/

CBinsights. (2020). The global unicorn club. *CBinsights*. Retrieved May 23, 2020, from https://www.cbinsights.com/research-unicorn-companies

CCN. (2018, July 4). *$731 Million Gained by Hacking Crypto Exchanges in 2018, Can it be Prevented?* Retrieved August 6, 2018, from https://www.ccn.com/731-million-stolen-from-crypto-exchanges-in-2018-can-hacks-be-prevented/

Černe, M., Jaklič, M., & Škerlavaj, M. (2013). Authentic leadership, creativity, and innovation: A multilevel perspective. *Leadership*, *9*(1), 63–85. doi:10.1177/1742715012455130

Chartered Accountants Australia and New Zealand. (2017). *The future of blockchain: Applications and implications of distributed ledger technology*. Retrieved June, 10, 2020, from https://charteredaccountantsworldwide.com/wp-content/uploads/2018/07/1216-07_Future-of-Blockchain_web_FA-1.pdf

Chartered Professional Accountants of Canada - CPA Canada & American Institute of CPAs – AICPA. (2017). *Blockchain technology and its potential impact on the audit and assurance profession*. Retrieved from https://www.aicpa.org/content/dam/aicpa/interestareas/frc/assuranceadvisoryservices/downloadabledocuments/blockchain-technology-and-its-potential-impact-on-the-audit-and-assurance-profession.pdf

Chartered Professional Accountants of Canada - CPA Canada & American Institute of CPAs – AICPA. (2017). *Blockchain technology and its potential impact on the audit and assurance profession*. Retrieved June, 10, 2020, from https://www.aicpa.org/content/dam/aicpa/interestareas/frc/assuranceadvisoryservices/downloadabledocuments/blockchain-technology-and-its-potential-impact-on-the-audit-and-assurance-profession.pdf

Chell, E., Nicolopoulou, K., & Karataş-Özkan, M. (2010). *Social entrepreneurship and enterprise: International and innovation perspectives*. Academic Press.

Chen, K. (2019). Information asymmetry in initial coin offerings (ICOs): Investigating the effects of multiple channel signals. *Electronic Commerce Research and Applications*, *36*, 100858. doi:10.1016/j.elerap.2019.100858

Chen, M. A., Wu, Q., & Yang, B. (2019). How valuable Is FinTech innovation? *Review of Financial Studies*, *32*(5), 2062–2106. doi:10.1093/rfs/hhy130

Chibba, M. (2009). Financial inclusion, poverty reduction and the millennium development goals. *European Journal of Development Research*, *21*(2), 213–230. doi:10.1057/ejdr.2008.17

Chiesi, A. M. (2001). The International Encyclopaedia of the Social &. *Behavioral Science*.

Choudhury, S. R. (2017, September 12). Governments want to control cryptocurrencies – but there's a danger to too many rules. *CNBC*. Retrieved March 3, 2020, from https://www.cnbc.com/2017/09/12/regulators-are-turning-their-attention-to-cryptocurrencies.html

Christine, L. (2018, June 22). *Estimating Cyber Risk for the Financial Sector – IMF Blog*. IMF. https://blogs.imf.org/2018/06/22/estimating-cyber-risk-for-the-financial-sector/

Cianci, A. M., Hannah, S. T., Roberts, R. P., & Tsakumis, G. T. (2014). The effects of authentic leadership on followers' ethical decision-making in the face of temptation: An experimental study. *The Leadership Quarterly*, *25*(3), 581–594. doi:10.1016/j.leaqua.2013.12.001

Ciuriak, D. (2018). *Rethinking Industrial Policy for the Data-Driven Economy*. Retrieved from https://papers.ssrn.com/sol3/papers.cfm?abstract_id=3223072

CNBV. (2018). *RegTech and SupTech: Where do we see the frontier?* Retrieved from http://pubdocs.worldbank.org/en/841991528990787287/04062018-RegTech-y-SupTech-Foro-Bernardo-Gonzalez.pdf

Coase, R. H. (1937). The Nature of the Firm. *Economica*, *4*(16), 386–405. doi:10.1111/j.1468-0335.1937.tb00002.x

Coelho, R., De Simoni, M., & Prenio, J. (2019). *Suptech applications for anti-money laundering. FSI Insights on policy implementation No 18. Financial Stability Institute*. Bank for International Settlements.

Cojoianu, T., Clark, G. L., Hoepner, A. G., Pazitka, V., & Wojcik, D. (2019). Fin vs. tech: determinants of fintech start-up emergence and innovation in the financial services incumbent sector. *SSRN Electronic Journal*.

Constitution of the Republic of France. art 34.

Courtney, H., Kirkland, J., & Viguerie, P. (1997). Strategy Under Uncertainty. *Harvard Business Review, 1*. Available from https://hbr.org/1997/11/strategy-under-uncertainty

Crawford, J., Dawkins, S., Martin, A., & Lewis, G. (2017). Understanding the organizational climate of unethical leadership in the Australian Football League. *The Journal of Leadership Studies*, *11*(2), 52–54. doi:10.1002/jls.21525

Crawford, J., Dawkins, S., Martin, A., & Lewis, G. (2020a). Putting the leader back into authentic leadership: Reconceptualising and rethinking leaders. *Australian Journal of Management*, *45*(1), 114–133. doi:10.1177/0312896219836460

Crawford, J., Kelder, J., & Knox, M. (2020b). What does it take to be a social entrepreneur?: Authentic leaders and their effect on innovation. In C. Dogru (Ed.), *Leadership styles, innovation, and social entrepreneurship in the era of digitalization* (pp. 282–310). IGI Global. doi:10.4018/978-1-7998-1108-4.ch011

CRD: Directive 2013/36/EU of the European Parliament and of the Council of 26 June 2013 on access to the activity of credit institutions and the prudential supervision of credit institutions and investment firms, OJ L 176, 27.6.2013, p. 338–436

Crossan, M. M., & Apaydin, M. (2010). A multi-dimensional framework of organizational innovation: A systematic review of the literature. *Journal of Management Studies*, *47*(6), 1154–1191. doi:10.1111/j.1467-6486.2009.00880.x

CRR: Regulation No 575/2013 of the European Parliament and of the Council of 26 June 2013 on prudential requirements for credit institutions and investment firms, OJ L 176, 27.6.2013, p. 1–337

CSBS. (2019). *Community Banking in the 21st Century: Seventh Annual Community Banking Research and Policy Conference*. https://www.communitybanking.org/~/media/files/publication/cb21publication_2019.pdf

Cusumano, M. A., Gawer, A., & Yoffie, D. B. (2019). *The Business of Platforms: Strategy in the Age of Digital Competition, Innovation, and Power*. Harper Collins Publishers.

Cyree, K. B., Delcoure, N., & Dickens, R. (2008). An examination of the performance and prospects for the future of internet-primary banks. *Journal of Economics and Finance*, *33*(2), 128–147. doi:10.100712197-008-9048-0

Czugan, M. (2017). Problemy otoczenia regulacyjnego rozwoju sektora fintech. In Regulacje finansowe: fintech - nowe instrumenty finansowe –resolution. Warszawa: C.H. Beck.

D.M. (2018). Sofi – an illustrative tale of why fintech disruption is so difficult. *Digital Innovation & Transformation.* Retrieved March, 3, 2020, https://digital.hbs.edu/platform-digit/submission/sofi-an-illustrative-tale-of-why-fintech-disruption-is-so-difficult/

Dai, J., & Vasarhelyi, M. A. (2016). Imagineering audit 4.0. [Editorial]. *Journal of Emerging Technologies in Accounting*, *13*(1), 1–15. doi:10.2308/jeta-10494

Dang, S., & Ahmad, P. H. (2014). Text mining: Techniques and its application. *The International Journal of Engineering & Technology Innovations*, *1*(4), 866–2348.

Das, S. (2019). The future of fintech. *Financial Management*, *48*(4), 981–1007. doi:10.1111/fima.12297

Davis, M. F. (2020). JPMorgan hires Capital One's Haus to lead digital technology. *Bloomberg*. Retrieved May 23, 2020, from https://www.bloombergquint.com/business/jpmorgan-hires-capital-one-s-haus-to-lead-digital-technology

Deboeck, G. J. (2000). Financial applications of self-organizing maps. *Neural Network World*, *8*(2), 213–241.

Deboeck, G., & Kohonen, T. (1998). *Visual Explorations in Finance with Self-organizing Maps*. Springer Finance. doi:10.1007/978-1-4471-3913-3

Deloitte. (2015). *Industry 4.0 – Challenges and solutions for the digital transformation and use of exponential technologies*. Retrieved from https://www2.deloitte.com/content/dam/Deloitte/ch/Documents/manufacturing/ch-en-manufacturing-industry-4-0-24102014.pdf

Deloitte. (2015). *Industry 4.0 – Challenges and solutions for the digital transformation and use of exponential technologies*. Retrieved June, 10, 2020, from https://www2.deloitte.com/content/dam/Deloitte/ch/Documents/manufacturing/ch-en-manufacturing-industry-4-0-24102014.pdf

Deloitte. (2017a). *The Future of Regulatory Productivity, powered by RegTech. RegTech position paper, Financial Service*. Available: https://www2.deloitte.com/content/dam/Deloitte/us/Documents/regulatory/us-regulatory-future-of-regulatory-productivity-powered-by-regtech.pdf

Deloitte. (2017b). The RegTech universe on the rise. *Inside Magazine- Edition*. Available: https://www2.deloitte.com/content/dam/Deloitte/lu/Documents/technology/lu_inside-regtech-universe-on-rise.df

Deloitte. (2018). *Digital Banking Maturity 2018*. Retrieved from: https://www2.deloitte.com/DigitalBankingMaturity

Deloitte. (2019). *RegTech Universe. Website*. Available: https://www2.deloitte.com/lu/en/pages/technology/articles/regtech-companies-compliance.html

Deloitte. (2019). *The Future of Cyber Survey 2019*. file:///F:/ali/hazik/us-the-future-of-cyber-survey.pdf

Deloitte. (2020). *What is digital economy? Unicorns, transformation and the internet of things.* Retrieved from https://www2.deloitte.com/mt/en/pages/technology/articles/mt-what-is-digital-economy.html

Deloitte. (n.d.). *What is blockchain.* Retrieved from https://www2.deloitte.com/content/dam/Deloitte/uk/Documents/Innovation/deloitte-uk-what-is-blockchain-2016.pdf

Demirgüç-Kunt, A., & Klapper, L. (2013). Measuring financial inclusion: Explaining variation in use of financial services across and within countries. *Brookings Papers on Economic Activity, 2013*(1), 279–340. doi:10.1353/eca.2013.0002

Demirguç-Kunt, A., Klapper, L., Singer, D., Ansar, S., & Hess, J. (2017). *Measuring financial inclusion and the fintech revolution.* The Global Findex Database, World Bank Group.

DESI. (2019). *DESI Report 2019.* Brussel: European Commission. Retrieved from https://ec.europa.eu/digital-single-market/en/desi

DESI. (2019). *Methodological Note.* Brussel: European Commission. Retrieved from https://digital-agenda-data.eu/datasets/desi/visualizations

Deutsche Börse Cash Market. (2019). *Eigenkapitalfinanzierung für kleine und mittlere Unternehmen (KMU).* https://www.deutsche-boerse-cash-market.com/scale/

DeYoung, R. (2001). The financial performance of pure play internet banks. *Economic Perspectives Federal Reserve Bank of Chicago, 25*(1), 60–75.

DeYoung, R. (2005). The performance of internet-based business models: Evidence from the banking industry. *The Journal of Business, 78*(3), 893–947. doi:10.1086/429648

DeYoung, R., Lang, W. W., & Nolle, D. L. (2007). How the Internet affects output and performance at community banks? *Journal of Banking & Finance, 31*(4), 1033–1060. doi:10.1016/j.jbankfin.2006.10.003

Di Castri, S., Hohl, S., Kulenkampff, A., & Prenio, J. (2019). *The SupTech generations.* Bank for International Settlements.

Directive (EU) 2018/843 of the European Parliament and of the Council of 30 May 2018 amending Directive (EU) 2015/849 on the prevention of the use of the financial system for the purposes of money laundering or terrorist financing, and amending Directives 2009/138/EC and 2013/36/EU, OJ L 156, 19.6.2018, p. 43–74

Dunning, J. H. (1981). *International Production and the Multinational Enterprise.* Allen & Unwin.

Dunning, J. H., & Wymbs, C. (2001). The challenge of electronic markets for international business theory. *International Journal of the Economics of Business, 8*(2), 273–301. doi:10.1080/13571510110051432

Dwolla. (2020). The programmable payments platform. *Dwolla.* Retrieved March, 3, 2020, from https://www.dwolla.com/

EBA Opinion on 'virtual currencies'. (2014). EBA/Op/2014/08. London: European Banking Authority.

Ehrentraud, J., Ocampo, D. G., Garzoni, L., & Piccolo, M. (2020). *Policy responses to fintech: a cross-country overview.* Financial Stability Institute BIS.

Eley, S. (2018). *RegTech and SupTech: Innovation, Risks and Opportunities.* 18th Annual WBG-IMF-FRB Conference on Policy Challenges for the Financial Sector, Washington, DC. Retrieved from http://pubdocs.worldbank.org/en/692151528989872128/2018-06-07-Session4-RegTech-SupTech-Slavka-Eley.pdf

Ernst & Young. (2015a). Innovating with RegTech. *EY's 2015 Global Governance, Risk and Compliance Survey.* Available: https://www.ey.com/Publication/vwLUAssets/EY-Innovating-with-RegTech/$FILE/EY-Innovating-with-RegTech.pdf

Ernst & Young. (2015b). Financial regulation of FinTech. *EY Global Financial Services Institute Article*, *3*(3). Available: https://www.ey.com/Publication/vwLUAssets/ey-financial-regulation-of-fintech/$FILE/ey-financial-regulation-of-fintech.pdf

Ernst & Young. (2019). *How FinTechs are a world of choice for small and medium-sized enterprises*, https://www.ey.com/en_kw/banking-capital-markets/how-fintechs-are-a-world-of-choice-for-small-and-medium-sized-enterprises

ESMA. (2019). *ESAs publish joint report on regulatory sandboxes and innovation hubs*. Retrieved from https://www.esma.europa.eu/press-news/esma-news/esas-publish-joint-report-regulatory-sandboxes-and-innovation-hubs

Euler Hermes. (2019). *European SME's: Filling the bank financing GAP*. https://ehrg.de/ver/studien/Studie_20190409.pdf

European Banking Authority. (2017). *Regulatory sandboxes. A proposal to EBA by the Banking Stakeholders Group*. EBA.

European Banking Authority. (2018). *EBA report on the impact of Fintech on incumbent credit institutions' business models*. Author.

European Banking Authority. (2019). *Guidelines on ICT and security risk management*. European Banking Authority.

European Banking Authority. (2020a). *EBA report on big data and advanced analytics*.

European Banking Authority. (2020b). *FinTech Knowledge Hub*. Retrieved from https://eba.europa.eu/financial-innovation-and-fintech/fintech-knowledge-hub

European Central Bank. (2013). Economic and Monetary Developments. *Monthly Bulletin*, 15–19.

European Central Bank. (2018). *Survey on the Access to Finance of Enterprises in the euro area*. https://www.ecb.europa.eu/pub/pdf/other/accesstofinancesmallmediumsizedenterprises201512.en.pdf?2c146594df6fe424c7adb001e1306c73

European Commission. (2015). *Communication from the European Commission on action plan on building a capital markets union*. https://eur-lex.europa.eu/legal-content/EN/TXT/PDF/?uri=CELEX:52015DC0468&from=EN

European Commission. (2018). *Action Plan on FinTech*. Author.

European Commission. (2018). *Distribution systems of retail investment products across the European Union*. https://ec.europa.eu/info/sites/info/files/180425-retail-investment-products-distribution-systems_en.pdf

European Commission. (2018a). *FinTech action plan: For a more competitive and innovative European financial sector*. Retrieved from https://ec.europa.eu/info/publications/180308-action-plan-fintech_en

European Commission. (2018b). *First meeting of the EU FinTech Lab*. Retrieved from https://ec.europa.eu/info/publications/180620-eu-fintech-lab-meeting_en

European Commission. (2019). *2018 SBA Fact Sheet & Scoreboard*. https://ec.europa.eu/docsroom/documents/32581/attachments/1/translations/en/renditions/native

European Commission. (2019). *EU Blockchain Observatory and Forum*. Retrieved from https://ec.europa.eu/digital-single-market/en/eu-blockchain-observatory-and-forum

European Investment Fund. (2019). *European Small Business Finance Outlook*. EIF Research & Market Analysis, Working Paper 2019/57. Luxembourg.

European Parliament. (2018). *The Proposal for a Regulation of the European Parliament and the Council on European Crowdfunding Service Providers (ECSP) for Business*. Author.

European Supervisory Authorities. (2018). *FinTech: Regulatory Sandboxes and Innovation Hubs*. EBA, ESMA, EIOPA. Retrieved from https://www.esma.europa.eu/file/49963/download?token=fN2J9ilC

European Supervisory Authorities. (2019). *European Forum for Innovation Facilitators (EFIF)*. Retrieved from https://esas-joint-committee.europa.eu/Pages/Activities/EFIF/European-Forum-for-Innovation-Facilitators.aspx

Eurostat. (2019). *Households and non-profit institutions serving households*. https://ec.europa.eu/eurostat/documents/499359/6246888/EN-Charts-and-Tables.xlsx/ed769615-8aa4-4f00-954e-550e765919a8

Evans, D. S. (1987). The Relationship Between Firm Growth, Size, and Age : Estimates for 100 Manufacturing Industries. *The Journal of Industrial Economics*, *35*(4), 567–581. doi:10.2307/2098588

Even Financial. (2019). Even financial CEO Phillip Rosen named "best fintech CEO" in 2019 fintech breakthrough awards program. *Even Financial*. Retrieved May 23, 2020, from https://evenfinancial.com/press/even-financial-ceo-phillip-rosen-named-best-fintech-ceo-in-2019-fintech-breakthrough-awards-program/

EY. (2015). *When finance moves into the cloud, will CFOs sleep better at night? Finance in the cloud*. Retrieved from https://www.ey.com/Publication/vwLUAssets/EY-finance-in-the-cloud/$FILE/EY-finance-in-the-cloud.pdf

EY. (2017). *EY FinTech Adoption Index 2017. The rapid emergence of FinTech*. Available from https://www.ey.com/Publication/vwLUAssets/ey-fintech-adoption-index-2017/$FILE/ey-fintech-adoption-index-2017.pdf

Ezell, S., & Swanson, B. (2017). *How Cloud Computing Enables Modern Manufacturing*. AEI/ITIF. http://www2.itif.org/2017-cloud-computing-enables-manufacturing.pdf?_ga=2.218587289.1802769062.1498483609-1058723113.1488819082

Fama, E. F., & French, K. R. (2002). Testing Trade-Off and Pecking Order Predictions About Dividends and Debt. *Review of Financial Studies*, *15*(1), 1–33. doi:10.1093/rfs/15.1.1

Fathi, E. (2018). *How artificial intelligence can help mend the UK's broken audit system*. Available: https://thefintechtimes.com/artificial-intelligence-audits/

Feng, W., Wang, Y., & Zhang, Z. (2018). Informed trading in the Bitcoin market. *Finance Research Letters*, *26*, 63–70. doi:10.1016/j.frl.2017.11.009

Ferreira, M., Reis, N., & Pinto, C. (2017). Schumpeter's (1934) Influence on Entrepreneurship (and Management) Research. *Revista de Empreendedorismo e Gestão de Pequenas Empresas, 6*(1), 4-39.

Fiedler, I., Ante, L., Steinmetz, F., & Häseler, S. (2018). Distributed Ledger Technology: A Possible Way Forward for Securities Clearing. *Binary District*. https://journal.binarydistrict.com/distributed-ledger-technology-a-possible-way-forward-for-securities-clearing/. Accessed 8 September 2019

Finance, U. K. Microsoft. (2019). *Artificial Intelligence in Financial Services*. Retrieved from https://www.ukfinance.org.uk/system/files/AI-2019_FINAL_ONLINE.pdf

Financial Reporting Council – FRC. (2017). *Audit quality thematic review – the use of data analytics in the audit of financial statements*. Retrieved June, 10, 2020, from https://www.frc.org.uk/getattachment/4fd19a18-1beb-4959-8737-ae2dca80af67/AQTR_Audit-Data-Analytics-Jan-2017.pdf

Financial Stability Board. (2017). *Artificial intelligence and machine learning in financial services. Market developments and financial stability implications*. Financial Stability Board.

Financial Stability Board. (2017). *Financial Stability Implications from FinTech. Supervisory and Regulatory Issues that Merit Authorities' Attention*. Available from https://www.fsb.org/wp-content/uploads/R270617.pdf

Financial Stability Board. (2017). Financial Stability Implications from Fintech: Supervisory and Regulatory Issues that Merit Authorities' Attention. Basel: Author.

Financial Stability Board. (2017). *Report Financial Stability Implications from Fintech Technology*. Author.

Financial Stability Board. (2019). *Third-party dependencies in cloud services. Considerations on financial stability implications*. Financial Stability Board.

Finriskalert. (n.d.). *Mercati, intermediari, istituzioni*. Retrieved from https://www.finriskalert.it/regtech-get-onboarding-the-challenges-of-compliance/

FinTech Australia. (2017). *Booming Australian fintech scene shown in new member ecosystem map*. Retrieved from https://fintechaustralia.org.au/newbooming-australian-fintech-scene-shown-in-new-member-ecosystem-map/

Fintechmap. (n.d.). *Explore the Swiss FinTech startup ecosystem*. Retrieved from https://fintechmap.ch/

Firth-Butterfield, K., Brent, R., & Grant, T. (2017). Virtual Currencies, Artificial Intelligence and Emerging Legal Questions. In Banks and Financial Crime (2nd ed.). Oxford University Press.

Fisch, C. (2019). Initial coin offerings (ICOs) to finance new ventures. *Journal of Business Venturing*, *34*(1), 1–22. doi:10.1016/j.jbusvent.2018.09.007

Fletcher, N. (2016). Dan Wagner and the fall of 'unicorn' startup Powa Technologies. *TheGuardian.com*. Retrieved May 23, 2020, from https://www.theguardian.com/business/2016/apr/18/dan-wagner-powa-technologies

Flint, G. D. (2000). What is the meaning of competitive advantage? *Journal of Competitiveness Studies*, *8*(1), 121.

Foo, J., Lek-Heng, L., & Ken, W. (2017). *Macroeconomics and FinTech: Uncovering Latent Macroeconomic Effects on Peer-to-Peer Lending*. https://www.researchgate.net/publication/320754864_Macroeconomics_and_FinTech_Uncovering_Latent_Macroeconomic_Effects_on_Peer-to-Peer_Lending

Fowers, B. (2015). *The evolution of ethics: Human sociality and the emergence of ethical mindedness*. Springer. doi:10.1057/9781137344663

Fox, D. (2008). *Property rights in money*. Oxford University Press.

Frame, W. S., & White, L. (2002). *Empirical Studies of Financial Innovation: Lots of Talk, Little Action?* Federal Reserve Bank of Atlanta Working Paper 2002(12). doi:10.2139srn.325800

Frame, W. S., & White, L. (2009). *Technological Change, Financial Innovation, and Diffusion in Banking*. Federal Reserve Bank of Atlanta Working Paper 2009(10). doi:10.2139srn.1434235

Freedman, R. S. (2006). *Introduction to Financial Technology*. Academic Press. Available from https://booksite.elsevier.com/samplechapters/9780123704788/Sample_Chapters/01~Frontmatter.pdf

Friedman, B., & Nissenbaum, H. (1996). Bias in computer systems. *ACM Transactions on Information Systems*, *14*(3), 330–347.

Frost, J. (2020). *The economic forces driving fintech adoption across countries*. BIS Working Paper 838.

Frost, J. (2020). *The Economic Forces Driving FinTech Adoption across Countries*. BIS Working Papers No. 838, 2020.

Frost, J., Gambacorta, L., Huang, Y., Shin, H. S., & Zbinden, P. (2019). *BigTech and the Changing Structure of Financial Intermediation*. BIS Working Paper.

G20. (2016). *G20 High-Level Principles for Digital Financial Inclusion*. G20.

Gabor, D., & Brooks, S. (2017). The digital revolution in financial inclusion: International development in the fintech era. *New Political Economy*, *22*(4), 423–436. doi:10.1080/13563467.2017.1259298

Gaidosch, T., Adelmann, F., Morozova, A., & Wilson, C. (2019). *Cybersecurity Risk Supervision*. IMF Departmental Paper No. 19/15.

Gambacorta, L., Huang, Y., Qiu, H., & Wang, J. (2019). *How do machine learning and non-traditional data affect credit scoring? New evidence from a Chinese fintech firm*. BIS Working Paper 834.

Gardner, W. L., Avolio, B. J., & Walumbwa, F. O. (2005). Authentic leadership development: Emergent trends and future directions. *Authentic leadership theory and practice: Origins, effects and development*, 387-406.

Garicano, L., & Posner, R. A. (2005). Intelligence failures: An organizational economics perspective. *The Journal of Economic Perspectives*, *19*(4), 151–170. doi:10.1257/089533005775196723

Gasser, U., Gassmann, O., Hens, T., Leifer, L., Puschmann, T., & Zhao, L. (2017). *Digital Bank 2025*. Available from https://www.alexandria.unisg.ch/publications/253962

Gerardi, K. S., Rosen, H. S., & Willen, P. S. (2010). The impact of deregulation and financial innovation on consumers: The case of the mortgage market. *The Journal of Finance*, *65*(1), 333–360. doi:10.1111/j.1540-6261.2009.01531.x

German Startups Association. (2015). *European Startup Monitor*. https://europeanstartupmonitor.com/fileadmin/presse/download/esm_2015.pdf

Goertzel, B., & Pennachin, C. (2007). *Artificial General Intelligence*. Springer.

Gomber, P., Kauffman, R., Parker, C., & Weber, B. (2018). On the fintech revolution: Interpreting the forces of innovation, disruption, and transformation in financial services. *Journal of Management Information Systems*, *35*(1), 220–265. doi:10.1080/07421222.2018.1440766

Goodwin, T. (2015). *The battle is for the customer interface*. Retrieved from https://techcrunch.com/2015/03/03/in-the-age-of-disintermediation-the-battle-is-all-for-the-customer-interface/

Gopalan, S., Jain, G., Kalani, G., & Tan, J. (2012). Breakthrough IT Banking. *The McKinsey Quarterly*, *26*(2). https://www.mckinsey.com/business-functions/mckinsey-digital/our-insights/breakthrough-it-banking

Götz, M. (2020). Attracting foreign direct investment in the era of digitally reshaped international production. The primer on the role of the investment policy and clusters – the case of Poland. *Journal of East-West Business*, *26*(2), 131–160. doi:10.1080/10669868.2019.1692985

Goya, C. (2018). These are the 25 most innovative Fintech startups in the world, according to KPMG. *Business Insider*. Retrieved May 25, 2020, from https://www.businessinsider.com/these-are-the-25-most-innovative-fintech-startups-in-the-world-2018-10?r=AU&IR=T

Goyal, A. (2012). The future of financial liberalization in South Asia. *Asia-Pacific Development Journal*, *19*(1), 63–96. doi:10.18356/81ba4404-en

Grab. (2020). Say hello to your everyday everything app. *Grab.co.sg*. Retrieved March, 3, 2020, from https://www.grab.com/sg/

Grant, M., & Booth, A. (2009). A typology of reviews: An analysis of 14 review types and associated methodologies. *Health Information and Libraries Journal*, *26*(2), 91–108. doi:10.1111/j.1471-1842.2009.00848.x PMID:19490148

Griffin, Z. (2012). *Crowdfunding: Fleecing the American Masses*. doi:10.2139srn.2030001

Grinblatt, M., & Longstaff, F. A. (2000). Financial innovation and the role of derivative securities: An empirical analysis of the Treasury STRIPS program. *The Journal of Finance*, *55*(3), 1415–1436. doi:10.1111/0022-1082.00252

Gunawardena, N. K. (2014). *Introduction to geographic information system.* Retrieved from https://www.researchgate.net/publication/264742771_INTRODUCTION_TO_GEOGRAPHIC_INFORMATION_SYSTEM

Gündoğdu, A., & Taskin, F. (2017). Analysis of the relationship between financial innovation and the performance of the Turkish banking system. *International Review of Economics and Management*, *5*(3), 16–32. doi:10.18825/iremjournal.280341

Gurney, K. (1997). *An introduction to neural networks.* CRC press. doi:10.4324/9780203451519

Gurung, N., & Perlman, L. (2018). *Use of Regtech by Central Banks and Its Impact on Financial Inclusion.* Available SSRN: https://ssrn.com/abstract=3285985

Hackman, T. (2017). *Leading change in action: Reorganizing an academic library department using Kotter's eight stage change model.* Academic Press.

Haddad, C., & Hornuf, L. (2019). The emergence of the global Fintech market: Economic and technological determinants. *Small Business Economics*, *53*(1), 81–105. doi:10.100711187-018-9991-x

Haldane, A. (2017). *Productivity Puzzles. Bank of England.* http://worldmanagementsurvey.org/wp-content/uploads/2017/03/boespeech_220317.pdf

Hannig, A., & Jansen, S. (2010). *Financial inclusion and financial stability: Current policy issues.* ADBI Working Paper, No. 259.

Han, S., Razaee, Z., Xue, L., & Zhang, J. H. (2016). The association between information technology investments and audit risk. *Journal of Information Systems*, *30*(1), 93–116. doi:10.2308/isys-51317

Harroch, R. (2019). 10 Key Issues for Fintech Startup Companies. *Forbes*. Retrieved 20 May, 2020, from https://www.forbes.com/sites/allbusiness/2019/10/12/fintech-startup-companies-key-challenges/#423154933e45b

Hayek, F. A. (1976). *Denationalisation of Money*. Institute of Economic Affairs.

Henderson, B. J., & Pearson, N. D. (2011). The dark side of financial innovation: A case study of the pricing of a retail financial product. *Journal of Financial Economics*, *100*(2), 227–247. doi:10.1016/j.jfineco.2010.12.006

Hennessy, C. A., & Whited, T. M. (2007). How costly is external financing? Evidence from a structural estimation. *The Journal of Finance*, *62*(4), 1705–1745. doi:10.1111/j.1540-6261.2007.01255.x

Henry, D. (2018, October 20). JPMorgan to build Silicon Valley fintech office. *Reuters*. Retrieved January, 16, 2020, from https://www.reuters.com/article/us-jpmorgan-tech-office/jpmorgan-to-build-silicon-valleyfintech-office-idUSKCN1MT2OL

Herzer, D. (2012). How does foreign direct investment really affect developing countries´ growth? *Review of International Economics*, *20*(2), 396–414. doi:10.1111/j.1467-9396.2012.01029.x

Hess, T., Benlian, A., Matt, C., & Wiesböck, F. (2016). *Options for Formulating a Digital Transformation Strategy.* Academic Press.

Hill, J. (2018). *Fintech and the remaking of financial institutions.* Available: https://ebookcentral.proquest.com

Hirakubo, N., & Friedman, H. H. (2002). Dot-bombs: Lessons from the dot-com debacle. *Journal of Internet Commerce*, *1*(2), 89–102. doi:10.1300/J179v01n02_07

Holden, K., & El-Bannany, M. (2004). Investment in information technology systems and other determinants of bank profitability in the UK. *Applied Financial Economics, 14*(5), 361–365. doi:10.1080/0960310042000211623

Holmes, C., & King, R. (2019). The evolution of business-to-business FinTech: What the future holds. *Journal of Payments Strategy & Systems, 13*(3), 217–225.

Holotescu, C. (2018). *Understanding blockchain opportunities and challenges.* Paper presented at The 14th International Scientific Conference "eLearning and software for education", Bucharest, Romania. Retrieved from https://www.researchgate.net/profile/Carmen_Holotescu/publication/324209739_Understanding_Blockchain_Opportunities_and_Challenges/links/5dac4f2c299bf111d4bf50f9/Understanding-Blockchain-Opportunities-and-Challenges.pdf

Holotescu, C. (2018). *Understanding blockchain opportunities and challenges.* Paper presented at The 14th International Scientific Conference eLearning and software for education, Bucharest, Romania. Retrieved June, 10, 2020, from https://www.researchgate.net/profile/Carmen_Holotescu/publication/324209739_Understanding_Blockchain_Opportunities_and_Challenges/links/5dac4f2c299bf111d4bf50f9/Understanding-Blockchain-Opportunities-and-Challenges.pdf

Hornuf, L., & Schwienbacher, A. (2018). Market mechanisms and funding dynamics in equity crowdfunding. *Journal of Corporate Finance, 50*, 556–574. doi:10.1016/j.jcorpfin.2017.08.009

Howard, A. (2019). The Regulation of AI— Should Organizations Be Worried? *MIT Sloan Management Review*, (July), 29.

Huber, R. (2018). *Apiax at Swiss Asset Management Day 2018: Introducing tax efficient investing.* Available: https://blog.apiax.com/apiax-at-swiss-asset-management-day-2018-introducing-tax-efficient-investing-4055b5c4bb49

Hughes, A. (1997). Finance for SMEs: A U.K. Perspective. *Small Business Economics, 9*(2), 151–168. doi:10.1023/A:1007971823255

Hull, I. (2019). *Big Data.* Machine Learning, and Quantum Computing at the Riksbank, Sveriges Riksbank.

IAIS. (2019). *RegTech and SupTech: Implications for Supervision Report of the A2ii – IAIS Consultation Call.* IAIS.

IBM. (2016). *Identifying API use cases: Banking industry.* Retrieved from https://www.ibm.com/downloads/cas/G4DVGRQJ

IDEA. (n.d.). *Big data and audit.* Retrieved from https://idea.caseware.com/big-data-and-audit/

IDEA. (n.d.). *Big data and audit.* Retrieved June, 10, 2020, from https://idea.caseware.com/big-data-and-audit/

ING. (2016). *The FinTech Index. Assessing digital and financial inclusion in developing and emerging countries.* ING Economics Department.

ING. (2020, March 2). Retrieved from https://www.ing.com.au

Institute of International Finance. (2016). *Regtech in Financial Services: Technology Solutions for Compliance And Reporting.* Available: https://www.iif.com/Portals/0/Files/private/iif-regtech_in_financial_services_-_solutions_for_compliance_and_reporting.pdf?ver=2019-01-04-142943-690

Institute of Risk Management. (2012). *Risk Culture. Under the Microscope Guidance for Boards.* Available from https://www.primo-europe.eu/wp-content/uploads/2017/06/Risk_Culture_A5_WEB15_Oct_2012.pdf

International Auditing and Assurance Standards Board – IAASB. (2016). *Exploring the growing use of technology in the audit, with a focus on data analytics.* Request for input. Retrieved June, 10, 2020, from https://www.iaasb.org/publications/exploring-growing-use-technology-audit-focus-data-analytics

International Federation of Accountants – IFAC. (2009). *International Standard on Auditing 240.* Retrieved from https://www.ifac.org/system/files/downloads/a012-2010-iaasb-handbook-isa-240.pdf

International Federation of Accountants – IFAC. (2009). *International Standard on Auditing 240.* Retrieved June, 10, 2020, from https://www.ifac.org/system/files/downloads/a012-2010-iaasb-handbook-isa-240.pdf

International Federation of Accountants – IFAC. (2019a). *Introduction to: ISA 315 (Revised 2019) Identifying and assessing the risks of material misstatement.* Retrieved from https://www.ifac.org/system/files/publications/files/IAASB-Introduction-to-ISA-315.pdf

International Federation of Accountants – IFAC. (2019a). *Introduction to: ISA 315 (Revised 2019) Identifying and assessing the risks of material misstatement.* Retrieved June, 10, 2020, from https://www.ifac.org/system/files/publications/files/IAASB-Introduction-to-ISA-315.pdf

International Federation of Accountants – IFAC. (2019b). *Technology and the future-ready auditor.* Retrieved from https://www.ifac.org/system/files/publications/files/IAASB-Tech-Talk-November-2019.pdf

International Federation of Accountants – IFAC. (2019b). *Technology and the future-ready auditor.* Retrieved June, 10, 2020, from https://www.ifac.org/system/files/publications/files/IAASB-Tech-Talk-November-2019.pdf

International Labor Organization. (2016). *ASEAN in Transformation.* http://www.ilo.org/public/english/dialogue/actemp/downloads/publications/2016/asean_in_transf_2016_r1_techn.pdf

International Monetary Fund & World Bank. (2019). FinTech: The experience so far. Washington, DC: Authors.

International Monetary Fund. (2018). Measuring the Digital Economy. Washington: International Monetary Fund. Retrieved from file:///C:/Users/eu/Downloads/022818MeasuringDigitalEconomy.pdf

International Monetary Fund. (2019). *Fintech, the Experience So Far.* IMF Fintech Policy Paper no. 19/024.

Ireland, R. D., & Webb, J. W. (2007). Strategic entrepreneurship: Creating competitive advantage through streams of innovation. *Business Horizons, 50*(1), 49–59. doi:10.1016/j.bushor.2006.06.002

Ismail, M. H., Khater, M., & Zaki, Z. (2017). *Digital Business Transformation and Strategy: What Do We Know So Far?* University Cambridge. Available from https://cambridgeservicealliance.eng.cam.ac.uk/resources/Downloads/Monthly%20Papers/2017NovPaper_Mariam.pdf

Issa, H., Sun, T., & Vasarhelyi, M. A. (2017). Research ideas for artificial intelligence in auditing: The formalization of audit and workforce supplementation [Editorial]. *Journal of Emerging Technologies in Accounting, 13*(2), 1–20. doi:10.2308/jeta-10511

Iszatt-White, M., Whittle, A., Gadelshina, G., & Mueller, F. (2019). The 'Corbyn phenomenon': Media representations of authentic leadership and the discourse of ethics versus effectiveness. *Journal of Business Ethics, 159*(2), 535–549. doi:10.100710551-018-3838-x

Jalil, A., Azam, F., & Rahman, M. K. (2010). Implementation mechanism of ethics in business organizations. *International Business Research, 3*(4), 145. doi:10.5539/ibr.v3n4p145

Jensen, M. C., & Meckling, W. H. (1976). Theory of the firm: Managerial behaviour, agency costs and ownership structure. *Journal of Financial Economics, 3*(4), 305–360. doi:10.1016/0304-405X(76)90026-X

Johne, A. (1999). Successful market innovation. In *Innovations management* (pp. 163–170). Springer.

Johnson, S., & Kwak, J. (2012). Is financial innovation good for the economy? *Innovation Policy and the Economy, 12*(1), 1–16. doi:10.1086/663153

Jovanović, S. Z., Đurić, J. S., & Šibalija, T. V. (n.d.). *Robotic Process automation: overview and opportunities*. Academic Press.

JPMorgan Chase & Co. (2020). History of our firm. *JPMorgan Chase & Co*. Retrieved May 23, 2020, from https://impact.jpmorganchase.com/about/our-history

Jude, C., & Levieuge, G. (2017). Growth effect of FDI in developing economies: The role of institutional quality. *World Economy*, *40*(4), 715–742. doi:10.1111/twec.12402

Kammoun, S., Loukil, S., & Loukil, Y. B. R. (2020). The Impact of FinTech on Economic Performance and Financial Stability in MENA Zone. In *Impact of Financial Technology (FinTech) on Islamic Finance and Financial Stability*. IGI Global. https://www.igi-global.com/chapter/the-impact-of-fintech-on-economic-performance-and-financial-stability-in-mena-zone/236809

Kane, G. C., Phillips, A. N., Copulsky, J., & Andrus, G. (2019). How Digital Leadership Is(n't) Different. *MIT Sloan Management Review*. Available from https://sloanreview.mit.edu/article/how-digital-leadership-isnt-different/

Kasiewicz, S., & Kurkliński, L. (2019). Konkurencja cyfrowa a kultura ryzyka w sektorze finansowym. In Bankowość emocjonalna. Cyfrowa transformacja banków a oczekiwania klientów. Warszawa: Wydawnictwo Poltext.

Kavassalis, P. (2018). An innovative RegTech approach to financial risk monitoring and supervisory reporting. *The Journal of Risk Finance*, *19*(1), 39–55.

Kavuri, A. S., & Milne, A. K. L. (2019). *Fintech and the Future of Financial Services: What Are the Research Gaps?* CAMA Working Paper No. 18/2019. Available SSRN: https://ssrn.com/abstract=3333515

Kellerman, B. (2012). *The end of leadership*. Harper Business.

Khanna, S., & Martins, H. (2018). *Six digital growth strategies for banks*. McKinsey. Available from https://www.mckinsey.com/business-functions/mckinsey-digital/our-insights/six-digital-growth-strategies-for-banks

Khan, S. (2010). Impact of authentic leaders on organization performance. *International Journal of Business and Management*, *5*(12), 167. doi:10.5539/ijbm.v5n12p167

Khant, A., & Mehta, M. (2018). *Analysis of Financial News Using Natural Language Processing and Artificial Intelligence*. Conference: International Conference on Business Innovation 2018, Sri Lanka.

Khiewngamdee, C., & Yan, H-D. (2019). The role of Fintech e-payment on APEC economic development. *Journal of Physics*, 1324.

Khurana, D., Koli, A., Khatter, K., & Singh, S. (2017). *Natural language processing: State of the art, current trends and challenges*. arXiv preprint arXiv:1708.05148

Kim, M., Zoo, H., Lee, H., & Kang, J. (2018). Mobile financial services, financial inclusion, and development: A systematic review of academic literature. *The Electronic Journal on Information Systems in Developing Countries*, *84*(5), e12044. doi:10.1002/isd2.12044

Kimura, R., Reeves, M., & Whitaker, K. (2019). *Winning the '20s: The New Logic of Competition*. BCG Henderson Institute. Available from https://bcghendersoninstitute.com/winning-the-20s-the-new-logic-of-competition-7c1500c5a187

Kling, R., & Lamb, R. (2000). IT and organizational change in digital economies. In E. Brynjolfsson & B. Kahin (Eds.), *Understanding the Digital Economy* (pp. 295–324). MIT Press.

KMPG. (2018). Three technologies that will change the face of auditing. *Forbes Insights*. Retrieved from https://www.forbes.com/sites/insights-kpmg/2018/07/16/three-technologies-that-will-change-the-face-of-auditing/

Knapp, G. F. (1923). *Staatliche Theorie des Geldes (4. Ausgabe)*. Duncker und Humblot.

KNF. (2019a). *Departament Innowacji Finansowych FinTech (DFT)*. Retrieved from https://www.knf.gov.pl/o_nas/urzad_komisji/dane_teleadresowe_struktura?articleId=61228&p_id=18

KNF. (2019b). *KNF Regulatory Sandbox*. Retrieved from https://www.knf.gov.pl/en/MARKET/Fintech/Regulatory_Sandbox

Koh, F., Phoon, K. F., & Ha, C. D. (2018). Digital financial inclusion in South East Asia. In Handbook of Blockchain, Digital Finance, and Inclusion, Volume 2 (pp. 387-403). Academic Press. doi:10.1016/B978-0-12-812282-2.00015-2

Kojima, K. (1975). International trade and foreign investment: Substitutes or complements. *Hitotsubashi Journal of Economics*, *16*(1), 1–12.

Konkel, M. (2020). Polskie firmy nie boją się sięgać obłoków (Polish companies are not afraid to reach the clouds). *Puls Biznesu*, *2020*(19), 16.

Kopp, E., Kaffenberger, L., & Wilson, C. (2017). *Cyber Risk, Market Failures and Financial Stability*. IMF Working Paper WP/17/185.

Kostro, M. (2020). *Bezpieczeństwo usług opartych o otwarte interfejsy programistyczne (API) w kontekście implementacji Dyrektywy PSD 2*. WIB Warszawa.

Kotter, J. P. (2012). *Leading change*. Harvard Business Press.

Kotter, J. P., & Schlesinger, L. A. (1989). Choosing strategies for change. In *Readings in strategic management* (pp. 294–306). Palgrave. doi:10.1007/978-1-349-20317-8_21

Koźmiński, A. (2004). *Zarządzanie w warunkach niepewności*. Wydawnictwo Naukowe PWN.

KPMG & Forbes Insights. (2017). *Audit 2025: The future is now*. Retrieved June, 10, 2020, from https://assets.kpmg/content/dam/kpmg/us/pdf/2017/03/us-audit-2025-final-report.pdf

KPMG. (2018). *Impact of new technologies on audit and assurance*. Retrieved June, 10, 2020, from https://home.kpmg/content/dam/kpmg/ng/pdf/advisory/Impact-of-New-Tech-on-Audit-and-Assurance.pdf

KPMG. (2018). *The Pulse of Fintech 2018: Biannual global analysis of investment in Fintech*. KPMG.

KPMG. (2018). *There's a revolution coming- Embracing the challenge of RegTech 3.0*. Available: https://home.kpmg/content/dam/kpmg/uk/pdf/2018/09/regtech-revolution-coming.pdf

KPMG. (2019). *The Pulse of Fintech*. Retrieved from https://home.kpmg/xx/en/home/campaigns/2020/02/pulse-of-fintech-h2-2019.html

Kraft, O. (n.d.). Financial RegTech: Opportunities and Obstacles. *CapTech*, 1–18. https://www.captechconsulting.com/uploads/whitepapers/financial-regtech-ebook-opportunities-and-obstacles-final-compressed.pdf

Kroll, J., Huey, J., Baroca, S., Felten, E., Reidenberg, J., Robinson, D., & Yu, H. (2017). Accountable algorithms. *University of Pennsylvania Law Review*, *165*(3), 633–707.

Krupski, R. (Ed.). (2007). *Planowanie strategiczne w warunkach niepewności*. Prace Naukowe Wałbrzyskiej Wyższej Szkoły Zarządzania i Przedsiębiorczości.

Kruse, K. (2013). What is Authentic Leadership? *Forbes*, (May), 12.

Kumar, N. (2013). Financial inclusion and its determinants: Evidence from India. *Journal of Financial Economic Policy*, *5*(1), 4–19. doi:10.1108/17576381311317754

Kurshev, A., & Strebulaev, I. A. (2015). Firm Size and Capital Structure. *The Quarterly Journal of Finance*, *5*(3), 1550008. Advance online publication. doi:10.1142/S2010139215500081

Laha, A. (2015). Association between financial inclusion and human development in South Asia: A cross-country analysis with special reference to India. *Journal of Economic Policy and Research*, *10*(2), 69.

Lahovnik, M., & Breznik, L. (2013). Innovation management and technological capabilities as a source of competitive advantage. *Management, Knowledge and Learning International Conference.*

Lambe, E., Micic, D., & Sosnovsky, X. (2019). *BIS initiative to build a big data Platform, presentation given at a workshop on computing platforms for big data and machine learning.* Bank of Italy.

Lane, N. (1999). Advancing the digital economy into the 21st century. *Information Systems Frontiers*, *1*(3), 317–320. doi:10.1023/A:1010010630396

Lastra, R. M. (2015). *International Financial and Monetary Law* (2nd ed.). Oxford University Press.

Laurent, P., Chollet, T., Burke, M., & Seers, T. (2018). The tokenization of assets is disrupting the financial industry. Are you ready? *Inside Magazine*, *19*(2). Retrieved from https://www2.deloitte.com/content/dam/Deloitte/lu/Documents/financial-services/lu-tokenization-of-assets-disrupting-financial-industry.pdf

Lee, T.-H., & Ali, A. M. (2008). The evolution of auditing: An analysis of the historical development. *Journal of Modern Accounting and Auditing*, *4*(12), 1–8.

Lei, M., Zhao, X., Deng, H., & Tan, K. C. (2013). DEA analysis of FDI attractiveness for sustainable development: Evidence from Chinese provinces. *Decision Support Systems*, *56*, 406–418. doi:10.1016/j.dss.2012.10.053

Lemoine, G., Hartnell, C., & Leroy, H. (2019). Taking stock of moral approaches to leadership: An integrative review of ethical, authentic, and servant leadership. *The Academy of Management Annals*, *13*(1), 148–187. doi:10.5465/annals.2016.0121

Lengnick-Hall, C. A. (1992). Innovation and competitive advantage: What we know and what we need to learn. *Journal of Management*, *18*(2), 399–429. doi:10.1177/014920639201800209

Lenka, S. K., & Bairwa, A. K. (2016). Does financial inclusion affect monetary policy in SAARC countries? *Cogent Economics & Finance*, *4*(1), 1127011. doi:10.1080/23322039.2015.1127011

Libra project – White Paper. (2019). *An Introduction to Libra – White Paper.* From Libra Association Members.

Library of Congress. (2019a). *H.R.2144 — 116th Congress (2019-2020).* Retrieved from https://www.congress.gov/bill/116th-congress/house-bill/2144/text?format=txt

Library of Congress. (2019b). *H.R.2154 - Digital Taxonomy Act of 2019.* Retrieved from https://www.congress.gov/bill/116th-congress/house-bill/2154/text

Linström, K. (2018). *Kommuner tar hjälp av AI I GDPR-jobbet.* Available: https://computersweden.idg.se/2.2683/1.697727/gdpr-kommuner-ai

Lin, T. (2015). Infinite Financial Intermediation. *Wake Forest Law Review*, *50*, 643–669.

Liu, H., Cutcher, L., & Grant, D. (2017). Authentic leadership in context: An analysis of banking CEO narratives during the global financial crisis. *Human Relations*, *70*(6), 694–724. doi:10.1177/0018726716672920

Li, Z. (2017). Will blockchain change the audit? *China-USA Business Review, 16*(6), 294–298.

Llanto, G. M., & Badiola, J. A. R. (2011). *Rural Finance Environment in Asian Countries: Policies.* Innovations, Financial Inclusion.

Lloyd-Walker, B., & Walker, D. (2011). Authentic leadership for 21st century project delivery. *International Journal of Project Management, 29*(4), 383–395. doi:10.1016/j.ijproman.2011.02.004

Lord, G. (2017). *Confidence in the future – human and machine collaboration in the audit.* PricewaterhouseCoopers. Retrieved June, 10, 2020, from https://www.pwc.co.uk/audit-assurance/assets/pdf/confidence-in-the-future-human-machine-collaboration.pdf

Lord, S. (2018). The future of the audit - The enduring importance of professional scepticism. *Accounting Today.* Retrieved from https://www.accountingtoday.com/opinion/the-enduring-importance-of-professional-skepticism-in-auditing

Lord, S. (2018). The future of the audit - The enduring importance of professional scepticism. *Accounting Today.* Retrieved June, 10, 2020, from https://www.accountingtoday.com/opinion/the-enduring-importance-of-professional-skepticism-in-auditing

Luca. (2018, January 28). *Financial Supervisors and Regtech: Four Roles and Four Challenges.* Retrieved from https://poseidon01.ssrn.com/ delivery.php?ID= 6871 0106 7008 1020 1701 7029 0040 6408 7090 0960 5505 8047 0230 4303 1088 0131 0908 7104 0290 8901 7121 0610 5300 0000 0330 9705 2117 0781 1803 1019 1080 6500 9094 0100 4501 4112 1170 0811 3118 0720 2509 5087 0410 0110 2031 0161 2208 2121 0900 8410 7122 0870 2511 9118 0070 0411 2102 0650 9300 4103 1020 8912 7&EX T=pdf

Luthans, F. (2002). The need for and meaning of positive organizational behavior. *Journal of Organizational Behavior: The International Journal of Industrial. Occupational and Organizational Psychology and Behavior, 23*(6), 695–706. doi:10.1002/job.165

Luthans, F., & Avolio, B. (2003). Authentic leadership development. In K. Cameron, J. Dutton, & R. Quinn (Eds.), *Positive organizational scholarship: Foundations of a new discipline* (pp. 241–258). Berrett Koehler Publishers.

Machiavelli, N. (2008). *The prince.* Hackett Publishing.

Ma, H. (2000). Competitive advantage and firm performance. *Competitiveness Review, 10*(2), 15–32. doi:10.1108/eb046396

Mani, M. (2016). Financial Inclusion in South Asia—Relative Standing, Challenges and Initiatives. *South Asian Survey, 23*(2), 158–179. doi:10.1177/0971523118783353

Mankesiöld, P. (2018). *Kommuner tar hjälp av AI I GDPR-jobbet.* Available: https://computersweden.idg.se/2.2683/1.697727/gdpr-kommuner-ai

Marchewka-Bartkowiak, K. (2020). *Rola piaskownic regulacyjnych w ograniczaniu ryzyka prawnego sektora FinTech, In Bankowość emocjonalna. Cyfrowa transformacja banków a oczekiwania klientów.* Poltext.

Mark, C. (2017). Cybersecurity: Risks and management of risks for global banks and financial institutions Mark Camillo. *Journal of Risk Management in Financial Institutions, 10*(2), 196–200.

Martino, P., Laurent, P., Hauman, S., Gavray, G. (n.d.). Process automation for the financial industry. *Inside Magazine, 13.*

Massachusetts Department of Revenue – Computer Assisted Audit Group. (n.d.). *A guide to computer assisted audit techniques.* Retrieved from http://www.mtc.gov/uploadedFiles/Multistate_Tax_Commission/Audit_Program/Resource/caat.pdf

Massachusetts Department of Revenue – Computer Assisted Audit Group. (n.d.). *A guide to computer assisted audit techniques*. Retrieved June, 10, 2020, from http://www.mtc.gov/uploadedFiles/Multistate_Tax_Commission/Audit_Program/Resource/caat.pdf

MathWorks. (n.d.). *Predictive Modeling*. Retrieved from https://www.mathworks.com/discovery/predictive-modeling.html

Matt, C., Hess, T., & Benlian, A. (2015). Digital Transformation Strategies. *Business & Information Systems Engineering*, *57*(5), 339–343. doi:10.100712599-015-0401-5

Mayfield, C., Perdue, G., & Wooten, K. (2008). Investment management and personality type. *Financial Services Review*, *17*(3), 219–236.

McKinsey. (2016). *Digital Finance for all: powering inclusive growth in emerging countries*. Author.

Mellino, E. (2019). Revolut insiders reveal the human cost of fintech unicorn's wild rise. *Wired*. Retrieved May 23, 2020, from https://www.wired.co.uk/article/revolut-trade-unions-labour-fintech-politics-storonsky

Mention, A. L. (2019). The Future of Fintech. *Research Technology Management*, *62*(4), 59–63. doi:10.1080/08956308.2019.1613123

Merton, R. C. (1992). Financial innovation and economic performance. *Journal of Applied Corporate Finance*, *4*(4), 12–22. doi:10.1111/j.1745-6622.1992.tb00214.x

Mesenbourg, T. L. (2001). *Measuring the Digital Economy*. US Bureau of the Census. Retrieved from https://www.census.gov/content/dam/Census/library/workingpapers/2001/econ/umdigital.pdf

Meyer, A., & Ante, L. (2020). *Effects of Initial Coin Offering Characteristics on Cross-listing Returns*. doi:10.13140/RG.2.2.10972.33920

Meyer, K. E., Li, C., & Schotter, A. P. J. (2020). Managing the MNE subsidiary: Advancing a multi-level and dynamic research agenda. *Journal of International Business Studies*, *51*(4), 538–576. doi:10.105741267-020-00318-w

Micheler, E., & Whaley, A. (2018). *Regulatory Technology*. Available SSRN: https://ssrn.com/abstract=3164258

MiFID II: Directive 2014/65/EU of the European Parliament and of the Council on markets in financial instruments, OJ L 173, 12.6.2014, p. 349–496

Mijwel, M. M., Esen, A., & Shamil, A. (2019). *Overview of Neural Networks*. Academic Press.

Minsky, H. P. (1992). *The Financial Instability Hypothesis*. The Jerome Levy Economics Institute Working Paper 74. doi:10.2139srn.161024

Mohamed, H., & Ali, H. (2018). *Blockchain, Fintech and Islamic Finance: Building the Future of the New Islamic Digital Economy*. De|G Press, De Gruyter.

Mohamed, H. (2020). The Future of FinTech in ASEAN. In M. Anshari, M. Almunawar, & M. Masri (Eds.), *Financial Technology and Disruptive Innovation in ASEAN* (pp. 63–79). IGI Global. doi:10.4018/978-1-5225-9183-2.ch003

Mohamed, H., & Ali, H. (2019). *Blockchain, Fintech, and Islamic Finance*. Walter de Gruyter Inc. doi:10.1515/9781547400966

Momtaz, P. P. (2020). Entrepreneurial Finance and Moral Hazard: Evidence from Token Offerings. *Journal of Business Venturing*. doi:10.1016/j.jbusvent.2020.106001

Mooney, S. J., Westreich, D. J., & El-Sayed, A. M. (2015). Epidemiology in the era of big data. *Epidemiology (Cambridge, Mass.)*, *26*(3), 390. doi:10.1097/EDE.0000000000000274 PMID:25756221

Moore, B., & Rose, J. (2000). Recovered paper trading—ready for the Web? PIMA's North American Papermaker: The Official Publication of the Paper Industry Management Association, 82(9).

Morash, E. A., Droge, C. L., & Vickery, S. K. (1996). Strategic logistics capabilities for competitive advantage and firm success. *Journal of Business Logistics*, *17*(1), 1.

Morgan, S. (2017). *2017 Cybercrime Report*. Academic Press.

Morningstar Inc. (2018). *2018 Fundamentals for Investors*. https://advisor.mp.morningstar.com/resourceDownload?type=publicForms&id=3f9dff3c-f085-47a1-98ba-0bc008df9f25

Moscatelli, M. (2019). *Corporate Default Forecasting with Machine Learning*. Bank of Italy.

Moscatelli, M., Narizzano, S., Parlapiano, F., & Viggiano, G. (2019). *Corporate default forecasting with machine learning (No. 1256). Economic Research and International Relations Area*. Bank of Italy.

Mujawar, S., & Joshi, A. (2015). Data analytics types, tools and their comparison. *International Journal of Advanced Research in Computer and Communication Engineering*, *4*(2), 488–491.

Mustafa, F., Khursheed, A., & Fatima, M. (2018). Impact of global financial crunch on financially innovative microfinance institutions in South Asia. *Financial Innovation*, *4*(1), 13. doi:10.118640854-018-0099-8

Nakaso, H. (2016). *FinTech – Its Impacts on Finance, Economies and Central Banking*. Remarks at the University of Tokyo - Bank of Japan Joint Conference in Tokyo on "FinTech and the Future of Money". https://www.boj.or.jp/en/announcements/press/koen_2016/data/ko161118a.pdf

Narodowy Bank Polski. (2019a). *Instrukcja uzupełniająca pakiet FINREP jednostkowy (FINPL) (Supplementary manual for solo FINREP reporting FINPL)*. Retrieved from: https://www.nbp.pl/statystyka/sprawozdawczosc/form/instrukcja-FINREP.pdf

Narodowy Bank Polski. (2019b). *Ocena funkcjonowania polskiego systemu płatniczego w I półroczu 2019 roku (Assessment of the functioning of the Polish payment system in the first half of 2019)*. http://www.nbp.pl/homen.aspx?f=/en/system_platniczy/Assessment_summary.html

Narodowy Bank Polski. (2019c). *Financial Stability Report. December 2019*. Retrieved from: https://www.nbp.pl/en/systemfinansowy/fsr201912.pdf

Narodowy Bank Polski. (2019d). *Financial Stability Report. June 2019*. Retrieved from: https://www.nbp.pl/en/system-finansowy/fsr201906.pdf

Narodowy Bank Polski. (2020). *Innowacje w sektorze banków komercyjnych w Polsce. Raport z badania 2019 r* [Innovations in the Polish commercial banking sector. Report from 2019 survey]. Retrieved from https://www.nbp.pl/systemfinansowy/Ankieta_innowacje.pdf

Nassiry, D. (2018). *The Role of Fintech in Unlocking Green Finance: Policy Insights for Developing Countries*. ADBI Working Paper 883. https://www.adb.org/sites/default/files/publication/464821/adbi-wp883.pdf

National Institute of Standards and Technology. (2008). *Special Publication 800-64 Revision 2 - Security Considerations in the System Development Life Cycle*. Author.

National Institute of Standards and Technology. (2010). *Special Publication 800-37 Revision 1 - Guide for Applying the Risk Management Framework to Federal Information*. Author.

National Institute of Standards and Technology. (2014). *Special Publication 800-88 Revision Systems. 1 - Guide for Media Sanitisation*. Author.

Newgenapps. (2018). *Random Forest Analysis in ML and when to use it.* Retrieved from https://www.newgenapps.com/blog/random-forest-analysis-in-ml-and-when-to-use-it/

Nickols, F. (2016). Strategy, strategic management, strategic planning and strategic thinking. *Management Journal, 1*(1), 4–7.

Nicoletti, B. (2017). *The future of fintech: Integrating finance and technology in financial services.* Available https://ebookcentral.proquest.com

Nicoletti, B., & Weis. (2017). Future of FinTech. Basingstoke, UK: Palgrave Macmillan.

Nicoletti, B. (2017). Financial services and Fintech. In *The Future of FinTech* (pp. 3–29). Palgrave Macmillan.

Nizan Geslevich Packin. (2018). RegTech, Compliance and Technology Judgment Rule. *Chi.-Kent L. Rev., 193.*

Noe, R., Hollenbeck, J., Gerhart, B., & Wright, P. (2017). *Human resource management: Gaining a competitive advantage.* McGraw-Hill Education.

Noorbakhsh, F., Paloni, A., & Youssef, A. (2001). Human capital and FDI inñows to developing countries: New empirical evidence. *World Development, 29*(9), 1593–1610. doi:10.1016/S0305-750X(01)00054-7

Nussbaum, A. (1950). *Money in the Law – National and International.* The Foundation Press.

Obłój, K. (2002). *Tworzywo skutecznych strategii.* PWE.

OECD. (2016). *Science Technology and Innovation Outlook, 2016.* http://www.oecd.org/sti/STIO%2010%20key%20technology%20trends%20for%20the%20future.pdf

Organisation for Economic Cooperation and Development – OECD. (2015). *G20/OECD Principles of Corporate Governance.* Paris: OECD Publishing. Retrieved from https://www.oecd.org/daf/ca/Corporate-Governance-Principles-ENG.pdf

Organisation for Economic Cooperation and Development – OECD. (2015). *G20/OECD Principles of Corporate Governance.* Paris: OECD Publishing. Retrieved June, 10, 2020, from https://www.oecd.org/daf/ca/Corporate-Governance-Principles-ENG.pdf

Organisation for Economic Co-operation and Development – OECD. (2018). *OECD Blockchain Primer.* Retrieved from https://www.oecd.org/finance/OECD-Blockchain-Primer.pdf

Organisation for Economic Co-operation and Development – OECD. (2018). *OECD Blockchain Primer.* Retrieved June, 10, 2020, from https://www.oecd.org/finance/OECD-Blockchain-Primer.pdf

Organisation for Economic Co-operation and Development. (2019). Initial Coin Offerings (ICOs) for SME Financing. *Organisation for Economic Co-operation and Development*, 1–72. http://www.oecd.org/finance/ICOs-for-SME-Financing.pdf

Osterwalder, A., & Pigneur, Y. (2010). *Business model generation: a handbook for visionaries, games changers, and challengers.* Wiley.

OVUM. (n.d.). *Assessing the role of Big Data in tackling financial crime and compliance management. Examining real use cases and its potential.* Retrieved from http://www.oracle.com/us/industries/financial-services/fs-big-data-fccm-wp-2861557.pdf

Ozawa, T. (1992). Theory of FDI as a dynamic paradigm of economic development. *Transnational Corporations, 1*(1), 27–54.

Palmer, M. (2020). Absence of leadership claim made against 'toxic' Triathlon Scotland, *The Times*. Retrieved May 22, 2020, from https://www.thetimes.co.uk/article/absence-of-leadership-claim-made-against-toxic-triathlon-scotland-mwt0tq967

Palmer, J. W., & Johnston, J. S. (1996). Business-tobusiness connectivity on the Internet: EDI, intermediaries, and interorganizational dimensions. *Electronic Markets*, *6*(2).

Panisi, F., & Perrone, A. (2018). Systems So Perfect That No One Will Need to be Good'? RegTech and the 'Human Factor'. *Orizzonti del Diritto Commerciale*. Available: SSRN: https://ssrn.com/abstract=3284636

Paradkar, A., Knight, J., & Hansen, P. (2015). Innovation in start-ups: Ideas filling the void or ideas devoid of resources and capabilities? *Technovation*, *41*, 1–10. doi:10.1016/j.technovation.2015.03.004

Park, C. Y., & Mercado, R. (2015). *Financial inclusion, poverty, and income inequality in developing Asia.* Asian Development Bank Economics Working Paper Series, (426).

Payment in Gold of Brazilian Federal Loans Contracted in France (Fr. v. Braz.), 1929 P.C.I.J. (ser. A) No. 21 (July 12)

Payment of Various Serbian Loans Issued in France (Fr. v. Yugo.), 1929 P.C.I.J. (ser. A) No. 20 (July 12)

Perić, E. (n.d.). *Industrija 4.0* [Industry 4.0]. Croatian Chamber of Economy. Retrieved from https://www.hgk.hr/documents/hgk-industrija-4058d8c59722f1e.pdf

Perić, E. (n.d.). *Industrija 4.0* [Industry 4.0]. Croatian Chamber of Economy. Retrieved June, 10, 2020, from https://www.hgk.hr/documents/hgk-industrija-4058d8c59722f1e.pdf

Perrewé, P. L., Ferris, G. R., Stoner, J. S., & Brouer, R. L. (2007). The positive role of political skill in organizations. *Positive organizational behavior: Accentuating the positive at work*, 117-128.

Peyton, A. (2018, May 22). Maybank makes a grab for cashless payments in Malaysia. *Fintechfutures.com*. Retrieved March 3, 2020, from https://www.fintechfutures.com/2018/05/maybank-makes-a-grab-for-cashless-payments-in-malaysia/

Pinsker, J. (2017, July 18). How in the world does Venmo make money? *The Atlantic*. Retrieved January 16, 2020, from https://www.theatlantic.com/business/archive/2017/07/venmo-makes-money-banks/533946/

Pollari, I. (2016). The rise of Fintech opportunities and challenges. *Jassa*, (3), 15.

Porter, M. E. (2011). *Competitive advantage of nations: creating and sustaining superior performance*. Simon and Schuster.

Porter, M. E., & Kramer, M. R. (2002). The competitive advantage of corporate. *Harvard Business Review*. PMID:12510538

Proctor, C. (2012). *Mann on legal aspect of money* (7th ed.). Oxford University Press.

Proposal for a Directive of the European Parliament and of the Council amending Directive (EU) 2015/849 on the prevention of the use of the financial system for the purposes of money laundering or terrorist financing and amending Directive 2009/101/EC COM(2016) 450 final

Puschmann, T. (2017). Fintech. *Business & Information Systems Engineering*, *59*(1), 69–76. doi:10.100712599-017-0464-6

PwC. (2016). *Turnaround and Transformation in Cybersecurity.* Retrieved from https://www.pwc.com/sg/en/publications/assets/pwc-global-state-of-information-security-survey-2016.pdf

PwC. (2017). *Na współpracy banków i fintech-ów skorzystają klienci.* www.pwc.pl›media›2017-06-08-na-wspolpracy-bankow-i-fintech-

PWC. (2018). *Canadian FinTech market map*. Retrieved from https://www.pwc.com/ca/en/industries/technology/canadian-fintech-market-map.html

Qamruzzaman, M., & Jianguo, W. (2018). Nexus between financial innovation and economic growth in South Asia: evidence from ARDL and nonlinear ARDL approaches. *Financial Innovation, 4*(1), 20.

Qamruzzaman, M., & Jianguo, W. (2017). Financial innovation and economic growth in Bangladesh. *Financial Innovation*, *3*(1), 19. doi:10.118640854-017-0070-0

Qamruzzaman, M., & Wei, J. (2019). Financial Innovation and Financial Inclusion Nexus in South Asian Countries: Evidence from Symmetric and Asymmetric Panel Investigation. *International Journal of Financial Studies*, *7*(4), 61. doi:10.3390/ijfs7040061

Quintane, E., Mitch Casselman, R., Sebastian Reiche, B., & Nylund, P. A. (2011). Innovation as a knowledge-based outcome. *Journal of Knowledge Management*, *15*(6), 928–947. doi:10.1108/13673271111179299

Rahmatian, A. (2020). *Credit and Creed: A Critical Legal Theory of Money*. Routledge.

Rajan, R. G., & Zingales, L. (1995). What Do We Know about Capital Structure? Some Evidence from International Data. *The Journal of Finance*, *50*(5), 1421–1460. doi:10.1111/j.1540-6261.1995.tb05184.x

Rego, A., Sousa, F., Marques, C., & Cunha, M. (2012). Authentic leadership promoting employees' psychological capital and creativity. *Journal of Business Research*, *65*(3), 429–437. doi:10.1016/j.jbusres.2011.10.003

Reuters, T. (2017). *Regtech 2020 and Beyond – What Does the Future Hold?* Author.

Robinson, B. (2016). *4 banking business models for the digital age*. Temenos. Available from https://www.linkedin.com/pulse/4-banking-business-models-digital-age-ben-robinson/

Rodríguez, C., Gómez, C., & Ferreiro, J. (2009). A proposal to improve the UNCTAD's inward FDI potential index. *Transnational Corporations*, *18*(3), 85–114. doi:10.18356/35d71cb5-en

Roh, C. (2018, July 5). *Cryptocurrency Exchange Theft Rising in 2018 According to CipherTrace*. Retrieved August 6, 2018, from https://cryptoslate.com/cryptocurrency-exchange-theft-rising-in-2018-according-to-ciphertrace/

Romānova, I., & Kudinska, M. (2016). Banking and Fintech: a challenge or opportunity? In *Contemporary issues in finance: Current challenges from across Europe*. Emerald Group Publishing Limited. doi:10.1108/S1569-375920160000098002

Rooney, K. (2018, September 14). After the crisis, a new generation puts its trust in tech over traditional banks. *CNBC*. Retrieved January 15, 2020, from https://www.cnbc.com/2018/09/14/a-new-generation-puts-its-trust-in-tech-over-traditional-banks.html

Rooney, K. (2019). *Wall Street banks are upping bets on their potential fintech competitors*. Retrieved from: https://www.cnbc.com/2019/09/15/wall-street-banks-are-upping-bets-on-potential-fintech-competitors.html

Roosenboom, P., van der Kolk, T., & de Jong, A. (2020). What Determines Success in Initial Coin Offerings? *Venture Capital*, *23*(2), 1–23. doi:10.1080/13691066.2020.1741127

Roth, J., Schär, F., & Schöpfer, A. (2019). The Tokenization of Assets: Using Blockchains for Equity Crowdfunding. *SSRN Electronic Journal*. doi:10.2139srn.3443382

Roubini, N., & Byrne, P. (2018). *The Blockchain Pipe Dream*. Project Syndicate. https://www.project-syndicate.org/commentary/blockchain-technologylimited-applications-by-nouriel-roubini-and-preston-byrne-2018-03

Rowley, J. (2016). Human Rights are Animal Rights: The Implications of Ethical Veganism for Human Rights. In *Critical Perspectives on Veganism* (pp. 67–92). Palgrave Macmillan. doi:10.1007/978-3-319-33419-6_4

Roy, S. (2018). *Regtech on the rise: Transforming Compliance into Competitive advantage*. Oliver Wyman. Available at: https://www.oliverwyman.com/our-expertise/insights/2018/may/the-rise-of-regtech.html

Royal Commission. (2019, March 4). Retrieved from https://financialservices.royalcommission.gov.au/Pages/reports.aspx#final

Rumelt, R. P. (2003). What in the world is competitive advantage. *Policy working paper, 105*(2003), 1-5.

Sahay, R., Čihák, M., N'Diaye, P. M. B. P., Barajas, A., Mitra, S., Kyobe, A., . . . Yousefi, S. R. (2015). Financial inclusion: Can it meet multiple macroeconomic goals? (No. 15/17). Washington: International Monetary Fund.

Sakalaki, M., Richardson, C., & Thépaut, Y. (2007). Machiavellianism and economic opportunism. *Journal of Applied Social Psychology*, *37*(6), 1181–1190. doi:10.1111/j.1559-1816.2007.00208.x

Saksonova, S., & Kuzmina-Merlino, I. (2017). Fintech as financial innovation–The possibilities and problems of implementation. *European Research Studies*, *20*(3A, 3A), 961–973. doi:10.35808/ersj/757

Sandrock, J., & Fringes, A. (2016), *Catalyst or threat? The strategic implications of PSD 2 Europe's banks*. Available from http://www.vivanest.com/wp-content/uploads/2016/09/Catalyst-or-threat-The-strategic-implications-of-PSD2-for-Europes-banks-.pdf

Sapienza, P., & Zingales, L. (2012). A trust crisis. *International Review of Finance*, *12*(2), 123–131. doi:10.1111/j.1468-2443.2012.01152.x

Sarma, M. (2008). *Financial inclusion and development: A cross country analysis*. Academic Press.

Sarma, M. (2008). *Index of financial inclusion* (No. 215). Working paper. Indian Council for Research on International Economic Relations (ICRIER).

Savigny, C. F. (1851). *Obligationsrecht I. als Theil des heutigen Römschen Rechts*. Berlin Veit und Comp.

Schindler, J. W. (2017). *FinTech and financial innovation: Drivers and depth*. Academic Press.

Schueffel, P. (2016). Taming the Beast: A Scientific Definition of FinTech. *Journal of Innovation Management*, *4*(4), 32–54. doi:10.24840/2183-0606_004.004_0004

Schumpeter, J. A. (1943). *Capitalism, Socialism and Democracy*. Routledge.

Schwab, K. (2016). *The Fourth Industrial Revolution: what it means, how to respond*. Retrieved from: https://www.weforum.org/agenda/2016/01/the-fourth-industrial-revolution-what-it-means-and-how-to-respond/

Schweitzer, M., & Barkley, B. (2017). *Is 'Fintech' Good for Small Business Borrowers? Impacts on Firm Growth and Customer Satisfaction*. https://www.federalreserve.gov/conferences/files/is-fintech-good-for-small-business-borrowers.pdf

Scott, S., Van Reenen, J., & Zachariadis, M. (2017). The long-term effect of digital innovation on bank performance: An empirical study of SWIFT adoption in financial services. *Research Policy*, *46*(5), 984–1004. doi:10.1016/j.respol.2017.03.010

SEC. (2019). *SEC Sues Alleged Perpetrator of Fraudulent Pyramid Scheme Promising Investors Cryptocurrency Riches*. https://www.sec.gov/news/press-release/2019-74

SEGOB. (2018). *Law to Regulate Financial Technology Institutions*. Diario Oficial de la Federación. Retrieved from http://www.dof.gob.mx/nota_detalle.php?codigo=5515623&fecha=09/03/2018

Sever Mališ, S., Tušek, B. & Žager, L. (2012). *Revizija - načela, standardi, postupci* [Audit - principles, standards, procedures]. Zagreb: Hrvatska zajednica računovođa i financijskih djelatnika [Croatian Association of Accountants and Financial Professionals].

Shanmuganathan, S., Sallis, P., & Buckeridge, J. (2004). Self-organising maps for integrating data across multiple scales. In *Bridging scales and epistemologies; Linking local knowledge with global science in multi-scale assessments International Conference by Millennium Ecosystem Assessment (MEA).* Bibliotheca Alexandrina.

Shäubli, T. (2018). *Apiax launches tax product, addresses key challenges of banks and wealth managers.* Available: https://blog.apiax.com/apiax-launches-tax-product-addresses-key-challenges-of-banks-and-wealth-managers-9bd0615aa9ff

Shevlin, R. (2019). Why did Chase Shut Down Finn? *Forbes.* Retrieved May 20, 2020, from https://www.forbes.com/sites/ronshevlin/2019/06/06/why-did-chase-shut-down-finn/#716002cf702b

Simon, H. A. (1979). Rational decision making in business organizations. *The American Economic Review, 69*(4), 493–513.

Sironi, J. (2016). *FinTech innovation: from robo-advisors to goal based investing and gamification.* John Wiley & Sons. doi:10.1002/9781119227205

Skinner, C. (2018). Digital Human: The Fourth Revolution of Humanity Includes Everyone. Singapore: Marshall Cavendish International (Asia) Pte Ltd.

Skinner, C. (2020). *Doing Digital.* https://calendly.com/chris_skinner/30min

Smith, C. W. Jr. (1977). Alternative methods for raising capital. Rights versus underwritten offerings. *Journal of Financial Economics, 5*(3), 273–307. doi:10.1016/0304-405X(77)90040-X

SoFi. (2020). How SoFi works. *SoFi.com.* Retrieved March 3, 2020, from https://www.sofi.com/how-it-works/

Solarz, M. (2017). FinTech – innowacje w obszarze usług finansowych. *Prace Naukowe Wyższej Szkoły Zarządzania i Przedsiębiorczości z siedzibą w Wałbrzychu, 43*(4), 233-250.

Spence, M. (1973). Job Market Signaling. *The Quarterly Journal of Economics, 87*(3), 355–374. doi:10.2307/1882010

Statista. (2020). *Global cyber security & insurance spending 2020.* Statista. https://www.statista.com/statistics/387868/it-cyber-securiy-budget/

Stavytskyy, A., Kharlamova, A., & Stoica, E. A. (2019). The analysis of the digital economy and society index in the EU. *Baltic Journal of European Studies, 9*(3), 245–261. doi:10.1515/bjes-2019-0032

Stec, A., & Rudke, M. (2018). *Prezes PKO BP Zbigniew Jagiełło: Będziemy firmą technologiczną z licencją bankową* [PKO BP CEO: we will be a technological company with a banking license]. Retrieved from: https://www.rp.pl/Banki/311139892-Prezes-PKO-BP-Zbigniew-Jagiello-Bedziemy-firma-technologiczna-z-licencja-bankowa.html?cid

Straessle, A. (n.d.). *FAQ - Business benefits - Do you offer an efficient solution for cross-border compliance? The Digital Marketplace.* MindBridge AI Auditor. Available: https://www.digitalmarketplace.service.gov.uk/g-cloud/services/464121930318123

Stripe. (2020). Our mission is to increase the GDP of the internet. *Stripe.* Retrieved May 23, 2020, from https://stripe.com/au/about

Sun, T., & Vasarhelyi, M. A. (2018). Embracing textual data analytics in auditing with deep learning. *The International Journal of Digital Accounting Research, 18*(1), 49–67. doi:10.4192/1577-8517-v18_3

Svanström, T. (2016). Time pressure, training activities and dysfunctional audit behaviour: Evidence from small audit firms. *International Journal of Auditing*, *20*(1), 42–51. doi:10.1111/ijau.12054

Swamy, V. (2014). Financial inclusion, gender dimension, and economic impact on poor households. *World Development*, *56*, 1–15. doi:10.1016/j.worlddev.2013.10.019

Swiss DLT-Bill: Bundesgesetz Entwurf zur Anpassung des Bundesrechts an Entwicklungender Technik verteilter elektronischer Register, https://www.admin.ch/opc/de/federal-gazette/2020/329.pdf

Symon, K. (2020, January 9). FinTech Scotland celebrates its second birthday with growing business numbers. *Insider.co.uk.* Retrieved January 14, 2020, from https://www.insider.co.uk/news/fintech-scotland-celebrates-second-birthday-21241330

Tan, J. (2001). Innovation and risk-taking in a transitional economy: A comparative study of Chinese managers and entrepreneurs. *Journal of Business Venturing*, *16*(4), 359–376. doi:10.1016/S0883-9026(99)00056-7

Tapscott, D. (1996). *Digital Economy: Promise and Peril in the Age of Networked Intelligence*. McGraw-Hill.

Techopedia. (n.d.). *Data Cube*. Retrieved from https://www.techopedia.com/definition/28530/data-cube

Tellis, G. J., Prabhu, J. C., & Chandy, R. K. (2009, January). Radical Innovation Across Nations: The Preeminence of Corporate Culture. *Journal of Marketing*, *73*(1), 3–23. doi:10.1509/jmkg.73.1.003

Teoh, C. S., & Mahmood, A. K. (2017). National Cyber Security Strategies for Digital Economy. *International Conference on Research and Innovation in Information Systems*. 10.1109/ICRIIS.2017.8002519

Thakor, A. V. (2019). *Fintech and Banking*. Available at SSRN: https://ssrn.com/abstract=3332550

The Hong Kong Monetary Authority (HKMA). (2018a). *Authorization of Virtual Banks*. Retrieved from www.hkma.gov.hk/media/eng/doc/key-functions/banking-stability/guide-authorization/Chapter-9.pdf

The Hong Kong Monetary Authority (HKMA). (2018b). *Guide to Authorization*. Retrieved from https://www.hkma.gov.hk/eng/regulatory-resources/regulatory-guides/guide-to-authorization/

The Hong Kong Monetary Authority (HKMA). (2019). *Open Application Programming Interface (API) for the Banking Sector*. Retrieved from https://www.hkma.gov.hk/eng/key-functions/international-financial-centre/fintech/open-application-programming-interface-api-for-the-banking-sector/

The Institute of Chartered Accountants in England and Wales – ICAEW & Dubai Financial Services Authority – DFSA. (2018). *Understanding the impact of technology in audit and finance*. Retrieved from https://www.icaew.com/-/media/corporate/files/middle-east-hub/understanding-the-impact-of-technology-in-audit-and-finance.ashx

The Institute of Chartered Accountants in England and Wales – ICAEW & Dubai Financial Services Authority – DFSA. (2018). *Understanding the impact of technology in audit and finance*. Retrieved June, 10, 2020, from https://www.icaew.com/-/media/corporate/files/middle-east-hub/understanding-the-impact-of-technology-in-audit-and-finance.ashx

The Law Library of Congress. (2018). *Regulation of Cryptocurrency Around the World. Global Legal Research Center.* Retrieved from https://www.loc.gov/law/help/cryptocurrency/world-survey.php

The Monetary Authority of Singapore. (2018). *Eligibility Criteria and Requirements for Digital Banks*. Retrieved from www.mas.gov.sg/-/media/Digital-Bank-Licence/Eligibility-Criteria-and-Requirements-for-Digital-Banks.pdf?la=en&hash=502B26B6D52B499200B4E95FA90ADDC983778655

The Telegraph. (2017). *The future of fintech*. Available from https://www.telegraph.co.uk/content/dam/business/spark/Fintech/Telegraph_Fintech_Report%202017.pdf

Thomson Reuters. (2019). English S. & Hammond S., Fintech, Regtech and the Role of Compliance in 2019. Thomson Reuters Report 2019.

Thomson, D. (2017). The Silent Crisis of Retail Employment. *Atlantic*. https://www.theatlantic.com/business/archive/2017/04/the-silent-crisis-of-retail-employment/523428/

Titman, S., & Wessels, R. (1988). The Determinants of Capital Structure Choice. *The Journal of Finance*, *43*(1), 1–19. doi:10.1111/j.1540-6261.1988.tb02585.x

Tomaszewski, R. (2019). *Adam Marciniak, PKO Bank Polski – O Chmurze Krajowej i jej współpracy z Google Cloud.* Retrieved from: https://fintek.pl/pko-bp-chmura-krajowa-google-cloud-wywiad/

Toplensky, R. (2019, September 10). Technology is bank's new battleground. *The Wall Street Journal.* Retrieved March 4, 2020, from https://www.wsj.com/articles/technology-is-banks-new-battleground-11568114378?mod=djemheard_t

Toronto Centre. (2017a). *FinTech, RegTech and SupTech: What They Mean for Financial Supervision.* Retrieved from http://res. torontocentre. org/guidedocs/FinTech% 20RegTech% 20and% 20SupTech, 20, 20.

Toronto Centre. (2017b). *Regulatory Sandboxes*. Retrieved from https://res.torontocentre.org/guidedocs/Regulatory%20 Sandboxes%20FINAL.pdf

Treleaven, P., & Batrinca, B. (2017). Algorithmic Regulation: Automating Financial Compliance Monitoring and Regulation Using AI and Blockchain. *Journal of Financial Transformation, Capco Institute*, *45*, 14–21.

Trilling, L. (2009). *Sincerity and authenticity*. Harvard University Press. doi:10.2307/j.ctvjhzrdp

Tsyganov, S., & Apalkova, V. (2016). Digital economy: A new paradigm of global information society. *Economic Review (Kansas City, Mo.)*, *45*(3), 295–311.

Tufano, P. (2003). Financial innovation. In *Handbook of the Economics of Finance* (Vol. 1, pp. 307–335). Elsevier.

U.S. Const., art. I. § 8., § 10.

Ukrainian Association of Fintech. (2019). *The Ukrainian Fintech Catalog 2019*. Retrieved from https://map.fintechua.org/en

UNCTAD. (2002). *World Investment Report: Transnational Corporations and Export Competitiveness*. United Nations Publication.

UNCTAD. (2004). *World Investment Report: The Shift Towards Services*. United Nations Publication.

UNCTAD. (2011). *World Investment Report: Non-Equity Modes of International Production and Development*. United Nations Publication.

UNCTAD. (2017). *World Investment Report: Investment and the Digital Economy*. United Nations Publication.

UNCTAD. (2019). *World Investment Report: Special Economic Zones*. New York, Geneva: United Nations Publication.

UNCTAD. (2019). *World Investment Report: Special Economic Zones*. New York: United Nations Publication. Retrieved from https://unctadstat.unctad.org/EN/

UNCTADSTAT. Retrieved from https://unctadstat.unctad.org/EN/

UNSGSA. (2019). *Early Lessons on Regulatory Innovations to Enable Inclusive FinTech: Innovations Office, Regulatory sandboxes and RegTech*. Retrieved from https://www.unsgsa.org/files/2915/5016/4448/Early_Lessons_on_Regulatory_Innovations_to_Enable_Inclusive_FinTech.pdf

Up. (2020, March 2). Retrieved from https://up.com.au

Valencia, J. C. N., Valle, R. S., & Jiménez, D. J. (2010). Organizational culture as determinant of product innovation. *European Journal of Innovation Management, 13*(4).

Vasarhelyi, M. A., & Romero, S. (2014). Technology in audit engagements: A case study. *Managerial Auditing Journal, 29*(4), 350–365. doi:10.1108/MAJ-06-2013-0881

VAT Directive: Council Directive 2006/112/EC of 28 November 2006 on the common system of value-added tax, OJ L 347 11.12.2006, p. 1.

Venet, B. (2019). FinTech and financial inclusion. In *A Research Agenda for Financial Inclusion and Microfinance*. Edward Elgar Publishing. doi:10.4337/9781788114226.00024

Vestager, M. (2017). *Google has to follow European rules*. Available from http://f24.my/youtubeEN

Vicuña, A. S. (2010). An Institutional Theory of Money. In M. Giovanoli & D. Devos (Eds.), *International Monetary and Financial Law: the Global Crisis*. Oxford University Press.

Villasenor, J. (2016). *Ensuring Cybersecurity in FinTech: Key Trends and Solutions*. Retrieved May 11, 2018, from https://www.forbes.com/sites/johnvillasenor/2016/08/25/ensuring-cybersecurity-in-FinTech-key-trends-and-solutions/

Virtual Currency Schemes – further analysis. (2015). European Central Bank.

Viscelli, T. R., Hermanson, D. R., & Beasley, M. S. (2017). The integration of ERM and strategy: Simplications for corporate governance. *Accounting Horizons, 31*(2), 69–82. doi:10.2308/acch-51692

Voshmgir, S., & Kalinov, V. (2017). *Blockchain – A beginners guide*. BlockchainHub. Retrieved from https://s3.eu-west-2.amazonaws.com/blockchainhub.media/Blockchain+Technology+Handbook.pdf

Voshmgir, S., & Kalinov, V. (2017). *Blockchain – A beginners guide*. BlockchainHub. Retrieved June, 10, 2020, from https://s3.eu-west-2.amazonaws.com/blockchainhub.media/Blockchain+Technology+Handbook.pdf

Vrgovic, P., Vidicki, P., Glassman, B., & Walton, A. (2012). Open innovation for SMEs in developing countries–An intermediated communication network model for collaboration beyond obstacles. *Innovation, 14*(3), 290–302. doi:10.5172/impp.2012.14.3.290

Vysya, V. N., & Kumar, A. (n.d.). Regtech: A magical entity from the fintech ecosystem. *Infosys*, 1–8. https://www.infosys.com/industries/financial-services/white-papers/Documents/magical-entity-finTech-ecosystem.pdf

Watanabe, C., Naveed, K., Tou, Y., & Neittaanmäki, P. (2018b, December). Measuring GDP in the digital economy: Increasing dependence on uncaptured GDP. *Technological Forecasting and Social Change, 137*, 226–240. doi:10.1016/j.techfore.2018.07.053

Watanabe, C., Tou, Y., & Neittaanmäki, P. (2018a, November). A new paradox of the digital economy: Structural sources of the limitation of GDP statistics. *Technology in Society, 55*, 9–23. doi:10.1016/j.techsoc.2018.05.004

Weber, M. (1922). *Wirtschaft und Gesellschaft*. Mohr.

Wehrmann, B., & Glavina, J. (2009). *Geographic Information Systems (GIS): the spatial dimension to development cooperation*. GT.

Wen Ooi, J. (2018). Big data and analytics will transform the audit profession - Here's what you must know. *Prospects*, 7. Retrieved June, 10, 2020, from https://www.prospectsasean.com/big-data-analytics-transform-audit-profession/

Wen Ooi, J. (2018). Big data and analytics will transform the audit profession - Here's what you must know. *Prospects, 7*. https://www.prospectsasean.com/big-data-analytics-transform-audit-profession/

Westerman, G., Soule, D. L., & Eswaran, A. (2019). Building Digital-Ready Culture in Traditional Organizations. *MIT Sloan Management Review*. Available from https://sloanreview.mit.edu/article/building-digital-ready-culture-in-traditional-organizations

Wheelock, D., & Wilson, P. (2011). *Do Large Banks have Lower Costs? New Estimates of Returns to Scale for U.S. Banks*. Federal Reserve Bank of St. Louis Working Paper 2009(054E), doi:10.2139srn.1493261

Wildcard. (2020, March 1). Retrieved from https://www.wildcard.money

Wishart, D., & Wardrop, A. (2018). What can the Banking Royal Commission achieve: Regulating for good corporate culture? *Alternative Law Journal, 43*(2), 81–88. doi:10.1177/1037969X18772153

Wong, C. A., & Cummings, G. G. (2009). The influence of authentic leadership behaviors on trust and work outcomes of health care staff. *The Journal of Leadership Studies, 3*(2), 6–23. doi:10.1002/jls.20104

World Bank Group & IMF. (2018). *The Bali Fintech Agenda*. Chapeau Paper, September 2018.

World Bank. (2018). *From Spreadsheets to SupTech: Technology Solutions for Market Conduct Supervision*. Retrieved from http://documents.worldbank.org/curated/en/612021529953613035/pdf/127577-REVISED-Suptech-Technology-Solutions-for-Market-Conduct-Supervision.pdf

World Economic Forum. (2017). *Beyond Fintech: A Pragmatic Assessment Of Disruptive Potential In Financial Services*. Retrieved from: http://www3.weforum.org/docs/Beyond_Fintech_-_A_Pragmatic_Assessment_of_Disruptive_Potential_in_Financial_Services.pdf

World Economic Forum. (2017). *Beyond Fintech: How the successes and failures of new entrants are reshaping the financial system*. Available at: http://www3.weforum. org/docs/Beyond_Fintech_-_A_Pragmatic_Assessment_of_ Disruptive_Potential_in_Financial_Services.pdf

World Economic Forum. (2017). *The Global Risks Report* (12th ed.). Author.

World Economic Forum. (2018). Agile Governance Reimagining Policy-making in the Fourth Industrial Revolution. Author.

Wyman, O. (2017). *Accelerating Financial Inclusion in South-East Asia with Digital Finance*. Asian development bank working paper series.

Yang, D. (2018). Evolutionary Approaches and the Construction of Technology-Driven Regulations. *Emerging Markets Finance & Trade, 54*(14), 3256–3271.

Yip, M., Shadbolt, N., Tiropanis, T., & Webber, C. (2012). *The Digital Underground Economy: A Social Network Approach to Understanding Cybercrime*. https://www.sigma.com.pl/pliki/albums/userpics/10007/Virtua

Zachariadis, M., Ozcan, P., & Dinckol, D. (2020). How is COVID-19 impacting fintech startups? *Fintech Magazine*. Retrieved May 23, 2020, from https://www.fintechmagazine.com/fintech/how-covid-19-impacting-fintech-startups

Zakrzewski, A., Tang, T., Appell, G., Renaud, F., Andrew, H., Nicole, H., Michael, K., Martin, M., Federico, M., & André, X. (2019). *Global Wealth 2019: Reigniting Radical Growth*. https://image-src.bcg.com/Images/BCG-Reigniting-Radical-Growth-June-2019_tcm9-222638.pdf

Zavolokina, L., Dolata, M., & Schwabe, G. (2016). *FinTech–What's in a Name?* Academic Press.

Zavolokina, L., Dolata, M., & Schwabe, G. (2016, December). FinTech transformation: How IT-enabled innovations shape the financial sector. In *FinanceCom 2016* (pp. 75–88). Springer.

Zekos, G. (2005). Foreign direct investment in a digital economy. *European Business Review*, *17*(1), 52–68. doi:10.1108/09555340510576267

Zemčík, M. T. (2019). *A Brief History of Chatbots. DEStech Transactions on Computer Science and Engineering*. 2019 International Conference on Artificial Intelligence, Control and Automation Engineering (AICAE 2019).

Zetzsche, D. A., Buckley, R. P., Arner, D. W., & Föhr, L. (2017). *The ICO Gold Rush: It's a Scam, It's a Bubble, It's a Super Challenge for Regulators*. doi:10.2139srn.3072298

Zhang, X., Tang, S., Zhao, Y., Wang, G., Zheng, H., & Zhao, B. Y. (2017, May). Cold hard e-cash: Friends and vendors in the venmo digital payments system. *Eleventh International AAAI Conference on Web and Social Media*.

Zhao, B. (2017). *Web scraping. In Encyclopedia of big data*. Springer.

Zhao, Q., Tsai, P. H., & Wang, J. L. (2019). Improving financial service innovation strategies for enhancing China's banking industry competitive advantage during the fintech revolution: A Hybrid MCDM model. *Sustainability*, *11*(5), 1419. doi:10.3390u11051419

Zhou, A. (2017). EY, Deloitte and PwC embrace artificial intelligence for tax and accounting. *Forbes Media*. Retrieved June, 10, 2020, from https://www.forbes.com/sites/adelynzhou/2017/11/14/ey-deloitte-and-pwc-embrace-artificial-intelligence-for-tax-and-accounting/#4ef48ee03498

Zimmermann, C. D. (2013). *A contemporary concept of monetary sovereignty*. Oxford University Press. doi:10.1093/acprof:oso/9780199680740.001.0001

About the contributors

Iustina Alina Boitan is Associate Professor at the Department of Money and Banking, Faculty of Finance and Banking, within Bucharest University of Economic Studies. She is member of several professional bodies, such as the Financial and Monetary Research Center (since 2008) and the Monetary Research Center within the University of National and World Economy, Bulgaria (research fellow since 2015). She has performed several documentation visits for sharing best practices in teaching and research (Complutense University of Madrid, Spain, 2014; University of Florence, Italy, 2018; University of Geneve, Switzerland, 2018; University of Zagreb, Croatia, 2019; Vienna University of Economics and Business, Austria, 2019) and ERASMUS+ stages (University of National and World Economy, Bulgaria, 2015; Tashkent Financial Institute, Uzbekistan, 2017; University of Dubrovnik, Croatia, 2018; Poznan University of Economics and Business, Poland, 2019). Her research interests focus on financial regulation and supervisory policies, banking systems' efficiency and competition, assessment of banking systems' distress, quantitative supervisory tools (such as the development of early warning systems), ethical or socially responsible banks, national promotional banks, crowd funding, social and financial inclusion, sustainable development, migration, labor market risks. She had been member of various research projects obtained through national competition or funded by the business environment.

Kamilla Marchewka-Bartkowiak is Associate Professor, Dr Hab, Director of the Institute of Finance at Poznań University of Economics and Business, 2016-2019 Dean of the Faculty of Economics, author of books and articles in field of banking, public finance, public debt management, public economy, regulatory economy, expert of finance at the Bureau of Research, the Chancellery of the Sejm (lower house of the Poland's Parliament), member of Working Group on Economic and Budgetary Affairs in European Centre for Parliamentary Research and Documentation, 2015-2019 member of Supervisory Board and Head of Audit Committee in Centralny Dom Maklerski Pekao S.A. (the biggest brokerage house in Poland).

* * *

Hassnian Ali is Assistant Director (Research) at International Center for Research in Islamic Economics (ICRIE) in Lahore, Pakistan.

Lennart Ante studied business administration at the University of Cologne, TU Clausthal and Universität Hamburg and works as a research associate at the University of Hamburg at the BMWI funded project ETIBLOGG, a project about making small amounts of energy tradable using blockchain technology to increase the efficiency of energy markets. He is convinced that the blockchain technology will have a sustainable influence on business models and society and would like to contribute with his research to develop positive potentials of the technology and assess possible barriers and risks. In addition to his research activities, he is a co-founder of STOKR, a company that offers corporate financing via blockchain technology. Has also co-founded the Blockchain Research Lab and leads the research projects "Entrepreneurship and Digital Finance" and "Literature and Bibliometrics". He is evaluating the use of blockchain technology across various sectors and is studying the implications and characteristics of cryptocurrencies and their respective markets. Of particular interest are topics related to entrepreneurial finance, such as startup financing with tokens and related digital markets and bibliometric analyses, which help to systematically prepare research on blockchain and cryptocurrency and make it understandable in context.

Teodora Cristina Barbu is Professor at the Department of Money and Banking, Faculty of Finance and Banking, within Bucharest University of Economic Studies. The professional experience and skills are the result of documentation at the University for Social Sciences Toulouse, France (1991-1992 and 2002); Marseille, France (1995); Hague University, Netherlands (1998); Orleans, France (2000); Universidad National de Educcation a Distancia Madrid, Spain (2002); University of Brighton, UK (2003). She published numerous papers indexed by Clarivate Analytics and other international databases which cover the following areas of interest: European integration and consolidated supervision; effects of bank recapitalization in the context of the current financial crisis; stock market consolidation; mergers and acquisitions in banking activity; the impact of monetary policy on the mortgage market; ethics and confidence in the banking business. The research projects won by competition or conducted jointly with several financial institutions were related on: capital market restructuring in Romania, Romanian banking system's European integration, management of operational risk in the Romanian banking system, restructuring loan portfolio during crisis and optimization of procedures for granting and guaranteeing mortgage loans. She is a founding member of the Financial and Monetary Research Center and of the Romanian Finance and Banking Association.

Mateja Brozović is an Assistant professor at the Department of Accounting, Faculty of Economics and Business, University of Zagreb, with a PhD in the field of audit of financial statements. She actively participates in teaching several courses (related to accounting, analysis of financial statements and audit) at university and professional study programs. So far, in addition to her doctoral thesis, she has co-authored a number of scientific and professional papers, presented papers at international and domestic scientific conferences, and participated in the writing of a university handbook. She is a member of the Project Team at the Faculty of Economics and Business in Zagreb. As a collaborator, she has participated in seven scientific projects, funded by the University of Zagreb, Croatian Science Foundation and European Social Fund.

Tessa Campbell is a third-year undergraduate studying a degree of business at the University of Tasmania, majoring in management and international logistics. Tessa's education and work experience has allowed her to understand the positive impact effective leaders have on the success of an organization, along with how they can make a positive contribution to society. This identification and acknowledgement has sparked an interest in researching the field, with future endeavours to research the relationship between effective leadership, motivation, and single gender dominated industries such as engineering and maritime logistics.

Anca Mihaela Copaciu (Paraschiv) is Economist within the Financial Stability Department of the National Bank of Romania and a PhD Student at Faculty of International Business and Economics, Bucharest University of Economic Studies. Her research interests are related to topics on Financial Stability, Financial literacy and Banking Networks. The results of Anca's research were published in different international research journals and proceedings of conferences.

Zi-Ying Anna Cui is a third-year undergraduate studying a degree of business at the University of Tasmania, majoring in management. Anna is interested in organizational leadership and its impact on various stakeholders, including the wider community. Anna believes that good leaders are foundational within organizations and for the health and wellbeing of society. Based on her own experience and skills in organizational management and leadership, Anna sees the need for continued research in the area of promoting ethical leadership in Australia.

Teresa Czerwinska is Professor of Economics at the Warsaw University. She specialises in finances and risk management. Since March 2020, she has held the position of Vice-President and Member of the Management Committee of the European Investment Bank (EIB). Prior to becoming EIB Vice-President, Prof Czerwińska was a member of the board of the National Bank of Poland since June 2019. Between January 2018 and June 2019, she was Minister of Finance of the Republic of Poland. In this role, she was also a Governor of the European Investment Bank. Before that, she held the position of Undersecretary of State responsible for the state budget at the Ministry of Finance (from June 2017 to January 2018) and still prior to that, at the Ministry of Science and Higher Education (December 2015 to June 2017) in Poland.

Luke DeJesus is a fifth-year undergraduate studying a double degree of economics and business at the University of Tasmania, majoring in marketing and economic analysis. Luke's upbringing, education and work experience has enabled him to understand the effect that authentic leaders have within the global economy and the social structure of firms and relationships. This recognition has motivated Luke to develop his knowledge by research in the expansive theory of authentic leadership. Luke will aim to use this knowledge to improve industry on a micro and macro level.

Marcin Flotyński is assistant professor, PhD, at the Chair of Economic Sciences, Faculty of Law and Administration at Adam Mickiewicz University, Poznań, Poland. He is an academic lecturer and author of over 30 publications on banking, capital markets, financial stability, derivatives and financial regulations. He was a speaker on numerous financial conferences. He gained experience at Poznań University of Economics and Business, Poland, the Aalborg Centre for Problem Based Learning in Engineering Science and Sustainability under the auspices of UNESCO, Denmark and Ivey Business School – Western University, Canada. He got a scholarship from the Foundation of the National Bank of Poland and was awarded by the President of the Management Board of the Polish Bank Guarantee Fund for his doctoral dissertation. He conducted a research project in the field of financial markets for the National Bank of Poland. He gained experience working as an analyst in financial institutions. He obtained the accounting certificate issued by the Polish Ministry of Finance. He is an active investor on the stock markets.

Adam Głogowski is a graduate of the Warsaw School of Economics. Since 2002, he has been working for the central bank of Poland (Narodowy Bank Polski), analyzing the financial system from financial stability and financial innovation perspectives. As the NBP's representative in various working groups at the ECB, ESRB and OECD, he has been contributing to the financial stability debate at international level. His professional interests focus on the area of macro stress testing frameworks, identification of systemic risks, formulating macroprudential policy, as well as dealing with the impact of the evolution of business models on financial stability.

Tomasz Gromek is an Adviser at Research and Financial Innovation Department, National Bank of Poland (NBP). For almost 20 years, his central bank career spanned across different business areas of the Bank, including: banking supervision, financial stability, macroprudential policy and ultimately – fintech. Before joining the NBP he had been member of the Polish delegation negotiating EU accession (the EMU/euro team). Since then he actively worked on many European projects as a member of various workstreams of the EBA, the ECB, and other European Institutions. He worked at the European Systemic Risk Board Secretariat in Frankfurt (2015-2018). Latest publications he co-authored, include: Resolving Non-Performing Loans in Europe (ESRB, 2017); Handbook on operationalising macroprudential policy in the banking sector – National flexibility measures under Article 458 CRR, and Reciprocity framework (ESRB 2015, 2017) and Financial Stability Report, December 2019 (NBP 2019, Box. 2.3 Expenditure on technological developments in the Polish banking sector). In his current role he is committed to bring data-driven analyses into policy discussions concerning fintech and financial system development.

Zsolt Halasz graduated Péter Pázmány Catholic University Faculty of Law and Political Sciences, Budapest, Hungary in 2000. He holds LL.M. from the same university (2002) and PhD from the University of Miskolc (Hungary), Faculty of Law (2011). In 2001-02 he worked as a lawyer in the CEO's Office of the Hungarian Development Bank. 2002-2005 he was in house lawyer in the Hungarian Investment and Asset Management Ltd. and 2005-10 legal referent in the Office of Parliamentary Commissioner for Human Rights (Ombudsman). 2010-13 he was director and head of CEO's Office in the Hungarian Development Bank, between 2013-16 advisor to a Vice-President of the European Investment Bank (EIB), and 2016-18 policy officer at EIB. Since his graduation, he has been continuously teaching financial law at Péter Pázmány Catholic University Faculty of Law and Political Sciences and in 2018 he has been appointed to associate professor and head of the Financial Law Department of the University.

Aneta Bobenič Hintošová is an Associate Professor of Business Economics and Management at the University of Economics in Bratislava, Faculty of Business Economics with seat in Košice, Slovakia. She holds master degrees in business economics and in law and PhD. in sectoral and intersectoral economics. Her teaching and research activities focus especially on international business and strategic management. Within her academic career, she worked as a vice-dean for international affairs, as well as a vice-dean for science and doctoral studies. She has completed many lecture stays abroad at several European universities. Her business experiences lie in performing consulting activities, especially for foreign companies allocating their investments in Slovakia. Currently, she is a member of the Ethics Committee of the University of Economics in Bratislava, member of the Scientific Board of the Faculty of Civil Engineering, Technical University in Košice and member of the Slovak Bar Association.

Humayun Kabir is a Lecturer at the Department of Business Administration, East West University, Dhaka, Bangladesh. His research interest includes dividend policy, financial inclusion, financial markets, and so forth.

Stanislaw Kasiewicz is Emeritus professor at the Warsaw School of Economics. Scientific Secretary of the ALTERUM Financial System Research and Analysis Center. The author of over 300 scientific publications, a member of editorial boards of scientific and financial journals.

Matthew Knox is a researcher of social sciences at the University of Tasmania, developing his knowledge through research in fields of behavioral, organizational and social psychology, as well as sociology and anthropology. Matthew is looking to consolidate his growing list of publications into his project on wellbeing during COVID-19. In a world fuelled by constructed images of the self, Matthew looks to investigate the impact authentic relationships have on the wellbeing of those suffering from the consequences of emotional labour. In doing so he looks to understand how to improve the world through understanding the people in it.

Lech Kurkliński is Professor at Warsaw School of Economics and Warsaw University (Ph.D., habilitation), specialist in banking, risk management, regulation impact assessment, cross-cultural management, director of ALTERUM Center for Research and Analysis of Financial Center, studied at Central School of Planning and Statistics, University of Virginia, University of Oklahoma City; since 1991 in banking: Managing Director of Craftsmanship Bank in Warsaw, CEO of Polski Bank Inwestycyjny SA, the management board member of BIG Bank Gdanski SA (Millennium Bank SA), Managing Director of Household International in Poland, head of consumer finance division and deputy CEO of HSBC in Poland, member of the supervisory boards e.g.: the Warsaw Stock Exchange, author of several publications: banking, regulations, foreign direct investments, risk management, cross-cultural management.

Sanja Sever Mališ is an Associate professor at the Department of Accounting and Vice dean for strategic partnerships and projects at FEB from 2018. She graduated in 2004 from Faculty of Economics and Business, University of Zagreb. She attended doctoral study in the field of economy and business economy at Faculty of Economics and Business and in 2010 she obtained Ph.D. degree by defending her doctoral thesis entitled "Internal control mechanisms in the function of financial statements auditing quality". She has published about 100 scientific and professional papers and participated at international and national scientific and professional conferences. Her research and professional interests include accounting, auditing and fraudulent financial reporting. She participated in several national and international scientific projects. From 2018 she is holding a position of the Vice dean for strategic partnerships and projects coordinating national and international research and expert projects at FEB.

Hazik Mohamed is a business strategist with substantial market research, operational management and start-up experience. He consults for MSMEs and MNCs on various business-related issues including market penetration, operational process trouble-shooting, investment management, and strategic execution. Specialized PhD research in behavioral research and analysis using game theory in view of conventional and Islamic economics perspectives. Its applications include understanding consumer/user behavior and viral marketing strategies as well as policy formulation and regulatory implementation through effective low-cost behavioral interventions. Other interests include region-wide strategic planning as well as implementation of innovative, disruptive and scalable technologies.

Shilpa Arora Narang is Assistant Professor (Accounting and Finance) from Institute of Innovation in Technology and Management, affiliated to Guru Gobind Singh Indraprastha University, throughout first class with distinction. She is MBA (Finance) from Guru Gobind Singh Indraprastha University. She is UGC-JRF/NET (Management) qualified. She possesses a rich teaching experience of 10 years. She is proactive in contributing research articles in peer-reviewed, refereed and indexed journals, magazines, edited books and conference proceedings.

Paweł Pisany is a Ph.D. in economics and finance; Economic Expert at Narodowy Bank Polski (Research and Financial Innovation Department) and assistant professor at the Institute of Economics of the Polish Academy of Sciences. In 2019 he completed doctoral studies at Warsaw School of Economics (SGH), previously Master's degree in finance and accounting at SGH (2014) and Master's degree in law at the Faculty of Law and Administration, University of Warsaw (2014). In 2019 he also completed post-graduate studies in Data Science at the Faculty of Economic Sciences, University of Warsaw. He carried out the research grant project regarding corporate bonds market in Asia, financed by the The National Science Centre (2016 - 2018). Currently he is involved in research on the ownership structure of banking sectors in developed and emerging economies, as well as entrepreneurship and financial innovation.

Alina Nicoleta Radu is Associate professor within the Money and Banking Department at the Bucharest University of Economic Studies. She gives lectures on topics like: Money, Credit Institutions, Capital Markets and Banking intermediation. Her research interests are related to topics on Crises Management, Resolution Mechanisms, Financial Stability issues, Moral hazard and Deposit guarantee funds. The results of own research were published in different international research journals and as chapters in books. The most representative paper is entitled Quantifying Recapitalization Fund Premium using Option Pricing Techniques, published in 2012 in the journal Economics Letters. At the same time, she is employed as an expert within the National Bank of Romania, International Relations Department. Her main duties are related to drafting specific documents on interdisciplinary issues regarding the relations of the central bank with international institutions and EU central banks, by liaising with similar departments of the Foreign Affairs and Public Finance ministries.

Josh Rowlands is a third-year undergraduate studying a double degree of business and arts at the University of Tasmania. Josh majors in business management and Mandarin with a minor in international relations. Josh's experience as an employee in a wide variety of businesses has inspired him to learn about effective leadership. With leadership having such a profound impact on business sustainability and long-term success, Josh has sought to research and contribute to the behaviors that produce valuable leadership. Josh chose to contribute to the current business literature in FinTech because it is an emerging industry that could benefit from sound leadership practices. After graduating Josh plans to operate his own Tasmanian business. He views engaging in business research as an advantageous opportunity to examine current leadership practices that can be implemented into his own business in the future.

Lajoš Žager is a Full professor at the Department of Accounting, Faculty of Economics and Business, University of Zagreb. As an author or co-author, he published more than 500 papers in field of accounting, auditing and financial statements analysis (expert and scientific books, textbooks, handbooks, dictionaries, lexicons, expert and scientific papers, projects, book reviews etc.). He participated in numerous expert and scientific conferences. At the Croatian Chamber of Auditors he was a member of an examination Commission for title certified Public Accountant and in Section of Internal Auditors he is the president of an examination Commission for a title certified Internal Auditor. Besides, he is vice President of Croatian Association of Accountants and Financial Experts. He is a member of different working groups improving national legislation of accounting and auditing profession.

Index

A

B

C

D

E

F

G

H

I

L

M

N

O

P

R

S

T

U

V

W

www.ingramcontent.com/pod-product-compliance
Lightning Source LLC
LaVergne TN
LVHW062143300926
849161LV00010B/2613